Introduction to
ECONOMICS

Other works by
Sir Alec Cairncross

Home and Foreign Investment 1870–1913 (Cambridge University Press, 1953)
Factors in Economic Development (Allen & Unwin, 1962)
Essays in Economic Management (Allen & Unwin, 1971)
Control of Long-term International Capital Movements (Brookings Institution, 1973)
Inflation, Growth and International Finance (Allen & Unwin, 1975)

Introduction to
ECONOMICS
SIXTH EDITION

SIR ALEC CAIRNCROSS
and
PETER SINCLAIR

BUTTERWORTHS
LONDON – BOSTON – DURBAN – SYDNEY
TORONTO – WELLINGTON

First published 1944
Second edition 1951
Third edition 1951
ELBS edition 1960
Fourth edition 1966
Fifth edition 1973
   Reprinted 1976
   Reprinted 1978
Sixth edition 1982

© Butterworth & Co (Publishers) Ltd 1982

British Library Cataloguing in Publication Data

Cairncross, Sir Alec
   Introduction to economics. – 6th ed.
   1. Economics
   I. Title
   330   HB171

  ISBN 0-408-71056-X
  ISBN 0-408-71055-1 Pbk

Typeset by Butterworths Litho Preparation Department.
Printed and bound by Richard Clay (The Chaucer Press) Ltd.,
Bungay, Suffolk.

Preface

This is the sixth edition of a textbook which, in its original form, was written in the 1930s. In successive editions the text has been extensively rewritten so that it is now a quite different book but the ordering of the subject matter and the level of treatment have remained unchanged. As explained in the preface to the fifth edition:

> I have always had in mind two classes of reader: those adults who are unlikely ever to tackle another textbook of equal length, but want to know what the subject is about; and those younger readers who are at the beginning of their study of the subject and may or may not persevere with it. For both groups it is important to have a look at the whole of the map so that they can take in quickly what ground it covers. Some of them may want subsequently to go over the ground conscientiously and in detail, while others are glad to be spared such an effort. But all of them can hope to learn a good deal that will hold together in their minds and give them a different outlook on events if they can take in most of what is in this book.
>
> The treatment remains general and non-mathematical, and I have emphasised leading variables – institutions, habits and attitudes – that do not lend themselves to mathematical specification and are usually more prominent in applied economics than in current economic theory. The sacrifice of theoretical rigour means that there are fewer hard and testable propositions to make a firm lodgment in the reader's memory; but I confess to some distrust of greater scientific precision in economics that the subject permits of. There is a good deal to be said for covering the ground once quickly *before* taking down the mathematician's kit of economic Meccano. Apart from anything else, those who are more at home in history than in mathematics may be encouraged to persevere by the comparative absence of symbols, formulae and equations and may be surprised how much that is essentially mathematical has taken root on the way to Part VII.

The revisions made to the present edition are more thoroughgoing than on any previous occasion. They have been made in collaboration with Peter Sinclair who will share responsibility for any future edition. In Parts I and II the old text has been abbreviated, two chapters (Chapters 2 and 6) have been removed altogether and the others have been brought up-to-date. In the later parts some chapters (Chapters 10, 21–23, 27–29 of the present edition) have been completely rewritten and many of the others have been given a thorough overhaul. In the interests of brevity (and with some regret) all appendixes except Appendix A have been cut out. The result is a more compact treatment in one volume of the entire subject, elementary enough for the general reader and yet abreast of current controversies and modern economic analysis.

Alec Cairncross

Contents

List of Figures

List of Tables

Part I

Introductory

Chapter 1

What economics is about

Economics is not a subject that can be learned, like mathematics, as a series of propositions that follow from one another with the neatness of a Chinese box. It is much more like medicine, compounded of imperfect knowledge, worldly wisdom, obscure jargon and scientific analysis. The student of medicine learns many things about the human body that are meant to improve his powers of diagnosis; but he can make mistakes, and his patients can disagree with him, sometimes quite violently. The student of economics is in much the same position. He learns a great deal about the economy of his country and of other countries. But since he is studying things with which everybody is familiar, such as production, trade, and income, and his conclusions about these things do not usually rest on an infallible logic beyond the comprehension of the ordinary man, he is wise to get used to the idea, right at the beginning, that there is room for disagreement in economic diagnosis and that people will disagree with him.

To make matters worse, when he passes from diagnosis to treatment, he finds an uncomfortable gap between the two. It is one thing to analyse what is going on in some branch of the national economy but quite a different thing to prescribe treatment, or in other words recommend the policy that ought to be adopted. There is very rarely one single treatment appropriate to an economic disease and the ultimate selection may have to be guided by entirely non-economic considerations. An economist may be confident, for example, that he knows what is causing inflation and yet feel that this does not entitle him to say what, if anything, should be done to stop it. Some economists go so far as to argue that policy is not their affair and that they should content themselves with outlining the probable consequences of particular policies without coming down in favour of any of them. Even if this seems overscrupulous, it is right to remember that, in matters of policy, economic and non-economic considerations may have to be weighed against one another and that, in such matters, there is no single answer. In this, economics differs from the physical sciences, where every difference of opinion can be put to the test of fact and, if the facts are known, resolved at once. Differences of opinion in the social sciences are not just differences about facts but may be differences about values. Everyone is entitled to his own view as to what matters most, and need not accept the pronouncements of experts if these pronouncements rest on a private conception of social priorities which he does not share.

All this is very confusing to a beginner who comes to economics in the hope of finding certainty. It is bad enough not to be quite sure what the subject is all about, or what the word 'economics' means, but completely devastating to be told at the outset that there is no simple body of doctrine to be mastered and that, whatever an economist says, somebody is pretty sure to disagree. It might seem a waste of time to study anything so apparently inconclusive; but nobody gives up studying medicine because doctors disagree. Economics may be unlike many of the physical sciences which have an appeal for the man who likes one answer to every question; but it is in the same boat as most other subjects that deal with human behaviour and are unable to reduce it to the kind of inexorable scientific laws that govern the behaviour of atoms.

How can one learn a subject that seems to have no beginning and no end? By reading systematically through a textbook? Perhaps; although it is not uncommon for the dawn of understanding to come a great deal later. Learning economics is not unlike learning to talk. A child listens and makes noises and after a good deal of gibberish, begins to talk intelligibly; a student of economics does much the same and takes about the same length of time to master the vocabulary. There is usually no fixed sequence in which the different parts of the subject are grasped; an understanding of each part is necessary to an understanding of the others, so that the student has to go over the ground two or three times rather fast before he can see the interconnection of ideas. Wherever he begins, he must make the round and come back again to where he started; he must not assume that he can understand everything completely as he goes along.

Plan of the book

The textbook writer must, however, begin somewhere and must at least appear to obey some logic in the order in which he moves forward. Here he comes up against a difficulty to which the reader should be privy. He can start by looking at the problems of the economy as a whole and encourage the reader to put himself in the position of the Chancellor of the Exchequer, faced with conflicting advice as to how to improve the standard of living, deal with a crisis in the balance of payments, prevent unemployment, stop prices rising, and so on; or he can start with more familiar, everyday matters, such as the things that shape the decisions of an individual business man about what to produce, what to charge for his product, when to install new machinery, and so on.

Some readers fancy themselves as Chancellor and everybody would like to know more about how the country is run, so that many economists plump for the first alternative and call Part I of their textbook 'Macroeconomics' (or the analysis of the economy in the large). Other readers find 'Macroeconomics' hard going because it has never occurred to them to think of national income, capital formation and a whole lot of other abstractions that lie at the heart of this part of economic theory. They prefer to be introduced to these abstractions more gently and only after they have accustomed themselves to the more elementary level of discussion with which they meet in 'Microeconomics' (or the analysis of the bahaviour of individual consumers and producers).

In this book, the second, less exciting approach is adopted. The reader is given a brief glimpse of the higher peaks that lie ahead of him before being led off in Part II for a spell on the foothills of economic theory; most of this Part is devoted to an analysis of the forces governing production in the individual business, taking for granted the existence of a market. In Part III production is looked at in terms of the way it responds to market forces, the connection between these forces and the wants of consumers, and the mechanism by which, in the economic system we know, the pattern of production is made to match the pattern of consumers' wants. Part IV analyses the influence of market forces on the productive resources at the disposal of society, their allocation between different uses, the incentives they are offered and the rewards they obtain. Then in Part V comes an introduction to macroeconomic problems, concentrating on fluctuations in economic activity and the forces causing them; this Part also deals with the role of banks and other financial institutions. Finally, Part VI discusses problems of international trade and payments and Part VII the general objectives of economic policy and the ways in which the state can contribute towards the achievement of those objectives.

What is economics about?

Now let us turn back to the beginning and ask what economics is about. This is a natural question to put; but the beginner will get little satisfaction from the answers that economists usually give. Some economists give a precise definition which usually conveys nothing at all to the newcomer to the subject and is thought too narrow or too misleading by the average professional. The best course is to accept that economics is what economists write about and then look to see what they write about by studying the tables of contents of some textbooks. For example, it is obviously about money, banking and international trade; about wages and profits; about production, consumption and the standard of living; and so on. An alternative course is to look at the examination papers that first-year students of economics are invited to answer. For anyone wanting to find out what professional economists think their subject is about, there is no surer method than looking through the examination questions that they put.

A definition in terms of illustrations is never satisfactory to the logical student. He wants to know what are the central problems of economics in the way that health and disease are the central problems of medicine. He is not particularly interested in exact definitions – after all, who would undertake to define health or disease with any precision? – but would like some working rule that tells him when he is well within or well outside the boundaries of the subject.

There are plenty of working rules. Alfred Marshall, the great Victorian economist, said that economics was about 'man in the ordinary business of life'; not about all aspects of human behaviour, but about man as buyer and seller, producer and consumer, saver and investor, employer and worker. This definition has the advantage of stressing that economics is a social science, concerned with social problems. A definition which may give the beginner a more useful clue to the scope of the subject is that economics studies the part played by money in human affairs. It is about the getting and spending of money; how men earn a living and what sort of living they earn; how money affects their way of life and their outlook on life.

If we pursue this definition we find that economics is really not so much about money as about some things which are implied in the use of money. Three of these – exchange, scarcity and choice – are of special importance. Let us take them in turn.

(a) Exchange

Money implies exchange. It is in fact the medium of exchange. In a primitive community, where exchanges are rare, we can dispense with money and resort to direct barter. Money is unnecessary so long as we are at the stage of trying to satisfy all our wants by our own efforts, growing our own wheat, milling our own flour, baking our own bread, and only now and again exchanging, say, wheat for a ploughshare or a calf for a millstone. But immediately we begin to specialize, and cease to produce goods for our own use, money becomes indispensable if exchanges are to take place smoothly. Exchange becomes triangular – we convert goods into money and money into other goods, instead of simply bartering goods for goods. If exchanges did not take place in this apparently circuitous way, no one who specialized in making bricks or bowler hats would relish a morning's shopping.

Nowadays, therefore, exchange rarely takes the form of direct barter. Instead, we do business with money. We buy what we want with money, sell for money, fix prices in terms of money, are paid our wages, salaries, or dividends in money, save money, and measure our wealth in money. But the problems which present themselves to us in terms of money are similar to the problems raised by direct barter. There is a surface difference between money-exchange and barter-exchange, but little difference in principle. Economics, therefore, does not limit itself only to money-problems but studies exchange-problems of all kinds. It is in fact, about exchange rather than about money, for exchange underlies the use of money.

When we exchange, we have stopped being self-sufficing and have become dependent on those from whom we buy and to whom we sell. Our fortunes are linked with theirs. If they are poor or unemployed then we are likely to be in danger of poverty and unemployment ourselves. Famine and flood in one part of the world can create scarcity and distress thousands of miles away by cutting off supplies of foodstuffs and raw materials. We are all within the circle of exchange.

(b) Scarcity

The use of money implies scarcity. Money itself must be scarce or it will cease to be used. If the supply of money is increased without limit it will soon lose value and in the end no one will accept it. Whatever passes as money, therefore, must necessarily be scarce. So also – and this is the important point – must be the things that money will buy. We only exchange one scarce thing for another. We do not pay for air and earth and water unless somehow they are stinted just as the supply of money is stinted.

The fact of scarcity makes it necessary for us to economize, i.e., to make the most of what we have. We have constantly to be counting the cost, weighing up alternatives, and going without one thing so as to be able to buy more of another. Nominally it is money that we economize, for what we have to decide is whether to spend money on this or on that. What we are really doing, however, is to economize the things that money will buy. We try to buy, with our limited income, the collection of goods and services which gives us most satisfaction. We are faced with the fact that these goods and services are scarce, and we have to accommodate this scarcity as best we can to our wants and needs. Similarly, in earning money we have to husband our scarce time and energy in order to obtain as large a return as possible (in money *or* in amenities and personal satisfaction) for our efforts. On some men, of course, the pressure of scarcity and want bears harder than on others. On the millionaire, for example, the pressure is negligible; he can almost always neglect considerations of cost. But for others the necessity of making ends meet enforces constant self-denial.

The economic problem   What is true of each of us is true also of society as a whole. There is an economic problem of making the *social* income go as far as possible. The goods produced in any country are limited in amount and insufficient to maintain a standard of more than moderate comfort. There are very few things that can be provided free of charge, even in a rich country like Britain. We can make as much use as we like of public libraries and roads. But we cannot help ourselves to books and motor cars, much less to food and clothing. The more of one thing is offered to us, the less can we have of other things. We cannot have more of *all* simultaneously. If A is free, B will be all the dearer.

The need to balance value against cost is forced on every country by the insatiability of human wants and the scarcity of productive resources. It has to be decided what commodities, and how much of each, should be produced; and the decision must rest, explicitly, upon estimates of cost and value. What costs a great deal and is of comparatively little value will not be produced at all; what is valued highly and costs little to produce will be provided first and in ample quantities; what happens with the large range of intermediate commodities will depend on the type of economic system and the way in which values and costs are measured.

It is as a result of our efforts to deal with scarcity (i.e., to economize) that exchange arises. We try to ration our limited means among the innumerable wants that compete for satisfaction and find that we can make our limited means go further by striking bargains with our neighbours. We give what we have in relative abundance – muscle or brain, professional knowledge or organizing ability – for what is comparatively scarce, what we could not do, or could not afford to do, ourselves. We sell our time and energies and spend our earnings on what others have laboured to produce.

In doing so, we are offering the goods or services in which our talents show to greatest advantage (or least disadvantage) for the goods or services which others are specially fitted to produce[1]. We are supplementing our deficiencies – our imperfect versatility, for instance – out of the proficiencies of others. Not only are we able to draw on the skill of others – skill which we may not possess at all – but we are also able to give our whole energies to a single task – one to which, either through practice or natural bent, we are far more fitted than those who engage in it only intermittently. By exchanging, we are making our efforts go further towards meeting our wants. We are reducing the pressure of scarcity and achieving economy. Exchanges arise, therefore, in order to alleviate scarcity, and scarcity is necessarily implicit in exchange.

(c) Choice

The use of money also implies choice. We have to choose between the many claims on our purse when we spend money, and between the many uses to which we might put our time and energy in earning it. We cannot spend the same evening in the cinema and in the theatre. We must choose one form of entertainment or the other. We may have to choose, also, between spending an extra pound or so on seats and spending the same pound later on cigarettes.

Our choice, of course, is not always made rationally. That is, we do not always weigh up carefully the possible ways in which we might spend our money. We are much more lighthearted and irrational in buying sweets, for example, than we are in renting a house. We buy, very often, impulsively or through habit or force of example. Or we may buy because our 'sales resistance' has crumpled at the sounding of some advertiser's trumpet. It is irrational to pay more than is necessary for a thing; and yet hardly a day passes but we buy goods without asking the price, or cannot be bothered to look for cheaper brands. We do not take the trouble to find out where prices are lowest; or we take excessive trouble to save a trifling sum, like the wealthy man who walks to save a penny fare. We do not budget for so much on clothes, so much on amusements, so much on food, so much on our savings account, and so on, but spend haphazardly so long as the money lasts. Or at least that is what large numbers of us do. Perhaps, however, the careful housewife – the tradition among economists is to think of housewives as the persons who hold the purse-strings – is more rational in her buying. The economic woman may be less of an abstraction than the economic man!

The way in which we make a choice is of great importance to the economist. For he cannot tell how much weight to place on the preferences expressed in the spending and earning of money until he knows how far these preferences are *rational* (i.e., self-consistent and giving due weight to all the facts). If, for instance, people persist in buying an expensive type of

---

[1] This must not be taken to mean that everyone is engaged in just that occupation for which he is ideally suited – that would obviously be nonsense. What is meant is that people tend to specialize, *so far as their limited knowledge and opportunities permit*, in the occupations which give fullest scope to their peculiar gifts and inclinations.

motor car it is important to know whether they buy it out of a liking for that particular type or because they are ignorant of cheaper makes with a similar performance or because of snob-appeal in the advertisements. Until the psychology of car-owners is explained to us, we cannot say whether the production and the sale of these high-priced cars involve a social waste. If car-owners are rational there *may* still be a waste (for instance, the price may be kept high by a monopoly). But if they are irrational, there is certainly a waste; they are paying more than the cost of other motor cars that would afford equal satisfaction.

In economics we begin by assuming that choice is rational. The so-called 'economic man' is simply one who is completely 'rational' in satisfying his wants, and pays no regard to the interests of others. It is, of course, an abstraction from the facts to assume that men are self-interested and rational. But to make this kind of abstraction is the only satisfactory procedure open to us. If we assume that people are self-interested and rational, we can predict how they will behave given a certain monetary inducement, and we can work out an analysis of action and reaction. For instance, if similar goods are on sale at different prices, or similar jobs advertised at different rates of pay, we know that men will, other things being equal, purchase the cheaper goods, and apply for the better-paid job. If we could not make such generalizations, if men were quite irrational, then we should never 'get anywhere' in economics. So we begin by assuming that choice is deliberate and rational, without, however, overlooking the part played by impulse, custom, and inertia. Later, we may study the psychology of choice more closely; analysing what shapes our expectations and desires, and sifting what is basic in our wants from what is superficial or conventional. But to begin with, we ignore these difficulties, take people's desires for granted, and assume that choice is rational.

In the economic system as we know it in Great Britain, choice rests largely with the individual. His preferences go to determine what is to be produced and what is not. Every penny spent on A is a vote in favour of the production of A; every refusal to buy B is a vote against the production of B. The free choice of individual consumers between the goods competing on the market helps to determine what industries can carry on at a profit. The industries that cannot show a profit are not carried on at all. Those that show excessive profits attract competition and expand until people's wants – as indicated by the price which they are prepared to pay – are more adequately met. That is, if competition is possible and effective. But if some commodity is monopolized, consumers may be powerless to get what they want (and will pay for) in the proper quantity. They show their readiness to cast votes for more of the commodity by offering high prices for it. But the election is disregarded. No one is willing to stand against the monopolist. So he is able to preserve an excessive scarcity by keeping people out of his line of business. He makes things scarcer than people want them to be and earns high profits by doing so.

Thus a country like ours does not deliberately decide what industries fit best with its advantages and needs and on what scale they should be carried on. The decisions that might otherwise rest with a central planning authority take shape instead in the market. One industry expands and another contracts as consumers alter their preferences and purchases. The scarce productive resources of the community are not rationed between the different industries by some Planning Commission. They flow into the channels lubricated by the expenditure of consumers.

But is it desirable that the individual should retain so much freedom of choice? What if consumers are irrational or incapable of judging between competing goods? Would it be better to appoint a State Planning Commission with power to decide what kind of goods should be produced and what kind of jobs workers should be encouraged to take up? Should each man's daily rations be assigned to him as the average man's daily work is at present? With whom should choice rest, and through what agencies is it best exercised? Here is a batch of problems for the economist.

The value of economic studies

For some people, the value of economics lies in disciplining them in sustained thinking about social problems. The student who is accustomed to a slipshod dogmatism, and is unaccustomed to tracing the consequences of admitted facts through chains of reasoning, stands to gain enormously from the discipline which the study of economics imposes on him. He comes to see what it is that he is assuming and becomes alive to the wider implications of those assumptions. He is forced to state his argument quite unambiguously, so that verbal misunderstandings are cleared away. He learns to be more impartial and look at all sides of the question; to generalize properly by distinguishing what is relevant from what is irrelevant; and to pay more attention to the average, inconspicuous case (as revealed, for instance, by statistics) and less to the few striking instances under his nose. For others, the value of economics lies mainly in shaking them out of an unreasonable complacency in their political philosophy. They may be all for changes in the wage system or in the money system which are either demonstrably impracticable, or practicable only if accompanied by further changes in which they are not prepared to acquiesce. Or they may be for no changes at all, without having weighed the case for and against. They may be roused to think for themselves on encountering the wide range of points of view which economists express, and accept less readily the dogma and propaganda purveyed so liberally by all the agencies which control public opinion.

Above all, economics is of value in allowing us to judge and frame policies in the light of full knowledge of how the economic system works. Everyone, willy-nilly, is an economist, for everyone has his view of how economic forces work, and what, if anything, should be done to control them. We all at some time or another maintain that workers should be paid a 'living' wage, or that there is a deficiency of purchasing power, or that rents are too high, or some such proposition. These are propositions which one must be an economist of sorts to debate. But, of course, 'economists of sorts' are not trained economists. The trained economist discusses propositions of this kind with the help of a whole apparatus of thought – what is called 'economic theory' – which has the same advantage over untrained common sense that medical science has over popular medicine: with this reservation – that the ordinary man has a much sturdier disbelief in the pretensions of economists than in the pretensions of doctors. He makes no claim to understand or dispense with the higher calculus; but economic theory, chiefly because of an exaggerated impression of the failure of economists to agree, is all too frequently dispensed with. The result is that elementary misconceptions flourish everywhere: in the conduct of business, in moral judgements, and in public policy. Economics is to these misconceptions what chemistry is to alchemy, or astronomy to astrology. It does not furnish a panacea or a creed. But it does serve the negative purpose of discrediting the crank and the charlatan; and it inculcates a technique of thinking without which a sound judgement of affairs is hard to come by.

One final point. It must not be supposed that economists are blind to everything but economy and efficiency. They may, privately, have a great liking for uneconomical and inefficient ways of doing things. But they assume that most people would prefer to work less hard or in more congenial occupations if they suffered no loss of income in doing so; that is, they assume that an economy of human effort is, in present circumstances, desirable, and that if there is some more efficient way by which the work of the world could be done, then it would be a pity not to try to discover it. They are interested mainly in *money* incomes and *money* costs – in making money incomes high and money costs low. But they do not suppose that every rise in incomes and every cheapening of goods and services is an advance in human welfare. For they know that the things that money will buy are not what men most desire; and that cheapness in money costs may conceal dearness in flesh and blood, in social amenities, in human needs and enthusiasms.

Economists, then, do not regard money and the things that money will buy with a special veneration. But they know more vividly than others, how enormously monetary considerations influence human conduct. They know that those who affect to despise money are generally well provided with it. They know that men tend to believe what it is in their interest to believe and that men's interests are inseparably linked with their bread and butter and the way it is earned. They know how unemployment and poverty can change men's minds as well as their bodies: how the course of our lives depends on the income and occupation of our parents: how the desire for power and mastery can be turned to acquisitiveness and greed. Knowing these things, economists are in no danger of underrating the economic factor in human affairs. But they can also avoid exaggeration. They have learnt something of the plasticity of human motives and ambitions and know that the hope of gain and the fear of unemployment have not always been the main incentives (and will not always be the most effective ones) for contriving that the work of society is done. Money and jobs are not the only human obsessions. It happens that the role which a man plays in life has come to depend more and more on the economic function which he performs and the social standing which his income obtains for him. But the time may come when prestige attaches to other and more important things than a man's income or his job, when the tiresome necessity of earning a livelihood has become less pressing, and qualities of spirit have come into their own.

Chapter 2

Production, consumption and trade

Whatever economics is about, it is certainly about economic activities and the main forms of economic activity are production and trade. Everybody thinks he knows what these terms mean but there are in fact many ambiguities in their normal use which it is important to clear up at the outset.

Production

It is common, for example, for the word 'production', and still more the word 'productive', to be used used rather narrowly. Some people think of productive work as work done on the factory floor or on the farm, usually involving manual effort and leading to the creation of some physical product like a piece of cloth or a crop of wheat. In the USSR, economic theorists exclude from production all services that yield nothing tangible and they measure the growth of production by an index composed entirely of physical products like coal and steel. Nor are the Soviet economists without some claim to orthodoxy because they derive their practice from the usage of the classical economists including Karl Marx and Adam Smith. In *The Wealth of Nations*, the foundation stone of modern economics, Adam Smith rejected as unproductive 'some of the gravest and most important, and some of the most frivolous professions: churchmen, lawyers, physicians, men of letters of all kinds; players, buffoons, musicians, opera singers, opera dancers, etc.' on the grounds that 'the work of all of them perishes in the very instant of its production'.

Consumption

This view of the matter might be justifiable if the sole object of production were the accumulation of reproducible wealth: the creation and enlargement of the means of production. But production is not something undertaken for its own sake or in order to increase production later on. Its prime purpose is to meet the wants of consumers; the test of what is and what is not productive is the contribution that is made to the satisfaction of those wants. Consumers don't want steel; they want the things into which steel is fashioned. In a sense, they don't even want these things; they want to *use* them, to enjoy the *services* they provide.

This may seem like a quibble. What is the difference between wanting a car and wanting the use of a car, especially when most people want the car for their own exclusive use? But that the distinction is a real one becomes clear if we ask ourselves how it is possible to consume a car year by year over its life. It does not disappear and, if well maintained, may not even deteriorate perceptibly. It is just as likely to be scrapped because it is out-of-date as because it no longer functions. We do not consume it by using it up in any physical way; we exhaust its utility, employing its services in a steady flow over its useful life until these services cease to satisfy us.

Utility

Now if, with this in mind, we look at production, the apparently solid distinction between productive and unproductive activities in terms of the creation of material goods, crumbles away. People do not so much make goods as make them more serviceable. They create, not material objects, but utility. When for example, a man makes a pair of boots, he rearranges pieces of leather from a *form* in which they are not wanted into a form in which they are wanted. When someone transports the boots from factory to warehouse, he is taking them from a *place* where they are not wanted to a place where they are wanted. When someone stores the boots in his warehouse, he is holding them over from a *time* when retailers do not want them to a time when they do. There is no essential difference between these activities. They all create utility, either of form, place, or time, and so improve the facilities for the satisfaction of our wants; that is, they are all productive.

In the same way, if we look at different occupations, there is no difference in principle between manual and other kinds of work: between the making of a violin and the playing of it in a concert hall. It can be argued that we are more dependent for the bare necessities of life on farm labourers and bricklayers than on shopkeepers, cinema stars and university professors. But such an argument makes very little sense as soon as we reflect that we enjoy a high standard of living precisely because it is not made up exclusively of the bare necessities of life and that nothing would lower it again so effectively as to require everyone to turn farm labourer or bricklayer.

Production, to sum up, is simply the creation of utility: that is, of the power to satisfy human wants. Consumption is the using up of utility when we come to satisfy our wants. When we produce goods, we build up a store of wealth upon which we can draw. But, stricly speaking, we do not produce or consume goods at all. We render and are rendered services, some of which are consumed on the spot, while others are stored in bread and butter, collars and ties, ships, houses, and so on, and are used up in periods varying from a few minutes to hundreds of years. Our efforts are productive if they are of service to someone. If they are not, then we may fairly call them unproductive.

Unpaid services

The economist usually narrows his study of production to that part of it which involves the making of goods for sale or the rendering of paid services. It is important to remember, however, that a great deal of productive effort goes on without payment: for example, within the household or in primitive communities where the circulation of money plays a very restricted part in the organization of production. It has been estimated that if one were to put a market value on the unpaid services of housewives, they would be equivalent, in the United States, to as much as one-quarter of the entire national income[1]. In subsistence economies, where the market is narrow and specialization limited, little money changes hands and yet the community makes a living by the same kind of exertions as would yield a substantial money income if trade with other areas were feasible. In the transition from a subsistence to a market economy, therefore, production in the narrow sense of actual sales increases more rapidly than production in the broad sense of total output, and the usual statistical measures of growth (in terms of the money income) exaggerate the improvement occurring in the standard of living. In the same way, comparisons between production in an industrial country like the United Kingdom and in a pre-industrial country like China exaggerate the gap between the two if they are made on the basis of monetary transactions. Estimates made by Professor Kuznets show that an apparent ratio of 12:1 between income per head in the United States and in China in the years 1931–1936, on a basis which is supposed already to take account of the greater reliance on subsistence production in China, differences in the cost of living, and so on, falls to a ratio of 7:1 or less if the full implications of the differences in economic structure are worked out[2].

Apart from unpaid services there is another set of economic activities which the economist usually excludes from his reckoning but which we all know to be important. In an industrial community we may not spend much of our time selling what we produce, especially if we can turn over our output to be marketed by others; but we inevitably spend a considerable time, as consumers, in buying. This represents an expenditure of effort not very different from the effort of production, although we may derive positive enjoyment from it just as we may derive enjoyment from our work. If we were completely logical we should deduct from the value of production some allowance for the trouble consumers have to go to in purchasing what is produced. Even if we think that this would be going too far, we should at least refrain from dismissing as unproductive efforts to save consumers trouble by incurring high selling costs through delivery services, advertising, etc. While these may be wasteful they may also be as valuable to consumers as costs incurred inside a factory.

Trade

It is axiomatic that if goods are made for sale there must be trade; production in the economist's sense cannot take place in the absence of trade. The connection between the two is extremely close not only in logic but as a matter of historical experience. It is arguable that the growth of

---

[1] S. Kuznets, *Economic Change* (London, 1954), p. 195.

[2] S. Kuznets, *Economic Change* (London, 1954), p. 189.

trade is a necessary preliminary to the growth of industry and that it is usually the expansion of markets that provides the main impulse to industrial development[1]. The process is one that can be observed at work in underdeveloped economies that are still acquiring commercial experience and have hardly yet begun to dabble in manufacturing. Speaking of West Africa Professor Bauer points out how trade

> promotes the growth of resources. . . . It widens markets and thus promotes specialization and increases production, both of export crops and of produce for local consumption. It serves to bring new commodities to the notice and within the reach of actual or potential producers of cash crops, making it worth their while to produce for sale, and, at the same time, providing a market for these products. This process encourages production and the extension of capacity, more especially the extension of acreage under cash crops. . . . The accumulation of capital and its productive employment are stimulated. . . . Trade also brings into prominence and influence a type of trade-entrepreneur accustomed to the ways of an exchange economy, notably the habitual and systematic use of money[2].

The structure of production

It may convey a more concrete idea of the make-up of economic activity if we look at the different ways in which people earn their living. The universal experience is that less than half the population is 'gainfully employed', i.e., works for money: more than half is not included in the labour force. This larger element is made up of children, students, old people, workers who have retired, married women, the incapacitated, and so on. The labour force includes those who are out of a job as well as those who are in one, whether as employers, self-employed, or employees. In most industrial countries the vast majority of those who constitute the labour force are employees, i.e. work for somebody else. But there are a considerable number of people who are self-employed (farmers, shopkeepers, professional men, etc.) and who may also act as employers.

If we look at the distribution of the labour force between different activities, it becomes clear that even in industrial countries industry plays a

[1] Compare, for example, Paul Mantoux, *The Industrial Revolution in the Eighteenth Century* (London, 1927), p. 93 (quoted by Youngson, *Possibilities of Economic Progress*, Cambridge, 1959, p. 111): 'Sometimes the advancement of industry, by forcing trade to find new outlets, enlarges and multiplies commercial relations. Sometimes, on the other hand, fresh wants, created by the extension of a commercial market, stimulate industrial enterprise. Nowadays, the first case is the more usual. . . . But is not this . . . one of the newest and most original features in the modern factory system? The fact that it is able to anticipate demand, to modify, or even sometimes to create it, is due to its extraordinary adaptability and to the rapid and incessant improvements in its technical equipment. . . . This was not the case with the old industry. Limited both by the slowness of technical improvement, and by the difficulty of communication, production was forcibly confined to the known wants of its habitual market. To manufacture for a clientele of unknown and distant possible consumers would have been considered an act of madness. In short, industry had to be regulated by the condition of trade connections. . . . In those days progress in industry was almost impossible unless it was preceded by some commercial development.'
[2] P. T. Bauer, *West African Trade* (Cambridge, 1954), pp. 28–29.

limited part. The figures in *Table 2.1* bring out the high proportion of employment in services in each of the four countries covered. Services of all kinds (e.g., transport, wholesale and retail trade, entertainment, public administration, education and health services) occupy up to half the working population. Industry, the other major employer, is taken in *Table 2.1* to include building, mining and electric power supply; but many people think of industry as what goes on in factories, i.e. as manufacturing industry. This rarely employs over one-third of the labour force.

TABLE 2.1. Distribution of working population in the United Kingdom, Germany, France and Italy, 1977

	UK	Germany	France	Italy
		(millions)		
Total population in private households	55.0	60.4	50.5	55.1
Labour force				
Employers and self-employed	2.1	2.3	2.7	4.0
Employees	22.1	21.6	17.2	13.3
Family workers	—	0.9	1.1	1.0
Unemployed	1.2	0.7	1.0	0.8
Total	25.4	25.5	22.0	19.1
		(%)		
Labour force as proportion of population over 14 years	58.1	51.3	54.9	44.2
Proportion of labour force:				
working part-time	16.9	9.6	7.3	2.5
with a second job	1.6	1.9	n.a.	2.9
Persons whose main occupation is in:				
Industry	41.5	45.0	37.6	39.5
Services	55.5	49.3	52.6	47.6
Agriculture	2.9	5.7	9.7	12.9

Source: Eurostat: Labour Force Sample Survey 1973, 1975, 1977 (Luxembourg, 1980).

In the United Kingdom the metal and engineering group of industries (including vehicles, shipbuilding, iron and steel, and so on) account for over half the total, with the textile and clothing group a long way behind and of about the same size as the building industry. Among the services, distribution (wholesale and retail trades, hotels, catering, etc.) is a very large employer and almost as many people are engaged in professional and scientific services (health, education, law, accountancy, etc.).

It is a great mistake to think of the factory or the farm as the typical productive unit; a shop, a government office, or a bus depot is just as typical. Even the common notion that industry lies at the centre of a kind of solar system while all other forms of economic activity are held in place like planets by the gravitational pull of industry is difficult to justify. There is some truth in the view that the *location* of factories has a strategic influence on the *location* of service trades, although the line of causation is often the other way round, factories going to the places that are well supplied with services. But there is no truth in the view that economic progress takes place exclusively inside factories while everything else jogs along in parasitic stagnation. Anyone who thinks of rising productivity as if it were purely a phenomenon of manufacturing industry should compare the throughputs of a self-service store and a booth in an Eastern bazaar. It is also not true that manufacturing tends to form a progressively larger proportion of total output; the proportion does increase as a country undergoes industrialization but it may begin to fall later if people spend more of their incomes on services as the standard of living improves. If mechanization were ever carried to the point at which all factories were fully automatic, the only employment they would afford would be like the employment created by a road system – in administration and maintenance.

The distinction between factory and other employments is also a highly misleading one. What do people do in factories? They move things around; they design and organize; they make arrangements to buy and sell; they fit things together or change the shape of materials. All of these things go on in non-industrial jobs. Transport, for example, is one of the most important of non-industrial employments; but there are probably more people whose occupation is to move or transport goods inside factories than are employed in transporting goods outside factories. Similarly, what do people do on farms? In a non-industrial country the mass of the population may appear to be employed in agriculture when half their time is really being taken up with buying, selling and transporting, and they may spend only a few weeks each year at work in the fields.

Business units

Production is organized in units that vary widely in size and complexity. The simplest type of unit is the *establishment*, which is the work-place of a single worker or a group of workers under common direction. A costermonger's barrow is an establishment; so is a shop, garage or hospital. In manufacturing industry the usual establishment is a factory; but some manufacturing establishments – for example, in the clothing trades – are private houses where the only machinery is a handloom or a sewing machine or there may be no more than a pair of knitting needles. A single factory may also house several establishments: under the 'room and power' system, a number of small textile spinners may divide one floor of a factory without so much as a partition between their spinning frames, and pay rent individually to the factory owner. There is an American factory making nuts and bolts that has let space to a cooperage undertaking from which it buys wooden containers for its products. A large American warehouse has gone so far as to form a separate company to acquire and maintain the fork-lift trucks that are used in the warehouse: so that there are two establishments in common ownership within the one building.

An establishment may be the sole place of business of a firm; but many firms own and operate several branches, so that there are fewer firms than establishments. The *firm* is treated in economics as the unit of control, in which decisions are taken about what is to be produced and how it is to be produced. It is the firm that hires labour and land, borrows or invests the necessary capital, purchases raw materials, organizes the process of manufacture, and markets the finished product. A firm may be a one-man show, like a taxi-driver; or a small unincorporated business, like a shopkeeper; or a partnership, like a firm of accountants; or a private company, owned by up to 50 different people; or a public company whose shares are dealt in on the Stock Exchange; or a public corporation running an entire industry, like the National Coal Board. Whatever its size and form of organization,it is a decision-taking unit, and anyone studying production and the behaviour of producers has to start from the firm.

When we say that the firm is a decision-taking unit, we imply that each firm takes decisions independently of other firms (although not without being influenced by their actions). This is not an altogether realistic assumption since there are often links between one firm and another in the form of understandings, agreements to cooperate in various ways, long-established trading relationships, interlocking directorates, common memberships of employers' associations, and so on[1]; this may make it difficult to say where one firm stops and another begins. An even closer association arises when one firm holds a block of another firm's shares; a quite limited holding may give the first firm effective control over the second, and if the holding exceeds 50%, the two firms are best regarded as parts of a single business unit. A *business unit* consists of a group of firms under a single control, although there may be minority holdings in any member of the group.

An *industry* consists of a number of competing firms or business units. The firms may be producing the same commodity (e.g., beer), or working on the same material (e.g., brass), or using the same process (e.g., building). There are thus three quite different bases on which we may group firms together into industries. Naturally this leads to difficulties of classification. Shipbuilding, for example, will be included in the steel industry if we use *materials*, and with building if we use *processes*, as a basis of classification. In practice, we rank shipbuilding as a separate industry, partly because it is big enough to justify the title, partly because its *product* is one in which many firms specialize. The crucial test is the way in which competition is delimited; and it is clear that shipbuilding firms are in active competition with one another, but are isolated from the competition of other firms which use steel or which are engaged in building.

It is exceptional to find all the firms in an industry confining themselves to the same range of products or processes or materials. Firms do not specialize along similar lines, but often compete in several different industries at the same time. A shipbuilding firm, for example, may engage in coal-mining and steel-making. Railways may own hotels, golf courses, and Atlantic liners. It is in a few industries only that firms confine themselves within the boundaries of their trade and are completely segregated from other industries. Again, even when the limits of an

---

[1] For an elaboration of this point see G. B. Richardson, 'The Organization of Industry', *Economic Journal*, September 1972, pp. 882 *et seq*.

industry are clearly defined, there may be little in common between two firms within it. Firms manufacturing buses no more compete with Rolls-Royce than British Airways competes with the Raleigh Cycle Company. Each firm within an industry has its own peculiar style or quality of product, or its own peculiar methods of manufacture, or uses its own peculiar materials. Sometimes these peculiarities are comparatively trifling (e.g., in cotton spinning), but in most industries they are of considerable and increasing importance. They make it very difficult to draw a clear line of division between firms which are in direct competition with one another (e.g., two firms making detergents), and firms between which competition is rather remote (e.g., an oil company and a pharmaceuticals producer). At best, the classification of firms into industries is a rough one.

The public sector

In conditions of private enterprise, most firms are privately owned and managed. Some undertakings however, have to be run by the state; the armed forces are an obvious example. The range of activities conducted by the state varies from country to country and in most countries has been greatly extended over the past generation. As matters stand in Great Britain, the public sector – that is, those economic activities that are conducted by the state or by agencies of the state – includes the nationalized industries, such as coal-mining; public corporations, like the BBC; local government undertakings, for example, municipal transport; the public social services, including education, the national health service, unemployment insurance, old age pensions, etc.; the work of the civil service, both national and local, and of the armed forces; and a large number of miscellaneous activities. About one worker in four is directly employed by the state in one capacity or another.

In these circumstances, it would be misleading to study the workings of the economic system as if it responded exclusively to the operations of private firms. In the past, however, it is on the private sector that the attention of economists has been concentrated. Even now, it is difficult to avoid giving disproportionate attention to the private sector, because the activities of the state have not been submitted to the same kind of systematic analysis as has the working of a system of private enterprise.

There is a sharp antithesis in the principles governing the public and the private sector, wherever the former involves the provision of services free of charge (e.g., education, medical treatment, etc.), or the employment of workers on tasks that yield no product measurable in terms of money (e.g., most of the civil service). There is nothing unique about such services. They are the same in principle as services provided within the family; but they differ fundamentally from the services provided by private industry.

No such antithesis arises, however, where the state is running an industry on commercial lines. An employee of the National Coal Board (which is a nationalized undertaking) might find that the British Petroleum Company (in which the state has a large interest) or Imperial Chemical Industries Limited (which is a private concern) came to decisions in much the same way about much the same things, were run with just as much regard for the public interest, and experienced much the same kind of muddles.

The market

A private firm – and this applies equally to a nationalized undertaking – requires to strike a bargain both with the factors of production which it employs and with the purchasers of its products. For example, it has to bargain with labour about the wages which it will pay, and with its customers about the price which it will charge. These bargains are driven in what is called 'the market'. The market, is should be clearly understood, is not a place – although bargains are still driven about wages at hiring fairs, and about prices on wheat, metal, and other exchanges. The market, in economics, is simply the network of dealings in any factor or product between buyers and sellers. These dealings may be regular and organized, or they may, as in the market in second-hand violins, be spasmodic and unsystematic.

It is round the market in this sense that the economic system under private enterprise revolves. Production is ruled by market requirements: if goods cannot be sold in the market they will cease to be produced. Men's incomes are governed by what 'the market' will offer for their services and for the hire of their capital. The vast impersonal force of the market shapes the environment in which we earn our livelihood: we are free only within limits set by the market. It is the business of the economist to throw light on these limits and to suggest how they may be thrust further back by a proper organization of our resources.

Chapter 3

The factors of production

Productive resources are usually classified by economists under three broad headings into labour, land and capital. The first of these represents human resources; the second, natural resources; and the third, man-made resources.

Factors as physical things

All three factors have a physical existence: they are tangible resources capable of employment for different purposes (or of being left unemployed). The labour force is made up of men and women working either on their own account or for pay; the stock of capital includes the physical assets that have been built up by human effort and thrift in the past – house-property, factories, power stations, railways, machines and so on; land consists of the free gifts of nature which are in human ownership and under human control, such as mineral deposits, forests, and agricultural land. It is not always easy to distinguish man-made from natural resources and for some purposes it is preferable to group them together as the external facilities which assist labour in production.

In any productive activity it is necessary to combine all three factors since land and capital can produce nothing unaided by labour – even if it is only the labour of reaping – and labour can produce nothing without some capital – even if it is only the capital out of which it maintains itself. There is no necessity, however, to combine the factors of production in a fixed way or for fixed purposes; and the business of organizing production, whether in a single establishment or in the whole economy, is largely one of deciding how to combine the factors and to what use to put them. This is a much more complicated business than it sounds since the units that have to be combined are not standard, homogeneous specimens of each factor, each interchangeable with every other unit of the same factor, but individual men and women, individual machines, or individual bits of land. It may suit the economist to adopt a Caesar-like division of the factors into three; but this should not conceal the infinite variety of each factor and the vastness of the jigsaw puzzle into which they are fitted.

Factors as services

It is possible to think of the factors of production in a quite different way: not as physical units but as services or as the sources of productive power. Knowledge, skill, organization, enterprise, and thrift, for example, have been among the most powerful factors in raising productivity and might accordingly be ranked as factors, of production. But while this usage would direct our attention to some of the keys to economic progress, the traditional classification seems preferable. We already take account of thrift when we include capital, since thrift is of no service unless it leads to an addition to the stock of capital. The first three items in the list are all attributes of labour: every worker possesses some knowledge, skill and organizing ability and it is, indeed, these things, the fruit of intelligence and judgement, that distinguish the human factor.

This is a proposition, which, however evident, is inconsistent with any attempt to identify labour with manual labour and the toil and exertion that manual labour frequently involves. Toil and exertion are far more characteristic of machinery, which can work on unremittingly for twenty-four hours a day. Even in agricultural communities it is horses and oxen, and not human brawn, that supply most of the necessary power. Work that does not call for the exercise of intelligence, and is purely mechanical, can (as the word 'mechanical' implies) be taken over by machinery. It may happen, of course, that the machinery is costly to make and operate, or that muscle-power is abundant and cheap, so that men continue to be used for what is literally inhuman work. But the more machinery is improved, and the scarcer brawn becomes relatively to skill and judgement, the more will toil-saving inventions be introduced. Muscle-power and machinery are in direct competition with one another and the one can replace the other. But the work of the human mind cannot be replaced. There are devices which, as we shall see, make a little intelligence and judgement go a long way in modern industry. But there are none which eliminate them completely from business any more than from the rest of life.

In saying all this, we are not assuming that the introduction of machinery is an unqualified good, or that it makes work somehow more 'human'. A man's muscles and imagination, to which machinery frequently gives little scope, are as much a part of him as his intelligence and nerves. When the machine sets the tempo and not the worker, there can be little opportunity for initiative and craftsmanship; and these are things the value of which is not exhausted within working hours. They enrich a man's personality in all his doings, and personality is a far more important product of industry than the goods and services which it is the humble duty of economists to discuss.

If it is judgement rather than toil that is labour's main characteristic, we can draw no sharp line of distinction between the labour of, say, a bus driver and the labour of the director of a bus company. There may not be the same technique of judgement in both jobs. The problems of negotiating a street corner are very different from the problems of negotiating for the purchase of a fleet of new buses. But both require intelligence and judgement. If the skills differ, the ingredients do not. For there can be just as much purposive control, planning, and adaptation of means to ends in driving a bus as in managing a company.

It is for this reason that there is no need to single out organization as a separate factor of production. There may be a number of people who call themselves managers or organizers and have rather more organizing ability or rather more scope for organizing than other workers have. But they are not a class apart. It may not be everyone who organizes *men* in industry, with power to give orders under threat of dismissal. But everyone, be he office boy, labourer, foreman, or works manager, has to organize either men or things. Moreover each worker – and not simply the general manager – will be paid more if his work involves the responsibility of organizing. The greater the skill and judgement he has to show, the more he can expect to earn. Some people draw higher incomes than others for their organizing; but everyone who is not doing completely mechanical work draws *some* income for what is really organizing.

Enterprise as a factor

It is rather more difficult to decide how to treat enterprise. It is clearly not a factor of production in the sense in which labour, land and capital are factors: it is not part of available resources. Yet when we look at the customary classification of the rewards of the factors of production we find a fourfold division into wages, rent, interest and profit and it is natural to expect a parallel and fourfold division of factors. Since profit can be regarded as a reward for enterprise, or successful risk-taking, there is something to be said for elevating enterprise to the apparent vacancy among the factors of production. This has, however, two important drawbacks, the second of which is decisive.

First of all, it is a mistake to associate enterprise with a single factor, capital, since capital is not the only factor that is exposed to risks and is paid for its enterprise. Labour runs risks too: risks, for example, of unemployment, slow promotion or physical injury. The steeplejack and the coal-miner may not risk any capital; but they risk their lives. There are risky occupations as well as risky undertakings; and part of the wages paid in these occupations might be classed as a return for enterprise, in just the same way as part of the return to investors in risky undertakings is classed as a return for enterprise. The peculiarity of capital – and this is the second and decisive point – is that it has usually a riskless alternative, since it is possible to lend one's capital with the virtual certainty that the money will be repaid. Pure interest is, in fact, interest on a debt that is free from any risk of default, and as soon as such a risk enters, the return on capital contains an element of profit as well as interest. This means that we ought to look on interest and profit as a joint return on capital with the element of profit increasing the greater the risk that the capital may be lost, and the element of interest representing the risk-free return that the capital could earn if transferred to some completely safe investment.

Financial assets as a factor

From this point of view, if we feel obliged to add a fourth factor of production, the strongest candidate is money and the whole range of *financial assets* in which we can invest our money: deposits with building societies, insurance policies, government bonds, mortgages, stock exchange securities and so on. These assets take the form of debts or titles to property rather than property itself. For the most part, they yield interest without any significant element of profit; but where the investor is more venturesome and buys shares on the stock exchange he expects to share in the profits of the company in which he has invested.

It is not immediately obvious how the pieces of paper which we call financial assets contribute to the productive process; it certainly cannot be assumed that the issue of more paper, whether in the form of money or securities, will enhance productivity or swell the national income. For present purposes, however, it is sufficient that many of the most important decisions that producers have to take are financial decisions involving the borrowing of money or the purchase or sale of stock exchange securities. Transactions in financial assets have a place in economic organization that can be as important as the place of transactions in physical assets.

Labour

Labour as a factor of production usually means the 'labour force', the group of workers who are either already in employment or are available for employment, given the opportunity. The use of the phrase 'manpower' conveys the same general idea of the human resources available to the economy. The size of the labour force is not fixed, nor is its effectiveness in producing goods and services; it obviously grows as population grows and improves in productive power with education and training.

Population

The size of the labour force is not a simple function of population. A varying proportion of the population is either too old or too young to work or is engaged in household and other duties and does not seek paid employment. In the United Kingdom, for example, the proportion of the population aged 15–64 increased from 59% in 1871 to over 69% in 1939 and has since fallen to about 65%. This means that the population of working age has fluctuated in relation to the population lying outside the age-groups from which most of the labour force is drawn. An important influence on the proportion of working age is the trend in the birth-rate, which fell from about 35 per 1000 in the 1870s to about 15 per 1000 in the 1930s; this resulted in a large reduction in the proportion of children in the population. Another important influence is the increase in expectation of life: in 1870 an Englishman had an expectation of life at birth of 40 years compared with nearly 70 today, and this increase in longevity has gradually raised the proportion of older people in the population. Emigration and immigration can also bring about important changes in age distribution since migrants usually include an abnormal proportion of men and women of working age: when emigration from Britain was at its peak something like half the migrants were aged 20–35 and this outflow tended to lower the relative size of the working population.

In underdeveloped countries where the working life is comparatively short, these considerations can be of special importance. An extension in the expectation of life from 30 to 45 may almost double the effective working life provided it results from a decline in the mortality of adults; and if it is accompanied by greater freedom from sickness and disease, the impact on the effective labour force will be still more pronounced. On the other hand, an increase in the expectation of life from 65 to 75 reflecting a fall in mortality at advanced ages will be unlikely to have any marked effect on the size of the working population. In practice, the experience of underdeveloped and industrial countries is not in such sharp contrast. Medical science has done little for many years to increase the expectation of life at ages above 55–60, while an extension of the average working life continues to swell the labour force in industrial countries; at the same time, the greatest triumphs in public health in underdeveloped countries have been in reducing the high mortality of babies and children and the immediate effect of this has been to raise rather than lower the proportion of dependants to the working population.

Working habits and working hours

The size of the labour force is also affected by changes in working habits. Between 1948 and 1957, for example, a further 1.4 million workers were added to the British labour force at a time when the population of working age showed little change, through the entry (or re-entry) into the labour market of married women and the postponement of their retirement from industry of large numbers of older workers. Both of these changes took place at a time when there was an acute shortage of labour and opportunities of employment were ample.

Another change that lends elasticity to the supply of labour is in working hours. In the nineteenth century, working hours were generally over 60 a week and often 66 or more. The fell progressively to 54 in 1913 and by 1939 were normally 48 or less. A further nominal contraction in hours to 40 in the post-war period has been consistent with the maintenance in most industries of hours of work (including overtime) not very different for the average worker from those of pre-war years. On the other hand, paid holidays have become increasingly common and the length of the holiday period has grown, so that man-hours worked per annum have diminished slightly.

All of these influences on manpower are in the long run subordinate to population growth. The importance of population growth is particularly obvious when it is rapid or when it is taking place in countries suffering from over-population; but even when population is stationary it is still necessary to explain why it is stationary and when there is no evidence of over-population it is still necessary to enquire how one can judge whether a country is over-populated or not. The influence of population growth on economic development is highly important.

The Malthusian theory

All subsequent thinking about population growth has been greatly influenced by the views put forward by the Revd T. R. Malthus in his 'Essay on

Population', the first edition of which appeared in 1798. This was the first scientific attempt to explain how changes in population came about; and although some of his fears and forecasts have since proved mistaken, the situation which he was analysing is not without its modern counterparts. Malthus was writing at a time when the growth of population, hitherto relatively slow, had suddenly accelerated, largely because improvements in personal hygiene, the growth of medical science, and probably also better nourishment, combined to lower the death-rate. This was not quite how it looked to Malthus who was more inclined to stress the influence of earlier marriages and a higher birth-rate. From his point of view the important issue was how the balance between births and deaths was preserved and how it would be re-established if, as a result of a divergence between the two, population started to grow or decline.

The record of earlier centuries is one of remarkable stability. World population is estimated to have doubled between the beginning of the Christian era and the middle of the seventeenth century: this represents a rate of increase of no more than 5% per century. Any divergence between birth- and death-rates must have been, throughout the ages, either almost insignificant or random and the conditions of life such as to perpetuate stability of population. In most countries birth- and death-rates probably varied little until recent times: both were very high by the standards of modern industrialized countries and the expectation of life was comparatively low. Literally half the children died in infancy and those who survived to maturity had to face the risks of disease, famine and war.

Positive checks

Disease, famine and war were Malthus's three 'positive checks' to population growth, their effect being to maintain the death-rate. They were reinforced by 'preventive checks' operating to keep down the birth-rate: postponement of marriage to later ages when fertility is lower, and deliberate birth-control after marriage. The essence of Malthus's argument was that if population growth was not checked by a low birth-rate it would be checked, sooner or later, by a high death-rate brought about by disease, famine and war. These positive checks would come into play because of the failure of the means of subsistence to grow at the same rate as population; only if mankind chose to make use of the preventive checks and regulated its numbers could pressure on the means of subsistence be kept at bay.

The fall in fertility

The acceleration of population growth in the eighteenth century was mainly the result of a sharp fall in the death-rate. This was followed, after an interval, by a drop in the birth-rate, beginning, in Britain, in the 1870s. There is evidence that the decline in fertility, as measured by births per married woman in the fertile age-group, had already turned downwards in the 1850s; and in the United States, where the birth-rate in the eighteenth century was much higher than in Britain (over 50 per 1000 or an average of 8 children per marriage), the decline started much earlier[1]. The decline in

[1] W. H. Grabill, C. V. Kiser, and P. K. Whelpton, *The Fertility of American Women* (New York, 1958), pp. 5, 17.

the birth-rate continued until the 1930s, when it reached 15 per 1000 in Britain and was for some years below 20 per 1000 in the United States. At those levels, less than half what had been customary in earlier centuries, it looked as if equilibrium had been restored between birth- and death-rates, and there was even talk of a declining population in Britain and other countries within a decade or two. However, the long-continued fall in the birth-rate not only came to an end but recovered a little while the death-rate continued its downward trend.

The lag of the birth-rate behind the death-rate caused population to increase: in the two centuries between 1750 and 1950 the population of Britain multiplied nearly sevenfold and throughout almost the entire period grew at a fairly steady rate of about 10% per decade. In other

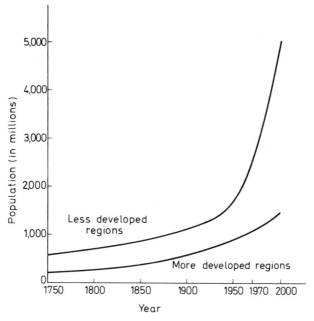

Figure 3.1 Estimated and conjectured size of past and future world population, 1750–2000 A.D., for more developed and less developed regions. Based on figures from *The World Population Situation in 1970* (United Nations, 1971)

countries an even faster rate of growth was recorded: in North America, for example, population grew from about 1 million in 1750 to 25 million in 1850 and 165 million in 1950, and in Latin America from about 10 million in 1750 to 162 million in 1950[1]. These rates of growth were due quite as much to immigration from Europe as to an excess of births over deaths. The United States alone received over 30 million immigrants in the 60 years before 1930.

For the world as a whole no very reliable figures exist. But the best estimates (on which *Figure 3.1* is based) point to a threefold increase in

[1] Estimates quoted from W. F. Willcox and the United Nations in S. Kuznets, 'Population, Income and Capital', in *Economic Progress* (ed. by L. Dupriez, Louvain, 1955).

population between 1750 and 1950 with rather faster rates of increase in the more developed regions (such as Europe and North America) than in the less developed regions such as Africa, Asia and Latin America.

The pattern of births that has emerged throws some light upon the forces that have caused the reduction in the birth-rate. There are now comparatively few large families of six or more children and fewer also of the childless and single-child families that were so common before World War II. A contraction in the number of large families continued in the post-war period whether the birth-rate was falling or rising. In the United States, three 'completed' families in five consist of two, three, or four children whereas families of this size were outnumbered in the 1920s by 'completed' families with one or no children. These facts demonstrate the importance in relation to current trends in the birth-rate of family planning and of the fashionable view of the optimum size of family. But what makes the fashion change? Here is a question that would require a book to itself: we should have to consider the influence on family life of an industrial and urban society, the emancipation of women, the mechanization of the home, the re-direction of acquisitve impulses, and a variety of other circumstances, the relative importance of which varies from one society to another.

Whatever the mechanism by which birth- and death-rates have been brought nearer together, it has not been the mechanism that Malthus feared. There has been no increasing pressure of population in industrial countries, no fall in living standards or return to the previous conditions of disease and undernourishment. On the contrary, if changes in the standard of living have formed part of the mechanism, it has been through their effect on the birth-rate rather than on the death-rate: the effort to maintain or improve their standard of living has made many families regard children as directly competitive with higher consumption and contributed in this way to the fall in the birth-rate. It is also difficult to maintain that the increase in population over the past two hundred years has simply diluted gains in productivity that would otherwise have been shared among fewer people. Part of the tremendous expansion in production that has taken place is directly attributable to the growth in the scale on which the economy functions and the increase in population has made an important contribution to this growth in the scale of operations.

When one looks at what is happening outside the industrial countries, however, Malthus's fears seem more justified. The improvement in public health through the elimination of malaria and other diseases by the systematic application of medical knowledge has had an immediate effect on death-rates far beyond anything previously recorded. There are some countries like Ceylon where the death-rate was reduced by over 50% in less than ten years; in some of the less developed countries the death-rate has fallen within a short period from 20–25 per 1000 to 10 per 1000 or less – rates which obviously cannot be maintained unless everybody lives to over 100. This sharp fall in death-rates has not been accompanied by any parallel reduction in birth-rates and in many parts of the world these remain at levels of 40 or even 50 per 1000 of the population. There is not, as yet, any convincing proof that birth-rates will follow death-rates down, as happened in western countries in the course of industrialization.

Meanwhile population is growing very fast – sometimes at rates of 3% per annum – under the impulse of medical rather than economic improvements, so that, while manpower is abundant, other resources in land and capital are lagging behind. It may be possible to enlarge the resource-base more rapidly in such countries, and to find new jobs and more food for the extra population. But even this will not restore equilibrium unless there is a change in attitudes towards fertility since unless at some point birth-rates start to fall the pressure of population is bound eventually to make itself felt.

Some economists faced with this dilemma argue that if only there is a special effort to make output rise faster than numbers, the resulting improvement in the standard of living will operate as it has done in the past to make people more inclined to limit the size of their family. If the effort fails, peole will have no higher standards at which to aim and will continue to reproduce themselves on a scale that will doom even their existing standard of living. Either the standard of living improves and the pace of population growth slackens or the standard deteriorates and population growth does not slacken. The change for the better or for the worse is cumulative since any slackening in population growth reinforces the improvement in the standard of living. This is an ingenious and plausible view, quite different from Malthus's, but it rests on a hypothesis that is as yet unproven. We cannot assume that fertility is governed in all continents by the forces that have governed it in Europe and North America; different societies entertain quite different ideas about masculinity, the importance of male heirs, the balance of power between husband and wife, and so on. It is also very much of an over-simplification to treat the fall in the birth-rate in Europe and North America as the direct outcome of an improvement in living standards; the mere fact that birth-rates have not fallen continuously but have recovered from their lowest levels during a period of great prosperity should be sufficient to suggest the complexity of motives affecting birth-rates.

Migration

If we turn from birth- and death-rates to migration from one country to another, we need have less hesitation in looking first to economic forces for an explanation. The large-scale inter-continental movements of population in the nineteenth century were dominated by hopes of economic advancement, although fears of racial or political persecution and the desire for a freer life also played their part. The largest movement, that to North America, brought over one million emigrants a year across the Atlantic in the first decade of this century. South America received fewer immigrants, but they formed a higher proportion of the population affected; in the Argentine, for example, the ratio of immigrants to the native-born population reached 30% in 1914[1]. In South-east Asia also, international migration was at its peak in the years before the First World War and some eight million Chinese, for example, were living abroad, chiefly in Malaya, Taiwan and the East Indies.

[1] W. Ashworth, *A Short History of the International Economy* (Longmans, London, 1952), p. 178.

Within countries, the movement of population has been on an even larger scale. In Western Europe, millions left the countryside for the towns during the nineteenth century and this process of urbanization still continues; in the USSR, for example, the urban population grew from less than 30 million (within the present boundaries) in 1926 to 100 million in 1959, while the rural population dropped from about 135 million to 109 million over the same period. In some countries a further shift has taken place into regions previously under-populated and little developed. In the United States, one-third of the population now lives west of the Mississippi where a century or so ago most of the area was thought to be a desert; in the USSR, over 30% of the population lives east of the Urals in an area once thought to be equally inhospitable, and the proportion is increasing rapidly[1].

Influences on labour supply

We have now identified a number of factors influencing the size and growth of the labour force in particular countries or places. It remains to put these various influences in perspective by indicating the order of magnitude of the changes they may produce.

First of all, the ratio of the labour force to total population (or *participation rate*) usually remains fairly stable because some of the factors influencing it offset one another. For example, the tendencies to longer schooling and to earlier retirement are offset by the tendency for married women to take paid employment. In the United Kingdom the labour force has varied over the past century between 68 and 73% of the population of working age and the proportion has never changed in any decade by more than 4% in either direction. Between one year and another, changes in working hours can be of much more importance; even over longer periods such as a decade they are capable of out-weighing all other influences on the effective labour force.

Population growth itself, as we have seen, may reach 3 or even 4% per annum through natural increase alone. Although it would be foolish to speak of a normal rate of increase, past experience suggests that such rates are exceptional and that it is more common for growth through natural increase to be limited to 1–2% per annum. There have been times when immigration has contributed on a similar scale to the growth of population and when emigration has removed over 1% of a country's population annually: annual immigration into Canada, for example, averaged 5% of the population in the years immediately before the First World War; on the other hand, emigration removed at least 1% of the Irish population in nearly every year from 1846 until the end of the nineteenth century. But these are highly unusual rates of migration and the only movements on a similar scale in recent years have been the inflow of Jewish refugees and migrants into Israel and the expulsions of population from central European countries that took place during and after the war. If we are looking to the future and not the past, we are probably safe in treating the balance

---

[1] 'Comparisons of the United States and Soviet Economies' (Joint Economic Committee, Congress of the United States, 1959), Part I, p. 61.

between births and deaths as the principal determinant of long-term changes in the size of a country's labour force.

Population projections

Of these two elements the greatest uncertainty attaches to the birth-rate. It is usually changes in fertility that upset the projections of future population growth made by demographers on the basis of their interpretation of the influences at work. In the United Kingdom, for example, the Government Actuary makes projections annually, in consultation with the Registrars General, of the likely size of the future population of the country, and between 1955 and 1965 increased his estimate for the year 2000 from about 53 million to nearly 75 million; only to bring it down again by 1970 to 66 million (which was not, of course, his last word). In other countries much the same thing happened. The main reason for these large swings in population projections lay in unexpected changes in the trend in births. These changes, and the revisions which they occasioned in the official projections, are illustrated in *Figure 3.2*.

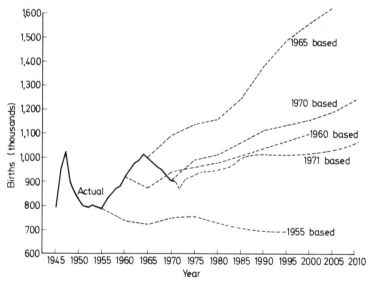

Figure 3.2 Actual and projected live births in the United Kingdom.
Source: *Population Projections No. 2, 1971–2011* (HMSO, 1972)

Whereas in 1955 births were expected to go on falling, the view taken ten years later was that by the end of the century births would have doubled since 1955. Only five years later, this projection had been drastically revised downwards to about half-way between the 1955 and 1965 projections. At the same time the actual level of births was showing a strong downward trend that made the 1970 projection itself open to considerable doubt.

This experience illustrates the difficulty of taking a dogmatic view about the long-term future of population size in an industrial country with reliable data. The difficulty is obviously intensified in less developed countries with inadequate data and much greater scope for large and unexpected variations in fertility[1]. Yet at the same time the growth of population must be of major importance to the economic prospects of such countries: so that the uncertainties faced by demographers are not matters of academic interest only, but affect fundamental issues of economic and social policy throughout the world.

Education and training

The human resources of any community are obviously not a matter of numbers alone; they vary with the capabilities of the working population and these capabilities can be improved by education and training. The importance of education lies partly in making the population literate and partly in making it more open-minded and capable of evolving or profiting from new ideas. Without literacy, the spread of knowledge is slow and many of the clerical, accounting and other tasks that occupy a large proportion of the labour force in an industrial country cannot be performed. The more advantage is taken of technological progress, the higher the level of education required, not only in the technologists themselves but also in those who employ them, or form their staff, or have business dealings of any kind with them. More important still for the mass of the population is the training and experience which it brings to its work. The complex tasks of modern industry frequently require relatively little formal education, but they presuppose a skill and competence that rest on thorough familiarity with the quirks and snags of the job, and on a social background in which there is both the incentive and the opportunity to pick up the necessary knowledge. All this may seem platitudinous in a country like Great Britain; but in a pre-industrial country with a low standard of living and a high rate of illiteracy, the problem of enlarging the experience and raising the level of skill of the working population is overwhelming.

Labour organization

Labour differs from the other two factors of production in the simple fact of its humanity. It is not a mere instrument of production but the mass of citizens engaged in their daily work. These are the same citizens who, in a different capacity, elect the government of their country and enjoy democratic rights to pronounce on the laws which they are expected to obey. They are, therefore, in a position to change the institutional framework within which they work and to lay down conditions that all employers (whether private firms or public corporations) must observe. As workers, they also show ordinary human reactions both towards one another and towards their employers. They are afraid of redundancy and unemployment; anxious to strengthen their bargaining power and improve their working conditions; jealous of any privileges they enjoy; proud of their skill; sensitive to encouragement and approval; moved by the desire

---

[1] Japanese experience is no doubt exceptional. But the fall in the Japanese birth-rate from 34 per 1000 in 1947 to 17 per 1000 in 1957 shows what *can* happen.

to stand well with their fellows. How they exert themselves depends on many complex factors as well as on the pay they receive: on the interest they take in their work, the notions of social justice they entertain, the accepted norms of effort, the need to maintain solidarity with other workers.

It is not possible, therefore, to treat labour as a mere aggregation of units or to confine an analysis of the supply of labour to the responses that follow changes in population or in pay. It is necessary also to take account of the influences governing industrial relations within the individual establishment and in the economy at large. It is also necessary to take account of the influence of workers' organizations – for example, of shop stewards and trade unions – because these organizations (and the corresponding organizations of employers) not only affect the terms on which labour is employed but help to shape industrial relations and are the agencies through which the pressures on both sides of the labour market tend to make themselves felt.

Land

Land as a factor of production has lost much of its former importance. In the days before the Industrial Revolution, perhaps two-thirds of the workers of Britain were employed in agriculture, against less than a twentieth at present. The owners of agricultural land drew in rent over a fifth of the total income of the country, whereas nowadays the proportion is barely 1%. A corresponding change has come over economic theory. The discussions of rent which fill the pages of Adam Smith and John Stuart Mill have dwindled sadly in the modern textbook.

What resources do we include in land? Generally speaking, all the free gifts of nature which yield an income: agricultural and building land, mines, fisheries, etc. We do not include sunshine, rain, and other natural agents, which assist in production, since these are not in anyone's ownership and control. They are resources over which we have no power of disposal, and which, therefore, we cannot economize.

Characteristics of land

(a) Fixity of supply

The characteristic of land on which economists have laid most emphasis is the fixity of its supply. Coastal erosion and flooding may reduce somewhat the land surface of the globe, while slight additions may be made through exploration, discovery, or the building of dykes. But broadly speaking, and with the possible exception of mineral deposits, no great change in the supply is likely to take place. If, however, we are thinking of fertile, cultivable, land this is much less true. Erosion, for instance, can lay waste millions of acres of arable land. Continuous cropping, neglect, and ignorance can all reduce the fertility of the surface soil. On the other hand, fertility can be increased by laying out capital on land improvement. Reclamation, drainage, manuring, irrigation – even afforestation – can make available a larger supply of cultivable land. Rich crops of cotton can be grown on land where sagebrush and cactus were once hard put to it to survive. It might seem, therefore, that to say that our land resources are fixed in supply is exaggerating a little. Fertility can be used up and it can be increased. There are no 'original and indestructible powers of the soil', or if there are, it is impossible to disentangle them from the powers which capital expenditure on land improvement has created.

From this it is an easy step to the conclusion that there is no fundamental difference between land and capital, and that there is no need to classify them as separate factors of production. Land, it is sometimes argued, is simply a piece of property with a very long life, and of a sort not easily added to. There is no need to separate it too rigidly from other pieces of property by pretending that it can never wear out and never be added to. Its supply is not rigidly fixed, but it takes an unusually long time for an increase or decrease to take place.

All this is true if by land we mean cultivable land, or simply fertility. But when a farmer uses land (and still more when a builder does) he has the use not only of the powers of the soil (indestructible or not) but also of a given area which enjoys an annuity of air, sunshine and rain and is in his exclusive occupation. Fertility can be changed by the farmer, but climate and situation cannot. We can improve site values, but we cannot multiply the sites themselves. As for mineral deposits, it is quite plain that we can do nothing to increase the supply, although we can do a great deal to make the supply more accessible (e.g., by prospecting, sinking shafts, building railways, etc.).

Thus in land as we find it there are two elements which in practice can rarely be separated, but in theory always. One is variable and the product of human effort, and one is constant and the gift of nature. It is the constant element – the advantages of climate, aspect, situation, etc., that come from the exclusive ownership and use of a site or of mineral deposits – which constitutes land.

It is this theoretical distinction which has led economists to treat land as a separate factor of production. But even if the distinction had never been drawn, it would almost have been necessary to invent some imaginary factor to take the place of land – a factor which, like land, would have been fixed in supply. In economics, we frequently have to distinguish between resources which are strictly limited in supply over the interval of time under discussion (e.g., machinery and plant) and resources which can readily be varied (e.g., semi-finished goods, labour, etc.). The first set of resources raises problems very similar to those raised by the use of land, and it is useful to be able to apply the theory that has already been worked out in connection with land.

To take a simple example. An important corollary of the fact that land is fixed in supply is that the owners of land are in a position of monopoly. They have exclusive use of resources without which our most urgent wants cannot be met. If those wants become more urgent (for instance, because population increases and more people have to be fed), no new land resources can be created to supplement the old, and landowners are put in a position to hold society up to ransom by charging higher rents. They profit, not because they have performed some additional service to the community, but because they happen to own resources which have become scarcer relatively to the community's need of them. They will continue to profit because the scarcity of land cannot be relieved by setting men to work to make more of it.

All this is true, not just of land, but of anything that is fixed in supply. If, for instance, there is a sudden, but sustained, demand for steel from the shipbuilding or automobile or construction industries, it will be impossible to expand the capacity of the steel industry for some time. Until new furnaces and rolling-mills come into production, the owners of the existing steel plants are in the same position of advantage as landowners faced with a rising demand for land. They may raise their price to the higher level which the market will bear, and reap an extra profit without extra effort. But theirs is not a continuing advantage, for the scarcity of steel can be overcome. After a time, high profits will encourage the construction of new steel-making plant, which will enter into competition with the old and bring down prices and profits. In the long run, the supply of plant can always be increased: high profits, therefore, tend to be self-extinguishing. But even in the long run, the supply of land cannot be increased: high rents, therefore, may continue indefinitely.

(b) No cost of production

A second characteristic of land is that it has no cost in production. No one paid a penny to have it created, and it costs no one a penny in actual outlay to allow it to be used. It is already in existence and awaiting employment. In this it differs from both labour and capital. Labour has to be reared – a troublesome and costly business – and does not offer itself for employment without a struggle; there are sacrifices to be borne by the parents of a worker in bringing him up and by the worker himself in seeking employment rather than yielding to the attractions of leisure. Similarly, capital has to be built up out of savings – which for most people means a sacrifice of present enjoyment. It is not, like land, indestructible, and can be used up and not replaced if the return to investment is not satisfactory. Thus while the provision of labour and capital is costly – in he sense that it puts us to some sacrifice either of leisure or of present enjoyment – there is no cost, no sacrifice of some desirable alternative, in providing land. The land is there for the owner to make the best of it, but labour and capital are not 'there'. How much of them exists depends largely on what they are paid, not on nature's bounty. We are not committed to saving some given sum, or working for so many weeks, or days, or hours at some fixed speed, irrespective of the efforts and sacrifices involved. We count the cost of working and saving. But the productive power of land is not of our making and puts us to no cost. If we choose to improve this productive power by sinking capital in land, then such man-made fertility has, of course, a cost of production. But naturally fertility and the advantages of climate and situation possessed by any particular piece of land have no cost of production.

From this it follows that an increase in land values must represent an increase in the wealth of individual landowners without the performance of any equivalent service on their part, unless the rise is due to the sinking of capital in improvements. On the other hand, a fall in land values represents a windfall loss to landowners with no offsetting gain. Generally, with an increasing population, we expect to see land values moving upwards. In ninetenth-century Britain, however, land values remained remarkably steady (taking agricultural land only). This must be set down to the opening up of vast tracts of land in America and elsewhere, and the consequent damping down of the pressure on British land. The land of the New World came into competition with the land of the Old, drawing off large numbers of emigrants, and sending back supplies of foodstuffs which, instead of becoming increasingly dear, became increasingly cheap. Nevertheless the fear remained that the needs of an increasing population would eventually force up land values and deposit an 'unearned increment' in the lap of British landlords. As for *urban* land values, they rose steadily as the towns grew in size, and there was never any doubt that the fortunate owners of sites in and around the towns were enjoying a substantial 'unearned increment'.

The fact that it costs nothing to supply land (as contrasted with the cost of labouring or saving) leads to a second important conclusion. For if it costs nothing to supply land, nothing is gained by making no use of it. Hence if the choice lies between letting land for an almost nominal rent and not letting it at all, it will pay to let it. The rent will be fixed by what the market will bear, not by cost, for the reason that there is no cost. It will always pay to obtain from land whatever income it will bring in, over and above the expense of farming it. Where land is not used for any purpose, it is presumably because it is too inferior in fertility or in situation to yield a surplus above the cost of farming it[1].

This reasoning can be extended to any productive agent where nothing is gained by failure to make use of it. A piece of machinery, for example, may depreciate no more rapidly when in use than when idle. If so, the real cost of using it (the sacrifice to which its owner is put) is nil, and it will pay to keep it in use so long as operating costs are covered. It is true that, unlike a piece of land, the machine costs something to produce, that the owner has hopes of recovering this 'sunk' cost, and that, if he does not, he will be unlikely to replace the machine when it wears out. But his past hopes and present chances are two different things. The cost of producing the machine has little connection with the cost of using it. The first was incurred long ago, and in economics one of the most important principles is that 'bygones are forever bygones'. The second is the cost of efforts and sacrifices which people are induced to make *now*; and the use of the machine involves no sacrifice whatever. The cost of using it is nil. We have here one more example of the analogy drawn above between land and durable capital.

(c) Heterogeneity

A third characteristic of land is its heterogeneity. No two pieces of land are exactly alike in fertility or in situation. Some are highly fertile and situated

---

[1] In the real world, where agricultural land depreciates when not in use (e.g., because it becomes overgrown with weeds) the reasoning given above is reinforced. It is doubly important to find a user for land if capital is lost as well as no rent is earned when the land lies idle.

near large urban markets, while some are on mountain tops and miles from anywhere. It is possible to arrange each piece of ground (or each deposit of minerals or each fishery) in descending order of value, ranging from those which it would pay to use in almost any circumstances to those which are unlikely ever to be used at all. We might have Manhattan Island at one end of the list and the South Pole at the other. A line can be drawn somewhere on the list between pieces of land which repay cultivation and those which do not; between pieces which are worth building on and pieces which are not; between deposits which can profitably be mined and deposits which can not; and between fisheries which it does and does not pay to exploit. This line is generally referred to as *the margin*. Land for which there is no remunerative use of any kind is called 'sub-marginal'; land which it is just worth while to cultivate is said to be 'on the margin of cultivation'; and land which yields a substantial surplus above farming costs is described as 'intra-marginal'. The margin, or line of division, is not, of course, fixed. It is pushed outwards, so as to include land that was formerly sub-marginal, if, for example, population increases and the demand for foodstuffs becomes more pressing. Or if, to take the opposite case, population falls,or people eat less food, or larger crops can be grown on the existing area under cultivation, the margin will press inwards and more land will pass into the sub-marginal, unused class. Similarly with mining. A fall in mining costs, for example, will bring pits which were previously uneconomic above the margin, while a rise in costs will force some pits over the margin into idleness, becuse mining operations have ceased to be worth while on the thinnest seams, or leanest ores, or deepest deposits, or in the most gaseous or flooded pits.

The margin of cultivation divides land which yields a surplus over costs of cultivation in any use (no matter what), from land which cannot be made to yield a surplus in any use whatever. A second kind of margin, the margin of transference, divides land which it pays to use for one purpose (e.g., dairy-farming) from land which it pays to use for another (e.g., cattle-rearing). We can range land used for dairying and cattle-rearing in order of what one may call 'relative suitability' for dairying, at current prices of milk and store cattle and at current levels of farming costs. There will be some land (e.g., rich pasture or land near the towns) for which dairying can easily outbid cattle-rearing. There will also be some land (e.g. hill-grazings and land in rather inaccessible places) where the advantage clearly lies with cattle-rearing. Land intermediate between these types can be allotted with more difficulty, and may pass from one use to the other, crossing and re-crossing the margin of transference, as milk prices rise or fall relatively to cattle prices. Land near to the margin of transference may be relatively well-suited to both dairying and cattle-rearing (and pay a high rent), or relatively ill-suited (and pay a low rent). The main point is that the pull on both sides, whether strong or weak, is roughly equal. If the pull of one side is strengthened (e.g., by a rise in the price of milk) more land is transferred across the margin, and a new margin, at which the pull on both sides balances again, comes into existence.

The third characteristic of land is one shared in by all the factors. The conception of the margin, which derives from this characteristic, can be applied, therefore, to labour and capital as well as to land. If pieces of land

are different from one another, so are workers and their tools. If there are
marginal tracts of sheep-land, there are also marginal shepherds and
marginal sheep. There is no conception in modern economics of which
such extensive use is made, or which is so fundamental to an understanding
of the subject, as the conception of the margin. We shall meet with it in
many forms from now on.

The law of diminishing returns

Reflection on the characteristics of land gave use, about 150 years ago, one
of the most famous of economic laws – the law of diminishing returns:

> Successive applications of labour and capital to a given area of land must
> ultimately, other things remaining the same, yield a less than proportion-
> ate increase in produce.

This 'law' is simply a generalization based on experience. If the law were
not true, if by doubling his outlay on labour and capital a farmer could
double his produce, every farmer could save nearly the whole of his rent by
giving up all but a small piece of his land and concentrating all his labour
and capital upon that piece. Instead of spending £10 on each of 50 acres, he
could multiply his outlay fiftyfold on a single acre and still grow as much as
before. Similarly there would be no point in having large herds of cattle if
every addition to the feeding stuffs increased the weight of the cattle at a
steady rate, without limit. A single bullock would supply the nation. But
the bullock, in point of fact, responds with constant or increasing returns
only if he has been half-starved, and with rapidly diminishing returns if he
has not.

A farmer may, *for a time*, work under increasing returns (that is,
additions to his outlay on labour and capital may yield a *more* than
proportionate increase in product). It may happen for example, that he
spreads his work over so large an area that he would gain by concentrating
his labour and capital on a smaller space. This may be the result of bad
organization; he may, for example, be sowing so lightly that his crops are
smothered by weeds. But it may also in the short run be due to the inability
of the farmer either to use less land or more capital. His land may, for
example, be understocked, in the sense that if he could raise the necessary
capital he could feed a larger herd of cattle and obtain a larger return per
pound of capital invested. In the same circumstances it would pay the
farmer to use less land (and so save rent) but the terms of his lease may
make this (for the time being) impossible.

Other things, too, must remain the same. The return to labour and
capital per acre of land may be raised and the law of diminishing returns
suspended if some new discovery makes land more fertile, or if, because
farmers are better trained or more skilled, they are able to put capital to a
better use than their less efficient predecessors. Fertilizers can treble the
weight of wheat crops: new brands of sugar can yield six times as much as
the old: new feeding stuffs can fatten cattle to weights undreamt of 200
years ago. But once a discovery has been made the law reasserts itself. At
Rothamsted wheat was grown on five plots, one receiving mineral manure
alone and each of the others various 'doses' of nitrogen. One dose of

nitrogen increased the yield by 10.3 bushels, a double dose by 19.4 bushels, three doses by 21.3 bushels and four doses by 21.8 bushels. The successive increments of nitrogen therefore conformed to the law of diminishing returns by yielding diminishing increments of product.

Many of these propositions can be more readily understood with the help of a diagram. In *Figure 3.3*, units of labour and capital applied to, let us say, an acre of land are plotted on the X-axis and the increments in product yielded by each successive unit of labour and capital are plotted

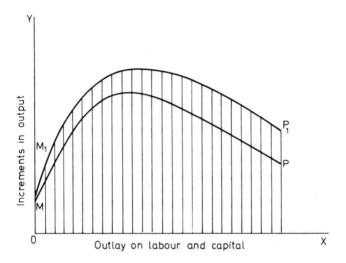

Figure 3.3 The law of diminishing returns

along the Y-axis. The total crop is represented by the sum of the increments, i.e., by the total area under the curve MP. At first, there are likely to be increasing returns: if twice as much labour and capital is used, the crop will more than double. Later, there will be decreasing returns: the increments (represented by strips of constant width) will become smaller and smaller. If an improved type of fertilizer comes on the market, the productivity of the soil will be increased, and the curve of productivity will rise from the position MP to the position M_1P_1. If labour and capital become scarcer and costlier, the distance along the X-axis which we will move for each £1 spent will shorten (i.e., the strips will be narrower) and the same crop will now cost more to grow. It will be observed that *Figure 3.3* shows actual quantities of product and not the cash value of these yields.

A tendency to decreasing returns is generally associated with a tendency to increasing cost. If equal applications of labour and capital yield diminishing increments of product, then each successive increment will be increasingly costly. The fifth pound's worth of fertilizer may add two bushels to the yield of an acre of wheat while the tenth pound's worth adds only one bushel. The cost of an extra bushel, therefore, will rise from 50p to £1 as cultivation becomes more intensive. In other words, the greater the quantity of foodstuffs which we try to raise on a given area of land, the more costly will these foodstuffs be. It is this conclusion, so enormously important to a country with a rapidly increasing population, that has made the law of diminishing returns so celebrated.

For a clear understanding of the laws of diminishing returns and increasing cost, it is essential to keep two points in mind. First, the laws have nothing whatever to do with *profits*. They relate only to cost, or to returns in the sense of physical product. In discussing the laws, our attention is concentrated on the production of goods without bothering about the price which the goods will fetch. Secondly, the laws do not tell us what will in fact happen to costs if output increases over a period of years. The cost of manufacturing a commodity may be falling steadily because of inventions, discoveries, and so on. But these influences are excluded by the clause 'other things remaining the same'. The fact that the cost of growing wheat *is becoming* less, or *will be* less ten years from now, is irrelevant to the question whether, under present circumstances and using existing methods of cultivation, wheat is being produced at increasing cost or not. If each additional bushel costs more to produce, other things remaining the same, then, whatever does happen or has happened in wheat-farming, the law of increasing cost is in operation.

Capital

When we speak of our capital we include two different things: our property (i.e., our goods and chattels and any business property we own) and our financial assets (including cash in hand and titles to wealth such as stocks and shares). Let us take these in turn.

Physical assets

Property or physical capital consists of a stock of assets possessing a money value. In the narrow sense of trade capital, it includes only assets in the hands of producers; in the broad sense, it becomes co-extensive with social wealth, and includes assets in the hands of consumers (dwelling-houses, motor cars, etc.) or belonging to the community.

Trade capital consists of the fixed instruments of production (buildings, ships, machinery, etc.), goods in process, and stocks of finished goods. The last two items are classed together as working capital, while the first is called fixed capital. The line of division is easily drawn, since fixed capital is not used up in a single use, whereas working capital is.

Social capital is something rather broader. It includes not only trade capital, but also non-commercial assets that possess a money value. These are productive resources equally with trade capital, since they have been accumulated with a view to satisfying human wants. We cannot, for example, rule out house-property from capital; for it is just as indispensable to meeting some of our wants as are railway carriages or blast furnaces to meeting others. Nor can we draw a satisfactory line of division between houses let to tenants, and bringing in an income of profit to their owner, and houses retained by owners for their own use and supplying them with shelter which would otherwise have to be bought.

The distinction between social capital and wealth is one of standpoint. Capital is an agent in *production*: it represents resources that can be used in the future. Wealth is a fund upon which we can draw in *consumption*: it represents stored up facilities for the satisfaction of future wants. But what are 'resources' to the producer are 'facilities' to the consumer. No one distinguishes as a private citizen between his capital and his wealth, except when speaking of his stock-in-trade (i.e., of trade capital). For society as a whole, the same identity exists so long as we think consistently of wealth and capital in real terms as a stock of assets, and ignore debts altogether.

Arguments about physical capital very often assume that it consists mainly of machinery used in factories. This assumption is, however, quite false. There is usually far more capital sunk in a country's house-property than in all the machinery used in its factories and mines. It is in buildings (including factory buildings, shops, etc.), in transport (roads, railways, ships, etc.), and in public utilities (gas, water, electricity, harbours and docks, etc.) that by far the largest proportion of a country's capital is invested.

Financial assets

(a) Money

So accustomed are we to include money in our capital that we do not always distinguish carefully between money and capital. The terms, in everyday speech, are used interchangeably. For instance, we speak of a millionaire 'leaving a great deal of money'. No doubt, by *our* standards, he did leave a fair amount of cash to his heirs. But his legacies probably consisted in the main of valuable property or of stocks and shares and other titles to wealth. Capital can always be given a money valuation. But there is a difference between reckoning capital in terms of money, and using the terms 'capital' (or 'wealth') and 'money' to mean the same thing.

When we seek to increase our capital, we do so firstly by adding to our stock of money. Normally it is money that we save and money that we borrow. Often, therefore, we talk loosely of wanting more money when what we really want is more capital. We want more money, not simply for ourselves, but, in our patriotic moods, for the whole country. We believe – quite mistakenly – that what is true for each of us must be true for all taken together, and that everyone would be better off if there were more money in the country. If there were more *capital* in the country, there would be a real gain to the community. But an increase in the stock of money would not, of itself, increase the stock of capital one iota. An increase in the supply of money – as David Hume argued two centuries ago – simply makes money less scarce and, therefore, less valuable. As the increased supply circulates, prices are driven up and money loses purchasing power. To be at pains to increase the supply of money (at any rate in good times) is rather like forcing food on a thin man who is already well-fed. Instead of making him fatter, you simply ruin his digestion.

The fact is that *any* stock of money will do to let the business of the world be transacted if prices and incomes are in line with the existing supply. An increase in the total stock is of service to the community only in special circumstances, whereas an increase in a person's stock of money is of service to him at any time. Money is capital to a person because it represents liquid resources which he can turn into concrete capital whenever he chooses. Money is not capital from the social point of view because society cannot use it to increase its stock of concrete capital, any more than Robinson Crusoe could have done so. Unlike a person, society cannot dispose of its money. A single country, however, can dispose of its gold holdings (and sometimes of part of its currency) to other countries, and might fairly treat its gold reserve as capital.

The confusion of money with capital and wealth might seem too crude to have played much part in history. But when we study the history of trade policy, we find that for centuries statesmen defended a policy of tariffs and trade restriction by arguments built on this confusion. They passed laws prohibiting the export of good English money under penalty of death. They took measures (such as tariffs on imports, and bounties on exports) to preserve a favourable balance of trade with foreign countries, and to force them to pay in treasure for the balance of their purchases. They believed, with Thomas Mun – an economist of the seventeenth century – that 'the ordinary means to increase our wealth and treasure is by foreign trade, wherein we must ever observe this rule: to sell more to strangers yearly than we consume of theirs in value'. This balance of trade doctrine chimed with the intense nationalism of the period – as it still does – and issued in beggar-my-neighbour policies which were designed to increase our stock of the precious metals and deprive other countries of theirs.

We have seen that money is not a factor of production in the sense that it forms part of our productive resources. And yet it is clear that money is constantly being converted into the concrete capital which does form part of our resources, and that concrete capital is always convertible and is constantly being converted into money. A manufacturer borrows money with which to build his factory (i.e., he converts money into concrete capital). A shopkeeper tries to sell his stock as fast as he can for money, with which he then buys more stock (i.e., he turns concrete capital into money and back again). A great many decisions about capital, therefore (e.g., whether we will add to it, whether we will hold it in a liquid form, and so on), are to all appearances decisions about money. In fact, however, they are really decisions about how we will use our real resources. Our decisions to save and invest money are decisions about how much concrete capital there is to be, and what form it is to take. So long as we hold money, we can dictate whether resources will be used to meet our immediate wants (e.g., by spending the money on opera seats) or whether they will be used in order to make an addition to our stock of capital assets (e.g., by investing the money in a new house). We have 'free' capital at our disposal. Once invested, however, capital ceases to be 'free'. It is sunk in a real asset like a house, and can only be 'recovered' (as money – or 'free' capital with its power of dispoal over liquid resources) as the assets wears out and the funds sets aside annually to cover depreciation mount up to the sum needed in order to replace it.

To make all this clearer, let us see in more detail what is happening beneath the veil of money when we decide to save. First of all, we refrain from spending money on services (e.g., on rail fares, cinema tickets, etc.)

or on goods for immediate consumption (food, clothing, etc.) – that is, on what are called 'consumption goods'. This means that we refrain from buying the services of those who make these goods. If we cut out buying chocolate, we deprive of a job the men, machines, and land which formerly supplied our want for chocolate. The first effect of saving, therefore, is to cause unemployment. Or, if as much chocolate as before is produced, stocks of unsold chocolate will accumulate, or will be disposed of only at unremunerative prices which impoverish the producer; neither of these things can go on indefinitely.

If, however, our savings are borrowed and expended on capital extensions, the borrower draws into employment men, machines, and land, paying out of our savings for the building of 'capital goods' (factories, machinery, houses, etc.). Thus a boom in the capital goods industries accompanies and balances a slump in the consumption goods industries. Saving throws butchers and bakers and chocolate-makers out of work; investment creates employment for bricklayers, riveters, engineers, etc. The savers accumulate claims to the services of the factors of production; the borrowers exercise these claims. The transfer of money from savers to borrowers is a transfer of claims on productive resources. Moreover if the claims are not exercised *pari passu* with their accumulation, the savings have been wasted. The whole purpose of saving is to release productive resources from the task of meeting our day-to-day wants in order to undertake the more important task of enlarging our stock of capital equipment. To save is to spare productive power; and if that productive power is not utilized when the saving is done, it does not survive to be utilized later.

It is not just when savings are running to waste that the goods 'saved' are not produced. As savings increase, a change comes over the organization of the labour force, so that more men are employed in the capital goods industries and fewer in the consumption goods industries. *Current* saving permits an addition to be made to concrete capital. Hence men work on new factories, new roads, new ships, new machines, etc. *Past* saving has accumulated a huge stock of concrete capital, which has constantly to be repaired and replaced. Hence new factories and roads and ships are needed because the old ones are wearing out; while an increasing number of men are engaged as engineers, plumbers, masons, roadmenders, etc., in maintaining the existing stock in working order. Production becomes more 'roundabout'. Instead of setting about making goods directly, men are called upon more and more to make goods to make the goods, or even to make goods to make the goods which make the goods – and so on, much as in the House that Jack Built.

(b) Securities

When money is lent, the burden of finding an outlet for savings in productive enterprise is transferred to the borrower. It is he who builds and owns the real asset that is added to our stock of capital. The lender retains only an expression of debt, a title to wealth, from which he expects to derive an income. Debentures or bonds, for example, will be added to his capital, while the companies to which he has lent build new factories or install more machinery. If we are thinking of capital as a factor of production we should include the machinery and the factories and exclude the bonds. But if we are thinking of capital, as we often do, as anything that yields us an income, debts will interest us just as much as real capital. If it were true that capital always yielded an income because it was a productive agent, then it would be easy to reconcile the two points of view. The income yielded by debts would be exactly equal to the productivity of the corresponding assets, and it would make little difference whether we regarded capital as income-yielding or as income-creating. But, in fact, debts are often unchanged when the value of the assets changes, or when the assets (like the munitions on which a large part of the national debt was expended) have been blown to smithereens.

What applies to bonds applies also to other titles to wealth. The buyer of shares in a public company, for example, becomes one of the owners of the company and of its assets and expects his investments to yield him an income. He retains a piece of paper in the form of a share certificate, and the expectation of dividends. Corresponding to the paper and the expectation is the property of the company, which may or may not yield a profit and allow dividends to be paid.

The factors of production and productivity

When production increases, it may be because of an increase in the quantity of productive resources employed or because of an increase in their productivity: that is, in output per unit of labour, land and capital. It makes a great difference which is the cause of the growth in production, since on this depends whether the increased output has to be shared between a constant or a larger number of units of the factors of production. If there is no improvement in productivity, the only ways in which the standard of living of the population can be raised are through the provision of fuller employment for the available manpower or through an expansion in the supply of the other two factors of production, land and capital. Indeed, if manpower outstrips these two factors, for example because of population growth, the effect may be a fall in output per head and so in the standard of living because some of the additional manpower may be left unemployed or because the failure of land and capital to increase proportionately brings into play the law of diminishing returns: land and capital may operate as bottlenecks as the economy expands. The more common situation is one in which capital grows faster than manpower but land remains relatively fixed. This might produce a gradual improvement in production per head, especially if capital could be used as a substitute for land (for example, through the use of fertilizers); but it could not bring about the rapid improvement that has in fact occurred over the past century or two. For an explanation of this improvement, we must look to the influences governing productivity, and particularly to the effects of scientific and technical progress.

In this chapter, it has been the supply of the factors of production that we have discussed, not their productivity. In the next few chapters we shall take the supply of the factors for granted and look at some of the influences on the efficiency with which they are used. We can observe those influences most clearly in the individual units, or firms, in which production is carried on; it is to the ways in which production is organized in such units that we now turn.

Part II

Industrial organization

Chapter 4

Growth, transformation and development

It would be possible to analyse the organization of industry in pure static terms as if the object of industrial activity were to organize a constant stock of resources so as to satisfy fixed wants by unchanging methods. Such an analysis would obviously be a travesty in any modern economy where resources, wants and methods of production are always changing and where the facts of economic growth and development dominate the environment within which production is carried on. Before we embark on a discussion of industrial organization, therefore, we must sketch, however briefly, the more important of those facts and the more obvious of their implications.

In a growing economy a great many things increase simultaneously. There is usually more labour, more capital, more trade, a higher standard of living, and so on. These purely quantitative changes we may call *growth*. Everything does not – indeed, could not – increase equally, so that different parts of the economy show different rates of expansion and some parts may even have to contract. The structure of the economy has thus constantly to be adapted in order to restore balance between the different elements in it. This process of structural adjustment we may call *transformation*. In addition, the process of growth gives rise to new situations of a different kind: new attitudes emerge, new techniques are discovered and new institutions are organized. These are changes in the things that shape economic activity; they are reflected in the economic magnitudes that register growth but they are themselves essentially qualitative. We shall refer to these elements of novelty as *development*.

Growth

We may begin by indicating the changes in some of the more important magnitudes to which we have just referred, leaving aside, until we come to the discussion on development, the causes of those changes.

1. First of all, total output grows progressively except in periods of intense slump. This expansion in output brings with it a parallel expansion in incomes and purchasing power, since the more a country produces the richer it is, and there is a corresponding growth in the size of the market.

2. Secondly, the increase in production is usually accompanied by, and is partly due to, an increase in population, so that output per head rises more slowly than total production. In some countries the increase in production may be exceeded by the growth of population so that output per head actually falls (see 6 below).

3. The increase in production usually requires a more or less proportionate increase in the stock of capital. The accumulation of the additional capital is facilitated by the growth of production, especially if production out-distances population and so leaves a larger surplus from which savings can be made.

4. There is in most countries a steady improvement in productivity, i.e. in the efficiency with which productive resources are used. This improvement, together with the growth of capital, is the source of a rise in output per head. It is not easy to measure the change in productivity but the growth of output per man-hour serves as a rough guide. Strictly speaking, this measures the gain in productivity only in relation to the input of labour, without reference to the input of capital. If capital keeps pace with production, the change in output per man-hour exaggerates the rate of improvement in productivity per unit of labour and capital, but it serves as an accurate index both of the direction in which productivity is moving and of any acceleration that is taking place in the movement of productivity.

5. The growth in productivity, measured in this way, normally yields a rather slower increase in output per head, a contraction in hours of work absorbing some of the gains from higher productivity. This increase in output per head brings with it an equal increase in income per head since, as we shall see[1], output and income are really the same thing seen from two different angles. Income per head is the index used by economists to measure changes in the standard of living (although they recognize that it is not always a trustworthy index and never a complete one)[2]. Rising productivity and a rising standard of living, therefore, go together.

6. Although growth is normally accompanied by higher productivity, there is nothing automatic about the association between the two. It would be possible for labour and capital to grow in such a way that each new factory duplicated existing ones, leaving output per head and per man-hour unaffected. The growth of population might also bring the law of diminishing returns into play by producing a growing shortage of land and natural resources. This would cause output per head to *fall* in

---

[1] See pp. 277 *et seq.*

[2] There are special circumstances such as war-time when a large increase in output per head may be absorbed by the state without any improvement in the standard of living. There are also major changes in conditions of life which may not show up either in total production or in income per head. For example, hours of work in Britain have contracted by about one-third over the past century; working conditions are very much better; people are healthier and have a far greater chance of surviving to old age. The improvement in health and education, in security from misfortune and in access to common enjoyments, is not adequately measured by the income expended on the social services that provide them. On the other hand, part of the rise in income per head might be regarded as offsetting some of the inconveniences of modern industrial life – smoke, noise, strain, fatiguing journeys to work, and so on – if these inconveniences were thought to be peculiar to the present day.

some of the principal economic activities such as agriculture and would pull against the effect of technical progress and other factors operating to raise productivity.

The magnitude of some of the changes in production over the past century is illustrated in *Table 4.1*. This summarizes recent calculations of the growth in total production, and production per man-hour in a number

TABLE 4.1. The growth of production, 1870–1980 (1913 = 100)

		US	UK	Germany (Fed. Rep.)	France	Italy
Total production	1870	17	39	30	51	55
(GNP or GDP)	1913	100	100	100	100	100
	1960	403	244	327	200	288
	1970	600	322	525	353	497
	1980	818	375	694	507	676
		Increase per cent per annum				
Total production	1870–1913	4.3	2.2	2.9	1.6	1.4
	1913–1950	2.9	1.7	1.2	0.7	1.3
	1950–1960	3.2	2.6	7.6	4.4	5.9
	1960–1970	4.0	2.8	4.9	5.8	5.6
	1970–1980	3.2	1.5	2.8	3.7	3.1
Production per man-hour[1]	1870–1913	2.4	1.5	2.1	1.8	1.2
	1913–1950	2.4	1.7	0.9	1.6	1.9
	1950–1960	2.4	2.0	6.0	3.9	4.1
	1960–1970	3.7	3.6	5.4	6.0	7.0
	1970–1980	2.8	2.5	4.1	4.7	4.5

[1] For 1960–1970 and 1970–1980 figures relate to manufacturing only. Figures for total production would be somewhat lower.

Sources: A. Maddison, *Economic Growth in the West* (The Twentieth Century Fund, New York, 1964); OECD, *Main Economic Indicators*; National Institute, *Economic Review*.

of countries since 1870. The estimates are given in the form of indices, using as a base the year 1913. The changes that have occurred are measured first in relation to the magnitudes applicable to 1913 and then, in the lower half of the table, as average annual rates of change over the periods 1870–1913, 1913–1950, 1950–1960, 1960–1970 and 1970–1980.

In all five countries shown, production has at least trebled since 1913; in the United States it has multiplied eightfold. The rate of increase has shown wide variations from country to country and in the 1960s varied between an average of 2.8% per annum in the United Kingdom and 5.8% per annum in France. The growth in productivity was particularly rapid in the 1950s and 1960s. In the 1950s it was 2% per annum or more in all five countries included and exceeded the secular average by a comfortable margin in all except the United States. In the 1960s, in manufacturing industry, productivity improved even faster and none of the five countries fell below 3.5% per annum. Little arithmetic is needed to show what a transformation in living standards would accompany the prolongation of such rates of improvement over several decades; if production per head grows at 3% per annum, it doubles every 23 years.

Transformation: changes in the pattern of economic activity

These rapid rates of growth are accompanied by large changes in the composition of final output and in the distribution of manpower and other resources between different industries and areas. Some of these changes are predictable and reflect the shift in spending patterns as people become better off. For example, there is a well-known generalization, known as Engel's Law, that the proportion of income spent on food tends to decline as income grows: a poor man is obliged to spend a great deal of his income on food, while a rich man, although spending a larger absolute amount on food, will devote a higher proportion of his income to other things. One implication of this Law is that, as *per capita* incomes rise, the industry which supplies us with food (i.e. agriculture) will tend to occupy a relatively smaller place in the economy. On the other hand, there are various services (e.g. professional services) on which a community spends a higher proportion of its income as it grows richer, so these services tend to occupy an expanding proportion of the labour force.

These tendencies can be illustrated from calculations made by Professor Simon Kuznets. In making these calculations, Kuznets divided the labour force (excluding unpaid family labour) into three main industrial groups in each of 38 countries, the groups consisting of agriculture, forestry and fishing (A sector); mining, manufacturing and construction (M sector); and all other activities and services (S sector). He then grouped the 38 countries in terms of production per head and worked out the relative size of A, M and S sectors in each of seven groups of countries with average *per capita* incomes ranging from about $100 in the poorest group up to $1700 in the richest. The A sector employed a much larger slice of the labour force in the poorest than in the richest group of countries, the variation being between 61% at the one end and 14% at the other. On the other hand, the

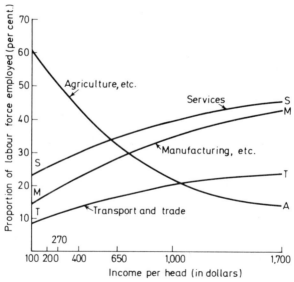

Figure 4.1 Industrial structure of the labour force in relation to income per head

M sector expanded from 15% of the labour force in the poorest group to over 40% in the richest, and the S sector from 24 to over 45%. Further sub-division of the S sector showed that the expansion was largely confined to two groups, one being transport and communications and the other, trade and finance. These two together accounted for only 8% of the labour force in the poorest countries and for 24% in the richest[1].

These figures and *Figure 4.1*, which is based on Professor Kuznets's data, illustrate the structural adjustments between different sectors of an economy to which economic growth gives rise. They bring out the dynamic character of specialization and the need confronting every economy to adapt itself not only to its failures but also to its successes. Manpower and other resources must be ready to abandon one specialized pursuit in favour of another; and the more rapidly the economy grows the more pressing is this necessity.

Development

Development is a more complicated business than growth and transformation. It overflows beyond the purely economic aspects of life and may alter radically the whole structure of society from the family at one end to the functions of the state at the other. The kind of economic development that has taken place since the industrial revolution has transformed work and leisure, changed the balance of political power, overthrown class relationships, introduced new educational needs and opportunities, and modified religious convictions and behaviour. Nor should one think of it as a once-for-all affair that gradually peters out; on the contrary, the pace of develoment is probably at least as rapid, even in the most 'advanced' countries, as in any previous period.

Techniques, attitudes and institutions develop

For present purposes, we must confine ourselves to a single aspect of development – its contribution to growth and particularly to the growth of productivity. From this point of view, development embraces the three broad elements which we referred to earlier as techniques, attitudes and institutions. These three elements interact with each other and with the growth of productive resources to produce growth. Apart from any advantages that flow from the sheer size of an economy and hence can be derived from a multiplication of the factors of production, and apart also from the discovery of fresh resources not hitherto charted, it is through development and development alone that productivity improves[2].

Development is innovation

This may seem a bold statement if the full compass of what is included in development is not understood. For development takes in all forms of

---

[1] S. Kuznets, *Six Lectures on Economic Growth* (Free Press of Glencoe, Illinois, 1959).
[2] This proposition does not apply rigorously to a single country since any one country may benefit from changes taking place abroad.

innovation: in technology, in personal conduct, in methods of organization, in laws and customs. It may be development in one country if the laws are enforced; in another, if cows cease to be sacred; in a third, if a man can make more money than his neighbours without having his house burned down or suffering other mischief. In an industrial country, it is natural to lay stress on advances in science and technology and on innovations in methods of production as the principal source of rising productivity. But even in such countries attitudes may be hostile to new techniques and unresponsive to financial incentives; business may be looked upon as rather degrading; and existing institutions – for example, company legislation or the machinery for financing new enterprises – may not be adapted to the needs of a developing economy. In pre-industrial countries, the need for social change to accompany technical change stands out far more clearly: in those countries attitudes and institutions lag quite as much as technology behind the practice of industrial countries, and the problem is not so much one of growth within an existing framework as of the replacement of one civilization by another.

How techniques, attitudes and institutions interact

The various elements that constitute development interact with one another and with the growth of productive resources. We can see this best in an underdeveloped country or by looking at the process of development in Western Europe over the past two or three centuries. A more experimental and secular temper in the population makes it possible for knowledge to grow more systematically, to acquire the force and universality of science and to issue in a cumulative and self-sustaining process of industrial innovation. The new methods and machines react on popular attitudes, creating new habits, new wants and new expectations; people become more willing to contemplate improvements, more perceptive of opportunities of improvement and more ready to take advantage of those opportunities. At the same time, the spread of new ideas and new attitudes, and the upheavals associated with industrialization and the growth of modern technology, work a revolution in social, political and economic institutions. New forms of organization have to be devised – the joint stock company, for example – and their introduction, like the introduction of newly invented machines, opens up fresh possibilities of growth. All of these changes may be accelerated by a simultaneous, and partly independent, expansion in productive resources through geographical and geological discovery, population growth and the accumulation of capital assets.

Capital accumulation and growth

The interconnection between the different elements is often overlooked when economists dwell on some one factor as the prime source of economic growth. They may, for example, lay stress on the accumulation of capital as indispensable to higher levels of output and productivity. It is true that in the early stages of industrialization there is frequently an acute shortage of physical assets to provide a framework for subsequent growth.

Such towns as there are may be small and poorly equipped to serve as centres for marketing and distribution; factory production may be almost unknown; there may be few sources of electric power and no adequate transport system. In such circumstances, capital can be a bottleneck and the growth of capital may permit a much improved organization of resources. In industrial countries too, more capital is usually required in order to take advantage of new processes and to produce new products, so that the forward movement of the economy pivots on the continuous accumulation of capital assets embodying the latest advances in technique.

The accumulation of capital, however, is not something completely autonomous and divorced from other social and economic forces. It involves an effort of saving and saving reflects an attitude towards the future[1]. This attitude is itself something that has to be developed: it depends upon social institutions – the assurance that property rights will be respected, the convenience with which savings can be invested, the emergence of intermediaries like banks and insurance companies – and it depends also upon the opportunities that exist for fruitful investment. In a society governed by custom and routine the need for savings and the incentive to save are alike reduced; but where innovation is rapid both are powerfully reinforced.

What produces innovation?

The process of innovation lies at the heart of economic development. But it is, as we have seen, a highly complex process. It rests first and foremost on the growth of knowledge and experience. The most important asset of any community is its intellectual, not its physical capital: not only the knowledge which it already possesses and the less communicable experience which it has built up, but the capacity to add to them both and to put them to use in commerce and industry, and the willingness to be guided by knowledge and experience rather than by dogma and received opinion. It is this intellectual capital that allows the community to discard old ideas and frame or learn new ones, and to profit from that substitution of new processes and products for old which issues in higher productivity and which we call technical progress.

The growth of knowledge, once scientific habits of mind take root, follows an inner logic of its own. But the application of scientific knowledge, and the direction taken by scientific research, are no more independent of social factors than is capital accumulation. Both respond to commercial incentives. Scientists and technologists may pursue truth for its own sake; but the firms who employ them or make use of their results do so in the expectation that they will profit by doing so. Spurred on by

[1] Cf. S. H. Frankel, *The Economic Impact on Underdeveloped Societies* (Oxford, 1953). 'The great growth of capital in the eighteenth and nineteenth centuries in Europe was due . . . to the emergence of new types of social activity. "Saving" was not a mechanical act but the result of new attitudes in social behaviour. To repair and maintain; to think of tomorrow not only of today; to educate and train one's children; to prepare oneself for new activities; to acquire new skills; to search out new contacts; to widen the horizon of individual experience; to invent, to improve, to question the "dead hand of custom", and the heritage of the past – in all these . . . lay the causes of capital accumulation.' (pp. 69–70).

competition, each firm is constantly reviewing the techniques which it uses so as to take advantage of new knowledge and, by superseding one process or method of production by a better one, reduce its costs and raise its productivity. When it makes an innovation in technique, it rarely takes over a ready-made invention, conceived and developed outside competitive industry by some individual scientist. There is usually a long and expensive process to be gone through before a novel idea, wherever originating, emerges as a working model and a still longer and more expensive process before the working model is translated into large-scale production. At each stage, money has to be provided and the readiness with which this is done will depend not only on the prospects of mastering the technical snags and producing an acceptable design but even more on the market possibilities for the finished product.

Innovation and technical progress

Technical progress should not be thought of in terms of the discontinuous introduction of major inventions, important though these may be. It consists, rather, in a continuous search for improvements in existing materials, machines and methods of production, a simultaneous scrutiny of market opportunities in the hope of devising new products or changes in existing products more to the liking of consumers, and, in addition, a combing through of the ideas flowing from scientific research in order to adapt these ideas to commercial applications. The pace of technical progress is faster the more rapidly knowledge spreads and is applied; and this brings us back once again to the social factors governing the numbers, alertness, power, and commercial ability of those who see advantage in innovation.

The expansion of overseas markets

If we look back on the steady and continuous growth in production since the industrial revolution, and leave aside the part played by the increase in population, technical progress and the accumulation of capital are bound to strike us as two of the dominant forces at work. But there was a third: the expansion of overseas markets. This was not independent of the other two, for it was largely made possible by the railway and the steamship on the one hand and by the investment of large amounts of capital abroad on the other. The settlement of countries overseas and the expansion in markets that went with it did, however, permit the industrial countries of Europe to re-deploy their resources and profit from a division of labour with other countries. A market grew up in Europe (and especially in Great Britain) for the foodstuffs and raw materials produced overseas and the newer primary producers were able to accelerate their development by specializing on exports to that market. In return, they imported manufactures and capital equipment from specialist producers in Europe. This trade not only expanded the scale on which industrial products were made in European factories, with the attendant benefits of large-scale operation, but enabled a country like Britain to give up producing some of its foodstuffs at high cost and transfer agricultural workers to industrial occupations in which they could earn substantially higher wages.

The growth of overseas markets also provided an additional stimulus to technical progress and innovation, which always flourishes under the influence of an expanding market. At the same time it reinforced the accumulation of capital by providing fresh outlets for investment and enriching the trading community. All three of the major influences at work interacted on one another to increase the contribution that each by itself could make to the more productive employment of manpower; and this increase in productivity in turn brought into play that process of transformation which we saw earlier to be a normal concomitant of a rise in the standard of living.

Trade, specialization and development

There are other circumstances in which the expansion of markets may play a similar role. For example, the emergence of a subsistence economy, isolated from markets, into a money economy, growing cash crops and exchanging them for imported manufactures, makes for an expansion of production and a higher return to the factors of production. It can also be the first step in the economic development of a backward country: the growth of trade and the specialization that goes with it is an indispensable preliminary to the operation of other factors increasing productivity. Robinson Crusoe could add to his resources and income by making for himself new bits of equipment and so accumulating capital; he could raise his productivity by acquiring new skills, finding better ways of organizing his time, and inventing new tools. But if he had a market for his output he would be able to make progress much more rapidly since he would acquire many things that he either could not make for himself or could make only with great difficulty. The development of a system of trading relationships in a money economy may thus be an important element in economic growth.

We may think of this element as production for a market, or as exchange and trade, or as specialization, because all three are facets of the same thing. When we exchange, we inevitably specialize. We limit the range of things we do and enlarge the range of things we consume; we give up variety in our work for the sake of variety when we come to spend the proceeds. The usual form of exchange is working for money in a specialized occupation, the money entitling us to the products of other specialists. The more of our time we give to working for money rather than to producing things for ourselves, the more we must specialize in making the products which we trade and the more dependent we are on a market for our services.

Once a money economy has emerged and full advantage has been taken of opportunities of trade, the growth of markets continues to be an important influence on production. But at this stage it is no longer an entirely new institution – production for a market – that is in course of development and exercising the stimulus to growth which, as we have seen, new institutions can exert. An expansion of markets, once trading relationships have been established, may be no more than the reflection of an expansion in output due to other factors, such as technical progress and capital accumulation. The more a country produces, the higher is its income and the wider the market confronting individual producers. This widening of the market may afford opportunities of specializing in different directions or to a greater degree; but it no longer makes the difference between an economy in which specialization is governed by market forces and one in which it is not.

In a sense, the growth of specialization is no more than a particular example of institutional development. But it is also something much more, since it is the basis of exchange and therefore of the economic activity which it is the business of economists to analyse. The various elements in economic development that we have been discussing would all be robbed of much of their importance but for extensive specialization. Take, for example, the introduction of rail transport which revolutionized production in the nineteenth century. Railways required a great deal of capital for their construction and the steam locomotive represented a major advance in technique. But the capital could never have been raised had there been no specialists in finance – promoters, bankers, issuing houses, etc. – to investigate, and to obtain support for, business propositions which might be made to yield a profit. Similarly, the steam engine could never have led to the railway had there been no division of labour between engine-drivers, engine-makers, guards, porters, signalmen, and so on.

Specialization in the firm and the industry

This sketch of the growth and transformation of production, and the ways in which economic development takes place, is on a wider canvas than the chapters which follow. In those chapters, instead of an aerial survey of the broad forces governing production and productivity, we take a worm's eye view of the operation of those forces within the individual firm and industry. Although the object is to explain the organization of industry as it exists rather than the way it changes over time, it is not possible to understand the problems of a firm or industry without some glimpse of the forces of dynamic change operating on it from outside and inside. A firm's markets change as the economy expands and the expansion of the economy is no more than the sum of the expansions that individual firms achieve. It is within firms that productive assets are accumulated and technical innovations are made. If economies grow and develop so also do firms and industries; and in judging whether they are efficiently organized we cannot do so in purely static terms. We must look not only to the way in which they use resources at a point in time but also to the scope which they offer for growth and devlopment in the future.

Chapter 5

Localization of industry

Districts, like persons, specialize. There is a geographical division of labour which leads each city, county and country to abandon some lines of production and extend others beyond local requirements. Each area restricts the range of its products, because such specialization enables it to obtain other products more cheaply by importing them. Through trade with its neighbours, the area is able to export what it has in comparative abundance in return for what it has in comparative scarcity.

Geographical specialization can be looked at from two different angles. We may ask why does a given area carry on some industries and not others? Or we may ask why is a given industry carried on in some areas and not in others? Economists have built up the theory of international trade – to which we will come by and by – in answer to the first question, and the theory of the location of industry in answer to the second. In the study of international trade, our attention is generally focused on the struggle which goes on between industries *inside* a country (or region) for the use of the scarce resources available there. We see how some industries survive while others are crowded out, and how the volume of industry expands if labour and capital are attracted to the country, and contracts if they flow abroad. In the study of localization, we start from the competition *between* regions for a given industry, or for industry as a whole, and discuss why one region can pull harder than another. These two lines of thought do not conflict with, but supplement one another.

The forces governing location

If we try to generalize the forces tending to bring an industry to a given area, we can adopt one of two courses. We can either think of the advantages offered by the area or we can start from the other end and ask what elements in the costs incurred by the industry would be affected by the choice of location. In the discussion which follows (pp. 61–66), the first course has been adopted; but we must first emphasize that the various advantages that an area can offer will only cause an industry to choose that location if they translate themselves into cost differentials in favour of the area.

Among those differentials it is usual to lay particular stress on two: transport costs and labour costs. If it makes a great deal of difference where an industry is located, it is usually because transport or labour costs could be materially reduced by the choice of one location rather than another. The influence of transport costs is discussed below (pp. 61–63) in relation to the convenience of an area as a point of assembly for raw materials or for the distribution of finished goods to their principal markets. The greater that convenience, the less the cost per unit of product of transporting materials from their source of supply or of shipping finished goods to their market. The direct importance of transport costs is often exaggerated, particularly in relation to consumer goods: the cost of delivery of such goods to their market is often less than 1% of the net selling price. The importance of transport costs is more apparent in the heavy industries and in industries that reduce their raw material to a less bulky or more easily transported form; but even in those industries raw materials have been exerting a diminishing influence over the past generation[1].

The direct influence of transport costs may also be reinforced or even over-shadowed by the direct influence of the factor of distance. This operates within individual firms against a dispersal of activities over different parts of the country. For example, it may deter the management from opening branch factories rather than extending the parent factory, or from separating the main factory from the sales organization, on the score of the greater difficulty of supervising and coordinating dispersed activites. On the other hand, if markets are dispersed, the management may be willing to consider decentralization to local units in order to save transport costs. This and other problems involved in the balancing of large-scale production in a central location against smaller-scale dispersal to branch factories are further discussed below (p. 67) and in Chapter 7.

The influence of labour costs on the location of industry within a country is generally limited. It might seem unlikely, unless the country is large, that there should be wide differences in rates of pay or in labour efficiency between different areas. But surprisingly large differences in earnings do persist even when trade union rates are negotiated on a country-wide basis; and it remains easier to find labour of the right type or with the right skills for a particular industry in one part of the country rather than another. The difference in labour costs can be such as to give a decisive locational advantage to an area; if wages are much below wages elsewhere, without any offsetting difference in labour efficiency, this may cause an industry to concentrate its expansion in the area, as happened between the wars in the American cotton industry. At other times, there may be a continuing lack of balance between the opportunities of employment open to men and

---

[1] See below, p. 62. A good example is provided by the oil industry: 'Forty years ago, only 30% of the crude oil was refined into a saleable product, kerosene, and so locating refineries on the oil fields saved large costs of transporting the 70% of crude oil destined to become waste product. At the present time, 90% of the crude oil is converted into saleable products, so that the advantages of locating refineries on the oilfields have been considerably reduced.' (R. S. Edwards and H. Townsend, *Business Enterprise*, p. 146, citing J. D. Butler, 'The Influence of Economic Factors on the Location of Oil Refineries', *Journal of Industrial Economics*, July 1953.)

women, and a chronic surplus of one or the other. In the coalfields and engineering towns, for example, there is normally a marked preponderance of jobs for men and a corresponding surplus of women seeking work. This leads to a migration of women to other areas; but it also gives rise to an inward movement of industries employing women, in order to take advantage of the surplus. Again, if there is a labour shortage in some parts of the country and unemployment in others, there is a strong locational pull towards the areas of unemployment, particularly if government policy is concentrated on eliminating any remaining pockets of unemployment.

We may now return to the first approach to location in terms of the advantages offered by different areas.

Natural advantages

First, there are the natural advantages of the area. These include its amenities – its possession of suitable sites and a suitable climate. Thus the flat, sunny country of East Anglia is far better suited than the wet glens of the Highlands to wheat-growing. Colour-printing is easier in a dry, and cotton-spinning in a damp, climate. And so on. The natural advantages of an area include also its access to sources of power and to raw materials and markets; these determine the savings in power and transport costs that it can offer.

(a) Power costs

Before the eighteenth century, power-driven machinery was rarely used, and cheap power was not an important localizing force. With the introduction of the water-wheel, factories – and especially cotton-mills – came to be built upon the banks of rivers with a good natural fall. Such rivers were most plentiful in the hilly parts of the country (i.e., in the north and west), and industries using water-power tended to become localized there. A great impetus was given to this movement when steam came into use as the chief source of power, for coal, from which steam was generated, was located in the districts in the north and west to which the textile industries were already gravitating. Of course, coal might have been brought by rail to the older centres of industry, but as it was expensive to transport, and none of its weight passed into the finished product, manufacturing costs were lower in the mining areas. As coal was used also as a fuel, as a reducing agent (in the metal industries), and as a raw material (in the chemical industries), the pull of the coal-fields was tremendous, and a whole network of industries grew up, attracting labour and capital from all over the country. This process is now being reversed. The development of new sources of power – particularly oil and electricity – has greatly weakened the dependence of industry on coal, and has led to a redistribution of industry in favour of the large urban markets (e.g., London), and at the expense of the mining districts (e.g., South Wales).

(b) Transport costs

Nearness to an industry's markets and its sources of raw materials very often pull in opposite directions, so that the advantages of one have to be weighed against the advantages of the other. Where there is great loss of weight in manufacture, or where the raw material is very bulky, and the finished product compact and easily transported, production will be carried on near the source of supply of the raw material. Thus, the crushing and concentration of ores is normally undertaken at the minehead, even when smelting or refining is carried on elsewhere. The pulping of wood, the pressing of grapes and apples, and the distillation of oil from coal are examples of the same tendency. If, however, the finished product is bulky, and loss of weight negligible, it will be the large markets which exert the biggest pull. The making of bricks, bread, bottles, and other bulky goods is generally carried on all over the country near each important market. Tinplate manufacture is more highly localized than any other industry; but the making of tins, cans and household utensils from tinplate is widely diffused, because it much cheaper to transport a box of plates than a pile of tins of various shapes and sizes. Similarly, the assembly of motor car parts is carried on in many countries in which the manufacture of these parts is uneconomical. The market has succeeded in attracting the later stages of manufacture because the final product is more costly to transport than are the parts.

Where several raw materials are combined in a single product, and their combined pull is strong (because of loss of weight or bulk) in relation to the pull of the market, the final location of the industry will represent the resultant of the pulls exerted by the various materials and will be such as to keep transport costs at a minimum[1]. The importance of each constituent in relation to others will depend upon what weight of it is used per unit of the final product[2]. If it is a weight-losing material, its pull, relatively to that of *other materials*, will not be any the greater; but of course the pull of all raw materials *vis-à-vis* the *market* will be strengthened. The steel industry has moved away from the coal fields, not because coal loses less weight in the smelting of iron ore, but because less coal has to be moved per ton of ore.

When the raw materials used include some that are available everywhere (e.g., water, sand, clay, etc.), industry is attracted towards the market. For if these materials are incorporated in the final product at the point of sale instead of elsewhere, the cost of transporting them is saved. Brewing, brick-making, and, above all, the manufacture of aerated waters, illustrate the working of this tendency.

When several markets have to be supplied, the location of the industry will again represent a compromise between conflicting pulls. A large market like London, with enormous spending power per square mile of area (high 'market density'), will pull a great deal harder then a country town or rural district. It will do so for two reasons: first, because production near a large market saves the cost of transport on goods sold locally, and these form a high proportion of output; and second, because large-scale production at a low-cost is easier when market density is high. We have seen already that the pull of London and the South-East has been growing because of the rise of new forms of power less highly localized than coal, and of new products less dependent upon localized materials.

---

[1] Other things (e.g., labour costs) being equal.
[2] And also, of course, on the distance it has to be carried.

We have now to add that the increased importance of large-scale production and the greater ease and comparative cheapness of transport have tended to concentrate industry near the chief markets, and especially London, since the outlying markets can be supplied more cheaply from a single point of manufacture.

Acquired advantages

The natural advantages of an area in any given industry are generally reinforced by acquired advantages. Transport facilities are provided or improved. Roads, railways, docks and harbours are built. Commercial services of all kinds – banking, warehousing, accounting, and so on – become available. Labour becomes familiar with the technique of the industry, and a high standard of workmanship is developed. Manufacturers are able to discuss problems of mutual interest, and in this way, or because of the appearance of trade and technical journals, improvements and inventions are stimulated. The district acquires a prestige which binds customers to it. An organized market for the product or for materials comes into existence. Subsidiary industries spring up in the neighbourhood, supplying accessories and parts, or making use of by-products.

(a) Vertical disintegration

At this stage a change comes over the type of specialization practised: as the industry obtains a firmer footing and grows in size, the process of manufacture often begins to 'disintegrate', the separate stages as they split off being taken over by a specialist firm or industry. The supply of machinery and material, the utilization of by-products, the organization of traffic and marketing may be undertaken by such specialist firms. Cotton firms, for example, no longer make their own machinery but buy it from engineering firms. Motor manufacturers buy in radiators, carburettors, electric equipment, chassis frames, and other parts from specialists who can produce very cheaply by supplying several firms at once. Shipbuilding yards assemble the products of dozens of industries. Similarly in building it is usual in large contracts for the steelwork, masonry, plumbing, air-conditioning, furnishing, and so on, to be contracted out to firms specializing in a single branch of the industry.

(b) Lateral disintegration

In a localized industry, 'disintegration' by *product* is also frequent. That is, neighbouring towns (or firms) specialize in supplying different markets, or use similar materials to make different products. In the West Riding of Yorkshire, for example, Bradford specializes in worsteds, Dewsbury in 'heavy' woollen cloths, Huddersfield in fine woollen cloths, and the Colne Valley in tweeds.

There is no *necessary* connection between the industrial disintegration which we have been discussing and the concentration of an industry in a given area. The first involves further specialization on the part of firms and industries, the second, further specialization on the part of geographical areas. In the world as we find it, however, both types of specialization very often occur together; and it is easy to see that, so long as the firms in a given industry are isolated from one another instead of being localized in a single district, they will be forced to do many things for themselves rather inefficiently, and will have to do without services which a specialist could supply to a localized industry. *One* cause of disintegration (but not the only one) is clearly localization. The more firms of the same type settle in the same locality, the more they tend to specialize and diverge from one another[1].

Acquired advantages not only strengthen the pull on an industry to a given area, but help the industry there when the natural advantages of the area have ceased to exist. There is no obvious reason why lace-making should be carried on in Nottingham or boot-making in Leicester except that both towns have acquired a long experience in their staple trades. A group of interdependent industries is even harder to unscramble; for even when one of the group might profitably start elsewhere it may be so knit together with surrounding industries that a change in location would be extremely costly. Changes in location, therefore, generally come about less through deliberate transference than through the rise of firms in a new area and the decline of firms in the old.

Comparative advantages

A clear superiority over other areas in natural or acquired advantages will not by itself attract an industry to a given location. Other industries may enjoy an even greater advantage in the same location; and this comparative advantage will allow them to compete successfully for the limited resources available in the area. In due course, if the area has such all-round advantages, there will be an influx of resources – including more workers – and a wider range of industries may be built up as the area prospers and grows. But at any one time the extent to which an industry locates itself in a given area will depend upon the competition for labour, land and capital within the area; and an industry will locate itself more readily in the area if it is not faced with a scarcity of productive resources due to the competition of other industries.

The competition between one industry and another that goes on within any given region can be observed also within smaller areas. Inside each town, for example, there is competition for sites. Some industries will pay high ground rents so as to be near to their workers, or to docks, warehouses and railway stations. Other industries, which have more difficulty in economizing ground space and need ample room for expansion, may prefer to move to the outskirts where ground rents will be much lower. The clothing and milling trades are examples of the first tendency, motor car and wireless manufacture of the second. The rough pattern into which the industries of a district sort themselves is in constant change as

---

[1] Industrial change may be in the direction of integration rather than disintegration. For a discussion of various forms of industrial integration, see below, pp. 126–132.

one industry yields space to others. One firm may vacate a site because the ground rent has become higher than it can afford: another firm may take over the site in order to extend its premises and retain a central location. There is a steady centrifugal pressure by which commerce squeezes industry from the inner parts of a town. The older factories near the centre are forced to re-locate themselves as hostels, offices, warehouses and shops creep outwards. The factories near the city boundaries may have to move farther out as the suburbs become built up.

Cumulative advantages

Once a great locational change is in progress and industry is on the move, the change will gain momentum from sympathetic movements of labour. There will be not only a re-shuffling of industries inside each area, but also a series of expansions and contractions of whole areas, in the sense that more labour will be put at the disposal of industries in expanding areas, and withdrawn from industries in contracting areas. This movement of resources will give the expanding areas a cumulative advantage, for it will both keep down some of the costs of firms trying to establish themselves there, and at the same time bring them a new local market when the immigrant workers begin to spend their wages. The contracting areas on the other hand will suffer from a cumulative disadvantage for they lose a customer in every migrant, and every customer lost may mean still another migrant.

The degree of localization

The more these advantages are monopolized in any industry by a small number of areas, the more highly localized will the industry be. At one extreme, we have the mining of gilsonite (which takes place only in Utah); at the other, services of all kinds (of shopkeepers, policemen, postmen, lawyers, bus drivers, etc.) which, being in demand everywhere and impossible to store, must be rendered everywhere.

The degree of diversification

The more outstanding are the advantages of a single industry or small group of industries, over other industries in any area, the narrower will be the range of industries in that area. In other words, industry will be highly diversified where the available resources, either in raw materials or in skill and experience, are varied, or when tastes and a wide market can be supplied; and it will be highly specialized when only a limited range of resources can be exploited, and when tastes are standardized and narrow. Ghana, for example, cannot readily turn from cocoa to other lines of production, and the American prairies have little alternative to wheat-growing. But in Britain industry is amazingly diversified, not only because of her varied resources – her coal and iron, her vast capital, long experience, and abundant skill – but also because her manufacturing centres, being within a short distance of the big ports, have easy access to the materials and markets of every other seaboard.

Depressed areas

When the degree of diversification in an area is low, it risks all the disadvantages of excessive specialization. If the main industry is depressed, the depression is communicated to the industries supplying local needs. There may be no other major industry to fall back on, and the difficulties of making a switch will then be enormously increased, since it is far harder to build up new industries than to build on old ones. Continued depression in the main industry will bring into existence a problem of long-term unemployment, especially amongst the older workers who can neither pick up a new technique nor move far afield in search of jobs. The younger workers may find employment in other areas, but their removal will unbalance industry more than ever. The social life of the community will suffer through the loss of many of its natural leaders, and through the chronic unemployment of a large fraction of its members. Unless invigorated from without, the whole community may throw up the sponge and wait apathetically for better things. In short, the problem of depressed areas comes into existence: the problem, that is, of persistent unemployment concentrated in pockets up and down the country. It is a problem which cannot altogether be got rid of so long as areas specialize at all. But it might be made a less serious problem if governments were to promote the diversification of industry in depressed areas, and indeed in any area too narrowly dependent upon a staple trade with an uncertain future.

The dynamics of location

It is one thing to try to explain the existing locational pattern: it is quite another to explain why individual firms pick on particular locations. The location of an industry might be rational even if the choice of location made by each firm in it was almost entirely haphazard[1]. Firms that made a bad choice would die off; firms that made a good choice would flourish and expand, until the industry was concentrated in the localities that they had selected. There is plenty of evidence that few firms engage in elaborate calculations before deciding where to go: particularly small firms – and most firms start small. There is also evidence that few firms ever want to move from their existing site so long as there is room for expansion, and that if they are obliged to move they like to stay in or near their home town.

[1] 'Mr Ford started to manufacture motor-cars in Detroit because it was his home town. Sir William Morris (later Lord Nuffield) chose Cowley because the school in which his father was educated happened to be for sale. Neither of these excellent motives can be regarded as promising certain success to those who imitate them. . . . Mr Ford and Sir William Morris either by acumen or by chance discovered places of production with great natural advantages.' E. A. G. Robinson, *Structure of Competitive Industry* (CUP, Cambridge, 1931), p. 152.

'Why is our glass industry concentrated in St Helens? Because the great-great-grandfather of the present chairman was apprenticed to a doctor in St Helens and in due time practised there, because his sons were brought up there, because they put some money into a glass works, the technical manager of which had to withdraw. This explains how they got in but not how they survived. Their survival was due to the general suitability of the area – the proximity of the port of Liverpool, coal, excellent sand (with low iron oxide content) and alkali close by.' R. S. Edwards and H. Townsend, *Business Enterprise* (London, 1958), p. 158.

When a firm decides to move to a new factory or to open a branch elsewhere, it may consider all the factors that we have already enumerated: the availability and cost of power; the convenience of the site in relation to raw materials on the one hand and markets on the other; the adequacy of local transport facilities and commercial services; the ease with which it can hire labour with the necessary experience, skill and drive; the competition it may have to face for the resources it requires; the momentum of expansion in the area to which it proposes to move. But it will also be influenced – and perhaps decisively – by other considerations, many of them arising out of the additional burden that such a move imposes on its limited managerial resources.

First of all, most firms do not have an unlimited amount of time and money to spend in looking for a suitable location. A management that is planning an expansion is probably already under some pressure to meet existing orders and may be unable to release staff to make a full investigation. If it makes use of the services of a consultant, it has still to find time to set out its problem and check the advice which it ultimately receives. It may confine itself, therefore, to a rather cursory inspection of a limited number of sites in the more obvious localities with the necessary physical characteristics. Secondly, the additional managerial effort involved in planning, building and operating a new factory will dispose an expanding firm to select a location that makes this effort less formidable. It will be disinclined to move to a remote site or one with which communications are difficult; it will avoid a location that lacks subcontracting facilities and specialist services, so that it is forced to extend its own responsibilities to tool-making, die-casting, and so on; it will, for the same reason, prefer to go where it can be sure of a regular supply of components, made to its specifications by local firms; it is likely also to try to confine the new factory to the manufacture of relatively simple products, requiring relatively little supervision and managerial effort. Finally, the need to transfer or recruit staff to manage the new factory will bias the firm in favour of locations which its staff will find attractive as places in which to live, because this will ease the task of managerial reinforcement. It will show a similar preference for locations which enlarge the knowledge and experience of its staff and improve their usefulness as managers. If the location is one in which the staff will be brought into frequent contact with new ideas, the latest scientific knowledge, and lively and stimulating associates, this will add greatly to its attractiveness, particularly in industries in which expansion is rapid and the shortage of capable managers is correspondingly acute.

The state and location

In post-war years a large number of new factories have been built in the areas of Great Britain remote from London – what before the war were called Depressed Areas, but have since been described as Development Areas. The location of these factories is generally assumed to reflect government pressure and government planning and there is no doubt that by control over factory-building, the offer of financial assistance, and in other ways, the influence of the government was powerfully exerted in favour of location in the Development Areas. It is arguable, however, that the shortage of labour elsewhere was at least as effective in inducing firms to choose new (and often less convenient) locations. The experience of war-time, when an acute shortage of labour developed in London and the Midlands while there was still a surplus in the outlying regions, demonstrated clearly the inertia of the existing geographical pattern of industry and the resistance to dispersion in response to any force less compelling than lack of manpower.

It is obviously desirable that an industry should be located where it can be carried on efficiently and at low cost. If it is located in some other area, the higher level of costs will mean a waste of resources and a loss of social product. On the other hand, it is also desirable that there should be a sufficient concentration of industry in each area to employ all the available labour. If industry moves from one locality to another, the first community may decay while the other prospers; no new industry may grow up to take the place of the old, so that chronic local unemployment results. There will then be a waste of resources that falls not on private firms in the shape of higher costs but on society in the shape of a bill for maintaining the unemployed, or, if they are successful in finding jobs elsewhere, in empty schools and dwelling-houses, and in local services that are no longer fully used.

There may thus be a conflict between the private and the social interest. If work is always brought to the worker, industrial efficiency may suffer; if the worker has to move in search of work he may remain unemployed or there may be a loss of social capital when he moves. The acuteness of the conflict depends upon the industry and upon the community. In some communities the social capital is hardly worth preserving and the chances of new industries succeeding are too faint. There are mining valleys, difficult of access, where the houses are old and the amenities poor; rather than rehabilitate these it would be better to provide more housing elsewhere. In some industries one location may be about as good as another; leather handbags, radio valves and typewriters may be examples. A push towards a depressed area would reduce unemployment there, and might put fresh life into the area, as well as providing a second line of defence at a later date against renewed depression in the older industries in the area. The more industries can be shown to be 'footloose', and oriented neither towards markets nor towards raw materials, the greater the ease with which they can be induced to move to new locations if public policy so requires, and the stronger the case for taking the work to the worker. If in addition most firms choose a new location rather haphazardly it is much easier to get them to change their mind and, if denied location in one area, to be content with location in another.

The state can bring influence to bear on the location of industry in a variety of ways. It can offer a good information service to assist firms in their search for a suitable locality and a suitable site. It can grant loans on favourable terms, offer investment grants or exemption from taxes, build factories for rent at cheap rates, and contribute to the cost of training schemes, provided firms will go to selected areas. It can encourage the setting up of factory estates in those areas and subsidize improvements in the transport system and other facilities. It can arrange to issue building licences or industrial development certificates more freely than in other areas. It can instruct government departments to try to place more contracts with firms in the selected areas. It can steer to those areas foreign firms wishing to set up branches in the country. The cumulative effect of measures such as these can be great, particularly when many firms are seeking to expand.

Yet it is pressure confined almost entirely to manufacturing industry; and in Great Britain manufacturing industry accounts for less than one-third of total employment. It is true that manufacturing industry is generally the magnet attracting industry, distributive and other services, and that as one industry grows it tends to attract others to the same locality. But there are other magnets: a convalescent hospital, a prison, the offices of a football pool, an insurance company or a government department – to take a few examples – can exert a locational pull just as strong and independent as the pull of industry. Even within manufacturing industry there are large sections – for example, in steel, wool-combing, heavy chemicals, and so on – where normal locational forces are too strong and the effective choice of locations is extremely limited. For these and other reasons, the amount of employment provided in the factories built in any one year in the Development Areas has been small in relation to the fluctuations in unemployment in those areas that occurred in pre-war years. Control over the location of new factories is no guarantee against severe localized unemployment; it does, however, make for a steady reduction in such unemployment when it might otherwise be steadily increasing.

Chapter 6

Large-scale production

Specialization, as Adam Smith pointed out, is limited by the size of the market. In a narrow market (e.g., in an isolated village), a worker must be able to turn his hand to many different jobs. The demand for his services in any one of these jobs will not be sufficient to keep him continuously occupied in it. In the same way, it will be impossible to use expensive machinery if it has to stand idle for long periods; or to introduce the elaborate organization – in management, costing, research, marketing, and so on – which is indispensable in a modern business of any size. Production must be on a large scale before full use can be made either of machinery or of specialists and specialized departments. This is true of the establishment (e.g., a single factory), of the firm (which may own several factories), of the industry (which consists of a number of competing firms), and of industry as a whole. As each of these expands in size, new opportunities of specialization, new types of machinery, and new kinds of organization make it possible to achieve economies which were impossible so long as production was on a smaller scale.

The economies of large-scale production – called for short 'economies of scale' – may be either 'internal' or 'external'.

Internal economies are those which are open to a single factory or a single firm independently of the action of other firms. They result from an increase in the scale of output of the firm, and cannot be achieved unless output increases. They are not the result of inventions of any kind, but are due to the use of known methods of production which a small firm does not find worth while. They are also not to be confused with any bargaining or monopoly advantages which large firms may acquire. These advantages may swell the profits of large firms and incite small firms to grow bigger; but they do not (except indirectly) make large firms more *efficient* than small ones.

External economies are those which are shared in by a number of firms or industries when the scale of production in any industry or group of industries increases. They are not monopolized by a single firm when it grows in size, but are conferred on it when some *other* firms grow larger. Whenever an increase in the output of one firm has a favourable reaction on the efficiency of other firms, either in the same industry or in other industries, these firms enjoy the benefit of external economies.

External economies

The chief types of external economies have already been illustrated in our discussion of localization[1]. There are:

Economies of concentration

When a number of firms settle in a single neighbourhood they enable each other to derive mutual advantages through the training of skilled work-men, the provision of better transport facilities, the stimulation of im-provements, and so on. Each employer has less difficulty in finding the kind of labour he wants, and can make use of special services – e.g., in merchanting his goods – which would not be available to scattered firms. In a country which has not yet been industrialized, economies of concentra-tion can be of special importance. Each new firm and each new industry attracted to the country help to build up a machine-sense, and a common stock of knowledge and experience on which each surrounding manufac-turer can draw.

Economies of information

In large industry it becomes worth while to issue trade and technical publications to which everyone has access. Manufacturers are thus saved much independent research which, in a smaller industry, they might be forced to undertake for themselves. It becomes possible also to set up research associations which will carry out research work on behalf of individual firms and publish the results for any firm to use. Economies of information are clearly of much more importance when applied to industry in general than when confined to a single industry. Cheap newspapers and information bureaux, an efficient weather-forecasting service, adequate provision for research, and so on, are of enormous advantage to industry as a whole, but far too much for a single industry to provide unaided. Thus it very often falls to the government to bear the cost of information and research services, the benefits of which are shared throughout industry.

Economies of disintegration

The growth of an industry may foster the splitting off of some process which can be carried on more efficiently by a specialist firm or industry. On this further specialization nothing need be added to what has been said above[2]. The economies which the specialist firms enjoy are internal economies and will be discussed presently.

What are external economies at one moment may be internal economies the next, if several firms unite with one another. To a village butcher, killing a few cattle a week, half of the animal is waste. But if the village grows into a thickly-populated urban district, with a large number of slaughterhouses, each of the local butchers will be able to dispose of this 'waste' at a good price. Specialist firms will 'make combs, buttons, knife

[1] See pp. 63–64.
[2] See pp. 63–64.

and cane handles from the horns and hoofs; glue from parts of the bones and cartilage; pipe stems, chessmen, dice, artificial teeth, crochet needles or electrical bushings from the bones; pharmaceutical supplies from the glands, artists' brushes from the soft hair in the interior of the ears[1]. The butcher will benefit from external economies. But exactly the same economies might be enjoyed if the butcher were to amalgamate with the specialist firms to form a large meat-packing concern. The economies which, in the British livestock industry, are still largely external to the slaughterhouses could be made internal by the adoption of the methods of the Chicago packers.

External economies, therefore, are not different in kind from internal: what are external, and what are internal, economies depend simply upon what operations it is profitable to combine under a single management. In the steel industry, for example, external economies are likely to be of less importance than in the textile industries, because the processes of manufacture must be integrated in the interests of conservation of heat in steel-making, but may be separated in the interests of efficient management in textile manufacturing.

Internal economies

Internal economies can be grouped together under five headings: technical, managerial, commercial, financial and risk-spreading.

Technical economies

Technical economies affect the size of the single establishment, rather than of the firm, which may own and operate several different establishments. An establishment may be anything between an ice-cream barrow and Ford's Rouge Plant at Detroit, covering over a thousand acres and employing 100 000 workers. In industries where technical economies of scale are great, the size of the typical establishment will tend to be correspondingly great; while in industries where size is of little technical advantage, and the methods of large plants can be easily duplicated on a smaller scale, the typical establishment will tend to remain small. In gold-mining, tinplate manufacture, and the generation of hydroelectric power, the large plant uses methods of far greater efficiency than are open to smaller units; in those industries, therefore, large plants are the rule. In agriculture, on the other hand, it often makes little difference whether a farm is large or small. The same farming methods may be used whether the dairy herd is one of thirty or three hundred and whether the sheep flock is numbered in hundreds or in thousands. If, therefore, we find many large dairy herds and sheep flocks, it will probably be because farmers are trying to take advantage of economies of scale which are not purely technical. It is only in arable farming that farm machinery (for example, the combine-harvester) gives the large unit a marked advantage in technique over the small unit.

Technical economies are of three kinds:

---

[1] S. H. Slichter, *Modern Economic Society*, p. 126.

(a) Economies of superior technique

Many types of machinery cannot be reproduced at all on a smaller scale, so that a small plant is driven either to install machinery which it cannot keep in continuous use, or to put up with less efficient machinery of a different type. A large motor-works can use giant presses, which turn out all-steel tops, body panels, and fenders in one piece, while in small factories a whole series of operations, more laborious and less mechanical, is necessary[1]. Only a large tin-plate works can make use of continuous strip rolling. Computers and calculating machines are economical in a large office, but uneconomical in a small one. A rotary printing press, linotype machines, and so on, are indispensable to most daily newspapers, but not to a small jobbing printer. Electrically-driven overhead cranes are in use in large engineering works and not in small. There are, in fact, few industries without some striking differences in technique between large and small establishments. The small establishments generally make more use of small machines worked by hand-power, while the large establishments make more extensive use of large machines worked by steam or electricity. From a technical point of view, these modern sources of power are superior and this superiority is communicated to large units of plant.

(b) Economies of increased dimensions

Even when a machine can be duplicated on a smaller scale, there is often a purely mechanical advantage is using large machines. There is an economy, for example, when size diminishes losses by friction, or evaporation, or cooling. The carrying capacity of a ship increases in proportion to the cube of its dimensions; the resistance to its motion increases, roughly speaking, in proportion to the square of its dimensions. The power required to drive a given weight through the water is less, therefore, in a large than in a small ship. Again, if we double the dimensions of a water tank by building one twice as long, twice as broad, and twice as high, it will hold eight times as much water as before. But the walls of the tank will have increased only four times in area, and since the loss of heat by radiation depends upon the area of the walls, and not upon the volume of water in the tank, the rate at which the water will cool will be greatly reduced. A large boiler, therefore, will be more efficient than a small one. Similarly, a large furnace has great advantages over a small one. These advantages are of special importance in the chemical and metal industries where there is great scope for the conservation of heat through an increase in the scale of plant.

There is further economy in the use of large machines. In spite of their greater output, they can generally be operated by a team no larger than is required for a much smaller machine of the same type. Whatever the size of a rolling-mill, a steam shovel, a locomotive or a concentrator, the number of men required is much the same. 'To turn a valve, to operate a switch, or to watch a gauge is no more arduous, though much more responsible, labour for a super-power station than for a tiny plant.'[2]

---

[1] That is, so long as there are no specialist firms from which the small factories can buy pressed steel parts.

[2] E. A. G. Robinson, *Structure of Competitive Industry*, p. 32.

Not only is the large machine cheaper to operate. It is also relatively cheaper to construct. An electric motor developing 20 hp does not require twice the material of a 10-hp motor, and takes little more labour to assemble. A double-decker bus is not twice as costly as a single-decker; the bodywork may be no stouter, and the engine, apart from a difference in horsepower, identical. In the building of a ship, a furnace, a factory, a telephone system, or a broadcasting station – to say nothing of the manufacture of pails and postcard albums – the size of the unit can generally be doubled without a doubling of labour and material costs.

It must not be supposed, however, that large mechanical units are *necessarily* more efficient than small ones; much depends upon what particular dimensions are increased, or what difficulties the increase in size is intended to overcome. The farmer who, impressed by the economies of increased dimensions, was silly enough to double the length, breadth and depth of his plough, found that it needed not one but forty horses – with a large gang of men in attendance – to drag it through the earth[1]. When a ship is very big, the resistance to its motion is greatly increased by skin friction, and size becomes a handicap. The large unit, too, may forfeit its advantages if there is no labour capable of handling it properly, or no raw materials of the quality required.

(c) Economies of linked processes

The operations of a single large machine are not likely to be the only ones undertaken in an establishment. There will be other operations, linked with those which the machine performs; and the more processes are linked together the larger, inevitably, will be the establishment. We must include amongst economies of scale, therefore, any economies resulting from this linking of processes.

The linking of processes in a single plant leads to many economies. There is generally a saving in time and a saving in transport costs, since two departments of the same factory are closer together than two separate factories. It is mainly for this reason that the editing and the printing of newspapers are generally carried on in the same building, and that most factories have their own repair, testing, and box-making departments. In coal-mining, the washing and screening of the coal takes place at the pit-head, partly because, since coals of different grades are sold in different markets, a saving in transport costs is effected. In short, wherever a process would normally be localized in the vicinity of the raw materials, there is a strong tendency for it to be carried on within the establishment where the materials are prepared.

There is a saving, too, in fuel and power wherever the physical conjunction of two processes makes for the conservation of heat. The most striking example is that of steel-making. In an integrated plant, the pig-iron is taken to the steel furnaces in a molten condition, and the steel ingots, once they have solidifed and have been re-heated in the soaking pits, can be rolled and re-rolled without being allowed to cool. The hot gases from

---

[1] J. M. Clark, *Studies in the Economics of Overhead Costs* (Chicago, 1931), p. 116.

the coke ovens and blast furnaces are used to heat the steel furnaces and soaking pits, and to generate the electricity which works the rolls in the rolling mills and the blowers in the blast furnaces. Thus the consumption of coal per ton of finished steel can be reduced from the 1913 average of over three tons to one ton in a modern plant.

The linking of different stages of manufacture is obviously not governed exclusively by technical considerations. It may be no more than the most convenient and profitable path along which a business can expand. Even when technical considerations are uppermost, they are often coupled with other motives such as the avoidance of uncertainty. A factory may decide to make rather than buy supplies of materials and components because it wants to be sure of obtaining what it needs at the right time, in the right quantities, and of the right quality. Any irregularity in the flow, or any failure to meet specifications in quality or design, will aggravate the managerial problem of organizing production efficiently and lead to higher costs. For reasons of this kind, an engineering factory will usually make its own screw nails and so remove any danger of unpunctual supply. Similarly, textile firms may spin their own yarn in order to be able to vary their material to suit the fabrics which they hope to market. Or, where a firm has a reputation for a highly individual product, it is likely to insist on supervision and control, often in its own premises, at each stage of manufacture.

Once several processes are linked within the same plant, it becomes necessary to *balance* them against one another. If the plant is to operate with maximum efficiency, the scale on which each process is conducted must not only exhaust the economies possible at that stage, but must be adapted to the demands of the succeeding stage. One machine, when working to capacity, may be able to handle 100 units of output; the capacity of a second machine may be 250 units, of a third 300, and of a fourth 2000. If each of these machines is to be kept in gear with the others, it will be necessary to use more than one model of each machine, and to produce more than 2000 units of output. The ideal solution would be to scale up output to 6000 units (i.e., the LCM of the capacity outputs of each machine) and use 60 machines of the first type, 24 of the second, 20 of the third, and 3 of the fourth. In the real world, however, capacity outputs do not fit together so neatly as in this example, and the LCM would often be impossibly high. Some possible economies, therefore, have to be sacrificed by overdriving one machine and running another below capacity. On the other hand, the risk of disorganization through breakdowns – especially at bottlenecks like our fourth machine – will tend to push normal output beyond the LCM, since the operation of a second unit will act as a safeguard against complete stoppage all along the line. Similarly, if routine repairs (e.g., the re-lining of blast furnaces) can be carried out when a large unit of plant stands idle, several units of the same type will usually be operated together.

Technical factors set a lower, not an upper limit, to the most efficient scale of operations: they create economies, never diseconomies. In any given state of technique, there comes a level of output beyond which no further reduction in costs can be obtained through the technical economies that size permits. But equally, there is no reason to expect a deterioration in technical efficiency with further growth since the most efficient units of plant can be duplicated and multiplied. If, therefore, there are other savings to be made – in management, in finance, in marketing, and so on – there is no reason why technique should set limits to expansion. We must look in other directions for obstacles to growth.

Managerial economies

Managerial economies may be effected either by increasing the size of an establishment or by grouping a number of establishments under one management. Both methods of expansion create opportunities for increased specialization. These opportunities are not confined to the managing staff but extend to the entire labour force. Workers can be kept fully employed on a narrower range of tasks. In a small garage, a man may be a mechanic, taxi-driver and petrol attendant. In a small office – e.g., in accountancy, banking or law – a clerk has generally more varied duties than in a large one. But it is mainly at the managerial level that specialization is carried further. This specialization is twofold.

(a) Delegation of detail

In a small business, the owner spends much of his time going to and fro in his shirt sleeves, superintending and assisting with the work of his factory. He has probably a thorough grasp of every side of the business and a strong hold on the loyalty of his workers. He may enjoy being worker, foreman, and manager combined, and have no wish to change. But if he is an able organizer, he will produce at lower cost – and incidentally make a larger profit – by expanding his business and delegating routine and details to subordinates. This will leave him free to concentrate on the more difficult work of organization. He will have time to make a full study of special problems, keep abreast of changes in technique, make influential 'contacts', and form a plan of campaign on the basis of adequate information. But all this will only be possible in a large business, where his time is not taken up with what a lower-paid worker could do equally well, and where his powers of foresight, initiative, and judgement are spread over the maximum volume of output to which they will stretch. Mr Ford and Lord Nuffield would have been wasted on a poultry-farm or the local cinema; they might even have failed disastrously. But they were far from being wasted on the Ford and Morris Motor Companies, where their organizing ability was given full scope, and could be paid for handsomely with advantage to the companies.

(b) Functional specialization

Division of labour can also take place, so to speak, horizontally. The work of management is split up through the creation of separate departments, each of which is put in charge of an expert administrator. One specialist becomes responsible for the organization of production, one for sales, one for transport, still another for the maintenance of machinery and buildings. There will be other departments engaged in costing and estimating, research, the hiring of workers, the purchase of materials, the preparation of new designs, the keeping of accounts, the arranging of finance, and so on. Each large department may be further sub-divided and its duties distributed between a large number of specialists.

The same division of functions takes place on the board of directors. The job of the directors is to guide the general policy of the business, much as Cabinet Ministers are supposed to govern the policy of government departments, without undertaking the detailed work of administration. One director may make himself responsible for finance, another for marketing, and a third for engineering problems. Thus the board of directors may be turned into an all-star team, in which are knit together widely different talents and experience.

The appointment of specialists and the setting up of specialized departments is economical only in a large business. A research chemist, an accountant, or a works manager may draw a salary which would make him much too expensive for a small concern and yet prove cheap at the price in a large one. A large business can afford a separate staffing department which will test applicants for vacancies, arrange for their training and assign them to posts for which they are suited[1]. Similarly with research: a small firm cannot possibly spend large sums on research and development, but a large one may spend several million pounds a year.

Marketing economies

Economies in the purchase of materials and sale of goods may be just as important as economies in manufacture. Raw materials may come to 50% or more of the cost of an article. Up to 60% of the cost of bread and 75% of the cost of cotton yarn goes on raw materials. Selling costs may reach even higher proportions. The costs of labour and materials in patent medicines is generally negligible in comparison with the price. Half of the price of milk goes to meet the cost of the distributor. In furniture, jewellery and luxury goods of all kinds, a distributor's margin of 50% and upwards is common. Clearly, a slight saving in the cost of distribution may be more valuable than a substantial cut in manufacturing costs. What we have to decide, however, is not whether there is room for economy, but whether there are more opportunities to make such economies in a large than in a small business.

First of all, the large buyer is able to obtain preferential treatment. He is quoted the lowest prices and offered discounts and rebates. He can obtain freight concessions from railway and road transport companies, liberal credit from the banks, and prompt delivery, careful attention, and special facilities from manufacturers. Even when others go short of materials, he is still able to obtain them. This preferential treatment is often the fruit of bargaining strength. Prices must be 'cut to the bone' because the large buyer might enter into competition with the firms from which he buys.

The bargaining advantages of large businesses make them profitable. But they do not make them *efficient*. A big firm may put money in its

---

[1] The small business, however, may be more successful in recruitment of new workers because the employer can pick recruits to suit his own requirements, see to their training, and detect misfits earlier than would be possible in a larger firm.

pocket by using its bargaining strength to beat down the price of materials. But it does so only at the expense of some other firm. The mere transfer of profit from one firm to another works no more improvement from the social point of view than the operations of gamblers or pickpockets. It is not a true economy at all. Similarly a big firm may find itself in a position of monopoly and mark up the price of its products, or sell an inferior quality at the old price. Here, too, there is no economy but only the exploitation of a monopoly advantage. Preferential treatment of large-scale buyers is a sign of economy in marketing only when it is offered by the seller in consequence of a reduction in his costs.

Such a reduction will normally take place when a large order enables plant to be run to capacity and without constant adjustment and frequent spoilage. A truckload will not cost twice as much to transport as two half-filled trucks. Steel sections rolled to one specification will cost less than an assortment of sections of the same weight, since the work will not be held up by the need to change the rolls. A large order which gives a factory steady work for six months is obviously more satisfactory than a series of small orders which provide work intermittently. In these and similar cases, better terms can be quoted for large orders than for small, and the firms which are big enough to place large orders make corresponding savings.

A reduction in costs also takes place because large orders enable the sales staff to be used to capacity. If customers double their orders it will not be necessary to double the sales staff. A traveller for one variety of tinned foods can book an order for 57 with little extra trouble.

The large firm, then, enjoys preferential treatment, partly because of the economies of large orders. It also enjoys other advantages in marketing. It can employ expert buyers, skilled in the selection and blending of materials. It can submit its materials to strict tests, grading them so that the final product is of uniform quality, and reducing the risk of waste from faulty materials. It can generally bide its time in buying and selling, and refrain from making purchases or sales when the market is unfavourable. Its customers will have the advantage of a better service of repairs and replacements than those who have bought from smaller firms. In making their purchases, they will have a wider range of choice, out of a greater variety of stocks, and will frequently be able to obtain immediate delivery from stock of goods which a smaller firm would require time to manufacture.

Financial economies

The large firm has also many financial advantages. It has a wider reputation and more influence amongst those who have money to lend or invest. It can borrow from bankers upon better security and raise capital more readily through the issue of shares and debentures than a small firm. There is a wide and regular market for these shares, so that shareholders can realize their capital without any of the trouble to which they would be put in a small private concern. Thus the cost of obtaining credit or of raising fresh capital is lower for a large than for a small firm.

This difference in the cost of borrowing might seem to be proof of a bargaining advantage rather than of true economy. But the lending of money in large quantities, like the bulk purchase of materials, is less costly than the lending of money in small quantities. A system of large-scale production allows capital to be raised with more convenience to the lender than a system where production is in the hands of a large number of small firms. This convenience to the lender – for instance, the greater ease with which he can recover his capital – is an economy of scale exactly like the convenience of supplying a large order rather than a series of small ones.

Risk-bearing economies

Large firms are often less exposed to risk than small ones. First of all, they are able to eliminate risks by grouping them. We can often predict what will happen *on the average* with fair certainty when the *individual* items defy prediction altogether. Thus we can say with some confidence that 5000 people will commit suicide in Britain next year, but we cannot possibly say who they will be. Similarly with births and deaths, motor accidents, burglaries, fires, and all the contingencies against which we can insure. The larger the number of instances, the less the risk of errors in judgement. In a large business, therefore, where the same operation is more often repeated than in a small one, uncertainty can be reduced.

The grouping of risks is of particular importance in finance. A large bank or insurance company, for example, tends to be more stable than a small one because it is less likely to be overwhelmed by a purely local catastrophe. The collective investments of a large bank are far more secure than investments of each of the branches. Similarly the insurance benefits payable by a large company vary less from year to year and can be more accurately foreseen than the benefits payable by a small company. Through their greater stability, large financial enterprises are able to command the confidence both of their customers and of their investors. Thus they are in a position to quote attractive terms for their services and to raise their capital comparatively cheaply.

When similar risks are grouped, the law of averages applies and uncertainty is reduced. When dissimilar risks are grouped, the advantage is less definite, but far from negligible. The spreading of risks is, indeed, one of the main preoccupations of modern industry. Firms may seek to spread their risks by diversifying their output, or markets, or sources of supply, or processes of manufacture. Such diversification makes the firm less vulnerable to sudden changes and allows it to remain a going concern where smaller, less diversified, concerns would be forced to give up business.

(a) Diversification of output

Where a firm is likely to be injured by a decline in the demand for its product, it will be likely to look round for other products which can be easily manufactured simultaneously with the first. In this way, it may be able to level out a slump in one product against a boom in another. Or if something happens to interrupt the manufacture of one, it will still be possible to carry on with the manufacture of the others. One of the main reasons why mixed farming has such a hold on British agriculture, for example, is that it is unusual for all branches of farming to be equally depressed, so that the farmer who is selling several different products can make ends meet by setting the profits from one against the losses on the others.

(b) Diversification of markets

Even when only one product is manufactured, increased sales, if there are to be a larger number of markets than before, may reduce the danger of fluctuations in demand. The sale of electricity for all purposes is less variable than the sale to industrial consumers only; the total sale to domestic consumers is more stable than the sale for heating, lighting, or cooking only. It pays distributors, therefore, to develop the domestic market; or, if they already supply electricity for lighting, to encourage consumers to use electric radiators, refrigerators, and cookers – to say nothing of radios, razors, and hair-wavers, all of which are, or should be, used at different times of day, and sum up to give a comparatively stable demand. In the same way, a railway which is largely dependent upon mineral traffic may find it worth while to develop suburban passenger transport. A firm which sells a new product in a local market may seek to make the demand broader and steadier by advertising it on a national scale.

(c) Diversification of sources of supply and of processes of manufacture

Here the same principle applies. Large firms may be better able to maintain output when some particular source of raw materials is cut off (e.g., by a strike), or when some particular process of manufacture becomes uneconomical or impossible. If, for instance, they use steam power as well as electricity bought from a central distributing agency (the 'grid'), a failure in the supply of electricity, or a rise in the price of coal will not hold up production altogether. A large business is likely to draw its supplies of raw materials from a wider area than a small one, and will be less exposed, therefore, to the danger of having its supplies cut off altogether.

It may seem strange to think of the spreading of risk as an economy; but if we mean, by economy, 'making the best use of resources, including human judgement', the term is quite properly applied to the spreading of risks that are known to be great. A firm which goes on producing regardless of risks may turn out goods at very low cost for a time, but if it is left high and dry by a change which might have been foreseen, and which other firms foresaw, its costs in the long run will work out above, and not below, theirs. For it will have sunk capital in an organization which is put out of action by a change which might reasonably have been predicted. It will have led resources, to put it vulgarly, up the garden path, and committed them to uses in which they are of little further value. It would have been more *economical* to spread risks at the start by sacrificing some of the advantages of specialization for the safeguards of diversification[1].

[1] This line of argument must not, of course, be pushed too far. There are limits to the advantages of spreading risks. What these are depends upon what view it is 'reasonable' to take of the future, and how strongly one may 'reasonably' hold that view.

Risk-spreading economies only make for large-scale production if they do not greatly complicate the business of management. But this complication is hard to avoid when products, processes, and markets are diversified[1]. Risk-spreading and managerial economies, therefore, very often pull against one another. Sometimes the net result is in favour of large firms; when, for example, two products with different seasonal peaks can be dovetailed under one management. At other times the spreading of risks can be accomplished only in comparatively small firms. A mixed farm, for instance, requires far more supervision than a wheat farm in the prairies, and is much smaller, in spite of the larger number of things which it produces[2].

Risk-spreading and technical economies are also in conflict with one another. A firm cannot obtain the full benefit of the technical advantages of large-scale production unless it sinks a great deal of capital in machinery and plant. If the plant can be run to capacity, so that it produces steadily on the scale for which it was designed, technical economies can be exploited up to the hilt. But if there is a risk of discontinuous operation, small firms using less expensive machinery, or less elaborately organized, may come into their own. In the steel industry, for example, it is very often the relatively small plants which survive an industrial depression most successfully. They are inferior, from the technical point of view, to large integrated plants designed to handle enormous outputs. But they have the advantage of lower standing charges on their machinery and plant, and have less difficulty, therefore, in making enough profit on a low output to cover these charges. They can also make savings more readily on operating costs if output has to be reduced below capacity. In a large interated plant, there is a nice balance between the blast furnaces and coking plant, the steel furnaces and the rolling mill. But this balance is completely upset if the plant has to run below the level of output for which it was designed. The heat supplied by the coking plant, or consumed in the soaking pit, cannot be halved to match a halving in the output of steel. If blast furnace gas is used to generate electricity, it will be impossible to damp down the furnaces and keep the rolling mill in operation. The team of men who work the plant at full capacity will be almost as large as the team required for an output 20% lower. In a small firm operating costs are more flexible. A firm owning no blast furnaces, for example, will find it easier to substitute scrap for pig-iron in its steel furnaces whenever scrap is comparatively cheap. It will also be more adaptable to quick *changes* in output. The costs of damping down and relighting furnaces, or of stopping and starting again in any other part of the works, are high in a large plant, where regular operation at a constant level of output is indispensable to efficiency. In a small steelworks changes in output are less disorganizing and can be made at less cost. Thus the risk of change, like the risk of operating below capacity, tends to halt the growth of the firm below the technical optimum.

---

[1] 'The more restricted the variety of the processes undertaken by a single business, . . . the simpler is the task of direction. The more simple the work of direction, the larger is the volume of output which can be efficiently controlled by a single mind. And the larger the volume of output the greater is the scope for the major economies of modern techniques.' F. Lavington, 'Technical Influences on Vertical Integration', *Economica*, 1927, pp. 27–28.

[2] Smaller, judged by the total value of what it produces, and not simply in point of area.

The spreading of risks through an increase in sales will normally also reduce marketing costs. This double economy in marketing and risk-spreading is always a temptation to firms to put new products on the market, especially when they have their own sales organization. A familiar example is the farmer who takes to raising chickens as a side-line and sells the eggs from his milk-cart. But risk-spreading, as we have seen, does not always make for an increase in output and sales. In mixed farming and steel-making, for example, risks are on the side of the small firm. Some marketing economies may have to be sacrificed, therefore, to permit of the spreading of risks by the small farm and steel-works. The large wheat farmer who changes over to mixed farming will find that his marketing costs have risen.

The logic of large-scale production

Many of these economies of large-scale production are illustrations of three general principles which have been named by Professor Sargant Florence: the principle of multiples, the principle of bulk transactions and the principle of massed (or pooled) reserves[1]. The first of these we encountered in discussing the economies of linked processes and the consequent need to balance the outputs of specialized machines at their lowest common multiple if the machines are to work to full capacity. The same principle underlies the employment of specialists and the full utilization of managerial ability[2]. Sometimes it is referred to as the principle of indivisibility since it rests on the impossibility of reproducing a machine on a smaller scale. The second principle underlies most of the marketing and financial economies that have been described: a large order or a large loan may involve no more trouble than a small one. But the principle also embraces what we have called 'economies of increased dimensions' which derive from having a big unit with the same mechanical properties as a smaller one. The same locomotive may either draw more trucks or bigger trucks: in either event the unit cost of transport will be reduced. The third principle, which is the most difficult to understand, can be regarded as the basis of what we have described as 'risk-bearing economies'. Professor Sargant Florence illustrates it in relation to the holding of stocks and shows that, with a large turnover, it is not necessary to increase stocks proportionately. One of the principal functions of stocks is to meet aberrations in demand but the greater the number of individual orders, 'the more likely are deviations to cancel out and to leave the actual average results nearer to the expected results'[3]. Thus the size of the stock held in reserve need not increase proportionately to output if orders are more numerous and the cost of holding stocks is correspondingly reduced.

---

[1] P. S. Florence, *The Logic of British and American Industry* (London, 1953), pp. 50–52.

[2] Cf. *ibid.*, p. 52: 'Any given specialization of equipment or men involves for balanced production a large scale of operation or production; but conversely it is only a large scale of operation or production that admits of specialization with all its well-known economic advantages. It is only large-scale production that will justify a special research organization, intensive costing, or the working up of by-products able to occupy researchers, cost accountants or by-product plant profitably for their full time.'

[3] Florence, *The Logic of British and American Industry*, p. 51.

Is size ever a handicap?

The economies of scale which we have described relate to particular commodities: the bigger the output, the greater the efficiency with which a single commodity can be produced. Economies of scale, and the consequent savings in costs, may be reaped at the level of a single plant, or in a group of plants owned by a single firm or, if they are external economies, they may involve a whole industry. Some external economies may be obtainable only when the total scale of output – not the output of a single commodity – is large either in relation to a particular area or over the whole economy. Indeed, they may, like some economies of information, be world-wide and dependent on the size of world markets rather than of the national market. At whatever level they are enjoyed, they are reflected in increased productivity, so that, as the market becomes larger and specialization can be carried further, costs of production fall.

We may reasonably ask, however, whether costs always fall with size or whether there may not be some countervailing tendency for size to become a handicap. This is a question that economists have usually discussed in relation to individual firms and commodities. It is not without interest, however, in relation to industrial areas as well, since size may begin to bring congestion and each newcomer may create inconvenience instead of adding to the facilities enjoyed by established firms. The reason why economists have concentrated on firms and commodities is that they have found difficulty in explaining why, if costs fall continuously with output, one firm should not succeed in capturing the entire market. If the odds are so heavily on the large firm by virtue of its size, how do small firms manage to carry on?

This is a question to which we shall turn in the next chapter. Three explanations have been put forward, one in terms of the difficulty of efficient management in large firms, one in terms of market limitations, and one in terms of the risk of loss from larger outputs. We shall deal here only with the first.

The optimum firm

The implication of this explanation is that, once a firm's production exceeds a certain volume it begins to encounter increasing difficulty in coordinating its activities and managerial *dis*economies creep in. The *dis*economies are sufficient to offset any remaining technical or other economies of scale so that eventually higher outputs involve it in higher unit costs. On this showing, there would be some optimum scale of production at which costs were at a minimum. Firms producing on a scale smaller than this (i.e., of less than optimum size) would be incurring higher costs, e.g., by sacrificing the use of expensive machinery without any compensating advantage. Firms of more than optimum size would also be incurring higher costs, e.g., because the organization was cumbersome and beyond the powers of its directors to manage properly.

A further implication would be that any concentration of production in a single firm, or in a nationalized industry, would run the risk of losing some of the advantages of large-scale production because of the comparative inefficiency of management in a very large productive unit. The maximum economy would be obtained by dispersing the total output over several firms of optimum size; and this would be true independently of any further gains that might result from the competition of those firms with one another.

Now there is no doubt that this line of explanation is in keeping with a great deal of everyday experience. It is common ground that the larger the firm, the more complicated, as a rule, are the problems of management. These problems manifest themselves in the difficulty of ensuring proper coordination between different departments and different people and in the need to devolve more authority on subordinates. It is harder to maintain speed of decision when there are more people to be consulted and harder to prevent misunderstandings as the chain of command lengthens.

The need for delegation

First of all, there is a limit to what one man can take in, reflect upon and decide about. It is impossible to supervise the work of more than a small group of immediate subordinates if only because it takes time to discuss matters with them and time is the scarcest commodity of which a top manager disposes. The more matters arise for decision, therefore, the more necessary it becomes to share or delegate authority. But this raises a fresh set of problems. Those who share authority, like the members of a Cabinet, must have confidence in one another's capabilities, good sense and above all loyalty. They must be willing to accept the decisions of their colleagues within the area of competence allotted to each and abide by the collective decision in all matters referred upwards for a joint review. Any reservations on this score are bound to lead to vacillation and delay, give rise to personal conflict and rivalry, and take from the efficiency of the whole organization.

Difficulties of delegation

Similar difficulties accompany the delegation of authority to subordinates: with this addition, that it may be more difficult to retain the loyalty of an able subordinate precisely because he may dislike being in a subordinate position. Moreover, the more complex the problems that create the need to delegate, the more awkward is the task of coordination. If every man's duties are precisely defined, he may show an excess of zeal not to usurp those duties and shirk responsibility for a decision. If his duties are not precisely defined, he may get to cross-purposes with his colleagues, indulge in empire-building, fail to maintain liaison with other departments, or just slack. If delegation is on a hierarchical basis, each man down the line taking responsibility for every aspect of the work of his department, from buying materials to training staff, there will be little scope for the specialists on each of these aspects. If it is on a functional basis, there is likely to be friction between the heads of the specialist departments: high specialization, in management as in everything else, means a looseness of contact between the specialists – between the sales manager and the works manager, the chief engineer and the head of the research department, the materials controller and the finance director – and those loose contacts can breed oversights, misunderstandings and demarcation disputes. Even when a staff is attached to a hierarchical line of command – in the line-and-staff system of organization – so as to feed in expert advice to each departmental head and undertake research, prepare plans or check results on his behalf, there are still a number of inherent weaknesses in a large organization: a tendency to red tape; a decline in the sense of urgency; failure in communications, both in the flow of information to those who need it and between those who are in charge of the organization and those whose work is being organized.

All this may be true; but it does not justify us in holding that firms become progressively less efficient the larger they grow, or that large firms are unable to survive competition with smaller firms because they have passed some managerial optimum. On the contrary, the biggest firms seem to be successfully maintaining their place in the economy and to be growing still bigger[1]. As a firm grows, it develops a new administrative structure appropriate to its size; this takes time and the fact that it takes time means that there is a limit to the *rate* at which a firm can grow without loss of efficiency[2]. It is quite possible also that the effort of growth may prove too much for a firm that has to make a rather large jump in size and that, before it has reorganized its administrative structure satisfactorily, it will make heavy losses and be wound up. There is no need to swing to the opposite extreme and suggest that large firms are immune from disaster. But, given time, they should be able to decentralize their organization sufficiently to permit of efficient operation[3].

Financial groups

A large firm may push decentralization to the point at which it consists of a group of separately organized businesses, enjoying almost complete autonomy. General Motors Corporation, for example, allows individual units in its system to compete with one another and seeks 'to make each separate unit self-contained, complete with all the functions essential to its full development'[4]. The companies in the Vickers group 'operate themselves very largely. Vickers Limited itself is a holding company, holding in almost all cases a 100% holding. It acts as the financial controller, and indeed the banker, in regard to all the financial requirements of the companies.'[5]

---

[1] See pp. 110–111.

[2] For a fuller discussion see E. T. Penrose, *The Theory of the Growth of the Firm* (Oxford, 1959), pp. 18 *et seq.*

[3] Cf. Florence, *The Logic of British and American Industry*, p. 64, 'The contention here is not that large organizations will inevitably be more efficient than small; but simply that it is *not* inevitable that larger organizations will eventually fail because of management. Corporate management may become *more* efficient with size owing to specialization of member managers, or if it becomes less efficient, its deficiency may in effect be counter-balanced by other factors. Sometimes admittedly there will be no counter-balance. Some firms fail with size because of management, if the immediate jump in size which they attempt is too great; or if the management is incapable of adapting its structure, or (and this is important for whole industries) if each unit transaction which management tries to undertake requires close attention to detail and quick adjustment to uncertain circumstances.'

[4] Annual Report, 1942, quoted by Penrose, *The Theory of the Growth of the Firm*, p. 175n.

[5] Evidence before the Committee on the Working of the Monetary System, Q11303.

Where companies are so loosely associated in a single group, bound together by financial control rather than as parts of a single administrative structure, it is difficult to see how size can present any real handicap on the score of managerial inefficiency. Yet as Mrs Penrose has pointed out, the tendency for the biggest firms to move in this direction is already perceptible.

> As an industrial firm becomes larger and larger, and its operations become progressively more decentralized with the lines of authority becoming more tenuous, permitting greater autonomy in the constituent parts, is it not possible that the firm will increasingly acquire the characteristics of a financial holding company, lose those of an industrial firm, and finally become virtually indistinguishable from an investment trust? And if this does happen, can we safely assume that the principles that govern the growth of an industrial firm are equally applicable when the organization is metamorphosed into an essentially financial firm?[1]

Is there an optimum size of firm?

These questions point to one of the weaknesses in the concept of the optimum size of firm. The concept makes sense only if it is applied to a group of firms making similar products, i.e., to an industry. A large firm may be a comparatively small producer of wooden furniture. Its efficiency as a producer of wooden furniture will be related, not just to its output of this one product but to the total scale of its operations as well. If we try to apply the concept of the optimum, therefore, we have first to decide whether it is wooden furniture and the scale on which it is being produced, or the actual firm, and the scale of its operations, that we have in mind. The firm may be a highly efficient producer of a wide variety of products, including wooden furniture, and may limit its production of the latter because it prefers to concentrate its resources in other directions. The scale of its production of furniture is low; but this is no proof that there would be little economy in large-scale production within a single firm of a different type. On the other hand, the total scale of production is high; but this is equally no proof that large firms, by virtue of their size, are particularly suited to the industry of furniture-making.

While we can analyse the economies that result from larger outputs of individual commodities, and the economies that result from the larger scale of operations of an individual firm, it is confusing to tie together the two types of economy as if all firms produced only a single commodity. Once we start comparing, not some idealized group of firms of varying size all producing the same article, but the large and small firms of real life, we have to take account of the changes in product-mix, and the simultaneous changes in administrative structure that go with size. This makes it very difficult to compare like with like and measure efficiency against some identifiable optimum; the satisfactory basis of comparison is cost of production or power to survive in free competition with other firms.

The structure of industry is highly complex, with different products integrated with one another in different firms and a fairly wide scatter in

[1] Penrose, *The Theory of the Growth of the Firm*, p. 19.

the scale on which they produce any one commodity. There may be an 'optimum' social output of the commodity: beyond a certain volume it may become increasingly difficult, without some rise in cost, to produce more of it. There may also be an optimum distribution of this output between different firms and a *minimum* scale of production below which efficiency is demonstrably sacrificed. There may, finally, be some weakness of organization to which large firms are more prone than small. But we cannot usefully talk of an optimum size of *firm* so long as firms of different sizes do different things and do them in different ways with a different administrative structure.

Influence of the industrial environment

Similarly, we cannot look at a firm in isolation from its industrial environment. Firms exist in association and in competition with other firms; they are linked organically with one another[1]. Their growth is conditioned by the play of opportunity on a given endowment of managerial ability, financial strength, and so on, just as the growth of organisms is conditioned by the play of environment on a given hereditary endowment. Firms grow by grafting and proliferation rather than as homogeneous units with which new units of the same kind are geared mechanically.

A firm, therefore, must be looked at against a background of market conditions from which we cannot abstract. Its costs depend not simply on how it does things (that is, on what is happening inside the firm), but also on what it has to do, and what it has to do depends upon the industrial environment. If the environment changes, the optimum changes, and the growth of the firm of itself may be sufficient to alter the environment.

If, for example, the growth of a firm reduces the competition to which it is exposed this may automatically ease the task of management: industrial combination might create an environment favourable to the operation of larger units that could survive intense competition – 'favourable' in the sense of making for lower costs, not just of making for higher profits. Many of the risks which keep the optimum firm comparatively small are themselves the product of competition. The individual producer must adapt his plans to the plans of his competitors without knowledge of their intentions. He is in the dark about the new models and new products which they mean to bring out, the output which they propose to market, and the methods by which they hope to market that output. Thus he is kept busy meeting their competition, retaliating in kind for invasions of his market,

[1] Compare A. N. Whitehead, *Science and the Modern World* (Pelican, London, 1938), p. 238.

'The trees in a Brazilian forest depend upon the association of various species of organisms, each of which is mutually dependent on the other species. A single tree by itself is dependent upon all the adverse chances of shifting circumstances. The wind stunts it: the variations in temperature check its foliage: the rains denude its soil: its leaves are blown away and are lost for the purpose of fertilization. . . . But in nature the normal way in which trees flourish is by their association in a forest. Each tree may lose something of its individual perfection of growth, but they mutually assist each other in preserving the conditions for survival. The soil is preserved and shaded; and the microbes necessary for its fertility are neither scorched, nor frozen, nor washed away. . . . A species of microbes which kills the forest, also exterminates itself.'

scheming to steal a march on them by some new agreement with distributors or some new advertising campaign, giving uncertainty for uncertainty. If all this competitive effort were inevitable, the optimum firm would remain small, since a large firm would lack the adaptability and thrustfulness necessary in a highly competitive market. But competitive secrecy and uncertainty are by no means inevitable. A monopoly gets rid of both. So also would nationalization – the formation of a state monopoly.

Competitive pressure may also induce a firm to make a wide variety of products, and this variety, by complicating the problem of management, tends to limit the growth of the firm. In a monopoly, however, it would be possible to carry specialization a good deal further, and to concentrate particular products on particular units. Similarly, although it tends to change the temper of management and create a more elaborate hierarchy than private enterprise, nationalization is capable of yielding important economies without the dangers to the public interest that a private monopoly would involve.

We cannot assume, therefore, that there is necessarily a loss in efficiency if an industry is taken over by a monopoly or if it is nationalized by the state; and this is true even in industries in which the typical productive unit is relatively small.

Chapter 7
Small-scale production

In Chapter 6 our attention was concentrated on the advantages of large-scale production, while the forces making for small-scale production were touched on very briefly. In this chapter we shall look at the other side of the picture and try to discover why small-scale production still holds its own.

The overwhelming majority of business units are extremely small; many are one-man businesses and many more employ only a handful of workers. There are, for example, about half a million shopkeepers and 300 000 farmers, while the total number of persons engaged in shopkeeping and farming is under three million. In the building industry at least 1 man in 10 works on his own account or as employer. In the professions, in road transport, and in a wide range of service trades from laundries to bookmaking, the small firm predominates. Even in manufacturing industry the number of really large firms is tiny. In 1963 there were only 100 firms in manufacturing industry in Britain employing over 5000 workers and about 1000 firms employing over 1000 workers. The smaller firms, however, did not account for more than a limited proportion of employment and output in the industries covered (which excluded public enterprises and building firms). There were about an equal number of workers in manufacturing firms employing over 10 000 workers and in firms employing between 1000 and 10 000 workers, and workers in each of these two groups were not greatly outnumbered by those in the smaller firms employing less than 1000 workers.

If we turn from firms or enterprises to plants or establishments, the picture is not very different. As will be seen from *Table 7.1*, which relates exclusively to the factory trades in 1975, there are about 100 000 establishments employing 7.5 m workers. Those employing over 1500 workers account for about 35% of all manufacturing employment: the much larger number of establishments employing between 100 and 1000 workers account for 45% of total manufacturing employment; the remaining 20% is accounted for by the large number of small establishments, nearly all of them separate enterprises, that employ less than 100 workers. Since output per head is higher in the bigger (and more mechanized) plants, these are in an even more dominant position in terms of output and sales than in terms of employment.

TABLE 7.1. Size of establishments in manufacturing industry in the United Kingdom in 1975

Average number employed	Number of establishments	Number of persons employed (000)	Proportion of total employment (%)	Proportion of net output (%)
1–10	53 993	259	3.5	
10–19	16 797	242	3.2	
20–49	14 562	447	6.0	} 16.7
50–99	7 443	521	7.0	
100–199	4 931	691	9.2	8.5
200–499	3 848	1 193	16.0	15.6
500–999	1 428	993	13.3	14.3
1000–1499	440	537	7.2	7.2
1500 and over	647	2 584	34.6	37.6
	104 089	7 467	100.0	100.0

Source: Census of Production for 1974 and 1975. Summary tables: Establishment Analyses

These figures understate the degree of concentration in the larger units since one firm may own several establishments and several firms may be controlled by a single business unit. There are literally scores of commodities – salt, mustard and cotton thread are familiar examples – produced exclusively or almost exclusive by one or two big firms. The degree of concentration in large units varies greatly from industry to industry; it is high in the chemical, metal and engineering group and low in the building and clothing industries. Over a wide span of industry, the typical situation is one of what we later describe as 'oligopoly': namely, domination of the market by a small group of sellers.

In a study of concentration in British industry Hart and Clarke found that in a sample of 132 industries the five largest concerns employed in 1973 an average of 42.5% of the workers in the industry and operated an average of 10 plants[1]. They also showed that the degree of concentration had increased quite markedly over the previous 10 years (in contrast to the United States where very little change seems to have occurred since the war). There is evidence that the degree of concentration in British industry was very little greater in 1951 than in 1935 and that the upward trend became rather steeper in the 1950s, very much steeper in the 1960s and then slackened again in the early 1970s[2].

In spite of this concentration in large units, the fact remains that there are small firms in most trades and that in some trades it is the large firm that is rare. How are we to account for this, in view of the economies to which large-scale production leads?

1. In some industries, the answer is a straightforward one: it is the absence of any major economies of scale. There may be little scope, for example, for highly capital-intensive techniques and no close links

[1] P. Hart and R. Clarke, *Concentration in British Industry 1935–75* (Cambridge, 1980), pp. 23, 45.
[2] *Ibid.*, p. 27.

between succeeding stages of manufacture. Technical economies may be realizable in a comparatively small plant and there may be no strong motives to combine different plants under a single control. Thus a small cafe does not suffer from the handicaps of a small aircraft firm.

2. A second reason is that the process of growth takes time. This is true partly because of imperfections in competition that give shelter to an existing concern and allow it to carry on in spite of comparative inefficiency; and partly because a large firm cannot grow without a great deal of effort, involving planned additions to its resources and their reorganization in a new administrative framework. Thus many small firms are able to survive for a time because the bigger firms suffer from indigestion if they try to gobble them up too quickly.

3. The fact that it takes time for big firms to expand helps the small firms in another way. Since the economy as a whole is growing, new opportunities of expansion are for ever being created and these opportunities are open to the small as well as to the larger firms. If the opportunities increase faster than the large firms are able to seize them, and if there is no special difficulty in entering the trade, there is obviously room for small firms to grow both in size and numbers even if they are unable to match the large firms in productive efficiency[1].

4. A fourth explanation is that there are always plenty of people ready to start a new business, many of whom must ultimately fail. Small firms are constantly being launched as new enterprises since it is usual in business, as in human existence, to start small and grow. These new enterprises show a high 'infant mortality' and may be operated for years at a loss before being finally wound up. The eventual failures – and, of course, the eventual successes – swell the number of small firms at any point in time[2].

5. Large firms that want to avoid being labelled monopolists may tolerate or even encourage smaller competitors. Similarly, orders may be placed regularly with high-cost small firms in order to keep them in business as an insurance against complete dependence on a single large supplier.

6. In addition to these reasons, there are the various obstacles to growth to which we referred in the previous chapter: managerial obstacles, market obstacles and financial obstacles. Managerial obstacles have already been discussed and they are also implicit in the second and third of the reasons given above, which lay emphasis on the effort of growing rather than on the additional managerial burdens that larger size may bring with it. We shall deal briefly with these burdens before turning to marketing and financial obstacles to growth.

---

[1] Cf. Penrose, *The Theory of the Growth of the Firm*, pp. 222–223, 'The productive opportunities of small firms are thus composed of those interstices left open by the large firms which the small firms see and believe they can take advantage of. If enough small firms judge their prospects reasonably correctly and act accordingly, then the rate of growth of the economy will exceed the rate of growth of the large firms. And if the existing small firms are unable or unwilling to fill all the interstices, there will be scope for the successful creation of new firms.'

[2] For example, American studies show that one or two retailers out of ten go out of business within the first year of operation and that in some cities less than half the manufacturing firms last as long as four years (Florence, *The Logic of British and American Industry*, p. 53). The death-rate appears to fall rapidly with size (*Ibid.*, p. 66).

Managerial obstacles

First of all, the range and complexity of the problems of management are greater in large than in small firms. In any industry, therefore, where there is need of constant supervision and rapid decision – where each firm must use a great deal of management, or 'decision-taking', per unit of product – small firms will predominate. Their advantages lie in the absence of divided responsibility, in the attention which they can give to detail, and in their ability to cater exactly for the wants of their customers. In retail shopkeeping, in farming, and in trades where the influence of fashion is great, or a very high quality of product is demanded, the small firm has no difficulty in holding its ground. But in trades that can be reduced largely to routine – the railways, the post office, etc. – or in which the range of problems is narrow – in cotton-spinning as compared with cotton-weaving[1], or in the worsted as compared with the woollen trades[2] – the advantage lies with the larger firm.

Given the range of problems in an industry, the large firm may be assisted by the development of new forms of organization and new methods of business management. The rise of cost accounting, for example, makes it easier to cope with the problem of tracing waste, and allows comparisons to be drawn between the efficiency of different departments and factories. The joint-stock system provides the large firm with facilities for raising enormous amounts of capital, and smooths the path of able men as they try to expand their business to the limits of their organizing ability. The spread of education and the growth of business morality makes it easier to delegate tasks to subordinates. Thus in industries where advantage can be taken of cost accounting, scientific management, up-to-date office equipment, and so on, even complex problems can be handled satisfactorily.

The managerial obstacle to growth is, in the last resort, a personal one. There is a limit to the range and complexity of the problems which a businessman, however able and however ably served, can tackle satisfactorily. The burden of detail becomes enormous, particularly in a business made up of scattered plants faced with their own special problems. If there is little devolution of responsibility to departmental and branch managers, they are deprived of initiative and degenerate into mere cogs in the machine. If, on the other hand, responsibility is delegated, subordinates of outstanding ability must be appointed and must be handsomely paid. These subordinates may, and frequently do, launch out on their own in competition with their former employers. The zeal and energy which they then show for their own interests may be out of all proportion to their previous efforts on behalf of their employers, for as salaried officers they have much less at stake, and are much less inclined to make sacrifices. From a mixture of motives – from a love of independence and uncertainty,

---

[1] Cotton yarns are spun by standard methods to standard specifications; in weaving, on the other hand, the mills generally produce a fairly wide range of product, differing in quality and pattern.
[2] The woollen trades call for much more skill in blending from a great variety of raw materials.

from pride or ambition, or the urge to create[1] – men may prefer to run a small business of their own rather than act as subordinates at a higher rate of pay. Their workers, too, may prefer to remain with an employer who knows their habits and history rather than move to a larger business where there can be no personal contact between employers and employed.

Some small firms are simply the large firms of tomorrow: not very many, because there are few large firms at any time. But in some of the newer industries, where a balance between large and small firms has not yet been struck, a rapidly expanding market often carries some of the small firms along with it, until what was initially the province of a host of small firms, many of them new, becomes dominated by the larger survivors.

There are other small firms that would be quite capable of expanding if the management showed more enterprise. These firms may not be organized to take full advantage of the opportunities open to them; they may be family businesses, content to jog along with a steady turnover, lacking the managerial resources to plan for expansion, and more afraid of prejudicing existing profits than attracted by the chance of doubling them.

From the point of view of management, therefore, small firms may survive, for one of three reasons. They may be large firms in the making; they may be capably managed by men who are indifferent to the possibilities of growth; or they may be managed by men who lack the judgement, experience, and organizing ability needed in order to manage a large firm. Similarly, large businesses may be dwindling because of imcompetent management; or they may be growing because of the enterprise of the management; or they may be changing little in size and be managed with more than average competence.

Market obstacles

Where the market is too narrow to permit of large-scale manufacture, the firm necessarily remains small. A firm might reduce its costs by doubling its output, but if the firm could not dispose of the extra output, there would be sense in producing it. It is only when the market is big enough that no economies of scale need to be sacrificed and firms can expand freely in size.

The market may be limited in various ways.

(a) Geographical

First, it may be limited by distance, as for example, the market of the local baker is limited. Rather than incur high transport costs (including waste in transit) by supplying distant customers, firms may prefer to produce on a small scale for local needs only. Whenever firms are distributing their products over a thinly-populated district, expansion will involve heavy

---

[1] One motive of some importance is the desire of the owner to leave to his son an occupation as head of his business and not just the capital which could be realized by selling out.

outlays on marketing to set against any savings in the cost of manufacture, and the firms will remain small. This is true also of sources of supply. If the raw materials of an industry are widely scattered, and are expensive to assemble at a central site, production will tend to be carried on in scattered factories drawing on local supplies. The milling of timber, grain, and minerals illustrates this tendency, while the furniture trade and the light castings industry illustrate the first.

The obstacle of high transport costs is all the greater when markets and sources of supply are not only diffused but also overlap. If production is carried on by small firms up and down the country, the cost of assembling and radiating supplies is greatly reduced, and since producers and consumers remain in close contact with one another, there is no need for a long chain of middlemen. In dairying, for example, there is an obvious advantage in having villages and small towns supplied with milk straight from the farm. But if the areas of production and consumption lie some distance apart, so that there is a bottleneck through which supplies must flow on their way to market, it will be easy for large firms, located at the bottlenecks, to drive small firms, situated on each side, out of business. This point can be illustrated from the live-stock industry. In countries and regions which export a large proportion of their meat (e.g. Argentina, New Zealand or Scotland), the points of export are bottlenecks through which the meat must pass. Thus the cattle can be assembled for slaughter in large meat-packing establishments. In a country like England, however, where both the market and the cattle are spread all over the country, the slaughterhouses are much smaller in size, since the cost of assembling the cattle for slaughter and radiating the meat to local butchers from a central site would be very high. In the United States the importance of the export market has declined, and with it the importance of Chicago and the large packers. The expansion of the home market has led to a decentralization of the industry in smaller plants set up in the leading cattle districts.

Thus the obstacle of distance is strengthened by an increased overlapping of the areas of production and consumption. It is strengthened also by a rise in transport costs and by a reduction in the density of the market or of sources of supply. The trend, however, is generally towards *lower* transport costs and *increased* density. We find bread-making, for example, concentrated increasingly in bakeries in the towns as a result of improved methods of distribution. An area whose bread used to be made in bakeries scattered through villages and suburbs is now supplied by a few large bakers. A further example is provided by the brewing industry, where the substitution of canned for bottled beer, by reducing transport costs, operates in favour of the large firm. Similarly a fall in coal freights, or in the cost of transmitting electricity, may lead to the erection of larger power stations. An increase in the consumption of electricity within a given area (i.e., an increase in the density of demand) will have the same effect.

Distance, in other words, provides the small firm with a sheltered zone which other firms can with difficulty penetrate. Each small firm, supplying a local market, is partially insulated from competition, but if it tries to push its way into more distant markets, it meets with keener and keener competition round the fringe of invasion. This market resistance to expansion checks the growth of firms to their optimum size. The check will be greater the higher the cost of transport, the more scattered the market and the sources of raw materials, and the more they overlap.

(b) Psychological

This line of reasoning can be extended from geographical to any other limitation of the market. Each firm, as we shall see, is normally marketing products which differ slightly from the products of its competitors. In the shoe trade, for example, no two firms cater for exactly the same shape of feet, specialize in exactly the same range of sizes, use leather of exactly the same quality, or market their shoes in exactly the same pattern and style, with exactly the same guarantees and advertisements. Each firm has a clientele of its own, just like the bakers in adjoining villages. The market is broken up, not only by distance, but by the tastes, habits, and prejudices of consumers. Miss A insists on clogs, Miss B on brogues, so they buy from different firms. Mr Broadfoot finds comfort in the shoes of Messrs C; Mr Narrowfoot will buy from no one but Messrs D. One firm supplies Lady Snooty, another Mrs Bourgeois, a third John Hiker, a fourth baby Jones, and so on. The market for each firm is limited by the requirements of the customers who are within its 'sphere of influence'. There is thus a market resistance to expansion which can be overcome only by finding new buyers or by invading the market of other firms. This puts the firm to the expense either of special concessions to its customers, or of an advertising campaign, or of the manufacture of new brands of product. It has to attract new customers by reducing its price, or by selling a better quality of product, or by persuading people that its products are 'superior', or by doing something equally costly. These costs of growth, like high transport costs in a scattered market, shelter the small firm by penalizing invasion of its market. The more varied the attachments which consumers form (the less the density of demand), and the less responsive they are to efforts to change their attachments (e.g., by advertisement, or by concessions in service, quality, or price), the more difficult will it be to dislodge small firms from their hold on the market[1]. It is only when consumers are indifferent from whom they buy, and what brands they buy – or when they actually have a preference for dealings with large firms – that the market ceases to be a major obstacle to expansion.

Branch factories

The market obstacle can, however, be circumvented in two ways: by setting up branch factories, or by manfacturing a wide range of products or brands of the same product. The setting up of branch factories is a way of circumventing the geographical limitation of the market; the manufacture of a wide range of products is a way of circumventing the psychological limitation. Neither of these 'dodges' is altogether satisfactory.

---

[1] A familiar example is retailing, where small shops have an intimate knowledge of the requirements of their customers, and can bind them by the use of credit even when large firms are charging much lower prices.

Branch factories under a central management can supply the adjacent territory without incurring the high transport costs and other marketing expenses of a single large establishment. They can specialize in the articles, brands, and sizes required locally, and supply orders promptly from a stock which is small in comparison with the stock carried by independent units. Each branch can participate in the technical improvements made by the others, and can detect and eliminate waste by comparing its accounts regularly with theirs. Risks are spread, since a period of bad trade in one district can be set against a period of good trade in another, while if production is held up at one plant by fire or strike, customers can still be supplied from other plants. These and similar advantages makes for the combination of scattered plants in a single firm when the individual plants are prevented from growing by market limitations.

Distance, however, sets a limit to the combination of plants just as it does to the size of the individual plant. The more scattered the units and the poorer the system of communication between them, the more insuperable are the difficulties of efficient supervision by the central office. If local circumstances differ greatly, responsible and expensive district managers must be appointed. Each plant must be given more latitude, and this makes it all the harder for the central office to keep them in step with one another, and frame a suitable policy. In short, branch factories sooner or later bump up against the managerial obstacle to expansion.

The range of products

The same obstacle, as we have seen, checks the multiplication of products, patterns, styles, etc., within a single plant. The work of management becomes more complicated, and at the same time the technique appropriate to the large-scale manufacture of a single product or style of product has to be abandoned. More than this, multiplication of products very often fails in its object. For if every firm adopts the same expedient and tries to supply the whole gamut of varieties sold by its competitors, it will end by producing everything on a small scale and selling in a market which has shrunk because of the universal rise in costs of production. The public will be offered a wide variety of styles, but it will be denied the benefits of large-scale production, for each firm will manufacture much the same varieties as its competitors, instead of specializing on a limited range of styles and turning them out on a large scale. Sometimes the economy of concentrating on a few special lines is small and confined to the time saved in re-setting machinery. But more often the failure of firms to specialize more narrowly causes waste from the social point of view, while market resistances to growth simply increase *pari passu* with the variety of output of the typical firm.

Apart altogether from the social waste involved, the production of a whole range of styles, while it may be forced – or appear to be forced – on each manufacturer by the action of his competitors, does not free a firm from the limitations of its market. The pressure to expand may be diffused over a wider area; but so, too, is the resistance to expansion. If one firm markets a new variety of product, other firms tend to follow suit. Even if they do not, they can threaten retaliation in other ways. Suppose, for example, that the new variety sells well. Then unless new layers of demand are tapped, sales will be mainly at the expense of the old varieties, and competing firms will find themselves in difficulties. They must either reconcile themselves to reduced sales or fight to retain their 'share' of the market. Very likely, they will fight – for instance, by cutting prices, or by spending more on advertising. The firm which took the initiative will then lose some of its original gains. So long as the threat of retaliation has to be faced, therefore, the marketing of new varieties of product is not greatly successful in overcoming market resistance to growth.

There is a market resistance to expansion on the side of supply as well as on the side of demand. A firm – or more frequently an industry – may find it difficult to obtain adequate supplies of one or more of the factors of production – adequate, that is, for optimum production. Labour, land, materials, or money capital may be scarce, so that larger supplies can be obtained only at increasingly higher rates of pay. A rise in output will then bring about a rise in costs. Rather than incur such additional cost, firms may be content to remain small.

Financial obstacles

An important reason for the survival of small firms is the difficulty of procuring sufficient capital. A small firm seeking to expand has generally to finance extensions of plant out of profits, or out of the personal savings of its owners and their friends. It is usually ignorant in matters of finance and unfamiliar with institutions other than the joint-stock banks from which it might borrow. If it does try to borrow, it has a difficult job of interesting possible lenders who know little or nothing of its affairs or the capabilities of its management, cannot judge how well it would use the capital and want to be sure of getting back what they lend whenever they need the money. The security that it can offer is limited, and it has usually to meet more than usually rigorous tests of creditworthiness. The more the owner borrows, the more he puts at hazard the entire future of the business, not merely the loss of some of its capital; if the investment which he makes turns out badly, he may be unable to meet his debts and be forced into a bankruptcy that slower growth would have avoided. If, instead of seeking a loan he were prepared to sell a share in the business, he might attract capital more readily; but this is a price that few owners with good prospects of expansion willingly pay. The very single-mindedness by which they thrive makes them reluctant to share control or run any risk of having to surrender it. Thus even when additional capital could be found, the owner may not know where to go for it, may not be able to offer adequate security or may not be willing to accept the conditions on which it would be provided.

These obstacles are greatest where it is long-term capital that is required. Medium-term capital can be obtained for some purposes on hire purchase without the need to pledge anything except the specific assets acquired. This is an expensive form of credit, but highly convenient from the point of view of the small producer; he is not troubled with elaborate enquiries from the lender and his credit in other directions remains undiminished. For short-term credit he can draw on the banks or, with less difficulty, on trade credit from suppliers. The cost of trade credit, in terms of interest charges (and possibly also in loss of freedom to buy elsewhere) can, however, be very high and such credit does not provide a very reliable foundation for long-term expansion.

Finance is a more important limiting factor in private than in public companies. Once a firm is sufficiently large to be floated on the stock exchange it is likely to find the task of raising additional capital a great deal easier. As a public company with its shares quoted on the stock exchange it can make an issue of capital to its own shareholders or to the investing public, using the machinery of the new issue market. The rise of the joint-stock system has thus removed some of the more important financial obstacles to growth. How it has done this, and how far it has been successful, will be discussed in the next chapter.

There remains one group of forces which we may call 'desire for competitive strength'. These forces occasionally limit the growth of firms, but more usually encourage firms to combine so as to increase their bargaining power or in order to establish a monopoly position. This group of forces will be left over for analysis in Chapter 9.

Chapter 8

The finance of large-scale production

Before the industrial revolution, the representative firm was tiny by modern standards, and was owned and managed by one man or by a partnership. The chief industries were carried on on a small scale in the fields or in the cottages, rather than on a large scale in factory and mine. It was only in foreign trade that there was much scope for the large firm. It was in foreign trade, therefore, that the need for large-scale borrowing first made itself felt; and it was in foreign trade that modern methods of finance (e.g., through the joint-stock company) were first evolved.

The channels into which savings could flow, or through which they could be borrowed, were narrow. The land-owners and the merchants had almost a monopoly of capital and used it on their land and property or in their businesses without much recourse to borrowing. There was little scope for expansion and little incentive, therefore, to accumulate capital or to borrow it. Improvements to property, social display, and mere extravagance swallowed up what the capitalists of later centuries, putting money before magnificence, would have sunk in stocks and shares, or factory buildings and plant. It was not until later, when the agricultural revolution began to create opportunities for investment, that thrift acquired its attraction and its virtue.

The inventions of the eighteenth and nineteenth centuries, and above all the coming of the railway, increased enormously the scale to which a business could profitably grow. But large-scale production without borrowed capital was impossible. The immense sums required exceeded the fortune of even the richest capitalist. Nor was the alternative method of raising capital through partnerships at all suitable. Partnerships are possible only between persons who have complete confidence in an one another, since agreements made by any one partner are binding on the partnership. Each partner, moreover, is liable without limit for the entire debts of the partnership, however small the stake which he has in it. If one partner wishes to withdraw, or dies, it becomes necessary for the surviving partners either to buy him out – perhaps at great trouble to themselves – or find a purchaser who is acceptable to everyone. These difficulties – the moral and financial risks of partnership and the danger of unexpected withdrawals – multiply rapidly as the number of partners, or the capital which they have put up, increases. It is impracticable either to raise small sums from a large number of partners, or large sums from a small number. It is necessary, therefore, to find some device by which persons can provide the capital required by a large business without running the risks to which partners are exposed. The limited joint-stock company is just such a device.

Public companies

A joint-stock company, or business corporation as it is called in America, is a body corporate with a common seal, carrying on business under the management of a board of directors and owned by a group of shareholders. After registration, the company enjoys certain privileges which enable it to overcome the legal obstacles to growth that beset the one-man firm and the partnership. First, the moral risk is removed. A shareholder, unlike a partner, cannot bind the company by his acts. The decisions which bind the company are taken by his representatives, the directors, or by the officials appointed by them. So long, therefore, as shareholders have confidence in their directors, they have little need of confidence in one another. Partners require to be in daily contact with one another. But shareholders can sleep soundly in complete ignorance of the identity, and hence also of the honesty, ability and intentions of their fellow-shareholders. Secondly, in a limited company, the financial risk is greatly reduced. Before 1855, when limited liability was introduced, shareholders were regarded by the law as partners, pledging the whole of their property against any debts incurred by the company. If the company failed, therefore, the shareholders might be ruined. In 1855, however, it became legal to limit liability to the nominal value of the shares, so that, as a rule, the maximum loss which a shareholder stands to make is represented by the capital which he has actually invested. Finally, withdrawals cease to be troublesome. Shareholders are at liberty to sell out whenever they choose, and can do so without disturbance to the work of the company. There is an organized market (the stock exchange) in which shares are readily negotiable, so that there is usually no difficulty in finding a buyer.

The joint-stock company makes it possible to tap the savings of a large number of people, without requiring them to take part in the management of the company. These people provide the capital of the company and receive in return stocks, shares, debentures, etc., entitling them to an income in the form of dividends on their stocks and shares or interest on their debentures. The terms on which the capital is supplied differ for different classes of shareholder. There are differences in income-rights, in the risks which shareholders run, and in the power of control which they can exercise. The least definite rights to participate in the profits of the company, the greatest risks, and the greatest powers of control are those attaching to ordinary shares. At the other extreme are debentures, which are loans to the company, not shares in it. They carry a fixed rate of interest, comparatively little risk, and no power whatever over the company so long as interest is paid regularly and the rights of debenture-holders are not threatened. Between these limits, as a kind of compromise, stand the preference shares.

Shares and shareholders

In theory, control of a company normally rests with the ordinary shareholders. They elect – or perhaps one should say approve – the directors, and can, by exercising their voting rights, supersede the retiring directors until, after a period of years, a completely new board has been appointed. The ordinary shareholders rank last in their claims on the property of the company, and participate in the profits only after other shareholders have received their share. Thus they bear the heaviest risks. Preference shareholders normally have voting powers only when it is proposed to alter their rights, or to wind-up the company, or when their dividends are in arrears. They are paid, not a fluctuating dividend, but a fixed rate of, say 6%. This dividend is not exceeded when the company is making large profits, however high the dividend earned by ordinary shareholders. It may not be paid at all, if the company is in difficulties and failing to earn a large enough profit. The dividends paid to preference shareholders necessarily vary less than the dividends on ordinary shares, and the risks run are correspondingly less. They are less also because preference shares usually rank ahead of ordinary shares if the company fails and its assets have to be liquidated. This difference in risk corresponds to some extent with the difference which there is in voting power and control between the two types of share.

The capital of a company is not provided solely by its shareholders. Borrowings are made through the sale of bonds or debentures, and this borrowed capital goes to supplement the share capital. Debenture-holders are not, like shareholders, proprietors of the company. They are creditors with no voice in the management and policy so long as they receive interest on their bonds. The debentures which they hold are generally repayable after a stated term of years at a fixed price, and form a first charge on the assets of the company.

Private companies

When the capital required does not exceed £1m it is more economical to raise capital privately, rather than by public subscription. A private company can be formed enjoying many of the advantages of public joint-stock companies, including limited liability. Private companies need not publish their accounts; they cannot have more than 50 shareholders; and the transfer of their shares is restricted. They can be converted into public companies if they want to raise additional capital by inviting the public to buy their shares or if the owners are obliged to realize their capital, for example because of heavy estate duties. The smaller firms in British industry are mainly private companies; they are 10 times as numerous as public companies but, being much smaller on the average, they control only half as much capital.

The capital market

The complex of arrangements by which new capital can be raised is called the capital market. This is not the same as the stock exchange, which exists to facilitate the exchange of existing stocks, shares and debentures between one investor and another; it refers rather to fresh borrowing and lending, either by a new issue on the stock exchange or by transactions outside the stock exchange altogether. The public joint-stock company may make an issue of shares or debentures for public subscription, or it may prefer to make an issue privately to existing shareholders. In a private company the capital is normally provided by the owners or by their friends and business associates. In all companies, an important source of new capital is profit and the reserves accumulated out of past profits: most successful companies rely heavily on self-financing of this kind as a means of expanding their activities. There are also various financial intermediaries – insurance companies and investment trusts, for example – to which a company may turn for additional capital. Working capital, to finance stocks and work in progress, is normally raised on short term from the banks in the form of bank advances. The state may also lend a hand and set up new financial institutions to remedy real or supposed deficiencies in the capital market.

Investment and risk

The joint-stock system, then, increases the supply of capital at the disposal of a single business, and so removes one of the chief obstacles in the way of large-scale production. But large-scale production requires that capital shall be available not only in large amounts, but for long periods, and for risky undertakings. Large businesses almost invariably use much fixed capital. This capital is, so to speak, highly specialized – that is, sunk in forms from which it will not be recovered for many years (ploughs as compared with seed) or in forms with a very limited number of uses (boilers as compared with crude steel). The longer the life of the fixed assets (the building and plant), the longer the period for which investors must part with their capital; and the more highly specialized are the fixed assets (either because they are durable or because they are not adaptable), the greater will be the risks which investors run. It may prove impossible to make regular use (or indeed *any* use) of the fixed capital over the period of its life; or it may yield a return lower than was expected; or it may yield a return which, while up to expectations, is less than might have been obtained by holding the capital in a more liquid, less specialized form and taking advantage of a change in circumstances favourable to some other line of investment. Whatever the *result* of sinking capital in fixed assets, the uncertainty is great; and the large firm, with the bulk of its assets fixed and specialized, has given an unusually high quota of hostages to fortune and has given them irrevocably for an unusually long time.

Add to this the risks of producing in advance of demand. Any large business – and many small ones too – supplies a market remote in time and space – a market whose requirements cannot be accurately foreseen. The wants of this market lie in the future and at a distance, but production must be undertaken here and now. The whole organization of the business, and not just its fixed capital, is built and operated in ignorance and uncertainty of the future demand. The owners must adventure their capital over the period of production and bear the risk of loss through error or misfortune.

There are thus two difficulties which the joint-stock system has to overcome. The first arises from the desire of the investor for liquidity. He wishes to be able to recover his capital quickly and without loss; but it has been sunk in durable plant, and can be recovered (in depreciation allowances) only over the life of the plant. How can the needs of the investor be met? The answer is that although the asset is illiquid, the investor's shares are not. There is a market in which they can be sold at any time (but not necessarily at their purchase price) – the stock exchange. The function of the stock exchange is to make stocks and shares easily marketable and so encourage investment in them. Since dealings are regular, the investor in a large company can sell at a moment's notice at a price which is uniform throughout the market. Since dealings take place over a wide area on local exchanges connected with one another by telephone and cable, very large blocks of shares can be sold without greatly depressing their price.

The second difficulty to be overcome is the disinclination of investors to expose their capital to risk of loss. This disinclination is reduced by a fourfold specialization in risk-bearing.

First, there is a specialization between directors and shareholders. Many owners of capital show little aptitude or inclination for the work of managing a business, while many capable businessmen have little or no capital. The joint-stock company, in divorcing ownership from management, simultaneously unites management with capital. Capital and business ability are brought together, and the resources subscribed by shareholders are put at the disposal of directors who are presumed to possess good judgement and organizing ability. The union of capital and business ability renders a double service. On the one hand, more money is saved because acceptable channels of investment have been created; and, on the other hand, the limits within which businessmen are able to exercise their judgement are expanded. There is more capital available, and more of it is loaned to, or invested in, large businesses.

Secondly, the practice of issuing different kinds of shares caters for the different dispositions to take risks of different classes of shareholders. There is a specialization in risk-bearing, not only between directors and shareholders, but also between debenture-holders and shareholders, and between preference, ordinary and deferred ordinary shareholders. This grading of bonds and shares according to the risks which the owners run allows the enterprise of investors to be harnessed more effectively in support of risky undertakings. The supply of risk-bearing, as it is sometimes put, is increased.

Thirdly, the participation of a large number of shareholders in each company limits and diffuses the risks which they run. A man with a total capital of £100 000 may scruple to sink three-quarters of it in a partnership with a dozen others. He may hesitate even more to invest the same sum in a company over which he has no control. But if, instead of being one of twelve, he is one of a hundred or two, and is asked to put up, not £75 000, but a few thousand pounds only, he will have much less hesitation. If he chooses, he can invest in a large corporation like the American Telephone and Telegraph Company with over half a million investors – more investors, indeed, than employees. He can then invest the rest of his capital in other businesses and spread his risks over a large number of shareholdings. His risks will be still further reduced by the limitation of his liability in each investment to the value of his shares. The shareholder, therefore, can limit his risks in three ways; by limiting his stake in each investment, by investing in a number of different companies, and by enjoying the protection of limited liability. This limitation of risk will once again make it easier for large or risky undertakings to raise capital.

Finally, there are various financial intermediaries which are enabled by the joint-stock system to borrow small amounts on good security and lend large amounts where the return is comparatively uncertain. The deposits of the joint-stock banks, for example, consist largely of small sums, withdrawable at short notice. The assets, on the other hand, include advances, for periods up to six months or a year, of very large amounts, and blocks of government bonds, often not redeemable for several years, running into hundred of millions of pounds. The banks' depositors lend their money in complete safety and without trouble; the deposits are lent by the banks after a great deal of trouble to discover which firms can offer satisfactory security, and not all of the loans are recovered in full.

Insurance companies and building societies perform similar functions. They receive a large proportion of the current savings of the public, the insurance companies in premiums on life assurance, and the building societies in repayments of principal on mortgages, or in deposits or from shareholders. These savings, when pooled together in this way, can be lent for longer periods, or in larger amounts, or to riskier undertakings, than when they were in the hands of individual savers[1].

Another agency in achieving these results is the investment trust. An investment trust aims at spreading the risks of its shareholders by distributing its assets over a large number of different shares – either in different companies or in the same industry and area, or, more commonly, in different companies scattered throughout the whole range of industry and over the whole area of the globe. The purchase of shares in an investment trust, therefore, allows a small capitalist to take an interest in a large number of enterprises exposed to a variety of risks, instead of linking his fortunes too closely with the one or two companies only in which he could otherwise afford to take shares.

These investment intermediaries, with the exception of the banks, either did not exist or were of negligible importance a hundred years ago. By 1980, the combined assets of the joint-stock banks, savings banks, building societies, insurance companies, pension funds and investment trusts amounted to over £200 bn. The current savings made through investment intermediaries, including the huge sums put to reserve every year by joint-stock companies of all kinds, form a high proportion of the total annual savings of the country.

Diffusion of ownership

Stock exchange securities are owned by three broad groups: by private persons, by investment intermediaries, and by companies as part of their reserves. Of these groups, the first is still the most important. The last,

---

[1] Building societies usually lend most or all of their money to private house-owners but may also finance property development (including commercial and office property).

unless acquiring a business investment in a subsidiary or allied company, is likely to confine itself to gilt-edged securities. An increasing proportion of industrial securities is held by investment intermediaries; in Britain their holdings of ordinary shares (or common stocks, as they are called in America) amount to about half of the total.

The number of shareholders is very often comparable with the number of employees so that the average stake of a shareholder in any one company is roughly equivalent to the amount of capital employed per worker in the company. This diffusion of ownership makes it easier to mobilize the necessary capital; but it also makes it difficult, if not impossible, for shareholders to assume the full responsibilities of ownership. They are, in the nature of things, absentees, and their interest in their property rarely extends beyond the return they can obtain from it.

Speculation

The owners of a company are not only absentees; they do not even remain the same absentees. They buy and sell again, not because death and necessity part them from their capital, but because they see a chance of a speculative profit. Their interest may be confined to the capital appreciation which they expect from a rise in the price of their shares over the next few days or weeks. At this stage, they have ceased to be property-owners with a stake in the company and entitled to the same rights as other property-owners, and have become speculators pure and simple.

Now speculation is inseparable from all investment; every owner of capital must 'take a chance' in whatever form he holds his capital. Risk is universal. Speculation, too, may be of immense advantage to society. Every pioneer of a new process 'speculates' his capital on its success. Every storer of wheat who buys the surplus of a bumper year speculates on a short supply in the succeeding years. Thus skilful speculation can work improvement in our use of scarce resources, or reduce the risks (e.g., of famine) to which their scarcity exposes us. The speculator is not just a gambler, but a specialist in risk-bearing, who, if he bears necessary risks wisely, saves us from those who are more imprudent, or less capable (through ignorance, or lack of capital, or excess of caution) of bearing the risks which they run. But the risks must be unavoidable, not the product of bad organization or a desire to encourage gambling; and the speculators must be well-informed and sound in judgement, not acting on 'inside' information which others do not share, nor seeking to spread rumours and false impressions, nor backed by such weight of capital that they can corner the market and reap monopoly profits.

How far are these conditions satisfied on the stock exchange? That the stock exchange is intended to reduce unavoidable risks we have already seen. It makes it less risky to lock up money for long periods, and thus increases the flow of capital into productive investment. But there are also risks on the stock exchange which are, so to speak, fictitious. The operations of the 'bears', who speculate for a fall in prices, are designed to alarm the public and create a sense of risk of which the 'bears' can take advantage; the operations of the 'bulls', who speculate for a rise in prices, are designed to makes risks appear less than they really are, with equal advantage to the speculators. Thus even if professional speculators, or those whose interest is predominantly speculative, were exceptionally judicious and capable of keeping market prices in correspondence with the real risks, they are not free to do so. It does not pay to steady market prices when by unsteadying them there is a better chance of profit. The real risks become overlaid by the fictitious risks, and wisdom dictates a forecast, not of what prices should be, but of what, given the psychology of the market, prices will be.

It is sometimes suggested that stock exchange speculation is pure gambling. But gambling only makes money change hands; speculation makes not only money but also stock change hands, and reacts on prices. When money changes hands, only the gainer and loser (and their dependants) are affected. But when the price of stocks and shares moves up or down, there is a long chain of repercussions on economic life. The investment of capital, the cost of living, the amount of unemployment, are all tied up with stock prices. Capital flows into those trades whose shares speculators are prepared to buy, and out of those trades whose shares speculators are pressing to sell. Men's jobs, too, depend upon the course of speculation. Where capital cannot be raised, men cannot find employment, and the ease with which capital can be raised depends on both the real prospect of return on it, and the mood of speculators.

Concentration of power

The joint-stock company was originally a democratic organization. In intention it is a democracy of capitalists, entrusting their surplus funds to a cabinet of their own choosing, and retaining an active interest in the use to which their capital is put. In practice, it has come to be the means by which financial and industrial power is concentrated in the hands of a small number of persons who are only vaguely and on rare occasions responsible to their shareholders.

This concentration of power is not the product of a simultaneous concentration of wealth; capital is not less, but more, equally diffused. Power has been concentrated because the bonds between ownership and control have been loosened. It is not necessary to own the entire capital of a company in order to control it. It is enough to have 'a controlling interest'. This may be secured through ownership of a bare 51% of the ordinary shares of the company. If, for example, capital is raised through the issue of debentures, preferred stock, and ordinary shares, each to the value of a million pounds, the comparatively modest investment of £500 100 in ordinary shares will carry with it control of the company's £3 m. Generally, however, a controlling interest can be purchased much more cheaply. The policy of the company can be dominated by a strong minority, holding perhaps no more than 10 to 20% of the voting shares, so long as there is no rival minority of equal or greater strength, and so long as the management is not antagonistic. The larger the number of shareholders, and the more diffused the shares of the company amongst them, the harder does it become to take concerted action to dislodge a powerful minority from control.

Many companies have reached such a size that control either by a majority or by a strong minority is impossible. The largest single interest may amount to no more than a fraction of 1% of the company's capital. In such companies, and in those where there is in fact no large and organized minority group, control normally rests with the management. The directors can remain quietly in power, procuring their own reappointment by the use of proxies. Shareholders who attack the management are put to the expense of preparing and issuing circulars, and run the risk of depreciating the value of their shares by criticism damaging to the company's reputation. Thus even large shareholders, rather than fight a policy they consider unfair and unwise, may prefer to take the easier course of selling out at a sacrifice price.

There are, in addition, various legal devices by which control can be concentrated. Of these the most striking is known as 'pyramiding'. One company may obtain a controlling interest in another, which in turn has a controlling interest in a third – and so on through a long chain of companies. The first, and some of the intermediate companies, will generally be holding companies, not engaged in production, but holding the securities of other companies, collecting the dividends on these securities, and in a position to govern the policy of the subsidiary companies.

Division of interests

The policy of any firm reflects a compromise between the various controlling interests. There are divisions of interest between large shareholders and small, between the owners and the management, between holders of shares and holders of debentures. How these divisions are reconciled depends upon the legal rights which each group possesses, and on the pressure which they can bring to bear on the company.

The large shareholders, for example, may seek to manipulate prices so as to increase the profits of some other company in which they have a still larger interest. The smaller their holding, the greater the temptation. They may exploit the company by selling materials to it at exorbitant prices or by forming a selling agency which draws handsome commissions for marketing the company's products. They may buy up or build small plants and re-sell them to the company at a profit. They can obtain inside information and use it in stock exchange speculation. If they control several companies, they can make their speculations doubly profitable by switching business from one company to another so as to mislead investors. There is no end to the ways in which those in control can, if they are so minded, exploit those who are not. The more diffused the capital of the company, the more helpless is the small shareholder.

Conflicts may also arise between the owners and the management. The officers of the company may reinvest profits in other companies so as to increase their own power, and without consulting the interests of their shareholders. Or they may offer higher wages to their workers, or better service to their customers, out of pride in their company – a pride which the shareholders, if they share it, may not wish to see indulged quite so generously.

The joint-stock company and the control of industry

The joint-stock company was one of the great social inventions of the nineteenth century. In a comparatively short time, it has come to be the predominant form of industrial organization in private enterprise economies and the prototype of the public corporation in mixed economies. The 2500 largest companies, raising their capital by public subscription, employ nearly half the workers in British manufacturing industry and earn about two-thirds of the total industrial profits; most of the remainder is accounted for by private companies. Outside the field of industry and public utilities, the company form of organization is less prevalent; in farming, in many of the service trades and to a smaller extent in distribution, the unincorporated business remains typical.

Like all thriving institutions, the joint-stock company shows great flexibility. Its primary purpose is to allow large capital funds to be put at the disposal of a single enterprise; in doing so it allows numerous enterprises to be linked together in a wide variety of ways. At the same time, it is a form of industrial government raising issues of social policy as well as of economic efficiency. It exercises authority over large groups of workers and controls the use of large blocks of the community's resources. In a democratic community it is a matter of some importance, therefore, who is in control of the larger companies and whether the joint-stock company is an efficient instrument for promoting the welfare of the community.

Control within a joint-stock company does not assume any standard pattern: the locus of control is often obscure and varies from company to company, but is rarely shared effectively among the body of shareholders. There is a divorce between ownership and control, between risk-bearing (which is inseparable from ownership) and risk-taking (which is the prerogative of control). Sometimes the divorce is absolute and no shareholder can hope to have any perceptible influence on the company's policy; sometimes it is far from absolute and the principal shareholders, even when in possession of only a minority of the shares, retain powers of control or at least of veto. When the government of the company is unmistakably in the hands of the management, there is still room for doubt as to the distribution of authority between the different elements in the management. The directors may have only nominal control; the chairman, the managing director, or some executive committee may be more influential than the board as a whole or any group of executive officers of the company. The directors, if they do exercise joint control, are subject to pressure from the government, from public opinion, and from their employees as well as from their shareholders; they may also find their powers restricted, when they wish to use them, by the need to conciliate others, the limitations of their own knowledge and time, and the inevitable delegation of authority to subordinates. Whatever the formal position may be, it is no easier to locate the effective voice in the government of a company than in the government of a country.

The use of the powers which the sheer size of the largest companies confers on them raises equally wide issues. There are, for example, the attendant dangers of monopoly either in the purchase of materials and components or in the sale of products. The large company may block, by unfair means, the efforts of smaller competitors to enter its markets. It may use its financial strength to drive them out of business or buy them up for the sake of a quiet life. It may gain a stranglehold on patents which it denies to other firms and does not use or carry further itself.

Against these and other dangers the state may take action by anti-monopoly legislation, not aimed specifically at public companies. It may reinforce this by company legislation, laying down conditions that all public companies have to satisfy, such as the publication of consolidated accounts. It may buy or acquire some of the shares of the larger companies or take them over and run them as public corporations. We shall discuss possible courses of action in Chapter 31. In the meantime we must look in more detail at the way in which the larger companies grow and consider how far the enlargement of their powers involved in the process of growth may be justified by the economies of scale that they are enabled to enjoy.

Chapter 9

The growth of business units

We saw in Chapter 4 that production in most industrial countries has been growing at a rapid rate. There has been a parallel growth in the size of the business unit; the typical factory produces a larger output than 50 years ago and the number of factories under the control of a typical business unit has grown. The share of the 100 largest manufacturing firms in total output has doubled (*Table 9.1.*).

TABLE 9.1.
Share of 100 largest British manufacturing firms in net output

Year	%
1909	16
1935	24
1949	22
1963	37
1970	40/41

Source: S. J. Prais, *The Evolution of Giant Firms in Britain*, p. 4.

In retailing, the evidence points to a steady increase in concentration of trade in the hands of the multiples and cooperatives at the expense of the independents (for the grocery trade, see *Table 9.2*), and this probably goes with a more or less corresponding expansion in the share of larger business units.

TABLE 9.2. Share of turnover by type of retail organization in the grocery trade (%)

Type of organization	1900	1930	1969
Cooperatives	15	20	15
Multiples	5	19	41
Independents	80	61	44

Source: Nielsen Researcher quoted by F. Bechhofer, B. Elliott and M. Rushforth, 'The Market Situation of Small Shopkeepers', *Scottish Journal of Political Economy*, June 1971, p. 169n.

Although large firms as a group may have increased their share of total production, this does not mean that *the same large firms* occupy the position in the market that they held earlier. The identity of the firms in any size-group is constantly changing and the biggest firms now are not the firms that were biggest at the beginning of the century; one need only think of the oil companies to recognize the truth of this. When the size of the average business unit grows, therefore, there is no uniform expansion that affects each existing firm in roughly the same way. What happens is that firms grow at a wide scatter of rates, unrelated in any definite way to their initial size; some fail to grow at all and shrink in size; some are absorbed by their competitors; and some go bankrupt, give up business or are wound up.

Motives and methods

A firm may seek to expand from two fairly distinct motives. It may be attracted by the prospect of lower costs of production (resulting from economies of scale), or by the prospect of higher prices (resulting from a bargaining advantage or the winning of a position of monopoly). At the same time a firm may seek to expand along either of two paths. It may extend its own plant and fight for a larger share of the market; or it may try to buy out, or combine with, other firms which have their own plant and organization. Between the two motives to growth and the two methods by which growth takes place there is no necessary connection. It is true that the monopoly motive is generally most prominent when a firm grows by combination, while the economy motive is generally the dominant one in growth by extension. But the difference is one of degree, not of kind. Firms may and do combine in order to reduce their costs; they may and do extend their plant so as to entrench themselves more firmly in a position of monopoly. Growth towards a larger and more efficient scale of operations or towards monopoly may take place along either of these routes.

Whichever method of expansion is adopted, both motives are commonly present. Monopoly gains are always an incentive to expansion; savings in costs can often be made simultaneously, so that the first motive is reinforced by the second. But sometimes the two come into conflict. For example, it may happen that expansion along one route is accompanied by lower costs, and along another by higher prices. A firm may hesitate between setting up small high-cost branch factories in outlying districts where competitors are at a disadvantage, and building extensions at low cost to its main plant alongside its chief competitors. Or it may have to choose between extending its plant and buying out some of its competitors. Plant extension may improve efficiency greatly, but it will also intensify competition and probably force down prices. Expansion by purchase, on the other hand, while it may be relatively costly and give rise to technical and managerial difficulties, is likely to strengthen the firm's hold on the market and maintain prices or even allow them to be increased. The extra expense of amalgamation must then be weighed against the higher prices and larger receipts which are in prospect. The two motives to expansion, becoming tangled up with alternative methods of expansion, come into conflict with one another.

When such a conflict arises, the social interest is comparatively clear. The monopoly motive is, in general, anti-social; while the economy motive is, in general, in the public interest.\So long, therefore, as we can readily distinguish between expansion aiming at monopoly and expansion aiming at economy, we can, by legislating against monopolistic expansion, allow firms to grow in size only when such growth is unmistakably in the public interest. But in practice the two motives to expansion generally reinforce one another rather than conflict with one another, and the public interest, therefore, is by no means obvious. The greater the economies of scale, the more closely efficiency and size coincide, until to have more than a single firm is to invite waste of resources and uneconomic methods of production. Efficiency and monopoly become inseparably linked, and we have to lump what we dislike for the sake of what we like. Alternatively, we have to resort to state control or state ownership, rather than leave in private hands powers which may be used against the common good.

The difficulty of disentangling the two motives has increased steadily with the constant improvement in industrial technique and business administration. So long as large-scale production offered only modest economies, the distinction between the two motives coincided broadly with the distinction between the two methods of expansion. The growth of independent concerns could be taken as a sign of superior efficiency from which the public would benefit in lower prices. Combination, on the other hand, was a device for getting prices up, not – except as an afterthought – for reorganizing production so as to get costs down. It was rarely a means of stepping up the size of the business unit in order to gain the benefits of large-scale production, but very often a short cut to monopoly. There was room for several competing firms and monopoly had to be reached at a bound or not at all. Broadly speaking, therefore, attempts at monopoly could be blocked by legislation against combination.

Local monopolies

Where the market was limited or scattered, however, there were local monopolies in the growth of which combination had played no part. Of these monopolies the local chemist's shop or the municipal gasworks were typical. These monopolies, free from the 'taint' of combination, were regarded as natural and advantageous. It was obviously stupid to have two chemists' shops or town gasworks, for the sake of competition, when one would do perfectly well. Competition involved wasteful overlapping of effort and duplication of capital.

It was from the railway that this lesson was first learnt. A railway system could not expand competitively, by building a line parallel to other lines, without great waste of capital. After the early years, the only rational method of expansion was by combination. But combination spelt monopoly, and no monopoly was more feared. The obvious advantages of a unified railways system had thus to battle against the Victorian horror of monopoly. A truce might have been called through nationalization – and this was in fact contemplated in the first railway bills – but private enterprise was held in too great veneration. In the end, safeguards against the abuse of monopoly power were worked out, and combination was allowed to proceed.

The lessons learnt from railway expansion have since been extended to many other industries. Monopoly is the price we have to pay for efficiency, if size and efficiency go together. From the social point of view, monopoly, redeemed by economies of scale and regulated by the state, becomes almost respectable; and a reflected respectability falls on combination, in which the motive of economy now mingles with the desire for monopoly. We cannot so easily single out combination for attack when its results cease to be wholly bad, and when exactly the same results might be achieved by the spontaneous growth of a large firm[1].

The more highly we rate the virtues of size, the better will we think of combination. *Either* method of growth will be more likely to win approval. But combination will be doubly attractive. For when firms are already large, it is difficult and costly to oust them from the market by competition, and comparatively easy and cheap to amalgamate. Especially if the market is narrow, shrinking or uncertain, and if the firms in the field are operating large amounts of durable, fixed capital, nothing short of combination will allow firms to grow. The alternative is to build and battle – to duplicate the plant of competitors, and try to annihilate them in a long-drawn-out cut-throat struggle. Thus as the minimum scale of efficient production keeps growing, and puts a steady pressure on firms to expand in order to keep pace, it is to combination rather than to plant extension that industry turns increasingly.

Motives to growth

The economies motive

The first motive to expansion – the prospect of reductions in cost because of economies of scale – has already been discussed. These economies, however, were looked at from the point of view, not of *growth* but of *size*. The angle from which they were approached was not the actual processes by which firms expand, but the comparative efficiency of large and small firms. But expansion is often arrested because the attraction of economies of scale is offset by obstacles to growth. Two obstacles – one marketing, one financial – are outstanding.

The obstacle of a limited market has already been touched on. It is difficult for a small firm to grow if it supplies a scattered market, or if it has to make its way against firms which have already a firm grip on the market – firms, for example, which have won the goodwill of dealers and

---

[1] Professor Jewkes, in a review of British monopoly policy, warns us against assuming too readily that size and efficiency necessarily go together in industries that are dominated by a large firm or group of large firms. 'In the ten reports in which the (Monopolies and Restrictive Practices) Commission has provided evidence of the relative costs and profits of different sized firms, there is only one, that relating to electronic valves and cathode ray tubes, where it was found that the largest producer showed the lowest costs. In other cases there seems to have been no evidence that size and efficiency moved together.' ('British Monopoly Policy, 1944–56', *Journal of Law and Economics*, Vol. 1, 1958, p. 18.)

consumers over a long period of years, or which can afford an expensive advertising campaign if their market is invaded, or which can bring pressure on dealers to boycott new competitors. This market resistance to growth is enormously stronger when a firm has to expand discontinuously, jumping from a size at which it can supply a local market to a size at which it has to fight for a national market. The risk of failure may deter many firms from sacrificing a comfortable profit to a 50–50 chance of death or glory.

Secondly, there is a financial obstacle. A severe setback in trade, against which every firm must guard, puts a very heavy strain on young and small firms, since they have limited access to credit facilities, and no large reserves on which to fall back if they are in temporary difficulties. Firms hesitate, therefore, to push on with schemes for expansion until they have firmly established their financial strength. This hesitation holds up the growth of the firm even when substantial economies are in prospect.

The monopoly motive

The second motive – the prospect of monopoly gains – has been identified up till now with profiteering – the charging of excessive prices. We have had in mind the pure monopolist, undiluted by any kind of altruism or by fear of retaliation by other firms. Such a monopolist, with exclusive power over the supply of a commodity, is able to make increased profits, not by rendering some special service or by producing more efficiently, but by selling less and charging more. He can force consumers to put money in his pockets, not because he gives them more, but because he gives them less. He simply exploits scarcity.

But monopoly power is generally sought from other motives than the desire to profiteer. First of all, the removal of the threat of competition may, on occasion, make possible genuine economies. When there are two or three firms in a market, each is 'kept guessing' by the manoeuvres of its competitors, and may spend more time and money in trying to defeat these manoeuvres than in improving the services which it offers to the public. Each firm tries to keep in step with the others in public (e.g., by offering 'backhanders', or discounts, or special terms of credit, or supplementary services). Sometimes the public gains from such competition in low prices and better quality, but occasionally it finds itself denied what it wants – a reduction in prices – and offered services it could well do without. At the same time, the competing firms are often forced by ignorance of their rivals' intentions into short-sighted policies from which the whole industry must ultimately suffer. They may each install more plant when prices are high, and then have to cope with the losses in which they are involved by the over-capacity of the industry. A single firm, with a secure hold on the market, is in a better position to take the long view; freed from the uncertainties of the competitive struggle, it can concentrate on making better and cheaper goods.

Against these economies of unity and stability must be set the temptation to slackness and apathy. There is no need to be enterprising and efficient when a comfortable profit can be made from a cautious dependence on routine. The stronger the monopoly, the less does it need to set its standard of performance against the standard of potential rivals. A firm whose control over any market is constantly challenged by other firms of equal strength must base its control on low costs. It may find competititon a nuisance, but is forced by the 'nuisance' to cater for its customers' wants with reasonable efficiency. Remove the nuisance and the spur of competition goes too. A very healthy baby, whose loss would be much lamented, may be lost sight of when the bath water of competition is poured away.

Secondly, firms may unite to form a monopoly in self-defence. They may be afraid of the entry into the market of a new competitor and hope to keep him out by presenting a united front. Two newspapers, for example, may meet a threat to start a third newspaper by amalgamating; in so doing, they take the risk of a fall in profits in order to escape the risk of an even greater fall if the threat to start a third newspaper is carried out. The defensive motive is specially prominent when the market is invaded by a large firm situated in some other part of the country or abroad. Two of the largest British companies – the Imperial Tobacco Company and Imperial Chemical Industries Ltd – were originally defensive combinations which aimed at meeting American and German trusts on an equal footing.

Self-defence may prompt other kinds of expansion. A firm which has to buy components from a monopoly may begin to manufacture them so as to reap a profit made, partly at its expense, by the monopoly. Sometimes the motive for this extension of scope is not so much self-defence against other monopolies as bargaining strength against competitors. For example, a firm which sells to shops and merchant houses which handle the products of other firms may extend its marketing organization so as to push its own sales. It may, like many firms in the clothing, boot, chocolate and druggist trades, open its own shops. Or, as in the electrical and engineering trades, it may have its offices or agencies in all the chief cities, abroad as well as at home. In the marketing of tea, petrol, etc., firms very often distribute direct to the retailer, partly from a desire to attach him to their interests[1].

Bargaining strength shades into the power to bully other firms. A large enterprise or combine with monopoly powers enjoys comparative immunity from retaliation and can, therefore, take unfair advantage of its business neighbours. It can cancel its orders with far less hesitation than a smaller firm, especially if it is not only a large buyer but the sole, or almost the sole, buyer in the market. It can allow delays in delivery or make delivery of inferior goods. It can threaten to cut off supplies from its customers and force them to give up buying from a potential rival. It may even squeeze out these rivals altogether by organizing a boycott, or by bringing pressure to bear on the firms which supply them with raw materials, or on the banks which supply them with credit[2]. Thus the bullying of other firms develops into the exclusion of other firms from the market. Although not protected from competition by its superior efficiency, or by laws granting powers of monopoly, a firm obtains a hold on the

[1] The same purpose may be served, *without* expansion of the sales organization, by the grant of an exclusive agency to a single retailer in each district.
[2] Some of these practices, and others such as exclusive dealing agreements, tying contacts, and deferred rebates, may be forbidden by law. For a discussion of the law governing restrictive practices see below, pp. 120–122.

market which it is almost impossible to challenge. In theory, any firm is free to compete; in practice, no firm will take the risk. Competition will be particularly difficult if the technical optimum is large or if the market is narrow. A new firm will hesitate to set up in opposition to established concerns if it can get a footing only by sinking an enormous amount of capital in plant, or in building up a connection. If there is only a limited market, it will be necessary to capture a share from a firm or firms which are already strongly entrenched. The new firm will have to face the task of attracting customers who are tied by inertia, ignorance, or fear to the monopoly. It has to offer not simply a better or cheaper article, but an article so much better or cheaper, or one so effectively advertised that the interest of the monopolist's customers is aroused. It has to make it worth while for these customers to risk the loss of patronage or supplies from the monopolist. It has to hang on through any price-war or boycott which the monopolist may initiate in an effort to smash competition. And all the time the monopolist may be trying to absorb his competitor, or to make terms which divide the market and restore conditions of monopoly in each part of it[1]. Even when a new firm succeeds in invading a market which is monopolized by a large firm, the net change from the point of view of the consumer may in the long run be precisely nil[2]. The form of monopoly disappears, but the substance remains.

Monopoly and freedom of entry

The exclusion of competitors from the market is the very essence of monopoly. Whatever form the monopoly motive assumes, the desire to impede entry into the market is always present. If there is unified control there *can* be no other firms in the market; self-defence is simply defence of a market against invasion by another firm; fighting strength is nothing but power to keep out other firms; even bargaining strength, in the last resort, is based on the threat to exclude some firm from a privileged market or to enter a market previously monopolized. It is this exclusion of competitors which makes profiteering possible.

But the danger of profiteering is not always equally formidable. The economies of unified control may even bring prices down; increased bargaining strength over other firms may simply produce a fresh division of the spoils, not higher prices to the consumer. It is only when firms combine for the sole purpose of raising prices, without making any attempt to change or coordinate their methods of production, that profiteering pure

---

[1] For example, the Monopolies and Restrictive Practices Commission reported it as the 'consistent policy, wherever possible' of the British Oxygen Company 'to take over or buy out other producers of oxygen and dissolved acetylene' and that it had done this 'primarily, though not solely, in order to extend and preserve its own monopoly in the supply of these gases'. *Report on the Supply of Certain Industrial and Medical Gases* (HMSO, 1956, para. 250).

[2] Indeed, prices may *rise*. The volume of business will be divided, so that the large firm will have to produce on a small scale, probably at higher cost. If neither firm sees any possibility of driving out the other, a policy of live and let live may be adopted with prices adjusted to the higher level of costs.

and simple takes place. But unless the firms continue to be separately managed and merely agree to raises prices in concert, such outright profiteering is generally diluted by economies both of scale and of unified control, and by the desire to build up a strong combine by stabilizing rather than raising prices.

Monopoly power and competitive strength

Monopoly power and competitive strength are the same thing looked at from different angles. Both are the product of expansion when expansion loosens the foothold of other firms in the market and makes the entry of new firms into the market more difficult. Strength, whether for bargaining, fighting or throttling, can be used, and is used, to put up prices against the consumer and to push down prices against the supplier of raw materials. It permits increased profits to be made without any improvement in efficiency. The desire for strength or monopoly, while not identical with the desire to profiteer, very often goes with it.

The desire for competitive strength has another side to it – it represents a revulsion against risk. There is the risk of wide fluctuations in prices, outputs and profits when firms with heavy overhead costs (e.g., railways, steamships, etc.) compete in a limited market. There is the risk of failure of supplies or of markets when either come under the control of a monopoly. There is the risk too, of recurrent disorganization of the market by in-and-out firms; these may be of the type which periodically dump a temporary surplus and then retire within their protected market; or they may be floated without adequate knowledge and backing, and meet disaster after a short-lived and ill-advised competition with established concerns. To protect themselves against these and similar risks, firms may seek strength through combination or expansion. No question of profiteering need arise; a reduction in any of these risks is, *so far as it goes*, a gain to society. But the question of profiteering does in fact constantly arise; it is hard to reduce the risk of excessive competition (the first risk cited above), or of intermittent competition (the third risk), without simultaneously raising barriers against competition of any kind. Society gets rid of undesirable competition, but only by sacrificing the main safeguard against the abuse of monopoly power. Once again, strength acquired for one purpose may be used for another; escape from risk may lead straight to profiteering.

The monopoly motive to combination is held in check by various forces of which the chief are public opinion and potential competition. Public opinion makes itself felt through the boycotting of the monopolist's products, or through anti-trust legislation designed to prevent (or at least to obstruct) monopolistic combination. Potential competition is an even more powerful check. If prices are put too high, consumers may turn from the products of the monopolist to substitutes of various kinds. New firms may begin production; old firms in foreign countries or in other lines of business may enter the market; satisfactory substitutes may be devised or may be already on sale. The wider the range of substitutes, actual or potential, the less is the power of the monopolist to charge extortionate prices and the less powerful, therefore, is the incentive to form a combine in the hope of making monopoly profits. If, for example, it is easy for new firms to get a footing in a market, a monopoly will always have the threat of competition hanging over it, and will only be able to maintain its position by superior efficiency. On the other hand, if new firms cannot possibly compete (e.g., because the monopoly holds important patents), it is comparatively safe to charge high prices and draw an inflated profit. In most trades new firms find themselves in an intermediate position – faced with great, but not overwhelming, difficulties in trying to establish themselves. These difficulties[1], which are constantly increasing, provide monopolies with a margin when they fix their prices. They can make their prices a little, but not too, excessive[2].

The power motive

The desire for size and strength may have its origin in a striving after power rather than after profit. Thus, in addition to the two motives to expansion which have so far been discussed, a third – the desire for economic power for its own sake – very often enters. A business is an instrument both for the making of profits and for the winning of personal power and a place in the sun. Its growth is governed, therefore, almost as much by the pride and ambition of its owners or managers as by the prospect of savings in costs or monopoly gains. Control of a large business is flattering to a man's sense of importance; he has scope for his energies, and freedom to plan and speculate and build after his own heart. His work is stimulating, because responsible and creative. It carries with it power and leadership over large numbers of workers; the excitement of a game; the satisfaction of a role in life; a sense of real achievement; the prospect of founding an industrial dynasty. These are incentives to which even the salaried administrators of joint-stock companies respond. Their eagerness to extend the operations of their company is shown both by the large sums which they put to reserve instead of distributing in dividends, and by the frequency with which they overreach themselves in trying to absorb other companies. The motive to expansion either out of undistributed profits or through amalgamation is very often power rather than prudence or profit.

Economic power carries with it independence. But love of independence by itself is an obstacle to growth. In a limited market, if one business is to expand, others must be pushed towards bankruptcy or must combine with the first. But if independence is highly valued, each firm may prefer to hang on stubbornly in spite of low profits rather than merge with an expanding competitor. Those who put independence before profit probably outweigh those who are willing to sacrifice profit to ambition, and on balance, therefore, the desire for economic power prevents rather than promotes industrial combination and the growth of the firm.

---

[1] For examples, see above p. 116.

[2] In comparison, that is, with the price which would satisfy a new firm if it could take over the monopolist's business.

The financial motive

When a firm expands by combining with other firms there is a profit to be made by *effecting* the combination quite distinct from the profits of the combination *once effected*. Hope of making a profit of the first kind is still another motive of expansion. How does such a profit arise?

Industrial combination is generally financed through the raising of capital on the stock exchange. There may either be a 'take-over' bid (i.e., an offer by one of the parties to the merger to the shareholders in the other), or a promoter may arrange the amalgamation on his own initiative and make a stock exchange flotation of shares in the merger. The second method, which used to be the more common, leaves the promoter with a profit if he is able to acquire the companies on better terms than those on which he can induce the public to subscribe. No one, not even the promoter, can predict accurately what the gains from combination will be. But it is possible to make great play with the various economies of large-scale production that may result, the reputation and business connections that have been built up by the undertakings which are being merged, the extensive and growing market which they serve, and so on. The earning power of the combination can then be capitalized generously so as to set a value on the assets in excess of their cost to the promoter, and investors, if in the right mood, will buy the shares.

Other motives

To these four motives to expansion might be added others of less importance. For example, a company may be forced to expand in order to comply with changes in the law. It may require either to add a new department or extend an old one or combine with some other firm. An Act requiring the compulsory pasteurization of milk would be likely to affect dairymen in one or other of these ways. Again, there is sometimes what might be called a 'fiscal' motive, when the exemption of a company's undistributed profits from tax puts a premium on expansion[1]. The shareholder has the alternative of seeing £1 put to reserve or receiving, say, 75p in dividend and investing it in some other company. Naturally he will be inclined to plump for the first alternative and approve – if his approval is sought – the building up of reserves for use in making extensions of plant or in buying up other companies. On the other hand, if profits put to reserve are subject to tax, an obstacle to expansion is created. The young and efficient firm which depends on high profits to provide capital for growth takes longer to overhaul the established firm which has already more capital than it can use[2].

---

[1] Such exemption does not exist in Great Britain, but the proposal for exemption has often been made. Limitation of dividends, whether statutory or voluntary, tends to operate in the same way.

[2] In some industries, however, a premium on expansion may persist even when all profits are subject to tax. Various outlays which help the business to expand can be charged, by judicious accountancy, to 'income account' (i.e., treated like other items of ordinary expenditure), and so escape tax, although the company benefits from such outlays in exactly the same way as from profits put to reserve. For example, no tax is paid on advertising outlay, but advertising helps to build up an important asset in the form of 'goodwill'.

Methods of growth

A firm may grow either by extending its plant or by combining with other firms. The first method involves an expansion in the capacity not only of the firm, but also of the whole industry; the second method produces a change in the pattern of ownership and control of the industry, but not in its capacity. Of the two, the second is much the more complex; combination covers a wide variety of methods of growth.

When we speak of two firms combining we generally think of two quite independent units coming under the same management. But how many firms nowadays are 'quite independent'? The management of one firm nearly always has a finger in the pie of other firms. Perhaps the directors have seats on the boards of other companies; or influential shareholders are equally influential shareholders in other companies; or friends and relatives of the directors, the shareholders or the staff hold positions of responsibility in other companies. Every company has personal links with others and these links limit its independence. The management is forced to show regard for interests outside the firm, and that regard may undergo little change once the forms of combination have been gone through. The same staff, the same shareholders, the same directors – even the same *policy* – may remain after 'combination'. What is generally called 'combination', in short, may be no more than a tightening of the links between two firms with common interests – more a gesture of recognition of mutual dependence than a destruction of independence.

Restrictive practices

A firm's independence or freedom of action may be limited not only by personal links, but also by trade etiquette or by understandings with other firms. In the eighteenth century, Adam Smith observed that 'people of the same trade seldom meet together even for merriment and diversion but the conversation ends in a conspiracy against the public, or in some contrivance to raise prices'. Nowadays 'conspiracies against the public' are as common as ever. In a large number of markets the prices to be charged and the areas to be supplied by each competitor are settled by gentlemen's agreements and informal understandings. In these understandings trade associations play an important part. By bringing businessmen into close personal contact, or by promoting the exchange of information on methods of cost accounting in use, prices charged, output, costs and so on, trade associations create an atmosphere of cooperation favourable, first to policies of 'live and let live', and later to joint action to maintain prices and restrict output. The information collected and exchanged provides a basis for a common policy and suggests the need for one. Very often, however, such a policy is narrowly conceived in terms of monopoly at its worst. It is designed to put an end to price-cutting and protect profits on invested capital. It does this, but only at the price of perpetuating inefficiency. There is neither the comprehensive planning and general overhauling of technical methods that might be expected to result from outright combination, nor the weeding out of inefficient firms and inefficient methods that might be expected to result from competition *à outrance*[1]. Instead, pressure is put equally on efficient and inefficient firms; the efficient firms are clamped down within their existing markets while the inefficient firms survive freely in theirs.

Understandings do not amount to combination in the narrow sense. But they represent a sacrifice of independence and a limitation of competition which are comparable in their effects with actual combination. Combination in the sense of concentration of control is a matter of degree rather than of kind, and understandings between competitors carry us a stage nearer to full concentration.

The next stage is a formal agreement to limit competition, for example by fixing minimum prices or introducing quotas on output. Such agreements were common in Britain before the war although, as contracts in restraint of trade, they were generally not enforceable at law. At that time, when most industries had a great deal of unused capacity and low prices might have ruined firms that had good long-term prospects, public opinion was sympathetic to restrictive agreements and the government itself encouraged, or even compelled, a number of industries to form marketing boards, centralized selling agencies and other price-fixing organizations, similar to the cartels described below. Since the war, with trade extremely active and prices rising continuously, there has been a change in the attitude of the public and of the government and new legislation has been introduced against restrictive practices.

The Monopolies and Restrictive Practices Acts of 1948 and 1953 brought into existence a Commission – now the Monopolies Commission – to which the government could refer for investigation any industry in which restrictive practices were suspected on the part of a firm or group of firms producing one-third of the total output. This Commission had no powers enabling it to require firms to desist from restrictive practices. Its functions were primarily fact-finding; but it could also report that certain practices were contrary to the public interest, and as the law laid down no criteria by which to judge the public interest, the reports of the Commission built up a kind of case-law on which later legislation could be drafted. Such legislation was introduced in the Restrictive Trade Practices Act of 1956, which required a wide range of agreements to be officially registered and set up a Restrictive Practices Court with power to decide whether the restrictive clauses in those agreements are in the public interest. The most important features of this legislation are that it places on those who enter into a restrictive agreement the onus of establishing, to the satisfaction of the Court, that it is in the public interest – not merely unlikely to be damaging, but of positive value to the public – and that, since each decision of the Court operates as a precedent with all the force of law, a few decisions are sufficient to put an end to a very large number of agreements. The Monopolies Commission remains in being to report on individual firms with monopoly powers but no longer investigates agreements between firms. Neither the Restrictive Practices Court nor the Monopolies Com-

---

[1] Competition does not always make for the survival of the efficient firm. The old and well-established (but inefficient) firm may ride the storm of trade depression more successfuly than the young and efficient (but poorly connected) firm.

mission has powers to investigate the activities of trade unions, national-ized industries or statutory bodies.

The Monopolies and Mergers Act introduced additional powers in 1965. Prospective or actual mergers can be referred by the government to the Monopolies Commission when the assets to be acquired exceed £5 m. Mergers can be held up until the Commission has reported; and the government can then either forbid or unscramble a merger or lay down conditions if the Commission finds it contrary to the public interest without imposing them. These powers were not initially used very extensively. For example, of 318 qualifying mergers up to the end of 1968, only eight were referred to the Commission; in three of the eight cases the Commission's verdict was against the merger. This was over a period when the assets acquired through takeovers and mergers by industrial and commercial firms grew from £500 m in 1966 to £1950 m in 1968[1].

British legislation is directed much more strongly against *agreements* than against *mergers* and in this respect is in contrast with American legislation. The chief preoccupation of American policy is with the danger of market control by a small group of large producers – what economists describe as oligopoly[2] – while the emphasis in Britain has been more on the danger of restrictive agreements between producers. American legislation has not prevented the emergence of very large firms nor a degree of industrial concentration at least as marked as in Britain. On the other hand, it is doubtful whether British legislation has yet succeeded in promoting as keen price-competition as exists in the United States. In both countries, the legislation has exercised great influence without fully accomplishing its declared purpose.

Whatever the present position, most British industries have had experi-ence of price-fixing agreements at one time or another. The usual arrangement is to fix minimum prices so as to prevent price-cutting. But whenever the temptation to price-cutting is great (e.g., under the stress of trade depression), the agreement tends to be evaded or openly violated. It can also be evaded by the offer of high discounts or of special concessions such as a low price for articles which do not come under the agreement.

Sharing the market

Price agreements frequently lead to agreements to share the market. Shipping conferences (i.e., associations of steamship lines), for example, not only agree to charge similar rates of freight but also arrange for the division of traffic by limiting each line to a certain number of sailings or to certain ports of sailing. When competition is by tender, arrangements may be made to share the market through an association which decides who is to make the lowest tender and take the contract. The other members either

---

[1] *Financial Statistics*, December 1971, Supplementary Table B. For a fuller account, see *Mergers* (HMSO, July 1969) and a critique by A. Sutherland in 'The Management of Mergers Policy' in *The Managed Economy* (ed. by A. Cairncross, Blackwell, Oxford, 1970); also, M. A. Utton, 'British Merger Policy' in *Competition Policy in the UK and the EEC* (ed. by K. D. George and C. Joll, CUP, Cambridge, 1975).

[2] See below, p. 182.

do not tender at all or put in higher tenders as a blind. Sometimes sharing the market is combined with a pooling arrangement.

Agreements to fix prices or to share the market are very often combined with agreements to limit output. Indeed, prices cannot be kept up in the face of falling demand *unless* producers cut down their output and offer a smaller quantity of goods for sale; if producers continue to press supplies on the market, prices *must* fall below the 'fixed' minimum, or the supplies will remain unsold. Similarly, sharing the market means that firms bind themselves to limit output to the needs of their own (reserved) market or to some fixed proportion of total trade. Restriction of output is implied, therefore, in agreements to share the market or to refrain from price-cutting; the responsibility of limiting its output falls on each firm individually. Sometimes, however, associations are formed to organize restriction of output for the industry as a whole. When an industry is depressed, for example, each firm may agree to work only a proportion of its plant. Or the aggregate output to be produced may be fixed by a central body and divided up between the members of the association in proportion to their output in the past. Each firm is allotted a quota. If this quota is exceeded, a fine must be paid into a pool in proportion to the excess; while, if a firm fails to reach its quota, a payment is made to it out of the pool. When this pooling system is not in operation, it is generally possible for producers to expand output beyond the limit set by their quota by purchasing the unworked quota of other producers. Later, when quotas are under revision, these purchases of quota can be used as a lever to procure a higher share of output under the new agreement.

One of the most obvious effects of quota arrangements of this kind is that the high-cost members of the association tend to be sheltered from competition while the more efficient, low-cost members can expand only with difficulty. They have to pay fines or buy quota so as to qualify for larger quotas when revision takes place, usually on the basis of past outputs. Their share of the market is not completely frozen; but the changes that would be brought about by free competition are slowed down and the public is denied opportunities of making purchases at lower prices.

Cartels

Associations which not only fix prices or allot quotas, but also undertake the business of marketing, are called cartels[1]. A cartel acts as a selling agency on behalf of its members, distributing orders between them in accordance with some agreed formula, and not interfering in any way with their internal management. The functions of producing and of marketing are separated, production being carried on by independent units under semi-competitive conditions, while all sales are made through the agency of a monopoly. The profits, or losses, of the sales monopoly are pooled and shared between the members in proportion to output. Sales in special markets (e.g., abroad) may be made at prices varying with the keenness of

[1] The term is frequently applied to some of the looser types of association described above. In the strict sense, however, a cartel means primarily a selling agency with monopoly powers acting on behalf of independent producers.

the competition that has to be met. Prices in the home market, for example, may be kept up while sales at cut-throat prices are made with a view to driving out competitors in some foreign market. Or a special levy per unit of output may be made on each firm so as to subsidize exports.

Trusts

The cartel, and the looser types of association which have been described so far, all stop short of actual combination. In this they differ from those financial groups which Americans call 'trusts'. A trust is simply a large firm formed by consolidation of independent companies, or a group of associated companies under the control of a single interest, the firm or group of firms being large and strong enough to exercise powers of monopoly. Trusts may take shape in a variety of ways – by 'take-over' bids, by acquisition of a controlling interest, by the formation of a holding company, and so on. The biggest of the British trusts – Imperial Chemical Industries – was formed by the issue of shares in exchange for those of four large companies, each of which was in a strong position in one branch or other of the chemical industry. Another example of a British trust is Unilever, which grew by absorption of competitors until it was producing 75% of the soap made in Britain. The subsidiary companies in a trust of this size generally retain a good deal of independence, and only the broad lines of policy – especially investment policy – are dictated to them.

When obstacles to centralization exist, trusts and cartels may differ little in their results, however much they differ in form. Each of them becomes simply a means of combining bigness in marketing (for the sake of economies of large-scale marketing or, more probably, for the sake of monopoly and competitive strength) with smallness in producing (for the sake of efficient management). When the obstacles to centralization are removed a real difference emerges between the trust and the cartel. The cartel is then a prop for units which are uneconomically small; trustification, on the other hand, may be used to bring units together so as to allow them to operate with greater efficiency within a single administrative structure. Like the cartel, the trust can integrate the price policy of the units, enforcing uniform prices; unlike the cartel, it can also integrate their methods of production, suppressing inefficiency, specializing plants to particular products or markets, standardizing varieties of product, and using wide powers of coordination over the whole field of production, research, marketing, and so on.

Combination, then, ranges from loose agreements at one end to outright amalgamation at the other. At each stage, control over price and over methods of production becomes more and more concentrated. First the monopoly powers of the combine are consolidated through more stringent agreements between the members; then the unit of management is expanded through the trustification of the members. Which method of combination is selected depends upon the advantages and costs of bringing about concentration of control.

Advantages of mergers

Let us take the advantages (to the combine, not necessarily to the public) first. Full concentration (e.g., in the trust) is to be preferred whenever economies of scale are in prospect. Management of large-scale units, for example, may have become easier, or technical changes may be making for expansion in the size of the business unit. Mere understandings and agreements generally do little to adapt industry to these changes, but tend rather to hold them up. Secondly, where the interests of producers differ widely, it may be hard to arrive at agreement between them short of amalgamation. Even if a looser agreement is possible, it may have to be too vague or too exposed to the risk of disloyalty to be of value. Consolidation in a trust, however, will ensure unity of control and a common policy. The vested interests which block the concentration of production in the most efficient plants will find the ground cut from under their feet, and at the same time each plant can be forced to charge a uniform scale of prices. Thirdly, full concentration may be the most effective method of suppressing competition. So long as firms are linked loosely together by agreements or understandings, they may find it harder to take concerted action against a new competitor than a large trust. Fourthly, it is generally easier for a trust than for a cartel to raise new capital when an industry needs to be re-equipped and re-organized. The new capital may be raised from the public when the trust is formed, or may be supplied by firms with surplus reserves when they are merged with firms in financial difficulties. Finally, the law generally puts more obstacles in the way of the cartel and agreements 'in restraint of trade' than in the way of outright combination to form a trust.

Limitations of mergers

Most of these advantages must be qualified, however. First of all, the economies of scale which can reasonably be expected from consolidation are often grossly exaggerated. It is too often assumed that the profits of a trust cannot be less than the joint profits of the firms out of which it was formed. It has repeatedly happened, however, that earnings after con-solidation have worked out far below previous earnings, in spite of the trust's monopoly advantages and in spite of the optimistic forecasts of promoters. Secondly, it is not to be supposed that disunity dissolves into unity whenever the wand of consolidation is waved. Sectional interests persist inside the trust, pushing the claims of one plant against another just as they might in a cartel, but generally with less vehemence and certainly with less power to threaten mischief. Thirdly, the strength of a trust is not necessarily greater than that of a cartel. A trust rarely controls the whole industry, whereas cartels very often do. The looser form of combination is the more elastic and comprehensive, and elasticity and comprehensiveness are often more essential to strength than unity. The monopoly of the salt trust – the Salt Union – was twice broken by new competition, but re-established successfully when it formed a cartel with its chief competi-tors. Finally, legal obstacles to trustification are sometimes at least as overwhelming as legal obstacles to other methods of combination. For the Big Four in banking to combine without Parliamentary approval and encouragement would be impossible.

These qualifications are reinforced by the comparative costliness of forming a trust. There are, first, the costs of arranging the merger itself.

These include not only lawyers' fees and bankers' commissions, but also the financial profits of the promoters. They include, too, excessive payments made to manufacturers for their plant – the cost, for example, of old and inefficient plants which are bought up only to be closed down almost at once; and the cost of firms which earn little or no profit for the trust, but which hold out successfuly for exorbitant compensation because they have a high 'nuisance value' – power, if left outside, to make things awkward for the trust. Secondly, there are the costs of meeting new competition attracted by the formation of the trust[1]. Manufacturers who have sold their out-of-date plants to the trust may invest their money in new factories, modern in design and the last word in efficiency.

In comparison with the cost of forming a trust, a cartel is inexpensive to organize and the cost of framing an agreement between trade competitors is negligible. A cartel, it is true, may be embarrassed by new competition much as a trust is, and may be forced to make terms (e.g., the grant of a large quota to new competitors) which are just as costly as purchase at an exorbitant price. But this new competition is not brought into play more or less automatically through the formation of the cartel; there is no displacement of management talent and capital, less publicity, and less need to shoulder the burdens of other producers by allowing them to share in the advantages of a stable market. The new competition which a cartel has to face is the penalty either of inefficiency or of exorbitance.

The view which producers (or promoters) take of these advantages and costs determines how far combination will go and what form it will assume. If the advantages are great (e.g., if important economies are likely to result) and if the costs are low (e.g., if producers are willing to surrender their independence cheaply) amalgamation will proceed rapidly. If the advantages are limited and if the cost of outright combination is high, then resort may be had to some other form of combination more in keeping with the special advantages hoped for, and the special obstacles met with. A wide variety of methods of combination may be considered, some concentrating control over price, some concentrating control over production also.

Direction of growth

The growth of a firm, as we have seen, may take place by either of two methods – plant extension or combination. Cutting across this division is another, based on the *direction* of growth. When a firm increases the size of its establishment, or combines with neighbouring establishments of the same type, it may continue to make the same products by the same processes on the same site. Generally, however, the growth of a firm, whether it takes place by plant extension or by combination, involves changes in the site or in the scope of the firm's operations.

---

[1] Such competition will be impossible if the trust has a monopoly of some essential raw material, a stranglehold on the channels of distribution, or legal protection through legal patents or franchises. In all other circumstances, competition will be possible, but not necessarily easy (see above, p. 116).

A firm may grow, therefore, along one of several routes. It may grow *horizontally* by combining with firms which make similar products; *vertically* by undertaking processes of manufacture in continuance of those which it already performs; *laterally* by extending the list of products which it turns out; *territorially* by operating over a wider area. But growth is rarely one-dimensional – it takes place, as a rule, along several of these routes simultaneously. A firm which sets up a branch factory, for example, grows horizontally if the new factory produces goods similar to those manufactured in the main establishment; vertically, if the new factory runs a repair department and the main establishment does not; laterally, if the range of products is slightly different; and territorially, if the branch factory is at a distance from the main establishment. Thus the pattern of growth is often woven from different types of integration. Sometimes it is woven, not from integration alone, but from integration mixed with disintegration. A firm may decide, for example, to increase the scale of output of standard lines (horizontal integration) and cease production of special lines (lateral disintegration). Or it may decide to abandon some processes of manufacture (vertical disintegration) so as to specialize on a larger scale on the remainder (horizontal integration). Or again, it may add a new stage of production at one plant (vertical integration) and close down a similar plant elsewhere (concentration plus horizontal disintegration).

(a) Horizontal integration

Horizontal integration leaves the range of a firm's activities unchanged. It may take the form of an extension of plant and an accompanying increase in output without change of product or process; or, alternatively, it may consist of the combination of firms making similar products. For example, an iron-smelting company may build more blast furnaces or combine with another iron-smelting company.

The normal method of growth is horizontal. The firm which is successful in one line of business naturally seeks to extend that line. The firm which is anxious to protect itself against price-cutting and loss of business tries to combine with other firms in its own trade. It is not only that businessmen like to stick to a trade with which they are familiar. Both the economies motives and the monopoly motive press far more powerfully horizontally than in any other direction. If a firm grows by widening the range of its operations rather than by simple expansion of output, economies of scale must as a rule be sacrificed. Similar, a combine of miscellaneous firms generally lacks the strength of a combine of similar firms.

(b) Vertical integration

Vertical integration is the union of a sequence of processes formerly carried on by separate firms. Two different varieties of vertical integration can be distinguished. First, an extension of the process of manufacture, backwards towards the raw materials or forwards towards the market. For instance, a steel firm may take over the previous stage of production and build its own blast furnaces, or combine with a company which is engaged in the production of pig-iron ('backward integration'); or it may continue processes already performed and build rolling mills or amalgamate with the firms which buys its steel ('forward integration'). Secondly, auxiliary goods and services required in the manufacture of a firm's main products may be provided within the firm instead of purchased from outside. For example, the firm may undertake its own repairs, generate its own power, or make its own tools or designs.

The motives to vertical integration differ with the type. The motive to forward integration, for example, is generally to find a market; the motive to backward integration is to secure sources of raw materials. Forward integration is not uncommon in times of depression, when firms are anxious to push the sale of their product and so reap the economies of operating at full capacity. Backward integration is to be expected mainly in times of boom when there is a danger of a shortage of raw materials. Thus a steel firm might buy over a shipbuilding yard when trade is bad, and blast furnaces when trade is good. Since combinations of all kinds are easiest to carry through in times of boom – the financial motive being very strong at such times – the antithesis is never quite so sharp as this. But there is a *relative* preponderance of forward over backward integration in times of depression, and of backward over forward integration in times of boom[1]. Similarly, the assumption of marketing functions is generally prompted by the desire for bargaining strength[2], whereas the motive to provide auxiliary services within the firm is more often to be found in the technical economies of linked processes[3].

Of the economies of scale to which vertical integration leads, two only are of much importance. The first – economies of linked processes – have been particularly striking in the steel and chemical industries, where it is essential to conserve heat by having each process in close conjunction with the succeeding one. In other industries, it is economical to link auxiliary services with the main process or processes (e.g., the making of machines, the generation of electricity, etc.). Generally speaking, however, it tends to be more economical to split up processes than to link them, since splitting (disintegration) allows specialist firms to carry on each process on a large scale. It is to the other set of economies – economies due to the spreading or avoidance of risk – that we have to look for the main force working against disintegration and in favour of integration.

The chief risk against which vertical integration safeguards a firm is failure of supplies. A firm which is unable to count on regular and punctual

---

[1] Whether combination is forward or backward must be judged from the position of the dominant partner.

[2] See above, pp. 77–78. The technical difficulties involved in integration of production with marketing are very great, unless the retailer handles only a narrow range of goods. The manufacturer of shovels, for example, will have no wish to retail them if he has to handle simultaneously everything from hot-water fittings to hearthrugs and even goats (cf. H. Smith, *Retail Distribution*, p. 94n, OUP, Oxford, 1937). Nor will the perplexities of drapers who sell cats' meat and ladies' underwear in Bethnal Green (*Ibid.*) appeal to the textile manufacturers of Lancashire. Evn when retailing is highly specialized (e.g., in shoes, oil products, motor-cars, etc.), it is rarely possible for the producer to defend his entry into retailing on grounds of efficiency. The real motive is generally the bargaining advantage which he obtains by building up a special market for his goods.

[3] See above, pp. 74–75.

delivery of raw materials runs the risk of being constantly held up by lack of supplies. It can protect itself against this risk by holding large reserves of stocks, but this procedure is both costly (since there are storage and interest charges to be met), and risky (since the price of stocks may fluctuate enormously). The firm may be forced, therefore, to secure direct control over the supply of its raw materials through vertical integration. Again, a firm may make its own materials in order to be certain that they are of good and uniform quality. Or it may undertake the manufacture of its materials as a precaution against a rise in their price, or against the danger that they may come under the control of a combine, and be monopolized. Vertical combination, in fact, is very often a counterstroke to horizontal combination.

A vertically integrated firm enjoys various other advantages. It can effect economies of unified control of the succeeding stages of production. If each stage is in separate ownership, the chain of independent firms may hang back from innovations which are in the common interest of the group, but from which the innovator derives little advantage. The design, quality and, above all, the durability which one firm looks for in its components may be unattractive from the point of view of the firm supplying them. Integration enables the conflicting interests of the various stages of production to be reconciled; each firm's special knowledge, and the profits which result from its use, can be pooled in the combine and new processes of common advantage can be introduced. Moreover, a policy which keeps each stage of production in step with the one before and the one after can be formulated. In the cotton industry, where there is little vertical integration, a change in demand must be transmitted gradually along the chain of independent firms, each of which, reacting in ignorance of what is happening further along the chain, easily misinterprets market tendencies and makes an excessive adjustment to the change in demand. In motor car production, on the other hand, each department is synchronized with the others, from the purchase of raw materials to the marketing of the finished product, and adjustment to reports by retail agents of a change in demand can be made quickly all along the line. Integration introduces more comprehensive planning.

Vertical integration is often a method of extending monopoly from one stage of production to another. In many industries there is some bottleneck, control of which carries with it control over the whole industry. Strategic importance may attach, for example, to mineral deposits, or to transport facilities, or to the channels of distribution. If any of these come to be monopolized, the monopolist can bring pressure to bear on producers at other stages, and can enter into competition with them so as to extend its monopoly advantage. The Standard Oil companies, for example, used to have a monopoly of pipelines for the transportation of crude oil from some of the American oilfields. Their refineries were given an advantage over independent refineries by charging the latter high transportation rates and by imposing onerous shipping requirements such as high minimum shipments of oil.

The trend towards vertical integration is much less powerful than the trend towards horizontal integration. It is obstructed by lack of familiarity with the technique of other stages of production and by lack of capital with which to finance vertical expansion[1]. Above all, it is obstructed by the forces which make for the specialization of firms on a narrow range of processes. Disintegration goes on side by side with integration as one industrial process after another reaches the scale at which it can be turned over to specialist firms. The medieval scribe is displaced by firms of publishers, printers, paper makers, machine makers, and a host of others[2]. The livestock industry breaks up into cattle breeding, cattle rearing, cattle fattening and the preparation of feeding-stuffs with all its ramifications. Even in the steel industry, heavy forging, the manufacture of stainless steel, and many other branches still resist integration.

(c) Lateral integration

Lateral integration is the turning out of additional products or styles of product. When, for example, a railway runs refreshment rooms, hotels, steamships, and so on, it is providing services which are connected *laterally* with rail transport; whereas, if it builds its own locomotives it is expanding *vertically*, since locomotives are essential to rail transport, while refreshment rooms, fortunately, are not. In this example, lateral expansion is undertaken in order to supply markets with which a connection has already been built up – railway passengers need refreshment, hotel accommodation, etc., and it is convenient and economical to have them provided by the railway. In addition, there is a spreading of risk, especially if a *competitive* service like road transport is integrated; total receipts from all the company's activities will be more stable than receipts from rail transport alone[3]. The use of the same raw material in a variety of products, or the fact that the same technical problems are involved, may also lead to vertical integration. A firm which produces motor cars, for example, may branch into aeroplane manufacture. Again, firms frequently take up the manufacture of new products which have been discovered by their research department or which have been brought to them by inventors unable to obtain a backing elsewhere. Sometimes a new department or branch factory is added, but more commonly a subsidiary company is formed to manufacture the new product. Lateral integration is also a line of retreat or of advance when competitive pressure changes. If, for instance, competition develops in the poorer qualities of a product a firm is likely to fall back on the special qualities in which its reputation and connections help to

---

[1] Cf. Marshall, *Industry and Trade*, p. 216: 'A firm with limited capital can seldom undertake considerable vertical expansions with success; for such expansions are not easily made by gradual steps. On the other hand, a business may proceed gradually and tentatively when extending its operations horizontally in the same stage.' (Quoted by Marquand, *Dynamics of Industrial Combination*, London, 1931, p. 44)

[2] Cf. Allyn Young, 'Increasing Returns and Economic Progress', *Economic Journal*, 1928.

[3] Integration of competitive services also introduces the monopoly motive, since control (or suppression) of substitutes is the basis of monopoly power. Railways may engage in road transport in order to protect themselves against competition from independent road transport companies. Lateral integration may also be a method, not of defending but of exploiting a monopoly advantage. A firm with a monopoly of one important product may put pressure on dealers to handle its entire line of products ('full-line forcing') by threatening to deprive them of its monopolized product. By extending its line of products, it can take full advantage of its bargaining strength.

insulate it from competition; in falling back, it is likely to look for new styles and brands which will compensate for its loss of trade in standard lines. A firm which is expanding may vary its output for similar reasons; once it begins to bump up against the limits of its market it may find it easier to make headway by branching out into new lines rather than by pushing on with the old ones.

Except in industries where the products are highly standardized, lateral growth is almost as common as horizontal. Indeed, if we put aside combination and the setting up of branch factories (both of which are predominantly horizontal), and think in terms of the establishment only, we shall probably find that change from one line of production to another plays at least as large a part in growth as horizontal expansion and contraction. This does not mean, however, that firms are tending to make a wider variety of products. Firms switch from one line to another, but do not necessarily add new lines to old.

(d) Territorial integration

The growth of the firm is frequently accompanied by geographical diffusion – the planting of branches over a wider area, or union with firms in other parts of the country. In some industries, indeed, diffusion and growth are almost indistinguishable. Chain stores, railways, electric supply companies, and other firms engaged in transport and distribution, find extension over a wider area much the easiest path of growth. In other industries diffusion is less attractive. The tremendous reduction in transport costs which has taken place over the last century has made it possible to concentrate industry in large central units which supply an area formerly served by a multitude of small local firms. The economies of large-scale production are often more than enough to compensate for the extra cost of drawing on a large area of supply, or of radiating output over a wide market. The big firm on a central site can do things more cheaply, in spite of the handicap of a bigger outlay on transport, than small local producers scattered through each village. A familiar illustration is the decline of farm butter- and cheese-making and the concentration of dairying in creameries.

The battle between economies of scale and market resistances[1], therefore, has gone heavily in favour of economies of scale, and by implication, it would seem, in favour of centralized production also. But the implication is incorrect. The improvement in transport and communications has made possible not only large-scale production on a central site, but also the union of scattered plants under the same management. The railways, the Post Office, and the telephone, make it easy for a firm to manage plants hundreds of miles apart – a feat which would have been almost impossible 200 years ago. Thus where the main economies of scale are not *technical*, and can be realized in a comparatively small plant, the firm tends to grow by diffusion, not by concentration. Again, if there are strong forces making for lateral or vertical integration, and there is a locational pull on the integrated products or stages of production towards different districts, firms will be forced to operate branch factories in each of these districts. If a firm which manufactures rubber tyres wishes to own rubber plantations

[1] See above, pp. 93–94.

and textile mills it will probably have to go to Malaya for the first and to Lancashire for the second. Similarly, it will be unlikely to carry on the production of golf balls or rubber cushions in the districts in which its tyre factory is located.

Growth and public policy

Without control, industry may evolve monopolistic forms of organization that pursue the interests of their owners to the detriment of the public interest, or it may leave in being a number of highly competitive units that maintain their independence only at the sacrifice of other social interests.

Those interests are primarily twofold:

1. The production of goods and services at the lowest possible real cost.
2. The progressive reduction of real costs through improvements in methods of business organization, techniques of production, quality of product, and so on.

There is a general presumption that those objects are most likely to be secured where consumers are free to choose between the alternatives open to them and producers are free to enter a market and offer wider alternatives or better terms; this is a presumption in favour of competition. This presumption is reinforced by the social importance of freedom of choice and the injustice that attends the exercise of monopoly power. On the other hand, there is a presumption in favour of large-scale production when this makes for efficiency; it may be better to have a narrower range of alternatives if they are also cheaper. This is a presumption which may justify some degree of monopoly, though not necessarily the uncontrolled exercise of monopoly powers. This presumption in turn is reinforced by the practical importance of assuring some private advantage, however temporary, to those who make improvements; patent legislation, for example, recognizes the need to introduce what Mr Downie called an element of 'grit' into the competitive process[1]. In addition, competition, like monopoly, has an unhealthy aspect when pushed too far and can deflect effort into a search for short-term gains at the expense of long-term development.

These conflicting presumptions cannot be reconciled in some simple formula for the organization of industry. In one industry, free competition may yield the best results; in another, a large producer held in check by potential rather than actual competition; in another, a public corporation exercising a statutory monopoly. Each industry must be looked at in relation to the techniques it uses and the market it supplies before any worth while judgement can be formed as to how its organization might be improved.

We shall be discussing the control of industry more fully in Chapter 31. In the meantime we must turn to consider competition and monopoly from the angle, not of industrial organization, but of supply and demand and the price mechanism by which they are adjusted to one another.

---

[1] 'There must be some, so to speak, grit in the system which prevents any advance of one firm from being immediately imitated with full effectiveness by all the other firms in the industry.' (J. Downie, 'How should we control monopoly?', *Economic Journal*, Vol. LXVI, December 1956, p. 575).

Part III

Supply and demand

Chapter 10

The price mechanism

In a market economy, few economic decisions are taken by government. Households and individuals decide what, where and when to buy. Decisions about production, employment and technology are made by managers of firms. Both sets of decisions are subject to various social influences, such as laws, advertising and patents; and they may be affected by limited information on the part of those taking them. These decisions are guided, too, by *prices*. A high price discourages purchases. Also, because it promises a large profit to the supplier, it stimulates production.

'The price mechanism' describes the system by which prices adjust themselves to the pressure of demand and supply and in their turn operate to keep demand and supply in balance. It is a mechanism resulting from the free association of consumers and producers in a market, each side concluding such bargains as it finds satisfactory at the ruling price. The price mechanism is the product of a 'market economy' in which consumers and producers exercise freedom of choice within the market, buying or not buying, selling or not selling, hiring or firing as suits their interests best. The more perfectly the market operates, the more each individual buyer and seller is powerless to alter the terms on which he can buy and sell or the less room there is for monopolistic pressure or for what Adam Smith called 'the higgling of the market'. The interests of buyers and sellers do not need to be reconciled by consultation, negotiation and awards; everyone has to accept the market price. This price faithfully reflects any change in the requirements of consumers or any change in the obstacles to supplying them, putting simultaneous pressure on the whole body of producers and consumers to modify their plans and their behaviour in the direction appropriate to the new degree of scarcity and abundance.

Capitalism

How do the terms 'capitalism', *'laissez-faire'*, private enterprise', 'market economy' and 'price mechanism' differ from each other? *Laissez-faire* was a slogan meaning 'Remove the schackles!' and summarized an economic philosophy; it dates from a period well after the main features of modern capitalism had already taken shape. Private enterprise is a convenient description of one feature of capitalism and the market economy of another; but it would be possible to have a great deal of private enterprise without rights of property or an organized market, and the market could still function in a socialist state. As for the price mechanism, it could fit into different types of economic system. There are many socialists who not only accept the theoretical virtues of the price mechanism but claim that without socialism it cannot function to the best advantage; in their view socialism would be a way of really giving effect to the rules of perfect competition instead of pretending that those rules are already in force under capitalism.

Capitalism embraces both the price mechanism and a particular set of institutions governing the ownership and control of property (for example, inheritance). If the institutions were different (if, for example, all property reverted at death to the state), the price mechanism might function as before but capitalism as an economic system would undergo a change. A panegyric of the price mechanism, therefore, is not a sound defence of capitalism since it sets on one side the social context (poverty and inequality, for example) in which the price mechanism operates.

The two main features of capitalism are the private ownership of property and freedom of enterprise. In capitalist society men have the right to accumulate property without limit for their exclusive use, and the right to dispose of it as they choose so long as they keep within the law. They have also the right to lend their capital or adventure it in any business, subject to such restrictions as the state imposes. These are not absolute rights; they rest upon the law, altering when the law alters. The state can tax transfers of capital, set a maximum to the property that can be owned by one man, lay down the terms on which money can be lent or invested, and so on. Rights of property and freedom of enterprise can be made to wither away until capitalism is no longer recognisable as such.

In the capitalist system as it exists at present these two features are associated with others; above all, with class divisions, and inequality of income and wealth. The ownership and control of property is heavily concentrated in few hands; on the other hand, the mass of the population owns little or no property and depends for its income on working for a weekly wage. There are also other classes to some extent intermediate between these two: for example, the self-employed, the salaried workers and small property-owners. While there is no clear line of division, however, between the various classes, there is no blinking the fact that for some people income comes mainly from work while for others an important, sometimes a major, contribution comes from property. Income from work varies widely, acording to seniority, age, hours of work, extent and type of skill; and also by region and industry. The system of taxes and benefits makes the distribution of incomes less unequal after tax than before it.

The price mechanism under capitalism

In the next few chapters the working of the price mechanism in a capitalist economy is analysed in some detail: not as it has been functioning, particularly in the recent past, but as it would function if state interference and (initially at all events) monopoly could be disregarded. These are rather large abstractions, and it is desirable to dwell on them at the outset.

The importance of monopolistic influences has already been stressed. To abstract from these influences might seem to imply a misrepresentation of the way in which capitalism works and an identification of it with free and effective competition. Obviously there is no such identity. Competition may operate more strongly under capitalism than under any other system of society. But even under capitalism competition is limited by elements of monopoly that can be very powerful. Conversely, if capitalism were to be replaced by some other economic system, competition in one form or another would continue. Because of the dominant role of competition in the capitalist system, however, an understanding of the system presupposes an understanding of the tendencies of competition; and these tendencies can be more readily grasped if they are assumed to work themselves out in abstraction from any elements of monopoly. This is generally expressed by saying that it is necessary to begin by assuming 'perfect' competition – a technical term meaning that no individual producer or consumer has any control over market prices. By starting from the extreme of 'perfect' competition, we can go on to study the ways in which competition is limited in the real world; whereas if we drop the thread of 'perfect' competition we shall find it hard to distangle the workings of competition and monopoly[1].

Government control

Unrestricted private enterprise, too, is something of an abstraction. It does not exist. Since Victorian times a range of devices has been developed for bringing pressure on businessmen to conform to the wishes of the government. The state can exhort or cajole; it can tax or subsidize; it can use statutory controls (for example, over raw materials or wage rates). The extent to which the state intervenes, and the methods of control practised, vary with the political system.

The controls exercised by the state tend to dampen the normal competitive reactions of industry. If a product becomes scarce, the government may control the price so that it does not become dear; the competitive incentive to produce more and relieve the scarcity is then weakened and may disappear. If the product does become dear, producers may be unable to expand for lack of the necessary licences. If, to take the opposite case, there is overproduction and some firms cannot sell enough to cover their costs, the government may come to their rescue with a subsidy or by restricting imports from abroad, so that the contraction to be expected under free competition does not take place.

In war, price-control is supplemented by rationing. This gets rid of the queue by converting one kind of shortage into another. Instead of allowing those at the front of the queue to be served first, rationing spreads the shortage over the body of consumers in order to guarantee everyone a minimum. Consumer rationing represents one form of limitation to the freedom of response of the price mechanism. If goods become scarce, the state may prefer to ration them rather than allow supply and demand to

[1] When economists believe that competition is, *in fact*, not far from perfect – once a fairly common belief – their theories can easily be interpreted as a complicated apology for the existing social system. We must be on our guard against being taken in by our own simplifying assumptions.

have free play. It will then become quite false to argue that scarcity drives up prices until the high prices choke off demand. The choking off will be done as a matter of policy by the government without any change in prices.

Thus the rewards and punishments by which the plans of producers and consumers are coordinated do not always arise from the operation of ordinary market forces; other incentives and other compulsions have been superimposed by the state. Market prices reflect government controls as well as the scarcity or abundance that the market would reveal in their absence. The influence of the government on prices, when its revenue is about two-fifths of the national income, would in any event be enormous; but it is greater than it would be if it acted merely as a large buyer or a large seller because it sets out deliberately to control the workings of the price mechanism. Few prices of any importance are nowadays unaffected by its decisions. Either it exerts its influence by direct controls over production, consumption or price or through taxes, levies, duties, subsidies, grants, etc.

This influence, however exerted, cannot be neglected; but the effects of intervention can best be gauged in relation to the results of non-intervention. We must start from supply and demand, and the workings of the price mechanism, if we are to see in what respects those workings are defective and require to be controlled and in what respects government control is unnecessary, dangerous or harmful.

The function of prices

An understanding of the mechanism by which supply and demand are balanced is fundamental in every branch of economic theory. This mechanism is generally referred to as 'the price mechanism' or 'pricing'; for it is about prices that supply and demand pivot. If supply increases, while demand remains constant, prices will fall; if demand increases, while supply remains constant, prices will rise. These movements in prices tend to restore the balance between supply and demand. If there is an excess of supply over demand, or of demand over supply, prices tend to move so as to wipe out the excess and bring supply and demand back into line with one another. It is this sensitiveness of prices that enables them to knit together the plans of producers and consumers. They can choke off an over-supply by falling below cost of production to levels unprofitable to producers; and they can choke off an excessive demand by rising to levels at which consumers do not think it worth while to buy.

In balancing supply and demand, prices perform an important social function. On one side, they reflect our 'values', our estimates of how much things are worth; on the other, they reflect the scarcity of things, and the cost of making them available to consumers. They preserve a balance between value and cost. But the balance may not be struck in the best possible way. Prices may reflect our wants imperfectly (for example, because of ignorance); and they may get out of line with costs (for example, because of monopoly). Market prices, that is, may diverge from those ideal prices which would accurately reflect our wants and the cost of meeting them. For some commodities the price will be too high and for others too low. Furthermore, since the price acts to ration a scarce commodity, and direct it to those who are willing and able to pay most for it, we are faced with the question: is the distribution of goods between consumers just in a society where incomes, and needs, differ?

The theory of price or value

We are faced, therefore, with two distinct sets of problems. First, we have to analyse how pricing does in fact work; and, second, we have to analyse how, ideally, it ought to work in the best interests of society. The first problem is one of explaining how the prices of different commodities come to be what they are. We have to ask questions like why can we buy several tons of coal for the price of a fur coat? Why are some prices above, and some below, cost of production?

The second problem discussed in the theory of price, or value, is that of what prices should be. This problem may be approached from two different angles: the angle of the just price and the angle of ideal output. We may ask: on what principles are we to decide when a given price is just and when extortionate? Or we may ask: on what principles of price-fixing will we secure an optimum allocation of productive resources between alternative uses? In short: how ought we to value the products of one industry as compared with the products of another?

It should be observed that the second problem lends itself to scientific treatment much less readily than the first. When an economist discusses how prices *are* determined in the real world, he will be wrong only if his reasoning is faulty, or if his pronouncements are based on inadequate or inaccurate observation. But when he discusses how prices *should* be fixed, or what principles *should* govern the allocation of resources between industries, he may find himself in disagreement with his colleagues, however careful and competent he is. For he will be raising questions of social justice on which no economist can claim to speak with authority.

The importance of social institutions

It is essential to study how prices are, or should be, fixed against the background of a given organization of society, in a given context of social institutions. We can assume institutions broadly similar to those with which we are familiar – private property, inequality of income, a wage and money system, recurrent unemployment, joint-stock enterprise, and so on – or institutions widely different from our own: the institutions, for example, of a South Sea island or a world of monopolies. It is natural, in a discussion of price determination, to assume the institutions of a capitalist economy, since the questions posed and answered would otherwise have little relevance to the society in which we live. This is not to say, however, that a discussion of the forces determining prices in other types of society is superfluous or uninteresting. Such studies might be of great assistance in enabling a decision to be made on the merits of alternative sets of institutions. An understanding of the way in which prices are arrived at in a prisoners-of-war camp, or of the methods by which prices are regulated in Soviet Russia, for example, may make it easier to judge what changes are practicable under capitalism.

If we are discussing how prices *should* be fixed, an institutional background is equally necessary. Consider such issues as whether to outlaw discrimination by sex or race in pay, whether to prohibit or tax the sale of narcotics or noisy motorcycles, what discounts (if any) to give children or pensioners on public transport fares. If there are prevailing social attitudes on these matters, it would be quite wrong for the economist to ignore them.

Price and value

The theory of prices is sometimes spoken of as the theory of value[1]. This alternative title is intended to make it clear that it is exchange values, or *relative* prices, that are under discussion. Suppose, for example, that pears cost 12p, plums 6p, and apples 4p. Then the exchange value of pears is two plums or three apples each. Suppose now that money loses half its purchasing power and that the price of pears goes up to 24p, of plums to 12p, and of apples to 8p. The exchange value of pears in terms of plums, apples and other commodities is unaltered. All that has changed is the value of money in terms of commodities. Thus a rise in the price of plums may reflect a change in their value relatively to other commodities or relatively to money. The theory of prices, therefore, is faced not with one problem but with two. It must explain what causes a change in relative prices or exchange values; and it must explain what causes a change in the value of money. The first problem is dealt with in the theory of value, the second in the theory of money[2].

Early theories of value were theories of what governs prices *in the long run*. Day-to-day fluctuations in price – fluctuations in 'the temporary or market value' of a commodity – were put down to 'the higgling of the market', or dismissed with a vague reference to supply and demand. Analysis was confined to 'normal' or 'natural' values – that is, to the long-run trend of prices, about which day-to-day fluctuations take place.

The labour theory of value and costs of production
Most early theories were variants of the labour theory of value. According to this theory the 'natural' value of a commodity depends on the amount of labour embodied in it – on 'the toil and trouble' bestowed on its production. The value of all commodities, it was argued, is reckoned in terms of money. Since the value of money is constantly changing, however,

---

[1] At least five different meanings of the term 'value' can be distinguished: moral good, aesthetic merit, utility, exchange value, and ideal exchange value. When we say, for example, that we 'value' freedom, we are using value in the moral sense. We think that freedom is something to which men are morally entitled, something that they should have; we are certainly not thinking in terms of supply and demand. Again, if we set a high 'value' on Shakespeare's plays or Beethoven's music our judgement is an aesthetic one. If we speak of water as being 'valuable', we mean that it answers to some well-known human needs, not that it fetches a high price; we are thinking of its utility. The 'value' of a house may refer to its selling or exchange value or to the price which some imaginary purchaser might or should be willing to pay for it (for instance, we speak of house property fetching less than its 'value'). In economics 'value' is sometimes used to mean exchange value, and sometimes to mean utility, or 'value-in-use'.

[2] A strict separation of the two problems is not possible. A change in relative prices, for example, may be sufficient to precipitate a change in the value of money; and a change in the value of money is invariably accompanied by changes in relative prices. In elementary economics, however, it is legitimate to assume that the two problems can be disentangled: otherwise no progress towards understanding either is ever likely to be made.

money cannot be the ultimate standard of value. But there must be *some* ultimate and invariable standard, some circumstance common to all commodities, by which exchange values are determined. Now we know that labour is needed in the production of almost everything of value, and that commodities 'are counted dear or cheap according as they can be had with much or little labour'. The effort expended in an hour's labour, moreover, will produce the same quantity of goods; labour is a reliable measuring rod, whereas money is not. Finally, it is clear that in a primitive community with little capital, exchange values will correspond fairly closely with the amount of labour embodied in each commodity. The laws of nature, which were supposed to apply in such a community, were often appealed to as a standard in the eighteenth century, and coloured much of the political and economic theory of the period. It seems to be in accordance with these natural laws that prices should correspond to the cost, in human effort, or producing commodities.

The labour theory of value is a special case of a broader result. If five conditions hold, the prices of goods depend solely on the quantities of a single factor of production (typically labour) needed to produce them. First, the unit cost of production must be independent of the scale of output; second, there must be no cases of by-products, or joint production, like beef and leather; third, the key factor of production must be uniform in quality and perfectly mobile between all uses; fourth, there must be no monopolies; and fifth, any additional factors of production must be either produced (like electricity), or free (like air), or combine with labour in the same proportion in every use[1].

This points clearly to what is wrong with the labour theory of value: its assumptions frequently fail to hold. A popular book is cheaper than a specialist one because a large print run spreads overheads. A large rise in the demand for beef could cut the price of leather shoes, as more cattle are slaughtered. Lawyers' fees will be high if there are only few of them. Monopoly generally makes for higher prices. The price of food depends on demand and the availability of suitable land, just as much as on man-hours consumed in farming. In short, it is not labour, but scarcity – or supply, which is just scarcity the other way round – that governs value – jointly, of course, with demand. Labour – toil or effort – is one thing among several that helps to moderate scarcity and so to create value.

Sometimes the labour theory of value is supported by an appeal to justice and the rights of man. It is suggested (for example, in the Marxian version of the theory) that labour alone creates value, and that, if market values are in excess of wage costs, then the labourer is being exploited and is receiving less than the value of his product. The surplus of rent, interest and profit falls to the capitalist class, not in return for any service which they perform, but because they happen to be the owners of the instruments of production. This is not so much a theory of value (i.e., of relative prices) as a theory of distribution (i.e., of the earnings of the factors of production). It is unnecessary, therefore, to discuss it in detail at this stage. The assumption in the theory that labour alone creates value is false, even if

[1] These five conditions form the basis of the Non-substitution Theorem proved by Samuelson. See 'Abstract of a Theorem Concerning Substitutability in an Open Leontief Model', in *Collected Scientific Papers of Paul A. Samuelson*, Vol. I, ed. by J. E. Stiglitz, 1966.

'labour' is interpreted broadly to include skill and judgement. The activities and risk-taking, for example, can be just as productive as labouring; they are almost as essential to the creating of value.

A more modern version of the labour theory is that prices are governed, in the long run, and in the absence of monopoly, by the cost of production. This seems plausible enough, and is in harmony with much that goes on in the business world. Nevertheless the theory breaks down, and for much the same reasons as the labour theory breaks down. First, it neglects the influence of demand. We have already seen that costs of production generally vary with the scale of output – that is, that there is no single cost of production for each commodity irrespective of the amount of it that is being produced. Now this amount is presumably equal to the amount that consumers want to buy, i.e., to the *demand* for the commodity. Until we know what the demand is, therefore, we do not know the scale of output of the commodity, and we also do not know its cost of production. But if we do not know the cost of production until we know the demand, it is useless to tell us that price is governed by cost. Demand (or utility) and supply (or cost) are like the two blades of a pair of scissors (to use Marshall's metaphor) – it is as idle to argue that one or other governs prices as to argue that it is this blade or that that does the cutting.

Secondly, the theory is emasculated by the qualifications 'in the absence of monopoly' and 'in the long run'. In modern business, it is monopoly that is the rule, free competition the exception. There are elements of monopoly in every trade, and it is these elements of monopoly that raise the most difficult problems in economic analysis. Such an analysis cannot proceed solely in terms of cost of production; there is nothing to compel a monopolist to fix his prices at or near to cost of production. We must bring in demand if we are to develop a theory of prices under monopoly. Similarly, it is not denied that prices may be above or below cost in the short run; the theory refers only to what takes place in the long run, given time for changes to work themselves out. But the short run is much more interesting than the long run; as Lord Keynes once reminded us, in the long run we are all dead. And we cannot say how far above cost, or how far below, prices will range in the short run until we have made a study of demand.

Thirdly, the theory gives only an incomplete account of the influence of supply. Cost of production seems simple and unambiguous enough. But in fact there are few phrases in economics so hard to interpret. Firms vary enormously in efficiency: some go on producing, year after year, at high cost, while others have costs consistently lower. In which firms are we to measure cost of production? Or again, when a firm produces several different commodities in the same building, how are we to distribute the overhead costs of the building between each of the different commodities? If sheep *will* persist in providing us with mutton and wool simultaneously, how are we to distinguish the cost of wool from the cost of mutton? To these questions, the cost of production theory returns no answer.

The deficiencies of the cost of production theory will become clearer when the modern 'marginal' theory of value has been explained. Before we turn to this theory, however, we must clear away some of the confusion that clings to the terms 'supply' and 'demand'.

Chapter 11

Supply and demand

The price of an article depends upon two distinct sets of forces, generally referred to as supply and demand. 'Supply' means the quantity offered for sale by producers and 'demand', the quantity that consumers are willing to buy. Thus the 'supply' of copper does not mean the amount of copper lying underground waiting to be mined (except, of course, in other contexts); it means the amount of copper which the copper companies are willing to put on the market at various prices. Similarly, the 'demand' for copper does not mean the amount of copper which people need, or would like to have, but the *effective* demand, the amount which people are willing to buy at various prices. It should be observed that we cannot speak of demand, or of supply without specifying some price. There is, for example, no such thing as *the* demand for copper. People will buy more copper when it is cheap than when it is dear. Similarly with supply. Copper producers will be more willing to mine and sell copper when the price is high than when it is low.

Thus demand and supply vary with price. But they also vary with other things – for instance, with people's tastes, or the standard of living, or the state of technical knowledge. The changes that take place in demand and supply in response to changes in these other things (what are called 'demand *conditions*' and 'supply *conditions*') differ, however, from the changes that take place in response to changes in price. Demand conditions and supply conditions are generally independent of one another whereas price affects demand and supply simultaneously. A change in the technique of copper-mining will affect the supply of copper, for instance by lowering the cost of mining it, but it will be unlikely to react directly on the demand for copper. A change in the price of copper, on the other hand, will affect both the supply of copper and the demand for it.

The fact that supply and demand both respond to changes in price means that supply and demand can be balanced if an appropriate price is charged. The higher the price, the more will be supplied and the less demanded; the lower the price, the less will be supplied and the more demanded. Any gap between supply and demand can be closed, therefore, by raising or lowering the price. If more copper is offered for sale than the market will absorb at the current price, the price of copper will be forced down until the surplus disappears, either through consumers buying more or because output is reduced. Similarly if consumers insist on having more copper, it will be through the offer of higher prices that they induce the mining of an increased supply. Given the state of demand (demand conditions) and the state of supply (supply conditions) there will be one price (the equilibrium price) at which demand and supply can be made to balance in the sense that every buyer is able to obtain as much as he wants and every seller to sell as much as he wants at the current price, and competition will drive the price to the balancing point.

Supply and demand curves

Thus, on the one hand, supply and demand depend upon, and vary with, price; and, on the other, price depends upon, and varies with supply and demand. The interrelationship between supply, demand and price can be illustrated by drawing a supply curve and a demand curve. These curves show how much of a commodity will be offered for sale at any given price, and how much of it consumers will be likely to buy at any given price. The supply curve will normally be sloping upwards from left to right, and the demand curve will slope downwards from left to right. Where the two curves intersect, demand and supply will be equal. The price at which this equality is achieved is known as the equilibrium price.

TABLE 11.1. Demand and supply schedules for oranges

Price of oranges (pence)	Number of oranges consumers would buy ('demand schedule') (millions)	Number of oranges offered for sale ('supply schedule') (millions)
3	8000	—
6	4000	—
9	2000	400
12	1000	1000
15	500	3000
18	200	5000
21	50	6000
24	10	6500

Suppose, for instance, that we are discussing the price of oranges. We can draw up schedules like those in *Table 11.1* to show how many oranges will be offered for sale, and how many will be bought, at any given price. As the price of oranges goes up, the number offered for sale goes up too; at first, very rapidly, because it will pay to stop growing other kinds of fruit and grow oranges instead; later, increasingly slowly, because there is a limit to the area on the surface of the earth where oranges can be grown. On the other hand, as the price goes up, the number of oranges bought begins to fall off. Some people will give up eating oranges because they cannot afford them; nearly everybody will buy fewer oranges and spend their money on other things that have not risen in price – apples, for example; the manufacturers of orange juice will restrict their purchases.

The schedule of supply and demand given in *Table 11.1*, when plotted on a graph (*Figure 11.1*), gives us the supply curve and demand curve for oranges. SS' (the supply curve) illustrates the changes in supply that are likely to result from a variation in the price of oranges, and DD' (the demand curve) the changes in demand. The curves intersect at P and the

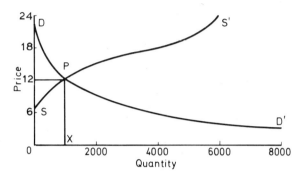

Figure 11.1 The orange market

equilibrium price PX is, therefore, 12p. This will be the price ruling in the market under the conditions assumed in *Table 11.1*. For 12p is the only price which balances demand and supply. At any price higher than 12p there is always an excess of oranges which can find a market only when they are offered for sale below the current price. At any price lower than 12p there will always be a shortage of oranges and buyers will make higher offers in order to obtain supplies. A low or high price at one point in the market will communicate itself – on the assumptions that we are making – to all other points in the market. Thus if dealings begin at some price other than 12p, they may be expected to oscillate for a time round 12p until it is clear that at this price a sufficient number of buyers will be forthcoming to take the whole supply of oranges off the market and that the requirements of buyers can be met in full. The price of 12p will then become the uniform price throughout the market and there will be no unsatisfied buyers and no unsatisfied sellers[1].

Changes in demand and supply

A change in price will come about whenever there is a change either in demand or in supply. Suppose, for example, that the public develops a liking for orange juice and is ready to buy more oranges than before at any given price. This will be represented by a movement of the demand curve to the right (see *Figure 11.2*). Consumers will be willing to buy LQ, not LP, at the market price PX and correspondingly larger quantities at any other price. At first, however, the quantity on sale will be unchanged and the

[1] This is not intended as a realistic description of how prices are fixed in a market like Covent Garden. The market spoken of above is not a place but a network of dealings (see above, p. 20).

price will be forced up steeply to RX. Once producers are able to respond to this rise in price, supplies will begin to increase and the price will fall to the point at which the new demand curve D_1D_1' intersects the supply curve SS', that is, to P_1X_1. This will be the new equilibrium price.

When a change takes place on the side of supply, for example because orange trees yielding a bigger crop are discovered, it will be the supply curve that is displaced: in the example given, it will move to the right because larger quantities will be put on the market at any given price. A new and lower price will then be established at which consumers make larger purchases than before.

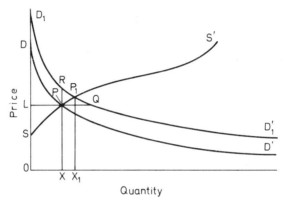

Figure 11.2 An increase in the demand for oranges

We must carefully distinguish between an increase in demand or in supply represented by a movement of the whole curve and an increase represented by a movement *along* the curve. Only the first kind of increase can initiate a change in price; the second is a reaction to a change in price and cannot be the cause of it. A change in demand in response to a change in price is not an independent change in the state of demand but simply the reflection of some antecedent change in the state of supply. If we fail to grasp this distinction we are apt to get in a muddle. We may argue, for example, that an increase in demand will push up the price but that at the higher price demand will fall off, so that the price will come down again, until we don't quite know whether the price will be higher or lower than before. This kind of muddle is particularly common when people start discussing the effects of a tax on a commodity. A flat tax or import duty of, say, 1p per orange will raise the supply curve by the same amount throughout its length and make it cut the demand curve nearer the origin; the demand, but not the demand curve, will fall and the equilibrium price will rise. How much the price will rise by will depend on the shape of the two curves. If, for instance, the supply curve is horizontal, the price consumers pay for an orange will rise by the full 1p.

Changes in price, in short, are initiated by a change either in demand or in supply conditions. This is represented by a displacement of one of the curves, which, unless compensated by an offsetting displacement of the other (a very unlikely occurrence) must force the price to a new equilibrium level. Put differently, if demand and supply are tending to get out of line with one another, they can be kept in line by an appropriate change in price. In the last resort it will be price that preserves equilibrium.

Elasticity

In order to understand how price balances supply and demand, we must study in more detail how each of these responds to small changes in price. The rate of response is measured by what is called 'elasticity'. The elasticity of demand for a commodity is the rate at which the quantity bought changes as the price changes, other things remaining the same. The elasticity of supply of a commodity is the rate at which the quantity offered for sale changes as the price changes.

These definitions are easier to understand in terms of the simple formulae:

$$\text{Elasticity of demand} = \frac{\text{Percentage change in quantity bought}}{\text{Percentage change in price}}$$

$$\text{Elasticity of supply} = \frac{\text{Percentage change in quantity offered}}{\text{Percentage change in price}}$$

In the schedules given in *Table 11.1*, for example, the elasticity of demand, when the price of oranges is 12p, lies between $\frac{5}{10}/\frac{1}{4}$ (i.e., 2) and $\frac{1}{1}/\frac{1}{4}$ (i.e., 4), according to whether we are considering an increase or a decrease in price. If we could consider infinitely small changes in price and quantity, the elasticity of demand would be the same whether we measured it in terms of a rise or a fall in price; but all that we can say from studying the schedule is that at the equilibrium price it lies somewhere between 2 and 4. The elasticity of demand is not the same at all points on the demand curve; when the price is 6p, for example, the elasticity lies between 1 and 2, and when the price is 18p the elasticity of demand lies between $4\frac{1}{2}$ and 9. In this particular example, the elasticity of demand is greater than 1 at all prices above 3p and increases as the price goes up; but it is easy to construct examples in which elasticity is less than 1, or in which elasticity falls with a rise in price. If it were true that people bought just as much salt at 8p as at 1p the elasticity of demand would not only be less than 1; it would be zero. If the only consumers of oranges left in the market when oranges rose above 24p were so well-to-do that they would go on buying almost as many at 27p or 30p, then the elasticity of demand would change abruptly at 8p and the demand would suddenly become relatively inelastic.

The elasticity of demand measures the ease with which people can put up with a small reduction in their consumption of a commodity, or alternatively the ease with which they can be induced, by a reduction in price, to consume a little more of it. If people buy the same amount of a commodity irrespective of the price, i.e., if they cannot do without *any* of the amount which they are buying then demand is absolutely inelastic (elasticity is equal to zero). If people cease to buy the commodity altogether when it rises slightly in price, then demand is perfectly elastic (elasticity is equal to infinity). These are the outer limits. Within these limits we can distinguish between demands that change more rapidly, and demands that change less rapidly than price. Just on the dividing line, a given change in price will lead to an exactly proportionate change in the quantity bought; elasticity of demand is then equal to unity. On one side of the line, elasticity will be greater, and, on the other side, less than unity. When elasticity is greater than unity – that is, when a given change in price leads to a more than proportionate change in demand – we say that demand is *elastic*. When elasticity is less than unity – that is, when a given change in price leads to a less than proportionate change in demand – we say that demand is *inelastic*. It will be observed that elasticity is a matter of degree and that, even when demand is inelastic, there are still some elements of elasticity. The five cases can be represented graphically as shown in *Figure 11.3*.

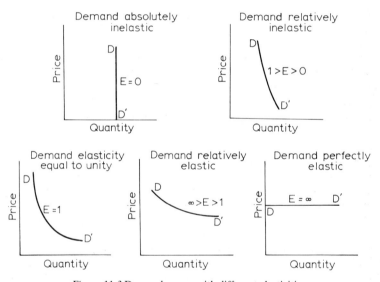

Figure 11.3 Demand curves with different elasticities

In the borderline case where demand is neither 'elastic' nor 'inelastic' but is equal to unity, the outlay of consumers will be constant as prices change, and the demand curve will take the form of a rectangular hyperbola. In this case, since by hypothesis the changes in price and in quantity bought are inversely proportional, the multiple of price and quantity (i.e., the amount spent) must be constant. Consumers will buy less of the article as its price rises but will pay more per unit of it and the rise in price will be exactly balanced by the increase in purchases, so that consumers spend the same amount of money as before. This allows us to formulate an alternative test of elasticity of demand: whether people spend more or less on an article as its price rises. If they spend more, demand is inelastic; if less, demand is elastic.

TABLE 11.2. The demand for oranges

Price of oranges (pence)	Total	Number of oranges that would be bought by		
		Working-class	Middle-class	Well-to-do
		(millions)		
3	8000	6500	1250	250
6	4000	2750	1000	250
9	2000	1000	750	250
12	1000	300	500	200
15	500	150	250	100
18	200	50	125	25
21	50	—	40	10
24	10	—	—	10

Price of oranges (pence)	Total	Amount spent on oranges by		
		Working-class	Middle-class	Well-to-do
		(million pence)		
3	24 000	19 500	3 750	750
6	24 000	15 500	6 000	1 500
9	18 000	9 000	6 750	2 250
12	12 000	3 600	6 000	2 400
15	7 500	2 250	3 750	1 500
18	3 600	900	2 250	450
21	1 050	—	840	210
24	240	—	—	240

Suppose, for example, that we divide the demand for oranges, expressed in the schedule in *Table 11.1*, into three elements, and distinguish the demands of working-class consumers, middle-class consumers and well-to-do consumers. The result might be something like that shown in *Table 11.2*.

Working-class consumers have a consistently elastic demand; they spend less money on oranges with each increase in price. Middle-class consumers have an inelastic demand up to 9p but an elastic demand at higher prices. The well-to-do have an extremely inelastic demand at low prices; they are prepared to spend more than three times as much on oranges at 12p each than at 3p each (although they get fewer oranges for their money). They have then a fairly elastic demand as the price rises to 21p; and thereafter their demand begins to be inelastic again.

The measurement of elasticity

The example given above is a hypothetical one. But economists have been able to make rough estimates of the actual elasticity of demand for some commodities by drawing up what is called a 'statistical' demand curve. In its simplest form this consists of a number of points plotted on a graph from observed prices and sales in past years (what statisticians call a 'scatter diagram'). The graph (*Figure 11.4*) shows how sales of potatoes in the United Kingdom varied in relation to their price in each of a number of pre-war years, each cross representing one particular year. The points lie roughly along a curve: and from the shape of the curve the elasticity of demand for potatoes can be calculated. The curve indicates that a rise in

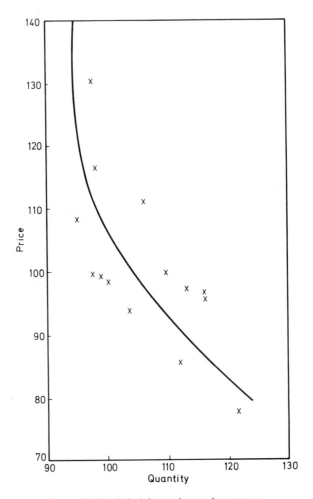

Figure 11.4 Statistical demand curve for potatoes

price by 1.5% reduces consumption by about 1%: that is, that the elasticity of demand for potatoes is about 0.7[1]. This statistical demand curve is valid if, and only if, we are entitled to assume that the supply curve has shifted up and down, and the demand curve has remained fixed in position.

---

[1] These estimates and the data from which *Figure 11.4* is constructed are taken from an article by Prof. K. S. Lomax on 'The Demand for Potatoes' in *The Manchester School*, May 1950.

Elasticity of demand and substitution

The elasticity of demand for a commodity depends mainly on the range of available substitutes. The better the substitutes available, the more elastic will be the demand for the commodity. If motor cars became dearer, the demand may not fall off very much, because people do not consider bicycles and buses very good substitutes for motor cars. But if the price of Morris motor cars goes up and there is a very similar model on sale (e.g., the Ford), demand will be transferred to the cheaper model and the sales of Morris cars will fall heavily; that is, demand will be elastic. In the same way, the demand for tea will be less than the demand for a particular brand of tea, because brands of tea are better substitutes for one another than cocoa, coffee, etc. are for tea. If there are absolutely perfect substitutes on sale (e.g., wheat of the same grade sold by different farmers), then the demand will be perfectly elastic; no one will be able to raise his price above the price paid to his competitors without losing his entire market.

The possibilities of substitution will be greater when there is a wide range of uses to which the commodity can be put. Electricity, for instance, is used for heating and lighting, for the supply of power, and so on. Hence it can be substituted for coal, candles, gas, petrol, wireless batteries, etc., whenever it becomes cheaper. As electricity falls in price in relation to other things, people find it worth while to reduce their expenditure on a great many different things and transfer this expenditure to electricity. Thus the demand for electricity is fairly elastic.

On the other hand, the demand for wheat is highly inelastic. Most people put wheat to a single use (i.e., they eat it), so that when wheat falls in price, they can only increase their purchases of wheat if they elect to eat more of it. This generally means a change of diet which is not very acceptable. So far, however, as wheat is used for other purposes (e.g., as a feeding-stuff) and so far as people are prepared to switch to wheat from potatoes, rye, oats, rice, and other substitutes whenever wheat is relatively cheap, the demand will retain some elements of elasticity.

Again, the demand for necessities is generally much less elastic than the demand for luxuries. The demand for potatoes, for instance, is far more inelastic than the demand for oranges. For necessities like salt or sewing thread, on which we spend a very small fraction of our income, demand will be particularly inelastic, since a rise of perhaps 50% in price may mean no more than a few pence on our annual outlay. Similarly, rich people have a less elastic demand than poor people. The poor man has constantly to be considering how he can spend his income to best advantage and is sensitive to changes in price; while the rich man, faced with a rise in price, may not bother to look for a substitute. The demand for pineapples will be far less elastic in Park Avenue than in Chinatown.

Elasticity arises in two different ways. Existing consumers will tend to buy more as prices fall, and new consumers will be tempted to make purchases. Sometimes, of course, only one source of elasticity is present. Practically everyone is already buying potatoes; new consumers cannot be found. On the other hand, it is rarely possible to persuade people to buy two copies of the same book; new consumers have to be found. Generally speaking, elasticity arises less through increased purchases by existing consumers than through the tapping of successive layers of demand from *potential* consumers as prices are brought down[1].

Practical importance of elasticity

The conception of elasticity is of great practical importance. Suppose that the railways are thinking of increasing fares. One of the first questions that they will have to reflect on is how much traffic will be lost? How many passengers will give up travelling by train and travel by some other means or not travel at all? This is the same question in another form as how elastic is the demand for rail travel? Similarly, if the government is thinking of putting a higher duty on tobacco it will have to form some idea of the impact on smoking habits, of the rate at which the demand for cigarettes and tobacco will fall off as the price goes up: that is, of the elasticity of demand. Manufacturers trying to work out the best price for a new line in stockings or hot-water bottles are faced with the same problem and will require to form some estimate of the elasticity of demand. They may not think in the precise terms in which elasticity has been formulated by economists. But there is no reason to suppose that their judgement is any the better for neglecting (or avoiding) the economist's formulation.

Elasticity of supply

The elasticity of supply of a commodity measures the ease with which producers can meet a small rise or fall in price by increasing or reducing supplies. Supply is said to be elastic or inelastic according as a change in price causes a more than proportionate or less than proportionate change in supply. *Figure 11.5* depicts various possible supply curves.

The elasticity of supply depends upon the range of alternatives open to the producer. If, for example, he is selling in several different markets his goods are likely to be in elastic supply to any one market; a fall in prices in that market will induce him to sell his goods elsewhere. Again, if he is producing several different goods, and can switch fairly easily from one to another, then each of his products will be in elastic supply. Or if the alternative of closing down his works and going out of business altogether will not involve him in heavy loss, then again supply is likely to be elastic. Finally, supply will be elastic if each producer's employees can readily obtain employment in other industries, if the materials which they use have alternative markets, and if their equipment is readily convertible to other

---

[1] Elasticity of demand, as discussed above, is sometimes called 'price elasticity' to distinguish it from 'income elasticity'. This measures the responsiveness of demand to a change in income. As people become better off, their consumption of some commodities grows much more rapidly than others: for example, they spend a smaller proportion of their income on food and a larger proportion on recreation and entertainments. This means that they have a low income elasticity of demand for food and a high income elasticity of demand for recreation. Just as the conception of price elasticity is of great importance in analysing fluctuations in prices, the conception of income elasticity is useful in analysing fluctuations in income. It is also valuable in a study of the dynamics of prices in explaining the tendency of some prices to rise relatively to others with increasing prosperity.

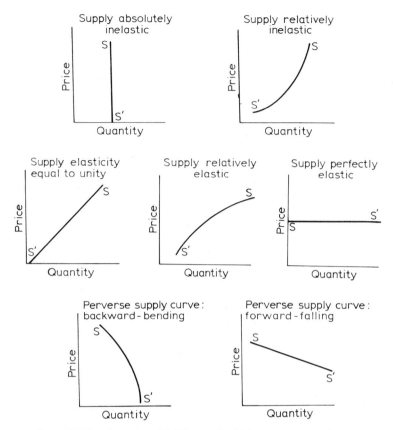

Figure 11.5 Supply curves with different elasticities; perverse supply curves

uses. The more attractive these alternatives, the less will be the incentive to continue in the industry when prices fall, and the greater, therefore, will be the contraction in output and in supply.

With supply as with demand, elasticity arises in two ways: through a change in the output of existing producers and through a change in the number of producers. There will be a full discussion of these changes in Chapter 13.

Elasticity and time

The response of consumers and producers to a change in price is generally spread over a period of time; some reactions are immediate and some delayed. If, for example, the price of cameras goes up, firms that are already making cameras may produce more and some firms outside the industry may decide to start producing cameras. But the new firms will take a little time before they can put cameras on the market; and the output of the industry as a whole may be limited by some common bottleneck such as optical glass, so that no expansion beyond a certain point can take place until the firms making optical glass have expanded their capacity, trained additional labour, etc. There will be a succession of adjustments as time goes on, all making for a higher level of output at some stage. The elasticity of supply, therefore, will grow with the passage of time. So also will the elasticity of demand. In the short run consumers may have no alternative but to pay higher prices; but in the long run the range of alternatives widens and substitution becomes easier. If railway freight charges go up, there may be no immediate reduction in traffic; but a great many businesses will make enquiries about alternative forms of transport and some will place orders for lorries or make trial shipments by water. The result will be a gradual transfer of freight away from the railways, the elasticity of demand increasing progressively[1].

Fluctuation in prices

Elasticity, whether of demand or of supply, makes for stability of prices. The price of a commodity like wheat, which is in inelastic demand, will have to fall drastically if a surplus has to be absorbed; whereas a comparatively slight reduction in price will be sufficient to secure the absorption of a surplus of oranges, which are in elastic demand. The more elastic the demand, the more stable the price. Similarly the price of commodities like rubber, which are in inelastic supply, will fluctuate more than the price of commodities like motor cars, which are in elastic supply. The more elastic the supply, the more stable the price. Where demand and supply are elastic – i.e., highly sensitive to changes in price – it will require no great change in price to keep them in step with one other. Prices will fluctuate more widely if either demand or supply is highly variable. The supply of strawberries varies enormously between December and June, and between one year and another, and this causes wide fluctuations in the price of strawberries. The demand for seaside holiday accommodation varies from one season to another, and resorts that are crowded one year may have plenty of room in later years; these fluctuations in demand are reflected in fluctuations in hotel and boarding house charges. When a commodity is both in highly inelastic demand and subject to wide variations in supply, the range of price fluctuations may be enormous. The farm price of potatoes, for example, may be £20 a ton one year and £100 a ton the next because large fluctuations in the crop encounter a highly inelastic demand.

Fluctuations in price are much more pronounced in agriculture and mining than in industry. Staple raw materials and foodstuffs such as wool, rubber, tin, wheat, sugar, coffee, and so on, undergo the most astonishing changes in price in a matter of months, while many manufactured goods are sold at the same price year in, year out, and many others change in price only at rare intervals and by comparatively short hops. This difference arises largely because the supply of agricultural and mining products is highly inelastic, so that it is not easy to match a change in demand by a corresponding change in supply, while the supply of manufactured goods is highly elastic and can be easily expanded or contracted in step with demand. One consequence of the difference is that the incomes of

---

[1] See also Chapter 15 for a fuller discussion of the influence of time on elasticity.

agricultural communities fluctuate more widely than the incomes of industrial communities. On the other hand, since the elasticity of supply in industry is only achieved by cutting down output and discharging workers when demand falls off, the comparative steadiness of prices in industrial communities is bought at the cost of relative unsteadiness of employment.

It may happen that a general fall in agricultural prices actually brings about an *increase* in agricultural output. The fall in prices cuts farmers' incomes; farmers may try to make up for the loss by extra effort; if they do, they will grow more farm produce and when the larger supply comes on the market it will drive prices still lower. The same kind of thing can happen in coal-mining; a shortage of coal tends to drive up prices and enables coal-miners to press successfuly for higher wages; the higher wages may make the miners disinclined to work so hard, since they will be able to earn as much as before in a shorter time; and, if this is the predominant reaction, the shortage of coal will be intensified, not reduced. Foodstuffs and coal would then display perverse, backward-bending supply curves. This is illustrated in *Figure 11.5*. If an increase in demand enabled the producer to supply an increased volume at a lower price because of a fall in cost per unit, the supply curve would again be perverse; but this time, it would be forward-falling. Again, *Figure 11.5* illustrates. Supply curves, however, typically are horizontal or upward-sloping.

Instability

This chapter has followed Leon Walras's approach to demand and supply. Walras's demand curve gives the quantity demanded at a given price. The supply curve, similarly, makes quantity supplied depend on price. When quantities demanded and supplied are equal, the market is in balance, and price will not change. Price rises if there is excess demand (quantity demanded outstripping quantity supplied). If there is excess supply, price declines. For Walras, the point of balance will be stable if a price rise can always be relied upon to lower excess demand or increase excess supply. When the two curves are normal (i.e., demand sloping downward and supply upward), and there are no lags, there is no danger of instability.

But a market could be unstable. Suppose producers respond now to current prices and decide next year's output on this basis. If the current price is high, it will tend to fall next year. If supply is more elastic than demand, not merely will it fall steeply next year but, all other things being equal, it will shoot above its present level the year after that. Explosive price fluctuations like this can be seen, now and again, in some primary commodity markets. They tend to stabilize in the end, partly because everyone learns how badly one year's price predicts the price in the year following. Yet fluctuations and trends are easier to tell apart with hindsight. Suppose now that buyers and sellers both treat current price movements as indicative of a trend. If prices rise, buyers will be prompted to buy more, not less, if the good in question can be stored cheaply or resold easily. Sellers, on the other hand, will cut back sales. So excess demand is intensified. Price rises accelerate. This is how a stock market bubble can start. Hyperinflation can be fuelled this way, too.

Difficulties in the construction of demand and supply curves

The drawing of demand and supply curves is not always such a simple matter as the discussion so far might imply[1]. How, for example, can we draw a demand curve for motor cars? What price are we to plot against the number of motor cars being sold to the public? Should it be the price of Fords or Rolls-Royces, of 10 hp or 90 hp cars, of second-hand cars 'in working order', or brand-new models fitted with the latest gadgets? Or if we try to calculate an average price for the whole group, how are we to average a fall in the price of some models against a rise in the price of others if the sales of each model do not respond equally to a given change in price? These practical difficulties make it impossible to represent the state of demand for motor cars with complete accuracy in a demand curve. A demand curve is intended to represent the demand for something uniform – for a commodity: but motor cars are a group of commodities rather than a commodity. Inside the group are cars which, from the point of view of producer or consumer, are about as far removed from one another as a power-house is from a television set. Other 'commodities' are just as heterogeneous. It is rare for the products of a large number of firms to be exactly alike, and it is correspondingly rare, therefore, for a demand curve to be possible that represents demand conditions exactly.

A supply curve may raise even greater difficulties. The curve is intended to show how much will be offered for sale at the market price. But what if there is no market price and each manufacturer can charge what he likes? Ford's do not enquire first after the price which their cars are fetching and then decide how many to sell. They try to make a market at a price which they fix themselves. They are willing to sell at that price far more cars than they are able to dispose of in practice; and if sales begin to increase, they are just as likely to lower as to raise the price of their cars. A supply curve of Ford motor cars, therefore, cannot possibly be drawn[2]. It is also impossible to draw a supply curve of motor cars in general. If we cannot tell how many cars a particular firm will offer for sale at any given price, we cannot tell how many cars will be offered for sale by the whole industry. The fact is that the drawing of a supply curve presupposes keen competition between a large number of firms, each taking the market price for granted and with no power to control it. There must be no trace of monopoly in the market – not even such limited monopoly as arises when firms make goods differing ever so slightly from the products of their competitors.

The apparatus of demand and supply curves must always be used guardedly. It suggests to many people a permanency in the state of demand and supply which is not in keeping with the facts: both demand and supply are in a constant state of flux. It suggests, too, that it is price, and price

---

[1] The assumptions underlying the drawing of demand and supply curves will be examined in more detail below (Chapter 13).

[2] It is, of course, quite possible to draw a cost curve of Ford motor cars. But a cost curve and a supply curve are two quite different things. The first relates to the firm; it is a curve of costs (i.e., of the expense to which a firm is put in order to produce a given output). The second relates to the industry; it is a curve of supply prices (i.e., of prices, expectation of which will induce sellers to put a given quantity of their product on the market).

only, that keeps demand and supply in line with one another – that price competition is the only kind of competition. For many things, this is planly not so. But, however one may question the legitimacy of drawing curves, they are an indispensable first step on the way to clear thinking about prices. The ladder may be rickety, and we may have to kick it out of the way later, but without it we will never reach the heights from which its shakiness becomes apparent.

Chapter 12

Demand

The major influences on demand

Unless mistaken or coerced, no one will buy something unless he expects to benefit by doing so. He must prefer the new bundle of goods and assets which includes this purchase, to the old one without it. Consumers' demand for goods clearly depends, then, upon preferences – but not only upon preferences. All too often, the consumer will find that he cannot afford to buy everything he would like. Purchases will be constrained by his budget. In this case, the price of an item he would like to buy is an important influence on his demand for it. Suppose his preferences are such that he plans to spend a given share, say one-third, of his income on food. With given preferences and income, his demand for food would double (or

TABLE 12.1. Influences on the demand for a good

| | Influences upon the demand for a particular good, X | |
	With given budget shares	In general
Income	Positive and equiproportionate (income elasticity of demand = 1)	Usually positive. If negative, X is an 'inferior good'
Weight in preferences	Positive (note: budget share must rise)	Positive
Price of X	Negative and equiproportionate (price elasticity of demand = 1)	Nearly always negative. Could be positive if X is an inferior good with a large budget share, and next to no substitutes; also possible if price rise leads directly to a change in preferences (ignorant consumers measuring quality by price; snob-appeal; expectations of future price changes in the same direction, if X can be stored or resold).
Price of Y (another good)	No effect	Positive if X and Y are substitutes, negative if complements

halve) if the price of food halved (or doubled). His demand for food would have an elasticity of one to the price of food. If income doubled, however, with given preferences and prices, the demand for food would double too. So income is (in this case) a positive influence on demand, with an elasticity of one. A change in his preferences in favour of food would also raise his demand for food, moving his demand curve for food upwards and rightwards, much like a rise in income. If the price of clothing changes, however, our consumer will not (as it happens) alter his demand for food: this is so because in our example the share of food in the budget is given independently of any prices, at one-third.

If preferences are such that budget shares for goods are given, then, the price of one good cannot affect the demand for another. In general, however, a rise in the price of one good can affect the demand for others, and in different directions. Dearer beef will mean lower demand for mustard (a complement) and higher demand for mutton and chicken (substitutes); dearer petrol will lower the demand for tyres and tourism, but strengthen it for bicycles, coal and pullovers. *Table 12.1* presents a list of influences on the demand for a good, and shows what effects they have, first if budget shares are given and then in general. It tells us that a rise in the price of X nearly always lowers the demand for X. In other words, the demand curve for X nearly always slopes downwards from left to right. The reason for this is the Principle of Substitution.

The Principle of Substitution

The Principle of Substitution states that if the relative price of two goods changes in such a way that a consumer with given preferences is neither better off, nor worse off, than before, any switch in demand must be *away from the good the relative price of which has risen*, towards the relatively cheaper good.

The truth of this can be seen clearly if we follow, to its absurd conclusion, the notion of its being false. Suppose, therefore, that a consumer were to substitute away from the cheaper towards the dearer good. Note that his real income must be held constant, since he is neither better off nor worse off than before the price changes. This means that he must cut his purchases of the now cheaper good by a higher proportion than he raises those of the dearer good. This implies, in turn, that the new bundle of purchases our consumer buys must have been available, and compatible with his budget, before the price changes took place. Before the price changes, the old bundle was preferred to the new bundle, since, if it weren't, it would not have been bought. But after the price changes, the new bundle is preferred to the old. So his preferences must have changed. But we are told that they had not. This contradiction can be resolved only by admitting that it must be false that the Principle of Substitution is false. So the Principle of Substitution is valid.

The Principle of Substitution cannot, however, establish that the demand curve for a good must slope downwards in all circumstances. If an *inferior good* falls in price, consumers' tendencies to substitute into it will be qualified by the fact that the price cut – in so far as it boosts their real income – will reduce the demand for it somewhat. It is just possible that this perverse 'income effect' could dominate the substitution effect. As noted in *Table 12.1*, there is also the chance that a price change could induce a change in preferences, for a variety of reasons. The combined effects of all these changes are ambiguous.

Indifference curve analysis

An indifference curve links combinations of different goods which give a consumer equal utility, benefit, or satisfaction. Suppose I am equally happy with three cups of coffee and one cup of tea each day, as with one cup of coffee and three cups of tea. If a diagram is constructed with cups of coffee and tea per day measured on the axis (see *Figure 12.1*), points A and B – depicting three coffee and one tea and one coffee and three tea – lie on

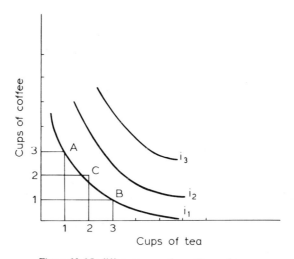

Figure 12.1 Indifference map for coffee and tea

what is termed an indifference curve. In *Figure 12.1*, this curve is labelled i_1. The other curves (i_2 and i_3) are indifference curves representing *higher* levels of utility – assuming, that is, that my desire for tea and coffee is insatiable, so that more is always preferred to less. If the commodities on the axes are both 'goods' (for which more is preferred to less), then the indifference curve must slope downwards. In *Figure 12.1*, the curves are drawn convex to the origin: point C, for instance, which represents two cups of both coffee and tea, lies on a higher indifference curve than i_1. Indifference curves are widely assumed to have this shape; this implies that mixtures are preferred. C is a half-and-half blend of A and B – presumably not in the same pot!

By themselves, indifference curves (which together form an indifference map) merely display the consumer's preferences. We cannot predict his actual purchases until we take account of income and prices as well. Suppose that my budget for coffee and tea together is strictly limited to £1

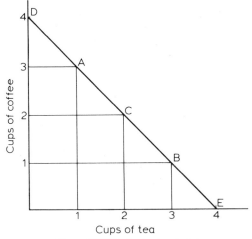

Figure 12.2 The budget restraint

per day, and that coffee and tea are both priced at 25p per cup and perfectly divisible. If all my £1 is spent on coffee, I can buy four cups. Similarly with tea. Call these 4:0 and 0:4 combinations D and E respectively. They are shown in *Figure 12.2*. D and E are limiting points of the budget restraint. Since

$$£1 = 2 \times 25p + 2 \times 25p = 1 \times 25p + 3 \times 25p,$$

points A, B and C in *Figure 12.1* also lie along the same budget restraint. Our perfect divisibility assumption allows us to make the budget restraint a *continuous* set of points; our assumption of given prices makes it a straight line. All points along DE represent an outlay of £1. Which shall I, the hypothetical consumer, actually choose? Our theory predicts that the consumer selects the point of tangency between the budget restraint and the highest attainable indifference curve. This is shown as point C, where DE just touches i*, in *Figure 12.3*. Any point on DE other than C

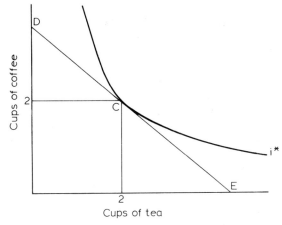

Figure 12.3 Tangency of budget restraint and indifference curve

represents a position where the budget restraint is crossed by an indifference curve of value lower than i*. So long as the two commodities are goods, not bads, and the indifference curve touches the budget restraint *on the outside*, this tangency point must give the consumer the highest possible satisfaction compatible with his limited means.

The effects of price and income changes are easily displayed. Suppose, first, that the prices of both coffee and tea double to 50p per cup, with no change in the budget in money terms. This is equivalent to a halving in the budget to 50p, at unchanged prices. What happens is shown in *Figure 12.4.*

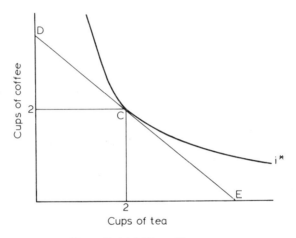

Figure 12.4 A fall in real income

The budget line is brought inwards from DE to FG, since the consumer can buy only half as much as before. FG and DE are parallel, since the relative prices of coffee and tea remain the same (one-to-one). The new point of indifference curve tangency is H. At H, tea consumption has fallen by one-quarter to 1½ cups, and that of coffee by three-quarters to half a cup. In this case, tea is a necessity, coffee a luxury. Before concluding that inflation stops people drinking coffee, however, we should notice two points: H was chosen at random (it could have been anywhere on FG); and more important, inflation generally raises peoples' money incomes in line with prices. Had the doubling of tea and coffee prices accompanied a doubling of the money value of the budget from £1 to £2, the consumer's budget restraint would have remained DE, and he would have continued to buy two cups of each drink per day.

Figures 12.5 and *12.6* both portray the effects of a doubling of the price of tea *only*, from 25p to 50p. Coffee stays at 25p a cup, and the budget remains £1. Point D on the budget restraint remains unchanged, since the budget continues to buy a maximum of four cups of coffee (when no tea is bought). But if no coffee is bought, tea purchases are sliced from four cups to two. So the budget restraint intercept on the tea axis moves in, from point E to point G. Both *Figures 12.5* and *12.6* show a fall in the amount of tea purchased: this is, as we have seen, an overwhelmingly likely effect, at least when preferences are given and the indifference map therefore stays

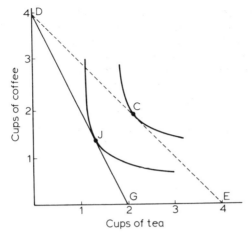

Figure 12.5 A rise in the price of tea when tea and coffee are complements

put. Where the two diagrams differ is in the extent of the fall, and in what happens to coffee consumption. If tea and coffee are complements, as in *Figure 12.5*, both purchases decline. Since less is spent on coffee, more is spent (out of a given budget of £1) on tea. So the demand for tea is inelastic. In *Figure 12.6*, tea is in elastic demand, since coffee consumption goes up. As coffee and tea are substitutes, the tea price rise raises total spending on coffee at the expense of tea. There is a borderline case between these two, in which coffee consumption is unaffected by the price of tea, and the elasticity of demand for tea (and also, incidentally, coffee) is one. This is what we analysed in the left-hand column of *Table 12.1*.

One important application of the complements–substitutes distinction shown in *Figures 12.5* and *12.6* is to the question of people's choice of

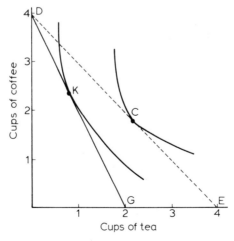

Figure 12.6 A rise in the price of tea when tea and coffee are substitutes

hours of work. Suppose the vertical axis stands for hours of leisure, not cups of coffee; D represents an 'endowment' of leisure of 24 hours per day. Let the horizonal axis depict not just tea, but all goods aggregated together (call them 'bread') which we bought with the proceeds from paid work. The budget line DE shows the restraint on leisure-cum-bread which the consumer will face, assuming that all his income is earned, and that the hourly wage rate and price of bread are given. C depicts the individual's choice of leisure and bread; the distance from D to '2' units on the vertical axis shows his hours of work, the remaining '2' units his leisure. Now consider the effects of a halving of the hourly wage rate (equivalently, a doubling of the price of bread, or a new flat-rate income tax at a rate of 50%). Each will swing the budget retraint from DE to DG. In both diagrams, the amount of 'bread' bought falls. In *Figure 12.5*, our individual works longer hours; in *Figure 12.6*, he works less. Both reactions are possible. Everything depends on whether leisure and bread are complements or substitutes. We can now see why coal and agricultural products might conceivably have backward-bending supply curves.

Some problems

At the end of the last chapter, drawing curves to explain prices was stated to resemble using a helpful but rickety ladder. It is now time to take stock of some important aspects of the behaviour of consumers that our analysis has not considered.

There are four difficulties with the budget restraint as drawn in *Figures 12.2* to *12.6*. First, there are not just two goods. There may be 10 000 separate items on the shelves of a single shop. Worse still, the question of time raises the choices between jam today and jam tomorrow, which are definitely different goods. Two-dimensional diagrams are at best drastic simplifications. Second, the consumer often does not know exactly what the price of a particular good is. In this and in other respects, ignorance reduces consumer behaviour to a complex guessing game. Third, many commodities are indivisible: most obviously houses, motor cars, airplane flights and the like. Indivisibilities turn the budget restraint into a set of disconnected dots. Finally, the price of a commodity may not be unique. The price of a millilitre of ink or tomato drink, for instance, depends on how much you buy. Non-unique prices make the budget restraint a curve or broken line. So the budget restraint is really a discontinuous curve of uncertain position in an infinite number of dimensions!

Then there is the problem of whether consumer demands are based on conscious choice and genuine preference, or reflect – in part at least – imitation, habit, advertising or limited information. Another psychological questionmark hangs over the 'goods' themselves: are they wanted directly as ends in themselves, or are preferences expressed over sets of *characteristics* that goods possess in varying amounts, such as proteins, vitamins, warmth, transportation, safety, ability to amuse? A further difficulty is the size of the consumer unit. This may be one person, a nuclear or extended family, or a much larger grouping such as a club or commune. When more than one person is involved, how are the group's preferences related to those of its members?

Appropriate refinements can be made to our analysis to deal adequately with some of these issues, while others are less tractable. But such refinements exact a heavy toll. The great virtue of the basic theory is its simplicity. It states simply that individuals or households will select their purchases of goods (and supplies of factors) in such a way that their budget restraint is tangential to the highest attainable indifference curve. Another way of expressing this is to state that purchases will be arranged so that, for each good that is purchased, the ratio of the marginal utility of the good to its price is set equal to the marginal utility of money.

Chapter 13

Supply: cost and price

In Chapter 12 we saw what governs the demand for a commodity. We have now to examine what determines its supply. Just as we tried to go behind the demand curve in order to study the preferences of consumers, so we must now try to go behind the supply curve to the costs of producers.

Cost controls supply in two ways. It controls the volume of output which each firm finds it profitable to produce, and it controls the number of firms that can carry on at a profit. If the cost of producing a commodity rises, other things remaining the same, the supply tends to contract for two reasons – first, because each firm will cease to manufacture units of output that no longer pay their way; and, second, because some firms will find it necessary, or advantageous, to abandon production of the commodity altogether. The rise in costs will press on supply at the margin – on units of output which it was just worth while for each firm to produce, and on firms which found it just worth while to carry on production of the commodity. Other (intra-marginal) units of output will continue to be supplied, and other (intra-marginal) firms will continue in business at the higher level of costs.

Marginal cost

Thus it is marginal, rather than average, cost that controls supply. Marginal cost is the net cost of a marginal addition to output. Strictly, it equals the change in the total costs of production when output is changed by a tiny (really negligible) amount, divided by that change in output. The marginal cost of a commodity is defined when the marginal costs of producing it are equal across all firms doing so.

Price and marginal cost can be equal. This will happen when two conditions are met, but otherwise generally not. These conditions are, first, that the firms concerned succeed in maximizing their profits, and second, that none of the firms is able to influence the price at which it sells. They are often not met. A firm may try to maximize profits but fail through error or imperfect knowledge. Or it may be more concerned with other goals, such as size, and not even try. Furthermore few firms face a selling price they cannot influence. One producer very often sells a substantial proportion of the total supply; his competition with other firms may be limited by understandings or agreements; and his powers over prices may be far from negligible. Producers, that is, are rarely able to take prices for granted and sell as much as they please at the ruling price. They have to regulate their output so as to keep from forcing down prices and spoiling their market. Similarly, a new firm may be unable to find a market without incurring special selling costs (e.g., by advertising). It has to build up a connection and 'make a market' for itself instead of simply offering its goods for sale at current prices.

In the special circumstances when firms act as profit-maximizing price-takers, competition will be 'perfect', that is, no single consumer or producer will control a sufficiently large proportion of purchases or sales, or enjoy sufficient 'pull' with his suppliers or customers, to be able to influence the market price. But if profits are maximized when there is a monopoly in the ordinary sense or monopolistic competition of one kind or another, price will be above marginal cost. A clear understanding of these propositions is extremely important.

Cost under perfect competition in the individual firm

We may begin by analysing the way in which cost and price are likely to be related, in conditions of perfect competition, within an individual firm. Let us assume that the firm is making a single commodity only and that, since it is by hypothesis able to sell as much as it can produce at the market price, it does not resort to advertising or any kind of sales pressure. These assumptions (which are obviously unrealistic) rule out a number of complications for which provision can be made later.

The Scribblo Propelling Pencil Company Ltd – to take a concrete example – is one of a large number of pencil manufacturers in keen competition with one another and the public likes its pencils as well as any. The price of pencils is 4p and the company is wrestling with the problem: how many pencils should it produce and sell in order to maximize its profits? It calls for a report from its accountants and they, after delving into all the facts and figures and throwing in a few guesses here and there to supplement the facts, submit the data shown in *Table 13.1*.

TABLE 13.1. Cost of production of Scribblo pencils

Output (million pencils)	Fixed cost (million pence)	Variable cost (million pence)	Total cost (million pence)	Average cost (pence)	Marginal cost (pence)
0	6.0	0.0	6.0	∞	
					3.5
1	6.0	3.5	9.5	9.5	
					3.1
2	6.0	6.6	12.6	6.3	
					2.9
3	6.0	9.5	15.5	5.1	
					2.8
4	6.0	12.3	18.3	4.6	
					3.0
5	6.0	15.3	21.3	4.3	
					3.2
6	6.0	18.5	24.5	4.1	
					3.5
7	6.0	22.0	28.0	4.0	
					4.0
8	6.0	26.0	32.0	4.0	
					4.7
9	6.0	30.7	36.7	4.1	
					5.6
10	6.0	36.3	42.3	4.2	
					6.6
11	6.0	42.9	48.9	4.4	

The accountants have divided Scribblo's costs into two elements: one, representing 'overheads', is fixed and does not vary with output; the other, representing the cost of labour, materials, and so on, increases as output increases. If the total cost at each successive level of output is averaged over the total output, it falls at first because of the element of fixed costs, which drags down the average. At a later stage, average cost begins to increase, for example because Scribblo's are working to capacity and having to pay overtime rates of pay[1].

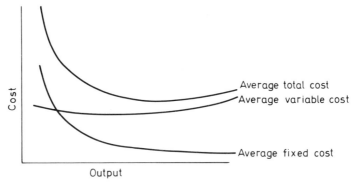

Figure 13.1 The cost of production of pencils

The relation between fixed, variable and total costs is illustrated in *Figure 13.1*. Fixed costs per unit of output take the shape of a rectangular hyperbola; variable costs per unit of output fall gently until capacity is approached and then begin to rise; total costs per unit of output (i.e., average costs) fall steeply at first but eventually begin to increase.

Marginal and average cost

Marginal cost of production is shown in the last column of *Table 13.1*. Marginal cost is the net cost of a marginal addition to output. To be more precise, it is the increment in aggregate costs when output is increased by one unit; or alternatively, it is the expense that could be avoided by reducing output by one unit[2]. The column headed 'Marginal costs',

[1] Even if Scribblo's were a new firm and had not yet installed its plant, its costs would show the same kind of variations. At first it would enjoy the benefit of economies of large-scale production and the larger the scale of production on which it decided, the lower would be its costs. There could come a point, however, at which a larger scale of production meant higher costs, either because the business was too large for efficient management or because output began to press on the supply of some scarce factor of production. If more workers were needed, for example, it might be necessary to offer higher wages so as to attract them from other districts and other trades, or alternatively to take on workers of less than average skill. For a fuller discussion, see Chapter 15.

[2] These two things are not necessarily identical. As a rule the difference will be insignificant. But if, before output can be increased further, a change has to be made in the organization of the firm, or in the layout of the plant, or in the machinery in use, there will be a discontinuous change in costs at that level of output. The net cost of an extra unit of output may then be much higher than the savings resulting from a cut in output by one unit. An additional complication is introduced by the time factor since the savings that result from a fall in output for a few weeks are very different from the savings that could be made if the reduction in output were for an indefinite period.

therefore, is derived from the column headed 'Total cost' by taking the increment in total costs as output rises from one level to the next. Strictly speaking, it should be calculated on the basis of *infinitely small variations* in output; but for practical purposes we can take the extra cost of producing one million pencils more, and divide the result by one million in order to obtain the marginal cost of a pencil at the level of output assumed. Marginal cost, as appears from *Figure 13.2*, is at first below average cost.

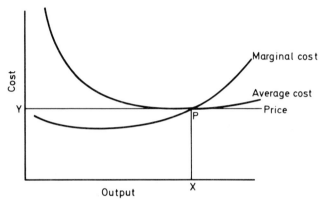

Figure 13.2 Average cost, marginal cost and price of pencils

The main reason for this is that marginal cost includes no element of fixed cost whereas average cost does. Even if fixed cost is left out of account, however, marginal cost will be below average *variable* cost so long as average variable cost is falling. Eventually, marginal cost begins to rise; but so long as it remains below average cost (i.e., so long as each additional unit costs less than the average) average cost continues to fall. When marginal cost exceeds average cost (i.e., when each additional unit costs more than the average) average cost increases. When marginal cost is exactly equal to average cost, average cost is neither rising nor falling but is at the turning point where it touches bottom. Thus the marginal cost curve in *Figure 13.2* intersects the average cost curve at its minimum point.

Marginal cost and price

Now the interesting thing is that this is also the point at which Scribblo's will make their maximum profit. Profit will be at a maximum if price and marginal cost are equal. If the price were above marginal cost, it would be possible to make an additional profit by putting on the market pencils that would add more to total sales proceeds than to total costs. If the price were below marginal cost, some units of output would not be paying their way; by ceasing to produce them Scribblo's could reduce their costs faster than their revenue. It is easy to test this by hypothetical examples. It emerges also from *Table 13.2*, although in a rather curious way.

If the price of pencils is 4p, Scribblo's can just cover their costs when they are producing between 7 and 8 million pencils but with any larger or

TABLE 13.2. Costs and profits of pencil manufacture

Output (million pencils)	Total cost (million pence)	Total revenue (million pence)	Profit (million pence)	Marginal cost (pence)	Price (pence)
1	9.5	4.0	−5.5		4
				3.1	
2	12.6	8.0	−4.6		4
				2.9	
3	15.5	12.0	−3.5		4
				2.8	
4	18.3	16.0	−2.3		4
				3.0	
5	21.3	20.0	−1.3		4
				3.2	
6	24.5	24.0	−0.5		4
				3.5	
7	28.0	28.0	–		4
				4.0	
8	32.0	32.0	–		4
				4.7	
9	36.7	36.0	−0.7		4
				5.6	
10	42.3	40.0	−2.3		4

any smaller production they will make a loss. At this level of output, price, marginal cost and average cost are all equal; Scribblo's costs are at a minimum; and they are maximizing their profits.

Average cost and price

Is this a coincidence? Does it mean that Scribblo's will close their doors and wait until their acountants come back with a new set of curves that obey a different geometry? Not a bit of it. The situation results directly from the assumption of perfect competition. For this implies that if pencil manfacturers make more than what we may call a 'competitive' or 'normal' profit, more firms will start to manufacture pencils and by their competition force down prices and profits to a 'normal' level. This so-called 'normal' profit is really part of cost of production since it is the minimum return that would induce Scribblo's (or a similar firm) to undertake the production of pencils. If the accountants have done their work correctly, therefore, the average cost of production already includes an indispensable provision for 'normal' profits. Average cost in this sense may be equal to price, and under perfect competition it cannot remain for any length of time below price, except in firms with some outstanding advantage over their competitors. But if price and average cost are equal and at the same time price and marginal cost are equal, average and marginal cost must also be equal and this condition is fulfilled only at a point where average cost is horizontal, as it must be at its minimum. In perfect competition, therefore, price must always equal marginal cost. There is also a powerful tendency for price to equal average cost as well: when price exceeds average cost, new producers are attracted into the industry; when less, some existing producers leave.

This rather involved reasoning and the conclusion to which it leads help to explain why economists are inclined to use perfect competition as a yardstick and to regard its outcome as an economic ideal. If perfect competition forces firms to produce at minimum cost and with no more than a 'normal' profit, it is certainly a highly desirable state of affairs; and even if it is impossible to create conditions of perfect competition it may be possible to borrow some of the rules that apply under perfect competition and try to make use of those rules in running a nationalized industry or in fixing prices.

Monopoly costs and prices

Let us now abandon the assumption of perfect competition and go to the other extreme. Suppose that Scribblo's produce a unique kind of pencil and that they have no competitors. This will mean that there is no established market price that they can take as given. They will have to decide both how much to produce and how much to charge; in addition to drawing a cost curve they will have to draw a demand curve. Under perfect competition the demand curve for Scribblo's output (whatever the shape of the demand curve for pencils in general) is perfectly elastic; it is represented in *Figure 13.2* by a horizontal straight line drawn through the price. Under monopoly the demand curve will be like the demand curve for any commodity, falling from left to right.

Let us assume that their costs are as before and that the demand schedule for their pencils is as given in *Table 13.3*. The demand schedule

TABLE 13.3. Demand for Scribblo pencils

Quantity (millions)	Price (pence)	Total revenue (million pence)	Marginal revenue (pence)
			12
1	12	12	
2	10	20	8
3	9	27	7
4	8	32	5
5	7	35	3
6	6	36	1
7	5	35	−1
8	4	32	−3
9	3	27	−5
10	2	20	−7
11	1	11	−9

shows an inelastic demand for Scribblo pencils up to 6p and an elastic demand at higher prices. If Scribblo's wanted to get the maximum *revenue* from the sale of their pencils they would charge 6p. But it is the excess of revenue over costs that they want to maximize, and this maximum is reached when the price is somewhat between 7p and 8p.

If it were possible to consider smaller variations in price we could narrow down the difference until it was negligible and so arrive at *the* price yielding maximum profit to the monopolist.

Price and marginal revenue

A firm's marginal revenue is the effect on its total revenue from the sale of a marginal (strictly, negligible) addition to output. It is the increment in aggregate receipts when one more unit is sold or the reduction in aggregate receipts when one unit less is sold. If Scribblo's (or any other firm) are producing on the scale of output at which their profits are maximized, an increase or decrease in output by one unit must leave profits lower than before. In other words, a marginal addition to output will increase aggregate costs by more than it increases aggregate revenue, while a marginal reduction in output will save less in cost than it sacrifices in revenue. Marginal cost cannot be above marginal revenue unless at least one unit of output is not paying its way; nor can it be below marginal revenue or there will be an extra profit to be made by making and selling at least one more unit of output. Marginal cost and marginal revenue must, therefore, be equal when profits are a maximum.

TABLE 13.4. Costs and prices of Scribblo pencils

Price	Total revenue	Total costs	Surplus of revenue over cost	Marginal revenue	Marginal cost
(pence)	(million pence)	(million pence)	(million pence)	(pence)	(pence)
12	12	9.5	2.5	12	3.5
10	20	12.6	7.4	8	3.1
9	27	15.5	11.5	7	2.9
8	32	18.3	13.7	5	2.8
7	35	21.3	13.7	3	3.0
6	36	24.5	11.5	1	3.2
5	35	28.0	7.0	−1	3.5
4	32	32.0	—	−3	4.0
3	27	36.7	−9.7	−5	4.7

The relationships between marginal and average cost, and marginal and average revenue (i.e., price) are illustrated in *Figure 13.3*. The demand curve slopes down steeply and the marginal revenue curve lies below it[1]. The cost curves are the same as in *Figure 13.2*. The surplus of revenue over costs is represented by a rectangle which has a maximum area in the position PQRS. This is the position in which marginal revenue is equal to marginal cost. Average cost is higher, and price higher still.

In *Figure 13.3* the curve of marginal revenue is consistently below the demand curve; marginal revenue is lower than price. The reason for this is that any attempt to increase the sale of pencils involves a reduction in price and this reduction applies to all pencils, not just to those which are bought because of the cut in price. The pencils previously disposed of at the higher

---

[1] As elasticity and slope are often confused it should be observed that in *Figure 13.3* the demand curve has a constant slope throughout almost all its length while demand changes from being elastic to being inelastic. The slope measures the ratio of an absolute change in demand to an absolute change in price; elasticity measures the ratio of two *percentage* changes. If the demand curve is a downward-sloping straight line, marginal revenue will fall twice as fast, and cross the horizontal axis halfway between the origin and where the demand curve cuts it. The elasticity of demand is one at the quantity where marginal revenue is zero.

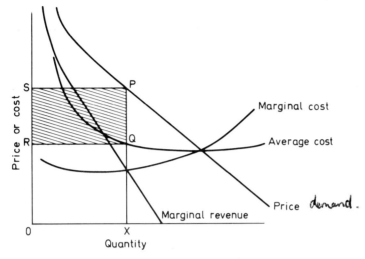

Figure 13.3 Price under monopoly

price bring in less revenue than before, and this loss of revenue has to be deducted from the price of the additional pencils that are sold before we arrive at the net increase in total revenue, or marginal revenue. Marginal revenue, that is, must fall short of price by an amount equal to the concession that has to be made to existing buyers to extend sales. This concession is small if demand is highly elastic, but is very great if the elasticity is not much greater than one[1].

Perfect competition as a limiting case

When competition is perfect, the difference between marginal revenue and price disappears. Increased sales can be made without any need to cut the price and so make a concession from which existing buyers gain. The demand for Scribblo pencils, under perfect competition, is perfectly elastic

---

[1] If the demand curve is represented by $P = f(X)$, then marginal revenue is equal to

$$\frac{d\,(PX)}{dX}$$

$$= P + X\,\frac{dP}{dX}$$

$$= P\left(1 + \frac{X}{P} \cdot \frac{dP}{dX}\right)$$

But elasticity of demand $\quad = -\frac{P}{X} \cdot \frac{dX}{dP}$

Hence marginal revenue $\quad = P - \frac{P}{E}$

and the excess of price over marginal revenue will be the greater, at a given level of price and output, the less is the elasticity of demand. A profit-maximizing firm would not produce at an output level where demand was inelastic, since a cut in output would raise total revenue and reduce total costs.

and the demand curve and marginal revenue curve coincide in a horizontal straight line drawn through the market price. The rule that marginal revenue and marginal cost are equal when firms are earning their maximum profit will still hold: but since price and marginal revenue will, for once, be equal, price and marginal cost will also be equal – as we discovered earlier. Perfect competition is thus a limiting case to which the more general rule still applies.

A measure of monopoly

We can, indeed, take the ratio of price to marginal revenue as an index of the degree of monopoly or competition in any market. The nearer the two approach equality with one another, the more nearly 'perfect' is competition and the less power of monopoly does a firm enjoy. The ratio of the two is governed by the elasticity of demand for the product of the firm[1]. Elasticity in turn is governed by the range of available substitutes. But these substitutes are simply the most closely competing products. So we arrive at the conclusion that the ratio of price to marginal revenue is a measure of the force of competition.

But this ratio, if the firm is maximizing its profits, will be the same as the ratio of price to marginal cost. Apart from the introduction of the word 'marginal', this is not a very novel conclusion. We all think of a monopolist as someone who can charge more than the cost of production for his goods. What the argument of this chapter shows is that the more a firm is able to use monopoly power in fixing its price, the higher, in general, will the price be in relation to (marginal) cost; and conversely, the more competition approaches 'perfection', the narrower will be the divergence between price and (marginal) cost. Where average cost is horizontal, indeed, marginal and average cost are equal. But if output is set where average cost is falling, price will exceed marginal cost by more than it exceeds average cost.

Price and average cost in a competitive industry

Up till now the discussion has been focused on the individual firm with occasional glances at the industry as a whole. But since output can vary either because of changes within existing firms or because of the entry of new firms into the industry there is a second type of marginal addition to output to be considered and a second meaning to be attached to marginal cost. There are marginal *firms*; and marginal cost may be used to mean the average cost of production in a marginal firm.

An industry is generally made up of firms varying widely in profitability. Some firms earn high profits because of the superior judgement or organizing ability of the management, others because their plant is well laid out and up-to-date, others because they have access to a large market or to cheap raw materials, and others again because of the skill or energy of

---

[1] Notice that we are talking about the demand for the product of a *firm*, not, as in Chapter 11, about the demand for a *commodity* (i.e., the product of an industry or group of firms competing with one another). For example, we are discussing the demand for Scribblo pencils, not for pencils in general.

the workers whom they employ. On the other hand, some firms earn comparatively low profits because they lack these advantages. In coal-mining, for example, there is a wide range of profits between one pit and another according to the depth of the coal seams from the surface; the thickness of the seams; the chemical composition of the coal; the presence or absence of water or gas; and a hundred other factors. Some pits rarely make losses while others rarely make profits.

The firms in the industry which we take to be marginal are those which, over a period of years, earn a profit just sufficient to induce them to remain in the industry. This minimum profit – which may be high or low – is really an element in the costs of these firms. A firm which has no prospect of earning a reasonable profit will ultimately close down, just as a man who sees no prospect of earning a wage commensurate with his abilities will ultimately seek employment elsewhere; the firm will have failed to cover its total costs.

Thus a marginal firm is one whose average costs (including 'normal' profits in the sense of the minimum profit discussed above) are just covered by price. If the price falls, marginal producers will be squeezed out and a new group of firms will find themselves on the margin of production. If the price rises, the margin will be pushed back as more firms find it worth while to come into the industry. The pressure of a change in demand and in price will cause the margin of production to shift inwards to firms whose costs are lower or outwards to include firms with higher costs of produc-tion. At a given level of demand the price will tend to equality with the average cost of production of the marginal producer. Other firms, in receipt of the same price, and producing at lower cost, will be able to earn a surplus profit – a profit higher than would suffice to keep them in the industry.

At any given moment, of course, price may fall below marginal cost. It is only over a period of years, averaging profits against losses, that the marginal producer will look for a certain minimum balance of profit. This makes it difficult and sometimes impossible to identify the marginal firms in an industry. We cannot always pick on the firms which are making the smallest profits or the biggest losses, for the firms which are making losses now may survive to make large profits in the future. They may, for example, be young and growing firms which have not yet solved their problems of organization and marketing, but are on the way to a solution. Even if they are firms which are certain to go out of business sooner or later, we may still hesitate to call them marginal firms. We may know that at current prices there will be a constant succession of firms which will take their place with no more success – that it is a normal feature of the industry, in fact, that there should be some firms in it which cannot show a profit at all, even in good times. Such firms are not marginal, but sub-marginal; their costs are higher than the costs of marginal firms, and will not be covered by price, even in the long run.

It must not be supposed that marginal firms are necessarily the least efficient firms. It may happen, for example, that some firms are efficient in manufacturing a number of different lines of product and that they are ready to abandon any one line whenever it is less remunerative than the others. A farmer may grow wheat, barley and potatoes at low cost and yet be a marginal wheat farmer because the profit which he makes from his wheat is barely enough to keep him from giving up wheat-growing in favour of barley- or potato-growing. He is on the margin of transference between wheat and other agricultural products.

Price, then, tends to be equal to the average cost of marginal producers and to exceed the average cost of other producers in proportion to any special advantages which they enjoy.

Price and average cost under monopoly

It might be thought that all this ceases to apply when we are dealing with a firm in a position of monopoly. So long as the monopoly lasts there can be no newcomers, and the only limit to the monopolist's profit is set by the elasticity of demand for his goods and the pressure of public opinion. In practice, however, so absolute a monopoly is rare. New firms could and would compete if the price were sufficiently attractive. But they are generally under a handicap of some kind in entering the monopolist's market – for example, they might have to go to a great deal of expense in developing a substitute and to more expense in advertising it. There is, so to speak, a cost of entry into the market and within the limits of this cost, the monopolist can raise his price without fear of competition. Looked at in this way, most monopolists are in the same position as other firms. They have potential competitors who can be regarded as marginal; and the monopoly price cannot be raised above the expected average cost of those competitors including the cost of overcoming any handicap or restriction on entry into the monopolist's market.

Although the tendency of monopoly is to raise prices above costs, this does not imply that prices under monopoly must be higher than under competition. The costs of the monopolist may be so far below the costs of the competing firms which might replace him that his price also is lower than theirs would be. This could not happen, however, unless there were pronounced economies of scale.

In short, the tendency of competition is to reduce prices to equality with cost – with the marginal cost of each firm, and with the average cost of a marginal firm. The tendency of monopoly is to raise prices above cost and profits above normal. In the modern world we generally meet with a mixture of competition and monopoly. There are substitutes, but not perfect substitutes, for each firm's products, and there is generally a threat of competition from newcomers.

The logic and the facts: cost-plus pricing

Many businessmen, comparing the logic of the foregoing argument with their everyday experience, would be inclined to dismiss the argument as academic. Few of them have heard either of marginal cost or of marginal revenue. Only a proportion of them have the costing machinery necessary for the estimation of average, still fewer for the estimation of marginal cost. Even if costing were in universal use, it would in many industries be extremely difficult to apply it to the estimation of marginal cost, while marginal revenue must almost always be a matter of guesswork. In many industries the usual procedure is to fix a price on the basis of average direct costs in labour and materials plus an allowance for overheads. This allowance is worked out so as to cover average fixed costs, not at the capacity level of output at which the plant was designed to operate, but at a rather lower level (say 80% of capacity) which takes into account fluctuations in activity and is treated as normal or standard for the purpose of costing. Sometimes the procedure is less elaborate: retail prices, for example, are often arrived at by adding a customary percentage margin to the wholesale price, irrespective of actual selling costs; and in manufacturing industry, firms may use a similar method, adding a uniform percentage mark-up above direct costs for a wide variety of products without any accurate assessment of the fixed costs attributable to each.

Both of these procedures are usually referred to as 'cost-plus pricing' and they are frequently cited as evidence of the disdain with which economists treat the elementary facts of business life. The economist on the other hand is sceptical about the 'facts' because they carry the logical implication that the businessman, almost as a matter of principle, charges less than he might. The way to make as big a profit as possible is to charge, not on the basis of cost, but what the market will bear; this means varying the price with *demand* on the one hand and *marginal* cost on the other, not deliberately ignoring both. How are we to reconcile the logic and the apparent facts?

1. Businesses may be reluctant to vary traditional margins because they are influenced by long-term considerations. They may fear the entry of new competitors that would result from exploiting an active market and feel that it would do none of the existing firms in the market any good to cut margins below the long-term norm in the middle of a slump. On this interpretation, margins and mark-ups are based, not on the costs of existing firms, but on the long-run costs of potential entrants.
2. Margins do in fact vary. Firms are prepared to discriminate (which is inconsistent with full-cost pricing), to shade their prices in order to get a contract or meet competition, to throw a large share of fixed costs onto items in which competition is relatively feeble, and so on. Even when they work out their standard costs, they have to take account of demand factors in deciding what level of output to treat as normal, and after establishing the 'full cost' of their product, they may and do decide from time to time to charge less for it.
3. Not only do margins vary, but costs vary. If prices are fixed on a cost basis, how can firms with different costs end by charging the same price? Yet in competitive markets, this is what happens.
4. The use of a fixed margin is not inconsistent with maximizing profits if it saves a great deal of trouble. In a firm turning out a large number of different products for a variety of constantly changing markets it would be a very formidable undertaking to work out a price appropriate to each transaction on anything except a simple and uniform basis. Pricing would be a very arbitrary affair if, for everything that was sold, a guess had to be made as to the maximum that could safely be charged; there could be no standard price-list, no guarantee that the same price would always be charged for the same commodity. It might be wiser to make

prices some multiple of direct costs, varying the multiplier to suit general market conditions.

5. Marginal and average cost in some industries lie close together. This is so, for example, in an industry like motor car manufacture where a large proportion of unit cost is represented by bought-in materials and components while fixed costs, although large in the absolute, are relatively small as a proportion of unit cost. Marginal cost, moreover, is often almost constant between, say 70 and 100% of capacity. In these circumstances, it would require a large change in demand to make prices alter perceptibly whether they were based on marginal or 'full' cost; and the price charged on the one basis would be fairly close to the price charged on the other.

6. In other industries marginal and average cost may differ substantially. This will happen if average cost is far from horizontal. But in this case the cost-plus pricing rule ('Calculate average cost; add a satisfactory margin for profit, to set price; produce what the market demands at that price') breaks down. Since average cost varies with output, a 'cost-plus' price can be arrived at only when a particular output range has been chosen.

These considerations suggest that the businessman may not be so illogical nor the economist so inobservant after all. The behaviour of prices and costs differs from one market to another, and what is true in one market is not true in another. It would be a mistake, therefore, to think that the few simple propositions to which this chapter has been devoted provide an adequate clue to the complexities of cost and market structure throughout industry; but they take us a little way along the road.

Chapter 14

Monopoly and competition

One is tempted to draw a sharp distinction between monopoly and competition. A monopolist, we say, is selling something different from other people. But how different? Must the difference be as great as that between milk and tea, or can it be as small as that between milk from one farm and milk from another, or beween one brand of tea and another? Are we to call Bovril and Oxo and Camp Coffee commodities and their manufacturers monopolists? If a single firm supplies us with 1000 cc motor cars while other firms confine themselvs to higher-powered cars, is the first firm a monopolist? The more we reflect, the more we are driven to conclude that practically every firm is *in some sense* a monopolist. Everywhere in business, firms are selling a product which is differentiated in style, brand, quality, location, size, etc., from the products other firms. Nonetheless, they *also* face competition. Their discretion in fixing prices is generally limited, and prices tend to be in broad correspondence with prices in other parts of the market. But the fact that firms have any power at all over prices is proof that they have acquired powers of monopoly within their special market.

The fact is that we never find monopoly undiluted by competition, and very rarely find competition undiluted by monopoly. In most lines of business there is a blend of competition and monopoly in which one or the other may preponderate. The difference between monopoly and competition is one of degree, not of kind.

Elements of competition under monopoly

Competition is fundamentally the offer of a substitute; monopoly is fundamentally the absence of substitutes. But there can never be an entire absence of substitutes. So long as our purchasing power is limited, everything on which we might be induced to spend our money is in a sense a substitute for everything else that we buy. If any one commodity becomes more expensive we can always give up using it and substitute some other commodity. We may continue to satisfy the same want if there are close substitutes (e.g., margarine for butter), or we may be driven to satisfy some quite different want so that the substitution becomes very round-about (e.g., we may buy a book instead of going to the cinema). What we obviously cannot do is to go on buying a constant amount of any one commodity, however high its price.

Even if competition within an industry is suppressed, therefore, the monopolized product has still to face the competition of other industries. Indeed, such competition as survives nowadays is more and more between industries and less and less between firms within an industry. As monopoly grows, prices are arrived at through bargains between organized industries, and the common interests of the firms in each industry come into open conflict with the interests of the allied firms in other industries.

The competition with which a monopolist is faced comes not only from other products already on the market but also from *potential* substitutes that might be made available to consumers if prices were to rise. High prices may drive consumers to devise new substitutes for the monopolized goods or tempt new firms to enter into competition with the monopolist. Such potential competition will tend to keep prices down, since the monopolist will have no wish to invite it and will have no confidence in his ability to meet it if he has lost the goodwill of his customers by overcharging. There can also be competition, actual or potential between different divisions, plants or branches of the same company.

The power of monopolists over prices, therefore, is limited by the competition of substitutes, actual or potential – in other words, by the elasticity of demand for the monopolist's product. The more elastic the demand, the more closely will price and (marginal) cost approximate to one another. The less elastic the demand, the greater will be the power of the monopolist, and the more excessive the price which he is able to charge. So we return to the conclusions reached in Chapter 13. Every producer is more or less of a monopolist; and many will attempt to maximize profits by equating marginal revenue and marginal cost. The more of a monopolist he is, the less elastic will be the demand for his produce; the greater, therefore, will be the ratio of price to marginal revenue; and the greater, finally, will be the ratio of price to marginal cost (at least in those businesses that do maximize profits).

Perfect competition

Perfect monopoly – unlimited control over the market price of a commodity – does not exist; perfect competition – competition purged of every element of monopoly – is rare, but it can exist. For competition in a commodity to be perfect, each individual buyer and seller of the commodity must regard the market price as entirely beyond his control. Buyers will have no incentive to restrict their purchases for the sake of driving down the price; sellers will have no incentive to restrict output or withhold supplies for the sake of maintaining or raising the price. Each buyer or seller will form his own judgement of the probable course of prices and will treat the price which he anticipates as unaffected by his individual purchases or sales.

Perfect competition on the side of buyers is common enough. The average housewife, competing with millions of other housewives, could not conceivably, by the impact of her purchases, budge the price of staple commodities. On the side of supply, examples of perfect competition are much harder to find. Wheat is one: the wheat farmer in the Middle West is hardly likely to hesitate about growing a few bushels more or less for fear of upsetting prices in the Chicago wheatpit. Gold is another example: the gold-miner is unlikely to be afraid of spoiling his market by dispatching an extra ounce or two of gold to London. Even in wheat and gold, however, competition is not altogether perfect. The price of wheat is greatly influenced by the operations of wheat pools, storage schemes, and so on, all of which introduce elements of monopoly into the market. The price of gold depends on how much the leading central banks think it is worth and their willingness to refrain from selling gold on the free market. Thus it is only from the point of view of the individual farm or mine that competition in wheat and gold is perfect.

When there is perfect competition, price ceases to be above marginal cost. Each firm can sell freely as much as it chooses without fear of spoiling its market; it can treat the demand for its product as perfectly elastic. If the firm tries to increase its sales, the additional supply put on the market is negligible in comparison with the total supply, and the fall in price, therefore, is so small that it does not enter into the firm's calculations. Price and marginal revenue are then necessarily equal, since each additional unit sold adds its full price to the total revenue of the firm; and if the firm is successful in equating marginal revenue and marginal cost, so as to maximize its profits, price and marginal cost must also be equal.

Perfect competition can be regarded, therefore, as the limiting case of imperfect or monopolistic competition. The more nearly competitive conditions approach 'perfection', the closer to unity will be the ratio of price to marginal cost: the greater the deviation towards monopoly the further will price rise above marginal cost. How do these deviations arise?

Elements of monopoly

Perfect competition presupposes two conditions: a large number of competing sellers and a perfect market. The first condition is easy enough to understand, but the second is less obvious. A perfect market is one in which buyers have no preferences as between the different units of the commodity offered for sale, sellers are quite indifferent to whom they sell, and both buyers and sellers have full knowledge of prices in other parts of the market. If markets were perfect, each firm would have to face the competition of products which were not only physically interchangeable with its own but which were considered by consumers to be perfect substitutes in every way. No firm would be able to charge more than the market price without losing the whole of its custom to its competitors, while no firm could charge less than the market price, since if it were to quote lower prices than its competitors, consumers would at once transfer their custom to it and other firms would be forced to come into line. There not only would be but *could* be only one price throughout the market.

The markets of the real world are rarely perfect. Firms seek to shelter themselves from competition by creating or supplying a special market in which they enjoy the goodwill of their customers. The existence of goodwill, however, is incompatible with the requirements of a perfect market since it rests on consumers' preferences for the goods of a particular seller. The number of firms competing with one another is also, as a rule, limited. If competition is restricted to a small number of firms the situation is described technically as oligopoly, just as when there is a single seller it is described as monopoly. The normal situation in business is one of market imperfection combined with oligopoly. In motor car manufacturing, for example, the big firms produce nearly all the smaller cars but do not make exactly the same model of car. Even in the textile industry, where the number of firms is legion, it will often be found that a particular product like bath towels or West of England woollen flannel comes mainly from a small group of firms, each with its own specialities.

Although market imperfection and oligopoly are generally combined, they are analytically distinct.

(a) Oligopoly

A market is an oligopoly if there are only a few sellers. Oligopoly has two essential features. First, no seller can know exactly where his average and marginal revenue curves lie. This is so, because if he were to raise his output or cut his price, how this affected his total receipts would depend upon how his competitors reacted. If they ignored his action, he would gain much more sales revenue than if they matched what he had done. Second, relations between the sellers are complicated by the fact that their interests are partly common, and partly opposed. If they act in concert, they can maximize their joint profits by behaving like a profit-maximizing monopolist with many plants: this means setting output rates where marginal revenue for the industry as a whole equals marginal costs of production in each plant. But in these circumstances, each seller has a powerful incentive to cheat his fellows by secretly producing more.

On the other hand, if oligopolists think (despite probable evidence to the contrary) that their own actions do not provoke their rivals to react, and behave in such a way as to maximize their own profits, there is a substantial measure of competition. The more numerous the oligopolists, the lower the selling price and the lower the profits they earn as a group. Perfect competition is one limiting case of this, when the number of firms tends to infinity; monopoly is the other, when it is only one. But while the oligopolists may think they are maximizing their profits, they are really not. As a group, they can never lose and will almost always gain by cooperating.

The highest profits are earned by a firm that acts unilaterally to produce a high output, when all its competitors have set theirs low in order to keep prices high. We saw that cooperation (or collusion) is flawed by the incentive it gives to overproduce; and that conflict (or independent competition) must waste opportunities for profitable cooperation. Few oligopolies, therefore, conform to complete cooperation or complete conflict. There are usually elements of both cooperation and conflict. Cooperation is likeliest when there are only two or three firms, and a single buyer of their produce (e.g., the government), the produce is of uniform quality, each firm's activities are easily monitored by the other(s), and marginal costs rise strongly with output. A multiplicity of firms complicates negotiations between them, while large numbers of buyers make it easier for a firm to offer secret price cuts; and product variety, falling marginal costs and inconspicuity encourage independence, high output, or both. The attitude of government is also important here; cooperation is often illegal, but may also be favoured in war or steep recession. Cooperation may take many forms: tacit or formal, temporary or permanent, covering prices, advertising, investment plans, technology, wages or political lobbying.

(b) Market imperfection

There are a number of reasons why markets are imperfect. First of all, there are imperfections due to ignorance. Buyers and sellers may be ill-informed about the terms on which dealings are proceeding elsewhere. Consumers, for example, generally know the price charged in a limited range of shops only, and buy from their regular suppliers without troubling to obtain other quotations. In the same way, they may go on buying a familiar brand in ignorance of cheaper substitutes on the market. Secondly, there are preferences due to the different suitability of competing goods for the purposes of different buyers. Each seller will try to cater for the special requirements of a given group of buyers, offering them goods of a quality, style, colour, etc., nearer to their taste than the goods offered by his competitors. Or he will try to carve out a special market by providing additional services – regular delivery, long credit, free insurance, gift coupons, etc. Some of his customers – those who are farthest away, or whose preferences are least satisfactorily met – will remain, so to speak, on the fringe. They will be marginal, in the sense that they can be most readily detached by competitors. Other customers – nearer geographically or in taste – will be firmer in their allegiance, and will desert to rival sellers only if the incentive is a strong one. Finally, the market may be imperfect because of preferences which do not originate in real differences between the products of each seller but in fancied differences or in habit. I may buy from Blank instead of from Blink from sheer force of habit, or because, after reading the advertisements, I am biased in favour of Blank's, or because, without making a thorough test, I believe that Blank's goods are better suited to my purposes.

Prices and cost under imperfect competition

Under imperfect competition the price will be above the marginal cost of production. How much higher will depend upon the market situation. If there is a monopoly in the ordinary sense, the products of the monopolist will be sharply differentiated from those of other firms, and the monopolist, by reducing his price slightly will be able to draw custom from a wide field. No other firms will be likely to feel the loss of custom sufficiently to be obliged to retaliate. We can then apply the ideas of marginal cost and marginal revenue in order to determine what price will yield maximum profits. Price will be above marginal cost and the ratio of the two will be governed by the elasticity of demand for the firm's product, if we assume that he does maximize profit.

The same formula will cover a situation in which there are many firms competing in an imperfect market so that one firm can extend its sales by cutting its price, but can extend them only to a limited extent and without having to reckon on retaliation by any of its competitors. If, however, there is oligopoly the formula will be far more difficult to apply. The competing firms will not be able, like the monopolist, to draw a tentative demand curve for their output, showing what will happen to sales at any given price. Each firm will be aware that if it cuts its price it will have to face retaliation; and it will have to puzzle out what will happen to its sales on various assumptions about their behaviour. This it can only do successfully if it has a shrewd understanding of the psychology of its competitors or long experience of their normal reactions. The oligopolist will have his eye as much on his competitors as on his customers and will be guided by his impression of *their* costs as much as by his knowledge of his own.

Price-competition and service-competition

When competition becomes imperfect, price ceases to be the sole consideration of consumers. A slight reduction in price by one seller, instead of drawing custom from all over the market, may pass completely unnoticed. A large reduction in price will certainly bring new customers; but if they come in large numbers from the clientele of rival firms, the reduction in prices is likely to spread throughout the market until most of the new customers are tempted back to their original suppliers. Price as an instrument of competition, therefore, becomes either increasingly ineffective or increasingly unpopular. It is condemned as foolish if it is unsuccessful, and as cut-throat competition if it succeeds.

Other devices for attracting custom may be used instead: advertising; improvements in quality or in service; the offer of a wider variety of goods. All these devices have this in common: that they represent an actual outlay with a view to increasing sales, whereas the device of lowering prices represents a sacrifice in *revenue* with the same end in view. When competition reduces prices, the gain to consumers is unmistakable: they save money which they would otherwise have had to spend. But when competition improves quality and makes services more lavish, the gain is more debatable; consumers get more for their money, but they might get still more if they could have the old quality and service at a lower price and were free to spend the difference in price on other articles of more utility. To the man who can barely afford a tourist fare in a transatlantic aircraft, the competition which drives each airline company to offer him the fastest possible trip is of less service than the competition which would bring down the fare.

Selling costs

We considered in Chapter 12 a firm which was free to vary the price which it charged and the amount which it produced. We reached the conclusion that the firm would try to equate marginal cost and marginal revenue. But we took no account of a third variable in the policy of the firm – selling costs. Selling costs include all expenditure designed to create, increase or maintain the demand for a firm's products. Advertising expenditure is the most obvious example, but improvements in quality, special services, etc., have exactly the same effect. They modify the preferences of consumers by making the firm's products, in appearance or in fact, better suited to consumer's requirements, and so increase the firm's sales just as advertising does. It is often very difficult in practice to distinguish between production costs and selling costs unless a firm is making a standard product that cannot be easily modified; the cost of making more units of the article gets tangled up with the cost of adapting it to suit new groups of consumer, or of advertising more widely, or of holding stocks in new markets. In principle, however, the distinction is clear: production costs have no influence on demand whereas selling costs are incurred *in order to* influence demand.

The existence of selling costs forces us to modify, but not to abandon, the marginal theory. The firm will push its sales costs, just as it pushes its production costs, up to the margin at which the last £1 spent on advertising, or on free gift schemes, or on any other kind of sales pressure, just repays itself by yielding a net increase of £1 in revenue (*net*, that is, after deducting the cost of producing the extra goods which are sold). Marginal sales cost, in other words, will tend to equal revenue from the last unit of sales outlay, just as marginal production cost tends to equal revenue from the last unit produced. With this reservation: that whereas the revenue from the last unit produced can occasionally be estimated with some confidence, the revenue from the last unit of sales outlay is much harder to predict.

We have seen that there are two margins – one of quantity produced, one of selling outlay. Two, however, is a gross understatement: there is a whole series of margins, cutting all the paths of policy open to the firm. The firm may consider, for example, a slight change in quality, or in finish, or in packaging, or in style. A change in any of these will involve an increase in outlay and in receipts, and the firm will move along the path of change until it reaches the margin at which a further move will add more to outlay than to receipts. *Any* marginal increase in outlay will, if maximum profits are being earned, involve a barely equal increase in receipts and marginal cost and associated marginal revenue will tend *everywhere* to equality.

Profits under imperfect competition

Under perfect competition the number of competing firms is large and, quite apart from this, new firms can enter the industry freely; there will also, as we have seen, be some high-cost firms on the margin of production, and some firms with slightly higher costs, just beyond the margin, ready to enter the industry whenever prices rise. But what if potential competitors are under a handicap, so that they are attracted into the industry only when prices are considerably above marginal cost? Marginal producers will then be making abnormal profits, while new firms that might produce at less cost and still make satisfactory profits will be debarred from competing. New firms will have to meet costs of entry as well as costs of production, while established firms, protected from competition, will have no costs of entry and will reap correspondingly high profits. These excessive profits, since they result from impediments to competition, are essentially monopoly profits.

In perfect competition, abnormally high profits act as a magnet to new firms. They are sooner or later competed away. This is what forces firms to maximize profit, or disappear. Restrictions to entry, by contrast, may permit existing firms to earn abnormally high profits indefinitely. It may also free them to pursue any non-profit goals, as well. Sales revenue will appear at least as attractive as profit to the salaried manager; sales revenue is usually linked more closely to the pay, power and prestige of the manager, especially if he has next to no shares in the concern. Although they can sell their shares when dissatisfied, shareholders lack complete knowledge of the manager's actions, and have at best limited control over them. Security, the growth rate of the company and the total wages bill should also appear as 'goods' to at least some members of the wide coalition that governs a large modern company. The stronger the emphasis on sales revenue or the wages bill among its objectives, the more the company will produce, and the lower its prices and profits will be. Nonetheless, the discretion to pursue these non-profit objectives must depend upon restrictions to entry.

Restrictions to entry

What are these impediments to competition? Sometimes they are due to legal restrictions. The Elizabethan monopolists, for example, were able to buy complete immunity from competition by a cash payment to the Crown. The holder of a patent enjoys a statutory monopoly for 16 years. The Traffic Commissioners can limit the number of licences issued to public service vehicles as they think fit, and can block competition from new transport companies very effectively. Some industries are nationalized and protected by the state in one way or another from competition.

When legal restraints are absolute, so that there is full private monopoly, prices might seem free to rise without limit. In fact, however, there is a double check. The monopolist will not wish to lose his monopoly by too obvious abuse of his powers; what the law has given, the law, under presure of public opinion, can take back. Secondly, excessive prices will lose not only goodwill but customers; there is a limit to what people will pay, as well as to what they will tolerate. The more elastic the demand, the sooner will this limit be reached, and the greater, therefore, will be the resistance to a rise in prices.

Legal restrictions make costs of entry infinite. So also does complete monopoly of raw materials; there was a time when the International Nickel Company, for example, had no need to fear competition from other nickel producers in fixing prices. But when the monopoly of raw materials is a local one only (e.g., the Aluminium Company's monopoly of bauxite deposits in the United States) then costs of entry become finite and measurable. They will, in fact, be equal to the cost of transport of alternative supplies from the nearest available point. Potential competitors are handicapped by distance from the local monopolist's market so that, if their costs are equal to the monopolist's and there are no economies of large-scale production, the monopolist can safely augment his price by the cost of transport from the nearest alternative source of supply. He will then make a surplus profit on each unit of output equal to this addition to his price. The surplus (or monopoly) profit will be equal to the cost of entry into his market or – what comes to the same – to the gap between price and the average cost of a marginal supplier.

Limitation of entry may also arise when existing firms have exclusive control over the channels of distribution. They may be able, for example, to black-list new firms and cut them off from the normal retail outlets. The mere fact, too, that existing firms have already built up a business connection gives them a strategic advantage over new firms, and may enable them to smother competitors who, although more efficient, have difficulty in gaining a foothold in the market. This strategic advantage will be particularly great where heavy capital outlay either on advertising or on fixed plant is necessary before production can be started. The newcomer must plunge boldly in instead of feeling his way. Hence he will run a heavy risk of failure without the chance to cut his losses. If the market is narrow he will have to face the additional risk of bringing down prices to levels unattractive to himself and unprofitable also to his competitors. One village cinema, for example, may find it easy to make a large profit. But a second cinema may introduce overcapacity and leave neither cinema with a satisfactory profit. Thus a firm which has the advantage of priority in a narrow market – particularly in industries using large amounts of fixed capital, like the steel or the railway industry – may continue to earn profits higher than a new firm of equal efficiency would consider adequate. There may be an appearance of free competition. But costs of entry, due to the narrowness of the market, the initial risks on a heavy capital investment in face of competition, and the hold of the established concern both on supplies of labour and materials and on the market, will combine to shelter the existing firm from competition and protect it in the enjoyment of a monopoly profit.

Conclusions as to profits under imperfect competition

The fact that there is imperfect competition does not necessarily mean that more than normal profits are being made. The level of profit depends upon whether there are restrictions on entry into the industry, even if those restrictions rest only on the narrowness of the market. It is quite conceivable that although every firm exercises some degree of monopoly power, in the sense that it has some control over its price, it earns no more in profit than it would in conditions of perfect competition. Monopoly in the first sense is far more persuasive than most people think; but in the second sense it is a great deal more rare. Price may be above marginal cost in the vast majority of firms; but it is rarely above, or appreciably above, the average cost of a marginal firm. Also, a monopolist who is able to restrict entry might earn only modest profits because demand is low, or because sales revenue is the dominant objective.

Aside from its possible effects on profits and, therefore, on the distribution of income, imperfect competition has few major differences from perfect competition that matter from a social standpoint. Two are possible advantages. Two are likely drawbacks. The first two are the cost-saving that comes from centralizing production, assuming economies of scale, in one firm or few firms; and the bonus to investment and growth from any long-term profit. The first drawback is the fact that output will almost certainly not occur where average cost is at a minimum. If, for instance, price equals average cost in a profit-maximizing firm with a downward-sloping average revenue curve, average cost must also be downward-sloping in the vicinity of current output. Worse, price generally exceeds marginal cost. This means that buyers would willingly pay more for an additional unit than it costs to produce. The allocation of resources is therefore less than perfect.

Chapter 15

Supply: cost in relation to output and time

The fact that cost of production varies with output is constantly over-looked. People speak of *the* cost of production of an article as though there were only one cost, irrespective of the *amount* of the article produced. But it is well known that in some industries (e.g., the motor industry) costs fall when a substantial increase in output takes place, while in other industries (e.g., wheat-farming) costs rise when output is increased. Why is this?

The reason why costs may fall as an industry grows bigger has already been explained. If the industry is to expand, either the constituent firms must produce on a larger scale or new firms must grow up alongside the old. The first method of expansion may well result in internal economies, the second in external economies. Economies of either type will reduce the average cost of production.

The reason why costs may rise is more obscure. The cost of any article *within each firm* may ultimately begin to rise as output expands. But this does not mean that sooner or later additional supplies of the commodity will only be available at increasing cost. For if all firms are alike and there is perfect competition, an unlimited number of new firms, of the same size and efficiency, will be ready to enter the industry and provide, at constant cost, for any increase in demand, however great.

In the last chapter we saw that firms are not, in fact, alike and that freedom of entry into an industry is generally limited. Here we have two possible explanations of rising costs. As an industry expands it attracts new firms which have either progressively higher costs of production or progressively greater difficulty in gaining a foothold. The second explana-tion, which will not be pursued here, turns on an increasing degree of monopoly; the first, which is by far the more important, turns on the scarcity and heterogeneity of productive resources.

The first explanation has so far been expressed in terms of firms; when prices rise, and the margin of production is thrust back, the new firms entering the industry are less favourably situated than the old. But it is not really the new *firms* that are more costly; it is the new *factors of production* attracted into the industry. If the cost of coal rises when the output is increased, it may be because sub-marginal coal deposits have to be mined, or because the new seams are worked by less experienced miners, or because the new pits are less ably managed. It makes no difference which factor is responsible for the rise in costs, and it makes no difference whether that factor is employed by new or by existing firms. The important point is that an *industry* can obtain command over additional labour, land, raw materials, managerial ability, etc., only by the offer of increasingly generous terms; by drawing in units of lower efficiency or with a higher supply price.

The industry must either use resources that were formerly left out of employment altogether, or bid against other industries for resources in their employment. Farmers, for example, can grow more wheat either on sub-marginal land or on land which would otherwise have been sown to oats or barley. Motor manufacturers can obtain more steel either by inducing the steel industry to bring more furnaces into production or by leaving less steel for shipbuilding, tinplate manufacture, etc. Expansion, in short, means the use of a larger share of the limited supply of productive resources, and these resources will be released by other industries only when they find themselves unable to bid high enough to retain them. Additional resources, therefore, can be commandeered by an expanding industry only at increasing cost.

The meaning of cost

This line of reasoning leads us to a new view of cost. The cost of producing any commodity is fundamentally the cost of *detaining* productive resources so as to make their services available to the industry producing the commodity *rather than* to some other industry. Now the cost of detaining resources is equal to the value of these resources for other purposes, plus the cost of transferring them from their existing employment to the most attractive alternative employment[1]. Cost, in other words, measures the pull of competing attractions. If the cost of any factor is not covered, that factor will move to some other industry, and the value of what it could produce in that industry is its cost in its present use. Cost, therefore, must always be considered in terms of alternatives. Cost measures what we could produce instead – what we forgo by using productive resources for one purpose rather than for another. Alternatively, it measures what we could save by not using the resources at all. If, for example, labour were employed for seven hours a day instead of eight, there would be a fall in the output of goods and services, but labour would enjoy more leisure and would be relieved from disagreeable duties. The sacrifice of leisure and the additional irksomeness in working for eight hours measures the cost of the additional goods produced in the final hour.

An illustration may help to make this view of cost clearer. When I give a friend the use of my car for the day 'at cost', how is he to decide how much to pay me? If he consults my garageman he may be told that £10 is a fair amount, since the garageman calculates that he could not afford to keep cars for hire for less than this. My friend may then point out that I already own the car, that I have to provide garage accommodation for it anyhow, and that if he had not borrowed it, it would not have been used at all.

---

[1] It may happen that other industries are paying resources less than their full value, so that the force of attraction is diminished. For the sake of simplicity, this possibility is ignored.

Provided the car is returned undamaged, I am not appreciably worse off by letting my friend have it free. The cost, apart from wear and tear on the road, is nil, because the *alternative* of letting the car stand idle would be just as expensive.

Cost and rent

It must not be supposed that every unit of resources is paid no more than its cost. It is, in fact, only the marginal units which earn just enough to keep them from moving to some other industry. Other units, which have a greater bias towards their present employment, will earn a surplus above their 'transfer cost'. This surplus, which is exactly similar to the surplus earned by intra-marginal firms, is called 'rent'. Thus the earnings of any unit of resources are made up of two parts – 'transfer cost' and 'rent'. The 'rent' element in earnings will be high where a factor is specially proficient in its present use, or suited to it temperamentally,or disinclined to move elsewhere. The idea of rent is one to which we will return in later chapters.

Scarcity, heterogeneity, mobility

We have seen that rising costs originate in the scarcity and heterogeneity of the factors of production. The tendency for costs to rise in any industry is the more pronounced the scarcer are the factors which it employs (i.e., the larger the proportion of the total stock engaged in the industry) and the more heterogeneous these factors are (i.e., the poorer the substitutes on which it can draw). In an industry like building, which employs a very large proportion of the bricklayers, masons, slaters, etc., in the country, there is a strong tendency towards rising costs; whereas in radio manufacture, which employs a comparatively small proportion of electricians, the tendency towards rising costs is almost negligible. Similarly, since the difficulty of finding more land suited to wheat-growing is greater than the difficulty of finding more land suited to dairy-farming, the cost of wheat tends to rise more steeply than the cost of milk. There is a third factor on which the tendency to rising costs depends – the mobility of productive resources. The greater the ease with which the factors of production can move from one industry to another, the less rapidly will costs rise. If, for example, labour is highly adaptable, or if most industries use a somewhat similar technique, then the cost of expanding any one industry will be much less than it would be if every worker were given a long and narrow training which fitted him for one job and one job only.

Relative scarcity

When an industry expands it may be specially difficult to obtain an adequate supply of some one factor. If no increase is possible, and there are no substitutes for the factor, the industry will be unable to expand further. But if there is some alternative technique which eliminates – in part or altogether – the use of the scarce factor, then expansion will be able to proceed at (presumably) rather higher cost. Resort to such alternative techniques, in order to meet a relative scarcity of some one factor, takes place every day. The problems raised by these changes in technique call for special consideration.

We start from two sets of facts – that great changes take place from time to time in the scarcity of one factor of production in relation to the others, and that corresponding changes take place in the use made of that factor relatively to the others. In some ages and countries labour is abundant and capital is scarce; methods of production, therefore, are such as to economize capital and use plenty of labour. In other ages and countries it is capital which is abundant and labour which has to be economized. The same services are rendered by combining the factors of production in very different proportions. Harvesting in China, where capital is scarce, is done with the scythe; in Canada, where labour is scarce, it is done with the combine harvester. In passenger transport there are endless possibilities of variation – from the labour-consuming rickshaw to the capital-consuming supersonic aircraft. The motor omnibus, the taxi, the railway sleeping car, the compartment for 8 *chevaux*, 40 *hommes* – all provide transport services with varying combinations of labour and capital.

When we say that the factors of production can be combined in different proportions we are really saying that they are substitutes for one another. We can produce the same quantity of product by using more capital and less labour (substituting capital for labour) or by using less capital and more labour (substituting labour for capital). The ease with which we change the proportions by substituting one factor for another varies from industry to industry. In some industries substitution is practically impossible; the technique of the industry is inflexible and dictates the use of productive agents in a fixed, or almost fixed, proportion. In the building of brick cottages, for example, both the materials required and the number of bricklayers, plumbers, carpenters, slaters, etc., are practically fixed once the plans are drawn[1]. In most industries, however, technique is fairly elastic, and a factor which has become specially cheap can be substituted for factors which remain dear. In the steel industry, for example, steel scrap and pig-iron can be substituted for one another in the making of steel whenever one of them becomes relatively scarce and expensive.

The law of diminishing returns

There are two general principles which govern the substitution of one factor for another. The first is that no one factor is a perfect substitute for another. This follows from the definition of a factor of production; if factors could be freely substituted for one another in all uses they would all belong to a single group of factors. The second principle, which is based on experience, is that substitution becomes progressively more difficult the more of one factor we try to substitute for another. We can easily do without a little of one factor and use a little of another instead; but we cannot easily do without a great deal of one factor and replace it by another. A small change in the pig-iron–scrap ratio makes little difference, but a large change creates great technical difficulties. The two principles,

---

[1] Even here there are possibilities of variation, e.g., by substituting more skilled for less skilled men, or high-quality for low-quality materials.

taken together, give us the 'law' of diminishing returns to the factors of production. This is simply a statement that, sooner or later, other things remaining the same, the combination of an increasing number of units of one factor with a given number of units of other factors must lead to a less than proportionate increase in output. The total product increases, but it does not increase so rapidly as the variable factor. The reason for this is just that some factors are not increased at the same time as the variable factor, and that increased supplies of the variable factor cannot entirely make up for this deficiency unless the variable factor and the fixed factors are perfect substitutes for one another.

The law is illustrated in *Table 15.1*. The first three columns of the table are hypothetical and provide the data from which the last two columns are calculated. Column 4 is obtained by dividing the total product by the number of units of A in use. If column 4 is increasing as output increases, the increase in output is more than in proportion to the increase in A; and if column 4 is decreasing, the increase in output is less than in proportion to the increase in A. In the first stage we have increasing, and in the second decreasing, returns. A third stage is also possible, intermediate between these two, at which output increases exactly in proportion to the increase in A, so that for a time column 4 remains constant. At this stage we have constant returns.

TABLE 15.1. **Variations in factor proportions**

Units of A	Units of B	Units of product	Average product per unit of A	Average cost of production when A = £20, B = £10
1	10	50	50	2.40
2	10	200	100	0.70
3	10	600	200	0.27
4	10	960	240	0.19
5	10	1270	254	0.16
6	10	1530	255	0.144
7	10	1750	250	0.137
8	10	1920	240	0.136
9	10	2070	230	0.135
10	10	2200	220	0.136

According to the law of diminishing returns we must ultimately reach the stage at which output increases less rapidly than units of A. But is there any reason why we need pass through the earlier stages of increasing or constant returns? If, for example, we can produce 1530 units of product with six units of A and ten of B, why isn't is possible to produce half as much (i.e., 765 units of product) with three units of A and five units of B, instead of the mere 600 units which our table gives as the joint product of three units of A and ten units of B? Why can't we save five units of B and still turn out 165 units more? Isn't there an obvious waste in using *any* of the first five combination, whatever the cost of the factors or the price of their product? Is there any reason, other than muddleheadedness, why these combinations should ever be adopted in the real world? The answer, to take the example we have just given, is that it may not be possible to use only five units of B, or find a market for 1530 units of product. If B is *indivisible* (i.e., if it cannot be duplicated on a smaller scale so that a smaller number of units can always be taken if desired) it may be necessary to use one of the earlier combinations of A and B so as to produce a limited quantity of product; and, secondly, it may be necessary to limit output because the market is narrow. A small motor-factory, for example, may have half the capital of a large one and, although employing more than half as many men, may turn out less than half as many cars. It is not of much use to recommend the small factory to adopt the methods of the large one and turn itself into a kind of half-scale replica, for it is only factories which are of a certain minimum size that can avail themselves of the methods of the large factory. Nor is it worth while to recommend the small factory to double its output and become a whole-scale replica of the large factory, for the increased output may not find a market. In other words, where there are economies of scale and market resistance to expansion we will find increasing returns operating, and continuing to operate.

Suppose now that units of A cost £20 and units of B £10. The tendencies to increasing and decreasing returns are then converted into tendencies to decreasing and increasing cost. The average cost of production falls until output is at 2070 units and rises for larger outputs. It will be observed that the output at which average cost begins to increase is considerably greater than the output at which returns begin to diminish. This is due to the spreading of the fixed cost of £100's worth of B over each output. Cost per unit of A is at a minimum when the return per unit of A is at a maximum. But cost per unit of A *plus* B continues to fall for some time. If a large amount of capital has to be sunk in a railway, the total cost per passenger will go on falling long after each additional train has begun to carry a smaller and smaller number of extra passengers.

The calculations of *Table 15.1* are intended to show how the substitution of one factor for another is, after a certain point, increasingly ineffective. It is assumed that only a strictly limited supply of one factor (B) is available, and that there is an unlimited supply of another factor (A). This assumption is obviously an extreme one. But if we remove it, and suppose instead that the supply of B is *more limited* than the supply of A, or that B is *relatively* scarcer than A, the principle illustrated in *Table 15.1* is unaffected. As output expands there will be a shortage of both A and B, and the cost of both will increase. But since B will be relatively scarcer and more expensive than A, it will pay to use a larger proportion of A and to economize B. The change in the proportion of A to B, whatever the absolute amounts of A and B used, will bring the law of diminishing returns into play, exactly as in *Table 15.1*. The substitution of the relatively cheaper for the relatively dearer factor can keep down the cost of production only within limits.

Thus if all the factors employed in an industry are perfectly divisible, and fully and equally available, there is no reason why one should be substituted for the other as output increases. The two will be combined in the proportion which makes costs a minimum, and if output has to be doubled, twice as much of each will be used. If every industry can draw freely on land, labour and capital at current prices, it can double its output without increase in cost; there will simply be two factories for every one there was before. So long as there is no reason to economize one factor rather than another, and so long as both are available in abundance at a constant price, costs cannot rise. If there is a limited supply of both factors, costs will rise because the factors are costing more as the industry seeks to attract increased supplies of each of them. If the supply of one factor is more limited than the supply of the other, so that the only units of the first factor that can be recruited are costly or second-rate, while the second factor can still be obtained in comparative abundance, then there will be good reason to substitute the second factor for the first. If such substitution were impossible and the factors had to be combined in a fixed proportion, costs would rise steeply. If substitution were perfect, and the second factor obtainable without limit at a fixed price, costs would not rise at all. In practice, as we have seen, the law of diminishing returns makes substitution imperfect and costs rise nonetheless. Thus it is because industries are forced to make do with the factors of which they *can* make increased use, meeting a deficiency of other factors as best they can, that diminishing returns come into play. Using a larger proportion of the factor which can be most easily increased is simply a method of economizing the other factors and avoiding the consequences of their scarcity.

Increasing and diminishing returns

Indivisibilities in the supply of factors of production make small-scale operation costly. It is these indivisibilities which underlie 'economies of scale'. If we assume that, by expanding output, a firm can never bring down the price at which it hires a factor of production, it is economies of scale, and economies of scale alone, that make costs fall as output increases in a given state of technical knowledge. The greater are economies of scale, the greater is the range of output over which costs will fall. If there were no economies of scale, increasing returns would disappear; and with increasing returns would disappear decreasing costs. Scarcity, combined with the law of diminishing returns, makes costs rise with output. Scarcity can be partially circumvented by substitution of one factor for another, but this substitution is limited by the tendency towards diminishing returns.

It is often said, for example, that agriculture is subject to decreasing, and industry to increasing, returns. But agriculture is full of examples of economies of scale – through the use of the combine-harvester, tractors, milking machines, and so on. It happens that the scale of production at which these economies can be realized is very small, while the market for agricultural products is very large. It is rare, therefore, to find any branch of farming working under conditions of increasing returns. Scarcity, on the other hand, makes itself felt in farming very markedly. There is a scarcity of fertile land; so that, if the output of all farm products has to be increased, farmers must either bring into cultivation sub-marginal land, or cultivate the existing area more intensively by applying to it an increased amount of labour and capital. The first expedient raises farming costs because sub-marginal land is inferior in fertility or in situation to the land already under cultivation. The second expedient raises farming costs because, if the proportion of labour and capital to land is increased, the tendency to diminishing returns comes into play. Each successive application of labour and capital, if the land has already been properly worked, yields a diminishing increment of product. If the output of only one farm product, e.g. wheat, has to be increased, scarcity will again force up costs. Land below the margin – this time the margin of transference – will have to be brought under wheat, and/or existing wheat land will have to be cultivated more intensively. The first expedient means paying a higher rent or renting inferior wheat land; the second brings decreasing returns into operation. If agricultural labour is also scarce, and the channels through which capital can be borrowed or credit obtained are narrow, then the rise in farming costs will be all the steeper.

In industry, on the other hand, the scale of production at which fresh economies cease to be made is enormous, and the market is comparatively narrow. Thus it is rare for an industry to be so placed that it could not more than double its output with the use of twice as much land, labour and capital. The average industry is producing under conditions of increasing returns. The pressure of scarcity, too, is less severe. The capacity of the industry can be increased by building plant exactly similar to the plant already in use. More workers can be found and trained much more easily and quickly than agricultural workers. Capital can be obtained in almost unlimited quantities. Thus costs of production rise only when output has to be increased very hastily, and when scarcity, therefore, is at its greatest. In the long run, costs in industry often fall when output is increased. Furthermore, experience of high output for some time may stimulate more cost-reducing innovations and improvements than a history of low output, or a sudden jump to high output.

The gradual approach to equilibrium

When there is a change in the conditions of demand or supply, the full effects of such a change are rarely felt immediately. Consumers may go on buying the same goods for some time after prices have risen and only gradually transfer their expenditure to other goods; producers may continue in business for years at prices which yield them a poor, or even a negative, return on their capital, and may only give up when their plant is completely worn out. Generally demand adjusts itself to changes in price much more rapidly than supply, and in the short run, therefore, dominates the course of prices; in the long run, however, supply becomes progressively more important as prices are pulled into line with cost.

A period sufficiently long to allow a full response of demand and supply to a change in prices is called 'the long period'. A period so short that there is no time for the 'capacity' of an industry (its fixed plant and organization) to alter appreciably is known as 'the short period'. But there are, of course, a whole series of periods, of increasing length, in which successively closer approximations are made to a full adjustment of demand and supply. This full adjustment, in which there is no further tendency for price to change, is described as 'equilibrium'. In the long period, therefore, price will reach its equilibrium level. Equilibrium is something which rarely exists, but is always coming into existence; price never has time to adjust itself finally to one change in demand or supply before another change interrupts progress towards equilibrium. The fact that a position of long-period equilibrium is never reached in the real world does not mean that the analysis of the last few chapters (which is almost exclusively in terms of long-period equilibrium) is quite futile. There are always long-period tendencies at work in each successive short period through which we live; and long-period equilibrium is simply the logical conclusion of these tendencies – their end-product, other things remaining the same. Moreover, if we understand what governs prices in the long run, we shall find it comparatively easy to apply the same line of reasoning to shorter periods.

The very short period

In the very short run – say, in the day's marketing – supply can be altered only by drawing on or adding to stocks. If the commodity is highly perishable there will be no stocks, and the influence of supply on price will be nil. In Covent Garden, for example, the supply of strawberries on sale every day will be fixed by the deliveries arriving in the morning, and will not respond to a rise or fall in prices during the day. The price of strawberries will be governed by the demand, in the sense that the price must fall to the level at which the whole supply will be bought. The demand is likely to be fairly elastic, since many buyers will be able to hold off until the following day if prices are abnormally high, and will be able to increase their purchases if prices are abnormally low. There will probably also be some minimum price at which sellers prefer to keep back their strawberries for disposal to jam manufacturers, and at this 'reserve price' supply will become extremely elastic since there will be a very elastic limit to the surplus from one day's sales that can be made into jam.

A similar example, covering a longer period of time, might be taken from potato-growing, where no increase can be made to the supply for almost a year after the crop has been harvested. The price is driven to the level at which the fixed supply can be rationed out amongst consumers so as to leave no surplus unsold. But amongst those consumers are the potato-growers themselves. For if prices fall too low they will feed their potatoes to stock instead of selling them for human consumption. Like the strawberry growers, they have a reserve price at which they withhold supplies from the market and below which, therefore, the market price cannot fall. In exactly the same way the price of commodities which are not perishable and can be stored cannot, in the short period, fall below the price which holders of the commodity expect to receive if they refuse to sell until later. This anticipated price (less carrying costs such as storage and interest charges) is their reserve price at which, so to speak, they enter the market on their own account.

The short period

In the short period, supply can be altered through a decision on the part of any firm either to make a marginal change in its output, or to discontinue production for the time being. The first decision will hinge on the relationship between marginal cost and revenue; the second on the relationship between total cost and revenue. But neither the marginal nor total cost of producing an article is the same in the short period as it is in the long. Suppose, for example, that I own a season ticket between Cambridge and London, and I stop to ask myself how much a journey to London is costing me. The answer, until the season ticket expires, is 'nothing at all'. I have paid in advance for as many journeys as I care to make. Suppose now that I am wondering whether I ought to renew my season ticket. Then the cost of a journey to London becomes something positive and calculable. It is equal to what I can save by not travelling. If I mean to make only a few journeys, for example, then the cost of each is clearly equal to the ordinary return fare. In the short period while my season ticket is unexpired, the cost of a journey is nil; in the long period, it may be as much as the ordinary return fare. In the same way the cost of using a piece of machinery, once it is installed, is often negligible, but the cost of using the machinery if it has to be hired every time it is used is by no means negligible.

The fact is that cost is not the same in the short period as it is in the long, because the alternatives open to us are not the same. In the long run we have the alternatives of *not* renewing our season tickets or the machinery which we have installed; in the short run, this alternative does not exist. A cost can only be a cost if it is something that can be avoided. But we cannot, in the short period, avoid the cost either of season tickets or of machinery; the cost of both has already been met, and since 'bygones are forever bygones' we cannot avoid the cost *now*. If the machinery depreciates more rapidly when in use than when it is idle, the *extra* depreciation can be avoided by not using the machinery and does, therefore, constitute a true cost, even in the short period.

It follows from this that costs which are fixed in the short period, and do not vary with output, are not really short-period costs at all. For example, firms cannot, in the short period, avoid payment of rates and taxes or debenture interest. Nor can they alter their fixed plant and organization and so avoid the cost of depreciation and obsolescence. These costs are fixed, whatever the level of output; they have to be met even if nothing is being produced. There is, so to speak, a cost of producing nothing. Now the cost of producing a given output is, as we have seen, what we could save by not producing it – what we could save by producing nothing. But the alternative of producing nothing may still involve us in expense. That expense, therefore, forms no part of the cost of what we do produce. It is only the additional *avoidable* outlay which is incurred that enters into the short-period cost of production.

Overhead costs

The cost of producing nothing is, for all practical purposes, the same thing as 'overhead' or 'supplementary' cost[1]. Overhead costs, therefore, are

---

[1] An alternative (and less novel) definition of overhead cost may be simpler to understand. Overhead cost can be taken to mean the difference between total cost and the cost of those factors of production (e.g., labour and materials) which vary with output in the short period. This alternative does not require any considerable modification of the statements made above.

fixed independently of output and have, no bearing on the questions: What output, if any, is most profitable now? What is the highest price that I can charge and the lowest that I can accept? In the short period it will pay to produce goods if they make any contribution whatever to overhead costs and fetch little more than their prime or avoidable costs; and in deciding what price to charge or to accept for his goods, a manufacturer will be guided more by his idea of what the market will bear than by the allowance which he thinks he must make for overheads. The plea that he must cover his overheads may be useful in mollifying his customers, and the suggested allowance for overheads may enable him to judge what price he can safely charge without inviting fresh competition from new firms. But it will be information on *marginal* costs – the cost of a few units more or a few units less – rather than on *average* prime and overhead costs that will be of most service to him so long as he remains in production. The allocation of overhead costs between different units of output, is, from the economic point of view, an irrelevant piece of ritual. In the long run, of course, overhead costs must be covered or manufacturers will stop producing. But they need not be covered consistently. Normally, some surplus over prime or variable costs will be earned. Sometimes this surplus will rise above and sometimes fall below overhead costs. It will fluctuate with the state of demand, increasing when an active demand allows prices to be raised, and decreasing when demand falls away and prices have to be reduced. The course of prices will govern the allowance that can be made for overheads.

The long period

In the long run, however, the position is reversed – the allowance that has to be made for overheads must ultimately influence prices. How does this come about?

The answer is that in the long period overheads are true costs. Outlay on overheads can be avoided by going out of business, or by closing down plant, which is idle and expensive to maintain, or by failing to repair and renew buildings and plant. In the short period these alternatives do not exist. A business will be willing to spend money in order to remain a going concern, producing nothing; it will be willing to meet the cost of producing nothing. It is only in the long run, when it has no incentive to remain a going concern, that it will prefer to produce nothing for nothing instead of at considerable expense. Similarly it will meet the cost of maintaining idle plant so long as there is a prospect that this cost of maintenance – not the original cost of the plant – will be recouped. The problem of replacements and renewals introduces even more elasticity for there will be some plant that falls due for renewal every year, perhaps even every month – and if prices are not high enough to justify renewal, output will immediately fall. What was a fixed cost in the lifetime of an old machine becomes a variable cost when the purchase of a new one is being considered, and all variable costs necessarily influence supply and price[1].

[1] It follows that when we speak of overhead cost we ought to specify some period of time during which cost remains fixed. Overhead cost is the cost of producing nothing in some given interval of time and in a given state of expectation (e.g., about future costs and prices). This interval of time will generally be one in which replacements of plant are negligible.

Marginal cost in short and long periods

We can now return to the two sets of decisions by which supply is altered in the short period. A marginal change in output may cost either more or less in the short period than in the long. A marginal reduction, for example, will save only the cost of labour and materials in the short period, while in the long period it will save part of the overhead cost of machinery and plant. On the other hand, a marginal expansion in output may, if the firm is working to capacity, be much more costly in the short period when there is no time to install additional machinery or train additional men, and the firm has to make shift by overdriving its machinery and overworking its employees. Especially if there has to be more overtime, with correspondingly high rates of pay, the short-period cost of a marginal expansion in output may be far in excess of the cost of a similar expansion over a long period.

The complications introduced by time make the problem of pricing an exceptionally delicate one. A firm has to weigh cost now and in the future against revenue now and in the future, trying to ensure that no marginal change in output will yield it a greater profit now without damage to profits in the future. It must hesitate, for example, to refuse a rush order from an important customer even when marginal cost is high – higher than price – if it fears that refusal will prejudice its sales in future years. Equally it must abstain from methods of production which leave a balance of profit now only by ruining all chance of producing at low cost in time to come.

Shut-down costs

The second set of decisions – to shut down temporarily or open up again – depends upon the relationship between total cost and total revenue: in other words, if we confine ourselves to the decision to close down, upon how big a loss firms are making. But the *amount* of the loss will not be the sole factor. We have also to ask, '*In what sense* is a loss being made?' If, for example, the firm is making a loss on total costs (including overheads) it is not likely to stop producing. If it cannot cover its debenture interest it may, of course, be forced into bankruptcy. But since a prime profit is being made (i.e., since the firm is making a profit over prime cost) it will generally pay the creditors to allow production to go on. It is better to have some return than none at all.

If a prime loss is being made, the action of the firm will depend upon three main factors: its financial strength, the view which it takes of future prospects, and the cost of closing down temporarily and opening up again.

1. The *ability* of a firm to make a prime loss will depend on its ability either to raise money on loan or to draw on reserves. No firm can go on disbursing more each week than it receives in the form of sales proceeds without running into debt.
2. The *willingness* of a firm to incur debt (assuming that lenders can be found) will depend upon its faith in such a revival in demand as will allow the debt to be repaid. A loss on prime costs is a species of investment on which a return is expected at a later date when the firm hopes to profit from having maintained its plant and organization in good condition.

3. The *wisdom* of continuing to make a prime loss will depend upon the costliness of the most attractive alternative. It may be cheaper, for example, to shut down temporarily, putting the plant on a care and maintenance basis. But this is a course which firms are reluctant to take, since it may mean the loss of business connections, disorganization of staff, and the dispersion of a reliable and carefully selected body of workers, trained in the ways of the firm. Frequently, therefore, firms prefer to work on a skeleton output in order to maintain contact with markets, staff and workpeople. Where shut-down and reopening costs, broadly defined, are high, firms will prefer to go on producing at correspondingly high prime losses.

Marginal firms in the short period

In the short period, as in the long, there will be some firms that are marginal and others that are intra-marginal. Marginal firms will be on the verge of closing down or opening up, and a small change in price will be sufficient to turn the scale. The average short-period cost of such a firm can be calculated by deducting from its total costs the alternative cost of closing down and producing nothing and averaging the residue over the firm's output. Below this average cost, price will not fall. Monopolistic influences may, however, succeed in maintaining prices above the average short-period cost of even the least favourably situated firm.

Summary

A change in price will have immediate and delayed reactions on supply. These reactions will be governed at each stage by the alternatives open to producers, and the range of alternatives will widen with the passage of time. Supply is more elastic the longer the period which we have in view.

This is particularly true of a *reduction* in supply. What is saved by contracting output in the short period is often small in comparison with what can ultimately be saved (e.g., by refraining from plant renewals). Especially when overheads are high, the adjustment of an industry to a *fall* in price is difficult and protracted. On the other hand, an industry generally attempts to expand its capacity quickly to meet a *rise* in price because short-period expedients for increasing output tend to be much more costly than the long-period expedient of installing more plant.

Chapter 16

Interrelationships of supply and demand

The effect of a change in price is never confined to a single product; there are repercussions on the prices of other products, linked with the first either in supply or in demand. These repercussions can be classified under five headings:

(a) Joint supply

There are some commodities which can only be produced in association with other commodities; familiar examples are wheat and straw, mutton and wool, gas and coke. These commodities are said to be in joint supply. Commodities are in joint supply whenever one commodity is a by-product of another, so that it is impossible to increase the supply of one without simultaneously increasing the supply of the other. If there is an increase in the demand for one joint product, therefore, the supply of *both* will increase, and, since there will be a larger supply of the second product to dispose of, its price will tend to fall. Similarly, a fall in the demand for one joint product will tend to increase the price of the other.

(b) Joint demand

Some commodities are wanted in association with other commodities, and when the demand for one increases, the demand for the complementary commodity increases simultaneously. For example, there is a joint demand for tea and sugar, collars and ties, bacon and eggs, whisky and soda. If any one of these becomes cheaper because of an increase in the supply, both joint products will be in greater demand, and the price of the second, which is no more plentiful, will tend to rise. Similarly, if one joint product becomes scarcer, the price of the other will tend to fall.

(c) Composite supply

Commodities in composite supply are substitutes for one another. Butter and margarine, for example, form a composite supply for the satisfaction of one want: tea, coffee, cocoa, etc., for the satisfaction of another. If, of two commodities in composite supply, one becomes cheaper, the demand for the substitute commodity will clearly be reduced, and its price will tend to fall, too.

(d) Composite demand

Commodities are in composite demand when they are wanted for several different purposes. Electricity, for example, is in composite demand for lighting, heating and cooking; for electric razors, clocks and wireless sets; and for driving electric motors in many different industries. If more electricity is needed for lighting, there will be less available for heating and cooking; an increased demand in one use will put pressure on the supply in alternative uses, and prices will tend to rise all round. In the same way, engineering labour is in composite demand for all the industries in which it can be employed. If, then, more engineers are urgently needed in one set of industries (e.g., the motor vehicle industries), the scarcity of labour in these industries will communicate itself to all industries employing engineering workers and engineering wages will go up all round.

(e) Derived demand

The demand for some commodities *derives from* the demand for other commodities. No one wants crude steel for its own sake; it is wanted for the manufacture of steel products. The demand for steel is a derived demand; yet from it, in turn, other demands derive – the demand for iron ore, coal, scrap iron and manganese. It is only when we reach the ultimate factors of production that the chain of derived demand comes to an end. At the other end of the chain are the final products of industry ready for sale to consumers. The demand for the services of the factors of production, therefore, is derived from the demand of the consumers of finished goods.

Inter-connections between demand and supply

These five relations sum up the inter-connections of different industries and different markets. One product is tied to others in the most unexpected ways, and without a vivid sense of these obscure ties we cannot lay claim to a real understanding of the theory of value. Consider, for example, the ramifications of a programme of rearmament. More steel has to be produced. Hence there will be a larger output of furnace slag – to take one by-product out of many – and the price of cement and of fertilizers, both of which can be made from slag, will tend to fall (joint supply). More munitions factories will have to be built (joint demand), and this may create a shortage of bricklayers, so upsetting the housing programmes of local authorities (composite demand) and forcing them to build timber and concrete houses (composite supply). At the same time rearmament will give a fillip to all the industries supplying raw materials for arms, from the producers of optical lenses for service binoculars to the makers of buttons for uniforms (derived demand). The reader will find it instructive to work out less obvious repercussions; to trace, for example, how recruiting and aerodrome construction create a shortage of agricultural labour, increase the demand for tractors and milking machines, and reduce the demand for horses and oats.

The marginal cost of joint products

When two commodities are interdependent in supply or demand, the task of disentangling the demand and supply of each looks daunting. We cannot produce wheat without straw; what, then, is the cost of the wheat and what the cost of the straw? If we know the joint cost of wheat and straw taken together, how are we to assign this cost between the two? This question can be answered satisfactorily only if we understand why it is ever asked. Information about the cost and utility of a commodity is of value only if it helps us to decide whether too much or too little of the commodity is being produced. That is, the information ought to bear on *marginal* units of the commodity and show whether there is a balance of gain or loss in producing these units. It is vital, therefore, for a firm to know the *marginal* cost of each of its products. But to divide up joint costs and distribute the total between each joint product is quite meaningless. The allocation of joint costs, while it may decorate a balance sheet and flatter the accountant's sense of propriety, serves no purpose whatever.

How, then, can we calculate the marginal cost of wheat? If wheat and straw are always yielded in a fixed ratio, so that we cannot increase the supply of one *at the expense of the other*, the answer is quite simple. The marginal cost of wheat is what can be saved by not growing a little of it, and this necessarily includes the cost of that inevitable concomitant of wheat-growing – straw. Similarly, the marginal cost of the straw includes the cost of the wheat that grows on it. The marginal cost of each is equal to the joint marginal cost of both. At the same time the marginal revenue of wheat will include the value of the straw which is produced simultaneously, while the marginal revenue of straw will include the value of the wheat which is produced simultaneously.

This may seem a very complicated way of explaining that the cost of wheat is neither separable nor different from the cost of straw. But observe how illuminating the explanation becomes if we *can* vary the proportion in which wheat and straw are grown – if, for example, we can grow wheat on a longer stalk or with a heavier ear. A marginal addition to the supply of wheat can then be made without sowing a larger acreage, for example, by sowing varieties of seed, or using types of fertilizers, or taking the kind of trouble over cultivation that will yield more wheat on a given weight of straw. There will be various marginal adjustments, that is, each of which will increase the yield of wheat without increasing the yield of straw proportionately – adjustments which, in other words, will substitute wheat for straw. Suppose that these adjustments are made in such a way as to yield the same quantity of straw as before and an additional bushel of wheat. Let us select that particular device by which this can be contrived at lowest cost. Then this lowest cost of producing an extra bushel of wheat gives us the marginal cost of wheat. When the marginal cost of wheat can be calculated in this way it is obviously quite distinct from the marginal cost of straw.

This is not a full solution to our problem. The price of wheat, even in the long run, may remain below marginal cost as calculated above. For although it may be *possible* to grow an additional bushel of wheat on the same quantity of straw, this may not be the most *profitable* expedient. It may be easier to grow a little more straw, and a good deal more wheat, setting the value of the additional straw against the increase in total costs. The price of wheat will then be governed by the rule that marginal cost tends to equal marginal revenue, the first including the cost of any additional straw and the second its value.

Joint products from the point of view of the firm[1]

The practical implications of these ideas may be clearer if we apply them to the problems that face the individual firm. Suppose, for example, that some machines, or some generator of power, or some piece of floor space is contributing to the output of several commodities. Then it will be a waste of time to try to allocate to each commodity its share in the joint or 'overhead' costs[2] of the machine, or the power plant, or the floor space. But it will be of the utmost importance to find what saving could be made on these overhead costs by reducing the output of any one commodity, and what additional outlay on overhead costs would be necessary in order to increase the output of that commodity. If there is no *measurable* saving or additional outlay attributable to individual commodities – if changes in overhead costs affect all commodities equally – then we must try to find out, on the assumption that overhead costs remain unchanged, what reduction in the output and sale of *other* goods is necessary in order to provide for an expansion in the output and sale of each individual commodity. For example, a shop which sells handbags and suitcases and has a fixed amount of floor space, may be able to estimate the loss in revenue from suitcases that will result from the stocking of more handbags and fewer suitcases. This loss in revenue can be regarded as the marginal cost of retailing handbags and should be weighed against the gain in revenue from the additional handbags that are sold. The problem of charging suitcases and handbags with their appropriate share of the cost of floor space (the rent of the shop) simply does not arise.

Handbags and suitcases are not only in joint supply, but also in a sense in joint demand: many customers normally purchase both in the same shop. A shopkeeper who reduces the price of handbags, therefore, will not only increase his sales of handbags, but will also attract custom in other lines, such as suitcases, and the profit which he makes on his additional sales of suitcases will go to reduce the margin required to cover the cost of retailing handbags. If handbags are sold at a specially low price, the sacrifice of profit on handbags may really be a species of advertisement designed to increase profits from the sale of other merchandise. Such a good is termed a 'loss leader'.

This parallel with advertisement and selling costs suggest that the principles governing selling costs apply equally to joint products. As before, once we define marginal cost and marginal revenue broadly, the rule that they tend to equality with one another holds. The position of

---

[1] Strictly speaking, joint products are products that must be produced simultaneously; the term is here more elastically to cover products that are in fact produced together.

[2] Notice that in this context overhead costs are 'costs common to a number of commodities', not 'costs fixed over a period of time'.

maximum profit, when several products are being produced or several markets supplied, will be one in which there is no commodity such that by producing more of it the additional net revenue exceeds the additional net cost. The net (marginal) revenue will include the rise in the proceeds of sale of the commodity, less the fall in returns from any commodity the output of which has had to be cut down, plus the rise in returns from any commodity which is in joint demand with the first. The net marginal cost will include net additional outlay plus any additional depreciation due to the expansion of output.

The same line of reasoning applies to the discontinuance or initiation of the production of some commodity in the long period. If there is a prospect of additional profit, taking into account all extra outlays and the balance of increase in receipts, then the commodity is *ipso facto* profitable. The problem of saddling the commodity with its 'share' of overhead costs, which are perhaps unaffected by this new departure, does not arise.

When the question of renewal presents itself, the considerations on which a decision should be based are similar. A machine may be used in the manufacture of several commodities. The manufacturer will, therefore, have to sum the various reductions in his receipts which failure to renew will involve and weigh the total against the annual charge for upkeep, depreciation and interest on a new machine. If there is some other method of production which promises larger profits, or lower losses, then the machine will not be renewed.

The fundamental point is that costs must be approached from the point of view, first, of alternatives, and secondly, of the margin. The changes which have to be analysed are generally marginal changes – repercussions of a suggested change must be worked out and the result compared with the existing position. The profitability of any output is thus purely relative. It may pay to make an apparent loss because an offsetting gain is being made, or is expected to be made, in consequence of the loss. To insist on making a profit everywhere may result in reducing profits all round.

Price discrimination

The practice of price discrimination offers an excellent illustration of this truth. Discrimination may arise whenever the products of a firm are in composite demand by distinct groups of consumers, each group being made to pay a different price for exactly the same product or service. For example, electricity is sold at different prices to households and firms. It can readily be shown that if a firm which is in a position to discriminate insists on making a profit in each market, its total profits may be less than they would be if the firm were satisfied with an apparent 'loss' in some of

	Price	Sales	Total receipts	Average cost
First market	£40	200	£8000	£30 (200 units)
Second market	£18	300	£5400	£20 (500 units)

its markets. Suppose, for example, that the firm possesses semi-monopolistic powers in one market (e.g., the home market) and is open to severe competition in another (e.g., the export market) so that it is more reluctant to spoil the first market than the second. The price in the first market may be £40, and in the second £18, while sales are 200 in the first and 300 in the second.

Suppose also that the average cost of production of 200 units is £30, while the average cost of $(200 + 300)$ units is £20. Then it might appear that every unit sold in the second market would lose the firm $£(20 - 18)$ or £2. In fact, however, refusal to sell in the second market results in the loss of £5400 in revenue, and saves only $£(500 \times 20) - (200 \times 30)$ or £4000 in cost. In other words, selling below (average) cost in the second market increases total profits by £1400.

Once again, thinking in terms of marginal cost and revenue saves us from confused reasoning. The marginal cost of output will depend mainly on the total amount produced and will be more or less independent of variations in the proportion disposed of in any one market. Now it will pay the manufacturer to make marginal cost and marginal revenue equal in *each* market, and since the gap between marginal revenue and price will be least in the highly competitive export market, he will tend to charge a lower price there than in the home market. If demand in the export market is so elastic that his power to depress or raise prices is negligible, then he will expand his sales abroad until marginal cost is equal to the world price, and since marginal cost will remain below average cost so long as costs are falling, price will also be lower than average cost.

It should be observed that the incentive to discriminate originates not in unused capacity as is sometimes suggested, but in the imperfection of competition. If competition acted with equal force in all markets, manufacturers would charge the same price all round, whether their costs were rising or falling. If it were impossible to separate one market from another, the same would be true. Discrimination can only be resorted to whenever groups of consumers can be separated out by geographical area, or income, or membership of some society, or propensity to visit particular shopping centres, or to buy particular qualities of product. There must also be some barrier to movement from one group to another. For example, goods dumped abroad may, if the price disparity is excessive, be reimported and bring down prices at home. British motor cars, if there were no import restrictions, could not be sold at one price in France and another in Britain.

Joint products from the point of view of society

Changes in market conditions have important social repercussions as well. Whereas the individual firm, in balancing cost against price, can confine itself to the limited range of products which it manufactures, and whereas the individual consumer, in balancing price against utility, can confine himself to the limited range of products which he buys, calculations of *social* welfare must embrace *all* goods and services. In private accounting there are many repercussions of our decisions to buy or sell that we can, if we choose, neglect; but in social accounting, allowance should be made for them. The producer of chemicals, whose waste gases pollute the atmosphere, does not reckon in pollution as part of his output. The consumer who burns raw coal in the domestic grate does not deduct the soot and dust which he created from the utility of the fire. Private costs and private preferences are partial and incomplete. Our private interests and the interests of society often fail to coincide.

To these points we shall return in the next chapter when we consider whether prices in a capitalist society adequately reflect the wants of the community.

Chapter 17

Social aspects of pricing

Now that we have seen how prices are fixed, it is time to turn to the more perplexing problem of how prices should be fixed. This is a question which people ask for several quite different reasons. They may want to know on what basis to decide whether a price is fair or just; they may be thinking of the problems of a war-time government armed with powers to fix prices and ration goods; or they may have in mind a socialist economy in which prices are not governed by market forces but have somehow to be 'planned'. It is unlikely that these different sets of questions can be given a single set of answers. St Thomas Aquinas and Stalin would hardly have seen eye to eye on the matter, and Lord Woolton, who was Minister of Food in war-time Britain, would have had good reasons for differing from them both.

A common-sense answer to the question would be that prices should be equal to cost of production. But, as we have seen, cost is a rather ambiguous concept: different firms have different costs; their short-run costs are not necessarily equal to their long-run costs; and the distinction between cost and profit tends, on closer examination, to become a little blurred. On top of this, cost may vary with scale of production, so that average cost and marginal cost are not necessarily equal. The common-sense answer, therefore, is not altogether satisfactory.

Marginal cost pricing

Nevertheless, it is in line with the general thinking of economists on the subject. They would be inclined to take the price that would rule under conditions of perfect competition as a useful point of departure, recognizing that this was not in all circumstances a satisfactory norm and that there might be good practical reasons for using some other basis of pricing. This would mean that prices ought, as a rule, to be equal to marginal cost of production. This formula would be justified by economists on the grounds that it would lead to an allocation of resources between different uses that was in keeping with the preferences of producers and consumers. Put briefly, the argument is that the price of a commodity measures the value that consumers set on an extra unit of it; its marginal cost measures the cost of producing such a unit. If price is above marginal cost, therefore, too little of the commodity is being produced. Equality between price and marginal cost secures the 'right' balance between value and cost and the 'right' output of the commodity.

To elaborate this argument at any length would take us too deeply into welfare economics, a disputed territory where even professional economists walk warily. But at the risk of confusing the reader, we may explain the gist of the matter as follows. Suppose that we need consider only two commodities A and B, that all resources are fully employed in the production of A and B, and that a marginal shift of resources between A and B can take place freely and without any cost of transfer. Suppose also that the marginal costs of A and B are equal. If in those circumstances the price of A is above its marginal cost and the price of B is not, a transfer of resources from B to A would leave consumers better off without injury to producers. By spending less on B, consumers would release resources that could produce just as much of A, for which they have to pay more than they do for B. They would therefore gain by an amount equal to the difference between the price and marginal cost of A. Similarly, if the price of A were below its marginal cost it would pay to transfer resources away from the production of A.

There are many services the output of which is not left to competition and which cannot be priced in this way. Even where competition does operate, an attempt to price on the basis of marginal cost would raise practical difficulties where costs fall with volume of output. In those cases, marginal cost would be below average cost and price would, therefore, also be below average cost; in other words, it would be necessary to run at a loss. This loss might be covered out of a subsidy from the state. There is nothing necessarily wrong about subsidizing an industry; but if the practice were to become very common, one might well conclude that the idea of pricing on the basis of marginal cost needed some re-examination.

Few economists have ever contemplated that the idea should be applied rigorously and systematically in a capitalist economy. If the state took responsibility for fixing prices, and introduced a system of levies and subsidies in order to balance out the profits and losses that resulted, it is almost inconceivable that it could escape taking control of the operation of the industries affected. If some industries were obliged to make consistent losses because their prices were held down by the state and subsidies were given in compensation, it would be necessary to have some guarantee that the losses were not made an excuse for slackness and that the subsidies were not unnecessarily large. There would have to be frequent adjustments in the rates of levy and subsidy – deliberate adjustments which would meet with vigorous resistance from the industries affected.

These difficulties might be overcome if the state had full and accurate knowledge of marginal costs in each industry; but it neither has nor could easily acquire such knowledge and any data that it collected would be open to conflicting interpretations.

The measurement of marginal cost is never a straightforward affair. There are ambiguities in the concept itself: it is relative to the period of time under discussion and the expectations that can reasonably be entertained about future developments. There are complications in its measurement whenever several commodites are produced in the same factory[1].

[1] See pp. 204–206.

There are further complications when, as often happens, a firm does not produce the same thing continuously for more than a year – or, like the local cinema, for more than three nights running – and when its efficiency depends far more on its success in improving or varying its product than in producing any single product at minimum cost. In some industries a firm may spend £1m in tooling-up and no more than a few pence in meeting direct costs per unit, only to re-tool after a limited run. In many industries (e.g., publishing) the number of price quotations runs into thousands. Experience of price-control in war-time does not suggest that the magic of a single golden rule will suffice to dispel the practical problems of pricing and leave industrial efficiency unaffected.

There are three further problems with marginal cost as a basis for pricing. First, the case for it must be valid if – and, depressingly, only if – every other related market in the economy is perfect. Suppose the output of beef is held down, below its ideal level, by monopoly or administrative error. If this distortion cannot be put right, the prices of substitutes for beef, such as lamb, should be raised above marginal cost, and those of complements for beef, such as mustard or hamburger buns, probably lowered to below marginal cost. These price changes would help to check the damage done by the overpricing of beef. Second, it is 'social', not 'private' marginal cost to which price should be linked. The private marginal cost of a call to the telephone company, in terms of electricity used and wear and tear on equipment, is trivial; but the social marginal cost, if my telephoning impedes other calls, could be large. Alcohol and tobacco are other goods generally priced far above private marginal cost of production, partly because of the social harm thought to accompany their consumption. Third, basing price on marginal cost for social reasons neglects completely another set of arguments for altering prices in a market economy: to affect a distribution of income between households that might be considered unjust. Holding down the prices of staple foods and urban rented accommodation will have other disadvantages, but it will bring some benefit to the poor; the same is true of price discrimination in favour of particular groups.

Nevertheless there are circumstances in which it would be both practicable and desirable to give effect to the logic of the idea. Suppose that a bridge could be built that would cost nothing to maintain after erection. The marginal cost of using it is nil so that, on the principle of marginal cost pricing, no toll should be charged. This might mean that a great many people used the bridge who would not use it if a toll were charged; and the total gain to the users might well exceed the cost of erection. Whether it would be right to build the bridge at the expense of the general tax-payer for the benefit of a limited group of users is another matter; if this decision *were* taken, there would be everything to be said subsequently for allowing the bridge to be fully used. Another example would be that of railway-building in a country still relatively thinly populated, where the marginal cost of railway services would be low in comparison with their average cost. However railway charges were fixed, revenue might be insufficient to cover costs and the fear of making a loss would deter private interests from undertaking the building of the railway. The social importance of having an adequate railway might, however, induce the state to provide the capital and, once the railway was in operation, pricing on a marginal cost basis would yield greater social gains than attempts to base charges on average costs.

It is clear that in these two examples, the case for marginal cost pricing rests on the desirability of making full use of some indivisible lump of equipment; it is because the cost of using this equipment is spread over an increasing volume of output that the cost curve is downward-sloping and marginal cost is below average cost. It is also clear that the key decision relates to the construction of the equipment in the first place rather than to its operation; it is the initial investment that needs to be subsidized. It would be possible to select other examples where the case for charging *more* than average cost rested on the undesirability of overloading existing fixed assets; if users were penalized by having to pay marginal cost, this would help to relieve a form of congestion. In such examples, it would again be the decision not to construct more of the fixed assets that was the critical one, since pricing on the basis of marginal cost would be a means of giving effect to this decision so as to minimize inconvenience to the consumer. Where there are no indivisible elements to give rise to unnecessary under-utilization on the one hand, or congestion on the other, and where resources are mobile and freely variable, costs will be constant and marginal cost will not diverge from average cost. Once this point has been grasped, it is much easier to see in what directions the principle of marginal cost pricing has a practical bearing; and there is less reason for supposing that at least the more glaring applications of the principle will escape notice and support.

Some wider considerations

The principle that price should be based on marginal cost is intended to secure that the wants of consumers receive the fullest possible satisfaction – if we are willing to sacrifice a little of A for the sake of a little more of B produced at equal cost, then our preference will be met by an appropriate transfer of resources from the production of A to the production of B. But what if we want to sacrifice a little of A for the sake of something not on the market at all? We cannot give effect, as individual consumers, to a preference for a less varied and cheaper selection of goods; or for economic progress rather than economic security; or for an increased national debt rather than increased unemployment. We have freedom of choice, but only within the limits of existing market conditions. If we want to change market conditions we must associate with other like-minded consumers in bringing pressure on the government. Our preferences find expression, not in the market, but in Parliament. But they are nonetheless preferences of which account must be taken in deciding what is to be produced and how it is to be produced. Preferences backed by voting power can be just as important in arriving at a just price or an ideal output as preferences backed by purchasing power; and as the market contracts they become more important.

Nor is this a trifling difficulty. For the deepest wants of man have little to do with the scarcity which economic activity is primarily designed to combat. Man craves most of all a sense of purpose, a role in life and in society. Deny him that, make him feel of no consequence, and he will take revenge by overturning any economic system, however well regulated. It is not enough to offer him value for his money in goods and services. He must have a place to match his sense of merit – something to admire and defend, entertainment and amusement, responsibility and initiative. Without these, goods and services are as dust and ashes, and any one output is as far from ideal as any other.

So long as we refuse to go behind man's wants to the inner motives which inspire them, the rules of pricing can be reduced to simple axioms. We can treat each want atomically as a demand for this or that service, and discuss choice as the balancing of one want against another. But immediately we begin to think of wants as fused by a sense of purpose, the tool of marginal analysis breaks in our hands. It is borne in on us that it is not just the surface wants that cry out for satisfaction, but the deeper urges which they often express. People buy goods not for their own sake so much as for what they symbolize. The African chief who, in fear of death at the hands of his tribe, seeks hair-dye of white travellers to prolong his youth and his rule: the *nouveau riche* who buys a country seat so as to impress his associates: the purchaser of cosmetics, parrots, or holy relics; all have resort to market agencies in order to satisfy wants that are denied satisfaction in other ways. And this is true not just of a few odd people or of a few odd purchases, but of practically everyone at some time and of the bulk of the purchases which most of us make at any time. We do not buy the cheapest article available and only those articles which are indispensable to living. We buy what appeals to our imagination under the pressure of social standards. In economic activity as in other spheres of life the motives which dominate us are rarely hunger and want in the narrow sense (except at a very low standard of living) but the desire for power, the desire to make others feel that power, to show off and keep up with our neighbours, to plan and build and dream. We seek distinction, for example, in our dress or in our profession; and power over others through our wealth or as their employers. To isolate individual buyers and sellers in some vacuum of choice, therefore, and discuss how industry can best maximize an ethereal utility is to misconceive the problem. We might as well discuss what combination of medicines will most promote health, without regard to the causes of ill-health or to the other remedies (fresh-air, exercise, good food, adequate clothing, and so on) that lie to hand. To substitute one assortment of goods and services for another may do far less for the people's welfare than the setting of new social standards or the direction of their energies into new and more acceptable channels.

Nor is this all. For the act of substitution of itself *changes* social standards and *creates* new demands. If, for example, we provide cheaper television sets we may reduce the demand for theatre seats and increase the demand for coal, since more prople will wish to stay at home and watch. Thus the balance between value and cost is upset and no one can say with assurance whether it is upset for better or for worse. We cannot assume, therefore, that if output is adjusted so as to keep prices in line with costs we are giving fuller satisfaction to the wants of consumers, for these wants are themselves affected by variations in output.

Again, many of our wants are shaped by the very system of production which exists to supply them. A man's habits of living and of expenditure depend partly upon the work which he is called upon to do. A worker in casual employment has a different scale of values from a worker in regular employment. A factory worker, a miner, an agricultural labourer, a stockbroker and a doctor have each their own outlook and make their own peculiar purchases. By changing methods of production, therefore, we can simultaneously change the demand of consumers. If we provide well ventilated and clean factories we can create a demand for well ventilated and clean houses. If we cut down overtime we may be able to reduce the demand for medical services – or for whisky.

Private and social values

In short, we cannot base prices solely on current market valuations because the money costs and values which find expression in the market are incomplete measures of social costs and values. Buying and selling go on against a social background from which we cannot abstract in estimating the value of what is bought or the cost of what is sold. Consider, for example, the building of a house. It costs, let us say, £35 000 and is valued at the same figure. But do we enter up in the cost the noise which the neighbours endure, the nuisance to passers-by from added traffic congestion, or the loss of amenities to other householders? Do we include in the value of the house its effect on our health and on the health of our children (matters of immediate interest to the community, which may have to support us if we fall ill, has to combat any infectious disease which we may help to spread, and is out of pocket on the cost of our education if we are unable to do regular work and to pay our taxes)? Do we include the effect which living in such a house has on our character and so on our work and friendships? Do we include the pleasure which other people derive from our garden? It is highly unlikely that we include any of these things. Yet they affect the cost and value of the house to the community just as surely as the cost in bricks and mortar and the number and size of the rooms.

Thus the machinery of the market – even when regulated so as to keep marginal utility and marginal cost equal to one another – is insufficient to make the output of each commodity ideal. We must supplement market competition, with its narrow perspective of self-interest, by some other kind of competition from which a broad judgement of social welfare will emerge. In democratic countries, this second kind of competition takes the form of competition for votes. It is the electorate which, in the last resort, has power to decide whether one industry is too small or another too large to be in the social interest.

Private values and state intervention

A wider question remains. Is it right to take demand for granted and give it the fullest possible satisfaction, without first deciding whether or not it *ought* to be satisfied? Clearly, there is no ideal output of drugs. But what of hundreds of other commodities which consumers buy ill-advisedly or ignorantly? Is the consumer the best judge of his own interests when he buys patent medicines, or petrol, or electric fittings? Still more important, should the value which he sets on milk or on opera or on education be the sole criterion by which the output of these things should be determined? In general, it is wise to leave the consumer to learn from his own mistakes and not to dragoon him too insistently into paths of wisdom and virtue prepared by a very fallible government. But there are times when, in fixing prices, the state may properly disregard individual valuations as shortsighted, mistaken or wrong, deny access to certain commodities in the quantities which consumers would be willing to absorb, and offer other commodities in larger quantities, in more attractive surroundings or backed by more advertising pressure, than free competition would provide. If technical experts are practically unanimous in praising one commodity and in condemning another, the state will be justified in setting aside any contrary verdict by individual consumers. It will be right to encourage, or even enforce consumption of the first, and to discourage or suppress the sale of the second. When informed opinion is seriously divided, however, or when important moral issues are involved, the state will be unwise to interfere unnecessarily with the free choice of consumers in order to impose upon them ideals which they do not share. To prohibit the drinking of methylated spirits is one thing; to prohibit the drinking of beer, quite another.

This is not, however, the end of the matter. The state's influence on prices extends far beyond a paternal anxiety to push the sale of milk and prohibit the sale of opium. The whole price system is honeycombed with the influence of the state, direct or indirect: a tax here, a subsidy there, the provision of facilities at one point, their denial at another. This influence is sometimes opportunist: it may reflect no more than the fact that it is easier to tax the smoker than the football pool enthusiast. Sometimes it expresses state policy towards a particular industry: the desire to encourage agriculture, for example. But to an increasing extent, it is the general economic policy of the state that guides its intervention: the objective of greater social equality may prompt it to subsidize foodstuffs or housing; the aim of full employment may induce it to control interest rates; the need to redress an adverse balance of payments may lead it to restrict the supply of imported goods of various kinds, with repercussions on their price. The action of the state is then based, not on any deliberate disregard of individual valuations of particular commodities or services, but on a positive policy related to those major objectives. Such action can only be satisfactorily judged, therefore, in relation to the state's objectives and policy. The issues involved will form the subject of Part VII.

Part IV

The distribution of income

Chapter 18

The distribution of income

There are two sides to the theory of distribution. One is concerned with the definition, measurement and explanation of economic inequalities: why some people have higher income or wealth than others. This is the theory of *personal* distribution. The other is the theory of *factoral* distribution. The factoral theory is the study of how, and why, the national income is divided between those who own the different *factors of production*, labour, capital and land. Of the two, the factoral theory is much the older and more developed. This chapter surveys the major ideas and issues inherent in these two sides of distribution theory. The two chapters that follow investigate two central areas with which both sides are concerned: the first, earnings (wages and salaries, and their distribution); the second, profits and wealth (profits, interest, rent, and the level and distribution of wealth).

Economic inequality

Perfect equality, and complete inequality, are quite straightforward concepts. But the vast area between these extremes is more complicated. Suppose £100 is to be divided among three people, A, B, and C. Perfect equality prescribes that each receive £33⅓. With complete inequality, one of them receives £100, and the others nothing. Now suppose A gets £50, B £30, and C £20. The distribution clearly become more equal if A transfers £1 to C (or, presumably, to B). But what if B loses £6, transferring £2 to A and £4 to C? B and C now both have £24: these two are more equal. The gap between A and C has also narrowed, proportionately and absolutely. But the gap between A and B has widened considerably: A now has £52, more than double B's £24. We cannot say whether the division £52, £24, £24, is more or less equal than £50, £30, £20. From the standpoint of the poorest, £52, £24, £24, is more equal; from that of the richest, less so. This little example shows why there is so often no clear general answer to questions such as 'Are incomes distributed more equally in West Germany than the US?', or 'Has inequality in UK incomes fallen in the past 10 years?' There are several different numerical measures of inequality, each imposing its own scheme of weighting income gaps at different points on the scale; and they can, and do, give conflicting answers to such questions. Much the same ambiguity attaches to comparison of investments by riskiness, or industries by degree of 'concentration' (i.e., monopolization by few firms).

Wealth and income are the two variables to which inequality is most often applied. Income is a flow, as it measures what a person or household receives in a period of time. Wealth is a stock. Wealth can be spent only once, while income is best defined as what you can spend if you keep the real value of your wealth intact. Of the two concepts, therefore, income inequality is perhaps the more important. Wealth and income do not necessarily go together: a retired man may have substantial wealth, if he owns his house, and the capital value of his pension rights is added in; but his flow of income, limited as it is to interest, dividend and pension receipts, may be modest. A younger person's earnings may give him a much higher income, while he may have next to no wealth. This example points to the greater usefulness of long-term averages, than of estimates of wealth at one date, or income in one short period. Short-period figures are more volatile and less informative.

Links between personal and factoral distribution

The link between the personal and factoral sides of the theory of distribution is provided by the distribution of ownership of the factors of production. The ownership of personal capital varies partly, as we have seen, according to age; it is affected, too, by government action, and by savings habits, and luck; and the dominant influence has nearly always been inheritance. In a society without slavery, everyone is born with labour-power and the ability to earn. Earnings ability varies, however, with age, education, training, natural ability, health, intelligence and sometimes, regrettably, sex and colour.

Once we know the personal distribution of ownership of factors of production, the personal distribution of incomes is governed solely by the earnings, or prices, of those factors. We shall turn now to what determines these earnings.

We shall assume, to begin with, conditions of perfect competition. We shall also assume conditions of full employment – meaning by this that the economic system is functioning so as to allow each factor as much employment as its owner wishes at the current rate of remuneration. By making these assumptions, and setting aside the influence of monopoly and unemployment, we are able to concentrate on a single issue: what are the tendencies of competition?

The price of any factor of production, like the price of a commodity, is governed by supply and demand. The scarcer the factor, the greater the demand for its services, the higher will be its earnings. The more abundant the factor, and the less urgently it is required, the lower will be its earnings. But this does not take us very far. What is it that governs supply and demand?

Supply

In early theories of value no importance was attached to demand. The only lasting influence on price was that of supply – in other words, of cost of production. This was true not only of commodites but also of factors of production; and just as an exception was made in favour of 'rare statues and pictures, scarce books and coins', where competition was powerless to increase the supply, so also an exception was made in favour of land, where again the supply could not be increased. The price of old masters depended solely on the demand: so also did the rent of land. But interest and profit, and above all wages, were governed by supply. The Subsistence Theory of Wages, for example – the so-called 'Iron Law of Wages' – was simply a statement that the price of labour tended to be just sufficient to cover the cost of production of the labourer. Wages, it was thought, must oscillate round a level that was just high enough to afford the wage-earner a bare subsistence. Higher earnings would induce workers to have larger families, the labour market would become overstocked, and wages would be forced down again. Similarly, if wages fell below the level of subsistence, workers would die off and the birth-rate would fall until the ensuing shortage of labour raised wages again.

This gloomy theory rested largely on the work of Malthus who argued that the human race had the power – and the propensity – to multiply its numbers more rapidly than the means of subsistence, that population was in fact increasing, and that this increase would inevitably lead to pressure on the means of subsistence resulting a high death-rate through famine, war and disease, unless mankind curbed its unruly instincts in later and less fertile marriages. Experience of the nineteenth century proved that Malthus's fears, although not altogether groundless, were exaggerated. The population of England and Wales, it is true, increased fourfold. But wages too increased fourfold; and instead of a rise in the birth-rate to match the increasing prosperity of the working class, the birth-rate began to fall and kept on falling. Far from high wages increasing the 'supply' of wage-earners, the reverse appeared to be true; the birth-rate was lowest in countries where wages were highest.

The fact is that, although the growth of population does depend upon the level of wages, the connection is by no means a straightforward one, and there are many other influences quite unconnected with wages. We may study these influence and try to forecast the future of population, and may study also how changes in population will react on wages. But this is a very different thing from laying it down that whatever happens to population, wages will tend to sink to the level of subsistence and that the demand for labour can, therefore, be neglected. A cost theory of wages along these lines must be ruled out.

Real costs: efforts and sacrifices

Wages are not related very closely – at any rate in an industrialized community – to the cost of 'producing' labourers (i.e., of rearing childen). But what of the cost of inducing labourers to work, putting up with hardship and discomfort for long hours with short holidays? Can we not say that each hour of work costs the worker something in the effort which he expends and the sacrifices which he undergoes? For those efforts and sacrifices wages are presumably intended to compensate, and high wages, therefore – whatever their effects on population – may be expected to call forth a greater supply of work by disposing the worker to make greater efforts and greater sacrifices. We decide how much work we are willing to do by weighing the wage offered against the subjective 'cost' of working; the wages must be high enough to overcome our disinclination to undertake disagreeable tasks. Indeed, we can go further. Provided we are free to choose which tasks we will do, the wage must be high enough to compensate us for the *most disagreeable* tasks. We balance the additional earnings which we can make against the additional hardship of working for one more hour, or at higher speed, or in less pleasant surroundings. It is the *marginal* disutility of work – the disagreeableness of those tasks which we are most tempted to decline – that governs the supply of labour.

This view of costs has two important disadvantages. In the first place, it suggests that a rise in wages will call forth greater effort from wage earners. But it often happens that a rise in wages, by making it easier for workers to reach their customary standard of living, induces them to work less energetically, or take longer holidays, or absent themselves more frequently from work. It is well known, also, that in times of trade depression when wages are falling, workers often respond by increasing their output, partly for fear of losing their jobs but partly also in an effort to maintain their old level of earnings. The more firmly workers cling to some fixed standard of living, the more likely it is that the supply of labour will move in the opposite direction to wages.

Secondly, the linking of wages with real costs suggests that wages are somehow *proportional* to real costs. But it would be ludicrous to suggest that the duties of a surgeon are four times as disagreeable as those of a coal-miner or blast-furnaceman, or that his income if four times greater than theirs because of the greater efforts and sacrifices which his training required. Earnings may be related, but are certainly not proportioned, to efforts and sacrifices. This is particularly obvious if we look at the earnings of the other two factors of production. The provision of land involves no sacrifice because the land already exists and cannot go out of existence. The provision of capital does involve a sacrifice since we can add to the stock only by saving, and saving means denying ourselves present enjoyments. The interest which we earn on our savings can be regarded as compensation for our self-denial. But no one would suggest that this self-denial is as great for the millionaire as for the wage-earner, although both are paid the same rate of interest. The stock of capital accumulated by past generations requires no fresh sacrifice, although it continues to earn interest. Clearly, then, the payments which are made to the factors of production bear little relation to the sacrifices by which they are earned.

Supply price: costs as relinquished alternatives

Payments to the factors of production are made, not in compensation for sacrifices, but as inducements to effort. These payments – the prices of the factors – must be high enough to provide an adequate incentive to the owners of the factors to continue to supply them. Each factor must earn its 'supply price' – the minimum price, expectation of which will just suffice to call forth the required amount of the factor – or its services will not be made available. This supply price will depend upon the pull of the alternatives open to the factor. If an hour of leisure is very attractive in comparison with an hour of work, then the supply price of labour will be correspondingly high. If we are little troubled by thoughts of a rainy day in the distant future, and weak against the fascinations of present enjoyments, then it will require a very high rate of interest to turn the scale in favour of thrift. Our time can be spent in work or in leisure, and our money can be spent or saved. The greater our preference for work, the lower will be the supply price of labour. The greater our preference for thrift, the lower will be the supply price of capital. The strength of our preference will make itself felt at the margin. The choice before us is one of a little more work or a little less, a little more spending or a little less. Thus it will be our marginal preference for work, as compared with leisure, which governs the supply of labour (in the sense of actual effort), and it will be our marginal preference for thrift which governs the supply of capital (in the sense of current savings).

The rate of wages and the rate of interest must be at least equal to the supply price of labour and of capital, and these supply prices are governed by our marginal preference for work and for thrift. In other words, the rates of wages and of interest measure the attractiveness at the margin of the alternatives which we relinquish by working or by saving. The value of these alternatives is the true cost of working and saving.

Supply price and transfer cost

This concept of cost, the cost of relinquished alternatives, is one which we have already met (see pp. 190–191). We saw how the cost of producing any commodity is equal to the value *for other purposes* of the factors engaged in producing it – what we called their transfer cost. Now 'transfer cost' is just another name for 'supply price'. But whereas in the present chapter we have been discussing the supply price of labour and capital *for any purpose*, what we discussed previously was the supply price of labour and capital to some *particular industry*. There is a distinction between the question what determines the total amount of labour and capital seeking employment? and the question what determines how a given amount of labour and capital will be distributed between competing industries?

This distinction is of great importance when we come to consider the third factor of production – land. The supply price of land in general is zero. There is no alternative to using land except not using it, and since there is nothing to be gained by not using it, its supply price is zero. The entire earnings of land, in the economic sense, therefore, form a surplus above its supply-price and it is by analogy with land that any excess of earnings over transfer cost or supply price is called 'rent'. On the other hand, the supply price of land to any one branch of agriculture is by no means zero. If, for example, land can be used either for wheat growing or for barley growing, then the supply price of the land to either industry will be its value under the other crop. The cost of using the land for wheat growing, therefore, is quite different from the simple cost of using the land; the alternative to be overcome is the comparatively attractive one of using the land for barley growing, not the quite unattractive one of letting the land go out to cultivation.

Rent and cost: an illustration

To illustrate this point in more detail it is necessary to elaborate the theory of economic rent. Economic rent is the payment made by a tenant for the use of land alone. The rent paid by a British farmer (contract rent) is generally greater than economic rent since it includes a payment for the use of buildings and fences and for other improvements such as clearing and ditching.

In general, economic rent 'does not and cannot enter in the least degree'[1] into price, but is itself governed by price. Yet this is true if and only if we are thinking of land in general. If it were possible to use land for a single purpose only, say for wheat growing, then the rent of land would have no influence upon the price of wheat. The supply price of land would be zero – that is, there would be no level of rent below which land would cease to be available for wheat growing. Rent, therefore, would be a surplus governed by the demand for wheat and the cost of cultivation. If the price of wheat were high it would not be because high rents had to be paid. The reverse would be true; it would be because the price of wheat was high that high rents could be paid.

The same conclusion holds for urban rents. Goods in Bond Street are dear not because the shops there pay high rents, but because customers are willing to pay high prices. These high prices increase the demand for shop sites in Bond Street, and so enable rents to be paid. Bond Street rents, in other words, reflect the differential advantages of sites in the centre of London over sites on the outskirts.

Suppose, however, that there are other crops than wheat and that Bond Street shops do not sell goods of the same kind. Then the supply price of land *for any one purpose* ceases to be zero. Land can be rented for wheat growing only if its use is denied to other crops, and the rent which it might yield under the most profitable of these other crops – the transfer cost of land – does enter into the cost and into the price of wheat. If this cost is not met, the land will cease to be available for wheat growing and will cross the margin of transference into the next most profitable use. Land on the margin of cultivation pays no rent; land on the margin of transference does pay rent. This rent enters into the cost of *particular* agricultural products because it enters into the cost of marginal producers; it is not a surplus over the cost of cultivation, but is itself part of the cost of cultivation, governing, not governed by, price.

The general level of rents, therefore, is governed by the demand for agricultural products as a whole and by the cost of cultivation at the margin; from the point of view of land in general, economic rent is a surplus, not a cost. The rent of a particular piece of ground depends, first upon the general level of rents, and secondly upon its differential advantages of fertility, situation, climate and so on, over other pieces of land; from the point of view of a single branch of agriculture, all or part of this rent is a cost, not a surplus.

[1] David Ricardo, *Principles of Political Economy* (Everyman Edition), pp. 40–41.

Demand

Given the supply of any factor of production, its earnings depend upon the demand for its services. Here the governing influence is productivity – the more productive a factor is, the greater will be the demand for it, and the higher it will be paid. The value of a factor to a profit-maximizing employer depends on what he expects it to add to his profits. Since in perfect competition the firm is a price-taker, this varies only with what he expects it to add to his output level. The effect on output of an additional unit of employment is known as the *marginal productivity* (or product) of labour.

Marginal productivity

As we are continuing to assume perfect competition, then, the earnings of any factor of production tend to be equal to the value of the marginal product of the factor. This may be thought of as the value of the contribution to output made by that unit of the factor which is engaged in the least productive task.

Suppose, for example, that a farmer is hiring workers all of whom are of equal efficiency and all of whom, as competition is perfect, will have to be paid the same wage. It may be worth £80 a week to the farmer to have the services of one ploughman, £70 a week to have the services of a second, and £60 a week to have the services of a third. The second ploughman will not be so indispensable as the first: if, for example, the farmer has no difficulty in laying down part of his land to grass but wishes to keep some minimum area under the plough; or if there are enough odd jobs about the farm to keep one ploughman busy in slack times but hardly enough for two. Similarly, the work done by the third ploughman will be less vital to the farm as an enterprise than the work of the second ploughman. There may also be other workers on the farm – cattlemen, shepherds, etc. – who are entrusted with tasks of varying productivity but who are all on the same level of efficiency. If the wage at which agricultural workers can be hired is fixed, the farmer will add to the number of men whom he is employing until the addition to the produce of the farm made by the last or marginal man just balances his wages. To employ more men would mean a needless sacrifice of profit; to employ fewer would be to miss an opportunity of a further small profit. Thus the marginal man will earn a wage equal to the value of the tasks which he performs, and other workers, being of the same efficiency as the marginal worker, will be paid the same wage whatever the value of the tasks on which they are engaged. If the workers are all interchangeable so that the farmer is quite indifferent which of them he employs, he will have no reason to pay a high wage to one man and a lower wage to another. He will pay all alike the value of the marginal product of agricultural labour.

What is true of one farm will be true of all. Each farmer will take on more men up to the point at which the marginal product of labour is equal to the wage that has to be paid. If, when all farmers are trying to do this, there is a shortage of labour, then farmers on whose land the marginal product of labour is above its wage will require to bid away workers from farms on which these workers are not being employed to the best advantage. This will force up wages; a variety of tasks which were previously undertaken by labour will cease to be worth while; the demand for labour will be reduced; and equilibrium between demand and supply will be restored at a higher level of wages and marginal productivity. On the other hand, if wages are so high that farmers do not find it profitable to employ all the workers who are looking for jobs in agriculture, it will be necessary for wages to fall, so extending the field of employment to include tasks which were previously sub-marginal, before the unemployed workers can find jobs.

The state of profits on any single farm will not, so long as labour can move freely from one farm to another, affect the terms on which that particular farm can hire its labour. This line of reasoning can, moreover, readily be extended to cover the whole of industry. If there is free movement of labour between industries – and this is far less likely than free movement between firms – then the wages paid to labour of a given grade of skill and efficiency will be the same in each industry. The state of prosperity of an industry will not affect the terms on which it hires its workers. Those terms will be governed by the marginal productivity of labour in a representative industry which is sensitive to the dominant trends in employment, expanding or contracting as the general level of employment expands or contracts.

The profit-maximizing, perfectly competitive firm will always set the level of employment where the marginal product of labour just balances the wage rate. Labour's marginal product is assumed to decline as more of it is employed. So, for the firm, marginal productivity explains the level of employment, not the wage rate, because the wage rate is taken as given. So what *does* determine the wage rate? And why have we been assuming that labour's marginal productivity declines as more labour is employed?

The wage rate, marginal productivity and substitution

The wage rate is the price of labour. The prices of goods are determined by the demand and supply. So, too, the price of labour. *Figure 18.1* presents a drastically simplified picture of the influences acting on the wage rate.

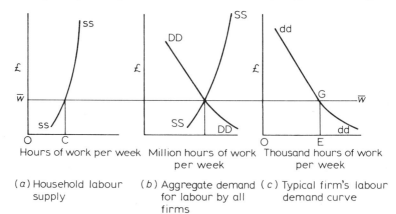

(a) Household labour supply

(b) Aggregate demand for labour by all firms

(c) Typical firm's labour demand curve

Figure 18.1 The determination of wage rates and employment

Panel (b) shows an aggregate supply curve of labour, SS. SS is derived by adding horizontally the labour supply curves of all households. SS is drawn highly inelastic. The typical household's labour supply curve is drawn in panel (a). For simplicity, labour is assumed to be of uniform quality, and there is just one commodity produced – call it corn – the price of which is conveniently £1. The curve DD in panel (b) depicts the aggregate demand for labour by all firms. DD is arrived at by summing horizontally the demand for labour by each firm. The typical firm's labour demand curve is shown in panel (c), as curve dd. dd shows the marginal product of labour. With the wage rate £w̄, our typical (perfectly competitive, profit maximiz-ing) firm chooses point G, where OE thousand hours are hired each week. The typical household chooses to work OC hours at this wage rate. As a whole, *Figure 18.1* shows individual consumers and producers choosing the *quantities* of labour offered and employment, while in aggregate they determine the 'equilibrium' price, £w̄. At any lower wage rate, there would be excess demand for labour, and upward pressure upon it; at any higher wage rate, there would be excess supply, or unemployment, in response to which one might expect wage rates to edge (perhaps very slowly) down-wards.

The curves ss (and SS) are based on the indifference curves, and hence preferences, of the households. The curve dd is also based on preference: the employer's assumedly unqualified preference for profits. Labour can increase profits only if it adds more to revenue than costs; and this ceases to be true to the right of point G. But dd also depends on other considerations. It would be raised (more northeastwards) if the firm had more of other factors (capital, or land, for instance) with which to work; or if the price of corn, which we have held at £1, were increased. Each of these changes would result, eventually, in a higher wage rate. The opposite would happen if population grew, or households preferred to work longer hours: by moving SS rightwards, these changes would bid down the wage rate *per hour*. Yet the question when dd slopes downward remains to be answered for a downward slope describes a diminishing marginal product of labour. The reason for the downward slope lies with the law of diminishing returns. We saw in Chapter 15[1] how successive additions of one (variable) factor to a given amount of other (fixed) factors would, sooner or later, lead to successively *smaller* additions to output. This is exactly what is shown in *Figure 18.1*, as the additions to output in this context are simply the marginal product of labour. The problem with increasing labour inputs alone is that labour is an imperfect substitute for the other factors that remain fixed. How quickly the marginal product declines depends on how imperfect a substitute labour is. If an industry can really operate only within a narrow range of ratios of labour to capital employed, for example, capital and labour are said to be complements; this industry is inflexible in its demand for factors; the marginal product of a variable factor declines steeply; there is a low 'elasticity of substitution' (between 0 and 1)[2]. If, however, capital and labour are substitutes (but less

[1] See above, pp. 192–195.

[2] The elasticity of substitution measures the degree of flexibility: it equals the proportionate change in the ratio of two factors employed, divided by the proportionate change in the ratio of their prices.

than perfect substitutes), the industry is flexible, diminishing returns set in
only gradually, and the elasticity of substitution is high (greater than one).

We must recall that *Figure 18.1* and the analysis behind it, only starts to
scrape the surface. We have assumed that labour is the only variable
factor, that there is only one type of good produced (corn), that labour is
uniform in quality, and that competition is perfect. In the sections that
follow, these unrealistic assumptions are removed. We should also note in
passing that households usually have little freedom in choosing hours of
work: the horizontal line in panel (a) of *Figure 18.1* is really a point, at 40
hours or so, for many workers. Income taxes, which means that the firm
pays a higher wage rate than the household receives, have also been
ignored.

Substitution with two variable factors and many goods

Suppose a profit-maximizing, perfectly competitive firm has £1000 each
week to pay for hiring labour and machinery. How does it decide how
much of *each* factor to employ? The marginal product of labour needs to be
equated with the wage rate; and the marginal product of capital with the
rental on machinery. So the ratio of the marginal product of labour, to that
of capital, needs to be equal to the wage-rental ratio. It is this equality
which is shown at point C in *Figure 18.2*. Let us imagine that labour costs
£4 per hour to employ, and capital is rented at £10 per hour. The firm has a
budget restraint, given by the line AB. If only capital were rented, £1000
would pay for 100 machines; if only labour were rented, it would yield 250
units.

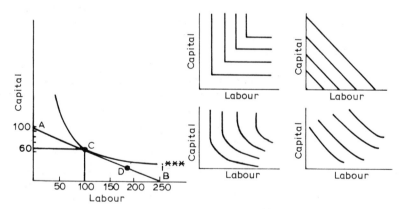

Figure 18.2 Prices and quantities of factors

The curves in *Figure 18.2* are known as *isoquants*. Each isoquant links all
combinations of the factors of production that yield a particular output
level. Isoquants are typically downward sloping and convex to the origin.
Profit-maximization calls for maximizing the revenue that can be earned
from the outlay (in our case, £1000). In perfect competition, maximizing
revenue means maximizing output. This is done at C, where the highest-
value isoquant, i***, just touches the budget restraint. So 60 machines and

100 units of labour will be hired; the wage bill will be £400, or two-fifths of total costs. The firm will not select another combination of inputs, for instance that shown by D, since that would entail lower output, lower revenue, and therefore (for given outlay), lower profits. The little panels to the right in *Figure 18.2* show various sorts of isoquant maps. If the factors of production are perfect complements, the isoquants are L-shaped; there is no flexibility whatsoever in the ratio with which capital and labour cooperate. In this case, the marginal products of the factors are not separately identifiable, and our theory breaks down[1]. If the factors are perfect substitutes, the isoquants are straight lines. Between these limiting cases, isoquants resemble the type of curves drawn in the other two panels.

Figure 18.2 can be stood on its head. Suppose, now, that a society is equipped with 100 units of labour, and 60 of machinery; there is still only one good produced; and if perfect competition prevails, point C will show the society's endowment of the two factors. Output will be maximized on isoquant i***. The gradient of the tangent to i*** at C – the gradient of the line AB – will tell us the *ratio* of the wage rate to the machinery rental that should prevail in equilibrium. That ratio is $\frac{2}{5}$. A rise in the ratio of machinery to labour, say from $\frac{60}{100} = \frac{3}{5}$ to 2, would tend to raise the wage-rental ratio. With labour scarcer and machinery more plentiful, the price of labour will tend to rise, while machinery rentals will tend to drop.

Now let us expand the number of goods produced, from one to many; and suppose that industries differ in their ratios of capital to labour. Some are capital-intensive, or relatively so; others (more) labour-intensive. If demand switches from a labour-intensive good to a capital-intensive one, there tends to be a lowering in the wage rate. As capital is now scarcer, machinery rentals are bid up. The change in consumers' preferences acts to damage the interest of labour, except in so far as labour is needed to construct new machinery; and when the new capital is installed, it will tend to bid wage rates up and machinery rentals down.

Supply and demand will also shape the differences in wage rates for different categories of labour. The relative earnings of doctors, lawyers and accountants will be sensitive to the numbers that are admitted into those professions. The fees earned by opera-singers will depend on the demand for opera, and how much of this is met by television.

When there are more factors than two, an increase in the supply of one factor may be of advantage to some and of disadvantage to others. If, for example, America were to admit a large number of Chinese immigrants, the wages of waiters, tailors, dock labourers, laundry workers, etc., would probably fall, while the middle classes would find themselves better off because they would be able to buy the services of Chinese workers more cheaply without suffering any loss of income either from property or from work. The immigrants would be almost entirely rival to the first group of workers, and almost entirely complementary to the second. There might also be an intermediate group of workers, such as farmers or semi-skilled factory workers who, on balance, would neither gain nor lose appreciably.

The conclusions reached above are very far-reaching in their implications. For example it will be in the interest of any group of people that

---

[1] For the similar problem of joint cost, see p. 204.

workers in other trades should be as numerous and hard-working and efficient as possible, while other workers in their own trade, or in close competition with it, should be as few, as lazy and as inefficient as possible. The first condition will make for cheapness in what they buy and the second for dearness in what they sell. Again, it will be in the interest of the working-class that capitalists should accumulate property as rapidly as possible rather than dissipate their income in private extravagance, since as the stock of property increases the return on it will fall, the earnings of labour will rise, and the share of labour in the national income will very probably rise also[1]. On the other hand, it will be in the interest of the propertied classes if the population increases rapidly, if hours of work remain long, and if wage earners work hard and save little. It is clear that the analysis of this chapter provides a clue to many serious conflicts of interest between classes and countries.

Marginal productivity and surpluses

It might appear that if one factor of production earned no more than its value in a marginal use, other factors of production would necessarily reap a surplus income; or that, if all the factors of production earned the value of their marginal product and no more, their joint income would fall short of the value of their total product. We have already seen, however, that under perfect competition price tends to equal average cost, including normal profit; and this leaves no surplus income accruing as profit to the entrepreneur. Price is also equal to marginal cost, and the value of a marginal addition to output is equal therefore to the joint earnings of marginal units of each of the factors, combined in the optimum ratio to one another. Average cost and marginal cost are equal when average cost is horizontal, as it must be at its minimum. Here, returns to scale are constant: and when this is so, the value of output will just equal the value of rewards to all factors of production, determined competitively.

Long-run influences on earnings

In order to give concreteness to the general theory outlined above, we may try to list the various influences which, in the long run, will make for an increase in the earnings of one of the factors of production. For this purpose we may concentrate on labour. In what circumstances should we anticipate a general rise in wage earnings?

We must first clear away two possible sources of confusion. The first is between money earnings and real earnings: that is, earnings adjusted for simultaneous changes in the cost of living. What makes money earnings increase is something we shall discuss below[2]. What makes real wages increase may be – and almost certainly is – quite different: it is only too obvious that if everybody is paid a higher money wage the main effect is

---

[1] This will, however, depend on the rate of increase of population and the elasticity of substitution between property and labour.

[2] See below, pp. 250–251. We return to the subject in discussing the causes of inflation (below, pp. 313 *et seq.*).

likely to be a rise in prices that goes part or all of the way to cancelling out the extra pay. What we shall be discussing in this section is what makes *real* earnings increase.

The second possible source of confusion is between short-term and long-term changes. In the short run the level of employment and economic activity fluctuates a good deal and earnings reflect these fluctuations: for example, in the amount of overtime worked. We shall be abstracting from these short-term fluctuations and assuming what is nowadays called 'a steady pressure of demand' over the longer-run. But of course we shall not be abstracting from all the long-run changes in working hours, labour participation rates, levels of employment, and so on, that obviously do occur. On the contrary, it is on these and other long-run changes that we shall be trying to fasten our attention.

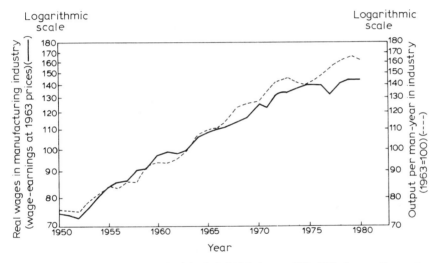

Figure 18.3 Real wages and productivity in British industry, 1950–1979. Source: *Economic Trends Annual Supplement*

Anyone who has ever looked at a graph of real wages covering a period of years is aware that real wages move in close agreement with the growth of labour productivity over time: that is, the dominant influence on the behaviour of real wages is usually productivity (see *Figure 18.3*). Anything said below has to be read in the light of that proposition. It implies that the real wage bill (real wages – in the sense of earnings – times the labour force) is usually a reasonably constant proportion of total output (output per head times the number of heads). While the influence of higher productivity is plain for all to see, the influence on real wages of almost every other factor is open to dispute and subject to qualification. Not that one should draw the conclusion that it lies with wage-earners to raise real wages by increasing their productivity. For the growth of productivity from which wage-earners benefit normally depends on forces such as managerial enterprise and skill in innovation that are not under the control of wage-earners, although within their power to weaken or stifle.

We can list five influences making for a long-run increase in wage-earnings, the first three of which would appear, in the light of what has been said above, to be of less importance, historically, than the last two.

1. Labour may become scarcer. This could happen for demographic reasons, such as a fall in the birth-rate or a higher rate of emigration to other countries. Or there might be a tendency to retire earlier. On the demand side, there might be a change in consumer preferences in favour of labour-intensive and away from capital-intensive industries (for example, there might be a bigger demand for the services of barbers, typists, traffic wardens, and so on, at the expense of jobs in chemical factories, power stations, etc.). Scarcity of labour tends to restrict the range of tasks on which it pays to employ workers, eliminating tasks of lower productivity and so raising the productivity of labour at the margin. Another effect is to stimulate labour-saving inventions and this is discussed below.
2. Land and capital may become less scarce or it may become possible to make more intensive use of the existing supply (e.g., by growing two crops where one was grown before or by running two shifts instead of one). This will reduce the marginal productivity of land and capital and induce employers to compete more eagerly for the limited supply of labour. There will be a larger *number* of tasks to be performed in conjunction with the additional supply of other factors, and it will be necessary, therefore, to reserve labour for the *kind of task* in which other factors cannot readily be substituted for it. The use of labour will be limited to tasks of higher productivity than before and the marginal productivity of labour will, therefore, increase. For example, if farmers suddenly found themselves with larger areas of land to cultivate, they would probably have to take men from work on the farm which just repaid itself and set them to plough the extra land. The work of ploughing being of greater productivity than the work from which the men were taken, farmers would be able to pay higher wages, and if they wished to retain the services of their workers in face of competition from other farmers, would be *forced* to pay higher wages.
3. Workers may work harder, or faster, or for longer hours than before. The supply of *work*, although not of *labour*, will increase; the range of tasks performed by labour will be extended, and the marginal productivity of work will be reduced. Workers will be paid less per unit of effort; but, if the demand for work is elastic, the total reward for effort (the wage *bill*) will increase, and since this total has to be divided amongst a constant number of workers, wages also will increase. A greater disposition to effort will be to the advantage of the other factors of production in the same way as an increase in the number of workers. From the point of view of the other factors it makes little difference whether labour is more abundant or more hard-working; either change increases the supply of work. It is only from the point of view of labour that there is a difference. If everyone works harder, and the demand for work is elastic, each worker will be paid more: if the number of workers increases each will be paid less. Conversely, if the demand for work is inelastic and there is a shortage of labour, workers will be able to earn

higher wages by showing a greater disinclination to effort. The other
factors of production will stand to lose from such a restriction of the
supply of work just as they stand to lose by a reduction in the number of
workers.

4. Workers may become more efficient, or better trained, or more skilful.
   Since these changes increase the productivity of labour, each of them
   will, in general, lead to a rise in wages. An increase in training or in skill
   will tend to raise wages, but an increase in efficiency may conceivably
   operate to reduce wages. Faster work, as we have seen, will reduce
   wages when the demand for effort is inelastic; and an increased speed of
   working is just as likely to result from greater efficiency as from greater
   application. Some *kinds* of increase in efficiency, however, are quite
   certain to raise wages. Greater efficiency in the use of property, for
   example, will reduce the number of breakages, fires, etc., and allow the
   supply of property to increase more rapidly. Greater efficiency in the
   use of loan-capital, by directing it into industries where it is less likely to
   be wasted, will have the same effect. Unless the property which is
   'salvaged' in this way is mainly of the type which is in close competition
   with labour (e.g., machinery), labour will necessarily gain from the
   greater abundance of property.

5. The productivity of factors other than labour may increase; for example, managerial competence and drive may improve or new inventions
   may be made. How do inventions affect wages? Do they make for a
   rising standard of living for everyone, or do they lead to unemployment
   and low wages?

Invention and wages

There is a tendency to think of the typical invention as 'labour-saving', and
it is true that many inventions do economize labour more than they
economize capital or land. We have to be careful not to think exclusively in
terms of machinery and of manufacturing processes. Some of the most
important inventions have been of new materials, such as synthetic textiles
and artificial fertilizers, that save land rather than labour; or have to do
with new sources of energy, such as electricity; or with new forms of
transport, such as railways, motor cars and aircraft. Very often, too,
inventions like safety-razors and dishwashers have helped the private
consumer to save his own time rather than someone else's labour, or have
provided him with new products and new uses for his time (like television).
It is rarely easy to judge until long after an invention is made whether the
net effect will be to reduce the demand for labour *relative to other factors*.
What one can say with some confidence is that the rise in the average
worker's standard of living over the past couple of centuries owes more to
invention and advances in technology than to any other cause.

The greater the economy of labour, the stronger will be the tendency to
unemployment and lower wages. But an invention may be labour-saving
and yet increase both employment and wages. The railway engine, for
example, has probably done more to save human effort than any other
single invention. Yet nothing did more to increase the volume of employment in the mid-nineteenth century than railway-building, and nothing

contributed more to the raising of the standard of life than cheap railway transport. Similarly, although labour-saving machinery may create unemployment and low wages in the industry into which it is introduced, workers in other industries are likely to derive a more than counterbalancing advantage from the fall in costs and prices to which the invention leads. The loss of jobs, however unfortunate from the point of view of the redundant worker, is not the end of the story and is in a sense a measure of the value of the invention in making some work unnecessary. When there is labour to spare, it is the government's responsibility to see that fresh job opportunities are created if they do not arise of their own accord (as they often do) out of the invention and to offer unemployed workers help and support while they make the necessary adjustments. The ultimate contribution to society of an invention that is purely and simply labour-saving lies in the additional output that comes from the workers dispensed with after they have been successfully reabsorbed. The only conditions in which inventions or innovations could reduce the demand for labour are a serious slump where output is held down by too little aggregate demand, or when they are labour-saving and applied in an industry with a very low elasticity of substitution between labour and other factors. Although possible in the short run, these effects become steadily less likely to persist as time goes on.

By and large, labour-saving inventions have generally done much more to raise than to lower the general level of wages, both by improving the worker's standard of living and by making labour less irksome. But if they have been of advantage to labour, they have been of considerable advantage to capital, too. It should be observed, too, that labour-saving inventions are rarely of equal advantage or disadvantage to all classes of workers. An invention may, for example, be skill-saving or toil-saving. If the invention is skill-saving, and strikes at an established handicraft such as hand-loom weaving, the earnings of skilled workers as a body will tend to suffer. If, on the other hand, the invention is toil-saving, and like the mechanical navvy economizes muscular effort, then it will be the earnings of unskilled workers that tend to be reduced. In either event, since greater mechanization is involved, machine-operators are likely to benefit.

Some inventions, however, are not labour-saving, but capital-saving or land-saving. Communication by wireless, for example, requires less capital than communication by telephone or by deep sea cable. Similarly a new fertilizer which increases the fertility of the soil economizes land, while urban sites are economized by improvements in the construction of skycrapers. These inventions, while they may increase the total earnings of capital and land, just as labour-saving inventions may increase real wages, will tend to reduce the *share* of capital and land in the national income[1].

If we ask which has gained most from invention, capital or labour, it is difficult to say. On the one hand, real wages are far above the level of a century ago and continue to rise at a rate roughly equal to the annual growth in productivity; whereas the return to capital is almost certainly

---

[1] It is perhaps unnecessary to point out that just as some workers gain while others lose by an invention, so some property-owners will gain while others lose. There is an obvious loss to those whose property becomes obsolete, and an equally obvious gain to those who own the invention or who use its products.

lower in real terms, even before tax, than it used to be in the nineteenth century. This strongly suggests that labour is the main beneficiary. On the other hand, there is now a great deal more capital per head than formerly, and this might, in the absence of invention, have lowered the return to capital very substantially. One way of throwing light on this problem is to look at pre-industrial economies and compare the shares of capital and labour in total income with the shares in industrialized economies. On this basis, the answer would seem to be indisputable. The share of labour has increased since industrialization took place and modern technology was absorbed into the normal operation of the economy: the stock of capital has kept pace with the expansion in output, but the share of capital in total domestic output has fallen. There are difficulties of measurement which should warn us against overhasty conclusions. Additional capital and new technology may, for instance, be inseparable, if the new technique requires a new machine. But it certainly seems that inventions and innovations *are* in labour's interest, at least in the long run.

Monopoly

Monopolistic influences on wages

We must now remove the simplifying assumption of perfect competition that has been made throughout this chapter. For a firm in oligopoly or monopoly, an increase in employment will usually call for a cut in the price of the product, for the extra output to be sold. By contrast, this price is given in perfect competition. Again, unlike perfect competition, increased employment may well mean that the firm must bid up the wage rate, probably for new and existing employees alike. The imperfectly competitive firm will have some monopoly power in his product market, or some *monopsony* power in his labour market, or both. Each power implies lower output and lower employment than under perfect competition. In perfect competition, profit-maximization leads to equality of wage and value of labour's marginal product, as shown in *Figure 18.1*. But in imperfect competition, additional employment brings a lower product price, a higher wage rate, or both; so profit-maximization implies a marginal product of labour higher than the wage rate. If a large firm tempers its desire for profits with a concern for sales, on the other hand, employment will be higher than if profits were its only goal.

Furthermore, the overall framework of wages is fixed in most industries by a process of collective bargaining between employers' associations and trade unions; sometimes by direct negotiations, sometimes by arbitration after argument of the case by both sides before an independent chairman; sometimes by an intermediate procedure of conciliation and discussion between the parties to the dispute with an added representation of independent or semi-independent opinion.

Collective bargaining, whatever the form which it assumes, is bargaining in which monopoly power is exerted by both sides; competition continues to influence the outcome, but the full force of competition is not exerted. For the trade union, the aim of the highest possible wage rate will be moderated by fears that the employers will lose business to the producers of substitute products, or to foreign firms, if their costs of production are too high. Similarly, employers may worry about the effects on morale and recruitment, in terms of quality as much as quantity, of very low wage rates. Within these limits, there may be a wide range of indeterminacy, within which bargaining power has free play.

On the tactics of the trials of strength that occur in wage disputes something is said in the next chapter.

Summary

The argument of this chapter has been conducted at a high level of abstraction from real life. But the problem of distribution is so complex that it must be approached in stages, and the first stage is to understand the tendency of competition. Setting on one side the implications of monopoly and monopsony, we have seen that the distribution of the national income between the factors of production is governed by the relative scarcity of the factors and by their marginal productivity. The supply of labour and capital depends upon our marginal preference for work and thrift, while the supply of land is fixed by nature. The ratios in which the factors are combined are determined by employers, who give effect to the twin principles of substitution and diminishing marginal productivity, varying their demand for any one factor until its marginal productivity is equal to its price or earnings. The removal of the assumption of perfect competition introduces an element of indeterminacy. It is to this and to other aspects of the theory of wages that we now turn.

Chapter 19

Wages

Competitive influences

The theory of wages deals mainly with two questions – what determines the general level of wages and the share of labour in the national product and why do wages differ in different places and occupations? An answer to the first question has already been given in Chapter 18. There it was assumed that all wage-earners were alike in efficiency, training and skill so that no employer would offer higher wages to one worker than to another. It was assumed also that all wage-earners were alike by temperament and taste, and that they worked under similar conditions in occupations and places that were equally agreeable or disagreeable, so that no worker would demand higher wages in one job than in another. On these assumptions we found that the tendency of competition was to make the general level of wages equal to the value of the marginal product of labour.

The second question arises as soon as we drop the assumptions. Wage-earners differ in efficiency, training and skill, and these differences are reflected in differences in wages. But even amongst workers of the same general calibre there are fairly large differences in wages. Why is this? Why do workers who are free to choose their occupation and place of work continue to accept low wages when they might move to better-paid jobs? Why do different industries and districts pay different rates of wages for the same grade of work? It is answers to these questions which provide us with explanations for much of the inequality in the *personal* distribution of incomes.

'Horizontal' differences in wages

We may begin with differences that arise when workers are alike in skill, training and efficiency, taking a kind of horizontal cross-section of labour. One source of such differences is that wage rates are generally expressed in terms of the full-time weekly rate of wages – sometimes called 'nominal wages'. But the nominal wages payable in any occupation may be greater or less than the average income which workers in that occupation can normally expect to earn. The cash wage may be supplemented by an allowance of free coal, or potatoes, or house-room, and these perquisites clearly form part of the 'real wages' payable to the worker. On the other hand, a deduction should be made from nominal wages in some occupations to cover any outlay on uniforms, overalls, travelling expenses, social display, etc., associated with the worker's duties. Nominal wages will also differ from real wages if overtime, short time or unemployment are normal features of an occupation. A bricklayer whose work is frequently interrupted by bad weather will not be so well off as a postman whose nominal wages are the same and who has the advantage of steady employment. As for unemployment, an occupation like shipbuilding which suffers from periodic slumps will require to offer fairly high nominal wages before the real wages obtainable in it over a period of years reach a moderate level. A final point of distinction is that whereas nominal wages are expressed in terms of money, real wages consist of the goods and services which this money will buy. Thus if we find a bus driver in London earning £120 a week and a bus driver in Glasgow earning only £110 a week we must not jump to the conclusion that wages are higher in London than in Glasgow, for it may cost £120 to buy in London what can be had in Glasgow for £110. Differences in nominal wage between occupations and places may be quite consistent, therefore, with equality of real wages.

Net advantages

Workers may accept comparatively low wages in one place or occupation because of some compensating advantage which they enjoy over places and occupations where wages are higher. There may be opportunities, for example, of alternative or supplementary jobs either for the worker himself or for his family. A textile worker may prefer to accept low wages in Lancashire, where all his family can find employment, rather than move to a well-paid job in Lincoln or Shrewsbury, where his family might earn little or nothing. Similarly, a married man with a young family may hesitate to give up agricultural work because of the ease with which he can find work for his children on the land. If he happens to have a great deal of spare time every winter, and can use this spare time for toy-making, his income from this supplementary work will be an added inducement to remain in agriculture. Evidence of rewards in the medical and legal professions shows that opportunities for rapid promotion and prospects of spectacular earnings will also compensate for lower initial earnings.

Compensation for a comparatively low wage may also be found in various amenities which attach to the job and enhance its attractiveness – what might be called the 'kudos other than cash' – which the worker enjoys. A man may prefer to seek employment in a poorly-paid job because the sacrifice in earnings is more than balanced by these non-pecuniary amenities. He may find the work more agreeable because it is carried on in the country, or in a well-ventilated factory, or with less danger to health. He may be attracted by the regularity and security of the job, or by the opportunities of leisure or absenteeism which it affords, or by the power and prestige attaching to it, or by the scope which it offers for the exercise of some special bent. On the other hand, he will avoid work which is exhausting (e.g., mining), or causes great discomfort (e.g., road-breaking), or endangers life (e.g., the work of the steeplejack, the sailor, etc.), or which is carried on in an unhealthy atmosphere (e.g., the roasting of copper ore, stoking, the manufacture of chemicals, etc.), or which is monotonous or excessively speeded up.

What determines the attractiveness of a trade, in other words, is not just the rate of pay, but all the characteristics of the job. Even when workers are alike in efficiency, and can move freely from one job to another, competition will not drive wages to the same level in all places and occupations. It will be the net advantages of each place and occupation that tend to equality. There are, however, a number of obstacles to the free movement of labour and hence to the equalization of net advantages. These obstacles, and the resulting immobility of labour, provide a second reason for difference in wages between places and industries.

Mobility and immobility

When an industry becomes comparatively overcrowded, it is not possible for workers to transfer themselves immediately to other industries. Movement would mean the sacrifice of an acquired technique, and a long irksome period of re-training. The older the worker, the greater the difficulty. The older men are less adaptable, and have more at stake in the revival of the industry. In it their industrial experience has taken shape, and in it they become accustomed to ways of life which they are reluctant to abandon. They are the more willing to wait in the hope of re-employment because their chances of employment in other industries are small. Employers will hesitate to start them on comparatively unfamiliar work so long as there is an over-supply of younger workers in the same district. The burden of change, therefore, falls on these younger workers. The same is true of geographical movement. If there is a depression in one part of the country, it will be particularly difficult for the older workers to move in search of employment. They are tied by family responsibilities and by old associations. They may own their house and be forced to sell it at a bargain price. On the other hand, they may have great difficulty in renting or buying a house in districts where there is no lack of work. The mere cost of transferring a family from one district to another may be enough to deter a married man from moving to a better-paid job. The young worker, with no family and no property, will move much more readily.

Thus changes in the distribution of labour between places and occupations come about more through the action of young workers in moving where prospects are good than through transfers on the part of older workers out of contracting industries and localities. Young workers are not yet in a groove. They have fewer commitments and more enterprise, and do not need to overcome the inertia of an earlier choice. The higher is the proportion of workers in the younger age groups, therefore, the greater is likely to be the mobility of labour.

Even the mobility of young workers, however, tends to be rather low. The range of occupations open to them, particularly in districts like South Wales, and towns like Bradford, is generally narrow, and the range of choice is often restricted by family circumstances. The need of working-class families for immediate income may force children into blind alley occupations. Or, by the force of example of parents and relatives, children may be induced to enter the industry with which their family is most familiar. This may, and does, happen even when the industry is in process of contraction and the older members of the family cannot find work in it. The tendency for boys to follow their fathers' footsteps is not due solely to bias towards the parental occupation, but quite as much to limited knowledge and limited contacts.

Immobility may result from the worker's disinclination to move – a disinclination originating in ignorance, uncertainty, poverty, family ties, or sheer inertia. But there are other, external, reasons for immobility; there may be impediments to the free movement of labour. A man cannot leave one country and enter another whenever he hears that wages are higher abroad; there are laws restricting immigration. Even within a country his movements may be restricted – an agricultural worker may require permission to take a job in industry, a teacher born in one county may be debarred from employment in other counties, or there may be discrimination by race, language or religion, limiting certain occupations to members of a single group. When such restrictions have not the force of law, prejudice, bias and custom may give rise to a boycott which is no less effective in limiting the field of employment. There are many occupations, for example, from which women have never been excluded by law, but in which, until recently, they rarely if ever found employment. This has partly been due to the pressure of trade unions and the rules of professional associations like the General Medical Council. These bodies, in an effort to increase their powers of monopoly, have not unnaturally sought to limit their numbers by erecting barriers against entry into their occupation or profession. Women – amongst others – have suffered since they have been forced to squeeze into occupations where entry is freer and which, as a result, are comparatively overcrowded. One reason, therefore, why women's earnings are lower than men's is just that they are not allowed to participate in the monopoly gains of 'protected' industries, but instead they have to crowd into the limited range of occupations which men have thought fit to surrender to them.

In some industries, all employees performing certain tasks must belong to a specified trade union. This is called a 'closed shop'. The closed shop may protect or improve its members' rates of pay, and their prospects of employment. But it will be detrimental to the job prospects of workers made redundant in other industries, if the trade union refuses to grant them membership.

In the world of the future a high degree of labour mobility will be more than ever essential, partly to secure speed of adjustment to violent changes in technique and in the direction of trade, and partly because there will be in the labour market a higher proportion of older and less mobile workers. The more we can increase mobility, therefore, the better.

The methods by which this can be done are well known. They include the provision of fuller and more accurate information to workers in search of alternative employment, grants towards the cost of movement and measures to improve or supplement training and educational facilities. A vocational advisory service, working in conjunction with the schools and the Jobcentres, can help juvenile workers to choose from a wider variety of careers. The Jobcentres may also assist industrial mobility by giving more prominence or preferential treatment to vacancies in industries where there is a general shortage of labour. The government has power to make payments of grants and allowances to meet the cost of removal from one district to another or of living away from home pending removal. It also runs a number of Training Centres which can concentrate their efforts on overcoming shortages of labour in particular trades or on helping unemployed or disabled workers to re-train for a new occupation.

High mobility and high employment go together. If there are plenty of jobs, people will change more readily from one job to another or from one district to another. But it is a thankless task trying to increase mobility when there are no jobs to be had: men generally prefer to be unemployed where they are rather than volunteer for re-training or transfer without the certainty of getting and keeping a new job.

'Vertical' differences in wages

So far, we have taken a kind of horizontal cross-section of labour and confined the discussion to workers of equal efficiency, training and skill. But when we think of differences in earnings we generally have in mind inequalities whose origin lies in 'vertical' rather than in 'horizontal' differences between workers. We think of lawyers and film-stars and company directors and compare their earnings with those of clerks and charwomen and navvies. We reflect that, far from these differences in earnings being compensated by differences in amenities, it seems to be the best-paid jobs that require least effort and afford most leisure. We may even ask ourselves why, if the jobs at the top are so attractive, so many people remain at the bottom. Three reasons suggest themselves – lack of ability, lack of training and lack of opportunity.

Differences between workers in natural ability are exactly like differences between pieces of land in natural fertility; just as the more fertile pieces of land command a premium over the less fertile, so the more able workers can obtain higher wages than the average. Indeed, economists often speak of a 'rent of ability' when comparing the earnings of superior talent with the earnings of mediocrity, so extending to labour the conception of rent as a differential surplus. This surplus, like land rent, is determined solely by demand. It is not enough to have rare gifts, superior to the gifts of others, in order to earn an exceptionally large income. It is necessary also to have those particular gifts which are most in demand. Few artists have ever made a fortune, or even a decent livelihood; just as few landlords have ever made money by improving the landscape. The ability of a stateman, a social reformer, or a philosopher is far more poorly rewarded – except in prestige – than the ability to cheat and dissimulate and take advantage of the ignorance of others. The most 'able' workers – like the most 'fertile' pieces of land – are those who can provide the services for which people pay, not those who, on a moral or aesthetic judgement, are most deserving of reward.

Differences in training also produce differences in earnings. If a worker has to sink capital in a long and expensive education (e.g., at a university) or in acquiring skill (e.g., in an apprenticeship), he will expect to be recompensed by appointment to a post which is either more agreeable or better paid than the posts open to him without training. A barrister, for example, has to spend many years, during which he earns little or nothing, preparing for examinations which he may never pass, and waiting for briefs which he may never be given. He has to pay stiff fees to examining bodies and to professional associations,and may also have a premium to pay on apprenticeship. Only the prospect of a high income – in cash or in amenities – will induce him to make the necessary sacrifices; he will look to be compensated, in the course of his career, for all his outlay, and for the long period of waiting and uncertainty – to say nothing of the cost of midnight oil.

So far as the cost of training is part of the supply price of labour – that is, so far as higher earnings are a necessary inducement to training – the extra earnings of trained workers will contain no element of rent corresponding to the rent of superior ability. But if at any time there is a shortage of trained workers, and apprentices cannot be trained quickly to meet the demand, the limited supply of trained workers will be able to obtain abnormally high earnings. Their earnings, in the short period during which no more workers can be trained, will be governed solely by demand and will be swollen by an element of *quasi-rent*. Quasi-rent resembles rent in that it is a surplus over cost or supply price, but differs from rent in that it disappears in the long run when supply is given time to increase[1]. Compare, for example, the earnings of a professor of mathematics and those of a bus driver. The professor can go on earning a high salary because few people are capable of expounding Einstein; but the bus driver can rarely earn much more than an unskilled worker, since there are large numbers of unskilled workers who could fairly easily learn bus driving. The high salary of the professor contains an element of rent – rent of ability. The bus driver's wage, on the other hand, could include quasi-rent only if it has risen because of a shortage of drivers. In the end this quasi-rent will vanish as more drivers are trained.

Inequality of earnings is also due to inequality of opportunity. Workers are not equally lucky in meeting with opportunities of earning higher wages. In particular, they are not equally lucky in their choice of parents. Some people are given a better start in life than others because of the superiority of their parents in character, or in education, or in wealth. The children of rich parents, for example, enjoy a more expensive education and a wider cultural background, have more freedom in their choice of occupation and better guidance in choosing it, and have more opportunity of making valuable social contacts. Thus they start with a fairly large advantage in income-earning power, and are generally able, given moderate ability, to keep ahead in the high-income group. Social mobility, therefore, is generally low. A worker tends to stay in the class into which he was born.

Just as there are often impediments to movement between places and occupations, so there are often impediments to movement between social classes. Under the caste system, for example, social mobility is nil. In countries inhabited by different races the dominant race often monopolizes positions of responsibility so that members of the subject-race cannot climb

---

[1] This use of the term 'quasi-rent' is to be carefully distinguished from its use in the following chapter to mean 'the earnings of an instrument of production'. On this second definition, the rent of a house is a quasi-rent.

to a higher status. The effect of these restrictions is to shelter a privileged class of persons from competition and to swell their incomes with a surplus or rent, akin to the surplus profits of a monopolistic producer. A somewhat similar surplus emerges when social mobility is limited by inequality of opportunity rather than of privilege. The differential advantages of birth in a rich family are as substantial, if not as secure, as the differential advantages of birth in a superior caste. Advantages of either kind are the product of institutions devised by man – the institution of inheritance or of the caste system – and the surplus income or rent corresponding to these advantages is called, therefore, 'institutional rent'. Since human institutions can be modified by appropriate legislation (e.g., by laws abolishing caste or limiting bequest) this source of inequality can be reduced at will (i.e., by the will of those who command political power). But it can never be entirely eliminated. It is impossible to contrive that everyone shall have exactly equal opportunities. We cannot, for example, equalize the ability of parents to bring up children, although we can see to it that the children are given more equal opportunities of education in schools and universities. We can increase social mobility, but we cannot make it perfect.

Bargaining influences

The rate of wages in any industries, then, depends upon the competitive pull which other industries are able to exert on its labour, upon the cost of moving to the most attractive alternative industry, and upon the strength of the workers' disinclination to move – that is, it depends upon the supply price of labour to the industry. It goes without saying that the rate of wages depends also upon the demand price of employers[1].

The rate of wages in an industry depends also upon a third factor – the strength of the organizations of workers and employers. In the trials of strength to determine where, within the limits of indeterminacy, wage rates are to be fixed, it is open to employers' association to threaten to lock out their workers and to trade unions to retaliate by the threat of a strike.

The tactical advantages of the two sides depend greatly on the state of trade. If there is severe unemployment a trade union will be in a relatively weak position: it may be in low water financially through having to pay benefit to its members; it may have less command over the loyalty of the workers, whether members or non-members, since they will be more afraid of losing their jobs; and if it adopts a truculent and uncompromising attitude, it may force some firms to close down that might otherwise keep going. On the other hand, with full employment there is a seller's market for labour and employers will be far more willing to make concessions in order to maintain their output and so profit from favourable market conditions. The trade unions will frequently wait before submitting wage demands until unemployment has fallen to a relatively low level, when expanding economic activity is beginning to be accompanied by rising costs. They will try by their intervention to cut down the lag that often occurs in such circumstances between the rise in costs and prices and the rise in money wages.

[1] The demand price of labour is the highest price an employer would willingly pay to hire it.

In bargaining over wages and conditions, the employers can enjoy certain definite advantages. Unless they face strong concerted union action, it will be easier for them to frame a common policy. They often have greater financial reserves with which to withstand a work stoppage, than the workers or their unions. An interruption to production need not be so damaging during a slump, especially in a labour intensive industry with surplus stocks.

Circumstances in which the employers' relative bargaining position will be weak are, above all, in full employment (when workers will be readiest to quit and hardest to replace); if the demand for the product is urgent as with newspapers; if the industry is capital-intensive, and has much to lose by a stoppage; and when the unions' strike pay, or national provision of unemployment benefits, is generous.

The economy of high wages

There are also economic factors disposing employers to pay higher rates of wages than they need. The economic interest of the employer is not in low wages but in low *wage costs*. He pays a certain rate of money wages and receives in exchange the services of his workers. The more favourable the terms upon which he can hire these services, the greater will be his profits. This does not mean, however, that it will pay him to offer low rates of wages; low-paid labour is often the dearest labour.

First of all, low wages mean a low standard of living, and this in turn means a low standard of efficiency. Workers who are not properly fed and housed, or who are left with little leisure, are unlikely to reach the outputs of more highly paid labour. They cannot stand up to the strain of modern industry so readily, or show the same initiative, or undertake as responsible work. When we find that workers in India and China are paid much less than British workers, therefore, we must not jump to the conclusion that wage costs are correspondingly low, and that competition with such countries is impossible. The fact that India is still one of Britain's biggest markets suggests that low wages have their disadvantages. On the other hand, we must not jump to the topsy-turvy conclusion that India would compete more successfully if employers there were to grant immediate increases in wages. Workers do not begin to work harder whenever their wages go up. Their first reaction is often to relax and either work *less* hard, so as to keep their earnings at much the same level as before, or spend less carefully, using the rise in their pay haphazardly and without advantage to their efficiency. It is some time before higher wages seep through to raise the level of efficiency, and since employers can rarely afford to take the long view – they may lose their workers at any time to their competitors – they are unlikely to pay high wages with an eye solely to their workers' standard of living. Particularly if this standard is already high, any gain in efficiency will appear small and speculative while the cost of a rise in wages will be large and certain.

There are, however, two further motives which are likely to be stronger in their appeal to the self-interest of the employer. The first is that by paying high wages it may be possible to 'cream' the labour market – that is, to attract workers of more than average efficiency. The second is that high wages may purchase the goodwill of a firm's employees, and create an atmosphere in which they are not deterred by suspicion and discontent from working wholeheartedly on behalf of the firm. Both of these motives, it will be observed, may induce a firm to keep wages high in relation to its immediate competitors in the district from which its labour is drawn; neither motive is sufficient to ensure that wages will be high *throughout* an industry or district.

Trade unions

The self-interest of employers is hardly the best guarantee of high wages. In order to secure improvements in their standard of living and conditions of employment, workers generally prefer to rely on their own organizations. The chief aim of these is to press for higher wages, shorter hours, and better working conditions.

This does not prevent the trade unions from exercising great political power. They have a profound influence on the thinking of both of the major political parties; their views largely inspire the programme of the Labour Party; many of their officials and members are Members of Parliament. Trade unions should also be seen increasingly as a counter-weight to government in its role as paymaster. Trade union membership in the UK is now far more strongly concentrated among employees of central and local government and the nationalized industries (over ¾, if defence and police forces are excluded) than in the private sector (less than ¼).

One of the prime objects of trade unions has always been to give the worker a sense of status – the feeling that he is one of a body of workers organized to protect their rights and interests, not alone and defenceless against the whims of employers. Again, trade unions, by employing skilled negotiators, can put the workers' case with more finesse, confidence and knowledge and can take his part in the hundred and one day-to-day grievances on things not covered by any formal contract. This is not without its advantages to the employer also, for it creates a regular channel through which grumbles can reach him, and allows him to enter into agreements which are binding on all his workers.

From the point of view of the community, too, trade unions serve a useful purpose in preventing employers from resorting in bad times to the attractive device of cutting wages as a means of cutting costs; and in bringing pressure on employers to examine carefully fresh methods of economizing labour. But the pressure of trade unions does not always make for increased efficiency. In the first place, when unions are organized on a craft (or occupational) rather than on an industrial basis, they are apt to have narrow demarcation rules and insist that given jobs should be done by members of their craft even when they involve little skill and could be done with much more convenience by other people. The cumulative effect of these rules in holding up urgent work and in perpetuating obsolete industrial practices is to cause a great deal of waste of time and labour contrary to the social interest, although very much to the monopoly advantage of the union. Rules limiting the number of learners and apprentices to be employed with each journeyman, or the number of women to each man, may have a similar effect. These rules are often no more than a safeguard against attempts by employers to get work done cheaply by learners who are not given an adequate training, and for whom no provision is made by the employer at the end of their time. But the tendency of such rules is plainly monopolistic and they are frequently pushed beyond the point at which they are in the social interest. Finally, if trade unions stick out for high wages over the whole field of industry, they may restrict the volume of employment exactly as a monopolist restricts his output of goods, and may achieve a high standard of living for those who continue in employment, quite as much at the expense of those who fail to get employment as at the expense of employers as a class.

Limits to the bargaining power of trade unions

Fear of creating general unemployment will not deter a particular trade union from pressing for higher wages. Trade unions in expanding industries will not regard it as part of their duty to keep wages low so as to ensure the rapid absorption of unemployed labour from less fortunate industries. Nor will a trade union necessarily be deterred if, by raising wages, it also raises prices and helps inflation along. Unemployment and inflation may influence the trade unions as a body, and each of the unions may abide loyally by decisions taken jointly through the Trades Union Congress not to press wage claims at certain times. Such decisions apart, trade unions will be guided mainly by the tactical position at the moment within the industry or industries which they cover and will, as a rule, give weight to the groans or expostulations of the public only in so far as they tend to weaken that position.

There are three major limitations on the power of trade unions to secure a lasting increase in wages in a single industry:

(a) Elasticity of substitution

The more readily employers can economize labour by using alternative methods of production, the more effective will be their resistance to claims for wage advances. The simplest expedient is to install more machinery; employers may re-vamp the layout of their plant so as to replace old-fashioned machines by more modern labour-saving types, or they may be induced, even in up-to-date plants, to turn over to more highly mechanized processes which were just not worth while when labour was cheaper. Either way, capital will be substituted for labour by a change in the proportion in which the two are used. The rate at which substitution proceeds – the rate at which the proportion of the two factors changes as their relative price changes – is called the elasticity of substitution; and the elasticity of substitution is the first damper on wages.

Substitution is not confined to the replacement of labour by capital; replacement of labour by labour, directly or indirectly, is quite as effective. If stonemasons extort a thumping increase in wages, for example, and bricklayers and carpenters are paid at the same rates as before, builders will tend to put up more houses of brick or wood and fewer houses of stone.

(b) Elasticity of supply of alternative factors

How far substitution can be pushed depends not only upon the ease with which technical changes can be made, but also upon the ease with which additional supplies of the substitute can be procured. In a boom or in war-time, manufacturers of machinery may be booked up for months ahead and practically all workers absorbed into employment. These are obviously favourable times for seeking wage advances. On the other hand, substitutes are in highly elastic supply during a depression and the bargaining power of trade unions is then at its lowest.

(c) Elasticity of demand

Consumers as well as producers can indulge in substitution, and the measure of their ability to find substitutes is the elasticity of demand for the product of the industry. Where demand is elastic, employers have difficulty in passing on an increase in wage costs to consumers and they tend, therefore, to offer more resistance to demands for high wages. A case in point is provided by the export industries which supply a fiercely competitive market and in which, between the two wars, even the strongest unions were hard put to maintain wages while the trend of wages in other industries was upwards.

These limitations of the bargaining power of trade unions are, in effect, limitations on the demand price for labour and are tantamount, therefore, to a threat of unemployment in the particular industry if wages are pushed too high. Apart from this ultimate sanction, there is generally a good deal of 'play' in wage rates depending on the current fortunes of the industry. If, for example, profits are high, and employers enjoy monopolistic or semi-monopolistic advantages, labour may be able to obtain a share in the swag and secure rates of pay which are well above the general run of wages in other industries. The employers may even go out of their way to make concessions to their workers in order to disarm criticism of their monopoly. A different kind of blackmail may be practised by a small but truculent union in an occupation which forms an indispensable part of large enterprises (e.g., the printing of newspapers). Rather than have the whole of the work held up from time to time by demands for higher wages from a relatively insignificant number of workers, employers may seek to forestall these demands and treat the extra outlay in wages as a cost normal in their line of business.

What do wage disputes really settle?

If the workers in an industry secure an increase in their wages and do exactly the same work as before, who is it that surrenders the income that the workers gain? That someone must be worse off is plain; the national income is no greater, and one section of workers is receiving more. Who, then, is 'squeezed'?

It is common to assume that the extra wages come out of profits and that it is the employers, therefore, who are the losers, but the margin available out of profits is a narrow one. All but one-tenth or less of disposable personal income in Britain consists of income from employment[1]. In any event, if employers can pass on the extra burden of cost in the form of higher prices, they can maintain their profits and it is then the consumer, not the employer, who is 'squeezed'. Now 'the consumer', when we are dealing with any large industry, includes other groups of workers as well as those who spend out of profits or rent. The gains of one section of workers, therefore, are likely to be in part at least at the expense of other workers. If wages rise all round, the cost of living will also tend to rise, and the real income of labour may be no greater than before.

If workers were unorganized and employers organized, wage disputes associated with the formation of trade unions might increase the share of labour in the national income. But if both sides are already highly organized, the chances of labour's gaining at the expense of capital through wage disputes are far less strong, except perhaps in the middle of an inflation in which wages are lagging behind the rise in the cost of living. Wage disputes are more likely to settle the distribution of the wage bill between one section of labour and another, or between one industry and another. As a rule, an increase in wages in one industry represents a levy on other industries and on the general consumer. If consumers cannot stint their requirements of the goods made by the industry, they have to meet the whole of the increase in wages in the form of higher prices. But if demand shows any elasticity, some part of the burden will recoil on employers in reduced profits and on the workers in reduced employment.

Broadly speaking, therefore, wage disputes are disputes over *relative* rates of wages. They do not fix the return on capital. But if not, what does? To this question we turn in the next chapter.

How the labour market works

Collective bargaining and the wage movements that result from it may dominate our thinking about the labour market to the exclusion of other important elements. When an industry is expanding its labour force, it does so primarily by offering more jobs, not necessarily by offering better pay. It may be able to meet its requirements merely by reducing turnover without an appreciable increase in the rate of hire. An average of one-seventh of the labour force changes its job annually, due to redundancy or, more often, voluntary quits. Shifts in the relative size of different industries may also be influenced by a kind of hierarchy of jobs. In a nineteenth century depression, workers used to stay in agriculture or go back to the land and then move to the towns to take an industrial job as the depression lifted. This phenomenon can be seen in developing countries

---

[1] 'If in 1968 all shareholdings had been sequestrated, no relief had been given to those who had lost retirement incomes and insurance policies, and the whole sum actually paid out as dividends had been used to raise pay, the average rise in pay, once for all, would have been under 15%, no more than the amount by which real pay has been rising within each six years at the rate of rise of productivity prevailing since the war. This rise in productivity remains the only fund out of which rises in the standard of living of the working population can be drawn progressively.' (Professor E. H. Phelps Brown, 'Inflation, Collective Bargaining and Public Opinion', *The Political Quarterly*, October–December 1972, p. 453).

today. In the UK other industries may now play the role of sponge, absorbing and then releasing labour, notably the distributive trades but to some extent also the armed forces and the building industry.

An industry may meet additional labour requirements by working overtime, by cutting down wastage or by absorbing unemployed workers from other industries without having to raise wages in relation to wages elsewhere. The increase in activity will itself provide a magnet in the form of more overtime pay, better prospects of promotion, greater security for retirement, and so on. When wages are increased in an industry that is short of labour this may be in response to pressure from the trade unions in face of rising profits and full order books, not because employers have decided to offer more pay as a way of attracting additional labour. Changes do occur in the ranking of different industries in the wages they pay, but they are usually remarkably small. As a rule, they take the form of an industry sinking down the league table over a long period of time while a surplus of labour is worked off and then experiencing a sharp revaluation as it returns to a more normal place in the table.

Wage rates, whether per hour or per week, may be the key factor determining what employees actually earn and employers actually pay. But they are not the only factor. Employers' contributions to national insurance and pension schemes may add one-quarter to labour costs in Great Britain – and in the Netherlands, and Sweden, as much as 60%; then there are perquisites, such as concessionary purchases or car privileges; and income tax which means that firms must pay considerably more than labour actually receives. The full cost of labour per unit of output depends, furthermore, on the productivity of labour.

Wage rates rarely equal actual earnings, either. Actual earnings generally exceed rates. They are also more volatile; and, on average, they grow faster. Why do earnings and rates behave so differently?

First of all, there is the incompleteness of national wage agreements. In Britain these are often extremely sketchy and may specify only one or two key rates leaving the others to be settled locally or on the shop floor on the pattern of the rates agreed nationally[1]. The engineering wage agreement, for example, includes only three rates: for fitters, semi-skilled workers and labourers. Negotiations at factory level may amplify the national agreement in such a way that wages 'drift' upwards or downwards in relation to the increases already fixed centrally. One example of this lies in the regular re-negotiation of piece-work prices which may lead to a progressive rise in remuneration, first for those who are on piece-work and later for other workers who are bound to draw comparisons with their own pay and try to catch up through fresh collective agreements.

Then employers may choose to compete for labour (especially skilled labour) by regrading jobs, or increasing holidays or perquisites, in ways not reflected in wage rates. This is frequent when the government is trying to hold down pay increases by an incomes policy in conditions when the labour market is tight.

[1] Things are very different in America, where wage agreements are embodied in documents running to a hundred pages or more, so that disputes are settled on a quasi-legal basis rather than by fresh bargaining or conciliation procedures.

Finally, workers may put in more overtime; and since this is paid at a higher rate than work done in normal working hours, earnings will outstrip rates. The greater the proportion of overtime in total hours worked, the greater will be the divergence between the two. This may constitute 'drift' as defined above or it may not. If the rise in overtime earnings goes with an extension in actual hours worked, no real change in wage rates may be involved and the spread between earnings and rates merely reflects fuller utilization of industrial capacity. But if, as has happened since the war, nominal hours fall (in Britain, from about 48 to 40) without an equivalent fall in actual hours, the contraction in nominal hours is to a large extent a disguised increase in wage rates. If the same job is done for more pay, the contraction in nominal hours is little more than a way of putting up wages.

Wages under full employment

The discussion so far has been largely in terms of wages in particular industries with occasional references to the state of trade and the demand for labour in the aggregate. The general level of wages has been assumed to be relatively stable. But in a world of full employment, this assumption can no longer be made. Whatever may be true of *real* wages – and their rate of increase is not likely to fluctuate a great deal if output is rising steadily – there can be no guarantee that free collective bargaining will maintain stability in the level of *money* wages or cause them to increase in line with the growth of productivity. On the contrary, there may be a continuous inflation in wage settlements throughout the economy, perhaps even at an accelerating rate.

There are a number of reasons why the rate of increase in money wages (i.e., in the general level of wages) is not determinate, particularly when the responsibility for preserving full employment has been shouldered by the government. At all times, bargaining between monopolists is a kind of game and we do not know in advance how the game will be played. With collective bargaining both sides will have an eye on the level of wages in other industries, current changes in the cost of living and in profits, and the trend in employment, output and new orders. But they will take different views of the available evidence, form different expectations, and attach different weight to different elements in the current economic situation as they see it. Even if a single centralized bargain could be struck over wages, there would be ample room for haggling and manoeuvring and no certainty, except within fairly wide limits, as to how negotiations would end.

In fact bargaining is fragmented, so that first one industry, then another, enters the game. Each wage agreement conditions those following it, and there is a strong tendency towards restoration of earlier differentials. Once a high rate of increase has been conceded in any major settlement, it tends to set the pace for later settlements. The converse appears to be less true: one relatively moderate settlement exercises a less powerful demonstration effect than an exceptionally high one. Even if this were not so, fragmentation tends to provide added momentum to an upward spiral in wages and prices; each new bargain improves the wages of one group of workers but almost entirely, as suggested above, at the expense of other groups that find prices raised against them once the higher wage cost is passed on. After they have had time to react by securing higher wages in compensation, the first bargain is on the way to being undone and frustrated in the eyes of the workers who gained initially by it. With fragmented bargaining there is no collective decision about wage differentials; and mutually inconsistent views among different groups of wage-earners can set off a process of inflation, as each in turn seeks to create or widen a differential in its favour by jacking up its wages ahead of the others only to see it disappear again as the wage round proceeds.

A third element in the situation is the relative bargaining power of the two sides. This has changed with the coming of full employment, the growing strength of the unions, and the rising cost of shut-downs. Employers have less reason to fear that higher prices will destroy the demand for their output, and more reason to fear that resistance to wage claims involving prolonged strikes will simply ruin them. Workers have less reason to hold back from pressing for higher wages because of fear that this may lose them their jobs: they can leave it to the government to prevent unemployment from spreading and disregard the danger that governments, torn between their simultaneous commitments to full employment and a stable currency, may come to waver and embrace this responsibility less wholeheartedly.

The nineteenth-century situation in which money wages rose very slowly, if at all, except when employers needed more labour and the labour market was already fairly tight, has given way to a new situation in which wage earners regard an annual increase in money wages as normal and can enforce their claims even if unemployment is increasing and the labour market is comparatively slack. The really interesting question is no longer why money wages go on increasing, but what sets a limit to the rate of increase. We return to this question in a later chapter[1].

The state and wages

In the United Kingdom it has been usual for the state to try to stand aside from the process of collective bargaining. Governments have laid down from time to time what is legitimate and what is not in a trial of strength between workers and their employers – whether, for example, peaceful picketing or a general strike is legal. The state has also passed legislation on how trade union funds can be employed – whether, for example, members can be obliged to subscribe to levies in support of a political party. But in general it has not attempted to decide particular disputes nor even to require that some particular machinery of negotiation be used.

To this an increasing number of qualifications are now necessary. Since 1909 the state has set up a number of Trade Boards, which were given extended powers and renamed Wages Councils in 1945, in industries where wages were unreasonably low or where the existing machinery of collective bargaining was inadequate. Separate legislation has led to the setting up of Wages Boards in agriculture and catering. The Wages Councils and Boards have power to fix minimum wages and other conditions of employment. In

---

[1] See Chapter 31, pp. 428–429.

all, statutory wage-fixing arrangements cover almost one-third of total employment, although in some industries these arrangements overlap with voluntary collective bargaining.

Apart from statutory regulation of wages, the state may intervene in an industrial dispute either in order to arbitrate at the request of both parties or to bring conciliation machinery into play at the request of either party. Any industrial dispute likely to lead to a stoppage of work must be brought to the attention of the Department of Employment; and if the danger of a serious stoppage is great, the government is likely to take part in the subsequent negotiations. Moreover, where voluntary arrangements have been made for the submission of disputes to arbitration or conciliation, the members of the Tribunals or Committees that are looking into the dispute will be guided to some extent by any general declarations of policy that have been made by the government. Finally, apart from intervention in particular disputes, the government may join with employers' and trade union organizations in a general compact that wage adjustments should be limited as far as possible to cases complying with a set list of conditions (e.g., industries where there is a labour shortage). When this stage is reached, collective bargaining has become subordinate to the wages policy pursued by the government as part of its general economic policy. So far from leaving wages to be settled freely by negotiations between employers and employed, the state, in those conditions, is influencing both the size of the wage bill and the changes in wage differentials. Above all, the state is the direct employer, or indirect paymaster, of a large and growing proportion of the labour force. Civil servants, soldiers, nurses, doctors and policemen are paid directly; many others, in nationalized industries, education and local government, indirectly.

So long as workers are free to strike and wage disputes continue, the rulings of wages councils, arbitration tribunals, conciliation committees, and so on, are obeyed only if they are not felt to be manifestly unjust. The various tribunals and councils in their turn may accept or reject any guidance offered to them by the government. The central organizations of employers and employed – the TUC and CBI[1] – may reach general agreement with the government on wages policy without preventing individual unions or employers' associations – and still more individual workmen and employers – from taking a quite independent line. Shop stewards may pull in one direction while trade union officials are pulling in another, so that official strikes give way increasingly to unofficial ones. The more the trade unions are associated with the government and with the employers in formulating a common line of policy, the more they are put in the position of apologists of that policy, and the more they are obliged to check the very propensity of their members to demand a better bargain on which their strength has been built up. However strongly the government wishes to regulate wages, and however closely it carries the TUC and CBI with it, it must still have regard to the movement of opinion among the workers if it is not either to discredit the trade unions or to deny them the right to strike. Even if the government is keen to avoid any direct

[1] Trades Union Congress and Confederation of British Industry

involvement in labour markets, moreover, it cannot abrogate its responsibility for rates of remuneration in the public sector; and it will face just these difficulties with the labour force there, if not perhaps in the rest of the economy.

The state and the distribution of incomes

In addition to its various roles as paymaster, conciliator and regulator of wages, the state has long employed other means of affecting households' incomes. Taxation and welfare benefits, taken together, are designed (in part) to alleviate poverty and reduce inequality in the distribution of personal incomes. The redistributive effect of income tax may be seen from these figures[1], relating to the 1972/3 fiscal year in Great Britain: the top 10% of income-recipients enjoyed 26.9% of the total of pre-tax incomes, but only 23.6% of post-tax incomes; the share of the lowest 20% was boosted from 5.8% of pre-tax incomes to 6.8% of incomes after tax. Taxes and transfers (welfare benefits) combined to reduce one particular measure of inequality of incomes between British households[2] by about one-fifth in 1973. Among other industrialized countries, it appears that the greatest inequality reductions are achieved by the tax and transfer systems in Scandinavia, and the lowest (at least until recently) in France and Spain. Subject to the qualification that both the data, and the concept of inequality itself, are distinctly ambiguous, the statistics suggest that inequality in British incomes is certainly not high by international standards, but has shown less of a tendency to fall, particularly since 1960 and in the lower half of incomes. Such equalizing forces as these have since the war included some 'catching-up' in pay by certain lower paid groups; workers in poorer regions, women, and above all unskilled workers, principally in the public sector. Policy measures towards welfare benefits and taxation implemented in and after 1979 will have increased after-tax measures of inequality in incomes.

[1] Based on 'Blue Book' data. See M. Sawyer, 'Income Distribution in OECD Countries', *OECD Economic Outlook Occasional Studies*, July 1976.
[2] This is the Gini coefficient. See M. Semple, 'The Effects of Changes in the Household Composition on the Distribution of Income', *Economic Trends*, December 1975. The fall in inequality due to taxes and transfers is slightly larger with the 1973 than the 1961 figures for household composition.

Chapter 20

Interest and profit

Interest

Interest is the price paid for the hire of loan-capital; more briefly, it is the price of a loan. This price is usually expressed as an annual rate, calculated on the principal of the loan. If, for example, I borrow £100 for one year on impeccable security, I am likely to be asked to pay back £105 at the end of the year – that is, interest will be charged at the rate of 5% per annum. But why should I be asked to pay interest? What has my creditor done to earn his £5 in interest?

The supply of capital

The immediate reason why interest is paid is that loan-capital is scarce. The amount of money which people are willing to lend every year falls far short of the amount which would be borrowed if no interest were charged. So it is necessary to ration the limited supply by putting a price on loans – that is, by charging interest on them. Only those borrowers who are willing to pay the current rate of interest will be able to obtain loans; those who cannot pay the price will be forced to go unsatisfied.

But why is loan-capital scarce? Why don't people lend more? There are three possible reasons:

1. Unless we are bankers, we cannot lend without going to the trouble of saving, and there is a limit to our willingness and ability to save. We can, however, lend to any single borrower without saving more; all we need do is to ask for repayment from some other borrower and lend the sum repaid.
2. We cannot lend without denying ourselves the use of our own savings. If we save more, therefore, we do not necessarily lend more; we may, instead, apply our savings to increase our stock of goods. For example, we may buy machinery for use in our business; or make a speculative purchase of raw materials to guard against, or profit from, a rise in their price; or store foodstuffs in fear of war; or buy a house, or a motor car, or some similar durable commodity. In other words, we may choose to

lend to ourselves rather than to other people, and hold our savings in the form of *goods* rather than in the form of debt.
3. We cannot lend without parting with our money for a period of time and leaving ourselves in a comparatively illiquid position during that time. Money is more convenient for many purposes than even the best of IOUs, and because of this greater convenience we are never willing to lend out all our money. In other words, we may prefer to keep part of our savings in the form of *money* rather than in the form of debt or durable goods.

Savings

Of these three reasons we shall, for the present, disregard the last, and treat the second as a variant of the first. We shall assume, that is, that when people save more they will also lend more. On this assumption, the only possible reason for the scarcity of loan-capital is the scarcity of savings. Upon what, then, do savings depend?

(a) The rate of interest

It might be supposed that the supply of savings, like the supply of oranges, depended mainly on their price, i.e., on the rate of interest. It is generally agreed, however, that although the payment of interest does offer an inducement to thrift, this inducement is subordinate to others. A low price would make us give up orange-growing, but it might require a *negative* rate of interest to make us give up saving. If the price of oranges rises from 8p to 10p we can be quite certain that more oranges will be put on the market. But if the rate of interest rises from 8 to 10% we cannot be certain that savings will increase. A man who wishes to save just enough to yield him £1000 a year in interest when he retires will save *less* at the higher rate; at 10% he will require to accumulate only £10 000, whereas at 8% he will need £12 500.

Similarly, life insurance companies may find that their premium income (which is a substantial part of the total savings of the community) is reduced rather than increased by a rise in interest rates. It is doubtful, however, whether many people have such rigid ideas about the future income at which they are aiming, and it is likely that, on balance, a rise in interest rates will increase savings. It certainly tends to depress spending on durable goods.

The nominal rate of interest is not an accurate measure of the *effective* inducement to saving. First we must deduct from the nominal rate of interest any taxes payable by the lender. If there is an income tax of 40p in the £1, I must pay this 40p whether I spend the £1 or save it. But if I save it, I shall later be asked to pay income tax on the interest. When the nominal rate of interest is 5%, therefore, the real rate to the saver is only 3%. His choice lies between spending £100 this year and having £105 less £2 in tax next year. On each £100 saved he gains only £3. Secondly, we must make provision for changes in the value of money. If I expect prices to rise by 6% over the year, I shall make a bad bargain by lending money at 5%, for £105 in a year's time will buy less than £100 does now. The *real* rate of interest will be *minus* 1%. On the other hand, if I expect prices to fall by 2%, and my expectations are well founded, the real rate of interest will be 5 plus 2, or 7%. A given rate of interest, therefore, offers a greater incentive to saving in times of falling than in times of rising prices. If we wished the real rate of interest to remain constant, we should require to raise the nominal rate when inflation was rising and lower it again with falling inflation. Nominal interest rates have displayed much more pronounced movements than real rates, especially in the 1970s. Real rates rarely stray outside the range between +3 and −2% per annum, when measured before tax.

(b) Social institutions

Savings depend upon the encouragement and reassurance offered to the saver by existing social arrangements and practices. If there are numerous outlets for savings, if lenders are brought readily into contact with borrowers, and if there is widespread approval of thrift as a civic virtue, the disposition to save will be immensely stronger than in communities where capital is little in demand, the capital market is inefficiently organized and the general temper of society is unfavourable to thrift. Habits of saving, therefore, vary greatly from one society to another. They were stronger under Queen Victoria than under Queen Elizabeth, and a great deal stronger than under Queen Boadicea. They are stronger in a stable capitalist society than in communities where the danger of repudiation or confiscation is serious, or where to possess capital is to court persecution or murder.

(c) Income

Every increase in our income adds to our ability to save. Of course, we are unlikely to save the whole of the increase, for when we become richer we generally scale up our standard of living. But neither are we all likely to spend the whole of the increase. Some of us will add to our savings – especially at first, while our customary standard of living is still unadjusted to the change in our income. Experience suggests that this part is generally fairly large, and that we tend to save not only a larger sum of money but also, in the short run at least, a *larger* proportion of our income.

(d) Wealth

An increase in our wealth enables us to save more only if there is an accompanying increase in our income. An increase in wealth unaccompanied by any increase in income will dispose us to save *less* of our income, since the more wealth we have the weaker is the motive to further accumulation. If our holdings of stock exchange securities rise in price (as generally happens when interest rates fall) we are likely to have less hesitation in spending out of our current income; while, if we feel ourselves impoverished by a fall in security values, we may spend our incomes less freely.

(e) Thrift

In a given order of society, at a given level of income, how much we save depends on the strength of the motives disposing us to thrift. These motives rarely induce us to make provision for saving by setting aside a definite sum; unless, of course, we are under contract to save – for example, by making repayment on a mortgage to a building society, or by paying an annual premium on our insurance policy. These payments apart, our expenditure is governed largely by the desire to maintain some customary standard of living. If our income is more than sufficient to maintain this standard, we save the surplus; if it is less than sufficient, we borrow the deficit (e.g., by running up debts to tradesmen or an overdraft at the bank) or live on our capital. In the short run, therefore, savings are a residue after meeting customary expenses. In the long run, however, people have standards of thrift as well as of expenditure. If they find that they are saving consistently more than they wish, they will raise their standard of living. On the other hand, if they find that they are running into debt, or are saving less than they think desirable, they will try to economize and reduce their expenditure. In the long run, savings cease to be residual and are fixed more and more deliberately.

Our standards of thrift vary with our preference for future as compared with present goods. If the rate of interest is 5%, we can choose between £100 now and £105 next year. Those of us who are thrifty will have a comparatively strong preference for £105 next year. We may be uncertain of the future and anxious to provide for emergencies; or hopeful of achieving a greater measure of independence and a higher standard of living; or eager to have more capital at our disposal to expand our business and back speculative projects; or full of ambition to build up a fortune and acquire social status; or we may have more foresight or be more alive than others to future needs and future pleasures; or we may want to accumulate money for its own sake out of sheer miserliness[1]. Other people, less concerned for the future, or attaching less importance to the possession of wealth, will discount future goods more heavily and be more attracted by £100 now. Everyone, whatever his motives to thrift, will modify his preference for future goods the larger the proportion of his income which he saves until at the margin he is indifferent whether his last pound is spent or left to accumulate interest – that is, until his marginal preference for future goods is measured by the rate of interest.

Recent years have seen a substantial rise in the proportion of their disposable income that households (on average) save. This was usually 5% or less in the 1950s; by 1975, it had climbed to 15%. Similar trends are visible in many other West European countries, but not in the United States, where it had fallen to 4% in 1979. In Great Britain, this 'savings ratio' has moved in curiously close harmony with the nominal rate of interest.

---

[1] Charles Booth drew an interesting contrast between the motives to thrift in rich and poor: 'With the working classes the object (of saving) is to render irregularity of income equal to the calls of a regular expenditure; with the rich this is reversed, and the aim is rather to make a comparatively fixed income meet the claims of a varying expenditure' (*Life and Labour in London*, Final Volume, 1890, p. 94).

Corporate saving

A large proportion of the savings of a modern industrial community are made by companies, not by individuals. Out of their profits, companies distribute part in dividends and retain the remainder in the business. Retained profits vary between 25% of national income in contemporary Japan, and 10% or less in the Netherlands, the UK and the US. Retained profits are treated as corporate saving, although they can also be thought of as saving by shareholders, to whom the retained profits really belong. The proportion of profits retained varies from period to period, firm to firm and country to country; it is often about one-half. So corporate saving varies strongly with profits. For the most part, it is used to finance companies' investment expenditure.

Government saving

The government has also, on occasion, made an important contribution to the savings of the country. It may do so, for example, by accumulating a budget surplus, rates of tax being so fixed as to leave an excess of revenue over current outgoings. Included in government savings will be any expenditure out of revenue that adds to, or improves, the capital stock of the country, and any payments (e.g., in respect of war damage claims) that will be treated by the recipients as capital. Current revenue that is paid out of capital (e.g., death duties) should be excluded. Apart from the budget surplus of the central government, there may also be a surplus in the accounts of the local authorities or of various public bodies, including the boards of the nationalized industries. Since 1970, there has been a strong tendency towards *dissaving* by the government in all industrialized coun-tries, including the UK.

The justification of interest, time preference and liquidity preference

We have seen that, for a variety of reasons, savings are scarce and command a price which we call the rate of interest. But does this *justify* the payment of interest? Can we, for example, regard interest as compensation for the sacrifice involved in saving as we can regard wages as compensation for the irksomeness of work?

Like the earnings of any other factor of production, interest is both a price and a source of income. Regarded as a price, interest performs a useful social function by rationing out a limited supply of savings between competing borrowers. Even in a socialist community, this is a function which interest might continue to perform, for it would still be desirable to determine the priority of schemes calling for the use of capital and to eliminate those schemes which showed an insufficient return. If the return could be measured in money terms the charging of a rate of interest would automatically secure this result, since it would give priority to schemes offering prospects of a higher return, and weed out schemes of lesser productivity. Regarded as a source of income, interest is less easy to justify. It is paid to some people rather than to others, because some people own loan-capital while others do not. If we wish to justify interest *payments*, therefore, we must first justify these differences in ownership. Secondly, we must show that without the offer of interest, capital would cease to be accumulated or cease to be lent. The first point raises issues too wide for treatment here.

The second point raises quite different issues. We know that it is only at the margin that the rate of interest has a decisive influence on thrift, and that the vast bulk of savings would continue to be supplied at lower rates. True, capitalists may *consume* part of their savings (or the savings of past generations) at low rates of interest, so that interest payments may be a bribe to dissuade them from this alternative. There is little doubt that capital consumption is in fact already being practised by the wealthy. It is arguable, however, that this arises mainly because of various disincentives to thrift, such as the tax on capital transfers and high rates of income tax. The real return to a wealthy person on a loan, given current rates of tax and an apparently chronic tendency for prices to rise, may be negligible and perhaps even negative. However that may be, a more immediate danger would make itself felt before low rates of interest caused savings to dry up or the total stock of capital to be run down – the disinclination of capitalists to *lend*.

This brings us to the second reason why loan-capital is scarce[1]. We have to overcome not only our reluctance to save, but also our reluctance to lend. Just as we may prefer present to future goods, and must be offered interest in order to overcome our 'time-preference', so we may prefer money now to the promise of money at some future date, and require the offer of interest before we can overcome our 'liquidity preference'. The phrase 'liquidity preference' sums up the various motives which prompt people to hold money rather than lend it at interest. The more we prefer money to IOUs of any kind – i.e., the greater our liquidity preference – the more difficult it will be to induce us to lend, and the higher, therefore, will be the rate of interest. By 'liquidity' is meant 'power to convert into other commodities or into something which is generally acceptable in final settlement of a debt'. Now money is of all things the most readily exchangeable into other commodities and the most generally acceptable in payment of a debt. Money, therefore, sets a standard of liquidity against which we can measure the liquidity of everything else. A preference for liquidity is a preference for money.

Assets other than money carry various disadvantages. Buying and selling are often expensive. There are dealers' commissions, and taxes, not to mention the nuisance and time involved. The dealers' margins may vary between 3% for bonds or shares sold or bought in large amounts, to 25% or more for antiques. Even deposits in building societies or savings banks, which are very close to being classified as money, may impose penalties or limits on withdrawals; and certainly there is some cost to the depositor, in transport and time, whenever he pays them a visit. In addition to all these different types of transactions cost many non-money assets have the major drawback of unpredictable disposal value. Most of us are averse to risk, and regard such uncertainties as disagreeable. Compensation for both transactions costs and risks is required, and given in the form of interest.

[1] See above, p. 255.

Differences in interest rates

There is no such thing as 'the' rate of interest. We have seen that interest rates may be expressed before or after tax, and before and after inflation ('nominal' and 'real'). But these are not the only differences. The rate of interest frequently varies with the length of loan. Rates on three-month loans to government (known in Great Britain and the United States as Treasury bills) are much more volatile, and at least as often as not lower, than rates on, for example five- or ten-year bonds. When the market expects three-month rates of interest to fall over the next six to eight quarters, the current rate of interest on one- or two-year bonds will probably lie below the current three-month rate. Expectations of rising short-term interest rates make for higher medium-term rates than short rates. If lenders prefer to lend over shorter intervals than borrowers wish to borrow, and both are averse to risk, shorter-term rates will be tilted downwards relative to longer-term rates: otherwise there would be excess demand for shorter-term loans and excess supply of the rest.

A second reason for differences in interest rates is that all borrowers cannot offer equally good security. Where the risk of default is negligible – e.g., on British government securities – loans will be made at rock-bottom rates. But whenever lenders feel doubtful of the borrower's honesty, or of his financial strength, they will be reluctant to lend, and will either refuse altogether or will insist on a higher rate of interest to cover the risk of default. They will charge a premium in excess of the rate payable by borrowers whose credit is irreproachable. This premium will vary with the standing of the borrower, his past record, and the pledges which he can offer as guarantees of ultimate repayment. It will vary, too, with the period for which loans are made, so that long-term loans are not only less liquid but also less secure.

Differences in interest rates may also be due to market imperfection. The capital market is made up of a great many sub-markets specializing in different kinds of loans and not always in close competition with one another. The banks cater for one kind of borrower, the building societies for another. The insurance companies cater for one kind of lender, the investment trusts for another. The market for short-term loans is cut off from the market for long-term loans. Thus borrowers and lenders, attached by habit or by ignorance to one sub-market, may raise or make loans on terms less favourable than the rates ruling in other sub-markets. Market imperfection is greatest when the obstacles to competition are geographical.

Finally, differences in marketability lead to differences in the interest payable on large and on small loans. A company which makes a small issue of bonds may have to pay a comparatively high rate of interest because, since trading in these bonds will be restricted, there will be greater difficulty in disposing of them at short notice when lenders wish to recover their money and also because, in a narrow market, the value of the bonds will tend to fluctuate more abruptly.

The demand for capital

Since borrowers are willing to pay interest, it is to be presumed that loans render some service at least equal in value to the interest paid. What is this service? By what process does the £100 which I borrow this year become the £105 which I shall be asked to repay next year? Do loans, in some mysterious way, increase the product of industry, or is the additional £5 paid out of the profits of exploitation by robbing workers of the full value of their labour? Few questions in economics have given rise to so much controversy.

The most famous exponent of the exploitation argument was Karl Marx. According to Marx, the only productive agents are human labour and natural forces. Machines, for example, are made by man from mineral deposits with the help of other machines; these machines in turn were made with the help of earlier machines. If we go back far enough to the first tools with which machines were made, these tools must have been the direct product of human labour. Machinery, therefore, is stored-up labour, and this past labour should be paid for at the same rate as present labour, without any addition of interest or profit. Capital is reducible to the labour and land which it embodies and renders no independent service. Nature, which partners labour in production, asks no compensation for its services. The full value of what is produced, therefore, is labour's by right; anything that goes in rent, interest or profit to the landowner, or to the capitalist, is seized from labour by exploitation.

This is a plausible argument, and one with a strong emotional appeal. But there is a flaw in it; it overlooks the value of time. Now time is precisely the service which is rendered to producers and to consumers by capital. We recognize this clearly enough when we are given credit – that is, when a loan frees us from the necessity of making immediate payment. For the privilege of paying at some more convenient time, we are willing to allow interest to be added to our bill; in other words, we are willing to buy time. But this is far from being the only kind of transaction in which time is of value. In nearly all productive processes an interval of time must elapse between the work which we do and the consumption of the finished product. There is an interval between ploughing and sowing, between sowing and reaping, between reaping and milling, between milling and baking. There is an interval between the commencement and completion of a house, a ship, or a machine, and a still longer interval before the full value of such durable goods is exhausted in the shelter or transport or manufactured goods which they yield over their years of service. Thus the efforts of a farmer or a builder bring in no immediate return; they fructify at some more or less distant date. It is necessary to *wait* for that fructification, and this waiting is possible only if someone saves. The farmer must support himself and his workers until his crop is sold, and if he is to obtain command of the necessary purchasing power he must either save himself – i.e., postpone consumption – or borrow from some other saver – or induce someone else to postpone consumption. To the work done by the farmer, therefore, there must be added the waiting done by the saver. Waiting is just as indispensable a constituent of production as working. Capital, which is the product of waiting, is as much a factor of production as labour, by which working is undertaken. To put the point another way; capital cannot be reduced entirely to past labour. For combined with the past labour which is stored up in machinery and other capital goods is the waiting that must be done before that labour repays itself.

The longer the interval of time between effort and return – what is sometimes called the 'period of production' – the more effectively we can work. Suppose, for example, that Robinson Crusoe (whom no one can exploit) goes fishing. The most primitive method which he can use is to catch fish with his hands, as boys do. Then he may use a more roundabout method – carve a spear, or take a day off to make a rod and tackle and look for bait. Instead of spending all his time fishing, he now divides up his time between making fishing gear and using it. Later, he may use still more roundabout methods, building a boat and making nets for himself before resuming his fishing. Each change of method involves the use of an increasing amount of capital – first a spear, then a rod, then a boat and nets. Thus an increasing amount of capital is the product of an increasing amount of waiting; Crusoe's exertions in building the boat, for example, add nothing to his catch until the boat is ready for the water. But these exertions will *ultimately* increase his catch by far more than he could ever have caught by more primitive methods in the time which he gave to the work of construction. He is more than compensated for this work because of the technical superiority of roundabout or capitalistic methods of fishing. But he can only use such methods if he is able to wait for the greater reward that boat-building will ultimately bring him. If, in a less deserted island, he could borrow enough to pay for a boat, he would be able to transfer the burden of waiting to other shoulders by the offer of interest, and this interest would come out of the increased catch which he could make with the help of the boat.

This illustration can readily be generalized. Most commodities can be produced by a variety of methods, some requiring a great deal of capital, some comparatively little. Producers can use first very primitive methods with easily constructed tools; then more elaborate methods with simple types of machinery; then power-driven machinery in expensive factory buildings. At each stage, output per man increases – not simply per man operating the machinery, but output per worker, including engineers, bricklayers, and all who build and repair the factory equipment. Although output per head is greater, the product is not available for consumption until a longer period of time has elapsed. The work which is done (e.g., by engineers) is directed to the satisfaction of wants that are increasingly remote as the period of production is extended. There is more 'jam tomorrow', but only if we are willing to wait until tomorrow. On the one hand, therefore, the use of capital increases the time interval between taking the first steps in production (e.g., making tools) and turning out the finished goods, and so permits of the introduction of more efficient methods. On the other hand, since these methods, far from increasing current output, are made possible only by the withdrawal of resources from meeting immediate wants – as one withdraws eggs for incubation – they cannot be adopted without sacrifice – the sacrifice involved in waiting or saving. Borrowers are willing to pay interest because of the technical advantages of lengthy and roundabout methods of production; they are forced to pay interest because the burden of saving which the community is willing to carry is a limited one.

Capital is required, then, because production takes time; by taking advantage of more roundabout techniques of production, a given number of men can produce more than twice as much at the end of two years as they can produce at the end of one, but they have to be maintained out of savings during the extra year. Capital may be required also for other reasons. First of all, goods may grow in value over time, without additional expenditure of effort. Given time, the forces of nature will cause wine to mature and trees to grow, unassisted by man. The function of capital here is not to allow the introduction of a more roundabout process, but to allow us to wait while nature does its work; the technique is of nature's devising, not man's. Secondly, capital may enable goods to be transferred from a time of plenty to a time of scarcity, or from a time when they are little in demand to a time when the need for them is comparatively great. Potatoes are plentiful in September and scarce in April; the capitalist, therefore, by buying potatoes in September and *waiting* until April, renders a service exactly similar to the services of traders in buying potatoes in *places* where they are abundant and carrying them to *places* where they are scarce. The greater scarcity of potatoes in April will raise their price and leave the capitalist with a profit, part of which is really interest on his capital.

Thirdly, capital may allow us to enter into immediate possession of goods which we urgently need. Not having sufficient capital ourselves, we borrow from other people and pay them a premium in interest for taking over from us the burden of waiting. The man who buys goods on the instalment system, the spendthrift who runs into debt, and the government which raises a war loan, share a common preference for present rather than future goods. They are disposed to dis-save, not to save; to anticipate their future income instead of trying to add to it. Each of them is using up saving, and none of them – apart, possibly, from the man who buys on the instalment system – is adding to the capital stock of the community as a whole. Nevertheless the loan of capital is of as real service to them as loans made for other purposes, and the interest paid is in recognition of this service.

The marginal productivity of capital

Capital, then, does render a service to those who borrow it; it *is* productive. Its productivity falls, however, as the supply increases; capital, like the other factors of production, is subject to diminishing marginal productivity, other things remaining equal. Each fresh extension of the period of production, for example, yields a diminishing increment of product. When capital is scarce, only those time-consuming methods of production which promise great ultimate gain can be adopted; when more capital becomes available it is possible to use methods which repay themselves less handsomely. With a little capital we can generate electricity from coal and obtain all the advantages of electric over labour power; with more capital we may reduce the cost of electricity by the construction of dams and of hydroelectric power stations. This tendency to diminishing productivity is almost universal. With more capital a merchant can keep a larger stock on hand, or a wider variety of goods; a manufacturer can use machines of better quality or more capitalistic techniques. But the additional capital yields a smaller return than the existing stock.

The productivity of capital, in this context, means the productivity of *loan* capital, i.e., the productivity of the things which can be bought out of a loan. The marginal product of capital is the additional return, after allowing for depreciation, which the borrower expects to obtain through the *use* of an additional unit of loan capital. The marginal productivity of capital varies, therefore, not only with the annual return expected on capital equipment, but also with the cost of such equipment. If, as capital accumulates, machinery becomes more costly in relation to the price of its product, the marginal productivity of capital will fall, both because the uses to which the additional machinery can be put will be less urgent, and because a greater investment of capital will be necessary for the purchase of the machinery.

In many uses to which capital is put its productivity is not easily measured. Who can say, for example, whether houses are more productive than roads, or roads then battleships? The measuring-rod of money can be applied to houses to give the annual return on the capital invested, but roads and battleships yield no monetary return. Are we to say, therefore, that houses alone are productive? Clearly, this would be absurd. What we must say is that productivity is measured by the borrower himself – sometimes, when he is producing goods for sale, with an eye to the judgements of productivity expressed by consumers in the prices which they pay; and sometimes, when he is meeting his own immediate wants, on the basis of his private judgement of how these wants can best be met. A businessman's judgement of productivity rests on his expectation of profit – which is measurable; a government's judgement rests on its conception of the needs of the community – which may not be measurable.

The marginal productivity of capital governs the rate of interest which borrowers are prepared to pay. Producers, for example, will put capital to uses in which the prospective return becomes progressively smaller as more and more capital is applied. Under perfect competition, they will increase their borrowings until, on a further loan, the prospective return over the period of the loan is a trifle less than the interest payable on it – that is, until the marginal productivity of capital and the rate of interest are equal. The return which producers balance against the interest cost of a loan is generally obtained through the conversion of the loan into concrete capital assets. Since the contribution made by these assets to the value of output extends into the future over the period of their life, the gross return is not certain, but must be estimated by producers on the basis of their experience of the past and their anticipations of the future; it is a prospective return. Since, however, capital assets depreciate over their life, provision must be made out of the gross return for the probable cost of depreciation; it is the *net* return which is balanced against the interest charge.

Under perfect conditions, a firm will be faced with an unfettered choice between buying a capital good and renting it. Its manager will arrange his affairs so that he is indifferent between these two courses. The rental charge on computers, for example, would be very high to reflect the fact that they are expected to fall in price as improved models come on to the market; and this would also be a drawback to buying a computer, instead of waiting for a better one. But with capital goods that are not expected to change in relative price, the rental rate in perfect competition will consist simply of two elements: the rate of interest and the rate of depreciation. Purchases, or rentals, will be taken to the point where the sum of these two rates just equals the marginal productivity of capital.

When competition is not perfect, a firm's marginal productivity of capital is likely to exceed the sum of interest and depreciation rates for two reasons. It will tend to limit its borrowings if faced with an upward sloping curve of loans, in order to contain borrowing costs. Second, if its product is sold in monopolistic or oligopolistic conditions, it will, given profit maximization, tend to restrict output. Marginal revenue and marginal cost will be less than price. Restricted output implies restricted inputs, of capital no less than labour.

Changes in marginal productivity

The demand for capital will increase or diminish whenever there is a rise or fall in the marginal productivity of capital. A rise may occur as a result of:

1. Invention; for example the invention of new means of transport (the railway and the steamship in the nineteenth century, the motor car and the aeroplane in the twentieth); or of communications (by cable, telephone or wireless); or of new sources of power (steam, electricity, petrol and oil).
2. Anything which makes concrete capital scarce relatively to the other factors of production – the destruction of property on a large scale in a earthquake or a war; an increase in population; an increase in the efficiency of labour; the discovery of new natural resources – minerals, oils, etc. – and the settlement of new and undeveloped countries; a long-term fall in savings.
3. A change in tastes from goods which require a low proportion to goods which require a high proportion of capital in their manufacture – for example, people may spend more on rent and move to larger houses, which require the investment of a great deal of capital, and spend correspondingly less on drink into which capital does not enter so largely. *Any* change in demand, indeed, will be likely to raise the marginal productivity of capital. For it will be necessary to provide more of one commodity and less of another; and since the machinery and plant used in the manufacture of the second commodity is unlikely to be adaptable for the manufacture of the first, more machinery and plant will have to be constructed if the output of the first commodity is to be increased. The demand for capital, therefore, will increase and the increase will be all the greater if a comparatively high proportion of capital to labour is used in the manufacture of the first commodity.
4. Anything inducing businessmen to take a more optimistic view of the future. If, for example, producers are in a more optimistic frame of mind, they will entertain more favourable expectations of profit; this will raise the prospective return on capital and stimulate borrowing. An important influence making for optimism is past experience of a steadily

expanding market. The marginal productivity of capital is higher in a world of expanding population and trade than in a world where population is tending to become stationary and trade restrictions accumulate. It is higher not only because businessmen tend to be more adventurous, but also because, whatever their mood, they can justifiably look forward to an expanding return from year to year.

The mobility of capital

The savings of the past have already been invested; they are fixed in the stock of concrete capital which society has accumulated. The savings of the present are still free and undecided in their use; they are available for financing additions to the stock of capital in those industries and districts where the demand for capital is most urgent. If the demand for capital increases in any one use, therefore, it is mainly out of 'free' capital that this demand is met. The rate of interest tends to be forced up, choking off demand elsewhere, and diverting savings to the expanding industry or district from other industries and districts in which these savings would normally have been invested. Just as the mobility of labour is greatest among new entrants, so the mobility of capital is greatest when capital is still free. But fixed capital, too, may be transferred from one use to another. If the production of one commodity is discontinued, the buildings and machinery used in its manufacture may be adapted for use in the production of some other commodity. The same plant may turn out a variety of products, any one of which may be substituted for the others without dislocation; shop space may be used for the retailing of a variable range of goods; a dismantled ship may supply a hotel with furniture and panelling, a coal-mine with machinery, and a steelworks with scrap. Thus one industry may decline and others take its place without drawing extensively on free capital. A third element of mobility arises through the conversion of fixed into free capital. As fixed capital wears out, a sum of money is set aside annually to provide for its ultimate replacement. These sums we may call 'depreciation funds', since they are supposed to provide for current depreciation. Now depreciation funds are really free capital. They can, if their owners so choose, be reinvested in *other* kinds of property – in other industries and districts – which are yielding a high return, instead of being applied automatically to the replacement of property which may be yielding a comparatively low return. There is no *necessity* to replace property as it wears out and so preserve unchanged the physical stock of capital. Indeed, it is very unusual for the new property to be precisely similar to the old; when plant is replaced an improved model is generally introduced. A nation's stock of capital is an amalgam of miscellaneous objects which differ in age, use, location and quality. This amalgam cannot be valued independently of the goods it produces and the other factors with which it works.

The rate of interest

So far we have made no attempt to formulate with any precision the forces controlling interest rates. We can discern basic, real forces that determine the central tendency that interest rates take, and shorter-term, chiefly monetary forces that account for the deviations.

The larger the supply of the various objects that make up the stock of capital, the lower rates of interest are likely to be. The greater the demand for capital, on the other hand, from greater population or a greater demand for capital-intensive goods perhaps, the higher the interest rates. These two sets of influences tend to shape long-term real rates of interest. Long-term money rates of interest will be approximately equal to these real rates plus the rate of expected inflation; but taxation is just one of several factors that make this approximation complex and inexact.

In the shorter-term, an increase in the supply of money will tend to ease credit conditions and lower interest rates, particularly short-term interest rates, whereas a rise in the demand for money (a rise in 'liquidity preference') will have the opposite effect. More detailed analysis of these and related points will be given in Chapter 21; there we shall focus particularly on how interest rates react with other macroeconomic variables.

Profit

Profit, as generally understood, is the difference between the total expenses incurred in producing or acquiring a commodity and the total revenue accruing from its sale. This difference may be expressed as a return on *capital*, the total profit over a year being related to the amount of capital employed; alternatively, profit may be expressed as the proportion by which the price per unit sold exceeds its cost, i.e., as a rate on turnover. A village chemist, for example, may be able to make a very large profit on turnover and only a moderate return on his capital; whereas a firm of wholesalers may make a comparatively trifling margin of profit on turnover, and yet obtain an abnormally high return on its capital. A third measure is the ratio of profit to value added. Our discussion will examine profit as a return on capital.

Gross and net profit

Profit as defined above is described by economists as *gross* profit, because it may include some items which are not really profit at all. The first of these is earnings of management. A joint-stock company includes in its expenses (and so excludes from profits) the salaries of those who undertake the work of management. But in businesses which are managed by their owner (e.g., farms, shops, etc.) the same kind of work is done without expense, and profits are swollen therefore, by the value of this work. The true or *net* profit can be arrived at only after deduction of the expense to which the owners of such businesses would be put if they had to hire the services of a manager; or, alternatively, after deduction of the salary which the owners might obtain by doing equal work for a joint-stock company[1]. Secondly, gross profit may include what ought properly to

---

[1] Strictly speaking, a rather larger deduction should be made. It costs something to bring capital and business ability together, so that an important advantage is lost by any businessman who lends out his capital and hires himself to a joint-stock company for a salary. This advantage, which is similar to the advantage of favourably situated land, gives rise to an element of rent which should be included in earnings of management rather than in net profit.

appear under the heading of interest. A business which uses borrowed capital counts the interest on this capital as an expense and excludes it from profit. Other businesses, using their own capital, include in profit the whole return on their capital. The proper procedure, if we wish to isolate net profit, is to deduct from the gross return on capital the interest which might have been earned by lending that capital on good security. A third item which ought properly to be excluded is the rent of land or buildings owned by the firm. A farmer, for example, might fail to reckon the rentable value of his land as a business expense in arriving at his profit on the year's working[1].

Distinguishing features of profit

Profit differs from other kinds of income in three ways. First, it may be negative. Neither wages, rent nor interest are ever likely to be negative, but every year there are some firms which make a loss and there are few firms which do not make a loss at some time or another. The evidence suggests that the *average* net profit which is earned in business (after deducting all losses and making provision for interest on capital) is comparatively small. Secondly, profit fluctuates more than any other kind of income. Between boom and slump there is comparatively little change in wage rates (and little more in labour earnings), or in rents; the brunt of the change falls on profit. Profit responds immediately to a change in price; other incomes are adjusted more slowly and less violently. Thirdly – and this is the crucial distinction – profit is not, like other kinds of income, a contractual and certain income, agreed on in advance, but an uncertain residue determined by the luck of events. A man's wage, for example, is predetermined and certain in amount; but the income of his employer is not. The man is paid now for goods produced in anticipation of future demand; and, since the future can never be foreseen with certainty, the goods which the employer obtains for a given wage-payment are of uncertain value. He *expects* to make a profit, but he may be unlucky.

The origin of profit

Thus profit originates in uncertainty. That uncertainty arises out of the responsibilities of ownership in a world of change and imperfect foresight. If everything could be reduced to routine, or if the future could be exactly predicted, there would be no uncertainty, no need to take chances, and no profit in the strict sense[2]. But in the world as we know it, there *is* uncertainty, the burden of which is all the greater because of our intricate economic system with its intense specialization and its production for

[1] The distinction between gross and net profit is by no means an academic one. When, for example, a tax is levied on profits, the usual basis of assessment is gross profit. This obviously discriminates against businesses managed by their owners or employing their owner's capital. There is also, as we shall see, discrimination against young, enterprising and growing firms in comparison with old and established ones. A tax on *excess* profit – i.e., on profit in excess of some 'fair' or 'normal' return – may also involve discrimination against firms which are making a high *gross* profit and only a normal *net* profit.

[2] There would, however, be *monopoly* profits; see pp. 185–186.

markets distant in time and space. The burden of uncertainty is one which *someone* must bear. To induce property owners to assume the burden of uncertainty the lure of profits is required; they will not run the risk of loss except in the hope of eventual gain[1]. There may be some people with such a liking for uncertainty that even the prospect of loss would not deter them from indulging their adventurousness; but most people take chances less from love of gambling for its own sake than from hope of making a profit if they are lucky. It does not follow from this that profit must be on the average a positive quantity. But it does follow that some people must make a profit and others a loss; there must be a prospect of profit which more than compensates for the risk of loss.

Profit and cost

People will take chances, therefore, only if they judge the chances to be in their favour – that is, only if they expect to make a profit. Before they will invest their capital in any industry they must have a sufficiently strong expectation of profit to overcome their fear of loss. This prospective profit is a cost exactly like wages, interest and rent. It is a necessary inducement without which adequate supplies of capital would not be obtainable. Prospective profit, therefore, enters into the supply price of finished goods; the price anticipated must be high enough to cover wages and interest charges and leave a margin which is considered adequate by businessmen to cover the various contingencies to which they are exposed. This margin will be larger for some businessmen than for others; those who are temperamentally cautious and averse to the assumption of risk will work to a larger margin than those who are more confident and venturesome. Those who take a gloomy view of the probable trend of prices will hesitate to take risks which seem moderate to more optimistic competitors. Thus there are marginal risk-takers, just as there are marginal savers and marginal workers; and it is the marginal risk-takers to whom expected prices must offer an adequate prospect of profit.

Although prospective profit enters into cost, realized profit does not. It is the reward for successful risk-taking and is a surplus governed by, not governing, price. At the same time, since men's expectations are generally grounded on their experience, prospective profit and realized profit are likely to move together. In the long run, if an industry consistently fails to yield a profit, businessmen will give up expecting it to yield one. By influencing expectations, therefore, and so controlling prospective profit, realized profit in the long run enters indirectly into price.

Realized profit is partly the result of luck, partly the result of good judgement – since some people take foolish risks – and partly the result of

---

[1] The burden of uncertainty is borne mainly, but not exclusively, by property-owners. An important part is borne by labour, since workers run the risk of injury, ill-health or unemployment. The burden on labour, however, has been relieved by schemes of social insurance and by state expenditure on the social services. Part of the burden on capital has also been transferred to the state, since it may be induced to offer special assistance to industries undergoing a severe depression and so relieve their owners of some of the risk of financial loss. In addition the state assumes the burden of uncertainty for all property in its ownership.

the skilful avoidance or elimination of unnecessary risks – i.e., of outstanding organizing ability. But if anyone shows evidence of good judgement and is right more often than other people, the return which he obtains on his capital is not all pure profit but a combination of profit and earnings of management. For a man of sound judgement can hire his services for a salary to people who have no faith in their own judgement or who recognize their own limitations. In the same way if one man is more skilful than his fellows in *avoiding* or *eliminating* risks because of his superior powers of organization he will earn a higher profit which reflects, not better luck, but greater talent. Once the return to superior organizing ability, like the return to superior judgement, has been transferred to earnings of management we are left with a residue of pure profit which is the net return to uncertainty-bearing and is governed solely by luck.

Trends and fluctuations in aggregate profits

Until the 1950s and 1960s few countries displayed any pronounced trend in aggregate profits, expressed as a proportion of national income or (as we have been considering them) as a rate of return on capital. There was some evidence of a gentle long-term downward drift in each, which often gathered pace in war-time; but no more than that. Since 1960, however, profits have registered a steep decline by some definitions in most large western countries (particularly the Netherlands, Scandinavia, the UK, the US, and West Germany). When measured before tax, but after depreciation and stock appreciation[1], there has been a real tumble, especially as a rate of return on capital. After tax rates, however, have held up much better: governments seem to have responded to the profit squeeze by transferring some of the burden of taxation from companies to wage-earners. Also, since the expansion of the capital stock has generally outpaced the growth of national income for much of the post-war period, profits by all definitions have held up better as a share of national income than a rate of return on capital. Indeed, it is probable that the large rises in all measures of the capital stock have themselves been responsible for much of the fall in the rate of profit.

Aggregate profits fluctuate chiefly because of the cycle in economic activity. If business is brisk and firms are operating at or near capacity, their average costs are likely to be not far from the minimum, while their sales are not far from the maximum. This conjunction generally causes profits to rise steeply, particularly if prices simultaneously begin to increase ahead of costs. On the other hand, at a low level of activity, with heavy standing charges and falling prices, profits tend to disappear and be replaced by losses. For industry as a whole, the same conclusions hold good. Aggregate profits move sharply up and down with boom and slump, inflation and deflation.

While an explanation of fluctuations in profit is necessarily wrapped up in the general theory of business fluctuations, the reasons why profit is higher in one industry than in another and why, over a long period, profits

---

[1] Stock appreciation is the increase in the value of companies' stocks of raw materials and work in progress excluding additions to their volume.

rise or fall, do not hinge entirely on such a theory and can be put quite simply. In what follows it will be assumed that we can disregard fluctuations in the total volume of economic activity but not fluctuations in particular sectors of activity.

Variations in profit between industries

The tendency of competition is to make profits highest in those trades in which the burden of uncertainty is felt to be heaviest. Profits are likely to be high in industries in which methods of production are constantly changing, so that there is need for continuous adaptation of technique; in industries supplying luxury products the demand for which fluctuates rapidly; in industries which are still too young for their prospects to be judged with assurance; in industries in which a long interval elapses between investment and return of capital; in industries in which the labour and capital employed must be more or less irrevocably committed to narrowly specialized tasks, and in industries exposed to specific risks the incidence of which is uncertain – agriculture, for example, with its dependence on weather conditions, or brewing, with the threat of prohibition or of higher duties hanging over it. There is no tendency towards equality of profits, but only towards such rates of profit as compensate for differences in the degree of uncertainty felt by investors in different industries.

Monopoly profit

Just as an element of rent may be included in wages or in interest, so profit may be maintained above the level which is necessary to induce capitalists to bear uncertainty. This surplus profit arises in trades into which entry is not free and in businesses which enjoy some monopolistic advantage over their rivals. The general level of profit may also be maintained at an artificially high level if there are any restrictions on new businesses in general, or any unnecessary impediments to the acquisition of command over capital by enterprising men.

The general level of profit

When there is great uncertainty the normal rate of profit tends to be high. In forecasting the future, people will leave themselves a wide margin of error, and in normal circumstances this will be reflected in a correspondingly high margin of realized profit *on the average*. For *individual* risk-takers, however, profit will range between a very large positive and a very large negative quantity; in a new industry, for example, some firms generally earn enormous profits while others lose their capital altogether. When uncertainty is comparatively negligible, the average margin of prospective, and of realized, profit will be correspondingly small and profit will range within fairly narrow limits; businesses supplying some staple article of clothing or of diet, for example, can generally predict their future profit with much more assurance than firms of shipbuilders and steelmakers. The correspondence between degree of uncertainty and prospective profit – and *a fortiori* between uncertainty and realized profit – is by no means perfect. Many people are more attracted by a spectacular chance of sudden fortune than by humdrum risks which are not likely to cause heavy loss and are equally unlikely to bring great gain; some outsiders, so to speak, are always more heavily backed than they should be. Thus profit is often highest in trades where risks are moderate – neither so negligible as to make risk-bearing almost superfluous, nor so enormous as to attract the incautious and the speculative. It was neither the railways nor the gold-mining industry which earned the highest profits in the late nineteenth century; it is neither the plastics nor the film industry nowadays.

The degree of uncertainty, and hence the rate of profit, will be higher the greater the rate of social change and the greater the degree of immobility of productive resources. The more rapidly change takes place, the more difficult and dangerous is the task of predicting the future and of undertaking the adjustment of resources to future wants. Whether that adjustment is planned by the state or undertaken by private enterprise a larger margin of profit will require to be added to present costs to provide for the uncertainties of the future. The task of adjusting resources to wants will be greatly complicated if these resources are specialized and immobile; for once they are committed to one use it will be difficult to adapt them for other purposes when new information or discoveries call for a change of plans. If resources are immobile the burden of uncertainty in deciding their use is heavy, and any acceleration of social change, by dictating more frequent and more drastic readjustment of resources to wants, will aggravate the burden. The risk of loss through sinking capital in forms no longer required is increased, and to overcome this increased risk of loss there will require to be a correspondingly higher expectation of profit.

Profits and development

The rate of profit, therefore, is intimately connected with what we have called 'development'[1]. A business contributes to development by pioneering new methods and new products. If its innovations are successful it reaps a profit; if it is unfortunate or injudicious it loses its capital. Because development means change, it creates uncertainty; and because development means increased efficiency it creates a prospect of profit. Development, therefore, is one of the chief forces maintaining the rate of profit and is itself one of the chief sources out of which profit is paid.

The personal distribution of non-wage income and wealth

The lion's share of national income is income from employment: wages and salaries. So the distribution of employment income between persons and households is a major influence upon the personal, or household, distribution of income. But it is not the only influence. Non-wage income is a

---

[1] See above, pp. 53–56.

consideration as well. The distribution of rent, interest and profit income between persons or households mirrors the distribution of wealth, from the ownership of which rent, interest and profit incomes are derived. The distribution of wealth is much less equal than that of income. This is partly explained by age differences. Young people have usually next to no wealth. Older people have accumulated savings and pension rights; but their incomes tend to be much more alike. Inheritance also plays a large role, probably a larger role, in explaining the inequality of wealth holdings.

Part V

Income, employment and money

Chapter 21

The national income[1]

Expenditure, production and income in a closed economy

What is bought is sold. The production of goods and services for sale generates incomes for those concerned with their production: wages, interest, rent and profit. Incomes, in turn, are spent on purchases. The three variables – expenditure, production and income – are clearly interdependent. More than that, they are actually *equal* to each other in a 'closed' economy (which has no transactions with the rest of the world).

We can look on E as demand and on Q as supply which are necessarily equal; and both must be equal to income Y in a closed economy. Expenditure (E) equals Production (Q), with two small provisos. E and Q must either both include sales taxes or subsidies imposed by the government (then they are measured at 'market prices'), or both exclude them (so that they are valued at 'factor cost'). Second, a rise in stocks of goods produced is defined as part of E, even if they have not yet been sold by their producer. The owner of these stocks has invested in them; and investment, whether in fixed capital or in stocks, is an element of E. Production Q equals Income (Y), again with some qualification. The measure of Q here must exclude sales taxes and subsidies; while Y is valued before income taxes have been deducted, and transfer payments made by the state (such as unemployment benefit) have been received. A second point to note is that Y includes two items that are at first sight surprising: retained profits by businesses (because they are in fact just as much part of the shareholders' income as dividends), and income generated from ownership of owner-occupied dwellings (the rent the owner –occupant effectively pays himself).

If E equals Q, and Q equals Y, then E equals Y; at least, Y equals E valued at factor cost. But though they are equal when defined appropriately, E, Q and Y are not synonymous. They are measured independently of each other. They are also conceptually distinct. It is the purpose of this chapter to examine what determines their size. There are three sets of influences at work. First, there are *real demand* influences on E. Then, there are the roles played by the supply of and demand for *money*; these also affect E. Lastly, there are important aggregate *supply* influences at work on Q. We shall look at each in turn. Throughout this chapter, we shall assume that the economy is closed.

[1] Readers may find this a difficult chapter to which they should return after completing Part V.

Real demand influences on expenditure

There are three groups of economic agent who contribute to E in a closed economy. There are households, producers and the government.

(a) Households' expenditure

Households' expenditure on new goods and services varies according to the durability of the item purchased. At one end, foodstuffs are purchased very regularly, in the main for almost immediate consumption. At the other, a car or a house is bought infrequently, and as an asset which will give a 'yield' of convenience, or imputed rent, for several years. In the national income accounts, houeholds' expenditure is called consumption, except in the case of house purchases. The purchase of new houses is classified as investment. The purchase of an existing house by family X from family U is, of course, an event of great importance to both families; but from the national standpoint, it is merely a swapping of title-deeds to existing assets, and has no bearing on total E.

Towards the non-durable end of household purchases, we can single out habit and prior commitments of various kinds as major influences. This implies that these sorts of spending exhibit inertia. They tend to repeat themselves, with little change, month after month so influences on them work slowly. Their composition will certainly display some sensitivity to relative prices, but even here the sensitivity will probably be more marked in the long run than on, say, a weekly basis. The scale of households' spending on non-durable goods will be affected by changes in the regular, or standard, income they expect to receive in a normal future period. An unexpected promotion of an income-earner to a higher-paid job, or a large unexpected rise in wealth with enhanced expectations of future unearned income, would be examples of phenomena that could cause a household to raise its level of purchases of these goods substantially and fairly quickly. By contrast, promotion or legacies which had been expected would not have nearly so much effect. Nor would a jump in income that the household believed to be purely transitory (a non-recurrent pay bonus, or a temporary cut in income tax rates, for instance). The household's current 'disposable', or after-tax, income has always been found to affect non-durable purchases to some degree, in a wide variety of studies. On average, it appears that a once-for-all increase in current disposable real income of £1 a week would raise it by between 10 and 30p per week in the current quarter, and between 30 and 50p per week in the current year; in the end, after two or three years have elapsed, it would rise by about 80p per week. Current income has a large role to play even in the short run, in certain circumstances: if households base their income expectations largely on current income experience (most appear not to, but some may); or if obstacles to borrowing and lending force people to try to synchronize spending with a time-pattern of income receipts over which they have little control. This latter possibility is especially likely in economies where credit markets are underdeveloped, and for the young and low-paid.

Durable purchases, on the other hand, are very volatile. Even at the aggregate level, there is often a negative correlation between purchases in one year, and those in the next. In the UK, registrations of new cars may be as much as 25–40% higher in boom years than in the troughs. By contrast, even the severest recession, by post-war standards, will rarely lower non-durable consumption purchases by more than 2½–3% below normal. Private sector housebuilding is even more volatile than the new car market; the demand for electrical houehold appliances, and furnishings, is somewhat less so. Evidence drawn chiefly from the US economy tends to confirm the importance of factors that theoretical reasoning would suggest as major influences on the level of spending on durables: interest rates (negative); credit availability, current income and changes in the level of real liquid assets held by households (all positive); the price of the durable good itself, and the amount of it bought in the recent past (both negative); expectations of inflation, or tax changes, that would raise the price of the good later (positive).

In the UK, total consumers' expenditure accounts for between three-fifths and two-thirds of national income. As a proportion of personal disposable income (after-tax income actually received by households, excluding such items as retained business profits) it is higher, falling from over 98% in 1950 to about 85% in 1975. The ratio of personal savings to personal disposable income rose about tenfold between those years. In the US, however, this savings ratio has been steadier, fluctuating between 5 and 10% for most of the past 150 years.

There is also a striking difference in the shares of food spending between the UK and the US. The food difference is explained by the fact that food prices are lower in the US and the demand for food is broadly inelastic to price; and also by the lower level of income per head in the UK, since food has a higher budget share for those with lower incomes. The savings difference is more of a puzzle. Part of the reason may be that interest payments, which are typically augmented by expectations of inflation when inflation rises and are hence exaggerated in the national income statistics, bulk more heavily among the income receipts of UK than US households; this could mean that the UK savings ratio looks higher than it really is. Secondly, expectations of inflation may have different effects in the US and the UK. In the US they seem to induce people to buy more, before the prices rise; in the UK, they may make people feel worse off and therefore spend less.

Generalizing and summing up, we must give pride of place to current income as the major influence on total consumers' expenditure. Except in the case of durable spending, it works with something of a delay; but its total effect, given time, swamps the influence of everything else. Its effect is, of course, positive. This is illustrated in *Figure 21.1* by the upward-sloping line CC, which has a gradient less than 1. CC is known as the 'consumption function'. Its gradient is called the 'marginal propensity to consume'. It gives the proportion of a rise in income that is devoted to increased consumption. In the long run, of course, CC is much steeper (and starts from a much lower position on the vertical axis) than in the short run, which is depicted in *Figure 21.1*. The position of the CC line will depend on the many factors, other than income, that we have encountered already. First, the positive influences that make for a high CC: households' wealth; their expectations of normal, future (or 'permanent') income;

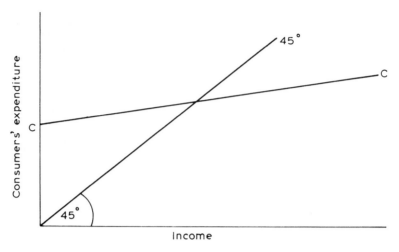

Figure 21.1 The consumption function

credit availability and holdings of liquid assets (especially important for durable purchases). Then the negative influences, which depress CC: interest rates, income tax rates; the price level; recent durable purchases.

Finally, we recall that households also spend on new houses, which is part of investment. This is best analysed, together with the quantitatively larger investment spending by producers, in the next section.

(b) Producers' expenditure

In addition to paying households or other producers for the loan of labour, land and capital – in the form of wages, rent, interest and shareholders' dividends – producers spend directly on goods and services. Much of this direct expenditure is devoted to raw materials and intermediate goods. The manager of a car factory will purchase components from other companies and plants, for instance; and other items, such as fuel and metals, will also be bought on a regular basis. But the components, fuel and metals will be used up in the process of production, and be converted into the output of the factory. If a producer's inventories of raw materials, intermediate goods, and final output are the same at the end of a year as at its beginning, he has invested nothing net during the year under the heading of 'working capital'. An increase in inventories, however, implies positive investment in working capital; a decrease, disinvestment. From the standpoint of total national expenditure, E, it is the *change in producers' inventories*, not the total of their gross purchases of raw materials and intermediate goods, that counts. We shall return to what explains changes in inventories below.

Producers' purchases of new capital equipment, new buildings and new plant are a different matter. As they represent acquisitions of newly produced final goods, they constitute part of total national expenditure, E. The purchase of an old building or a second-hand machine is not part of E: it is merely an exchange of title-deeds to an existing asset, like the change in ownership of an existing house.

Producers' expenditure is best considered under three headings: investment in new plant and machinery; investment in buildings (and
households' investments in new dwellings can be subsumed conveniently
under this head); and investment in inventories.

Investment in new plant and machinery is an addition to the stock of
plant and machinery. Why should a firm wish to increase this stock? The
simplest explanation is because its managers presumably expect it, on
balance, to add to profits. This it will do (assuming that the costs of the
investments are borne earlier on average than its receipts arrive) if the rate
of return on it proves to exceed the cost of capital. From this reasoning, it
appears that a rise in the cost of capital could be expected to delay or lower
investment spending, while an increase in the expected rate of return
should have the opposite effect. The cost of capital is the cost of
borrowing, at the margin, if the producer has to borrow. If he is able to pay
for the investment project from internal sources (retained profits, plus
funds set aside for depreciation) the relevant cost is the financial return the
producer would have earned by not committing these funds to the project.
The lower these rates of interest are, it appears therefore, the larger the
stock of plant and machinery which the producer will wish to possess; and
the larger the required stock of plant and machinery, the greater the
probability that he will wish to add to his existing stock while the greater
this existing stock the less he will wish to add to it.

Probably still more crucial to the explanation of investment than interest
rates, are the producer's expectations of the rate of return. A firm demand
for the commodity that the plant and machinery produce is an absolute
requirement for profitability. In competitive industries, expectation of firm
demand means the expectation of high prices relative to costs in the years
that follow the installation of the new equipment. In monopoly, it means
the opportunity to charge appropriately high prices in these years, on the
output levels now being planned or expected. For want of more reliable
information on the state of future demand, producers may treat present
and recent past sales figures as a useful guide. An unexpected jump in sales
in the recent past may cause them to revise upwards estimates of future
receipts on hypothetical investment projects not yet undertaken; this is
quite likely to increase their assessments of capital stock requirements,
which in turn must raise the probability of investment. Another factor
which will have a key bearing upon the expected returns from investment
in plant and machinery is the acquisition cost of the piece of equipment
itself. The cheaper it is to the firm buying it, the more of it the firm will
want to operate.

Summarizing so far, we may say that producers' demand for new plant
and machinery will be affected: negatively by interest rates, by the price of
the equipment, and by the stock of equipment it already possesses; and
positively by the expected demand for the commodity it will produce (and
for this, present sales figures may be a partial proxy). Furthermore, there
may be a lag of six months or more before any influence on investment
takes effect. There may also be other influences discernible. If a firm finds
that the borrowing rates of interest are above those for lending (this is
typical for small companies), the timing of profit receipts will play a large
role in determining the timing of investment spending. The exact timing of

spending on new plant and machinery should also be influenced by expectations of prices, both for the equipment itself and the commodity produced. If both are expected to ease back for a year or two, and then rise strongly, it will appear much wiser to postpone the project for, say, fifteen months. Investment is also highly susceptible to changes in technology. There is also replacement investment, which depends chiefly on the size of the capital stock and the speed with which it depreciates. Finally, the maximization of profit is a highly questionable assumption for producers. Nationalized industries' investment will be subject to frequent and complex intervention by government, and often follows quite different paths from those of private industries. In private industries, managers' aversion to risk may well mean that investment is slower and smaller than it would otherwise be, while the emphasis on other objectives, such as growth, could imply the opposite.

Investment in buildings by companies is subject to the same influences, for the same reasons, as investment in plant and machinery. As a whole, it is often more volatile, perhaps because it is more subject to the vagaries of the weather, and to indivisibilities. Housebuilding investment by households is also highly volatile. The UK has traditionally witnessed a 25–30-year cycle, with housebuilding booms in the 1870s, and the years 1895–1904, 1925–1935 and 1953–1965. There have also been quicker fluctuations, particularly since the Second World War, which can be put down largely to monetary conditions. Low interest rates and easy credit from building societies and banks make for a high demand for houses, high house prices, and a high level of 'starts' of new houses.

Lastly, investment in inventories of working capital. Although small as a share of total E (rarely as much as $1\frac{1}{2}\%$), they are liable to large fluctuations. There is a lag of some weeks before a change in final sales is transmitted back to producers. In the meantime, inventories of unsold goods in shops, warehouses and factories can rise or fall substantially. Eventually, production responds, and this may induce a sudden hiccup, up or down, in inventories of raw materials. Sometimes production may diverge from, or even lead expenditure, again causing temporary additions to (or depletions from) inventories. Inventories are a buffer between output and demand; in manufacturing industry, they act as a temporary substitute for price changes: an excess demand for strawberries or equities will lead to an immediate rise in prices, but an excess demand for cars will lead, initially at least, to a run-down in stocks of cars awaiting sale.

(c) Government expenditure

Central and local government make five kinds of payment to residents of the home country. First, they make payments to each other, which are generally of no significance for E. Second, they may acquire existing assets from households or producers – for example, when a business is nationalized. Again, E is affected neither by this, nor by the third type of payment, a transfer payment such as unemployment benefit paid to households or producers. This third type is best treated as a negative tax. But the last two kinds of payment are counted as part of E. These are payments for current goods and services purchased by central or local government and purchases of capital assets, such as newly constructed council houses, warships and hospitals. The current goods and services include the salaries of the armed forces, doctors and school-teachers, and current supplies of goods and services to maintain defence, hospital, educational and other establishments.

The primary explanation for spending by government is that only government can secure an appropriate provision of *public goods*. Public goods have two characteristics: they can be consumed by everyone in a society and no one can be excluded from them. Defence is a perfect example. All of us may experience the benefit (if benefit it be) of a warship or a squadron of fighter aeroplanes. And no one can be prevented from receiving this benefit. If I buy and drink a litre of milk, on the other hand, no one else can drink it; and I can deny access to others to my milk easily, before I drink it. So milk is a pure 'private good'. A public park is somewhere on the borderline; some of its appeal comes from the solitude the visitor finds there, and to this exent it is a private good; and access may be denied by fencing the park off, and charging entry through a turnstile. If society is composed of numerous egocentric individuals all acting independently, (approximately) enough milk will be provided for everyone taken together; there will be a fair amount of park space, but probably rather less than there should be; and there will be far too little spent on defence. Everyone will rely chiefly upon defence provision by others for his own wants, and place no value on the benefits others receive from his own provision of defence. In order to secure release from this unsatisfactory state of affairs (which is an example of the 'Prisoners' Dilemma', a state of conflict between what seems best to each and what is best for all), society needs a government to take decisions upon defence spending, and the involuntary tax payments that inevitably accompany it.

Other justifications given for government spending include the 'merit-good' argument that peoples' preferences may not accord exactly with their best interests, so that some goods (perhaps libraries, health and education) should be given free and/or compulsorily, or at least subsidized; and also the political 'income-distribution' argument that government provision of certain goods (low-rent housing, for instance) may reduce poverty or inequality. All three arguments have one element in common. This is the hypothesis that, left to itself, a free-market economy can malfunction.

Total expenditure

Expenditure by consumers, producers and government is added together to form E. If consumption spending is C, and government spending G, investment spending by producers and by households in purchases of new houses may be labelled I, from which we may state $E = C + I + G$. I and G may be added vertically to the CC line for consumers' expenditure that was presented in *Figure 21.1* to form the line EE in *Figure 21.2*. EE depicts the real level of expenditure, for each level of income. Like the CC line, it slopes up, but at a gradient of less than +1. If total I is affected positively by national income, and G is independent of it, the EE line will be steeper than CC. The EE line may be called the Total Expenditure Function. The position of EE will depend, amongst other factors, upon:

1. positive influences: the level of government spending, producers' expectations of future output prices; the availability of credit and supply of liquid assets; consumers' wealth and *expectations of future income*;
2. negative influences: tax rates; rates of interest; the current price levels of all goods.

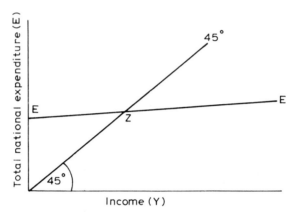

Figure 21.2 The total expenditure function

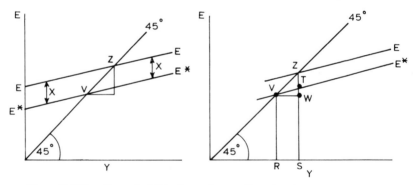

Figure 21.3 The effects of a fall in the total expenditure function, and the multiplier

Now two lines are drawn in *Figure 21.3*: the EE line, and a 45° line from the origin. The latter represents the equality between Y and E which we saw earlier to follow by definition, if one of two assumptions were made. In *Figure 21.3*, therefore, there are two relationships at work: a necessary equality between E and Y (the 45° line) and a dependence of E upon Y (the EE line). If both must be true, the levels of E (and Y) must be determined where the two lines cut, at Z. Y could not be higher than this, because production would then outstrip expenditure (this is known as a 'deflationary gap'); nor lower, because the opposite would then be true (an 'inflationary gap').

Suppose, now, that the line EE dropped by the vertical distance x. There could be many reasons for this: a rise in the value of any of the negative influences on EE, or a fall in that of any of the positive influences. Perhaps the easiest example to consider is a fall in government spending. A lower value of EE (at E*E* in *Figure 21.3*) would mean that the point of intersection between the 45° line and the total expenditure function fell from Z to V. The right-hand panel in *Figure 21.3* illustrates this in more detail. Y must fall from S to R. This drop in income equals the horizontal distance from W to V. How large is this in relation to x, the vertical distance between the old EE line and the new, depressed, expenditure line E*E*? The fall in $Y = SR = VW = WZ$ (since VZ is on the 45° line). Now $WZ = ZT + TW = x + VW \cdot TW/VW = x + VW \cdot e$, if e is defined as the gradient of the expenditure line. But since $WZ = VW =$ the change in Y, we have

Change in $Y = x + e$. Change in Y

$$\therefore \text{ Change in } Y = \frac{x}{1-e}$$

$$\therefore \frac{\text{Change in } Y}{x} = \frac{1}{1-e}$$

Now this last expression $(1/1-e)$ is known as the 'multiplier'. It tells us how much income will change, given a one-unit change in expenditure for a given level of income, assuming that all the other influences on expenditure are given. Since e lies between $+1$ and 0 by assumption, the multiplier has a value greater than $+1$. The example of a cut in the level of government spending illustrates the workings of the multiplier. If the government cuts its road-building programme, for instance, the income of road-builders will be reduced; they will tend to lower their own expenditure on goods and services; this will set in motion a sequence of cuts in other people's expenditures. These indirect falls in expenditure are shown in *Figure 21.3* by the distance *TW*.

There are, however, a number of important qualifications that must be introduced. First, the curve EE moves over time: it registers little sensitivity to Y in the short run (within a year, for example), and is represented more accurately by a very gently upward-sloping line in this period. Furthermore, its position is only gradually altered by changes in any of the many influences we have considered upon it.

Second, we have ignored the role of exports and imports; our economy is closed. We take account of this later, in Chapter 28.

Third, the role of supply has so far been ignored. In fact, the society's endowments of natural resources, capital, and labour will place clearly defined limits, given the present state of knowledge, upon the level of output that can be produced. *Figure 21.2* should be amended, as in *Figure 21.4*, by the insertion of a vertical limit $\bar{Q}$, illustrating the ceiling set by productive potential. If the EE line and the 45° line cut at a level of Y less than $\bar{Q}$, there will be underproduction, and underemployment or unemployment of labour, capital or both. This is shown in the right panel of *Figure 21.4*. If these two lines intersect even slightly to the right of $\bar{Q}$, the economy is likely to be subject to suppressed or open inflation: this is illustrated in the left hand panel of *Figure 21.4*.

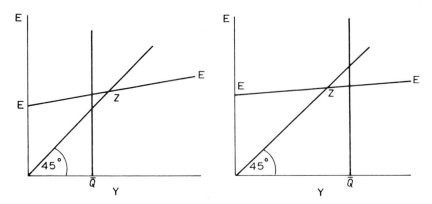

Figure 21.4 The productive potential barrier: excess demand at productive potential, and underemployment/unemployment due to demand deficiency

Finally, it is clear that the position of E depends upon several factors which cannot be treated properly as variable, determined 'outside' the system. Two factors in particular cry out for inclusion in a more complete view of the way the economy works: these are the rates of interest, and the level of prices. It is the purpose of the next two sections to tie up these important loose ends, and provide that more complete view.

The role of money and interest rates in determining aggregate demand

This section takes a preliminary look at the demand for and supply of money, and at how they fit into the determination of aggregate demand. A more thorough treatment will be given later, in Chapters 24 and 25. At this stage, we shall make some simplifying assumptions, which enable us to get to grips with some of the salient issues.

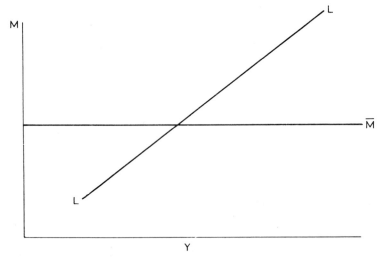

Figure 21.5 The demand for money as a function of real income with given interest rates and price level

The supply of money, let us suppose, is a unique, readily definable variable controlled by the government, and pre-set at a particular value in money terms at $\bar{M}$ (e.g., £60 000 000 000). The demand for money varies positively with the price level and with income (since both of these must influence the average levels of bank balances and cash that households and firms wish to hold for the purpose of making transactions). But the demand for money varies negatively with the rates of interest available on alternative assets. The higher the yield available on building society deposits or government bonds, for instance, the stronger the incentive to cut down on balances of relatively unremunerative money. Two final assumptions: the demand for money and supply of money are always equal, as a result of sufficient flexibility of interest rates or other variables; and, lastly, there is only one kind of asset in addition to money – call it A – with a unique rate of interest (symbol: R) upon it.

Figure 21.5 illustrates the workings of the monetary part of our economy. The vertical axis shows the stock of money, M: the supply of M is a horizontal line, $\bar{M}$: and the demand for money (symbol: L) is an upward-sloping curve LL. Strictly, one LL curve may be drawn only if R and the price level are given: for a rise in the price level must raise LL, while a rise in 'the' interest rate, R, must lower it, to the right. If the price level is given at $\bar{P}$, therefore, we may show a family of LL curves, all drawn for different values of R: this is done in *Figure 21.6*. The higher the rate of

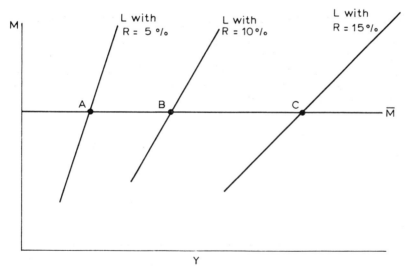

Figure 21.6 The demand for money as a function of real income with different interest rates but a given price level

interest, the higher the value of income compatible with equality because the demand for and supply of money. This is so because a high interest rate discourages people from holding money, thus permitting a given money supply to support a larger value of transactions. Put another way, a rise in income will tend to raise interest rates if the supply of money is fixed: the rise in the demand for money can only be choked off by the rise

in interest rates. Points A, B and C in *Figure 21.7* illustrate positions of
'equilibrium' between R and Y.

Figure 21.7 links up our brief monetary analysis with the expenditure
analysis in *Figures 21.2* and *21.3*. First, however, we must recall that the
position of the line EE varies with R: a rise in 'the' rate of interest must
lead to a fall, to the right, in the height of the total expenditure function
itself. This is shown in the top panel of *Figure 21.7*. The bottom panel
reproduces *Figure 21.6*; and the middle panel depicts the two separate links
between R and Y: the upper panel link shows a negative relation between
Y and R (a higher rate discourages investment and durable purchases,
implying a low value of expenditure) while the lower panel link has a
positive relation (a high R releases money balances for supporting a high

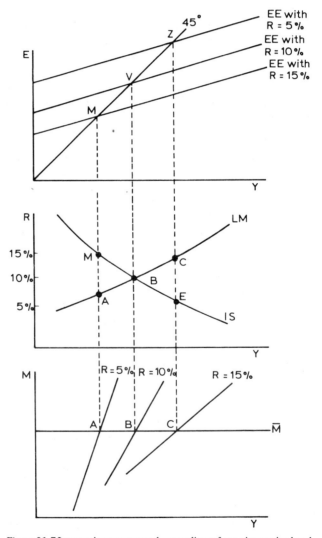

Figure 21.7 Integrating money and expenditure for a given price level

value of transactions, hence a high level of income when the price level is given). The first, negative link is called 'the IS curve' and shown by the downward sloping curve in the middle panel connecting points M, V and Z. The second, positive link is known as 'the LM curve'; this is the curve connecting A, B and C in the middle panel.

The interest rate, and the level of income are now simultaneously determined, in the middle panel of *Figure 21.7*. In the example, R is 10%, and Y is at the value B, or V in terms of the upper diagram. We now consider the consequences of some changes in the government policy instruments, G and $\bar{M}$. A rise in G would mean a rise in the family of EE lines in the upper panel. Each would cut the 45° line at a higher level of Y, for any given value of R so the IS curve in the middle panel must move out to the right. This must entail (1) a rise in the rate of interest, unless LM is horizontal, which may tend to 'crowd out' at least a little of the level of investment that would otherwise have occurred; and (2) a rise in the level of income, unless LM is vertical. A vertical LM will imply that only the interest rate rises, and that the rise in G is fully offset, within an unchanged level of Y, by falls in C, I, or both.

Alternatively, consider a rise in $\bar{M}$. This leads to a higher level of $\bar{M}$ in the bottom panel of *Figure 21.7*. $\bar{M}$ cuts each demand for money curve at a higher value of Y, for a given value of R. So the LM curve must move downward to the right, in the middle panel. This must entail (1) a fall in the rate of interest, unless the LM curve is horizontal (in the relevant range, at least) and (2) a rise in the level of income, unless the IS curve is vertical (which would imply that E, taken as a whole, was unaffected by a change in interest rates). Finally, the rise in $\bar{M}$ would, in fact, also affect the total expenditure functions in the upper panel, in all probability raising them, albeit perhaps slightly and rather slowly. The reason for this last effect is the dependence of at least consumers' expenditure on durables upon liquid assets and credit availability.

These important conclusions are, however, not final. This is so because we have not considered the effect that these changes may have upon the price level. The increases in G and M might have much, even most, of their effect spent in raising prices. In the next section we complete the picture by introducing an aggregate supply curve which will tell us the extent to which this will be so. For the present however all we have is an analysis of aggregate demand. We know that all the curves in *Figure 21.7* were drawn on the assumption that the price level was given. How would a price rise affect them, and, in consequence, the level of real aggregate demand? *Figure 21.8* portrays the answer to this central question. In the upper panel, the rise in the price level will tend to discourage spending by consumers, and possibly also producers on investments goods, for reasons already seen. Consumers' wealth falls in purchasing power, and households are induced to retrench in consequence. This effect cuts the expenditure function to EO, if R stays at 10%. In the lower panel, the rise in prices must increase the demand for money. If R were to remain at 10%, the demand for money curve would move upward to the left to LO. The new IS and LM curves are drawn as IS* and LM* in the middle panel. In the event, the middle panel shows that R must move; in our example, R must go up to 12% (it might have fallen, had the IS curve effect dominated

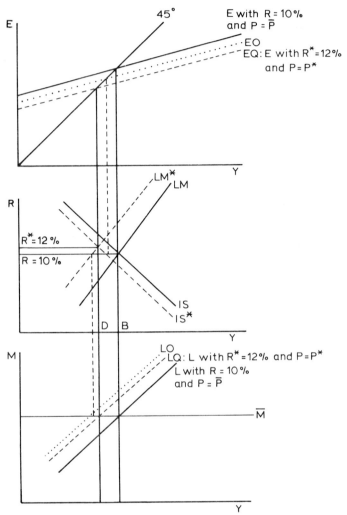

Figure 21.8 The effects of a rise in the price level from P̄ (the original price) to P* (a higher price)

the effect of the higher price level on the LM curve); and so new EE and demand for money curves (EQ and LQ), appropriate to the 12% interest rate as well as to the higher price level P*, are drawn in the top and bottom panels. Most importantly of all, the level of Y sinks from B to D. Notice what we have discovered: a rise in the price level tends to lower real aggregate demand, for two reasons. First, it cuts real wealth and lowers expenditure directly. Second, it raises the demand for money; this pushes up interest rates, in response to which expenditure falls back. At one extreme, real aggregate demand would be virtually independent of the price level, if the spending effect from a change in real wealth were negligible, and if either the LM curve were horizontal (this would occur with a 'liquidity trap' where interest rates are effectively independent of the supply of or demand for money, or if the *supply* of money were infinitely elastic to the rate of interest) or the IS curve were vertical (illustrating independence of E from interest rates). This extreme may be referred to as the Ultra-Keynesian Special Case[1]. At the other extreme, which we may call the Ultra-Monetarist Special Case, the LM curve is vertical, and the level of real aggregate demand is determined exclusively by: the supply of money, $\bar{M}$; the demand for money, L (which is simply an institutionally-determined completely predictable, multiple k of the price level and the level of real aggregate demand, Y)[2]; and the price level, P. These two possibilities are illustrated in *Figure 21.9*.

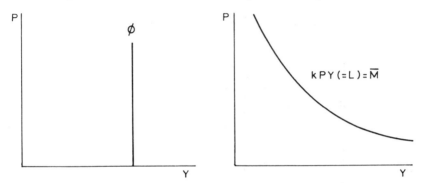

Figure 21.9 The ultra-Keynesian and ultra-monetarist special cases for the aggregate demand curve

A less extreme presentation of aggregate demand is shown in *Figure 21.10*. This allows aggregate demand, f, to be affected by the money supply *and* by government spending, as we saw in the discussion that followed the presentation of *Figure 21.7*. The arrows drawn above $\bar{M}$ and G show that following a rise in either, f moves in a northeastward direction. A rise in the demand for money (L), on the other hand – such as might be occasioned by a sudden fear that asset prices could fall – would push f southwestward. A large role is reserved for expectations. A deterioration in expectations of future profits would, for instance, threaten to reduce investment; this would lead to a leftward movement of the IS curve in *Figure 21.7* and, unless the LM curve were vertical, to a fall in the level of real aggregate demand, Y, for a given price level. So f would move leftward, except in the Ultra-Monetarist Special Case. An opposite direction of movement might be expected if there were an increased expectation of inflation, although much of the effect of this would be shown by a fall in L; and it is possible, given our earlier discussion, that the

[1] Aggregate demand is depicted by ϕ, a vertical line: the price level has no effect on aggregate demand. The position of ϕ is also independent of the money supply, $\bar{M}$. It is governed instead chiefly by G, and the habits and expectations underlying C, I, and L. These views are an extreme version of the ideas presented by J. M. Keynes, *The General Theory of Interest, Employment and Money* (Macmillan, 1936).

[2] Aggregate demand is presented as a rectangular hyperbola, of Y against P, the position of which depends simply on the ratio of the money supply $\bar{M}$ to the institutionally-determined k. This follows from assuming that the demand for money is always a multiple k of the price level and Y, and that it must equal the supply of money. This is the simplest version of the traditional Quantity Theory of money, as described by Irving Fisher, see pp. 313–314.

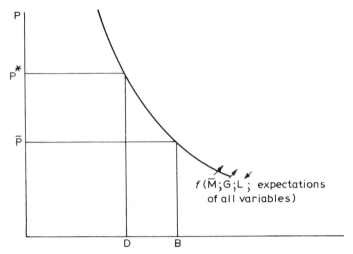

Figure 21.10 The aggregate demand curve: the general case

UK consumers' reaction (unlike that of the US consumers) could greatly mitigate the northeastward movement in f which would otherwise occur.

The aggregate demand curve, whatever its shape and however sensitive it is to other variables, tells only half the story of output and the price level. Even the question raised above, about how prices react to changes in M or G, cannot yet be answered. We have only one relationship linking P and Y. Before further progress can be made, a second link must be found. That second link is the aggregate supply curve.

Aggregate supply

Let us suppose that our economy produces just one commodity. Labour is the only variable factor of production. There are diminishing returns to it. The money wage rate is given, as are the stocks of fixed factors, such as capital, and the level of technology. The commodity in question is produced by numerous competitive firms.

In these circumstances, there will be a positive relationship between the price level and the level of output. A rise in prices will be needed to encourage the firms to hire more labour, since the money wage rate is given and there are diminishing returns to labour. More labour will be hired if, and only if, the real wage rate is lowered. This requires a rise in the price level. If more labour is hired, more output will be produced. So the link between an increased price level and an increased level of output is proved.

Our assumptions are, of course, highly artificial: national output consists of a vast number of different products, many (perhaps all) produced under imperfect competition; there are many different types of labour and capital; capital is rarely completely fixed, and labour is rarely freely variable; and the set of money wage rates is rarely static. But artificial as they are, our assumptions do provide the basis of a clear answer to our earlier questions of what determines the extent to which rises in G or M raise prices as opposed to real income. Everything depends on how elastic output is to the price level. Under our assumptions, the elasticity of aggregate supply will be

$$\frac{\text{elasticity of substitution between}}{\text{labour and the fixed factor(s)}} \cdot \frac{\text{labour's share of income}}{1 - \text{labour's share of income}}$$

Figure 21.11 illustrates three possible types of aggregate supply curve. Panel (a) shows it almost horizontal. In panel (a), we need a high elasticity of substitution, or a high labour share, so that diminishing returns to labour only set in very slowly. In panel (b), the aggregate supply curve is unit-elastic: this it would be if, for example, the substitution elasticity were one and labour's share of national income were one-half. Panel (c) displays a very inelastic supply curve, illustrating strong complementarity between labour and the other factor(s), or a low labour share, or both. In case (a), a rise in aggregate demand (occasioned, for example, by a rise in M or G) would have most of its effect in increasing real output, and raise the price level rather little. In panel (c), however, it would be the price level that increased much more than the real income level, since aggregate supply was so inelastic. One factor which must make the aggregate supply curve vertical at some point is the barrier to production reached when available labour is fully employed. This causes a kink in the aggregate supply curve, shown in panel (a) of *Figure 21.12*.

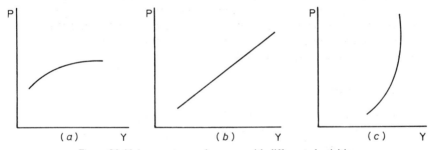

Figure 21.11 Aggregate supply curves with different elasticities

Figure 21.11 shows how a shift in the level of aggregate demand can alter prices and output. But the aggregate supply curve could also move. There are three chief influences upon it: the size of the capital stock, the level of technology, and the level of money wage rates. A rise in the stock of capital, as a result of a period of heavy investment, would move the aggregate supply curve southeastward, and (all else equal) cut the price level and raise that of output. If aggregate demand were elastic, the second effect would predominate; if inelastic, the first. A technical improvement would also tend to bring output up and prices down, for the same reason. A rise in the money wage rate, however, would have the opposite effect. By increasing the marginal costs of production, firms would respond by hiring less labour, and producing less output, at a given price level; so the aggregate supply curve would move northeastward. This movement would tend to cut output and raise prices, in proportions dependent upon the elasticity of aggregate demand.

The picture changes drastically if it is the real wage rate, rather than the money wage rate, that is assumed to be given. In this case, the aggregate supply curve will be vertical. This is so because only one level of employment will be consistent with a particular real wage rate: this is where the real wage rate equals the marginal product of labour (which is itself assumed to decline continuously as employment is increased). If a fixed real wage rate fixes the level of employment, it also fixes the level of output (since the stock of capital, and level of technology, are assumed given).

Keynesian and monetarist views about aggregate demand and aggregate supply

We are now in a position to portray visually the different beliefs inherent in *Keynesian* and *monetarist* views of the workings of the economy. In the Keynesian view, aggregate supply is rather elastic, and typically a good deal more elastic to the price level than aggregate demand. It follows from this that increases in M or G (particularly the latter) will be reasonably effective in increasing output, provided at least that there is some unemployed labour to be hired; but while increases in output will be associated, at least as often as not, with changes in aggregate demand, a rise in the price level can be attributed chiefly to a rise in money wage rates unaccompanied by a sufficient rise in labour productivity. Hence the Keynesian policy prescriptions: fight inflation with incomes policy, constraining the growth of money wage rates; sustain the growth of output by expansionary policies of demand management. This Keynesian view is shown in panel (a) of *Figure 21.12*.

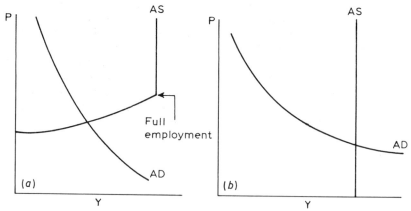

Figure 21.12 Keynesian and monetarist views of aggregate demand and aggregate supply: (a) The Keynesian view; (b) The monetarist view

In contrast, the monetarist argues that aggregate demand is more elastic, much more elastic, than aggregate supply. The aggregate supply curve is drawn vertical, on either of two assumptions: either the real wage rate is fixed, which we saw earlier meant that employment and output were independent of the price level; or there is a pronounced tendency to full employment, brought about by a high degree of flexibility of money wage rates to any shortages or imbalance in the labour market. The vertical aggregate supply curve implies that changes in M have no effect at all on the level of real output or employment. All that follows from a rise in M, at a given level of real income, is a rise in prices. A rise in real income depends on forces acting on aggregate supply: investment which adds to the stock of capital, or technical change that increases the output that can be derived from given inputs, would both lead to higher output. So would a rise in the labour force, or an increased willingness to supply labour on the part of existing workers (e.g., in response to tax changes), if the full employment explanation of the vertical aggregate supply curve were given; while if the real wage rate were given, a fall in its level, however this came about, would lead to a rightward movement of the aggregate supply curve. The monetarist policy prescription is to keep the growth of the money supply as low as possible, if inflation is to be avoided.

The issues on which controversy turns are:

1. the role of interest rates in influencing the demand for money;
2. the volatility of the demand for money;
3. the role of interest rates, and money holdings, in influencing expenditure; and
4. the rapidity with which money wage rates change, and what causes them to change; and
5. what causes the money supply to change.

The typical monetarist view is that (3) is much more important than (1); that there is no argument or evidence for (2); that money wage rates change rapidly in response to excess demand or supply for labour, and fully incorporate expectations of inflation; and, on (5), that changes in the money supply occur only because the central bank permits them. In contrast, the typical Keynesian view stresses the stickiness of money wage rates (at least under conditions of unemployment); it emphasizes the possibility of 'endogenous' changes in the money supply, for example in response to interest rate changes, with the consequence that the LM curve in *Figures 21.7* and *21.8* may be more elastic, and the AD curves in *Figures 21.9–21.12* less elastic; it believes that (1) is much more important than (3); and it maintains that (2) is a serious possibility. The chapters that follow explore these (and related) issues in more detail.

Chapter 22

Fluctuations in the national income: unemployment and the trade cycle

The national income fluctuates, sometimes violently and with terrible consequences for large groups of people. Between 1929 and 1932 the national income of the United States fell, in money terms, by over 50% and the wage and salary bill by 40%; between 1938 and 1942 national income doubled and wages and salaries almost doubled. In real terms the fluctuations were rather less severe because prices fell in the first of those periods and rose in the second; but even in real terms the changes in the level of economic activity were enormous.

Unemployment

These changes were not due to some temporary aberration in productivity such as a fluctuation in harvest yields but reflected a failure to make full and continuous use of the productive resources available. This failure was most conspicuous in relation to manpower. The outstanding feature of the periodic slumps of pre-war years was the waste of productive power in unemployment that accompanied them. The loss due to unemployment in the United States in the 1930s was at least as great as the loss suffered in war-time through the absence of millions of men in the armed services and the diversion of manpower to the production of munitions. In Britain the loss of income in the decade before the war through failure to find a use for the energies of the unemployed can be put at not less than 10%.

The evil of unemployment is not to be measured in purely economic terms any more than is the cost of making war. It was the unemployment of one German industrial worker in three in 1933, as much as any other single thing, that gave Hitler his chance of power. The social strain of intense and protracted unemployment could overturn any economic system. Even in personal terms, unemployment cannot be equated with mere loss of income. A long spell of unemployment ruins a man's self-respect by depriving him of an honourable opportunity of earning a living; it creates a sense of frustration and finally of uselessness; it saps his powers of concentration and his capacity for normal enjoyments; it makes for tension within the family and within the community; and it leaves men apathetic to ordinary social activities and duties, or ready to lend a willing ear to violent expedients for regaining status and a sense of purpose.

The worker's attitude to his job is also perverted. He goes in fear of losing it and yet in fear of excelling in it: he can neither afford to be conspicuously inefficient nor to be conspicuously efficient. 'So long as there is a scramble for jobs, it is idle to deplore the inevitable growth of jealous restrictions, of demarcations, or organized or voluntary limitations of output, of resistance to technical advance. . . . Failure to use our productive powers is the source of an interminable succession of evils.'[1]

Frictional unemployment

Even in war-time, when the demand for labour is intense, unemployment never entirely disappears. A residue remains which, in more normal circumstances, may reach quite considerable dimensions. This residue includes, first of all, seasonal unemployment. There are few industries in which it is possible to maintain steady employment all the year round; either there are seasonal peaks in demand (e.g., in the manufacture of umbrellas, toys and motor cars), or weather conditions hold up work at certain seasons of the year (e.g., in agriculture and building). These seasonal irregularities do not necessarily create unemployment. Sometimes it is possible without excessive inconvenience to make use of the services of married women in peak periods, or to provide off-peak employment for regular workers by dovetailing one kind of work with another (e.g., by making straw hats and bowler hats in the same works). Some workers, too – the salaried staff, for example – may be able to cope with seasonal pressure by working harder, slacking off again once the rush is over – a practice of particular importance in peasant communities where the problem of seasonal unemployment tends to be transformed into one of *under*-employment during the winter months.

Unemployment also arises in industries in which demand fluctuates erratically. A dock labourer, for example, may work at high pressure for a few hours or a few days when a large number of ships put in, and find himself unemployed for the rest of the week when the berths are empty. Anyone who is engaged in repair work, or in making goods influenced by fashion, is likely to have a similar experience. Bad organization, accident and failure of supplies may also lead to unemployment.

It is common, too, for some days or even weeks of unemployment to elapse between the conclusion of one job and the discovery of another. This interval will probably be affected by the level and type of unemployment benefit, and no doubt, too, by the quality of information available to those seeking and offering jobs. There may be vacancies in plenty of other places and industries, but none of them, given human immobility, quite suitable. However well-organized the labour market, therefore, and however keen the demand for labour, some unemployment will persist.

Sructural unemployment

Hardly less avoidable than frictional unemployment, and sometimes classified with it, it unemployment caused by changes in the structure of

---

[1] Lord Beveridge, *Full Employment in a Free Society* (London, 1944), p. 248.

industry: by changes in industrial organization and technique, by the decline of major industries, and by the migration of industry from one region to another. All of these played an important part in the unemployment problem which Britain and other countries had to face in the 1920s and 1930s. Technical progress was extremely rapid and displaced workers who could not always be re-absorbed in other industries. The heavy industries, such as iron and steel, engineering and shipbuilding, in competition with the expanded war industries of other countries, were obliged to contract. The new and growing industries, such as motor car manufacturing instead of expanding alongside the older and declining industries and absorbing unemployed workers in the vicinity of their homes, grew up in the very parts of the country where there was least unemployment, and created a major problem of labour transference from contracting to expanding areas. No group of workers suffered more from these changes than the coal-miners. Of 325 000 workers who had been continuously unemployed for over a year in June 1936, no less than 81 000 were miners, and many more must have had only occasional spells of employment during the year.

Structural unemployment of this kind represents the 'hard core' of unemployment. It is not intermittent like other types of unemployment, but results from a permanent change in opportunities of employment to which workers have to adjust themselves. Men engaged in work of one kind or in one place find themselves shut out from their customary employment and forced to change their occupation or domicile. The more immobile they are, and the greater the structural change in progress, the greater is the resulting unemployment. In pre-war Britain, the changed balance between export and home markets, between capital and consumption goods, and between north and south, put a heavy strain on the adaptability of industry. Structural unemployment, therefore, was unusually high. Structural unemployment arises partly because the structure of wage rates responds only slowly to the decline in the demand for particular types of labour.

Full employment

When people talk of 'full employment', they do not mean that no one is out of a job. In almost any circumstances, some unemployment will persist and is really unavoidable. How much is unavoidable depends on all the things that have just been discussed: on whether big structural changes are going on, whether demand in export markets is fickle or failing, whether labour is mobile, and so on.

At the end of the war Lord Beveridge suggested that it might be possible to maintain an average unemployment rate of 3%, this figure being made up of 1% to cover seasonal unemployment, 1% as a 'margin for change of employment incidental to progress', and 1% to provide for fluctuations in overseas demand[1]. How do these figures compare with past experience? Since the war the unemployment rate in Britain has tended to rise from an average of under 2% in the 1950s to one of over 4% in the 1970s. Before

[1] Lord Beveridge, *Full Employment in a Free Society* (London, 1944), p. 128.

the war, the rate was much higher than this, averaging 14% between 1921 and 1939; further back still, in the 50 or 60 years before the First World War, the average was probably slightly under 5%, and in many years the rate was much higher[1]. No one would regard the rate of unemployment between the wars as anything but intolerably high; even in Victorian times the record was far from one of continuous full employment on any definition. The early post-war record was so much lower that it is natural to hesitate before accepting it as a norm. Many other countries have experienced similar trends in unemployment: a steep decline during and after the Second World War from very high rates in the 1930s, followed by a gradual, irregular rise in the 1960s and 1970s.

Even when unemployment remains constant the identity of those who are unemployed does not; there is no 'standing army' of the unemployed. The vast majority of those who are unemployed on any given date have been in work at some time within the preceding year and will be in work again at some time in the succeeding year. But when unemployment is on the pre-war scale the normal lag between losing one job and finding another is greatly increased. In 1936 one man in four of those registered as unemployed had been idle for at least twelve months.

Fluctuations in unemployment

The fluctuations that have taken place in the last 45 years are illustrated in *Figure 22.1*. In the 1920s unemployment was almost continuously in excess of 1 million and reached a peak of nearly 3 million in 1931. In the 1930s it hardly ever fell below 1.5 million. Then in the first two years of the war it melted away and was latterly under 100 000. Once the war was over and the special compulsions of war-time were relaxed, unemployment increased slightly, oscillating in the succeeding years between 250 000 and 500 000. A more serious and obstinate increase took place after 1966 and the total, adjusted for seasonal and other special factors, reached a peak not far short of 1 million in the winter of 1971–1972 before falling again in the upswing that began in 1972. Unemployment fell for two years and then rose steeply to over one million in 1976 and 1977. After dropping back somewhat in the next two years, the total of those out of work climbed very steeply in 1980, back to pre-war levels.

The consequences of full employment

Full employment, however defined, means a fundamental change in the position of the worker. Before the war, perhaps one worker in two had learnt what it was to be out of work at some time or another, not because of a personal failing, but because there were not enough jobs to go round. Whether he was in work depended on his luck as well as on his free choice. He was in a buyers' market for labour, in which employers could choose

---

[1] These figures are not strictly comparable. A much larger number of workers are now included in the national insurance scheme than were included in the pre-war unemployment insurance scheme. The nineteenth-century figures refer only to members of a small group of trade unions.

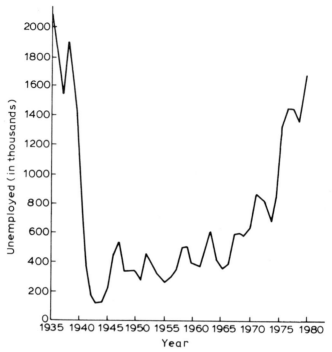

Figure 22.1 Unemployment in the United Kingdom, 1935–1980.
Source: *The British Economy Key Statistics 1900–70* (London
and Cambridge Economic Service, 1971) and *Economic
Trends*

their men, but workers were not so free to choose their employers. The
threat of unemployment, therefore, could be used like a whip to make a
worker conform to the standards of his place of employment. With full
employment, all this is changed: the buyer's market for labour becomes a
seller's market. Where the employer was in a position to say: 'If you don't
want the job, there are plenty of others who do,' the worker can now say:
'If you don't want to employ me, there are plenty of others who will.' In
terms of labour relations this means that new ways of preserving industrial
discipline have to be worked out. Secondly, since labour is scarce, new
methods of production become worth while in order to economize it (for
example, the greater use of mechanical appliances). Most important of all,
the bargaining position of labour is strongly reinforced so that trade unions
are put in a favourable position to force up wages and – if full employment
continues – keep forcing them up. Since each increase tends also to raise
prices, this can easily precipitate a general inflation. If high employment
brings on continuous inflation because the advantages of a sellers' market
are abused, there may be nothing for it but to retreat somewhat from a
high level of employment. Indeed, if unemployment stays beneath some
critical level, the result may be not just that money wage rates and prices
rise, but that they rise at an *accelerating rate*. This will certainly happen if
expectations of inflation keep rising at the same time.

The causes of unemployment

When there is substantial unemployment, this may indicate that labour costs too much and that the remedy lies in a fall in real wages. Alternatively, it may mean that there is a deficiency of demand which only an increase in real expenditure can cure. *Fluctuations* in the level of employment are clearly associated with fluctuations in demand. Rises and falls in national unemployment figures tend to follow, with a lag of six to twelve months, falls and rises in total real expenditure.

If we are to learn how to maintain full employment we shall do well to study the causes of unemployment in the past. Many of the same forces are still at work but the momentum that they can develop can only be gauged by looking at past events when they were allowed to get out of control. Full employment is far from being so normal that we can take it for granted or assume that unemployment is easily mastered, given the will.

The trade cycle

Nowadays it is natural to think of fluctuations in economic activity primarily in terms of changes in the level of employment and unemployment. When economists first began to study those fluctuations, however, there were no official figures of employment and output and it was the movement of prices, which could be more readily measured, on which they concentrated their attention. In looking at price indices, economists became aware of a more or less regular alternation between boom and slump and gave to this phenomenon the name 'trade cycle'. The oscillations that took place were not confined to individual prices or particular industries or groups of industry, although some parts of the economy were more affected than others. It was apparent that the *general* level of prices and of economic activity was alternately raised and lowered over a period varying in length from six to ten years, all, or nearly all, industries being simultaneously prosperous or depressed. In periods when the long-term trend in prices was downwards – for example between 1874 and 1896 – the cycle appeared to lengthen and become more severe; in periods of rising prices – such as occurred after 1896 – the cycle appeared to be shorter and less violent. In the first of the two periods referred to, there were booms in the United Kingdom in 1873, 1882–1883 and 1890 while in the second period the booms were closer together, in 1900, 1907 and 1913. Booms in other countries did not occur in exactly those years; trade cycles, although common to all industrial countries, did not synchronize perfectly in all of them. Differences in timing, however, steadily diminished and it was increasingly rare for one of the leading industrial countries to experience a different cyclical pattern from the others.

Although the trade cycle manifested itself in a periodic and fairly regular fluctuation in prices it was primarily a cycle in activity, whether measured by employment or output. It also showed up in many other economic and social phenomena: profits, for example, and wages; exports and imports; the birth-rate, drunkenness and crime. A common cyclical pattern stamped itself on many things between which there was obviously little direct connection – the classical example is the marriage-rate and the consumption of beer – suggesting causal relationships where none existed.

Whether the trade cycle is now a thing of the past is more debatable. Between the two world wars there were turning-points in the United States and in the United Kingdom in 1920, 1929 and 1937 but it is difficult to regard the two latter years as booms and the intervening slump was of quite unprecedented severity. The instability of the pre-war period seems to have been due to special circumstances calling for a rather different explanation from the Victorian cycle; and the comparative stability of the post-war period equally requires a special explanation. Since the Second World War there has been a brief, mild cycle in aggregate demand around a strong upward trend in real national income (which grew on average by nearly 3% per year). The post-war peaks have been 1951, 1955, 1960, 1964, 1968/9, 1973 and 1978/9. The periodicity, or average duration of the cycle, has been fairly steady at about 4½ years. Most of these cycles appear to have been amplified by the monetary and fiscal policies of governments. In what follows, we shall examine how violent fluctuations in aggregate demand could arise of their own accord. While there is little evidence of this having happened in the UK since the Second World War, it clearly did so before this, and could again.

The cumulative process

The main characteristic of the trade cycle is that in the upswing there is a *cumulative* expansion and in the downswing a *cumulative* contraction. An essential element in the process derives from the simple fact that one man's expenditure is another man's income. Suppose that, at the bottom of a depression something happens to increase effective demand for goods and services. It may be that consumers spontaneously begin to spend more, or, more probably, that larger orders are placed with manufacturers in order to re-build stocks or to renew or extend capital equipment. To fill these orders manufacturers will have to engage more workers and the newly-employed workers will spend more freely out of their increased incomes. This will cause further orders to be placed to replace the goods that have now found a market and these extra orders will give a fresh stimulus to production. As fast as more goods are dispatched for sale to new consumers, more income will be generated and out of the additional income more goods will be bought. If production is shrinking, the reverse process will operate, every reduction in output and employment limiting the market for the goods produced and setting off a fresh contraction in output.

The multiplier and the accelerator

This kind of instability is the basis of the *multiplier*. As we saw in Chapter 21 (p. 285) the idea is that, the more people spend out of any increase in their income the more any initial change in spending is multiplied in its repercussions on the level of income of the community. A second concept – that of the *accelerator* – can be illustrated from another source of instability which is superimposed on the first. If businessmen find their market reviving, they may decide to place orders that are larger than the sales they have just made and are related instead *to the rate of increase* of those sales. For example, they may try to build up stocks in the expectation that sales will go on increasing or to add to their capacity so as to be ready to meet the level of sales which, given the current trend, they expect to make at some later date. On the other hand, when the trend in sales is downwards they may think it unwise to place orders that match current sales and may cut their orders so as to take account of the trend. Similarly they may postpone additions to capacity or even the renewal of some of their equipment because the trend in sales leads them to take a pessimistic view of the future level of demand. Action of this kind represents a change in what the economist calls *investment intentions* (plans to add to stocks or to fixed capital) and accelerates the impact on output and employment of a given change in effective demand. We examine how the multiplier and accelerator may combine to bring fluctuations in aggregate demand below (pp. 305–306).

Prices in the trade cycle

There is no reason in principle why a change in the level of aggregate demand should provoke a change in output and employment. If prices of all goods and factors were perfectly flexible, it would be prices, rather than output, which would bear the effect of changes in the level of aggregate demand. But if prices and money wage rates are sticky, changes in output will occur.

The role of the banks

There are several other features of the trade cycle on which economists have laid stress. One is the role of the banking system. The fluctuations between boom and slump have often been aggravated by the creation of bank credit in the boom and restriction of credit in the slump. How much importance should be attached to changes in the money supply is by no means clear. Some economists take the view that unless the banks help to finance the expansion in activity by creating more credit it will never get very far; others are inclined to doubt whether the banks do more than add fuel to the fire. There is perhaps more agreement about the influence of the banks on the turning-points in the cycle. A rise in interest rates in the later stages has at times been the means of breaking the boom by creating a liquidity scare: that is, by making businessmen alarmed that they might not have enough cash to meet their forward commitments. Such a rise in interest rates may occur if the boom gives rise to an unfavourable balance of payments and by producing a loss of reserves of foreign exchanges causes the monetary authorities to restrict credit in self-defence.

Economic instability and foreign trade

Fluctuations in economic activity has so far been explained in terms of a closed community, not in terms of a single country engaging in trade with other countries. But it not infrequently happens that unemployment originates in a country's export industries through a failure of demand abroad; the cause of unemployment then lies outside the country and not in some maladjustment within it. Indeed, for most industrial countries other than the United States, the main practical problem is how to guard against the instability of foreign markets and prevent the infection of unemployment spreading to their own. It is only when foreign trade occupies a quite subordinate place in a country's economy, or when, as with the United States, a country possesses sufficient economic strength to draw world markets along with it, that it can disregard changes in economic activity and in demand in other countries.

There are few countries where this is so evident as in the United Kingdom. In the nineteenth century it was the common experience that the export industries were the first to feel the effects of a slump and the first to show signs of a recovery. This was not in conflict with the theory that fluctuations in investment are the main source of instability in employment. On the contrary, it was precisely because investment by Britain *in countries overseas* developed a cyclical pattern that exports to those and other countries fluctuated cyclically. If British capital was used to speed up the economic development of, say, Canada, by financing railway construction, new opportunities of employment were created there, the income of the country increased and the demand for goods of all kinds was swollen. Part of this demand overflowed on to imports, and British goods – locomotives, textiles, etc. – found a market either in Canada itself or in other countries which profited from the stimulus of expanding activity in Canada. Nor was this the end of the story. For the prosperity of the British export industries gave a fillip to shipbuilding and set off a boom in the home market. Even when Britain occupied a dominant economic position, therefore, she was highly sensitive to changes occurring abroad, and the level of employment that she experienced was closely dependent on the prosperity of foreign markets.

After the First World War this dependence was painfully evident. In the mid-1920s the volume of exports remained far below the level that had been reached in 1913 and the export industries underwent a corresponding contraction, leaving heavy localized unemployment in the areas that had specialized in the manufacture of exports[1]. Then came the slump that began in 1929; in three years total employment in the export trades fell by nearly one million[2]. In a single year (1931) the fall was probably not far short of a half a million. The unemployment of those years was obviously dominated by international factors. The slump of 1929–1932 was one of unusual severity; but later experience showed that it was by no means exceptional in the speed with which it affected British exports. In the brief recession of 1938, for example, the volume of exports fell by one-eighth in a year, or the equivalent of over 200 000 workers.

It would be foolish to pretend that any action taken by a single government could prevent serious dislocation and distress in the face of a sudden slump in exports of this magnitude. Effective action must be international.

---

[1] The volume of exports in 1924 was about 25% below the volume in 1913. If, as has been estimated by Dr E. C. Snow, the total manpower employed in exporting in 1924 was 2.4 million the consequential reduction in employment may have been of the order of 800 000.

[2] E. A. G. Robinson, 'Sir William Beveridge and Full Employment', *Economic Journal*, April 1945, p. 73.

The interaction of the accelerator and the multiplier

The accelerator postulates a functional relationship between investment and *the rate of growth* of income. It assumes that the stock of capital will always be adjusted to the output that has to be produced, and that if output expands, productive capacity will be expanded too. An increase in productive capacity or in the stock of capital is the same as investment: so investment will take place where output is growing and will be the greater *the more rapidly* output is growing.

If K is the stock of capital, and v the ratio of capital to output, then:

$$K = vO$$
$$= vY \tag{1}$$

and
$$I_t = K_t - K_{t-1}$$
$$= v(Y_t - Y_{t-1}) \tag{2}$$

where the suffix t denotes a period of time, so that I_t is investment during a period t and I_{t-1} is investment during the preceding period, and so on. What equation (2) says is that investment in a given period will be a fixed multiple of the growth in income between one period and the next, provided that the ratio of capital to output, v, is fixed.

Ambiguities in the accelerator

A moment's reflection will show that it is extravagant to assume a fixed relationship between investment and changes in income. Nobody who is conscious of all the complex influences on investment decisions would think it realistic to suppose that they are designed to bring capacity instantaneously into accord with the current level of sales. We may all agree that, *taking the long view*, the most powerful incentive to expand capacity is an increase in sales. But in the short run when decisions are actually made, there are many other influences at work and many reasons why we should expect time-lags in the adjustment of capacity to current output.

There is, for example, a good deal of elasticity about 'capacity'. It is possible to increase output quite considerably above the normal level without enlarging the stock of capital, although in the course of time continuous operation without a normal margin of spare capacity will drive producers to order more equipment. Similarly, there is no difficulty about under-utilizing capacity and when this happens producers need not necessarily cancel their plans of expansion even if they are free to do so. It is increasingly common for manufacturers to frame long-term investment programmes, to which they try to adhere in the face of unexpected changes in demand; the accelerator principle is obviously inapplicable to investment by such firms. Even in firms that do revise their investment plans when sales and output take unforeseen turns, the adjustment may be delayed until the trend in sales is unmistakable or until it is possible to obtain additional plant or until outstanding arrangements for expansion have been completed. There is nothing instantaneous about the reaction.

There are further qualifications. While income can drop very sharply, the stock of capital cannot contract rapidly: a limit is set by the rate of depreciation and obsolescence. Although investment can be negative – when no new capital assets are constructed and the existing assets continue to wear out – it cannot be so negative that capacity falls at the same pace as output does in a severe slump. Furthermore, there are other variables which are known to have a substantial effect upon producers' demand for capital goods, and upon the speed of investment. The demand for capital will be related negatively to interest rates and the prices of capital goods, and positively to the expected price levels of goods produced. Profits should also have a major effect on the level and timing of investment.

Let us put these qualifications on one side for the moment, and assume that equation (2) holds. Suppose now that output, Y, consists only of investment and consumption, C, and that C is a linear function of Y:

$$C_t = a + bY_t \tag{3}$$

$$C_t + I_t = Y_t \tag{4}$$

Equations (2), (3) and (4) form an unstable system as they stand: Y will be in equilibrium, with no change in its value, (i.e. $Y_t = Y_{t-1}$ so that $I = 0$) where

$$Y = \frac{a}{1 - b}$$

but the slightest disturbance will send Y moving further and further away from this value. A floor may be provided where gross investment is zero, and a ceiling where all available resources are fully employed.

If (2) and (3) are replaced by *lagged* equations, however, different results follow. If

$$I_t = v(Y_{t-1} - Y_{t-2}) \tag{5}$$

and

$$C_t = a + bY_{t-1} \tag{6}$$

we derive, with (4), the result

$$Y_t = a + (b + v)Y_{t-1} - vY_{t-2} \tag{7}$$

which can generate cycles (provided b is sufficiently small). If v is unity, such cycles in Y, once initiated by a disturbance, would be exactly self-repeating.

In a model of this kind, fluctuations could be cyclical and very violent – far more violent than in the real world since in every slump net investment would plunge below zero. A more realistic model would, therefore, have to introduce some of the damping factors and lags that help to keep investment steady in relation to output changes and maintain it except on rare occasions like the slump of the early 1930s, above the level of capital consumption.

There is a great deal in this brief summary that one might elaborate or qualify and there are many learned works in which the reader will find ample elaboration and qualification. But there is neither room nor necessity for them here, and many of the more important points are implicit in what we have already said. The ideas of the multiplier and the accelerator are fascinating to the mathematician who can produce cycles from them with the dexterity that others show in producing rabbits out of hats. To the layman, less impressed by constants which turn out on examination not to be constants at all, and more troubled by the lack of empirical evidence for a relationship like the accelerator, it is enough that the ideas provide a clue to an understanding of the instability of the economy. The models of the mathematicians may not explain everything; but they show us where to begin in interpreting economic fluctuations. There are two central ideas that underlie the trade cycle: fluctuations in aggregate demand, which can be spontaneous and self-aggravating within limits; and inflexibility, particularly downwards, in wage rates and prices. Nonetheless, prices do change, and can sometimes rise very rapidly. It is to this subject that we now turn.

Chapter 23

Inflation

The importance of monetary stability

There are serious inconveniences in using money that fluctuates in value. Such fluctuations may be unavoidable or may result from policies that are desirable on other grounds; they may benefit particular groups in the community and even serve, for a time, as a stimulant to total production. But if a reasonable measure of stability in the value of money is not preserved, the whole basis on which economic activity rests is threatened. It is in monetary units that we plan our expenditure, comparing the values of alternative purchases. It is in monetary units that our incomes and expenditure are measured and in monetary units, therefore, that we strike a balance between them, planning how much to spend and how much to save. It is in monetary units also that producers compare the relative costliness of different factors of production, planning methods of production which will substitute relatively cheap for relatively dear factors.

Finally it is in monetary units that producers plan their future volume of output, forming their expectations of profit by comparison of present with prospective money prices. It is of great importance, therefore, that monetary units should be as stable in value as possible. Without reasonably stable units in which to plan, we cannot hope to plan accurately.

Even comparatively small fluctuations in the value of money may create a state of uncertainty damaging to sound enterprise. Our forecasts of the future may be thrown into confusion because the monetary units in which these forecasts are expressed change unexpectedly in value. Producers may find, when the value on money falls – and when prices, therefore, go up – that they have made a larger profit than they expected. When the value of money rises – that is, when prices fall – they may make equally unexpected losses. Neither the profits nor the losses can be foreseen so long as changes in the value of money are unforeseen. Changes in the value of money, therefore, create additional uncertainty and make the already difficult task of planning still more difficult. If such changes could be avoided, so that we were able to plan with a stable and dependable measuring rod, economic activity would be steadier and more wholesome.

Furthermore, inflation makes it more difficult to manage the economy. It destroys the framework of conventional expectations about rewards and incentives and calls in question income differentials that were previously taken as given but have become visibly responsive to pressure. Thus it excites resentment, greed and an aliveness to anomalies and injustice which are quickened with each large change in prices and incomes. Once moral indignation is fretted, the technical economic elements in managing the economy come to play only a subordinate role. The task of management also becomes more difficult for more complex reasons. For example, once the domestic value of the currency begins to slide, the external value may slide faster and the interaction between the two forms of depreciation may make both of them less amenable to control.

The pace of inflation has varied from country to country. Nowhere has it quite equalled the fine careless rapture of the Hungarian pengö as it whizzed across the financial sky in 1946, multiplying itself 300 000 million million million million times.

In comparison with nineteenth-century experience, post-war instability in the value of money has been abnormal. In Britain, for example, the maximum fluctuation in the value of money, one way or the other, was probably not more than 20 or 30% in the 90 years before 1914. Prices fell steadily, but very gradually, from the end of the Napoleonic Wars until 1896, with a short interval of rising prices in the 1850s and 1860s. After 1896 prices began to rise again, but until 1914 the rise was no more rapid than the previous fall. What produced rapid inflation, in 1914 as in 1939, was war; the changes in the value of money in peace-time were all within limits that now seem relatively narrow.

Index numbers

When the pace of change is slow, the movement is not so easy to observe and, as some prices may be rising while others are falling, it may be difficult to say whether, on the average, prices are going up or coming down. We may rely on personal impressions and point to a number of particular changes in price as indications of the general trend. But it is obviously desirable to have a more exact measure, and this is provided by what are known as 'index numbers', which are indices of the average changes in price.

Index numbers measure changes in the value of money for particular purposes or to particular groups of people; but money has a different value for different purposes and for different people. An index number of the cost of living, taking some base year in the past as 100, aims at measuring changes in the value of money used by a typical consumer for the purchase of finished goods; or, to look at things the other way round, in the price level of goods and services sold to consumers. But money is used in order to buy other kinds of goods – raw materials, semi-finished goods, machinery, exports, imports, stock exchange securities, and so on – and its purchasing power over these goods may change in a different direction or to a different degree from its purchasing power over finished goods. Instead of a single price level – the price level of finished goods or the retail price level – there is a whole host of price levels corresponding to the different groups of things that we can buy for money: for example, the wholesale price level, the export price level, the price level of capital goods, the price level of bonds, the wage level and so on. A separate index number can be calculated to measure changes in each price level, and the method of constructing these indices is exactly the same as that used in constructing a cost-of-living index number.

Different price levels do not move exactly in parallel with one another and this is one reason why changes in the value of money are so important. A general movement of prices up or down causes some prices to run ahead of others: wholesale prices, for example, outstrip retail prices, and wages and other costs may lag behind both. Normal profit margins and price relationships are upset, and strains and stresses are set up in the price structure. The pressure on productive activity at various points can be gauged by the use of price indices to measure the spread between price levels. By comparing any two indices we can see where normal price margins have been disturbed, and on what scale the disturbance has been. A comparison of indices of export and import prices, for example, shows whether a country is obtaining imports more cheaply in terms of the exports which it sends in payment. Similarly, a comparison of indices for farm products and manufactured articles shows how much more heavily a fall in price bears on farmers than on the rest of the community. Index numbers of prices sum up the changes that re-orientate business activity; they make it easier to interpret these changes intelligently and to control them.

The consequences of changes in the value of money

Because different price levels do not move together, a change in the value of money is accompanied by windfall gains and losses to particular classes in the community. Some people find that the goods they buy are rising faster in price than the goods they sell; others find that their money incomes do not change, or change slowly, when the value of money changes. The shifts in purchasing power that result can generate social discontent on a formidable scale. Their impact on the distribution and production of wealth is also far-reaching.

Effects on distribution

Incomes, as we saw on p. 268, are either fixed by contract or variable with market prices. The income of labour, supposing no change in employment, is fixed by a number of wage bargains, the majority of which can only be revised slowly and after much bickering. Income from loan capital is fixed for periods varying with the duration of the loan. Income from ownership of land and of dwelling-houses is also slow to change, either because rents are fixed for a number of years ahead or because custom inhibits the raising of rents to existing tenants. Profit, on the other hand, is free to vary as prices move up or down.

There is, first of all, a transfer of wealth from creditors to debtors if prices rise, and from debtors to creditors if prices fall: when debts can be discharged in money that has fallen in value, the real burden of debt is diminished, while if money has risen in value, the real burden of debt is increased. By far the largest debtor in the community is the government; inflation is therefore not without its attractions to governments that have debt obligations. No one supposes that the great inflation in every major country over the past generation can be attributed to a deliberate effort to lighten these obligations. Nevertheless the gain to governments and the corresponding injury to their creditors, the unfortunate holders of public debt, has been one of the outstanding consequences of the inflation. In the United Kingdom, for example, although the net debt of public authorities to all private creditors increased nearly fourfold between 1935 and 1960, the national income, mainly because of inflation, rose even faster and the service of the debt, after the most costly war in history, was a smaller element in the budget than before the outbreak of war.

In the private sector the largest debtor are financial institutions like insurance companies and commercial banks; and as they are creditors at the same time, they have losses to set off against their gains when the value of money falls. This is true also, although to a much smaller extent, of industrial and commercial undertakings: in so far as they work with borrowed capital they are clearly beneficiaries of a fall in the value of money; but part or all of this advantage may be offset if they simultaneously hold large liquid reserves which depreciate in value in a period of inflation. Among private persons, the rentier whose money is invested in fixed interest securities, is bound to suffer an uncovenanted loss as prices rise and the real value of his income falls, because he is helpless to protect himself by seeking a revised loan contract. Other private persons, who have a mortgage on their house, stand to gain. With persons as with businesses, inflation operates in favour of the *net* debtor and deflation in favour of the *net* creditor: there is a transfer of real income to or from those whose debts exceed their holdings of other people's debts, including the debt of public authorities (i.e., government securities), insurance companies (i.e., insurance policies), building societies (i.e., deposits with those societies) and banks (i.e., bank deposits).

These transfers from debtors to creditors result from past contracts between the two and reflect *unforeseen* changes in the value of the money in which the contracts are expressed. But if money goes on losing its value, expectations become adjusted to the fall and loans are made on terms that take into account the chances that it will continue. For example, lenders will insist on higher rates of interest to compensate them for the expected depreciation in value of the repayment obligation they receive. These higher (money) rates of interest need not imply any change in the real cost of borrowing but may amount only to a restoration year by year of that part of the real value of a debt which inflation has cancelled. So long as inflation conforms to expectations and there is no unforeseen acceleration or deceleration, there will be no windfall gains or losses on *new* debt contracts.

A second transfer of income results from the lag of some prices behind others; this type of transfer, unlike the first, does not survive a change in the value of money but continues only so long as the change is in progress. Landlords, for example, may be in a weak position to put up the rent of land or buildings when other prices are rising but find it comparatively easy to resist a fall in rents when other prices are falling. Wages may lag behind the prices of finished goods because it takes time for workers to bring pressure to bear on their employers for an increase in good times, and employers find it difficult or impossible to cut wages in bad times. Either lag confers a bounty on one party at the expense of another: on landlord or tenant, employer or wage-earner. While there is plenty of evidence for transfers between landlords and tenants occasioned by inflation or deflation, it is much more difficult to find satisfactory evidence for transfers between employers and wage-earners that can be attributed to monetary factors. The strongest evidence relates to periods of heavy government spending in war-time; at other times it would seem that profit margins are comparatively steady and that, whether because of the competition of employers for labour or because of the pressure of trade unions, wages do not lag much behind prices during an inflation, while the steadiness of wages prevents a sharp fall in the price of manufactured goods during a deflation. Primary produce, on the other hand, fluctuates widely in price and is usually relatively dear in a period of inflation and relatively cheap in a period of deflation. There is, therefore, some transfer of income to and from primary producers as prices fluctuate – a transfer which has very important consequences for countries that depend heavily on the export of primary produce.

Effects on production

If rising prices reflect growing pressure of demand, as they do in a boom, they are likely to go with expanding turnover and higher profits. But once full employment or other capacity limits are reached, the stimulus to production exhausts itself and any further increase in demand will merely push up prices faster.

Where inflation has taken hold on a continuing footing and costs and prices both go on rising from year to year, almost regardless of the margin of idle resources, the effects are different. There is then no guarantee that a faster rise in prices necessarily implies a wider profit margin since the impulse behind the rise in prices may come from wages, materials or other costs, not from any expansion in sales. Even if profit margins are maintained, producers may encounter cash flow problems because of the higher cost at which materials, components and fixed assets will have to be replaced. By following accounting rules appropriate to a regime of stable prices, producers may find inflation a threat to their solvency rather than a fillip to expansion.

Falling prices, unless accompanied by falling costs of production, mean falling profits and unemployment. Producers are unable to cover their costs and try to protect themselves by curtailing output. Part of the burden is thus passed on to the wage-earner, who loses his job or is put on short-time. A smaller quantity of goods is produced so that the national output is diminished. Deflation, therefore, is generally more creative of social distress than all but the most rapid inflation. If inflation tends to wipe out savings and inflict hardship on special classes, deflation can be far more disastrous in causing unemployment amongst those whose resistance to it is the weakest, in driving businesses into unmerited bankruptcy, and in impoverishing the community by throwing productive resources into needless idleness.

The causes of inflation

Economists have put forward a number of different explanations of inflation. The traditional explanation, until it was challenged by Keynes, was the Quantity Theory of Money which goes back at least as far as David Hume. The Keynesian explanation has in turn been challenged by the monetarists, notably Milton Friedman, who have reverted to an explanation in terms of the money supply.

The Quantity Theory is based on the simple fact that, like the value of everything else, the value of money depends upon how much there is of it. If the government debases the currency or makes excessive use of the printing press, inflation is bound to result. The influx of gold from the New World in the sixteenth century and the gold discoveries in the nineteenth century provide historical examples of the way in which an increase in the quantity of money made prices rise.

The theory as usually expounded 50 years ago took the form of an equation (devised by Professor Irving Fisher). If for the supply of money we write M; for the velocity of circulation, or average number of times a unit of money is spent, we write V; for the volume of transactions or of goods exchanged, we write T; for the price level we write P: then it is easy to show that:

$$MV = PT$$

MV represents our money outlay, the flow of money on to the market for goods, while PT represents what we buy, the flow of goods coming forward for sale against goods; and these must necessarily be equal.

The next step is to rewrite the identity so that it reads:

$$P = \frac{MV}{T}$$

We then make P refer unambiguously to the price level of finished goods and define T correspondingly to mean the real national income (i.e., we exclude transactions in raw materials, semi-finished goods, stock exchange securities and so on). Strictly speaking, we ought also to limit M to money held by receivers of final income and V to the number of times a unit of money held by income-receivers changes hands in the course of a year. P, T, M and V would then be defined in mutually consistent terms.

At this point the Quantity Theory moves from being an identity to an assertion of causal connections. It asserts than an increase in M will *cause* an increase in P. By implication it denies that a change in M might be offset by an opposite change in V or a parallel change in T. It regards V and T as relatively stable, and M as the prime source of inflationary tendencies.

Now it is not immediately obvious that V and T are stable in the absence of a change in M and by no means universally accepted. Taken in conjunction V and T reflect the demand for money in contrast to M which represents the supply. If money circulates more rapidly, this means that we need less of it in relation to the transactions in which we engage, i.e., our demand for money has fallen. If output is lower, fewer goods have to be exchanged; there is less work for money to do and again the demand for money falls. We cannot take it for granted that the demand for money is stable; but if it could be shown empirically that it was, then any instability in prices would be traceable to instability on the supply side, i.e., in the quantity of money.

In attacking the Quantity Theory, Keynes started by insisting on the need to concentrate on the behaviour of output and employment rather than of the price level. He might have been prepared to concede that under conditions of continuous full employment, the price level would sooner or later reflect changes in the quantity of money. But at lower levels of employment the Quantity Theory was in his view seriously misleading since it did not allow for the effect of increased spending on the level of output. An increase in the flow of expenditure (MV) might or might not require an increase in M; but even if it did, the response in additional output might involve little or no rise in price, depending on the shape of the aggregate supply curve. If expansion continued, bottlenecks would develop as capacity came under pressure and at that stage, with the supply curve bending more steeply upwards, the danger of inflation would become more acute. But this stage was unlikely to be reached before the economy was within sight of full employment; and the more serious danger then was that workers might take advantage of their more powerful bargaining position and demand higher wages so that prices began to be pushed up by higher costs rather than by the pressure of demand.

What this comes to is that Keynes regarded the driving force behind demand inflation as MV without accepting that V could be relied upon to remain constant; and left open the possibility, which the Quantity Theory excludes, of cost inflation, i.e., of an upward thrust in costs in which demand factors play little or no part. We shall deal in more detail presently with cost inflation. But we must first consider the more sophisticated version of the quantity theory associated with monetarism.

Monetarism

Monetarists start from the proposition that 'inflation is always and everywhere a monetary phenomenon'. Prices can only go on rising if there is enough money to keep pace. Even if the monetary authorities don't start off the inflation by pumping out more money they must 'accommodate' it by allowing the money supply to expand or it will peter out through financial stringency.

Next, the monetarists rest their view of inflation on the quantity theory of money. They regard fluctuations in money income and expenditure (MV) as dominated by fluctuations in the money supply (M). They claim that the velocity of circulation (V) and the demand for money (not just the stock in the hands of final consumers but the total stock of money) are relatively stable since they are determined by things that either change slowly like the interval between receipts and payments, normal income, and so on, or are comparatively weak in their influence like interest rates.

They would not dispute that an increase in interest rates would to some extent compress the demand for money because it involves those who continue to hold money in a bigger sacrifice in the form of interest. They accept that money lies at one end of a long chain of liquid assets between which substitution can and does occur whenever one or other gains or loses in relative attractiveness and scarcity: for example, when the rates of interest they bear are altered or are expected to alter. But they insist that money must be differentiated from these other financial assets, that variations in interest rates do not in practice have much effect on the velocity of circulation and that they do not, therefore, upset the close association between money and prices. The money supply lies within the control of the monetary authorities and this control is the key to the avoidance of inflation. The authorities should set and publish in advance long-term targets for monetary growth which they should have no discretion to vary whatever the changes from month to month or year to year in private sector spending.

Like most other parts of monetarist doctrine, the stability of the velocity of circulation is regarded by other economists with some scepticism. Experience suggests that it is stable neither in the short run nor in the long. In any event things which are normally quite stable may cease to be stable just when their stability is taken for granted. When money becomes tight new ways of economizing it may come into play.

Although monetarists have been inclined to make light of the variability of the demand for money, the substitutability of financial assets from which it arises provides them with a useful explanation of the process by which changes in the money supply work through to changes in prices. If there is more money about while the supply of other financial assets is unchanged, people will begin to revise their asset preferences and try to reduce their holdings of money in favour of interest-bearing financial assets or real assets such as house-property. This will tend to raise the price of these assets and set in motion expansionary forces that will extend the rise over wider sections of the economy. Ultimately the general price level will be raised to the point at which the additional money has been fully absorbed and is once more in keeping with current requirements.

An analogous argument relates to the influence of the money supply on the rate of exchange. If monetary expansion is excessive it will be reflected in a deficit in the balance of payments which, in the monetarist view, is simply the difference between domestic credit creation and the country's requirements for money. With a floating exchange rate, the deficit will push down the rate, the price of imported goods will increase correspondingly and this will set off increases in price in other parts of the economy. So, apart from any direct effect of monetary expansion on domestic prices there will be a powerful indirect effect through depreciation of the currency. The more one country expands its money supply in relation to other countries, the less value its currency will have and the more its prices will rise in comparison with other countries.

Monetarism does not concentrate, as Keynes did, on fluctuations in output and employment. It assumes, as Keynes's predecessors did but Keynes himself did not, that the private sector of the economy is self-regulating and that fluctuations in output will be short-lived and limited in amplitude so long as the money supply is kept stable. Additions to the money supply will have no lasting effect on the 'real' performance of the economy but will serve only to raise the price level. Fluctuations in output may result from monetary fluctuations or may be due to miscalculation; but if mistakes do occur, they will be recognized for what they are, prices will adjust and the situation will soon rectify itself. Underemployment of labour will continue only if workers insist on rates of pay in excess of the value of their net product and so price themselves out of a job. The same applies to other resources whose use may be limited under monopolistic conditions through the charging of excessive prices.

Economists of all persuasions agree that an increase in the money supply will initially have a dual effect, partly on output and partly on prices, but they differ as to the relative importance of these two effects and the changes to be expected subsequently. Keynesians would insist that the main effect comes through MV not M and would expect most of the effect to be on output (except in the vicinity of full employment) with only the residue affecting prices and the rate of inflation. Monetarists would argue that while there would be an initial expansion in production, the effect of any addition to the money supply would soon begin to show itself in a steeper rise in prices which in due course would take up the whole of the addition, leaving production at the level from which it started. The full effect on prices (according to the monetarist interpretation of past experience which other economists would dispute) would not be apparent until after a lag of about two years.

The difference of view is sometimes expressed in terms of what is known as 'the Phillips curve'. An investigation by Professor A. W. Phillips of the behaviour of unemployment and prices in Britain from 1860 onwards showed that there was a strong correlation between the level of unemployment and the rate at which the price level changed. Annual observations plotted on a curve, with unemployment measured along one axis and the rate of change in prices along the other, showed low levels of unemployment going with a high rate of inflation, and high levels of unemployment with a low rate of inflation. A simple-minded interpretation of these results would be that labour becomes dearer as it gets scarcer. But this is not the only possible interpretation. The data reflect the workings of the trade cycle, with business conditions governing the changes in unemployment and prices simultaneously. All that one can conclude is that unemployment tends to be lower and wages to rise faster when trade is good. We cannot deduce that prices would rise faster *in the long run* if the same fluctuations took place round a lower average level of unemployment. Nor can we be sure that the experience of the nineteenth century yields conclusions that still hold true under the different conditions of the late twentieth century.

In current economic controversy, however, the Phillips curve is widely accepted as providing a link between inflation and unemployment, and as implying some trade-off between the two. Monetarists would deny that such a trade-off can be more than transitory. They argue that, while there may be a short period over which lower unemployment can be traded against a higher rate of inflation, that period can last only so long as workers suffer from 'money illusion' and do not adjust their wage claims to allow for the falling value of money. Once their expectations take account of the inflationary process there is nothing to be gained in lower unemployment by letting prices rise a little faster. In the long run, the monetarists maintain, the Phillips curve is a vertical straight line and the trade-off between unemployment and inflation disappears.

The importance of expectations under inflationary conditions can be expressed in terms of the 'expectations-augmented Phillips curve'. If, for example, we write Δp for the rate of inflation, Δp^e for the expected rate of inflation, u for some measure of slack or under-employment, and v for all other influences on the price level, then the relationship in terms of such a curve would take the form:

$$\Delta p = au + b\ \Delta p^e + v$$

The first term in this equation corresponds to the Phillips curve relationship provided the parameter a is negative: prices will rise more slowly in a given state of expectations, the greater the amount of slack. The second term expresses the influence of expectations: monetarists would put the value of the parameter b at unity and would argue that since expectations are moulded by past experience a constant rate of inflation would come to be fully anticipated. Other economists, while admitting that expectations would catch up with experience, would attach a lower value than unity to b and would therefore leave open the possibility that a diminishing but still positive gain in employment could result from a higher rate of inflation. They would also contend that some of the most important sources of inflation in particular circumstances – for example, a sudden, large increase in the price of oil – remain concealed under v[1].

One of the difficulties about the Phillips curve approach is that it does not explicitly introduce the influence of collective bargaining in a fragmented labour market. Keynes's formulation of the relationship between output and prices assumed that wage cuts were not only impracticable but largely ineffective because, in the absence of measures to expand demand, prices would fall in line with wages and leave no fresh incentive to increase employment. Real wages, in the Keynesian system of ideas, cannot be raised or lowered by manipulating money wages except to the extent that this reacts on demand. A Keynesian, therefore, does not think of the problem in terms of a trade-off between inflation and unemployment. He enquires how unemployment can be reduced without raising the pressure beyond the point at which inflation accelerates. The Holy Grail of which he is in search in the Non-accelerating-inflation-rate-of-unemployment or *Nairu*.

The monetarist has a rather similar concept: the natural rate of unemployment. By this he means two things which rarely if ever coincide. One is the rate of unemployment at which the labour market is in balance in the sense that there is neither such a shortage that wages are rising faster than productivity nor such a surplus that they are failing to keep pace with the growth of productivity. The other is the lowest rate of unemployment at which the economy can function smoothly, given the residue of frictional, seasonal and structural unemployment likely to remain as the

---

[1] The argument of this paragraph is based on D. Laidler, 'Monetarism: an Interpretation and an Assessment', *Economic Journal*, March 1981.

economy approaches its full potential. On the first definition the natural rate of unemployment in Britain must have been over two million in the 1930s since wages and prices rose steadily from 1933 onwards, while unemployment did not drop below two million until near the end of the decade. Yet in the late 1940s when the rate of inflation was not very different, unemployment averaged about 300 000. Does it make any sense to apply a term such as 'natural rate of unemployment' to such widely different circumstances? Similarly if one thinks of the natural rate as a kind of irreducible minimum, we have to explain how it was possible for the rate of unemployment in Britain to fall to a mere 80 000 in war-time while there were symptoms of acute labour shortage in 1973 when unemployment was still about 600 000 and continuing evidence of labour shortage even in 1979 when unemployment was about 1 400 000. One might be tempted to conclude that the natural rate of unemployment is whatever the actual rate has been for the past few years.

So far we have looked at inflation in terms of the quantity of money, the flow of expenditure, the amount of slack in the economy and expectations of further inflation. But we have taken little stock of all the factors under v, including shocks like a harvest failure or a doubling of oil prices, acts of policy like a substantial increase in VAT or other indirect taxes, and changes in institutions or in behaviour such as greater trade union militancy. Many economists would regard these as of greater importance in an explanation of inflation than changes in the money supply; and some would indeed go much further and argue that it makes more sense to explain changes in the money supply in terms of the flow of expenditure, as affected by those factors, than to make the money supply the starting point for an explanation of inflation. It is not at all obvious that wages and labour costs dance to the tune of the money supply rather than the other way round.

If all inflation could be shown to be demand-led there would be probably little disagreement over its causes. The major disagreement is over the role of costs. Where costs are determined, as in the case of many raw materials, in a competitive market in which price responds freely to changes in supply and demand, they can exercise no independent influence on prices unless there is some exogenous change in supply conditions. The same would be true of wages if they too were fixed in markets that cleared automatically so that there was no involuntary unemployment. Some monetarists, without asserting that this is how the labour market does in fact behave, have developed an analysis of inflation on the *assumption* that the labour market clears, workers making up their minds between leisure and work and accepting or rejecting offers of employment on the basis of what are called, rather fancifully, 'rational expectations' as to how prices and other variables will move. Even monetarists who are sceptical of this approach would still deny that there is any such thing as cost inflation. They would maintain that workers who continue to press for higher wages than are consistent with price stability are pricing themselves out of a job and that efforts to bring them back into employment by increased government spending will only result in inflation.

We shall return presently to cost inflation. Before doing so let us see what recommendations for policy flow from monetarist doctrine. On the positive side it is claimed that inflation could be stopped by an appropriate monetary policy and by that alone. Some monetarists, such as Professor Hayek, think that it could and should be done at a stroke whatever dislocation, bankruptcies and unemployment resulted. But they sometimes couple this with the reservation that the powers of the trade unions must first be limited or abandoned, without much of an indication how this could be brought within the realm of practical politics. Others, like Professor Milton Friedman, would prefer a progressive deceleration so that the money supply expanded at a diminishing pace and inflation was gradually eliminated. If the government announced its programme in advance and made clear its firm intention to stick to it, expectations of inflation would cool off and this in itself would help to reduce the pace. Whatever their differences on this point, all monetarists would be confident that the rise in prices *would* be brought under control if the supply of money were rigorously controlled.

They would also unite in seeking to limit the discretion of the monetary authorities in exercising this control. They are usually very distrustful of governments and central banks and anxious to see them tied down in the way they were tied down under the gold standard by the need to maintain adequate reserves. One prescription is for a gradual expansion in the money supply at a steady rate matching the growth in productivity in the economy as a whole. This prescription would come into force once inflation had been eliminated. Until then there would be a series of published monetary targets on a diminishing scale: the central bank would be required to keep the increase in the money supply over the next 12–18 months within defined limits and the proportionate increase permitted would be revised downwards every year.

Targets for the money supply have been adopted by nearly all the leading industrial countries. But of course the monetary authorities have no way of exercising direct control over the money supply: the main instrument at their disposal – control over interest rates – operates indirectly and sometimes perversely. The injunction to adhere to a monetary target may seem simple enough: but in practice it can be a matter of the utmost complexity to keep the money supply within even fairly broad limits, as the experience of central banks has demonstrated. It is just as difficult to 'fine tune' the money supply as it is, by demand management, to 'fine tune' the level of demand. It is something of a paradox that those who see no value in the one set such store by the other.

The stress on monetary targets is not due entirely to the insistence of the monetarists on the primary importance of the money supply in causing inflation. It also reflects a belief, which others share, that the monetary authorities tended to concentrate too much on short-term objectives such as avoiding wide swings in interest rates, preserving stability in financial markets, and so on. These are not unimportant objectives but they can be pursued too far if the price is a large increase in the money supply. What is more open to question is whether it was a major error – as the monetarists maintain – to frame monetary objectives in terms of price (rates of interest) rather than quantity (the money supply).

If the authorities do elect to use quantity targets they need some unambiguous measure of quantity. But there are various measures of the money supply and there is no unique definition of money that allows us to exclude all but one of these measures. Money narrowly defined (M1) can diverge and has diverged quite widely from money broadly defined (M3). These divergences cannot be waved aside. Is it constancy of M1 or M3 that assures steadiness in the value of money? Or is it M1 at one time and M3 at another? Whichever is selected by the authorities will, for that very reason – because it is the object of control – begin to behave differently. If they operate on one group of assets and call it money, that group may then follow a different path from other monetary assets so that the target ceases to be appropriate.

Once we examine monetarism closely, much of its apparent simplicity disappears. It appears to provide the authorities with a formula they can apply automatically. But in fact their task is at least as complex and demanding as before. If they apply the formula too rigidly, the result may be disastrous. Above all, the forces that manifest themselves in inflation in the 1980s may have little to do with the supply of money and may lie much deeper in group attitudes and aspirations.

A Quantity Theory approach to inflation concentrates attention on the force which, in the past, has dominated the course of prices; it hangs out a warning against the fatal expedient of making money too plentiful. Its weakness is that it does not provide us with an adequate picture of the *process* of change. We can see in a general way that changes in the quantity of money will work through to the price level; but if we want to make a closer study of the machinery of change we find ourselves beginning to discuss wage rates, interest rates, expectations of profit, and other variables which find no place in the formula. We can still construe everything – with some difficulty – in terms of the formula; but only when we have worked out, by another route, what is happening. We do not learn from the formula; we read into it what we have already discovered.

Demand inflation and cost inflation

The Quantity Theory, in its simplest form, seems a natural application of the theory of value – the greater the supply of money, the less its value. But what from one point of view is a change in the value of money, is from another point of view a change in the price level of commodities. Now a change in the price level of commodities can come about only through a mass of changes in the prices of particular commodities. And if we ask of the theory of value why the price of any *particular* commodity should change we receive an answer which has apparently no connection whatever with the explanation given by the Quantity Theory why prices in general should change. We learn that the price of a commodity will rise if there is an increase in the demand for it or an increase in its cost of production. Corresponding to this distinction there are two possible ways in which inflation may come about: there may be a demand inflation caused by pressure of demand or a cost inflation in which the pressure is exercised on the side of costs. The first type of inflation can be represented by a movement of the demand schedule for goods and services and the second type by a movement of the supply schedule.

Demand inflation

Let us for the moment put aside the possibility of a spontaneous movement in costs and see how a demand inflation develops. The simplest example is that of an increase in government spending financed by the banking system. Additional expenditure brings additional orders and causes businesses to buy more materials and components, hire more labour, work more overtime, and make preparations to expand their plant. The multiplier comes into play and demand presses more strongly on available resources of materials, manpower and capacity. So costs begin to rise. The primary impulse being on the side of demand, producers can more than recoup the rise in costs and can, if they choose, widen their profit margins or if they decide otherwise still enjoy higher profits from an expanding turnover. Rising profits distinguish a demand inflation from a cost inflation in which the primary impulse to the increase in prices comes from costs.

The role of money in this process is to finance the initial burst of spending. But once the additional money is there it permits the expansion to go on unchecked by financial stringency until the extra money is fully absorbed, i.e., until the higher level of activity and the higher level of incomes make demands on the money supply to match the increased stock.

It would be possible for some expansion in demand to take place – for example, in response to a boom in export markets or heavier capital expenditure or simply consumer spending out of savings – without being sustained by a larger money supply. But in the absence of a change in the velocity of circulation of money, such an expansion would be likely to prove transitory unless facilitated and sustained by additional credit creation on the part of the banks, i.e., by an addition to the money supply. A demand inflation of any duration is likely to require a parallel expansion in the money supply.

Cost inflation

What then of an inflation of prices that originates on the side of costs? There are two major sources of cost inflation, one imported materials and the other, money wages. We have seen that demand inflation will drive up the price of materials and the level of wages so that if we are seeking to isolate the influence of cost inflation we must begin by leaving such increases out of account and concentrate on exogenous changes in the price of materials and labour.

So far as materials are concerned, a country relying primarily on supplies from abroad can regard an increase in import prices as a form of cost inflation. Whether the increase reflects higher costs abroad, or a decision by some powerful group of producers such as OPEC, or a rise in activity and demand somewhere else in the world, or a devaluation of the currency, is largely irrelevant: the higher cost of materials will come to be reflected in the prices of finished goods irrespective of any change in domestic demand. Moreover, since changes in raw material prices can be very large and abrupt, this form of cost inflation is frequently of great importance by itself and may in addition be reinforced by wage inflation when the higher cost of materials begins to affect the cost of living. If imports become dearer, somebody has to meet the cost through a sacrifice in living standards; and the more a reduction is resisted, the greater will be the eventual inflation of wages and prices.

It is of course possible that the original rise in material prices may have had its origin in a *world* demand inflation to which each country contributed. It may then look to individual countries as if they were struggling with cost inflation that radiated from world markets for primary commodities and not from their own inflationary policies. But in fact they would have brought the inflation on themselves by expanding demand.

It is also possible that over-expansionary domestic policies may generate inflation by leading to a devaluation of the currency that pushes up import prices. Higher import prices will then be blamed for a cost inflation that seems independent of government policy but is in reality a by-product of the prior expansion in domestic demand.

Whatever the sources of higher import prices it can be argued that they need not occasion a general inflation and would not do so if the money supply were held constant. When some prices go up, ought not other prices to come down, particularly if people have the same purchasing power as before? The fact is, however, that some prices – wages, for example – hardly ever come down but only move upwards. There is an asymmetry in the system, beyond the power of the monetary authorities to correct, which makes the price level unstable in an upward direction.

Wages and inflation

This brings us to the second source of cost inflation: wage increases. It must be emphasized right at the start that it is money wages and not real wages that we are discussing. As we saw in Chapter 19, a rise in money wages across the board may leave real wages unaffected once employers adjust their prices to the higher level of costs. If they succeed in maintaining existing profit margins, wage-earners will find that they have gained nothing when they come to spend their higher money incomes. The value of money will have fallen but the real value of wages will be unchanged.

We have also seen that demand inflation, by increasing the demand for labour and later by pushing up prices and the cost of living, tends to be acompanied by rising money wages. Extra spending by itself inflates the level of costs. Indeed, it may set off a wage–price spiral in which successive increases in wages and prices follow one another, each fresh rise in prices provoking renewed demands for wage increases while these, if granted, raise costs and prices still further.

It is not altogether easy to distinguish such a situation from one of cost inflation proper. In principle, what distinguishes the latter is the absence of any change in the pressure of demand. If the steam has gone out of demand inflation and profit margins are tending, if anything, to narrow, a continuing rise in wages is evidence that pure cost inflation is taking over. Employers may be reluctant to concede claims for higher wages under such conditions. But they will hesitate less if they know that their domestic competitors will follow suit, if they have learned that what they concede is not likely to differ greatly from what other employers throughout the economy will concede and if they can expect to see any substantial rise in domestic costs and prices offset by a corresponding fall in the external value of the currency so that their foreign competitors will gain no continuing advantage. If there is a very firm wage structure that changes little over time whatever happens to wage settlements at this point or that, individual wage bargains will tend to perpetuate this structure and the average increase from year to year will be very much at the mercy of events.

The likelihood of wage inflation, unrelated to any prior change in the pressure of demand, depends on the strength and structure of employers' organizations, their mood and outlook, the leadership they enjoy, the political background, and so on. But even when these are known, the rate of wage inflation is hard to predict. The size, timing, generality and vehemence of the wage demands that are put forward and the readiness with which they are conceded are governed only to a very limited extent by the state of the labour market. There is no simple and dependable trade-off between inflation and unemployment with more of the one yielding less of the other as is sometimes thought to be implied in the 'Phillips curve'. Very heavy unemployment, for example, does not necessarily stop wages from increasing and rising unemployment and rapidly rising prices can go together. The most one can say is that when unemployment *is increasing* and workers are concerned that they may lose their jobs, they are less likely to press demands for higher wages as strongly as they would if they felt their jobs secure. This is a very different proposition from one that makes the *level* of unemployment a check to wage inflation.

There are likely to be some industries in which wages are already moving upwards well below full employment in the economy as a whole; and employment may either expand over a wide tract of the curve without much acceleration of this movement, or, at other times, a sharp and widespread increase in wages may occur at a much earlier stage. Moreover, we cannot realisticially treat employment as changing discontinuously from one level to another, and prices as changing simultaneously in step with marginal costs; we have to take account of the *rate* at which the change takes place, the expectations that develop of *further* changes, the *continuous* advance and retreat of economic activity, that prevent output and prices from settling at any given level. The movement of wage rates may be very different at the same level of output if the tempo of expansion and the attitudes that accompany it are different. We have also to be on our guard against the convenient assumption that full employment and the virtual disappearance of unemployment are the same thing: employment in Britain grew between 1949 and 1957 by 1½ million workers while the number of unemployed workers remained unchanged at 250 000 and the population of working age rose comparatively slowly. An acute shortage of labour may draw more workers into the labour market, given the time necessary for the creation of new industrial capacity. The *shape* of the cost curve may be altering while output is in course of expansion.

Thus if we ask whether there is some critical level of employment at which cost inflation will occur, and the growth in wage rates will exceed the normal rate of improvement in productivity, we are unlikely to find such a level from simple observation. We may, nonetheless, find that cost inflation is unlikely to take place below a certain level of employment and unlikely to be avoided above some higher level, and regard the intervening belt of employment as an area of indeterminacy. Even this conclusion may not be open to us. It may happen, for example, that after years of continuing inflation, workers become conditioned to expect a periodic round of wage increases and are prepared to strike in support of fresh wage claims although output may have been stationary for a long time or is actually contracting. In such circumstances the resulting inflation cannot be ascribed to any current change in effective demand and is undeniably cost inflation. Experience suggests that a situation of this kind is by no means altogether imaginary and that when demand inflation has spent itself cost inflation may take over.

Chapter 24

The demand for money

In the preceding chapters we have taken for granted some understanding of the place that money occupies in the modern world: what money is and what it does; what governs monetary habits; how control is exercised over the supply. By jumping ahead in this way we were able to see how monetary influences affect production by making access to finance easy or difficult: the supply of money reacts on interest rates which in turn react on investment and so on effective demand. We must now turn back to examine the role of money more clearly.

A definition of money

What distinguishes money from other commodities is its acceptability, or – to use a term introduced in Chapter 20 – its liquidity. Money is anything which, by custom or law, is generally acceptable without question in payment for goods and services or in final settlement of a debt. We accept other commodities for their own sake because we wish to consume them; if we do not wish to consume them, we have to go to the trouble of finding a buyer for them. Money, on the other hand, we accept not necessarily for its own sake, but because we know that other people will accept it; we know that there is never any trouble in finding a 'buyer' for money – people will take it in exchange for goods of any kind at almost any time. We can never be stranded with money as we can be stranded with other commodities.

Money performs four distinct services: it is a medium of exchange, a store of value, a measure of value and a standard of deferred payments. Let us take each of these in turn.

Money as a medium of exchange

Men will specialize, as we saw in Chapter 4, only if the limited range of goods which they produce can be exchanged quickly and conveniently for the much wider variety of goods which they wish to consume. But exchange is quick and convenient only if some commodity is singled out as the standard medium of exchange – that is, as money. The alternative of direct barter leads to endless delays and inconvenience. The use of money, in fact, arises out of the inconvenience of direct barter in a community of specialists. A good monetary system, by facilitating exchange between producers, allows them to carry specialization further, just as a good transport system, by facilitating exchange between different regions and countries, extends the area of dealings and promotes regional specialization.

Money as a store of value

It is a short step from using money as a means of payment to holding money in reserve against *future* payments. Some of these payments may have to be made in the very near future – when we go shopping, for example. We do not wish to be without money when we board a bus, or when we see a bargain in a shop window, or when someone calls to collect the rent. Other payments may be more distant. There will be various bills to be met; or we may be saving up in order to buy a motor car or a house. In addition to the payments which we already contemplate there will be some against which we must guard but which cannot be foreseen – payments due to unexpected illness, or to sudden requests for money from relatives, or to miscalculation of the patience of our creditors. We will generally keep a margin of cash in excess of prospective payments in order to provide for these unforeseen contingencies. Again, since it is in money that our incomes are paid, we may not trouble, because of the expense or inconvenience involved, to invest what we feel to be surplus to our requirements. Or we may decide to hold a store of money in preference to alternative investments, such as bonds, shares or property, because we do not feel confident in the stability of the value of these investments or because we take the view that their value will fall. From all these motives we try to keep by us a stock of money as a reserve of liquid purchasing power. We want money to hold, not just for paying away immediately.

Money as a measure of value

Money is not only the *thing* with which we pay for goods and services; it is also the *scale* in which we measure their value. Money provides a scale of pounds and pence by which we can make comparisons of value, just as a thermometer provides a scale of degrees centigrade by which we can make comparisons of temperature. Even if we had to resort to a barter system some such scale would be indispensable. We could not possibly carry in our minds a complete catalogue of exchange values, expressing the value of each comodity in terms of a different amount of every other commodity. We should want some common denominator of exchange values and this common denominator would be money. It would not be money proper – the thing which we exchange. It would be money-of-account – the abstract unit in which price quotations are made and in which debts are expressed. In Great Britain the pound note is money proper, while the pound sterling is the money-of-account. No one has ever seen a pound sterling – any more than anyone has ever seen a degree centigrade or a mile or any other unit of measurement. What we do see, from time to time, are Bank of England pound notes, with which undertakings to pay one pound sterling may be discharged. The pound sterling does not exist; it is an instrument of thought to assist us in making comparisons of value. The pound note, on the other hand, does exist; it is a piece of paper, fairly constant in value, and generally acceptable in payment for goods priced at one pound sterling. The pound sterling is very ancient; it goes back to Charlemagne. The Bank of England one pound note, on the other hand, dates only from 1928.

As a measure of value money makes possible a system of prices. Exchange values, instead of varying between one transaction and another, become coordinated and regularized into market prices. A 'market' for each commodity comes into existence and the gain from sales and purchases becomes more calculable. The existence of the market, and the greater calculability which it permits, encourage increased trading, and with this increased trading goes increased specialization. Once again the use of money lies at the root of specialized production.

Money as a standard of deferred payments

Besides being the unit in which we measure prices (present payments), money is also the unit in which we measure debts (future or deferred payments). A debt is an undertaking to pay something – usually money – at some future time; and what has to be paid is measured in terms of some standard unit – the money-of-account. In Britain, for example, contracts of debt are expressed in terms of the pound sterling, but what is actually paid is hard cash – either banknotes or a cheque.

Just as dealings in commodities would be exceedingly complicated without a measure of value, so borrowing and lending would be exceedingly complicated without a unit for the measurement of debts. Instead of borrowing general purchasing power and buying with it such goods as we required, we should be forced to hire or rent the desired selection of goods, returning them (or similar goods) at the end of some agreed period, together with an additional payment of goods as rent. We should be unable to reduce the goods borrowed to a common measure and make repayment in *other* goods of equal value or in a single generally acceptable commodity. It would be impossible also to set debts to a given value against credits to the same value and so to cancel out payments between different traders. Every transaction would stand by itself. Dealings in debts – the work of the stock exchange, the insurance companies, building societies, commercial banks and other financial intermediaries – would cease.

By providing a unit in which debts can be measured, money makes borrowing and lending enormously easier. A capital market can come into existence in which debts are traded just as goods are traded in commodity markets. With the capital market come large-scale production and increased specialization. Here, therefore, is yet another link between money and specialization.

The demand for money

Because money acts as a medium of exchange and a store of value, there is a demand for it for its own sake. People want to hold a stock of money just as they want a stock of clothes; they carry about with them or hold at the bank a quantity of purchasing power on which they do not, as a rule, earn interest but which offers them the compensating advantage of liquidity. The sum of the individual money balances held must be such as to add up to the total supply since all the money in the country must obviously be *somewhere*: and if more money is put into circulation, *somebody* must add to his stock of purchasing power. If the supply of money is unchanged and one group of people want more of it, they can only acquire it by persuading another group of people to run down their money balances, for example in exchange for stock exchange securities; ownership of the existing supply of money is then redistributed. The total stock that people hold has a purchasing power than can be represented as a fraction of the national income or as sufficient to buy, say, K units of goods. If the demand for money balances were to increase, this would show itself in a rise in the ratio of the money supply to the national income and in the quantity of goods (K) that total money balances would purchase.

The demand for money, measured in this way, is simply the inverse of the velocity of circulation (V) which we discussed in Chapter 23. If we start from the formula $MV = PT$ and write $V = PT/M$ then, on one set of definitions at least, we can identify PT with national income and V becomes the ratio of the national income to the money supply while K, as just defined, is the ratio of the money supply to the national income. An increase in the demand for money can be thought of, therefore, either as a fall in V or as a rise in K.

Whoever holds money (including businesses) must presumably have some motive for doing so, since he could, if he chose, earn interest by lending it. What are the motives which prompt people to hold money? Upon what, in other words, does K depend? There are, broadly speaking, three sets of motives:

(a) The receipts and payments motive

First, we may hold money in order to bridge over the gap between the time when we receive money and the time when we pay it away. We receive our incomes in the form of money, as wages, salary payments, dividends, and so on, and pay them away in exchange for goods and services of all kinds. If receipts and payments were simultaneous – if, for example, we ran up accounts and paid them off as our income reached us – we should require very little money. But if we are paid only once a quarter, and have payments to make at a steady rate, we shall be left at the beginning of the quarter with a large cash balance which gradually diminishes until it is replenished at the next pay-day. If we are paid weekly, our income will reach us in smaller lumps and we are not likely to hold so large a balance. The time intervals which separate income payments, therefore, have an important influence on the amount of money which the community normally holds. The same is true of the time intervals which separate payment for goods and services. If income tax, for example, is paid half-yearly it will be necessary to build up a cash balance every six months so as to be able to pay the tax, whereas a tax payable weekly would not add very appreciably to the normal stock of money held by the taxpayer.

The gap between receipts and payments is not enough of itself to prompt consumers to hold money. The gap must also be so short that it is not worth the consumer's while to lend his spare cash and earn interest on it. If the interest which he could earn is small (e.g., on deposit account with a bank), the mere trouble of arranging a loan may be counted too great in comparison; and even if the interest is appreciable (e.g., on industrial debentures) the cost of making the loan (commissions on sale and purchase) may cancel most of the prospective gain.

The same time intervals between receipts and payments which induce consumers to hold a stock of money exist in business. Businessmen, too, therefore hold money balances to provide for any large payments which are in prospect or as the residue of receipts not yet expended. Indeed, in an industrial community, the balances held for business purposes may be just as large as the balances held by consumers against future payments. The cash requirements of business will vary with trade activity, rising in a boom and falling in a slump. In a boom, when higher profits are being made, larger balances will be required to provide for increased dividend disbursements, and to finance extensions to buildings and plant. Other payments and receipts will also be higher in value, partly because of expanding trade, partly because of rising prices, so that, if the time intervals between receipts and payments remain as before, businesses will find themselves holding, or requiring to hold, more money. In a slump, all these tendencies will be reversed, and businesses will hold reduced money balances. Consumers respond to fluctuation in trade in the same way. The higher their income, the more money they will hold, and the higher prices are, the more money they require to hold in order to make their normal purchases. When trade is good, and incomes and prices are rising, consumers will increase their stock of money; and in a depression, with incomes and prices falling, they will diminish it. Thus the strength of the first motive to hold money depends mainly upon the level of incomes and prices, and upon the normal time intervals between receipts and payments.

(b) The speculative motive

The second motive is an expectation that prices – especially the prices of stocks and shares – will fall. This expectation will lead people to hold money instead of using it to buy goods which they hope to obtain later at lower prices. If the expectation is sufficiently widespread it will *cause* prices to fall and so produce its own justification. But the expectation cannot be universal or prices will fall at once into line with the general market expectation; for consumers will not pay prices which they think too high, and producers, sharing the general opinion, will have no motive to hold out for existing prices. The fall in prices will remove the divergence between fact and expectation, and unless *some* consumers expect a further fall, the second motive to hold money will disappear. In other words, the second motive presupposes divisions of opinion on the future trend of prices. One group of people, satisfied with existing prices, continues to buy. Others, anticipating a fall, reduce their purchases and add to their bank balances instead. But prices at any given moment are always low enough to clear the market of all goods offered for sale, an addition to stock being regarded as a purchase by the holder.

When prices begin to rise, and are commonly expected to rise further, the second motive to hold money is transformed into a motive to get rid of it. No one wants to hold money, a depreciating asset, longer than is necessary, and it is passed on hastily like a bad penny. In a major inflation, people keep by them just enough money to meet day-to-day expenses and do all they can to reduce the normal intervals between receipts and payments. Thus the store of real purchasing power which they hold in the form of money (K) falls heavily. At the end of October 1923, the note issue in Germany had increased 400 millionfold in comparison with 1913; but in spite of this enormous inflation, which raised the printing of notes to the status of a major industry, the real purchasing power of the note issue in terms of gold was less than a fortieth of the purchasing power of the pre-war note issue.

(c) The precautionary motive

The third and final motive to hold money springs from uncertainty. We can never be quite certain in what payments the future will involve us, nor what receipts we shall ultimately obtain. Lacking certainty, we arm ourselves with money against emergencies – against calamities like illness and death, and the expense to which they put us; against sudden calls on our charity; against opportunities of purchase on favourable terms; against delays guessed at or unforeseen in the receipt of income. The money that we hold gives us security; it makes us *liquid*. The motives to liquidity are particularly strong when it is the price of securities about which we are uncertain. Even if we do not expect that security prices will fall – that is, even when the second motive to hold money is absent – we may have too little confidence in our judgement to come in and buy. We may prefer to hold a large part of our wealth in money until the future course of prices is less in doubt.

Hoarding

A demand for money from the second or third motive is primarily a demand for money to hoard. We want the money, not for some specific purpose but as a safeguard or as the best investment open to us. For the time being we want to keep it idle. To suggest therefore – as is so often done – that there is something heinous about 'piling up idle deposits in the banks' is to misunderstand completely the functions of money. It is the business of bank deposits – other than those held from the first motive – to be idle. Nor does it lie within the power of the general public to alter the total volume of bank deposits, except by devious ways such as stuffing their pockets with notes; the level of bank deposits depends upon the policy of the monetary authorities. Nor, in point of fact, are bank deposits at an abnormally high level in the years of depression when 'idle deposits' are most lamented; they are generally *below* the level reached in more prosperous years. What is true, and what does lend colour to the complaints, is that a larger proportion of bank deposits is hoarded in a depression – that is, is held exclusively from the second and third motives.

But the remedy lies not so much with the public as with the banking system, which, by creating more money, can satisfy the increased desire for liquidity. The public might, of course, spend more, and give money more work to do, but this would change, not their aggregate bank balances, but their savings.

Liquidity and interest rates

The increased 'hoarding' that takes place in a depression shows itself, as a rule, in an increase in K – the ratio of the money supply to the national income. An increase in K is likely to occur in war-time: in the years 1940–1947, for example, the supply of money grew faster than the national income because of heavy government borrowing on short-term (which inflated the money supply) and the exercise of controls over various types of expenditure (which checked the inflation of incomes). People built up large liquid balances which they could not spend at once but which they intended to use once the war was over. The war-time rise in K was followed by a gradual decline as people brought their money balances into closer relationship with their more normal requirements. These movements are illustrated in *Figure 24.1* which shows the ratio of the net deposits of the

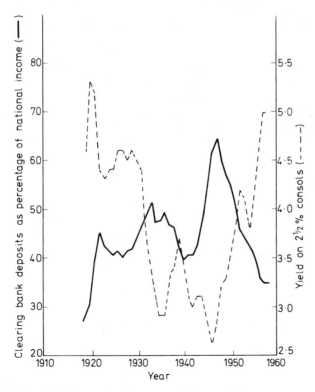

Figure 24.1 The supply of money and the rate of interest.
Source: F. W. Paish, 'Gilt-edged and the Money Supply',
The Banker, January 1959, p. 18

London clearing banks to the British national income in the years 1919–1958. It will be seen that there are three peaks in K, one after each of the two world wars and one at the bottom of the depression in 1933.

Figure 24.1 shows the fluctuations over the same period in the long-term rate of interest as measured by the yield on consols. The rate of interest appears to have varied inversely with K as if the fluctuations in the one have an important influence on the other.

There are two possible lines of explanation of this phenomenon, one in terms of the speculative motive, one in terms of the precautionary. We have already seen that the speculative motive results in efforts to economize money balances when they are expected to depreciate. The same expectation of inflation will also make people avoid fixed interest securities since a constant money return will represent a diminishing yield in terms of future prices; this loss of favour sends down the price of fixed interest securities and raises the rate of interest. As K falls, the rate of interest rises.

The first line of explanations is thus in terms of a diminishing demand, under inflationary conditions, for money and bonds. It lays stress on the effects of a general loss of confidence in the future value of money but does not presuppose any exact correspondence from year to year between changes in interest rates and in the real value of money balances. What happens in any one year will depend on the way in which the authorities try to stem inflation. There may well be some recovery in the gilt-edged market while prices go on rising and the money supply undergoes little change, so that, for the time being, interest rates and K both decrease.

The second line of explanation is in terms of the motives to liquidity which, as we saw in Chapter 20, are linked with interest rates. Our demand for money is a function of our preference for it in comparison with less liquid alternatives such as consols. If we are anxious to remain liquid we are prepared to sacrifice the interest that we might earn by buying consols and the more anxious we are the more interest we will forgo. In a period when the money supply is not expanding as fast as the national income, there is less money in relation to the work is has to do, people are less liquid, and they are less willing therefore to lend money or buy government securities and run down their cash balances. In other words, interest rates rise as a reflection of a higher liquidity preference. Conversely, if interest rates rise, the cost of remaining liquid rises too and some people will be tempted to lend their money or exchange it for fixed interest securities[1].

At this point we rejoin the main stream of argument. The demand for money, together with the supply, helps to determine the complex of interest rates and through interest rates the level of economic activity. An increase in the demand for money acts as a brake on investment while a decrease makes investment easier and cheaper to finance.

---

[1] This second line of explanation can be modified so as to make the argument turn on the behaviour of short-term interest rates. These reflect monetary policy and at the same time react on long-term rates. A restrictive monetary policy will operate to reduce the money supply in relation to national income, will involve high short-term interest rates, and will produce a sympathetic rise in long-term rates.

Chapter 25

The supply of money

Bank money

Many people think of money as currency (i.e., notes and coin). But there is another kind of money of far greater importance as a means of payment – bank money. Unlike currency, bank money, or money deposited with a bank, is not a commodity. There are, it is true, ultra-cautious depositors who make periodic visits to their bank to see for themselves that their money is still there, and who are handed banknotes (a commodity) by the teller. But the banknotes which they inspect are not the same thing as their bank account. Banknotes are oblong pieces of paper decorated with a promise to pay whereas a bank account is an entry in a ledger. This entry gives us the right to ask the bank for a specified amount of currency – a right which, if we make all our payments by cheque, we shall never use. The entry also gives us the right – if our balance is held on 'current account' – to draw cheques directing the bank to transfer money from our account to some other person's account. So long as the bank remains solvent and our cheques continue to be accepted freely, we can use our bank balances almost as effectively as notes to make a purchase or to settle a debt. In times of crisis the risk of banking failures may cause people to insist on payment in notes; notes, being legal tender, are absolutely liquid, but a bank account may be frozen if the bank is unable to meet its obligations. In normal times the difference in acceptability or liquidity is small; we may even prefer payment by cheque to payment in banknotes.

Cheques themselves are not money: they are devices for transferring the ownership of bank money from one person to another. But chequable bank deposits, or current accounts, can normally be classed as money. So also may other bank deposits – deposit and savings accounts. Unlike current accounts, these cannot be drawn on at any moment; the depositor requires to give notice of his intention to draw on them and they are less liquid, therefore, than current accounts. But they are so much more liquid than other assets, and are so commonly classed with current accounts when we are mentally contrasting money with alternative investment, that any sharp line of division between current and other accounts would be false to the facts.

Money and other liquid assets

If we include savings accounts in money where are we to stop? Is money lent to a savings bank, money? Or money invested in bills of exchange? Or money used for the purchase of consols? For an answer to these questions we must go back to our definition. Money, we said, was anything generally acceptable without question in payment for goods and services or in final settlement of a debt. Now acceptability is a matter of degree.

Unless something is much more acceptable than all possible substitutes, we cannot draw a hard and fast line between what is money and what is not. All we can do is to arrange things in order of liquidity and stop at the first big gap that we come to. We might think that bills of exchange and consols could be ruled out because they are debts, not money. But some kinds of money are simply debts. Pound notes, for example, are promises to pay – acknowledgements of debts; current accounts are debts due to us by our bank. Pound notes, it might also be suggested, are a perpetual debt; the Bank of England is never likely to be asked to redeem its promises. But the same is true of consols; they, too, are a perpetual debt unlikely ever to be redeemed. What then is the difference? Is it that consols bear interest while money does not? Not at all; interest-bearing notes were used as money for over a century. The only ultimate difference is one of degree. Consols are a less liquid asset than money; they are not generally acceptable as a means of payment. Similarly, bills of exchange and savings bank deposits should be excluded; they stand on the other side of the gap that separates money from less liquid assets.

Definitions of the money supply

In practice the money supply may be defined narrowly or widely, depending on what counts as a bank and which liabilities are included. The Bank of England, for example, uses two statistical series, M1 and M3 (M2 was discontinued). The first of these includes notes and coin in circulation with the public plus sterling current accounts held by the private sector only. The second, which is easier to estimate, also includes notes and coin but covers *all* deposits held by United Kingdom residents in both the public and the private sectors, whether denominated in sterling or other currencies[1]. Changes in the money supply can look very different according as one or other of these definitions is used. For example, between the first quarter of 1972 and the first quarter of 1974, M1 increased by less than 14% and M3 by nearly 59%.

Bank money and credit creation

The convenience of using bank money is so great we could almost manage without currency altogether, receiving our incomes by cheque and paying them away by cheque or credit card. No money would ever change hands; we should simply instruct our bankers to reduce our balance and increase

[1] *Sterling* M3, which is most commonly used, excludes foreign currency deposits (see below, pp. 347–349). Both definitions of the money supply exclude 60% of the net value of transit items within the banking sector (e.g., cheques in course of collection).

our creditor's balance correspondingly. Money would consist entirely of claims on the banks, transferable by cheque, and all payments would be made by appropriate entries in bank ledgers. From this day of universal reckoning in bank ledgers we are still, however, some distance away. We do not all go shopping with cheque books (or even with credit cards), and we are not all successful in running up bills (to be settled later by cheque) with tradesmen, landlords and others. We pay for most of our smaller purchases in cash. Hence we still need currency. But currency plays a minor part in modern business. A century ago, it was spoken of as 'the small change of credit'. Today, with the rapid growth of banking and the cheque system, the predominance of bank money is even more marked. In 1980 the British public held nearly five times as much on deposit with the banks as it held in notes and coin.

If most of the money in use is bank money, the supply of money must depend upon how bank money is created. Indeed, we can leave coin and notes entirely out of account because the supply is expanded nowadays to keep pace with the demand. If anyone is short of change he can draw on his bank balance for the coin or notes that he needs; the output of coin from the Mint and of notes from the Bank of England's printing press is governed by the public's desire to hold money in this form rather than in the form of bank money. If a member of the public wants more bank money, on the other hand, he cannot, as a rule force the banks to create more of it. He can, it is true, pay more notes across the counter and so increase his own bank balance. But this will not necessarily add to the total of all bank balances since some other person may be withdrawing notes and running down his bank balance; only if there is a *general* reduction (or increase) in the total of notes in circulation can the public act on the supply of bank money. Such a reduction, in point of fact, is rarely accompanied by an expansion in bank balances; more commonly the note issue and bank deposits contract (or expand) together. Presumably, therefore, a change in the supply of money is initiated, not by the public but by the banks.

We start, therefore, from a paradox. Everyone is free to decide for himself how much money he will keep on deposit with the banks; but the public as a body has little or no influence on the total volume of bank deposits. To understand how this can be so we must look at the way in which the banks conduct their business.

Manufacturing money

The primary function of banks, which is to mobilize savings, has become entangled with a second, and quite distinct, function – that of creating the means of payment. Ever since the introduction of banknotes, banks have been able to *manufacture* money. At first they did this by issuing notes in excess of the valuables deposited with them. By increasing their loans they could put more notes into circulation, the loan being drawn upon and paid away in banknotes. Similarly, by calling in their loans (that is, by 'restricting credit') they could reduce the notes in circulation and hence the supply of money. At this stage in the evolution of banking, the notes put into circulation were limited only by the reserves which the issuing banks thought fit to keep. If, for example, they held rigorously to a reserve ratio of 20% (i.e., if they held £20 in gold against every £100 in notes), they issued notes to the value of five times their gold reserve. Whenever an additional deposit was made with them, they could lend five times the value of the new deposit and so add four times its value to the amount of money in circulation. A withdrawal of deposits reacted automatically to reduce the note-issue in the same proportion by forcing the banks to call for repayment of their loans.

When gold disappears from circulation, and the issue of notes is limited or taken over by the government, the power of the banks to create money does not by any means come to an end. Just as they were once able to vary their note issue by increasing or diminishing their loans, so the banks can now vary their deposits by exactly the same technique. By lending more freely they can *create* deposits, and by restricting credit they can extinguish them.

The mechanism by which they do this depends upon the reserves which they hold against their deposit liabilities and the ratios which they maintain between reserves and deposits. Suppose, for example, that it is regarded as good banking practice to keep a cash reserve of 10% against deposit liabilities, and that this ratio is adhered to by every bank. Then total deposits will necessarily be equal to ten times the cash reserves of the banks as a group, and a change in the money supply will come about whenever these cash reserves are expanded or contracted. In a monetary system of this kind, the money supply will be a function of what is usually called 'the cash base'.

The cash base

Let us make the simplifying assumption that cash reserves consist entirely of till money, and that till money consists entirely of notes. Let us also assume – it not a very extravagant assumption – that the public wants to divide its money in a fixed ratio – say 5:1 – between bank deposits and notes. Finally, let us assume – again without much departure from fact – that the government has an exclusive right to issue notes. Then the supply of money will expand whenever the government puts more notes into circulation (e.g., to pay for the construction of new roads): at first by the amount of the additional notes but eventually by much more. The initial increase in notes will exceed what the public wants to hold at the current level of income and some of the notes will be deposited with the banks, where they will swell the cash reserves. This will dispose the banks to lend more freely (or to add to their investments) and as a result of their loans (or purchases of securities) bank deposits will expand. The process of expansion will continue until the banks are obliged to limit their lending by the insufficiency of their reserves. Once the additional notes have been absorbed and there is no scope for further creation of credit without infringing the normal reserve ratio of the banks, the public will again be holding five times as much bank money as notes and the total supply of money will have expanded by much more than the initial injection of additional notes: on the particular assumptions that we have made, by four times as much[1].

Credit creation and bank profits

This brief description of credit creation may suggest that banking is a highly profitable pursuit since banks can literally make money out of nothing. In fact, however, it is by no means inevitable that banks will make higher profits when the money supply is expanding than when it is contracting. When a bank 'creates money' it adds simultaneously to its assets (loans and investments) and to its liabilities (deposits, i.e. bank money); whether it makes a higher profit depends upon what inflation does to the return on its assets and the interest it has to pay on its deposits, not just upon what inflation does to the magnitudes on each side of the balance-sheet. It is not unknown, for example, for interest rates to increase during a period of inflation and for this increase to cause a serious depreciation in the value of the gilt-edged securities that form a large proportion of bank assets. At the same time, the changes in interest rates may be more pronounced on the liabilities side than on the side of bank assets, though this is not likely to happen except in rather special circumstances.

Banks and other financial institutions

There is, however, a more fundamental misunderstanding about the role of the banks in credit creation. Banks are financial institutions, in many ways like other financial institutions. They are dealers in financial assets – loans and debts – borrowing from some people and lending to others, hiring money and hiring it out again. This is what all financial institutions do: building societies, insurance companies, investment trusts, discount houses, finance houses, and so on, all raise money and lend or invest it. There are, of course, differences between these institutions in the sources of their funds and in the purposes to which they are applied. There are also differences between banks: some draw their funds mainly from the shareholders, others mainly from depositors; some lend mainly to industry, others mainly to public bodies, including the central government; some deal in short loans, borrowing and lending for short periods, while others deal in long-term loans, borrowing and lending for comparatively long periods. But all banks and all financial institutions have this in common: that by incurring fresh liabilities they can acquire additional assets. A building society can take steps to attract larger deposits and lend the proceeds on mortgage to householders; an investment trust can raise

---

[1] Let B = bank deposits, N = notes held by the public, T = notes held by the banks.
Then $B = 5N$, $B = 10T$, so that $N = 2T$.
Of the increase in notes (X), two-thirds will ultimately be retained by the public and one-third will be held by the banks as till-money, providing backing for a tenfold expansion in deposits.
The increase in the money supply will eventually be $\frac{2}{3}X + \frac{10}{3}X = 4X$, or four times the initial expansion in the note issue.

money on the stock exchange and invest it in securities. The distinguishing feature of a bank, or at least of a deposit bank accepting money on deposit from the public, lies in the character of the liabilities it creates. These liabilities, unlike deposits with a building society, shares in an investment trust, insurance policies, etc., are themselves money: not just something capable of being turned into money, or forming security for a loan of money, but money-at-the-bank.

It follows from this that banks are not alone in their power to create credit if by credit we mean liquid assets. The liabilities of most financial institutions are relatively liquid in the sense that they can be readily disposed of at little cost and without much sacrifice of their face value. They differ from money, but the difference is a matter of degree. If the liabilities of financial institutions other than deposit banks are increased, the money supply remains unaffected but something happens that is very much akin to an increase in the money supply: the economy becomes more liquid and less in need of bank money. If people have more on deposit with the building societies, or hold more savings certificates or bigger insurance policies, they have less motive for holding a large balance at the bank; their need for liquidity is satisfied in other ways. Now all financial institutions are in competition with one another for money and the banks are not immune from this competition; they may lose ground to savings banks, building societies, and other competitors. If this happens, the place of the banks in the whole financial structure will alter and so will the place of bank money in relation to other kinds of liquid asset. The changes taking place in the supply of money will then be a very misleading guide to the changes taking place in general liquidity and it is the latter that are significant in the management of the economy. Changes in the supply of money are no more than a means of acting on liquidity; and deposit banks are only one group of financial institutions capable of generating additional liquidity.

Moreover if we look at the process of credit creation through the eyes of an individual bank, its behaviour does not seem very different from that of other financial institutions. It balances it books just as they do, entertaining fresh applications for loans or buying additional securities only if there is a surplus above normal reserve requirements. If it decides to hold a rather larger or rather smaller reserve against its liabilities, it is again making a decision that other financial institutions may take when they think it prudent to increase their liquid reserves or are content with a narrower margin in hand. A bank can no more afford to increase its liabilities without regard to its reputation than can any other financial institution.

We must not push these arguments too far. While it is true that other institutions create credit, and that a great deal of credit is given by one business to another or by one person to another without the intervention of any institution, the banks occupy a central position in the creation of credit and liquidity. They do so for three reasons. First of all, banks as a group usually have command over larger resources than other financial institutions. In the United Kingdom, pension funds and building societies equal only the insurance companies and the clearing banks in the size of their assets, but insurance policies lie far apart from bank money in point of liquidity. This illustrates the second reason for the key position of the banks: their liabilities are more liquid – generally much more liquid – than those of other financial institutions. While bank money is not the sole source of liquidity it is a much more satisfactory source than most other liquid assets. Thirdly, the banks offer a relatively convenient instrument of control over general liquidity: if the authorities can control the supply of bank money, they have a very powerful lever for controlling general liquidity.

Bank money and the cash base

This brings us back to the main issue which we set out to discuss: what determines the supply of money? We have seen that the general public has only a very limited influence, exercised through a switch between notes and bank deposits; that individual banks have little power to initiate a change except by altering their customary reserve ratio; but that, if the cash base changes, the banking system will expand or contract credit proportionately. This seems to make everything turn on the size of the cash base and direct attention to the factors operating upon it. In the example which we took, the cash base consisted entirely of notes in the till, and these notes were the residue of the total issue after providing for the requirements of the public. The money supply depended on the size of the note issue, the state of preference of the public for notes in relation to bank deposits, and the reserve ratio maintained by the banks.

In one respect this example was a highly artificial one: it made no reference to any central bank such as now exists in most countries – for example, the Bank of England in the United Kingdom or the Federal Reserve Board in the United States – yet it usually rests with the central bank, in association with the government, to regulate the supply of money. The real power to create or contract credit is exercised, as a rule, by the monetary authorities, a term which is used to cover the central bank (if there is one) and any agencies or departments of government (such as the Ministry of Finance or the Treasury) that exercise control over monetary policy. The powers and techniques used by the monetary authorities to control the money supply vary from one country to another, and the relationship between the central bank and the government also varies. The position in the United Kingdom is discussed more fully in Chapter 26 on British financial institutions: what is said below is intended to be of general application. In order to avoid a detailed description of banking institutions, however, the argument is set out in terms of central banking operations and the monetary authorities are identified, for simplicity, with the central bank. The central bank is assumed to control, with the concurrence of the government, the size of the cash base and hence, given fixed reserve ratios, the total volume of credit.

Where there is a central bank, the commercial banks normally keep part of their reserves in the form of a balance with the central bank. They may be required to do so by law or by a convention that has the force of law. But there is also an obvious convenience to the commercial banks in the centralization of their reserves; if they all hold balances with the central bank, they can settle surpluses and deficits at the clearing by a simple book entry, the banks with a deficit making a transfer from their balances to the banks with a surplus. From the point of view of the central bank, the advantage of centralization is the power which it confers over the cash base: it puts the central bank in the same relationship to the commercial banks as the commercial banks occupy in relation to the public. The public holds money in deposit with the commercial banks which in turn hold money on deposit with the central bank.

Open market operations

Just as the commercial banks can create deposits with themselves, so also can the central bank. It may lend directly to the commercial banks (although this never happens in the United Kingdom), or it may lend indirectly (as when it helps out the discount market at the same time as the commercial banks are withdrawing funds from the discount market), or it may buy government securities, paying with a cheque drawn on itself. If it chooses the third course, and resorts to 'open market operations', the cheque will be paid into a commercial bank by the seller of the securities and the proceeds credited to him. This bank in turn will be credited by the central bank with an increase in its balance there. The action of the central bank causes the public to switch from government securities to money and to hold additional deposits with a commercial bank; simultaneously it adds to the cash reserves of the commercial bank and puts it in a position to initiate a cumulative expansion of credit of the same type as would result from an increase in the note issue.

If the central bank wants to initiate a contraction of credit, it reduces its lending or sells securities. This forces the commercial banks to part with some of their reserves either in repayment of loans or in settlement, on behalf of their customers, of the securities which they have purchased. The loss of reserves, in the form of balances with the central bank, sets in motion a general contraction of credit as the commercial banks try to restore their reserve ratios.

In what has been said so far, no reference has been made to till money which was treated earlier as the entire cash reserve of a commercial bank. In practice, cash reserves are made up partly of till money, and partly of balances with the central bank; sometimes they also include balances with other banks and gold. In most countries the variable element in reserves consists of balances with the central bank and no real violence to the facts is involved in concentrating exclusively on this; but in some countries, particularly those where there is no central bank, the situation is rather more complicated.

Methods of credit control

Even where such complications can be disregarded, the central bank does not rely exclusively on open market operations and variations in its loans to commercial banks in order to control credit. It may operate directly on the commercial banks by varying the reserve ratios which they are asked or required to maintain or (which comes to much the same thing) by calling on them to make additional or 'special' deposits with it. This has the same effect on the banks as a change in the size of their reserves without the embarrassments that sometimes accompany open market operations (e.g., if the central bank wants to sell government securities it has to find buyers for them and the presence in the market of a large seller may be discouraging to possible buyers). The central bank may also operate through interest rates: it may, for example, raise its lending rates, rather than simply restrict its loans, and take what action it can to force a general increase in rates. Any restriction of credit is likely to involve a rise in interest rates but there is a choice between raising the cost of credit so as to limit the demand and reducing the supply of credit, knowing that this will raise the cost. A third weapon which the central bank may use is selective credit control: it may require a limitation by the commercial banks of lending for some purposes which are deemed to be of low priority, or it may make borrowing for those purposes more difficult or more onerous. An example of such action is an increase in the margin which purchasers of stock exchange securities have to provide from their own resources when seeking bank accommodation for the remainder. Similarly, importers may be asked to make cash deposits before being granted permission to import some types of commodity, these deposits increasing the cost or difficulty of financing the transaction. Credit control of this kind, while qualitative in form, has a quantitative effect and it may be this effect which the authorities most desire.

Credit control in Britain

In the United Kingdom there is an unusual relationship between the central bank and the commercial banks since there are few direct dealings between the two. In particular, the commercial banks do not borrow from the Bank of England although they do hold deposits with it and can be called upon by the Bank to make additional ('special') deposits if credit has to be restricted. What makes the British systems unique is the use of the discount market as a buffer. When the (commercial) banks need to replenish their reserves their first recourse may be to what is called 'the inter-bank market', i.e., they may borrow from other banks with excess reserves until any slack of this kind has been taken up. Thereafter if money becomes tighter, they will have to fall back on their next line of defence, which (depending, of course, on the movement of borrowing rates in the different markets) is likely to be a reduction in their lending to the discount market, and not, as in most countries, direct borrowing from the central bank. The discount market will then be 'forced into the Bank'; in other words, the discount houses will be obliged to borrow from the Bank at what they will regard as penal rates.

There is a further point of difference: the cash reserves of the British banks are not nowadays the pivot of the monetary system and respond to changes in the money supply instead of controlling it. It is true that the cash reserves of the banks form a steady ratio to their deposit liabilities but this is because the banks can obtain more cash from the Bank of England (or part with excess cash to it) by varying their other liquid assets, not because total deposits move up or down in step with cash reserves.

The Bank has at various times since the war sought to make use of a different ratio by specifying the liquid assets to be included in reserves and requiring the banks to maintain a minimum ratio between their reserves so defined and their deposit liabilities.

The liquid assets base

At first this ratio was 30%; later it was reduced to 28%. At that stage only the clearing banks were under any obligation to observe a minimum liquid assets ratio and this ratio was thought to reflect their customary practices and so impose no great hardship. Liquid assets were more broadly defined than they were later (for example, till money was included) and bank liabilities were confined to sterling liabilities without any similar reserve requirement, then or subsequently, in relation to foreign currency deposits (see below, pp. 347–349).

An important change took place in 1971 when all British banks were required to observe a minimum asset ratio of 12½% between eligible reserve assets and sterling deposit liabilities. This change was intended to put the clearing banks on a footing of greater equality with other financial institutions that were in competition with them for funds and had been growing more rapidly over the post-war period, partly because they were free from the controls exercised over reserve requirements. At the same time other changes were made that put an end to the maintenance of agreed uniform rates of interest on bank deposits and were intended to encourage greater competition in banking and free the banks from direct controls over their lending. The minimum ratio was reduced in stages from 12½ to 10% in January 1981 and finally abandoned in September 1981.

So long as specified reserve assets formed the base of the British monetary system their significance was similar to, but by no means identical with, the cash base in other systems. The difference is that while commercial banks cannot themselves create cash, they can generate additional liquid assets or substitute one kind of liquid asset for another if the monetary authorities seek to restrict the supply. It was open to the Bank of England to operate on the liquid assets base either directly by varying the minimum ratio or, less dramatically, by regulating the supply of liquid assets available to the banks. In practice it relied almost exclusively on the indirect method. Sometimes use was also made of an intermediate device by a call for 'special deposits', i.e. by requiring the banks to increase the balances they normally hold with the Bank of England. But if the banks had a surplus of liquid assets or if they could liquefy some of their existing assets, for example by selling government securities for cash, this method of control was not likely to be very effective.

Bank rate

In 1981 further important changes took place. The minimum reserve asset ratio was abandoned: all that banks and other licensed deposit-takers are now required to do is to keep ½% of eligible liabilities at the Bank. At the same time the use of Bank Rate, or as it had come to be called in the 1970s the Bank's minimum lending rate (MLR), was suspended. This was the *minimum* rate at which the Bank discounted first-class bills or made advances to a discount house against eligible paper. It governed the movement of market rates of discount, although these usually remained below bank rate by a margin which fluctuated but was rarely large except in a depression. Many administered interest rates, such as the rates on clearing bank deposits and advances, moved with bank rate, partly by custom, partly (up to 1971) because of a bank cartel that rested on government support. A rise in bank rate, under those conditions, stiffened the terms on which the discount market could obtain cash in the last resort from the Bank of England, and produced a sympathetic rise in the rate of discount on bills held in the market and in other rates of interest traditionally associated with bank rate. The greater return on Treasury bills and other liquid assets was an inducement to the non-bank public (including businesses and foreigners) to switch out of cash; and this involved the banks in making a switch in the opposite direction, i.e., in parting with liquid assets to their depositors.

The new arrangements introduced in August 1981 leave the Bank free to announce its minimum lending rate in special circumstances. It remains the money market's lender of last resort. Normally, however, the Bank seeks to keep short-term interest rates within a target band which it does not announce publicly; nor does it announce any decision to change the band. In making such decisions the Bank is guided by targets for the money supply laid down in advance in agreement with the government.

Under these arrangements the operations of the Bank are conducted largely through open market purchases and sales of bills rather than through direct lending to the discount market. The Bank acts directly on short-term interest rates to keep them within the target band but leaves the market to set the rates without the kind of guidance previously given by MLR. The Bank's open market operations produce an expansion or contraction of the money supply by adding to or reducing the liquid assets held by the money market and hence the reserve of liquid assets held by the banks. The fact that the reserves are held voluntarily on prudential grounds rather than in some required ratio to deposits does not prevent a contraction in reserves from producing a contraction in deposits even if the size of the contraction is likely to be less predictable. But the success of the Bank in keeping control of the money supply obviously depends on the effectiveness of changes in short-term interest rates in limiting the market's access to liquid assets.

This effectiveness in turn must rest either on a contraction in the supply of bills (e.g. by inducing the government to borrow less on short-term and more on long-term) or on a redistribution of outstanding bills between the banks and the public. If neither of these processes is very sensitive to changes in short-term interest rates it will be necessary to vary the rates widely in order to keep to a fixed monetary target, especially if it is thought necessary to scotch erratic departures from the target path from month to month or even from week to week. The translation of monetary targets into appropriate interest bands is no easy matter; and a steady growth in the money supply may well require great volatility in interest rates. In the end it may be the reaction of interest rates not on bank reserves but on the level of economic activity and so on the *demand* for money that is the ultimate determinant of the money supply.

It is partly for this reason that some economists who see dangers in wide fluctuations in interest rates (and hence in the price of financial assets) would prefer to see central banking policy concentrate on maintaining or altering the complex of interest rates, letting the money supply adjust itself to those rates. Others, attaching more importance to changes in the money supply, would like the monetary authorities to content themselves with expanding or contracting the credit base, letting this work its way through to the supply of money and so to market rates of interest.

We have left on one side the influence of interest rates and credit conditions abroad. But efforts to redistribute liquid assets between the banks and the public have to reckon with the inclusion of the whole of the rest of the world among 'the public'. In a world where capital flows are very large and sensitive to interest differentials it may be impossible to vary the rate of interest without producing an international movement of funds that largely nullifies the intended change. Where capital is completely mobile and rates of exchange are fixed, no country can have a really independent monetary policy or set and achieve monetary targets that ignore what is happening elsewhere in the world.

Direct operations on the banks

Although the Bank of England relies primarily on open market operations the monetary authorities can still, if they choose, make use of more direct instruments of control. They can, for example, deprive the banks of some of their liquid assets by bringing pressure on them to exchange Treasury bills for short-dated bonds which do not rank for inclusion in their liquid reserves; on two occasions in the early 1950s and again in 1971 such a conversion operation took place. They can, as already explained, require the banks to make 'special' deposits with the Bank of England over and above their normal cash holdings and so freeze some of the banks' liquid assets. Finally, the monetary authorities may limit bank *lending*, for example, by putting a ceiling on bank advances. They are likely to do this in order to make it more difficult to obtain command over money rather than with a view to limiting its supply; but a check to expansion in one of the main assets of the banks (their loans to customers) may simultaneously check expansion in their liabilities, especially if the principal alternative outlet for their funds, namely government securities, happens to look unattractive because they are falling in price.

Bank assets and liabilities

It may be worth dwelling for a moment on this point. The money supply has been defined as the deposit liabilities of the banks; and since bank assets and liabilities must match one another, the money supply can also be regarded as the total of bank assets. This means that it must be the sum of government debt taken up by the banks and loans made by them to private (mainly business) borrowers. The money supply can be held constant, therefore, if the government does not resort to additional borrowing from the banks and if at the same time bank advances to the private sector do not increase. On the other hand, if the money supply does expand this must imply either that the government has possessed itself of additional purchasing power out of bank loans or that the private sector has been enjoying additional credit facilities. This way of looking at things may be more revealing than trying to work out the implications of changes in the money market although it will not be of much help in trying to unravel the chain of cause and effect.

The money supply and the PSBR

The influence of government borrowing on the money supply is obviously very important. Historically it has been the dominant influence, especially in war-time when the need to finance additional government expenditure is most urgent and the printing press provides an easy way out. But there is also a good chance that in peace-time, too, governments will over-spend and then try to finance the resulting budget deficit by borrowing from the banks. The link between the budget deficit and any increase in the money supply that results is, however, far from automatic.

It is usual, in discussion of this link, to begin from the deficit, not of the central government alone, but of the entire public sector. This cash deficit does not imply a corresponding borrowing requirement because of various transactions in existing assets: for example, the need to meet maturing debt obligations will add to the borrowing requirement while capital receipts from asset disposals will diminish it. Once these adjustments have been made the public sector borrowing requirement, or PSBR, emerges. This may be financed in any one of three ways. First of all, the debt may be monetized: that is, it may be taken up by the banking system through an increase in the money supply. Alternatively, the government may try to avoid recourse to the banks by issuing more gilt-edged securities through the capital market. A third possibility is that some of the debt may be externally financed. While the first of these has usually been the largest, this is not necessarily so. How far the Government relies on the banks and how far on other forms of borrowing depends ultimately on the monetary policy pursued.

If, for example, the government is anxious to keep interest rates steady, sales of government securities will be limited to the purchases the public is prepared to make at existing prices as its wealth increases and the whole of the residue will have to be taken up by the banking system. On the other hand, if the government is determined not to add to the money supply it has to be prepared to see the price of its bonds fall until sales are sufficient to ensure this result. Since the public may show some initial disposition to hold off buying when bond prices fall (and interest rates, therefore, increase), the fall may have to go a long way before a quite modest increase in the PSBR is absorbed without resort to the banking system. So, on the one hand, the government may have to choose between allowing the money supply to expand and accepting the attendant risk of inflation and, on the other, holding the money supply fixed at the cost of big swings in interest rates and credit conditions that may have serious consequences for investment, employment and financial stability.

In the United Kingdom monetary policy moved away in the 1970s from emphasis on interest rates to emphasis on the money supply; and the practice developed of announcing monetary targets for the coming year (in the 1980 budget, for the next *four* years). These targets, which indicate the range (e.g., 7–11%) within which it is intended to confine the increase in the money supply, are partly intended to influence public expectations of the future rate of inflation. They have not been implemented completely rigorously in the sense that there has usually been some departure from target; but they have inevitably obliged the authorities to manage the public debt in such a way as to rely more heavily on changes in the level of interest rates. At the same time the once close relationship between the budget deficit, the PSBR and the growth of the money supply has become progressively looser. High interest rates have made government securities a more attractive investment not only to British investors but also to investors abroad and there have been quite wide fluctuations in the take-up of government debt by both groups.

It is of course possible that the more successful the government is in meeting its borrowing requirements without recourse to the banking system, the more the private sector is 'crowded out' from its normal sources of finance and forced into the banks. It would be at least a useful first approximation to suppose that, if the money supply is held constant, additional borrowing from the market by the government is likely to be balanced by diminished borrowing by private undertakings. But if their credit is good these undertakings may be able to borrow from the banks so that the money supply resumes its expansion. Companies may not be able to go on borrowing indefinitely from the banks; but the extra interest cost will not be a major deterrent if additional credit is urgently needed.

It may be asked why, if the growth of the money supply is dominated by government and private borrowing, it is not brought to a halt by a lack of reserves. How are the banks able to go on lending without infringing their fixed reserve ratios? The answer is that with large holdings of maturing government debt the banks need merely let some of the debt run off and use the repayment to buy Treasury bills or add to their balance at the Bank of England. Once there is an ample supply of government short-term debt the credit base of the system is assured, and instead of the base determining the money supply, it is the money supply that rules the credit base. The money supply is limited only by the disinclination of the government to use bank credit and the lack of demand from creditworthy borrowers in the private sector.

International influences on the money supply

Money is no more immune from international influence than any other aspect of economic life. So far we have disregarded this influence and we shall defer a full discussion of it until Chapter 28; but it may be useful to indicate briefly how it makes itself felt.

Just as a commercial bank has to be ready to settle any deficit at the clearing by drawing on its cash reserves, so the central bank of a country has to be in a position to settle an external deficit in the balance of payments by drawing on its reserves of foreign exchange. The parallel is not complete because the central bank may make use of exchange control to ration the supply of foreign exchange between importers and preserve a balance between what is paid in by exporters and what is taken out by importers without allowing its reserve to be drawn upon; or it may stand aside from the market in foreign exchange and let fluctuations in the rate of exchange take the strain, hoping that private dealings will help to balance supply and demand without too violent a movement in the rate. But if it wants to peg the rate of exchange at a fixed parity and to allow free dealings at that rate, it has no alternative but to come forward when necessary and either release enough foreign exchange to bridge a deficit in the balance of payments or absorb enough to clear a surplus. For this purpose, it has to maintain a reserve of internationally acceptable currency.

Foreign exchange reserves

This reserve may take one of three forms. It may consist of gold, which has long been the most acceptable means of international payment; it may consist of some currency such as sterling or dollars which is extensively used in international commerce and can be expected to remain relatively stable in value; or, finally, it may consist of deposits with some international banking organization or an automatic line of credit from such an organization. Liabilities of international institutions such as the International Monetary Fund, although still relatively small, seem destined to play an increasingly important part in the settlement of international accounts.

   If a drain of gold and foreign exchange takes place, the automatic effect is a reduction in the money supply since those who make payments abroad with the gold and foreign exchange acquire it by drawing on their bank accounts and so extinguish deposits to an equivalent value. The central bank may then, if it chooses, offset this reduction by open market operations; or it may, in alarm at the loss of reserves, reinforce the reduction in the money supply by setting in motion a further restriction of credit. Here, therefore, is a second point at which the reactions of commercial banks to a loss of cash reserves find no parallel in the reactions of a central bank. Commercial banks hold to a more or less steady reserve ratio and are very unlikely to meet a fall in their reserves by an expansion of credit. A central bank, unless required to do so by legislation, has normally no fixed ratio by which to regulate its behaviour and unless it has some reason for anxiety about the absolute level of its reserves is under no compulsion to contract credit when a deficit occurs. What it decides to do depends upon its diagnosis of the reasons for the deficit and upon other elements in the situation that make it appropriate or inappropriate to bring monetary weapons into play.

Euro-currencies

Money is usually thought of in national terms as the medium of exchange in use among the residents of a particular country. But non-residents have bank accounts too and they may even arrange to lend the money in their ownership to other non-residents. In the late 1950s there began to grow up, mainly in London, a market in externally held dollars that subsequently assumed unexpectedly large proportions. These Euro-dollars, as they are called, are deposits with banks outside the United States, including foreign branches of American banks, that are denominated in dollars and on-lent to non-bank borrowers, perhaps after one or more redeposits from one bank to another[1].

The growth of the Euro-dollar market, which is now a highly developed international market in bank credit with participants from all over the world, can be traced to a number of factors. These include, first of all, restrictions on both sides of the Atlantic. British banks found themselves prevented by exchange restrictions from granting sterling credits to borrowers outside the sterling area but free to bid for dollar deposits for this purpose since foreign currency borrowings were not subject to the same restrictions. At the same time there was a relatively wide spread between the maximum rate payable on deposits in New York and the minimum lending rate that New York banks charged their customers. There was thus a strong incentive to banks in London and elsewhere to work within these limits by offering slightly higher rates for dollar deposits and charging slightly lower rates for dollar credits. In addition, businesses in several European countries, particularly Germany and Italy, were attracted to the Euro-dollar market by lending rates that compared favourably with the rates payable to domestic banks.

A second important influence in the early days of the Euro-dollar market was the willingness of Soviet and Eastern European banks to hold their dollar balances in London or Paris and their unwillingness to hold them in New York. This meant that the Moscow Narodny Bank, for example, was able to enter the market as one of the main lenders. In due course this group of countries became substantial borrowers, along with Japan and Britain, while Latin America and the Middle East assumed the leading role as lenders.

A third factor in the growth of the market was the long-continuing deficit in the American balance of payments which increased foreign holdings of dollars. But it is a mistake to suppose that Euro-dollars must increase or decrease automatically according as the American balance of payments is in surplus or deficit. On the contrary, total Euro-dollar balances have gone on increasing whether there was a surplus or a deficit. The fact that there is a deficit need not imply any addition to external private holdings of dollars since the deficit may arise on the other items in the balance of payments and be settled between one central bank and another; but the deficit would certainly be inflated (on a liquidity basis at least)[2] if, for example, American residents transferred funds abroad that were then fed into the Euro-dollar market.

---

[1] Euro-dollars are not, as is commonly assumed, a post-war phenomenon. They existed in the years before 1939 when the movement of funds from the United Kingdom to the United States was '. . . believed to have included, in relatively substantial amounts, the acquisition by British banks of dollar deposits held for the account of foreign, especially French, clients' (A. I. Bloomfield, *Capital Imports and the American Balance of Payments 1934–39* (Chicago, 1950), p. 9).

[2] See below, pp. 384–385.

The Euro-currency market had expanded by 1981 until the gross total of foreign currency deposits was over $1 300 000 m ('gross' because there is an unknown element of double-counting in the total resulting from the on-lending of dollar deposits from one banker to another before they reach a non-bank borrower). The total includes foreign currency deposits in several non-dollar currencies, including sterling, francs, marks, lire and Swiss francs, but Euro-dollar business was far greater than business in any other Euro-currency.

Euro-dollar loans are made for various periods, from overnight to a year or more, at rates of interest varying with the period. There is also a rapidly expanding medium-term syndicated business in Euro-dollar loans. An international capital market dealing in Euro-bonds has also come into existence and most of the bonds issued are denominated in dollars.

The significance of these developments is twofold. On the one hand they reflect a closer integration of national economies and an expansion in international capital flows that limits the freedom of action of national monetary authorities. On the other hand they inject a large and elastic element of private liquidity into the international financial system. The growth of this stock of private international liquidity may prove stabilizing or de-stabilizing; it may make the task of managing the international economic system easier or more difficult. One cannot but be a little uneasy, however, when a new kind of money has come into existence while no national or international authority accepts responsibility for regulating

Chapter 26

British financial institutions[1]

We now turn to examine in more detail the financial institutions of a single country, the United Kingdom, and to the way in which these institutions affect the flow of funds into investment in real assets. We shall draw attention as we go along to any marked peculiarities of British institutions and refer from time to time to the institutions of other countries, particularly the United States.

We have already seen that from the point of view of anyone wishing to hold his savings in liquid form, there are a number of alternative types of investment, varying in liquidity and competitive with one another. From the point of view of anyone wishing to obtain command over liquid resources, the various financial institutions, such as banks, insurance companies and investment trusts, again provide a series of alternatives. There is a capital market in which financial institutions compete for funds and through which they make funds available. The market is not perfect because lenders prefer to make use of customary channels, and borrowers, as the Radcliffe Committee remarked, 'do not turn readily or without difficulty to alternative sources of finance. There are, as it were, faults in the structure of the market which are difficult to cross, partly because of ignorance, custom or prejudice, and partly because of the greater inconvenience or cost of using a different type of financial institution.' But there is nonetheless 'an underlying unity in the market for loanable funds'[2].

The truth of this may be checked by reflecting on the way in which the head of a small business obtains his capital. If he needs more he may, and usually does, draw more heavily on his own savings, ploughing back a larger portion of his profits, realizing some of his investments or drawing on his bank balance. He may also go to his bank for a bigger overdraft, mortgage his house or borrow money on his insurance policy, buy some equipment on hire purchase, take fuller advantage of credit from his suppliers or put off paying his bills, or try to raise money from an institution that specializes in advancing long-term capital to small businesses.

[1] A full account of the working of British financial institutions is given in the *Report of the Committee to Review the Functioning of Financial Institutions* (Cmnd 937, 1980).

[2] *Report of the Committee on the Working of the Monetary System* (Cmnd 827) para 319 (1959).

Self-finance

The most important single source of capital is self-finance: just as the private householder relies heavily on his own savings when he buys capital equipment such as a motor car, a washing machine, or a bedroom suite, so the average business usually turns first to appropriations from profit as a source of capital. There are no figures for all British businesses, but if we take companies alone and exclude companies in insurance, banking and finance, the total appropriation that they made to reserves (other than tax reserves) in 1979 was a little under £6000 m. About half of this sum represented an allowance for depreciation and so for the renewal of capital assets rather than for additional investment. But even if company saving were measured net of depreciation it would still stand out as the largest source of funds for new investment in real assets.

The new issue market

For public companies the next most important source was the new issue market. Issues of stocks and shares through the new issue market cannot be made by private companies since the flotation, unless it takes the form of a private 'placing' of shares with no provision for their subsequent sale to the public, has to be accompanied by an application to the stock exchange for permission to deal and no dealings in the shares of private companies can take place on the stock exchange. Issues in 1979 by quoted non-financial companies (i.e., excluding companies in banking, insurance and finance) totalled £1507 m. Most of this was raised in large issues, often in the form of 'rights' issues to existing shareholders at a price below the market quotation at the time of issue. Some small issues can be made down to about £1 m. On grounds of cost, these are rarely accompanied by a prospectus inviting the public to subscribe but are usually 'placed' with an insurance company or other institutional investor but such investors will normally take only a limited share of a company's capital so that even small issues can be made only by fairly large companies. The facilities of the new issue market are almost entirely confined, therefore, to the larger public companies.

Trade credit

Next in order of importance, but for very different purposes, is trade credit. Most businesses have at any one time large amounts outstanding to their credit for goods supplied and at the same time owe large amounts for goods they have received. The credit which they give and take is one of the leading causes of fluctuation in their liquidity and in their need of funds, and these fluctuations may, and do, give rise to insolvency. Apart from credit given by public companies to one another, a large amount of credit is given by exporters to their foreign customers and by retailers and others to private persons.

Personal credit

Some of the credit received by private persons is for house purchase and for this purpose they may go to their building society, their insurance company, their local authority, or their bank; building societies are by far the chief source of finance. Durable consumers' goods bought on hire purchase absorb a further large amount of credit: these sales are mainly financed by specialized institutions, the finance houses, which in turn raise the necessary funds from the banks and from deposits made by private persons, or, more commonly, by businesses with cash to spare for a limited period.

The main financial intermediaries

To obtain a more complete picture of the functioning of the capital market, we must look at each of the main financial intermediaries through which a large part of the flow of credit is channelled. The relative size of these institutions is shown in *Table 26.1*.

TABLE 26.1. Liabilities of British financial institutions

£m

	1960	1978
Major deposit banks	8600	36 100
Discount houses	1200	4 100
Accepting houses: resident*	130	3 800
non-resident	250	3 000
Other banks: resident*	250	20 100
non-resident	1100	103 500
National Savings Bank	1700	3 000
Trustee Savings Banks	1300	5 300
Finance houses	700	2 600
Building societies	3200	39 700
Investment and unit trusts	2150	11 400
Insurance offices	6350	46 800
Pension funds	3300	29 000

* Excluding UK banks' holdings of non-sterling currency deposits

Source: Mervyn Lewis. *'Rethinking Monetary Policy', Lloyds Bank Review, July 1980, p.42.*

The banks

Since the banks are the most important group of financial institutions we deal with them first and in some detail. In Britain as in other countries there are several types of bank and it is not easy to know where to draw the line between what is and what is not a bank. For example, some of the smaller finance houses call themselves 'industrial bankers' although not generally regarded as forming part of the banking community; on the other hand, the old-established 'merchant banks' of the City of London are usually referred to as 'accepting houses' although no one would dispute that they are banks.

We shall not discuss the various British *savings* banks, such as the National Savings Bank and the Trustee Savings Bank, which invest their funds exclusively or almost exclusively in government securities. We shall also make no reference to *mortgage* banks, which play an important part in some countries in providing capital on mortgage for real estate: in Britain somewhat similar functions are performed in relation to housing finance by the building societies, which we discuss in a different context, and in relation to farming by the Agricultural Mortgage Corporation and the Scottish Agricultural Securities Corporation, which make loans to farmers for periods of up to 60 years at fixed rates of interest. Finally, we shall make no specific reference to *development* banks, the main business of which is to finance new enterprise by providing long-term capital: these banks often play an important role in developing countries where there is only a limited and rather imperfect capital market. In Britain, in contrast to the European continent, the deposit banks take little direct part in the provision of long-term capital to industry or public utilities and prefer to limit themselves to credit for the finance of working capital. Most of the ordinary banking business of the country is transacted by the deposit banks and, as we have seen, their liabilities form the major part of the money supply.

The clearing banks

The banking business of England and Wales is largely in the hands of four banks, Barclays, Lloyds, the Midland and the National Westminster (the 'Big Four'), which, together with two smaller banks, Coutts and Williams & Glyn's, enjoy clearing facilities through the London Clearing House. The six clearing banks had total sterling deposits at the end of 1980 in excess of £40 000 m and in addition owned a number of subsidiaries with substantial funds.

Of the four Scottish clearing banks, with sterling deposits of £4000 m at the end of 1980, the Clydesdale is owned by the Midland Bank and the British Linen by Barclays, while Lloyds has an interest in a third, the Royal Bank of Scotland. Only the fourth, the Bank of Scotland, has no affiliation with any of the large English banks.

Other banks

There are also a number of small banks, of which the Co-operative Bank is the largest, which do not have access to the London Clearing House, a group of merchant banks to which we refer below, and some very large banks, operating mainly abroad or as exchange dealers, but with offices in London. Some of these overseas and foreign banks are British companies like Barclays Bank International (a wholly owned subsidiary of Barclays Bank Ltd), with their head office in London and their branches in other countries. Others are foreign or Commonwealth banks, the most important being American and Japanese. Taking all these together, including the Scottish and Northern Irish banks, their sterling deposits are roughly equal to those of the London clearing banks so that for the banking system as a whole, including the offices of foreign and Commonwealth banks, sterling deposits were over £80 000 m at the end of 1980.

The total deposits of the banks are much larger than this since they include deposits in foreign currencies which are used, in roughly equal amount, to make loans or investments in foreign currencies, mainly to overseas borrowers. About three-quarters of these foreign currency deposits, which exceeded £200 000 m in 1980, are with overseas banks, mainly American and Japanese. They are of great importance to the international business done in London and are further discussed below under the heading 'Euro-dollars' but can be left out of account for the present in a consideration of the British capital market. The sterling deposits of the overseas banks form only about 10% of their foreign currency deposits.

American banks

The banking system of the United Kingdom is in striking contrast to that of the United States. There are some 14 000 American banks, of which 9000, chartered under federal law, are national banks and 5000, authorized under the law of one of the 50 states, are called state banks. Whereas in Britain the two largest banks have over 2000 branches each, in the United States the *total* number of branches does not exceed 4000, most of these being sub-offices in the home town[1]. This difference arises because American legislation is dominated by fear of a banking monopoly – 'money trust' – and either prohibits branch banking (as in many of the states) or submits it to stringent limitations. While the British system puts a small number of very strong banks in a semi-monopolistic position, the American system runs the risk of extensive bank failures. Between 1921 and 1933 no less than 10 000 American banks closed their doors. The events of those years are not likely to repeat themselves, and the system is now far more capable of weathering a financial crisis; but the risk of bank failures is still far greater than in Britain[2].

Bank deposits

About 40% of the deposits of the London clearing banks are on current account: these earn no interest, are withdrawable on demand and can be drawn upon by cheque. The remaining deposits are held on deposit account: these earn interest, can be withdrawn only at seven days' notice and are not directly chequable. In practice, banks are usually prepared to allow money to be transferred from time to time from deposit to current account without notice but subject to loss of interest, so that deposit accounts are not appreciably less liquid than current accounts. The distinction between current and deposit accounts is not unlike the distinction in other countries such as the United States between 'demand' and 'time' deposits; but in those countries there are usually more competition

---

[1] In Chicago, for example, there is no branch banking at all. On the other hand, in California branch banking is allowed anywhere in the state; and in New York there are a number of very large branch banks with offices in various parts of the town. (R. S. Sayers, *American Banking System* (Oxford, 1948), pp. 21–23.)

[2] America is the only country of importance in which there is no developed system of branch banking. In France, for example, there are three large deposit banks (all three publicly owned) with their head offices in Paris and branches all over the country. In Germany, there are three major 'universal' banks carrying out all banking functions and a network of savings banks, some very large, moving increasingly into general banking.

and more variety in the terms on which deposits are accepted and a wide range of periods of notice and rates of interest is offered.

In the United Kingdom the rates paid on deposit accounts and the periods of notice used to be fixed by agreement among the banks, but since 1971 these arrangements have ceased. The banks compete with one another both in rates and in the services they offer. Some of these services are advisory and book-keeping: the banks are willing, for example, to act as trustees to collect dividends, and to execute wills. Their principal services to their customers, however, consist in facilities for making payment by cheque or standing order and for borrowing from time to time on overdraft. These facilities attach to the current rather than the deposit accounts of their customers whose deposit accounts are merely a convenient reserve of liquidity supplementing their slightly more liquid chequable deposits.

Bank advances

The principal use to which the British banks like to put their funds is in advances to customers and these are also the most profitable of bank assets. A small proportion of these advances consists of fixed loans but by far the greater part of them are made on overdraft. Borrowers on overdraft are allowed to withdraw money up to an agreed limit and are charged interest on the outstanding balance. The security for the advance varies with the customer: the most usual collateral consists of stock exchange securities but advances are also made against life insurance policies, commodities, personal guarantees or the unsupported credit of the borrower. The rate of interest charged also varies with the customer: for well-established public companies the rate is normally 1% above the bank's base rate but for private individuals may be 2 or 3% above.

From the point of view of the average borrower a bank overdraft is usually much the most convenient and generally also the cheapest source of credit. His financial position can be more readily explained to his bank manager than to other institutions with which he has less frequent and intimate contacts and he can either make repayments or add to his outstanding debt, within the agreed limits, without any need for renegotiation of the loan. The most important drawback, if he is faced not with a seasonal but with a continuing need for credit, is that bank overdrafts are reviewed annually so that he may be called upon to reduce his overdraft at an awkward moment. Banks do, however, lend for periods much longer than a year – for example, for the purchase of a farm or a house or to finance an extension of plant – and although they are rarely willing to make the loan formally one extending over several years, they may give an informal undertaking not to call for repayment so long as they are satisfied that they hold adequate collateral or can count on the gradual elimination of the overdraft out of current earnings.

Term loans

There has been a growth in what are called 'term' loans – fixed loans for a definite term of years, rarely extending beyond ten. This practice has the virtue of certainty and allows the borrower to make firm plans for the use of the borrowed money; but it may involve him in higher rates of interest, and offer less flexibility in repayment. The borrower may also be confident that a less formal arrangement, renewed from year to year, will not lead to any embarrassment so long as his affairs are in good order, since the banks do not like to abuse their dominant position and have every incentive to keep the goodwill of their customers. For this reason the banks like to maintain their other assets in a sufficiently liquid form to be able to refrain from calling in their loans and to meet any unexpected increase in the use made of overdraft facilities or in the pressure to expand them.

In principle the British banks do not like to lock up their money in long-term investments. They are particularly averse to investments that involve them in exercising control over the management of industrial and commercial undertakings although their directors may themselves also sit on the boards of such undertakings. This attitude derives partly from the relative importance of deposits as a source of their funds and partly from the comparative ease with which industrial expansion could be financed in England in the formative years of banking development. In some of the continental countries where the capital market was less highly developed, the links between banking and industry were closer from the start because the finance which the banks were able to mobilize was indispensable to some of the larger and more capital-intensive projects upon which industrialization depended.

Self-liquidating advances

The general preference of the British banks is for advances which help to tide over a temporary shortage of funds. The shortage may be a seasonal one as in agriculture where the farmer is faced at harvest-time with a heavy outlay in wages which he will recover only when his crop is sold. In the same way merchants may make use of their overdraft facilities as stocks rise to a temporary peak and make repayment as they sell off the surplus and let their stocks run down again to a normal level. An industrialist may deal with a temporary divergence between outgoings and receipts in the same way and so also may a private consumer faced with large demands for payment of income tax. Bank advances can thus be turned over from one use to another, relieving financial pressure in a succession of different parts of the economy. There is a continuous process of repayment and renewal of bank indebtedness as each transaction is brought to a close and succeeded by others.

Not all bank advances, however, conform to this self-liquidating pattern. Many businesses maintain a substantial overdraft throughout the year and would be highly embarrassed if obliged to repay the entire amount within twelve months. There are also various forms of medium-term financing in which the banks now engage: they provide credit to exporters for periods of up to five years against guarantees from the Export Credits Guarantee Department; they have made loans for a term of years for purposes such as tanker construction; they are shareholders in Finance for Industry, which makes long-term investments in industry, and they own or control most of the larger hire purchase finance houses; they make personal loans for the purchase of motor cars and other durable goods by consumers; and they have long made a practice of lending to farmers and house-holders for the purchase of farms and house property. Their preference for short-term, self-liquidating advances is not allowed, therefore, to govern their lending policy to the exclusion of medium and longer-term loans.

This preference originated in the days when a small bank might have to meet a sudden run on its deposits and had to be ready to turn its assets quickly into cash. Even in those days the banks by no means confined their lending to short-term requirements and often participated in investment in railways and similar enterprises. In present circumstances, the chances that a bank's deposits will suddenly melt away can be regarded as negligible and the main justification for preferring short-term to long-term advances is that it is easier for a bank manager to assess the creditworthiness of a customer over a limited period than to gauge his long-term prospects.

Limits to bank advances

There is a limit to the proportion of a bank's assets which it can safely employ in advances to customers. Whether they are self-liquidating or not, bank advances are not a particularly liquid asset. They cannot be sold because there is no market in them; an advance involves a personal assessment of the borrower's credit – of the security which he offers, of his character and ability, and of the prospects of his business – and the bank manager's assessment is not one that other people unacquainted with the borrower could make with the same confidence. There are also difficulties in the way of contracting bank advances either by refusing to renew loans or by calling them in. The denial of overdraft facilities is a very personal transaction, unlike the sale of Treasury bills or gilt-edged securities on the market to the most willing buyer. It may mean the loss of a customer; it may even push a customer into bankruptcy; and it is quite likely, if too sudden and pressing, to force the borrower to realize some of his assets at far below their true value. Thus if a bank finds it necessary to contract credit, it is likely to play for time by selling off investments rather than reduce its advances too rapidly. Similarly, if a bank finds itself accumulating large surplus funds it will generally invest them in government securities, rather than relax too far the standards of security which it requires from borrowers.

Bank credit forms a more important element in the calculations of small borrowers than large. It is true that the accounts of public companies do not show much variation between small and large companies in the ratio of bank credit to total net assets; it is also remarkable that this ratio averages, for all quoted industrial and commercial companies, no more than about 10% – a reminder of the limited role of bank credit in industrial finance. But the indebtedness of a company to its banker, as shown in its balance sheet, does not measure the degree of its dependence on bank credit when it is in difficulties or is trying to expand. Large public companies, and even smaller ones, have a much wider array of alternative sources of finance than small private businesses, which would normally turn first to their banker for additional credit.

Investments

The investments of the banks are more liquid than advances, in the sense that they can be realized at short notice, but less liquid than other bank assets because realization may involve a capital loss. They used to include a large proportion of long-term government securities but these have now virtually disappeared from bank portfolios. Such government securities as are held by the banks are confined to short bonds which are more stable in value but not always easy to sell in large blocks because the banks between them hold such a large proportion of the outstanding issues.

The banks regard their investments as a residual use of funds so long as advances are below the level at which they would consider themselves fully lent. In recent years they have formed a relatively small proportion of total bank assets.

Liquid assets

The clearing banks used to treat cash in hand and balances at the Bank of England as their first line of reserve, and it was this cash reserve rather than total liquid assets or eligible reserve assets that was significant for monetary policy. Today, however, the action which the banks take in order to restore their cash reserves has ceased, for technical reasons, to be of major importance. They need only exchange one liquid asset for another, and so long as their total liquid assets are unaffected, the money supply will be unchanged.

The next item, money at call and short notice, consists mainly of money lent on a day-to-day basis to the discount market, which in turn lends much of it to the government by holding Treasury bills or short-dated government bonds. The special significance of call money in the British monetary system will become apparent when we deal with the discount houses.

Treasury bills

Finally, the banks are large holders of Treasury bills and commercial bills. Treasury bills are government securities with a maturity that is usually of 91 days and occasionally of 63 days. They are issued by tender every week, allotment being made to the highest bidder, and as the price at which they are sold is below their face or redemption value, the difference, or discount, provides a return to the holder and is the effective yield on the bill. The practice of the clearing banks is not to tender on their own account (although they do so for customers) but to acquire bills by purchase from the discount market. It is also the practice of the banks so to arrange their portfolio that some bills mature every week or even every day.

The supply of Treasury bills varies with the fiscal requirements of the government and its success in selling longer-term securities to the public. If more Treasury bills are issued and taken up by the banks and the discount market, the liquid assets of the banks are augmented either directly through their purchases of bills or indirectly through increased loans to the discount market. The credit base is thus enlarged and the money supply is free to grow correspondingly.

Bills of exchange

We have referred above to the commercial bills held by the clearing banks and we shall find that these bills are also of some importance in the operations of the discount market and the accepting houses. The legal definition of a bill of exchange is that it is 'an unconditional order in writing, addressed by one person to another, signed by the person giving it, requiring the person to whom it is addressed to pay on demand or at a fixed or determinable future time a sum certain in money to or to the order of a specified person or to bearer'. The person to whom it is addressed 'accepts' the bill by signing it, usually on the understanding that the drawer will put him in funds by the date the bills falls due and pay him a commission for acceptance. This commission is in recognition of the added marketability that the bill enjoys when it carries the name of an acceptor of undoubted creditworthiness. Most bills are drawn for a period of three months and are a means of obtaining credit for that period, the bill being sold, or 'discounted', after acceptance so as to enable the drawer to obtain payment at once. Other bills ('sight drafts') are payable on presentation and are primarily a means of settlement of international transactions.

Although some bills continue to be used to finance purchases from another part of the country ('inland bills'), most bills arise in connection with imports and exports. An importer of wool, for example, may pay with a bill of exchange drawn on his bank or on one of the London acceptance houses: the exporter will turn the bill over to his bank (together with various other documents) and ask to have it discounted in London after acceptance. The bill is purchased on the strength of the acceptor's standing in the market and the exporter is paid from the proceeds while the importer obtains credit from the holder of the bill. By the time the bill falls due, the importer will have sold his wool and be able to send the acceptance house the funds necessary for paying the bill.

Discount houses

One of the unique features of the British monetary system is the discount market. The assets of the discount houses are invested mainly in bills and short bonds issued by the British government or local authorities. To finance these holdings, the market operates largely on borrowed funds, nearly all supplied by the banks, including overseas and foreign banks. In view of the fluctuations in their cash position it is a convenience to the banks to be able to employ a temporary surplus of cash in this way by lending it on a day-to-day basis to the discount market. The alternative of lending to other banks through the inter-bank market is less attractive not only because they prefer to lend against paper but above all because the paper counts towards the eligible reserve assets which they are required to hold (or were until 1981).

The special importance of the discount market arises because it is through the market that the Bank of England acts in its capacity of 'lender of last resort'. If there is a shortage of funds, it is the discount houses which are able to go to the Bank of England and borrow against eligible paper[1]. The commercial banks are not able to do so but can transfer any squeeze on their own cash position to the discount market by reducing their loans to it. The market thus acts as a buffer between the central bank and the commercial banks. This had its convenience in circumstances when the central bank was content to exercise pressure almost exclusively through the bill market and when it was anxious to keep its distance from the market, as a lender of last resort, rather than operate continuously in it. The arrangement is less satisfactory in present circumstances when monetary policy involves a much closer coordination between the operations of the central bank and those of the commercial banks.

Because of its position as the most sensitive element in the bill market, it is in the discount market that any pressure on funds first makes itself felt. This pressure is reflected in the movement of short-term interest rates and the market occupies a strategic place, therefore, in the determination of those rates. If the Bank of England makes open market sales of securities, the immediate effect is to reduce the cash reserves of the commercial banks, force them to replenish their cash at the expense of the discount market and oblige the market in turn to come to the Bank for assistance. If the discount houses are forced into the Bank on relatively onerous terms, they inevitably stiffen the rates at which they themselves are prepared to tender for Treasury bills. The same effect can be (and is) obtained by simply increasing the size of the weekly tender, since this amounts to putting more bills on the market, so producing a fall in the price and a corresponding rise in the rate of discount. Even if the market merely expects an increase, the expectation will be sufficient to cause a precautionary rise in discount rates. New bills acquired at current prices will not mature for three months and any rise in interest rates over that period would involve a fall in their value; any strong expectation of such a rise, therefore, makes the market reluctant to tender except at a rate which is sufficiently high to discount the danger of a further increase.

Since pre-war days a major change has taken place in the relations between the Bank of England and the discount market. An understanding now exists that the discount houses will always 'cover the tender' for Treasury bills while the Bank of England will ensure that the market has adequate funds for this purpose. This means that the Bank is less of a 'lender of last resort' and that the market is much more frequently 'in the Bank'; it also means that the power of the Bank to control the movement of interest rates is exercised more directly, whether by 'smoothing' purchases and sales of bills or by regulation of the tender issue of Treasury bills.

In comparison with other countries, however, it is one of the features of the British system that the market does not expect to draw its resources to any appreciable extent from the central bank. It is the regular practice elsewhere, but not in Britain, for the commercial banks to obtain funds by

---

[1] Eligible paper consists either of Treasury bills or gilt-edged securities with less than five years to run ('short bonds') or of first-class commercial bills that satisfy certain conditions laid down by the Bank of England. In other money markets, the central bank is usually prepared to re-discount bills but in Britain it prefers to lend against collateral.

rediscounting bills, promissory notes and other 'eligible paper' from the central bank, and it is largely through its control over the supply of such funds that the central bank exerts its influence on the money supply.

Accepting houses

Among the financial institutions which accepts bills of exchange are the accepting houses. These are sometimes referred to as 'merchant bankers' and most of them were originally merchant houses engaged in trade before specializing in financial operations. Their standing as traders made it advantageous to have their name on a bill, so that from accepting their own bills they were induced in course of time to accept bills for others. Their name on a bill, together with one other British name, makes it a Bank bill, eligible for discount at the Bank of England, and ensures that the drawer will be able to discount it on the most favourable possible terms.

In addition to their acceptance business, all of the accepting houses do ordinary banking business on behalf of their customers. This largely arises out of their accepting and other business and is ancillary to it. Their deposits, for example, are drawn largely from foreign banks and companies or from long-established domestic customers. These deposits differ from the deposits of the clearing banks in that they are for fixed periods and are bid for by the accepting houses. In recent years a high proportion of the sterling funds invested has taken the form of short loans to local authorities.

Apart from foreign exchange and other business, the accepting houses act as issuing houses and investment advisers and have come into prominence as company advisers in take-overs and mergers. They are by no means the only issuing houses but include many of the largest.

Issuing houses

The function of an issuing house is to sponsor and guarantee a new issue rather than to find the money out of its own resources. The issuing house first discusses the terms of the issue with its client and satisfies itself that the amount sought is reasonable and likely to be forthcoming on terms acceptable to the borrower. Since its own reputation is involved in the making of the issue, the issuing house has to study both the financial needs of its client and the general economic outlook with a view to choosing the best method of raising fresh capital and the best time at which to go to the market. This expert examination assists the borrower in getting satisfactory terms and at the same time gives the investor confidence that the issue is a well-considered one and made under reputable auspices.

Once the issuing house has agreed to make the issue it makes itself responsible for the underwriting and sets about arranging the sub-underwriting with insurance companies, investment trusts and other institutional investors[1]. It also prepares the prospectus, draws up the advertisements that are required, and carries out all the necessary negotiations with the stock exchange authorities. If it is desired to save the cost of a

---

[1] An underwriter guarantees, for a commission, to take up any part of a new issue for which the public fails to subscribe at the price of the issue.

prospectus issue, the issuing house may 'place' the issue privately with financial institutions.

Not all issues in Britain are made by issuing houses. For example, the large issues by the British government and by the nationalized industries make no use of the services of an issuing house and are handled directly by the Bank of England. The main clients of the issuing houses are public companies and local authorities. But even public companies may dispense with an issuing house and use an issuing broker, who does not have the same close and continuous contacts with his clients.

Insurance companies and pension funds

The importance of the insurance companies and pension funds in the British capital market can be judged from the rate at which their assets are increasing – by £7500 m in 1978 or 7% of personal income after tax. This increase reflects both the saving undertaken by individual policy-holders and the spread of group schemes designed to provide pensions for the employees of business firms and other corporate bodies.

In post-war conditions, government bonds were a relatively unattractive investment because of the steady fall in the price of fixed interest securities, and equities were correspondingly attractive. A large proportion of the current accretion to their funds was therefore invested in equities – about 30% in the early 1970s. Later, with the great expansion in high-yielding gilt-edged stocks, life insurance funds were again directed mainly to gilts: equities in the later 1970s took only 14%, while gilt-edged securities absorbed 62% of the flow of new insurance funds into investment. The pension funds, however, have continued to show a preference for equities which form over half the total market value of their investments.

The life insurance and pensions funds dominate the market in securities, purchasing nearly half the issues of gilt-edged securities and about three-fifths of all the company securities on offer. Their holdings represent about 40% of all UK securities outstanding in either group. Institutional investors are gradually replacing individual private investors as the main source of capital.

The insurance companies and pension funds are also large lenders to local authorities, usually for periods of ten years or longer. Another substantial proportion of their funds is invested in real property and mortgages (especially mortgages on offices, shops, flats and similar blocks of property).

The insurance companies are interested only in the return which they obtain on their investments, rarely in the control or management of the companies whose securities they acquire. The prefer to limit their stake in any one company so as to avoid having to exercise such control as well as to ensure the marketability of their holding.

Investment trusts

An investment trust invests the money entrusted to it by shareholders (or borrowed on debenture) in a diversified range of securities so as to obtain for them a higher or more secure return than they could obtain through individual investment. The portfolio of the investment trust may be varied at the discretion of the management – as in the older type of 'managed' trusts – or it may be restricted to a list of securities set out in the trust deed – as is usual with 'unit' trusts. The subscriber to a unit trust does not buy shares in a limited liability company but is issued with a certificate at a price that reflects the market value of the underlying securities held by the trust, and can sell the certificate back to the managers at a price that is calculated in the same way but leaves a margin for operating expenses. Additional certificates can be sold by the management whenever there is a demand for them, without the need to issue a special prospectus or, indeed, make any anouncement.

The early success of British investment trusts was attributable to the skill of their managements. This was particular evidenced in the investments which they made in other countries, about whose affairs they were more knowledgeable than was the average private investor. Their later popularity owes more to the continuance of inflation. Nearly the whole of their portfolio is in equities and it is the conviction that a diversified holding of ordinary shares is the best hedge against inflation that has created so ready a market for unit trust certificates.

Like insurance companies investment trusts act as underwriters and like them do not usually seek to exercise control over the companies in which they invest. Some investment trusts, however, have links with companies specializing in the finance of promising small businesses which they intend later to float on the stock exchange, and some trusts also make investments in the unquoted securities of smaller companies. The total amount of money provided to industry in these ways is relatively small and not comparable.with the substantial holdings of the investment trusts in freely marketed industrial securities which in 1978 amounted to over £11 000 m.

Building societies

The building societies are keen competitors for small savings, which they apply mainly to the finance of house-ownership. The money deposited with them amounted in 1978 to some £40 000 m. Most of this represented 'shares' rather than deposits; but shares in a building society are in practice almost indistinguishable from deposits in spite of the formal requirement to give one month's notice (or longer) of withdrawal. There is usually a steady inflow of new funds which is supplemented by repayments by borrowers, and these funds are used to make loans on a first mortgage within the United Kingdom. Over two million property-owners have building society mortgages which they are in process of paying off over a period of years; most mortages are for periods of 20 years or more, but because borrowers are able to accelerate the rate of repayment the average period for which mortages are outstanding is well under 20 years. The vast majority of the borrowers are private house-owners and it has been estimated that the societies provide finance for about two-thirds of private house-building. Some of the societies lend to builders as well as to house-owners and a few of them have also engaged in the finance of commercial property development, not always with satisfactory results.

The rates of interest payable to their shareholders and depositors is governed by the competition which the societies have to meet. They generally defer an increase until they find the inflow of funds affected by the offer of more attractive terms by local authorities or by other institutions such as the Trustee Savings Banks or the hire purchase finance companies. If, on the other hand, the inflow is becoming embarrassingly large, they may limit the amount which they are prepared to receive annually from any one person. The lag in their borrowing rates is parallelled by a lag in their lending rates. These are not fixed for the entire period of a mortgage, as are other long-term rates, but can be revised upwards or downwards with market conditions; the societies are not in so vulnerable a position, therefore, as one might expect from the liquidity of their liabilities and the illiquidity of their assets. They are naturally reluctant, however, to make frequent changes in mortgage rates and if faced with a shrinkage of funds are inclined to limit their lending by introducing more stringent conditions rather than make immediate adjustments in the rates at which they borrow and lend.

Consumer credit

Instalment credit or hire purchase finance is mainly of importance in the United Kingdom in the sale of durable consumer's goods. Of the total amount of credit outstanding (about £6000 m at the end of 1978) about half has normally been advanced for the purchase of motor cars and commercial vehicles, and about a quarter for furniture, most of the remainder being for electrical equipment of all kinds, such as radio and television sets, washing machines and so on. Comparatively little hire purchase credit is used in Britain for purchases of business equipment, but there is evidence that it is extensively used by small and growing firms for the purchase of vehicles, plant and machinery.

About half of this credit is provided directly by retailers and dealers and the other half of it comes from a specialized group of institutions – the hire purchase finance houses. There are a very large number of those institutions, most of them relatively small; of the larger ones which are members of the Finance Houses Association, several are linked with, or controlled by, one of the clearing banks. These larger finance houses draw their funds partly from their own capital, partly from the commercial banks, and partly from unsecured deposits by business concerns and others.

The Bank of England

We come finally to the most important of British financial institutions, the Bank of England. It is not possible to give more than the briefest account of its work, but something has already been said in Chapter 25 and in the discussion, which was presented earlier in this chapter, of the banks and the discount market.

The Bank of England is first and foremost a central bank whose prime responsibility is to put into effect the monetary policy of the country. As is true of nearly every other central bank, the Bank is publicly owned and acts as the government's bank. but it was a central bank long before it was nationalized and for many years it has acted in close consultation with government departments, especially the Treasury. For the policy which it pursues, the government takes ultimate responsibility; but it is inevitable that in the formulation of that policy the Bank should play a leading part. In giving effect to the policy, the Bank is brought into contact at many points with the entire financial community and enters also into close association with the financial institutions of other countries and with various international institutions.

In its domestic business, the Bank acts as financial agent to the government, managing the note issue and the national debt and supervising the issue of all government loans. It is the government's banker, keeping both the central account of the government – the Exchequer Account – and a number of other official accounts. It also provides the government with expert financial advice both on the technical problems of day-to-day monetary operations and on the longer-term issues that arise in connection with those operations.

In its external business, the Bank stands equally close to the government. It manages the Exchange Equalization Account, engaging in dealings in foreign exchange so as to hold the rate of exchange within whatever limits have been set by the authorities: it may also conduct both spot and forward transactions at its discretion. The Bank has also extensive dealings with the central banks of other countries and with international financial institutions of which the United Kingdom is a member, such as the International Monetary Fund and the Bank for International Settlements. These dealings embrace both actual operations, such as the purchase and sale of gold, and the exchange of information and discussion of financial and trade policy.

In addition to its relations with governments and government agencies, the Bank exercises great influence over the operations of British financial institutions. It holds the cash reserves, other than till money, of the clearing banks and provides them with the kind of facilities in making payments to one another that an ordinary bank customer enjoys from the use of his bank account. There is also frequent and regular contact on monetary operations and policy between the Bank and representatives of the clearing banks, and the Bank is the normal channel of communication between the Treasury and the clearing banks. It acts as banker to the discount houses, which have to maintain working balances with it and are dependent in their operations on the power which they enjoy to obtain cash from the Bank by borrowing against eligible collateral. It is also in close touch with the acceptance houses in order to satisfy itself as to their liquidity.

The contacts of the Bank with other financial institutions are not simply of the banker–customer type nor confined to an exchange of views or an exposition of government policy. They arise to a much greater extent because of the involvement of the Bank in actual dealings in the bill market and in the gilt-edged market. Through its command of the issue of Treasury bills it is by far the largest operator in the money market and through its command of new issues of government bonds it is by far the largest operator in the gilt-edged market. Its operations are not confined to sales since it can, if it chooses, buy bills, and it regularly engages, for technical reasons in large-scale switching operations in bonds. We have already seen (pp. 345–346) the close connection that exists between monetary policy and debt management; this connection finds expression in the United Kingdom in the combination of functions which makes the Bank of England manage the public debt as well as carry out all the other duties of a central bank.

The Federal Reserve Board

In this the situation in the United Kingdom differs from that in the United States where the functions are divided between the Treasury on the one hand and the Federal Reserve Board on the other. There is also a different relationship between the commercial banks and the central monetary authorities. There is no American bank corresponding to the Bank of England. Instead, there are twelve Federal Reserve Banks, one in each of the twelve Federal Reserve districts and a Board of Governors of the Federal Reserve System sitting in Washington. The Federal Reserve Board acts as a central bank but it does not have the same range of executive responsibilities as the Bank of England and is much more of a policy-shaping body. In some way the counterpart of the Bank of England is the Federal Reserve Bank of New York, which is the main executive agent of the system, while the Federal Reserve Board has more in common with the Finance Division of the British Treasury.

The Federal Reserve Banks act as bankers' banks for their members who include most, but by no means all, of the commercial banks. They hold the cash reserves of the member banks, rediscount bills for them and lend to them, provide them with clearing facilities, and act as a link between their members and the Board of Governors in Washington. They also issue about two-thirds of the total note circulation of the United States. The powers of the Board of Governors were originally supervisory but were greatly strengthened in 1935. They can prescribe the minimum reserve ratio to be preserved between the cash deposits of member banks at the Reserve Banks and customers' deposits at the member banks; they can fix maximum rates of interest on deposits, whether with member banks or non-member banks; and they have final authority over discount and other interest rates charged by the Reserve Banks. A separate body, although all the Governors are members – the Federal Open Market Committee – controls purchases of government securities by the Reserve Banks. The Federal Advisory Council, which is composed of twelve representatives of the member banks, advises the Board of Governors on the views of member-bankers. Lastly, there is the United States Treasury itself, sometimes in sharp conflict with the Federal Reserve System, and armed with ample powers (particularly over gold and foreign exchange) to intervene in its operations if it wishes to do so.

Part VI

International trade and finance

Chapter 27

International trade

The reasons for international trade

International trade occurs because those conducting it see profit in it. A commodity is exported from one country to another because its price is – or would otherwise be – higher in the second country than the first. As a rule, traders buy cheap and sell dear. A region or a country therefore exports the goods it does because these are less scarce, in terms of the goods it imports, than in the country that imports them. There are three principal reasons that can explain why they should be less scarce.

One is that the exporting country, and the firms and workpeople within it, have a relative lead in efficiency in manufacturing them. This explanation gives pride of place to *technological differences* between countries. What is needed for trade is not that the exporting country have an *absolute* advantage over the importing one in converting its resources, such as labour, to the exported good. Rather, it should have a *comparative* advantage. The exporting country should have a higher *ratio* of labour productivity in its exported good to that in its imported good, than the other country with which it trades. In addition to the hypothesis of comparative advantages in technology, there are two other reasons why prices could differ between countries before trade occurs: *differences in endowments of factors of production* and *differences in the pattern of demand*. A country well endowed with labour may export labour-intensive goods, for instance, since wage rates should tend to be low. Also, if there is much higher demand for a commodity overseas than at home, it might well be cheaper at home than abroad; and this would encourage traders to export it. Differences in technology, factor endowments and demand patterns lie at the basis of international trade.

Let us look more closely at the hypothesis of comparative advantages in technology.

The hypothesis of comparative advantages in technology

To illustrate this hypothesis more fully, let us suppose that there are only two countries. Anywhere and Nowhere, that each produce only two commodities, sugar and salt, and that the only factor of production in either country is labour (land being free and of uniform quality). Let us also suppose that Anywhere is better suited to the production of sugar and Nowhere better suited to the production of salt. For example, let:

10 days' labour in Anywhere produce 100 units of sugar
10 days' labour in Anywhere produce 80 units of salt
10 days' labour in Nowhere produce 50 units of sugar
10 days' labour in Nowhere produce 200 units of salt

Before trade begins, sugar in Anywhere will sell at four-fifths of the price of salt, while in Nowhere it will fetch four times the price of salt. There will be obvious advantage to both countries, therefore, if Anywhere exports sugar in exchange for salt at any price within these limits. What price will actually be established will depend upon the strength of the demand for sugar and salt in the two countries. Let us suppose that, the cost of transport being negligible, the price in both countries settles down after the opening of trade at two units of salt per unit of sugar. Then Anywhere by exporting 100 units of sugar will obtain in return 200 units of salt; so that, by 10 days' labour in sugar production, it saves 25 days' labour in the production of salt. Similarly, by exporting 200 units of salt, which it took 10 days to produce, Nowhere obtains 100 units of sugar which it would have taken 20 days to produce; 20 days' labour in the two countries produce as much salt and sugar as formerly required 45 days' labour.

In this example, Anywhere has an absolute and also a comparative advantage in the production of sugar, while Nowhere has an absolute and also a comparative advantage in the production of salt. But suppose that 10 days' labour in Nowhere produce, not 200, but only 50 units of salt. Then Anywhere will have an absolute advantage in the production both of sugar and of salt. It will still be worth its while, however, to trade with Nowhere, for Nowhere retains its comparative advantage in the production of salt; it can produce as many units of salt as of sugar per day's labour, whereas Anywhere can produce only four-fifths as much. At any price between four-fifths and one, both countries will gain from trade. Suppose, for example, that the terms of trade fixed by the joint demand of both countries for sugar and salt are 10 units of sugar for nine units of salt. By expending 10 days' labour in the production of sugar and exporting it in exchange for salt, Anywhere can obtain in return 90 units of salt which would otherwise have taken 11¼ days to produce. Similarly, instead of spending 10 days' labour in producing 50 units of sugar, Nowhere can obtain just as much by trade through nine days' labour in salt production. The only real difference from the first example – apart from the smaller gain from trade – is that the lower productivity of labour in both industries in Nowhere reduces wages there below the level in Anywhere. In our first example, wages must be exactly equal in both countries since 100 units of sugar (produced by 10 days' labour in Anywhere) are assumed to be equal in value to 200 units of salt (produced by 10 days' labour in Nowhere). Given terms of trade more favourable to sugar, however, wages will be higher in Anywhere, and given terms more favourable to salt, they will be higher in Nowhere. In the second example, it is easy to calculate that wages in Anywhere will be nine-fifths times wages in Nowhere. Here again, however, relative wage-rates depend upon the terms of trade between sugar and salt, and may lie anywhere between ten-fifths and eight-fifths.

The two examples may be illustrated diagrammatically. In both cases, labour is the only factor of production, and there are constant returns to scale in both the sugar and salt industries, with no joint production. Under these assumptions, we can be sure that the production possibility frontiers for Anywhere and Nowhere are straight lines. Suppose that both Anywhere and Nowhere have a million days' labour. If all its labour is applied in Anywhere to sugar production, the output of sugar will be 10 million; if to salt, 8 million units; if half goes to sugar and half to salt, 5 million and 4 million units respectively. In the first example, Nowhere's maximum output levels are 5 million for sugar and 20 million for salt; in the second, in which 10 days' labour in Nowhere produce 50 units of salt, they are 5 million for sugar and 5 million for salt.

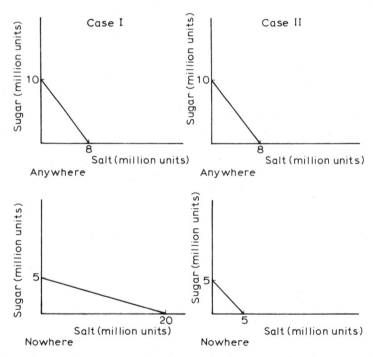

Figure 27.1 Production possibility frontiers showing comparative advantage

All that is needed for mutually profitable trade is that the gradients of the two production possibility frontiers *differ*. This will mean that the price ratios differ before trade takes place. This will provide the incentive to trade, provided, of course, that the difference in gradients is large enough to outweigh any trading and transport costs.

The hypothesis that countries have comparative advantages in technology has much to commend it. International differences in technology are undoubtedly important in explaining much of the pattern of international trade. But they do not provide the only explanation. Differences in

demand patterns could also be a contributory factor, at least when
countries' production possibility frontiers are bowed outward so that
demand can influence pre-trade prices. More important, there are differences in international factor endowments; there is more than one factor of
production; and commodities differ in the proportions in which factors are
employed. This has two implications for countries' production possibility
frontiers. It tends to make them bowed outward, as in *Figure 27.2* because

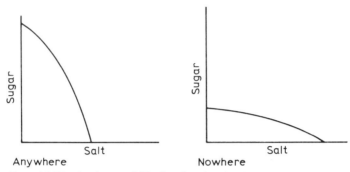

Figure 27.2 Production possibility frontiers showing the effect of
different factor endowments

increasing use of any one factor makes it more expensive; and it makes
their shape depend not only on technological considerations (as in *Figure
27.1*) but also upon factor endowments. In *Figure 27.2*, sugar is likely to be
cheaper, in terms of salt, before trade takes place, in Anywhere than
Nowhere. The reason for this could well be that Anywhere is better
endowed than Nowhere with the factor used intensively in the sugar
industry. It is this rival explanation for trade that we consider next.

International trade and diversity of resources

International trade, like other kinds of trade, originates in the scarcity and
diversity of productive resources. The resources of each country are
limited, and they differ from the resources of other countries. By trading,
therefore, a country enlarges the range of its resources, drawing on the
bounty of other countries instead of contenting itself with home-produced
articles. By refusing to trade and seeking after self-sufficiency it denies
itself access to resources which are relatively scarce – or cannot be found at
all – within its borders; it deliberately restricts its 'Lebensraum' or
'living-room'. That this is so of raw materials is generally agreed; everyone
sees the advantage of importing essential raw materials. But what is true of
natural resources is equally true of labour and of capital. If one country is
well endowed with skilled labour, while in another skilled labour is
relatively scarce and unskilled labour plentiful, then it will be to the mutual
advantage of both countries if the first sells commodities embodying much
skilled labour in return for commodities embodying much unskilled labour.
Similarly, countries in which capital is scarce relatively to labour can trade
profitably with countries in which labour is scarce relatively to capital. It is
differences in *relative* scarcity which gives rise to trade, and these differences are by no means confined to raw materials.

Consider, for example, the international trade of Great Britain. Britain is a thickly populated country with abundant skilled labour and capital and comparatively little fertile land. Britain, therefore, finds it worth while – enormously worth while – to specialize in the production of manufactured articles which make full use of its skill and capital, and to leave the production of roughly half its food to countries like Canada and Australia in which land is abundant and industrial skill and experience relatively scarce. By exporting machinery, high-quality manufactured articles, and the services of its banking houses, insurance companies and mercantile marine, it receives in return foodstuffs which it could not produce at comparable cost on its own soil. Not that agriculture in Britain or industry in, say, Australia is wiped out. Distance affords adequate protection to perishable and bulky products, such as milk and vegetables, and gives partial protection to others, such as fresh meat. In the same way, many of the lighter industries in Australia are sufficiently insulated by distance from foreign competition to thrive naturally, without protection from the state. But it is not only distance which enables British agriculture to survive. There is also an adaptation of farming methods to the comparative scarcity of land. Since land is scarce relatively to labour and capital, it is also relatively dear. There is every incentive, therefore, to economize land and use a high proportion of labour and capital per acre; in other words, to farm intensively. In Canada and Australia, on the other hand, land is relatively abundant and therefore relatively cheap. As a result, farming is extensive, with a low output per acre and a high output per man.

It must not be supposed, however, that Britain's trade is simply a bartering of manufactured goods for foodstuffs. She has always had an extensive trade with other manufacturing countries such as Germany and the United States. For many years she has imported more from the United States than from any other country, and has found in the United States one of her most important markets. In 1913 she imported more from Germany than from any other country except India, and sold to Germany twice as much as she sold to Australia. Part of this trade with other manufacturing countries is in raw materials – cotton imported from the United States, coal exported to Germany. But a large proportion is in finished goods in the manufacture of which one country or another is particularly proficient. No manufacturing country has workers of optimum skill in all industries; some countries excel in the manufacture of chemicals, some in textiles, some in glassware, some in engineering and shipbuilding. Thus within the range of skills at each country's command there are, so to speak, interstices into which trade fits the special skills of other countries. It is not only in the relative scarcity of land, labour and capital that countries differ, but in the relative scarcity of types of land, types of labour and types of capital equipment. These differences, equally with the broader differences, give rise to trade of mutual advantage to both parties.

To summarize the argument so far. Wherever some factor or sub-factor of production is relatively abundant, it is also relatively cheap. Goods into the manufacture of which that factor or sub-factor enters largely will also be relatively cheap, especially as methods of production will be adapted so as to make extensive use of the cheap factor. On the other hand, goods into the manufacture of which other and relatively scarce factors enter largely will be relatively dear. There will be a tendency, therefore, for the first set of goods to be exported and for the second set to be imported. The resulting exchange of goods will be of advantage because the imports relieve the pressure on the supply of relatively scarce factors, while the exports will provide a vent for the relatively abundant factor.

This argument can now be amplified. First, it should be observed that it is based upon differences in the comparative cost of the factors of production in the trading countries. If the absolute cost of each factor is the same in all countries, the incentive to trade disappears. For the object of trade is to take advantage of the *comparative* cheapness of commodities in other countries; and if the factors of production are everywhere paid alike, costs of production will be the same everywhere and no commodity will be cheaper in one country than in another. If, for example, there is only one factor of production, labour, which is equally efficient and equally versatile in every country, then no worker will have any reason for trading with other workers either in his own country or abroad. It is only when workers differ from one another, or (what comes to much the same) when there are several factors of production available in different proportions in different places, that trade is worth while. For then there are differences in the relative costs of the factors of production, and differences in the relative prices of their products. Some goods are relatively cheap in one country and some relatively cheap in others, so that there is an all-round advantage in exchanging one set of goods for the other. The volume of trade increases until – setting aside transport costs – prices are brought into line in all countries.

But the earnings of the factors of production are not brought into line. Trade does not make wages equal in all countries, nor interest rates, nor rents. In India, for example, labour continues to earn low wages (even in relation to its low efficiency) because of its abundance relatively to the capital and natural resources of the country. In Britain, capital continues to earn a comparatively low return because there is much more of it per worker than in most other countries. In the leading manufacturing countries, labour earns comparatively high wages because it is skilled and plentifully supplied with capital in a world in which skill and capital are relatively scarce. If the factors of production moved freely from one country to another, these differences could not persist. Workers would emigrate from countries in which wages were low to countries in which wages were high, and capital would flow out to countries, in which it is relatively scarce, until the return to labour and capital was equal all over the globe. Since international mobility is low, these movements do not in fact take place. Each country continues to have a relative abundance of some factors and a relative scarcity of others, so that the first factors earn less than elsewhere and the second factors more.

Although trade does not equalize the earnings of the factors of production in different countries, it often tends to reduce differences. In the absence of trade, there would be a greater superfluity of labour and a greater scarcity of capital than ever; wages would fall still lower and interest rates rise still higher. Trade has the effect of bringing wages nearer to the level in other countries. The pace is set by the export industries which, having the advantage of cheap unskilled labour, are able to

undersell competitors abroad and, by drawing more and more workers
from domestic industries, lever up wages all round. This process could be
seen at work quite clearly in pre-war Japan where the demand for exports
created a corresponding demand for labour in the export industries and
brought wages nearer to the level in foreign countries. The movement of
goods between countries is, in fact, a substitute for the movement of
factors of production. Instead of making use of Japanese labour by
allowing it to immigrate, people make use of it at long range by buying its
products. Thus they admit it to competition with their own labour only
under the handicap of distance. In the same way, unable to borrow British
capital for their own industries, other countries can make use of it
indirectly by buying British exports in the manufacture of which a great
deal of capital has been used. Wages in Japan are raised – although not as
much as they would be by direct emigration; and the return on British
capital is maintained – although not perhaps so successfully as it would be
by investment abroad.

In practice, differences in technology and in factor endowments should
be seen as complementary explanations for the pattern of international
trade. Differences in technology between countries may be recreated as
fast by new discoveries, and the beneficial effects of experience upon
productivity, as they are undermined by the process of diffusion of
knowledge. Equally, there is clearly more than one factor of production;
industries differ in their factor proportions and countries differ in their
factor endowments.

The gains from trade and the terms of trade

Having considered what causes trade, we turn now to its social effects. In
what sense does a society gain from trade?

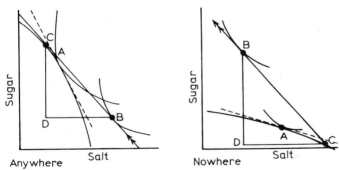

Figure 27.3 Consumption and production before and after trade. The
dotted lines represent the pre-trade price natio and are tangential to the
curves. BC represents the international price ratio after trade.

International trade allows the community as a whole to consume beyond
the bounds of its production possibility frontier. To see this, we need to
introduce demand into our analysis. This can be done, given some rather
strict conditions, by displaying the community's preferences by a set of
indifference curves. Social consumption can then be contrasted, before and
after trade. This is done in *Figure 27.3*. In both panels, point A depicts

production and consumption for each country *before* trade takes place, assuming that perfect competition or good luck ensures that there is no waste or unemployment of resources. The double-tangents to the indifference curve and the production possibility frontier differ in the two countries: the fact that it is steeper in Anywhere than Nowhere shows that sugar is relatively cheap in Anywhere, salt in Nowhere. When trade occurs, the relative prices of sugar to salt will be driven toward equality in the two countries. The new, common, international price ratio of sugar to salt is the *terms of trade* for the two countries. It is shown in *Figure 27.3* by the slope of the line BC in both panels. A country's terms of trade is the ratio of the (average) price it obtains for its exports to the (average) price it pays for its imports. A rise in import prices relative to export prices is a deterioration in the terms of trade, and brings with it a reduction in the community's real income; a relative rise in export prices brings an improving terms of trade. In *Figure 27.3*, the terms of trade lie between the two pre-trade price ratios for sugar to salt: trade makes salt relatively cheaper in Anywhere, and sugar relatively cheaper in Nowhere.

Point C shows the ideal point of production for sugar and salt after trade in each country; point B depicts post-trade consumption for each society. Each country has exports of CD (of sugar in Anywhere's case, salt for Nowhere); and imports of BD (salt for Anywhere, sugar for Nowhere). In each country, international trade allows the community to lift its total consumption outside the limits of the production possibility frontier. Before trade, A was as far as consumption could go.

Nonetheless, we cannot conclude that society as a whole must be better off trading than not trading: unless, that is, we are prepared to say that the losses of those people who may lose as a result count for less than the gains of those who gain. There are three categories of people would could lose. First, the switch in production from A to C will lower the rewards to owners of *fixed* factors employed in the contracting sector (salt in Anywhere, sugar in Nowhere). Workers who have become specialists in Anywhere's salt industry will, for example, have to face a spell of unemployment, or a wage cut. Second, there is the long-run tendency for the reward to owners of the factor of production hired *intensively* in the contracting sector, to decline. Suppose this is land, in Nowhere's case: the sugar industry is land-intensive. As we have seen, trade will in this case tend to lower the rent on land throughout the economy in Nowhere. So Nowhere's landowners will suffer. Finally, there is the possibility that people who own some of both or all factors of production could suffer if they have a really pronounced bias in demand toward the good which the society is starting to export: international trade will make importables cheaper, but exportables relatively dearer. It requires a very strong value judgement to declare that the losses of these three possible types of loser are necessarily overbalanced, in social terms, by the undoubted gains of groups who gain (owners of fixed factors in, or intensively-employed factors in, the expanding sector, and those with two or more sources of income and a taste bias towards the importable good). The sense in which society must be better off in international trade than self-sufficiency is that international trade provides *an opportunity for all groups to gain*, if programmes to compensate any losers are put in train.

Trade restrictions and trade policy

The move from self-sufficiency to free trade brings the possibility of gain to everyone in society; and although there will usually be some who lose, there must certainly be others, quite likely a large majority, who gain from the move. Every country in the world trades with others. But many restrict their trade, by tariffs or quotas on certain categories of imports, by taxes on imports, by imposing regulations which tend to reduce imports, or by other methods. Why are these trade restrictions imposed?

The possible reasons for trade restrictions are well illustrated by the tariff on imports. *Figure 27.4* shows a small country – too small to affect its terms of trade by any policy it conducts – imposing a tariff at rate AB upon imports of a particular good. Because it is small, the world price remains unchanged at w. The domestic price rises from B to A. Home production of the importable good rises, along the domestic supply curve SS; home demand falls, along the domestic demand curve DD. There is a double-edged squeeze on imports. Before the tariff was applied, the value of import payments was e + f + g; after the tariff, this shrinks to f. Areas e and g represent the direct effect upon imports: a fall, which leads to an improvement in the current account of the balance of payments.

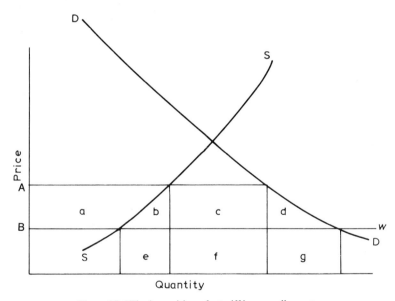

Figure 27.4 The imposition of a tariff by a small country

At home, there is an increase in the volume and value of output of the good. The total increase in value is a + b + e. Of this, b and e are balanced by the reduction in the value of production of other goods at home that will occur under ideal conditions (such as full employment). But area a represents a new surplus, which will be paid to owners of factors hired intensively or exclusively in this particular industry. Area a is called an increase in producers' surplus. Another source of gain is area c. This is the addition to government revenue, since the height of rectangle c is the tariff rate, and its base, the surviving volume of imports; so c is the proceeds from the tariff. Against areas a and c of gain, however, we must consider the loss in the welfare of consumers. The total value that they place on the commodity can be illustrated by the area under the demand curve for it, taken from the origin rightward to the level of actual purchase. The excess of this area over what they actually pay is called consumers' surplus. In *Figure 27.4*, the tariff reduces consumers' surplus by areas a + b + c + d. Subtracting the producers' surplus gain of a and government revenue gain of c from this leaves two little triangles of net loss: b and d.

Figure 27.4 tells us, therefore, that under ideal conditions a small country can only lose as a result of imposing a tariff upon imports – assuming that different groups' gains and losses can be aggregated and netted out in the simple way we have been doing. Even if such aggregation and netting out is not permissible, it will still be true that a move back from restricted trade to free trade will create a theoretical opportunity for *everyone* in the society to be better off, if compensation to losers is paid. It is this point that provides the cornerstone of the argument for free trade. But *Figure 27.4* also points to a number of reasons why a government might choose to impose a tariff notwithstanding. One reason could be to improve the balance of payments on current account. Another might be to raise production and employment, when the economy suffers from unemployment: in this case the curve SS will exaggerate the true social marginal cost of production, and there is a strong case for raising output of this commodity (and, presumably, others). A third might be the need to generate government revenue, for the provision (for instance) of public goods. All sources of taxation have disadvantages: they create distortions and inefficiencies, they blunt incentives, they interfere with transactions people willingly enter into, and they could even increase inequality. For developing countries in particular, the damage done by a system of modest tariffs on imports may be relatively slight. Then there is the possibility that the government actively seeks the income redistributive effect of area a, the increased producers' surplus. France and Germany have traditionally applied tariffs on imported wheat and dairy products – policies continued under the Common Agricultural Policy of the EEC – partly because of the political strength of the agricultural interest representing farmers, landowners and agricultural workers. A further argument for the tariff may be the fact that it allows an increase in the output of a domestic industry which would be (at least temporarily) commercially unprofitable, but socially advantageous, at free trade prices. This is an aspect of the 'infant industry' argument for a tariff: without the protection it gives, an industry which should be set up would not be set up or would be kept too small.

There are two further arguments for tariffs which go beyond what can be illustrated in *Figure 27.4*. First, it may be wise to have a tariff purely for bargaining purposes, so that other countries could be induced to remove theirs in a multilateral agreement on free trade. Secondly, a large country can gain from a tariff in reducing the international price of a good it imports, if it has monopsony power. If the United States, for instance, placed a tariff on imports of oil, the world price of oil would drop; and this would bring a terms of trade improvement to the United States (at the expense of oil exporters). Similarly, a country, or group of countries, may have monopoly power in the international markets for their exports. If so, they will gain from an export tax, which raises the international price of their exports. The recent actions of the Organization of Petroleum Exporting Countries provide a graphic illustration of this.

Finally we have to take account of dynamic influences on the international division of labour. If specialization is on the basis of existing skills and market opportunities it will be governed by today's comparative costs, not tomorrow's. But in an economy in process of development, it may be desirable to anticipate later changes and to build up industries for which the long-term prospects are good even although, in the short run, they are unable to cover their costs. Where we are dealing with marginal changes within an existing framework the price mechanism is a fairly reliable means of bringing them about; when an economy is undergoing the great structural upheavals associated with industrialization, it is not nearly so satisfactory. It allows individual producers and consumers to make their choices without looking too far ahead or taking into account the total effect of what they do. If, however, the principal object of economic policy is to transform the economy and to make it grow faster, the long view may differ widely from the short and the outcome of individual decisions may run counter to collective needs.

The force of this argument was recognized long ago when the champions of free trade themselves advanced the infant industry argument for a tariff: the argument that an industry might have to be nurtured for a time by protection before it was sufficiently established to stand on its own feet. Nowadays the scope of the argument has widened and it is applied to the economy as a whole: not in the sense that anyone suggests protection for every economic activity – since that would be self-defeating, protection for any one activity reducing the advantages enjoyed by all the others – but rather in the sense that economic development is no longer regarded as best accomplished by competitive forces and without active encouragement by the state. Where economists differ is on the form that such encouragement might usefully take and on the extent to which it need involve restrictions on trade with other countries.

The tariff is rarely the best instrument for securing the advantages alleged to follow. As we shall see in the next chapter, there are other instruments available for improving the balance of payments, some of which (such as devaluation) are widely thought to be more powerful than import restriction. Although a tariff would tend to reduce unemployment, by raising the demand for labour in the domestic industry directly affected, a general subsidy on production or employment would produce greater net benefits. The infant industry argument also constitutes a case for subsidy rather than a tariff. Any income redistributive benefits can often be secured at less cost by other means, as well: a production subsidy to agriculture for instance, will avoid some of the sacrifice of consumers' surplus that a tariff would otherwise entail.

Chapter 28

The balance of payments

Payments between countries generally differ from domestic payments in that they involve the exchange of one kind of money for another. Each country has its own money, which is not freely accepted abroad, but must be changed into foreign money at a rate which may be either fixed or variable. The rate of exchange, whether fixed or variable, is a price; and, like any other price, must be such as to balance supply and demand. At any given rate, sales of foreign exchange must be equal to purchases; the payments made by foreign countries must be equal to the payments made to them. If the balance of payments is tipped against a country, there will be increased pressure to buy foreign exchange, and, if the rate of exchange is free to vary, the price of foreign moneys will rise – that is, the currency of the country will depreciate. If the balance of payments is favourable to the country, there will be increased pressure to sell foreign exchange, and this pressure will tend to raise the value of the country's currency; or, in other words, cause it to appreciate.

This idea of a balance of payments which may be either favourable or unfavourable is fundamental to the whole theory of foreign exchange and requires careful explanation. Strictly speaking, since payments on both sides of the account must balance in the sense that sales and purchases are necessarily equal, they can never be out of balance in the sense that there is a deficit on all items taken together. A deficit, or unfavourable balance, must relate to a partial balance leaving out some item or items; for example, any sales of gold from the reserve of the central bank which may preserve equilibrium in the foreign exchange market for the time being but cannot continue indefinitely.

The expression 'balance of payments' is in fact used in several different ways, depending upon what is left out as a residual or balancing item: and the more one examines different usages the more apparent it becomes that what matters is *how* a balance is preserved rather than the size of the deficit or surplus on any particular definition.

There are three balances in common use that merit explanation.

(a) The balance of trade

In speaking of an unfavourable balance of payments we may have in mind an excess of imports of merchandise over exports. Since details of these imports and exports are published monthly, and since merchandise forms a large proportion of total trade, this 'balance of trade' figures very prominently in most popular discussions. But that it is of limited importance is clear from the fact that Britain had an unfavourable balance of merchandise trade almost continuously for over a hundred years without any unfortunate consequences.

(b) The balance of payments on current (or income) account

In addition to merchandise exports and imports there are various 'invisible' exports and imports whose value is not officially recorded although estimates are made. For example, large sums are earned every year by the British mercantile marine in carrying goods and passengers from one foreign country to another, or between British and foreign ports. The Board of Trade records the value of British exports 'fob' (free on board – that is, at the port of embarkation), and the value of British imports 'cif' (cost, insurance, freight – that is, at the port of landing). Thus its returns exaggerate the adverse balance by leaving shipping earnings out of account. Since foreigners require to make additional payments to cover sea transport charges on exports carried in British vessels, and since Britain is spared from making payments to foreigners to cover sea transport charges on imports carried on British vessels, the earnings of British ships in carrying goods to and from Britain go to reduce any visible adverse balance of trade. Further deductions must be made in respect of the fares of foreign passengers in British ships, transport of goods between foreign ports, and disbursements of foreign ships and sailors in British ports. On the other hand, disbursements by British ships in foreign ports (for example, for fuel or in payment of port dues) add to any unfavourable balance.

A second 'invisible' item is interest and profit on foreign investments. Interest and profits represent a kind of 'invisible' export; they can be regarded as payments for the hire of British capital just as freight payments are payments for the hire of British ships. Similarly, interest payments on capital invested in Britain are 'invisible' imports. Before the war about a quarter of Britain's net imports came in payment for past investments of capital in foreign countries. The disposal of foreign investments during the war and the debts then incurred greatly reduced the size of net earnings under this heading, the average in the years 1956–1958 being only £235 m compared with imports in the same years of nearly £3500 m. The loss of investment income was a main cause of Britain's post-war balance of payments difficulties.

To these two items may be added a large number of others. There are, for example, disbursements by tourists abroad, remittances to friends and relatives in other countries, grants to other governments, and so on. Yet against these payments must be set similar payments by foreign countries, including the commissions earned on marine underwriting, insurance and acceptance business, etc.

Once all these items have been included we reach a quite different balance, representing the difference between the value of goods and services currently produced in Britain and sold abroad, and the value of foreign goods and services bought from abroad. This balance is usually called 'the balance of payments on current account' (see *Figure 28.1*). It was consistently favourable to Britain all through the second half of the nineteenth century and did not become unfavourable (apart from the war years 1914–1918) until 1931. Thereafter the balance on current account was not markedly favourable or unfavourable, but oscillated between small positive and small negative quantities until the outbreak of war in 1939.

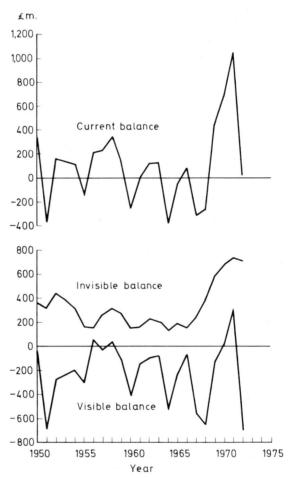

Figure 28.1 United Kingdom balance of payments on current account, 1950–1972.
Source: *United Kingdom Balance of Payments 1972*

During the war it was increasingly in deficit, and the deficit continued into the post-war years. By the middle of 1948 equilibrium had been restored and in 1950 there was, for the first time for many years, a substantial surplus. Apart from a large deficit in 1951 and a smaller one in 1955, a surplus continued to be earned throughout the 1950s. In 1960, however, the current account was again in deficit and after an improvement over the next three years it was in heavy deficit in 1964–1968. Once the devaluation of 1967 had had time to take effect, a surplus reappeared in 1969 and the immediately following years only to disappear again in 1972. After a record deficit in 1974, the current account gradually improved, thanks partly to the replacement of imported oil by North Sea oil, but remained weak.

(c) The balance on current and long-term capital account

The balance of payments on income account is of limited significance. It provides a measure of the addition that a country is making to its net overseas assets (including its reserves of gold and foreign exchange): for if it is selling more goods and services to foreign countries than it buys from them it can lend or invest the difference. Indeed, the only way in which the account can be equated is by a capital transaction that offsets the current account surplus; or rather, the net outcome of all the capital transactions must exactly offset the net outcome of all the current transactions. Now it may be a matter for disquiet if the balance on current account is in deficit and the country is having to borrow abroad; but there is nothing necessarily undesirable or 'unfavourable' in such a state of affairs. Some countries such as Canada – to say nothing of many of the less developed countries – have run a deficit on current account year after year almost as a matter of course, borrowing abroad to finance development at home.

Suppose, for example, that a country is engaged in building up a merchant navy and that its own savings are inadequate to finance the work. By borrowing from other countries it can make purchases of ships abroad and pay for these purchases not by equal exports, but out of the borrowed funds. In the same way, if Britain has an unfavourable balance on income account, this may simply reflect unusually active investment at home; she may be drawing on her accumulated foreign investments in order to finance a building boom or the construction of nuclear power stations. A country can choose between investing its savings at home or abroad. The more it inclines to home investment the less favourable will be its balance of payments as measured by the difference between exports and imports; for it will have less resources to spare for the manufacture of exports and it will be more anxious to draw on the resources of other countries by importing from them.

Although there is nothing necessarily unfavourable about a negative (or 'passive') balance of payments which is covered by *long-term* borrowing abroad, a negative balance which is met either by short-term, 'makeshift', borrowing, or by exports of gold, is quite another matter. Long-term borrowing designed to finance the construction of capital assets can go on with impunity for very long periods. But short-term foreign loans are generally obtained only if there are good prospects that the loans can be quickly repaid. A country can borrow on short-term to tide over a temporary deficit in its balance of payments; but it cannot continue to add to its short-term borrowings without simultaneously taking measures to correct the unfavourable balance. Similarly, it can finance a deficit in its balance of payments by the sale of gold or dollars; but, since its stock of gold and dollars is limited, the loss cannot go on indefinitely. Short-term borrowing and sales of foreign exchange, therefore, are palliatives which, so long as they continue, keep the rate of exchange from depreciating, just as the sale of goods from stock keeps their price from rising when demand increases. Both expedients are danger signals as well as palliatives. They usually indicate that, unless action is taken to correct the unfavourable balance and so reverse the inward flow of credits or the outward flow of foreign exchange, depreciation is inevitable.

Considerations of this kind direct our attention to a different balance, sometimes referred to as the 'basic' balance, which adds together the balance on current account and the net balance on long-term capital account. The latter includes direct investment inwards and outwards by business undertakings as well as portfolio movements involving the sale or purchase of bonds and stock exchange securities. This balance on current and long-term capital account is necessarily equal in magnitude to the balance of all other transactions, since total sales and total purchases of foreign exchange must be equal to one another.

Even this, however, may not be the significant balance if what we are trying to isolate is some measure of external disequilibrium: the amount of accommodating finance that bridges what would otherwise be a deficit in the balance of payments. Movements of short-term funds *may* represent flows of 'hot' money of a purely temporary kind, liable to sudden reversals. But they may also reflect longer-term influences that make it convenient to accumulate funds or obtain finance in some particular centre such as London or New York. It would be going too far, therefore, to regard a net inflow of short-term funds as a temporary substitute for a run-down in the reserves: the net inflow may be as stable an element in the balance of payments as any other and just as capable of exerting an independent influence on the level at which balance is achieved. There is in fact no single, precise way of measuring the size of an external deficit in the sense used above of an almost passive response to the difference between the other 'active' items.

For this reason there is no universally agreed convention observed by all countries. Many countries measure their surplus or deficit in terms of the balance on current and long-term capital account. The United States used to follow a practice that made its deficit larger than on this definition by the amount of any net outflow of United States private short-term capital. On this so-called 'liquidity' basis of measurement, the net inflow of short-term capital from abroad was not offset against this outflow on the grounds that such an inflow gives rise to liquid liabilities to foreigners and is better regarded as a way of financing a deficit rather than as a straightforward capital receipt. This treatment is open to the objection that it is asymmetrical and that if every country adopted it they might all find themselves in deficit simultaneously. The Bernstein Committee, reporting on this in 1965, suggested the inclusion of all short-term capital flows, inwards and outwards, in the American balance of payments, subject to one exception: inflows from abroad representing an increase in liabilities to foreign central banks and other monetary authorities and hence in the reserve assets (in the form of dollar holdings) of those authorities[1].

---

[1] The Balance of Payments Statistics of the United States, Report to the Bureau of the Budget, April 1965.

The current American practice is to use two definitions, one called the *'net liquidity balance'* and the other the *'official reserve transactions balance'*. The first of these is made up of the basic balance of payments (on current and long-term capital accounts), plus flows of short-term non-liquid private capital inwards and outwards, plus allocations to the United States authorities of SDRs[1], plus errors and omissions. This is taken to be 'a broad indicator of potential pressures on the dollar resulting from changes in (the United States) liquidity position'[2]. The second concept differs from this in including changes in private liquid claims and liabilities. With this addition the balance obtained is necessarily equal to the *'official reserve transactions balance'* or *'balance on official settlements'*, i.e., the sum of all drawings on, or additions to, official reserve assets and all net transactions with foreign monetary authorities. Much the same concept is used in the official presentation of the British balance of payments. But what other countries call the *balance on official settlements* is given in the British accounts the vague and rather misleading title: *'total currency flow'*.

Reserves

When there is a deficit in the balance of payments two problems arise. The first is to settle the deficit and the second is to get rid of it. The second problem is discussed in Chapter 29. The settlement of the deficit, except in so far as short-term borrowing takes place, must be in some internationally acceptable means of payment. The most obvious example of such a medium is gold; but there are various currencies, notably the pound and the dollar, that are used internationally and it is likely that in course of time other international assets such as balances held with the International Monetary Fund or Special Drawing Rights on the Fund will be of increasing importance. Whatever the means of settlement between countries, they are usually held by the central bank and constitute its reserves of foreign exchange. The purpose of these reserves is to provide ammunition against an unfavourable balance of payments and allow time for corrective action to take effect. Since reserves represent an investment of capital that could be used for other purposes there is a limit to the amount that countries are prepared to accumulate, particularly if, like gold, it brings no revenue.

In Britain some of the reserves are held in gold and there is also a working balance of dollars. The normal method of settlement is in dollars and when the Bank of England intervenes in the market the currency which it buys or offers for sale is the dollar. The reserves are held in an Exchange Equalization Account set up after Britain left the gold standard in 1931. This is managed by the Bank of England on behalf of the Treasury, and is financed by the issue of Treasury bills. During periods when the balance of payments is in favour of Britain, the Account adds to its stock of gold and foreign exchange, issuing more Treasury bills in order to raise the sterling necessary for its purchases; when the balance of

---

[1] Special drawing rights issued by the IMF, sometimes referred to derisorily as 'paper gold'.

[2] David T. Devlin, 'The US Balance of Payments: Revised Presentation', *Survey of Current Business*, June 1971, p. 24.

payments is unfavourable, it sells gold and foreign exchange for sterling and pays off a corresponding portion of its sterling debt. ⟋

The object of the Account in the 1930s was not to maintain a fixed rate of exchange; it could use its discretion in allowing the rate to depreciate or appreciate. Its aim was to reduce fluctuations in the rate by supplementing the supply of foreign exchange when there was a danger of depreciation and by making purchases of foreign exchange when the pound was appreciating. When there was a persistent movement against sterling the Account was powerless to control it since its holdings of foreign exchange were limited. It had to content itself with preventing fluctuations due to speculation, and to keep them from affecting trade and credit without trying to prevent fluctuations attributable to more fundamental 'real' causes. It had a further aim of attempting to insulate the British money supply from the effects of payments surpluses and deficits.

The system in use was thus intermediate between one of fixed exchanges and one of freely fluctuating rates. The range of variations in exchange rates was steadily narrowed in each successive year from 1933 onwards. From the outbreak of war until the devaluation of 1949 the pound–dollar exchange rate was held constant at $4.02 = £1; the rate then remained fixed at $2.80 = £1 until the second post-war devaluation in 1967 to $2.40 = £1. In this respect, therefore, the post-war system represented a return to pre-1931 conditions, although in many other respects it differed widely from it. Apart from a six-month period after December 1971, sterling has been floating since August 1971. But even under this floating exchange rate regime, there has been frequent intervention by the Bank of England to affect the exchange rate.

International liquidity

If international reserves consisted exclusively of gold this would obviously create a danger of excess or shortage in relation to the scale of international trade and payments. The stock of gold increases slowly in comparison with the growth of the world economy and this could give rise to a powerful deflationary drag on monetary policy if it created widespread anxieties in the leading countries about the adequacy of their reserves. Just as no one would wish to tie the growth of the domestic money supply to the amount of gold mined every year, so it would be unfortunate if the growth of international means of payment were to be governed by the same irrelevant factor.

Just as gold and other precious metals have to be supplemented by paper money for use in transactions *within* countries, so paper currencies came to play an increasing role in transactions *between* them. But the international use of paper money came later, and more gradually. In the late nineteenth century sterling accounted for a growing proportion of international reserves. In the twentieth century this role was increasingly played by the US dollar, especially after 1945.

The fact that reserves have in fact grown rapidly since the war is due to special circumstances. In the early post-war years when the United States was in overwhelming surplus it did not drain every other country of its gold reserves but tried to reduce the imbalance between North America and the rest of the world through the Marshall Plan. Then in the early 1950s the American balance of payments moved into deficit and it continued in deficit for the next 20 years of so. This meant:

1. That the major deficit calling for the use of reserves fell on a country amply supplied with them.
2. That so far as the deficit was met in gold, the rest of the world was able to increase its monetary holdings of gold at a more rapid rate than would have been possible from newly mined gold alone.
3. That so far as the deficit was not settled in gold, the rest of the world was able to acquire an acceptable means of international payment in the form of dollars.

These favourable circumstances could not, however, continue indefinitely. On the one hand the United States gold reserves fell heavily. This aroused expectations that the United States might run out of gold, or that the dollar might cease to be convertible into gold, or that the dollar price of gold would be raised: all expectations calculated to make gold seem a more attractive asset and the dollar a less attractive asset. On the other hand the central banks of the world found themselves in possession of an increasing stock of dollars; and their willingness to go on accumulating the currency of a country in chronic deficit was clearly not unlimited. By the autumn of 1971 the dollar holdings of central banks outside the United States were far above their holdings of gold and four or five times as large as the gold reserve of the United States. Long before this, the United States had progressively limited the access of foreign central banks to its gold stock, more by informal pressure than by formal arrangements, and although the official dollar price of gold remained at $35 an ounce, this was not so much the selling price as the price at which the United States did *not* sell gold. Gold exports were not formally suspended until 15 August 1971.

Table 28.1 shows how international reserves grew over the twenty years preceding this suspension. In 1951 gold was still by far the largest component, with sterling next in importance. Holdings of sterling did not change very much over the 20 years, and when expressed in terms of dollars showed a fall. The supply of gold increased only gradually and an increasing proportion of the annual increment was absorbed by industrial uses. From the late 1960s onwards the stock of monetary gold (i.e., gold in the hands of the monetary authorities) was actually falling.

All this brings out the reliance of the rest of the world on the use of the dollar as a reserve currency. It was the large expansion in dollar reserves that enabled central banks to increase their total reserves more or less in line with the growth in world trade and payments. Except at the end of the period, moreover, the form taken by the increase in reserves accorded with the preferences of central banks which needed large working balances of dollars as an 'intervention currency' (for regulating their market in foreign exchange) and found the interest which they earned on their dollar holdings a powerful counter-attraction to the lure of gold. To the extent that they were firmly held, and not liable to be switched without notice into some other reserve asset, it could be claimed that dollars acquired by

TABLE 28.1. World monetary reserves, 1937–1980

$1000 m

	1937	1951	1961 End of year	1971	1980
Gold in hands of monetary authorities[a]:					
United States	12.8	22.9	16.9	13.2	188.5
Other countries	12.5	10.7	22.0	26.0	480.1
Total	25.3	33.6	38.9	39.2	668.6
Dollars (US liabilities)	2.3	4.2	11.8	50.6	365.8
Sterling (UK liabilities)	(2.5)	8.2	6.4	7.8	11.0
Reserve positions in IMF	—	1.7	4.2	6.9	11.3
SDRs	—	—	—	6.4	22.2
Residual[b]	—	1.3	1.0	18.9	—
World Total	30.1	49.0	62.3	129.8	1078.9
ECUs (European Currency Units)	—	—	—	—	41.9[c]

[a] Valued at $35 an ounce except at the end of 1971 when the dollar value was $38 and the end of 1980 when it was $589.5.
[b] Including holdings of currencies other than United States dollars and sterling; also the effects of any discrepancies between figures of assets and liabilities.
[c] End 1979

Source: IMF International Financial Statistics.

central banks were not really part of the United States deficit at all, but were catering for the international need for acceptable liquid assets. 'One man's money', as it has been aptly put, 'is another man's debt; one country's money is another's debt[1]'.

But this is just the trouble. Nobody can be very happy to see the richest country in the world creating international money at no cost to itself. Nor does experience with reserve currencies make it a safe assumption that their holders will refrain from switching out of them in a crisis. What possible ways are there of working out a satisfactory system of international reserve-creation?

A dollar standard

One possibility would be to go over to a dollar system in spite of these objections. A dollar system in this sense would be one in which international accounts were settled in dollars without the option of demanding gold: gold would be demonetized although it might continue to play a subsidiary part, like sterling or other national currencies, in settlements between countries still willing to accept it. A system of this kind could not be imposed. The final test of what is and what is not money is acceptability, not government declarations, and this is as true of the international money used by central banks as of the national money used by the ordinary man. As the currency of by far the most powerful national economy, dollars seem likely to remain highly acceptable, especially when prices in the

[1] F. Hirsch, *Money International* (Pelican edition, 1969), p. 119.

United States are at least as stable as anywhere else and interest can be earned on highly liquid money market paper. But the urge to hold all or part of a country's reserves in gold is not easily suppressed and will be sustained by the continuing private demand, including industrial demand, all over the world. There would also be strong opposition to leaving to the United States the undisputed power to create international money to its own national advantage, and fundamental doubts as to the wisdom of abandoning gold as an objective source of discipline in international finance.

A resumption of the gold standard

At the other extreme it might be possible to go back to gold as the principal reserve asset, leaving to the dollar its post-war role as an 'intervention currency' held by central banks as a means of regulating fluctuations in the exchange rate of their currency against the dollar. Such a state of affairs might require a large increase in the price of gold to enable it to take the place of the dollars which the United States undertook to retire from circulation. Both of these changes – the increase in the price of gold and the liquidation of dollar liabilities – would create a considerable upheaval and would affect different countries very unequally. They would also meet with opposition from those who feel that gold has had its day and that, in international as in domestic affairs, it is no longer indispensable to monetary management. The strongest case against the resumption of the gold standard is perhaps the needless waste of resources to which it would give rise. Keeping gold stocks in official reserves prevents them from being applied to other uses – industrial, ornamental and dental. This is not true of paper money. The one advantage of a true gold standard, however, is the natural brake it provides against inflation.

An IMF unit

A start has already been made with a new system of international payments through the International Monetary Fund. All members of the Fund enjoy certain borrowing rights which allow them to draw foreign currencies from the Fund against deposits of their own money. While it is not quite so convenient to have larger overdraft facilities as to have more cash in the bank, both serve much the same purpose in helping to tide over pressure on liquidity. Borrowing rights are sometimes described as 'conditional reserves' (because there are usually pre-conditions to any loans) as distinct from 'owned reserves'; but in practice the distinction can become rather a fine one. If, for example, the IMF allows a country to borrow up to 25% of its quota without question and does not set limits to the period over which it must be repaid, it is hard to distinguish such borrowing rights from ordinary reserve assets. The more freely countries could make use of their borrowing rights the more liquid they would be. But freer access by borrowers would only be possible if there were simultaneously a greater willingness on the part of creditor countries to allow themselves to be

[1] For an account of the International Monetary Fund, see below, pp. 403–405.

drawn upon by the IMF. If, for example, they were prepared to regard a claim on the IMF as part of their reserves and could use such a claim in due course to settle a deficit with other member countries, this would be a great step forwards towards a more satisfactory system of international payments.

In 1968, after a long debate, agreement was reached on a scheme for the creation of Special Drawing Rights, or SDRs to supplement existing reserves and perhaps eventually grow into a substitute for them. Each member of the IMF had its account credited with a share of the total issue of SDRs in proportion to its quota in the Fund. SDRs were given a value equal to one United States dollar's worth of gold and carried interest at $1\frac{1}{2}\%$. They could be used to buy the currencies of IMF member countries so as to settle a deficit in international payments, and each member of the IMF agreed to accept SDRs up to an amount equal to three times its own cumulative allocation.

The first issues of SDRs were inevitably on a limited scale, since they were intended to allow international reserves to grow in step with the need for international liquidity. It happened that there was no need for anxiety on this score since the issues were made during a period of very heavy deficit in the American balance of payments and a correspondingly large absorption of dollars into the reserves of some of the major trading countries. But once started, the scheme is obviously destined to continue. Derided as 'paper gold', SDRs hold out the prospect of fulfilling the original functions of gold without the need for gold-mining, and without making world liquidity dependent on the vagaries of the supply of gold.

It would be a mistake to think that the appearance of yet another reserve asset, however splendid its eventual role, will eliminate crises from the international financial system. It will exist for many a day side by side with gold, dollars, sterling and a host of *ad hoc* methods of settlement, from currency swaps to barter deals. The plurality of reserve assets may free the world from any danger of a shortage of international liquidity; but it is likely to create awkward problems of confidence in one or other of these assets unless the rules governing conversion of one into another are carefully worked out.

We should also not overlook the connection between the need for international reserves and the ease with which countries are able to get back into balance. If the process of adjustment to an external deficit is hard and prolonged, countries will have more need of reserves than when they are confident that they will be able to get rid of a deficit quickly. Chapter 29 discusses how adjustment takes place and what can be done to bring it about.

The mechanism of international adjustment

Pressures on the balance of payments

The balance of payments may become unfavourable because of pressures on it from inside or outside the country. It can act as a safety valve to domestic inflationary pressure as more imports are sucked in until the resulting loss of foreign exchange obliges the monetary authorities to take corrective action. We have also seen that inflation in the outside world may put strains and stresses on trade and payments and tug at the prices of goods entering into international trade[1]. It drives up the price of imported goods, including foodstuffs and raw materials and spreads to domestic costs of production as money wages chase the cost of living upwards, so that both material and wage costs are inflated. Just as inflation spreads from one part of a country to another, so it can very easily spread from one country to another.

Deflation abroad is equally contagious. If purchasing power collapses in overseas markets, the export trades begin to suffer from unemployment; at the same time imports may be swollen by distress sales of goods that have fallen disastrously in price and cannot find a market elsewhere; the balance of trade will become unfavourable and the central bank will find its reserves oozing away to cover the deficit. Few countries are strong enough to preserve internal financial stability if world markets are slumping.

A country may decide to concentrate either on internal balance or external balance. Short of complete autarky – the abandonment of all trade – it cannot afford to neglect either; but it may give preference to the one over the other. If it tries at all costs to maintain a fixed rate of exchange and free convertibility of its currency into other currencies – the two main features of the gold standard – it has come down heavily on the side of external balance: it is prepared to let its prices follow world prices, come what may. If, on the other hand, it allows exchange rates to fluctuate freely and tries to keep domestic prices steady, it is plumping for internal rather than external balance: it is hoping to be able to insulate itself from movements in world prices by letting the rate of exchange take the shock.

---

[1] Above, pp. 321–322.

It may go further and bring all transactions in foreign currencies under exchange control, seeking to manipulate payments and receipts by requisitioning (in return for its sterling equivalent) the foreign exchange earned by exporters and rationing the foreign exchange required by importers; this will hedge foreign trade and payments around with difficulties and complications but will give the monetary authorities more latitude in dealing with domestic financial problems.

It might seem from this that the choice lay between a high volume of trade and a smaller one: and that some countries deliberately restricted their trade for the sake of greater domestic stability. There are no doubt countries that are faced with such a choice. It is also true that, whatever is decided, the decision will be influenced by the risk of a contraction in trade. But the real choice relates, not to the volume of trade, but to the *method* by which an adverse balance of payments is eliminated – by forcing prices and incomes into line with prices and income elsewhere, by allowing exchange rates to fluctuate or by direct action on payments and receipts.

The mechanism of adjustment in the balance of payments

Pressure on the exchanges may arise for one of three reasons:

1. It may be due to a large volume of purchases of imports or sales of exports.
2. There may be a change in the terms on which imports and exports are exchanged (i.e., in the terms of trade) and therefore in the average price of imports in relation to the average price of exports.
3. Even when current transactions are stable in value, there may be a transfer of capital across the exchanges because of heavier borrowing from, or lending to, foreigners.

If the current and capital accounts of the balance of payments combined were in balance before the change, they will now (taken together) be out of balance. There will either be a surplus or a deficit. A surplus will imply a world-wide excess demand for the home country's currency, and a tendency for its reserves to rise or its exchange rate to float upwards; a deficit will imply an excess supply of the currency in the world as a whole, in response to which either the reserves or the exchange rate will fall. If the exchange rate is freely floating, it will be the exchange rate itself that absorbs the pressure of surpluses or deficits. Under a fixed exchange rate, the level of reserves will react. We are now confronted by a crucial question: can surpluses or deficits be relied upon to be self-eliminating?

The answer to this is a heavily qualified 'yes'. There are several mechanisms at work which will, or may, tend to remove the surpluses or deficits. But some work much more slowly than others, and all operate only in specified circumstances.

To some extent pressures on the exchanges automatically correct themselves through changes in incomes and prices. This is true in each of the three cases listed above.

First of all, let us take the case where foreigners are buying more British goods and the rate of exchange is fixed. The increase in demand will raise British incomes and have a multiplier effect exactly like that analysed in

Chapter 21. The people who find jobs in the export industries spend more out of the higher incomes they earn; this creates more jobs for other people in the home market; these newly employed workers are also able to spend more; and so the process goes on. But at each stage in the cumulative process of expansion there is, so to speak, a leak of purchasing power to expenditure on imports. The increase in imports might even counterbalance the original increase in exports without other intervention if the expansion in incomes proceeded far enough.

This does appear to happen in some primary producing countries. It is not uncommon for the exports of those countries to fluctuate violently and for those fluctuations to be accompanied by equally violent fluctuations in imports. There may not even be any perceptible lag in imports behind exports; for if it is plain that export prices are rising sharply, importers will know that their customers are having a good year and will take action at once to stock up with suitable commodities. It happens that in many primary producing countries there is a high income elasticity of demand for imported manufactures (i.e., a high proportion of any increase in income is spent on those imports) and this speeds up the process of adjustment. Where the appetite for imports is less easily stimulated (or inhibited) the flow of expenditure is concentrated on the domestic market; but since, as a rule, output in primary producing countries is highly inelastic, the immediate effect is a sharp, all-round inflation of prices. This inflation accomplishes what the increase in incomes by itself failed to accomplish: it makes imports seem relatively cheap and attractive and widens the market for them. In the end, therefore, the same adjustment takes place but at a higher level of money incomes.

In a manufacturing country this kind of automatic adjustment would operate through swings in employment rather than in price. If, for example, exports fell off, this would first be reflected in unemployment in the export industries and the depression in the export industries would then be communicated to other industries as the volume of demand contracted. The resulting depression would reduce the current off-take of imported materials and would also react on the demand for imported foodstuffs and finished goods of all kinds. In the absence of government action, this process would continue until the deficit in the balance of payments disappeared.

A movement of capital can also be self-correcting but in a rather different way. It might result, for example, from a decision to build new fixed assets abroad rather than at home, although such decisions are rare and not typical of the normal decisions that lead to an export of capital. The fall in British investment would release resources in Britain while the rise in investment abroad might increase the demand for exports of capital goods from Britain, so that a shift in the employment of British resources into the export trades earned the foreign exchange necessary to accomplish the financial transfer of capital.

This kind of situation was more likely to arise half a century ago when the United Kingdom was both the major exporter of capital and the chief supplier of most of the capital-importing countries. But even at that time, the mechanism of adjustment was usually a great deal more complicated. The main effect of an increase in the export of capital was to make it more difficult to finance investment in Britain, so that it helped to depress the level of domestic investment. At the same time, foreign countries tended to borrow from Britain at a time when British exports were high, so that the pressure on the export trades compensated for the lack of pressure on the building industry. This made it possible to transfer capital without giving rise to recurrent crises in the balance of payments; but there was nothing in the nature of things that made this inevitable.

So far we have left out of account the monetary effects of a change in the balance of payments and any action that the monetary authorities may take to speed up or delay the process of adjustment. These efforts differ according as dealings in foreign exchange are free or restricted, at a fixed rate or at a fluctuating rate. We may begin by taking the case where dealings are free and at a fixed par of exchange. The fixed par is usually defined in terms of the price of gold, or of some currency convertible into gold, and the classical example of a system of fixed parities is that of the gold standard.

The mechanism of adjustment under gold standard conditions

Conditions under which countries rely mainly on gold as a means of settling surpluses or deficits with one another are the hallmark of the gold standard. These conditions might obtain even if there were no central bank so long as there was some means of converting currency freely into gold and shipping it abroad in settlement of debts. But there is a second and perhaps more important characteristic of the gold standard: convertibility of currency into gold *on fixed terms*. It is this characteristic that explains the use of the word 'standard': gold acts as the standard of value in the sense that its price is fixed in terms of the unit of account, e.g., the pound sterling.

If gold coins are in circulation and all other kinds of money, such as bank notes, are promises to pay gold then free convertibility into gold at a fixed price is automatically secured. Even if, as in Britain between 1925 and 1931, there is no gold currency but only a law instructing the central bank to purchase all gold offered to it at a fixed price, and to sell gold bullion at a slightly higher price, the condition is still fulfilled. It is also fulfilled if the central bank is instructed to buy and sell at fixed prices not gold, but the money of some other gold standard country; for this money is itself convertible into gold at a fixed price. The first kind of standard was the one generally adopted up till 1914; the second, the gold bullion standard, came into use after the war of 1914–1918; while the third, the gold exchange standard, was adopted by countries like India which could not afford a full gold standard, but which preferred instead to link their currencies with sterling, and so, indirectly, to link them with gold.

The gold standard was a means of preserving constant, or almost constant, exchange rates between different countries. If the United States and Great Britain were both on the gold standard, the dollar and sterling prices of gold would both be fixed, and the terms on which pounds and dollars exchange would, therefore, also be fixed. Suppose, for example, that the mint price of gold in New York is $35 an ounce and in London £7 an ounce. Then the mint par of exchange will be $5 to the £1. It will be foolish for an American to offer more than $5 for £1 since by buying gold and shipping it to London he can obtain pounds at this rate. On the other hand, no American will sell pounds for less than $5, since by buying gold in London and bringing it to New York he can convert his sterling balances into dollars at this rate. But the shipping of gold in either direction puts him to some expense, and various obstacles may be put in his way by central banks which do not like to lose gold too easily. If he can buy pounds on the market for foreign exchange, therefore, he will be willing to pay rather more than $5 to save himself trouble and expense, and if he has pounds to sell he will be willing to accept rather less than $5 for the same reason. Thus the gold standard did not entirely eliminate variations in exchange rates; but it sets narrow limits to them. For each country there was a maximum price of foreign exchange above which gold began to flow out ('gold export point') and a minimum price below which gold began to flow in ('gold import point').

The gold standard provided a common medium of exchange, with which, in the last resort, international payments could be made: but only in the last resort. While the balance of payments was in equilibrium, and total exports were equal to total imports, there was no need for gold to move at all. It was only when imports and exports got out of line with one another that some residual transfer of gold was necessary in order to balance the two. Gold flowed in when exporters had more foreign exchange than importers would buy (so that its price dropped to gold import point) and flowed out when the supply of foreign exchange was insufficient to meet the demand (so that its price rose to gold export point). The gold was purchased by, or obtained from, the central bank which, since it was its duty to keep the price of gold constant, had to hold a substantial stock of it, adding to the stock or drawing on it whenever the balance of payments was favourable or unfavourable.

The central bank of a country on the gold standard had to do more than hold a stock of gold and relieve any pressure on the exchanges by appropriate purchases and sales. It had also to be able to safeguard its stock by taking action to check any drain of gold. To some extent it could rely on the flow of gold to reverse itself automatically, but a large flow one way or the other called for active intervention.

In the United Kingdom, for example, the automatic effects were set on foot through the financing of the excess of payments by purchases of gold or other international assets from the Bank of England. Those purchases were paid for in the ordinary way by cheques on a commercial bank and the Bank of England, on receipt of the cheques, debited them against the bankers' balances which it held. This had two consequences. The first was a contraction in total bank deposits and so in the supply of money. The second was a fall in the cash reserves of the commercial banks and in their reserve ratios. Unless the Bank of England took action to restore bankers' balances by open market operations, therefore, a contraction of credit ensued exactly like the contraction that would follow the sale of government securities by the Bank of England. The commercial banks were forced to call in their loans to the discount market and reinforce the immediate fall in their deposit liabilities caused by the purchases of gold by a further reduction through credit restriction. This made money 'tight' and brought about a rise in interest rates.

The earliest and largest increase was in discount rates, since it was the money market which felt the immediate impact of credit restriction. The higher rates of discount made London a less attractive source of short-term credit and reduced the flow of bills sent for discount on the London market. To a lesser extent it also increased the demand for sterling funds in order to take advantage of the higher return obtainable in London. The combined effect of a reduced demand for foreign exchange and an increased demand for pounds was to move the rate of exchange away from gold export point and to bring to a stop the outward flow of gold.

If the deficit in the balance of payments was a temporary one – due, for example, to seasonal pressure – this effect was adequate to correct it. If the deficit arose because the level of costs and prices in Britain was rising relatively to costs and prices elsewhere, or because the pressure of demand was becoming excessive, the rise in interest rates might be sufficient either to moderate the pressure or give time for the divergence in prices and costs to correct itself. But if the source of disequilibrium was more deep-seated, the effect of higher interest rates on the flow of international credit could only be a stop-gap. So long as foreign borrowing was curtailed or foreign balances continued to be attracted to London[1], imports could remain in excess of exports without any movements of gold. But immediately no further change in the flow of credit took place, gold exports had to be resumed. Or if, for any reason, the deficit had made foreigners fear devaluation – as in those days never happened – and a flow of 'hot' money out of sterling had begun, the pressure on sterling would have been greatly aggravated. A continuing deficit could be cured only by a fall in imports or a rise in exports.

To this cure the rise in interest rates and the restriction of credit contributed. They operated in the same direction as the automatic influences on employment and incomes which we discussed above and were not easy to distinguish from these influences. Dear money discouraged investment and limited demand so that there was an incentive to ship to foreign markets goods that could not be sold at home. At the same time, the fall in incomes that accompanied the lower level of investment reduced the demand for imports of all kinds. By depressing economic activity, it was possible to bring imports and exports back into balance with one another.

Eventually, yet another effect might make itself felt. The depression in activity tended to drive down the level of costs and make Britain a relatively cheap market from which to buy and a difficult market in which to compete. This fall in costs might arise simply from lower profit margins or from a closer attention to more economical methods of production by manufacturers facing keener competition; or there might, in conditions of intense depression, be reductions in wages forced on workers under

---

[1] There was, of course, no *physical* movement of foreign money into London. All that happened was that foreigners bought pounds and sold foreign money in exchange; this foreign money was then used in payment for excess imports. In the same way, when we talk of money leaving the country, no money (except gold) moves: it is its ownership, not its situation, that changes. Some people sell pounds (which other people buy) in return for foreign moneys.

pressure of unemployment. Whatever the cause, lower costs would allow exports to rise, drive down imports and reverse the unfavourable trend in the balance of payments.

So long as a country remains on the gold standard or maintains fixed exchange rates, therefore, equilibrium in its balance of payments tends to be maintained by a number of different forces some of which come into play automatically while others are released by monetary forces. The monetary forces operate through interest rates, first on the flow of credit to or from the country, then on the level of economic activity, and finally on the level of costs and prices. This is true, whether as we have supposed, the disequilibrium expresses itself in a deficit or takes the form of a surplus: a fall in interest rates sets off changes that are similar, but in the reverse direction, to those set off by a rise in interest rates.

The extent to which monetary forces are brought into operation depends upon the policy of the central bank and on the urgency with which it seeks to wipe out a deficit or surplus. The forces arresting a loss of reserves, for example, may be slow in gathering strength, while the effects on the size of the reserves are immediate and serious. If the reserves are already small, and little in excess of the minimum legal requirements of the bank, there is a danger of panic. Foreigners, afraid that the country may be forced to devalue, and that gold or foreign exchange will then be obtainable only at a much higher price, rush to withdraw their balances, and by increasing the pressure on the reserves add to the very danger which alarms them. The bank, therefore, may be forced to take drastic action in self-defence. Alternatively, if it has reason to believe that the loss of reserves is temporary and that no tightening of credit is necessary in order to secure their return, it may seek to counteract and alleviate the direct impact on the money supply of the loss of reserves.

This it can do by open market operations. By buying government securities it can prevent a contraction of credit just as, by selling them, it can reinforce it. Whatever assets the central bank acquires – government securities, gold, Treasury bills – it creates deposits with itself (generally in favour of the commercial banks), broadens the base of credit, and gives the whole monetary system an inflationary impetus; whatever assets it sells, and whatever loans it calls in, it cancels deposits with itself, narrows the base of credit, and applies deflationary pressure to the commercial banks. The purchase of one asset is equal and opposite in its effects to the sale of another. A loss of gold, therefore, can be offset by the purchase of government securities; an inflow of gold can be offset (or sterilized) by the sale of government securities. By keeping its total assets constant the central bank can insulate the whole credit system from the effects of gold movements; but only so long as it still has gold or other reserve assets to sell when the flow is outwards or government securities to sell when the flow is inwards.

Fixed exchange rates leave some scope, therefore, for monetary man-agement. There is still need for discretion and judgement in deciding what action to take when reserves are flowing in or out. The central bank has to decide whether to offset or reinforce the movement; it has to reconcile, as best it can, the credit requirements of domestic industry with the state of the foreign exchanges; it has also to avoid unnecessary embarrassment to other central banks and seek their cooperation in its own policies. But the need to preserve a fixed par of exchange sets narrow limits to management of the currency, and may face the central bank with many unpleasant dilemmas. In some circumstances, as we have seen, it may even be obliged to acquiesce in severe credit restriction that can only result – and is intended to result – in a deflation of output and incomes.

If a country has to impoverish itself by restricting output and incomes so as to retain fixed exchange rates, it is hardly likely to feel much enthusiasm for the system. It is even less likely to accept a standard that obliges it to bring its costs into line with those of other countries by periodic cuts in money wages since downward adjustments in wage rates are notoriously difficult to bring about. On the other hand, there are undoubtedly great conveniences to a trading country in a stable and fixed rate of exchange. It is natural to ask, therefore, whether some relaxation of the system might not allow adjustment to take place at less cost and with less harshness and without sacrificing the advantages of a stable exchange rate. One such relaxation – if it may be so described – is to be ready, in appropriate circumstances, to change the par value of the currency. If the alternative is to try to bring about a sharp adjustment in domestic prices and incomes, devaluation (or, in the opposite case, revaluation upwards) is likely to be preferable.

Devaluation

Devaluation means the adoption of a new and lower parity of exchange; the price of gold in terms of the currency is increased and the value of the currency, therefore, in terms either of gold or of other currencies is reduced. The effect of devaluation is, as a rule, to wipe out the unfavourable balance and to convert it ultimately into a favourable balance. Suppose, for example, that the pound falls in value from \$3 to \$2. Then British exports to the United States which were previously sold at \$3 can now be sold at \$2 without any reduction in the number of pounds received by the exporter. By quoting the same price in terms of sterling, therefore, British exporters will be able to undersell their foreign competitors; this will give a fillip to exports and reduce the unfavourable trade balance. On the other hand, if exporters quote the same price in terms of dollars, they will still sell as large a quantity of goods as before and the sterling value of exports will again increase. Similarly, imports into Britain will require to be sold at prices 50% higher if the proceeds in terms of dollars are to be maintained; for each pound will now fetch only two instead of three dollars. The rise in the price of imports will cause a reduction in the volume of purchases and also, if the demand is elastic, a reduction in the value of imports. This will reinforce the improvement in the balance of trade and relieve the pressure against sterling. When imports consist very largely of foodstuffs and raw materials, however, they will be in inelastic demand and devaluation, far from reducing their value, will actually increase it. In such circumstances devaluation may be comparatively ineffective as a means of correcting an unfavourable balance; it is even conceivable that it might aggravate the unfavourable balance. In practice, a country's demand for imports and the foreign demand for its exports rarely fail to be elastic enough to produce a contraction in imports and an expansion in exports. Devaluation turns the balance of payments in its favour and relieves the pressure on its exchanges.

Devaluation works by raising the price of goods imported from overseas, and their domestically-produced substitutes. It acts like a tariff on imports, curbing demand, and stimulating domestic supply of these substitutes. It also tends to raise the home price of goods exported to foreign markets, once again squeezing home demand and increasing domestic output. There are, however, conditions under which these effects (on the balance of payments and on output) will be neutralized. This is especially likely if devaluation is accompanied by large increases in money wage rates and in the domestic money supply.

Devaluation can hardly be a recurring expedient. If a country devalues its currency every time it suffers from an unfavourable balance, it will destroy the confidence of traders and speculators in the fixity of its exchange rate and lead them to expect further depreciation. Without that confidence, half the value of fixed exchange rates in facilitating international trade and investment is lost; the country has moved halfway from a system of fixed to a system of freely floating exchange rates.

The mechanism of adjustment with floating exchange rates

Let us now suppose that the authorities allow the ordinary forces of the exchange market – the pressures to buy and sell foreign exchange – to govern exchange rates. Where will the exchange rate settle? Will it really settle at all, even within wide limits? And how will exchange fluctuations help an adverse balance of payments to correct itself?

For an answer to the first of these questions – what determines the normal equilibrium rate of exchange – we must study the country's balance of short-term indebtedness. If the country is losing gold and foreign exchange reserves or is selling foreign balances or is being forced to borrow on short-term in order to finance its imports, then its exchange is overvalued and is likely to depreciate. But if the country is gaining reserves of gold and foreign exchange, because it is not importing on the same scale as it is exporting, then its currency is undervalued and is likely to appreciate. It is not necessarily true, however, that the equilibrium rate of exchange is one at which no change in the country's short-term indebtedness will be taking place. The country may be a centre in which there is an increasing and natural tendency for the short-term funds of other countries to find investment. Or the country may be trying to make a gradual addition to its holdings of gold and foreign exchange in order to safeguard itself against the effects of violent fluctuations in its exports.

Purchasing power parity

A rather different, and more easily applicable, test of equilibrium in the rate of exchange has been put forward in the 'purchasing power parity' theory[1]. It has been suggested that exchange rates tend to be pulled into

---

[1] The 'purchasing power parity' theory is generally associated with the name of Professor Gustav Cassel, but the gist of the theory was put forward a century earlier during the controversies over the Bullion Report of 1810.

line with their 'purchasing power parities'. Sometimes this is taken to mean that if £1 has the same purchasing power in Britain as $2.4 in America, then the equilibrium rate of exchange is £1 = $2.4. Sometimes with more justification, the theory is modified so as to refer, not to a comparison between the purchasing power of the pound and the dollar at any particular time, but to a comparison between the *changes* in their purchasing power since some base date. If, for example, the purchasing power of the pound has been halved while the purchasing power of the dollar has been doubled, then, it is argued, the dollar will tend to exchange for four times as many pounds as before. In other words, changes in the external value of a currency (its value in exchange for other currencies) tend to reflect changes in its internal value (its purchasing power over commodities).

The first version of the theory is clearly untenable. Every tourist knows that it is cheaper to live in some countries than in others and that, since prices are lower in America than in Britain, he can buy less with £1 than with the $2.4 for which it exchanges. Some prices, the prices of traded goods, must be more or less in line in both countries; but other prices – fares, hotel charges, lawyers' fees, etc. – need not correspond because there is no way by which people living in one country can take advantage of cheap services provided in another. The second version of the theory is more reasonable. It is clear that if prices rise in any country (so that its currency loses purchasing power) there will be a strong tendency for exports to diminish and for imports to increase; the balance of payments will become unfavourable, and exchange depreciation will result. There is a presumption, therefore, that changes in purchasing power will be followed by similar changes in exchange rates. But this presumption must not be interpreted too rigorously; the changes in purchasing power and in exchange rates need not be in exact accordance with one another.

If we take the price of any staple traded commodity, such as wheat, we are likely to find that, converting at current rates of exchange, this price is the same in all countries, allowance being made for transport costs and tariff barriers. So long as the rate of exchange is $2.5 = £1, wheat selling at a dollar a bushel in Chicago will sell at rather more than 40p a bushel in Liverpool. If the Liverpool price rises, more wheat will be shipped until the local scarcity disappears. In the same way a fall in the Liverpool price will reduce imports until parity with the Chicago price is re-established. Or if the rate of exchange depreciates to $2 = £1, the Liverpool price – failing any change in price in Chicago – will be marked up automatically to 50p a bushel. What is true of wheat is true also of other traded goods. Prices in each country must conform to one another at current exchange rates whatever these rates happen to be. Thus it is useless to compare changes in the purchasing powers of two currencies over *traded* goods as a test of equilibrium. For unless freights or tariffs have altered[1], these changes in purchasing power *must* be equal whether exchange rates are in equilibrium or not. It is the prices of traded goods which are pulled into line with

---

[1] A rise in British tariffs or in freight charges on British imports will increase the margin between the price of traded goods in Britain and abroad. Prices will tend to rise in Britain, but since purchases from, and payments to, foreigners will fall, the balance of payments will be more favourable and the rate of exchange, instead of depreciating, will probably appreciate. Thus purchasing power and exchange parities will diverge from one another.

exchange rates rather than exchange rates which are pulled into line with the prices of traded goods.

When we turn to domestic goods – that is, goods which do not enter into international trade, such as house-room, milk, services of most kinds – we find nothing to couple their prices in one country rapidly and automatically with prices in other countries. If, for example, domestic goods double in price in Britain and remain unchanged in the United States there is no obvious reason why the sterling–dollar exchange rate should immediately fall by 50%. Purchasing power parities measured in terms of domestic goods, therefore, may certainly diverge from exchange parities. But can the divergence *continue*? Is the divergence a measure of disequilibrium in exchange rates and a safe basis on which to forecast their future course?

It should be noted, first of all, that the divergence can equally well be expressed as a divergence between the price levels of domestic and traded goods. The link between exchange rates and the price level of traded goods must also bind the general price level unless domestic goods fail to keep in line with traded goods. If the price level of domestic goods lags behind the price level of traded goods, the purchasing power of the currency will also lag behind movements in exchange rates. And if equilibrium requires an equal change in purchasing power and in exchange rates, it must also require, therefore, an equal change in the price levels of domestic and of traded goods.

Now there are strong forces linking together these two price levels. If either group of commodities becomes dearer, the most likely cause is a rise in the cost of wages and materials which, if it is at all great, is fairly certain to spread to the other group of commodities. A persistent rise in wages in the export industries, for example, will soon lead to a sympathetic rise in wages in allied industries supplying the home market. First of all, domestic workers in the same craft will share in the rise, then workers in the same grade of labour, and finally workers of greater or inferior skill. Similarly, with raw materials. A rise in the price of steel affects ship plates for export equally with girders for offices and shops at home. Prices are stitched by competition into a fabric which resists distortion. Pressure at one point is felt on all sides, and, although the fabric may give for a time, the old price relationships are soon restored.

It is to inertia in price structure that we must turn if we wish to justify the purchasing power parity theory. If the prices of traded and non-traded goods keep in step, so also will exchange rates and purchasing power parities. But we must be careful not to exaggerate the stability of the price structure. Dissimilar changes in the level of output, the unequal incidence of invention, the immobility of labour, and the imperfections of competition make for irregular movements in wages and in prices in different industries, and even in large groups of industries. The test of purchasing power parity will then break down.

A similar breakdown takes place whenever there is a change in a country's terms of trade. Suppose, for example, that of two countries each consumes equal amounts of its own and of the other country's goods. A fall in the price of one country's exports will then affect prices (but not incomes) similarly in both countries, and will at the same time cause a depreciation in the rate of exchange parallel to the fall in export prices.

That is, the rate of exchange will alter without any similar alteration in purchasing power parity.

A divergence between the rate of exchange and purchasing power parity may also arise because of international capital movements. If a country is lending large sums abroad, or if speculators are transferring balances to other financial centres, heavy sales will be made of the country's currency and its value will depreciate. But prices – at any rate, domestic prices – will not be directly affected by these transfers of capital, and the depreciation in exchange rates will not be accompanied by an equal fall in the purchasing power of the currency.

Once the appropriate qualifications have been made, the purchasing power parity theory loses much of its precision. It is an unsatisfactory short-period theory because it makes no provision for the influence of speculation, capital movements, and so on; and it is an unsatisfactory long-period theory, because it fails to take account of the fact that wages and prices in different groups of industries do not move together. The behaviour of the sterling–dollar exchange rate between 1977 and 1980 provides a very good illustration of how the purchasing power parity theory can fail to explain facts. Sterling rose by 40% against the US dollar over the period despite the fact that Britain was experiencing faster inflation than the United States.

Cumulative movements in exchange rates

Although a fall in the rate of exchange generally serves to improve a country's balance of payments, there are circumstances in which it may actually aggravate an existing deficit. Suppose, for example, that the country's exports are in inelastic demand in foreign markets and that they are also in inelastic supply. These conditions will apply if the country has a limited range of exports, consisting largely of staple products, and if it is the principal supplier of those products. A fall in the rate of exchange will automatically reduce the price of exports in terms of foreign currencies, while the volume of exports will show little response either because of difficulties in expanding the supply or because of the inelasticity of demand in world markets. The net result, therefore, will be a reduction in the amount earned in foreign exchange. If there is a similar inelasticity on the side of imports – for example, because they consist largely of foodstuffs – a fall in the rates of exchange may do little to diminish their volume and their costs in terms of foreign currencies. The excess of imports over exports will then be higher than before. Moreover, since imported goods will rise in price in terms of the local currency, there will be a strong tendency towards a general inflation of prices and a strain throughout the whole financial system. A cumulative process of exchange depreciation and internal inflation may be started off, the balance of payments getting steadily worse, not better.

For a fall in the exchange rate to add to an already adverse balance is rare, except where the elasticities involved are abnormally low. Even when the balance of payments is slow in swinging round, speculative forces generally come into play at an early stage and these forces help to sustain the rate of exchange by a transfer of funds into the depreciating currency as soon as it appears to be undervalued. Not all economists, however, would agree with this judgement; and there have been a number of elaborate calculations purporting to show that, in international trade, the elasticities involved are often surprisingly low.

Whatever the truth of the matter, there is no doubt that most countries are afraid that *in their case* the elasticities will be low and are full of good reasons for not allowing their currency to depreciate in spite of a persistently unfavourable balance of payments. A country that lowers its rate of exchange is deliberately accepting less favourable terms of trade, since import prices in the country's currency will rise relatively to export prices. It may feel, therefore, that it would have to make a large concession (for example, in additional exports) for a small gain in its balance of payments. For this reason, and also for reasons of prestige, few countries devalue except from sheer necessity. On the other hand, few carry this reasoning to the point of deliberately *raising* their rate of exchange.

Exchange control

When a country is unwilling to allow market forces to operate unchecked on its rate of exchange, or fears that market forces will not operate to restore equilibrium in its balance of payments, it can institute a system of exchange control. The banks will then be allowed to supply foreign exchange only to make payments approved by the government while all receipts in foreign currencies will have to be handed over to the banks. A system of exchange control was established in Britain at the outbreak of war in 1939 and was put on a statutory basis by the Exchange Control Act, 1947. It was dismantled in 1979.

The mere canalizing of receipts and payments through a control would make little difference if there were not a simultaneous limitation on the transactions permitted by the government. The first such limitation was on capital movements. Loans to foreign countries, purchases of securities from foreigners, even transfers of money by emigrants, came under strict control. There may also be limitations on current transactions. The machinery of import licensing imposes a ceiling on imports of particular goods, or fixes quotas for imports of the goods from each country. Tourists may be given a ration of foreign currency which they must not exceed. Various other transactions involving payment in foreign currencies can be made illegal or subject to licence.

Because exchange control is more mysterious or more remote than other types of control many people are disposed to accept it as more effective. But it is subject to the same limitations. There is the same scope for administrative muddle; there are black markets in foreign exchange as in commodities; there are flights of capital even when capital movements are forbidden. It only requires a minor delay on the part of exporters in surrendering foreign exchange and a minor scurry on the part of importers to meet their obligations in foreign exchange to create a disconcerting divergence between the excess of exports over imports and the excess of receipts over payments. The terms of credit which importers enjoy or for which exporters are asked depend upon the confidence of foreigners in the currency: if their confidence is shaken, the terms of payment will move against the country and the balance of payments will reflect this move without any transgression of the law or any change in imports and exports. Speculative movements of funds may have been driven out of the door; but they have a way of coming in again at the window.

During the Second World War and for many years thereafter sterling's convertibility into foreign currencies was suspended. Sterling became freely convertible again in December 1958. But exchange control was retained for a further 21 years, chiefly to limit British residents' overseas investment.

The International Monetary Fund

The International Monetary Fund (IMF) was created to foster international monetary cooperation. The IMF is worldwide in scope, its members including the United States, the United Kingdom, and all the countries of the Commonwealth.

The IMF was planned at Bretton Woods in 1944 and was brought into existence after the war 'to assist in the establishment of a multilateral system of payments in respect of current transactions between members and in the elimination of foreign exchange restrictions which hamper the growth of world trade'. The principal aim of the Fund, like that of the gold standard, is to secure a general convertibility of currencies as stable rates of exchange; unlike the gold standard, it tries to combine with this aim the preservation of internal economic balance and a high and stable level in the member countries. It is possible, however, to accept convertibility, fixed exchange rates and internal balance as objectives of policy without specifying in what sequence each should be approached, in what order of priority they should be ranked, or by what means they should be achieved. In practice, the Fund laid emphasis on the early declaration of fixed parities of exchange and the early removal of exchange restrictions, without contributing a great deal during the critical post-war period towards establishing conditions in which these things were appropriate.

The emphasis on fixed rates of exchange was in reaction against the experience of the 1930s and designed to prevent competitive depreciations. Until 1971, every member was required to keep its rate of exchange within a margin of 1% of the gold parity declared to the Fund and to consult the Fund before changing this parity. Such changes were allowable in principle if the country was in a state of 'fundamental disequilibrium' (presumably when it had a chronic deficit – or surplus – in its balance of payments). The British depreciation of 1949, however, was decided upon without any real consultation with the Fund (although it was delayed so that the Fund could be informed); other countries have adopted multiple exchange rates or fluctuating exchange rates without prior consultation with the Fund. Thus the general principle that rates should only be varied (by more than 10%) after consultation and with the concurrence of the Fund is largely a dead letter.

Convertibility of currencies was supposed to be achieved by the end of a short transition period. A distinction was drawn between capital transactions which could continue to be restricted and current transactions which could be restricted only during the transition period. This distinction arose largely out of the 'hot money' movements of the 1930s – movements which were patently de-stabilizing in their effects. The distinction, although clear in principle, was much more difficult to apply in practice since capital movements could take place through the medium of current transactions and were correspondingly difficult to control in the absence of a simultaneous control over current transactions. For many years, however, the distinction had little practical importance since both types of transaction were controlled and the transition stretched out indefinitely. It was not until 1958 that a decisive step towards external convertibility was taken.

The fixed exchange rates of the 1950s and 1960s gave way in the 1970s to a much looser regime of exchange rates. Sterling floated from August to December 1971, in company with many other currencies; since June 1972 it has been floating continuously. Other countries to adopt floating exchange rates for much or all of this period include Canada, France, Italy and Japan. The decade closed with the creation, in 1979, of a new regime of fixed exchange rates which included all EEC currencies except the pound sterling. This is known as the European Monetary System.

The Fund tries to help its members in various ways to reconcile internal and external balance. This it can do in two ways: by penalizing countries that remain persistently in surplus and by giving credit to countries in temporary deficit. It can, for example, declare a general scarcity of a currency if the country concerned is draining away other countries' reserves and throwing them out of balance; it can also declare a currency scarce on the more technical ground that its own holdings of the currency have been exhausted through loans to its members. In fact, the Fund has never declared any currency scarce on either ground and it is highly unlikely that it ever will. It has relied instead on the advance of credits to its members.

These credits take the form of purchases from the Fund's pool of foreign currencies, to which all members have contributed. The amount contributed to this pool by each country (and its voting rights in the Fund) is governed by its quota, one-quarter of the quota being payable in gold or dollars and the rest in its own currency. Each country can withdraw up to the first quarter more or less without question, but drawings in excess of this have to be justified by progressively stricter criteria and the maximum that can be drawn, with the Fund's agreement, is 125% of the country's quota. The credits are repayable in gold or convertible currencies and bear charges that become increasingly onerous the larger the amount outstanding and the longer the period for which they are outstanding.

In the early post-war period, the difficulties of monetary reconstruction were bigger and more enduring than the Fund could have hoped to overcome, even if it had been trying to do the right things. To re-establish world trade on a multilateral basis, free from exchange restrictions, nededed more time, more resources and more deviousness than had been imagined. Once this aim had been achieved, there was a chance that the IMF might come into its own; but it is still possible to doubt whether the resources at its disposal are adequate to maintain international equilibrium.

Part VII

Economic policy

Chapter 30

The role of government

The market and the state

The first task of an economist is to explain how the economy works; once he has got that far, he can do on to discuss how it might be made to work better. Both tasks make it necessary to consider what governments do or might do. Governments are not only important elements in the functioning of the economy but enjoy political as well as economic power and can use that power to make deliberate changes in the economic system. Anyone disliking the way in which the system is working or who thinks his interests threatened or damaged can agitate for action by the state to protect his interests or alter the system. Side by side with the market in which economic transactions between buyers and sellers take place and economic power is exerted there is a political system in which the pressures are of a different kind and are intended to lead to intervention by the state. Money is the currency of one system and votes of the other. Since the two systems interact, it is necessary for the economist to take account of both.

Economists usually start by analysing an economy in which market forces are paramount and the state does little except maintain a framework within which those forces can operate freely. The limitations of a market economy are then examined and a need for state action to remedy these limitations is deduced. As economists have become increasingly aware of the defects of market forces this need has been spelled out in more and more detail. But the state is still seen as a kind of *Deus ex machina* which can be relied upon to make good any weaknesses in the system brought to light by the analysis. There is little or no analysis of the state as an economic agent or of *its* peculiar weaknesses; and it is generally taken for granted that the defects of the market economy *will* be overcome by state intervention.

At the opposite extreme we have Communist regimes in which the state is paramount and it is market forces which lead a kind of subterranean existence within permitted limits. Recognition of the difficulty of organizing economic activity through state action alone drives such regimes to allow more scope to the operations of the market. But although the value of market forces is usually recognized, they are viewed with suspicion as calculated to subvert the political system within which they operate.

Thus we can either examine the economies of the real world in terms of market forces qualified by state action or of state action qualified by market forces. Whatever procedure we follow, we are bound to recognize that every economic system is, in one way or another, a mixed system relying on the market for some purposes and on the state for others.

Market forces and economic organization

Alongside the antithesis between the market and the state is a second, allied, antithesis between a system in which economic activity is organized exclusively through the uncontrolled operation of market forces and one in which it is organized directly within separate units which may be as large as the state or as small as a household and include businesses of all kinds from multinational corporations to the corner shop. In principle, under the first arrangement market forces might dissolve all forms of business organization into a multitude of one-man businesses trading with one another and organizing their own activities freely in response to the movement of market prices as happens at an auction. Equally, it is conceivable, in principle, that the state should undertake to organize every detail of economic life, leaving the individual no freedom to buy or sell, or to opt for work or leisure, or to move from one job to another. Both of these extremes are far removed from reality. Market forces are not in practice a complete alternative to deliberate organization and planning; and even within most organizations some matters are settled by bargaining. But there is a choice, extending over the whole area of economic activity, between letting decisions be taken by individual units in the form of responses to market signals and managing or planning what is to be done within the units of decision-taking that we call firms; and this choice extends also the degree to which the decisions of those units are themselves free responses to market signals or are subject to management and planning by larger units, either privately controlled or agents of the state. The bigger the average size of business unit the more is organized and planned rather than left to the operation of market forces; and the prevalence of bigger units in business itself facilitates, prefigures, encourages and ultimately dictates a parallel expansion in government planning and control.

Every economic system, therefore, is a blend of market forces and organization and planning. But the organization and planning may take place privately, within the firm, or publicly through the state; and this still leaves open how the two forms of organization, the firm and the state, should be married and what scope is allowed by each of them for harnessing market forces to the public advantage.

Laissez-faire

We have already studied in considerable detail how market forces do operate. Unqualified enthusiasm for the market and distrust of the state led in the nineteenth century to the triumph of *laissez-faire*. The market, so ran the argument, allowed producers and consumers to associate freely, on an impersonal basis, without the need to consult any interests but their own. There was no need for bargaining or negotiation; in a perfect market the price did not respond to the pressure of individual buyers or sellers, but only to the total pressure of all buyers and sellers, and was automatically such as to allow all who were prepared to do business to transact all the business they wanted at the market price. The weighing up of alternatives, the acceptance or rejection of offers for sale or purchase, the initiative in seeking improved ways of producing or in meeting wants in a more economical way, were left to producers and consumers who could be supposed to have an unrivalled knowledge of their own affairs. There was no need for argument or compulsion before a price moved up or down, a new technique of manufacture was adopted, or greater economy in a scarce product was practised: the silent pressure of the market settled prices, forced the inefficient out of business and steered the limited incomes of consumers away from expensive towards other, less costly, products. If a producer wanted to make things differently from his competitors he was free to do so and, if successful, might see them all obliged to follow suit, not from rivalry, but in self-preservation. If a consumer wanted to indulge some personal idiosyncrasy he, too, could do so without permit, licence or extra coupons. Individual preferences were given the maximum scope; innovation and capital accumulation were given the maximum encouragement. The cost of living was kept down because the inefficient went out of business and because, thanks to free trade, the maximum advantage could be taken of the willingness of foreigners to offer goods that could only be made at high cost in return for goods that could be made comparatively cheaply.

Thus whatever might be true of distribution, the market was an admirable and automatic technique for controlling production. It was unnecessary for the government to regulate and plan industry because prices already balanced supply and demand, cost and utility; the price mechanism was an adequate substitute for planning. It was also unwise for the government to intervene; governments were incapable of improving upon the delicate machinery of the market, and were likely, by their intervention, to throw the machinery out of gear, or to impose the dead hand of routine, or to act as the puppets of 'sinister interests'. By devolving the tasks of enterprise upon the business community, they could enlist stronger motives and more intimate knowledge in the planning of industrial output. And that output, produced at the lowest possible cost, would conform to the free choice of consumers as expressed in their purchases, not to some ideal imposed by an authoritarian government.

The case for *laissez-faire* was a strong one; it was realistic in its appeal to experience, and idealistic in its appeal to individualism. Historically, too, *laissez-faire* was a highly successful, if unnecessarily harsh, policy; the material progress made in the nineteenth century was immense, and it would be foolish to belittle it. But the policy had its drawbacks and the arguments on which it rested, their flaws.

The long-term trend towards regulation and control

Laissez-faire was a dogma rather than a fact: the state never yielded entirely to the general bias against intervention in industry. In particular, it showed more reluctance to leave domestic trade uncontrolled than to adopt free trade in international economic relations. The subsequent extension of government control, however, particularly over the last 50 years, represents something of a revolution in economic policy and it is no longer possible to treat such control as exceptional and running counter to the general temper of the age.

The decline of *laissez-faire* and the corresponding rise of government control, although gaining momentum after the First World War, date from an earlier period. There had been intervention against the abuse of monopoly power: railways, gas and electric power companies, for example, were not free to fix their charges, and were subject to various restrictions over dividends, new construction, and other matters. There had been intervention in sectors of the economy of critical importance to policy; the Bank Charter Act of 1844, for example, was designed to prevent the financial system from getting out of order. There had been intervention also because the market ignored fundamental wants or was incapable of bringing them satisfaction. Public health legislation provides many examples: infectious diseases, like cholera, could not be got rid of by competition in any form but could be got rid of by better sanitation, and this involved common arrangements on behalf of all citizens, independently of their power to contribute to the cost. Ignorance was potentially as great a danger as disease; common arrangements had, therefore, to be made for the schooling of the population at the state's expense. Roads, public parks and libraries met other, communal, wants. In course of time the vast machinery of the social services was built up to meet common dangers, provide common enjoyment, and succour those who fell below a common minimum standard.

With all this there went a decline in the philosophy of individualism and an increased stress, partly under the influence of German writers and statesmen, first, on social ties and secondly, on the state as the means by which those ties could be preserved and fostered. It was realized that the state had a positive part to play in creating a social framework and in keeping enterprise in check where it might otherwise do injury to the common weal. This change in outlook contributed to the growth of free secondary education, the introduction of insurance against unemployment, old age pensions and other social services: these services were recognized as needs of a thriving community for which it was the responsibility of the state to cater. Direct restrictions on freedom of enterprise also increased. The state defined more narrowly the terms on which business of any kind could be carried on (e.g., in the Factory, Truck, and Marketing Acts). It legislated on maximum hours of work and gave Trade Boards power to fix minimum wages. But at this stage the state rarely sought to *replace* the market; it preferred to re-shape the market conditions, retaining the motive forces of competition through the price mechanism and redirecting it into channels where it would serve the public interest, not clash with it. This meant a recognition that private enterprise did not uniformly promote the public interest; but it also meant a reliance on private enterprise within the leading-strings of legislation. The Bank Charter Act, for example, was not directed against the automatic operation of the money market and intended as a preliminary to a managed monetary system; its object was rather to make the financial system function *more* automatically, but function in the right way. To prohibit the employment of women in coal mines did not affect the ownership and control of the mines but merely ruled out one technique of operation. A protective tariff tilted market conditions more in favour of the industry protected without altering the basis of competition within the industry. The state could both limit the range of permissible activities and encourage desirable activities within that range without violence to the price mechanism or serious limitations on enterprise.

Once the path of control and regulation had begun to be trodden, however, it was difficult to halt. The very idea of social control, in an age of science, had attractions that would have puzzled an earlier generation. The fascination of a system that worked automatically to the advantage both of individual and society gave way to the fascination of a system in which everything was planned in advance by a conscious effort. Those who had been taught to accept the verdict of the market on their services as a thing unalterable, saw the market itself under control. They began to learn that appeal could be made to the state, and that the decision of the state could be swayed in ways that did not operate through the market: by propaganda, by influence with a political party, by obstinacy in a national emergency. There was also less distrust of the government machine: the civil service had ceased to be corrupt, lazy and arbitrary and was capable of assuming wider duties whereas a century earlier its inefficiency and corruption argued powerfully for a limitation of its responsibilities.

The justification of an active economic policy

Government intervention has developed piece-meal, each measure being adopted on its merits and only rarely in order to give effect to some theory of economic organization. No one can claim to have foreseen, much less planned, the present blend of private enterprise and state control, although a mixed system of some sort has long been recognized as desirable and indeed inevitable. The growth of state intervention has to be explained and justified, therefore, at least as much in terms of the practical reasons that have brought it about as in terms of the theoretical arguments by which it can be justified. It is important to distinguish these two lines of approach. It would be quite wrong to suppose that the transformation of capitalism into a managed economy has resulted primarily from a demonstration of its theoretical imperfections; it has resulted far more from everyday necessities. It would also be wrong to suppose that theories of state intervention are always based on a faithful rendering of the kinds of intervention that are in fact practised, of the motives that govern them and the success that they achieve.

War and state intervention

The practical reasons for state intervention include the upheavals of two world wars and the various legacies that these wars have left. A modern war cannot be fought by relying on the price mechanism to mobilize resources effectively; if the economic system has to be geared to winning the war, and not to giving the consumer the highest possible standard of living, some conscious redirection of resources is necessary, and this redirection can be undertaken only by the state, since it is the state that is responsible for the waging of the war. The price mechanism can play an important part in procuring the necessary redistribution of resources; the movement of workers into the munitions trades, for example, can be accelerated by the offer of higher wages, and changes in the pattern of production can be facilitated by corresponding changes in the pattern of prices. But when the sudden and intense scarcities of war-time have to met, it is impossible to rely exclusively on price adjustments: prices would swing too violently, and might get out of control altogether, instead of guiding demand and supply gently towards a new equilibrium. To speed up responses on the side both of supply and demand, compulsion in various forms has to be used; to ensure that the responses are in the right direction and fit into a general economic strategy, the state has to embark on comprehensive planning of production and consumption.

The reasons for intervention do not end when war ends. What can be done in war-time can be done in peace-time: all kinds of inhibitions about the functions of the state have been removed by experience of prolonged state intervention in the course of two world wars. To finance a war, the state is obliged to tax the rich; to prevent disaffection, it has to aim at the maintenance of a minimum standard of living for everyone. Why then should it not turn its weight as powerfully in peace-time in favour of the masses and against the wealthy? The spectacle of easy riches made by profiteering or on the black market weakens respect for private property as an institution. The moral objection to the use of the state to make transfers of income from one set of people to another is deprived of much of its force. The eyes of the disadvantaged have been opened to their power to insist on such transfers; and once a power has been seen to be used, it is not lightly relinquished.

The emergence of a managed economy

Although war gave a fillip to state intervention, the trend towards economic management probably owes more to the deficiencies of the system as revealed between the wars in large-scale unemployment and waste of resources. No one living through those years could fail to absorb the lesson that the economy was not self-regulating. But if it was not, no agency other than the government could regulate it, and assume the responsibility of maintaining continuous full employment. This responsibility could be discharged, according to the ideas of Keynes and others, through the management of demand: that is, by using monetary and fiscal policy so as to regulate the pressure of demand on available resources, especially manpower.

From this point of view, management of the economy was concerned primarily with stabilization policy and with the short-run, since stabilization is by definition a short-run affair. The simultaneous growth of the welfare state involved longer-term aims. It extended the scope of economic management by adding enormously to public expenditure on health, education and housing as well as to social security benefits, pensions, family allowances and transfer payments of all kinds. A further expansion in management resulted from the nationalization of a large sector of industry, which brought under public control what had previously been part of the private sector in form if not altogether in substance.

The growth of the public sector in these various ways posed problems of management more akin to those of a large business. In a country where one man in four is employed by a public authority, public investment exceeds private investment, and the combined expenditure of all public authorities (including the capital expenditure of the nationalized industries) is one-half the size of the national income, the economy has to be managed as a whole and not just as a group of uncoordinated activities. The total impact of public authorities on the rest of the economy is too compelling to be neglected in the calculations of private industry and must itself be the subject of management.

Management of a national economy has to have regard to external as well as domestic balance. One of the major problems of government in a managed economy is to cope with pressures on the economy originating abroad and producing fluctuations in the balance of payments. A whole catalogue of devices, from exchange controls to import quotas and surcharges and agricultural protection, has been used for this reason and these devices have been justified as methods of preserving domestic balance in the face of external imbalance. Whatever may be thought of them, they are evidence of the preoccupation of governments with one of the central problems of economic management: adjustment to external pressures.

Management and planning

Management is not the same thing as planning although the two ideas have much in common. Management can be regarded as adjustment of the affairs of a single enterprise or an entire economy in the light of signals coming from the market while planning involves an effort to change the framework within which market forces operate. The main aim of management is the preservation of short-term balance, whereas comprehensive economic planning is usually designed to bring about long-term structural changes in the economy, often with a view to more rapid economic growth. There are many different forms of planning: indicative planning in France, for example, had little in common with the Soviet Five-Year Plans.

Governments are obliged to engage in some form of planning because they have a revenue to raise, expenses to meet and property to administer: in short, because they have a budget. But they are also responsible for the economic life of the country: they are pledged to maintain full employment; they must try to secure the most effective use of all available resources; they must ensure that adequate provision is made for the future through additions to the stock of capital; they have to give effect, as best they can, to the demand for social justice. Any one of these objectives may involve a great deal of government intervention, and if this intervention is to be successful, the various 'controls' that the government employs must be coordinated, i.e., planned.

Alternative systems of economic planning

In framing its plans the government may follow one or other of two courses. It may allow consumer spending to influence what is to be produced without itself planning production; or it may leave the consumer free to spend his money as he chooses, but only on such products as it allows to reach the market. The first alternative is the one adopted under a system of private enterprise, which confers on a great many individual producers the power to decide how the factors of production shall be employed, but submits these producers simultaneously to the compulsions of the market and the need to find willing buyers at prices to cover their costs. The second alternative involves comprehensive economic planning by the state and the setting of production targets that may bear little or no relation to current market shortages or surpluses.

There is a sharp antithesis between the two systems because the one is organized round market forces and prices and works through incentives of profit and loss, while the other sets out to organize production and supply by administrative decision. In a sense, the one system is the individual consumer writ large while the other is the individual firm writ large. In the one, planning is geared to demand, to the price mechanism, to discovering what consumers want most and letting them have it provided they can pay the price; there is a corresponding emphasis on selling and marketing – an emphasis which offends those critics of market forces who distrust the consumer's power to make sensible decisions under sales pressure. Under the other system, planning is looked at with the eye of a producer – one might almost say an engineer – aiming at an ever-expanding output and not much concerned about the demand for it; the task that is set each unit of production is not how to find a market for the goods that it can produce but how it can carry out its part of the plan, almost irrespective of the level of costs or profits; and the detachment of the plan from any necessary link with the spending of consumers gives to it a dictatorial character, quite apart from any drastic sanctions by which its fulfilment may be secured.

This sharp antithesis is often less acute in practice than it seems in theory. Under a system of private enterprise, there is already a large public sector in which the state is directly responsible for the planning of production and investment. Through taxation, moreover, it can abstract purchasing power from private consumers and apply it to purposes of which they, or rather the electorate, may only vaguely approve when they come to vote at the next election. It may also 'rig' market forces by taxes, subsidies, tariffs, and so on, in order to check some outputs and encourage others, until the result is almost indistinguishable from that obtained by central planning of production. In the last resort, it is because the consumer is also an elector rather than because of any difference in the role of the price mechanism that the two systems remain quite distinct.

Similarly, if one looks carefully at a centrally planned economy one finds that market forces are by no means disregarded and that individual producing units are not simply given a plan and told to carry it out; consumers' wants do influence production and producers still have to sell, if not their output, their view of what the plan for their factory should be. Just because an economic system is centrally planned, we need not assume that it does not respond to consumer values and that the consumer has to take whatever he is given; planners do not always dictate but try also to foresee what consumers will buy. Equally it would be unrealistic to assume that all economic decisions are taken administratively and that what goes on among producers in a centrally planned system does not have a great deal in common with what happens under private enterprise; the plan may reflect what producers are doing and will continue to do in response to prices, costs and market opportunities rather than represent a set of marching orders imposed from outside.

Incentives and compulsion

In war-time the government is able to make many of its plans effective by compulsion and direction. It conscripts men for the Armed Services, it directs workers into jobs which they would not otherwise select, it introduces an array of prohibitions and licences all backed by the force of law in Statutory Rules and Orders. Yet it does not neglect the use of economic incentives. In civil industry men continue to be paid wages related to the value of the work they do; goods continue to be made for sale and to be sold at prices intended to yield a profit. The market continues to function, within narrower limits and subject to more controls, as an agency for coordinating the wants of consumers and the resources available for their satisfaction. Even when the government has complete power over the allocation of raw materials it charges a price for them and generally relates this price to its costs; it uses the market even when it is also using compulsion.

In peace-time, reliance on compulsion is unpopular and the government's plans necessarily rest far more heavily on price incentives. The government may, for example, decide to spend more heavily so as to put more purchasing power in the hands of consumers. No one is compelled to respond, but if there is more money to be had there are likely to be plenty of takers. Compulsion enters as soon as the government brings the other side of its budget into play and imposes fresh taxes: the payment of taxes *is* compulsory. Not, perhaps, in the same sense as direction of labour is compulsory: it is possible to avoid income tax by abandoning any attempt to earn an income above the tax exemption limit, and no one need pay tax on a commodity like tobacco as long as it is possible to exist without smoking.

The British government has not been in the habit of stopping short at the use of price incentives and taxation as its only weapon for securing the fulfilment of its plans. It has rationed consumers, maintained a strict control over imports, allocated raw materials, licensed new building, and prevented workers in industries like agriculture and coal-mining from leaving the industry. All of these involve a partial supersession of the price mechanism, due to a disinclination to rely on prices to bring about the changes desired. Very often, the controls have been used on the grounds of 'shortage'; that is, because it was felt that a rise in price might do very little to speed up an increase in supply and/or might have to be undesirably large to restrict demand to the extent necessary. As the 'shortages' were mastered, the controls were abandoned. Whatever the reason for them, controls spell compulsion. If meat is rationed, it means that no one is allowed to buy more than the ration; if imports are licensed, it means that no one is permitted to import more than the government has decided; and so on.

The mere fact of compulsion need not make us shiver; all law involves compulsion. Moreover, in a democracy compulsion cannot be arbitrary: plans do not pass into law and are not framed by a government unless they would be likely to command a wide measure of approval. But the more extensive the field of economic planning, the greater the temptation to resort to compulsion and either short-circuit or by-pass the market with its free association, freedom of choice and interplay of incentives.

Central economic planning

The case for central economic planning of production rather than planning through the central budget is strongest when it is desired to bring about large or sudden changes in the structure of the economy. The price mechanism, while a valuable instrument for securing marginal adjustments, is comparatively ineffective when the pattern of supply and demand has to be radically or quickly transformed. If the priorities of consumers change abruptly, existing prices will not serve as a guide to the reallocation of resources that is called for; and if market forces are allowed free play, they may effect the necessary changes too slowly and only after violent fluctuations in prices and production. The larger the adjustments to be made and the lower the elasticities of demand and supply the greater is this danger. A sharp rise in prices may set in motion forces that will ultimately cause a bigger adjustment in output than is desired while in the short run the adjustment may be much too small. In those circumstances, the swing in prices is liable to thwart the very approach to new equilibrium of supply and demand which it is its function to promote.

This type of situation is most apparent in war-time when central economic planning is fostered by an independent set of circumstances. It is not merely that priorities suddenly change but that the priorities of civilian consumers are subordinated to a new objective to which only the government can give effect – the objective of winning the war. A single consumer, the government, may be employing half the total reserves of the country directly and be willingly accorded a prior claim on any resources that will assist the war effort. The more wholehearted this effort, the more the government is obliged to plan production in conformity with a single set of priorities laid down by itself for the effective conduct of the war[1].

Planning in underdeveloped countries

The same kind of situation arises where the economic effort of the community is directed, not so much towards satisfying the conflicting wants of a multitude of consumers as towards accomplishing some overriding task such as industrialization. This task imposes priorities of its own which it

[1] Cf. E. Devons, 'Economic Planning in War and Peace', *Papers on Planning and Economic Management* (Manchester University Press, 1970).

may be difficult to reconcile with consumer preferences through ordinary market mechanisms. Direct controls may be necessary in order to speed up industrial growth and assist the coordination of economic activity. These controls short-circuit the price mechanism so as to bring outputs directly into line with the plans of the authorities. Elasticity is obtained, not through spontaneous reactions to price changes, but through administrative measures and compulsions: where the government wants output to expand, it can transfer resources from other, less urgent uses, and where it is not prepared to allow output to expand, it can throttle down demand through rationing and allocation arrangements.

The idea of central economic planning has a particular attraction for underdeveloped countries. There are several reasons for this:

1. In terms of the argument set out above, it is in these countries that large and rapid changes in the structure of the economy are most commonly required.
2. Market forces in many underdeveloped countries work less powerfully than they do in industrial countries; elasticities are lower and the adjustments to price changes are less calculable and continuous.
3. When development takes place, it is more difficult to isolate the change taking place within a single firm from the changes occurring outside it than it usually is in an industrial country. One firm's actions overflow more readily so as to affect other firms. Any new departure in technique may have cumulative effects; any fresh investment may make it significantly easier for existing enterprises to expand; any training of one firm's labour may improve the prospects of attracting other firms. It is more difficult, therefore, to leave development to a number of independent enterprises and more tempting to the government to take in hand a coordinated programme of development.
4. Governments that are anxious to speed up industrialization find it useful to dramatize the process. The preparation of a plan has dramatic appeal. Central economic planning for industrialization usually goes with heavy capital expenditure financed to some extent out of taxation. The government has to show the taxpayer why it needs more money and a plan at least allows it to hold before the taxpayer the prospect of jam tomorrow while the tax-collector gets on with the job of collecting jam today. It can also be argued that one of the main needs in an underdeveloped country is to extend the time horizon and bring home to the average man the social importance of providing for posterity. This a plan helps to do when less drastic action might fail.

The technique of planning

There are four principal aspects of any plan. First there are the objectives which the plan is designed to fulfil. Next there is the time horizon by which it is bounded. Thirdly a plan has to be based on an appreciation of the existing situation and the way in which it is likely to develop. Finally a plan should set forth the measures by which it is intended to take a grip of the situation forecast and mould it so as to realize the stated objectives.

There are many possible objectives of economic planning. They are different in war and in peace, in an industrialized and pre-industrial country, in circumstances of hyperinflation and of slump. But as a rule the two principal objectives are stability on the one hand (including external stability) and growth on the other. The first of these is normally a short-term objective since stability, if achieved, is continuous from one year to the next. The second is necessarily a longer-term objective since economic growth is a fairly gradual process. While the time horizon for a stabilization plan is unlikely to be much above a year, the time horizon for a plan of economic development is likely to be at least three years and may be anything up to seven or ten.

Short-term economic planning is discussed in the next chapter. The stability at which it aims is stability in the pressure on economic resources or, what comes to much the same thing, continuous full employment. It does not aim at stability in the level of economic activity, for there is an underlying upward trend in any progressive economy either because its resources in manpower and capital are expanding or because productivity is steadily rising. This underlying trend means that more can be produced each year without any change in the intensity of employment of available resources.

Short-term planning is based on short-term forecasting. This is a highly skilled activity involving an assessment of the existing economic situation and the changes to be expected in the main elements in effective demand over the coming year or so. The diagnosis of current trends is inevitably complicated by deficiencies in the statistical material, which may not be very up-to-date, is bound to be subject to seasonal and other influences, and usually presents an incomplete and rather self-contradictory picture of what is happening. Separate forecasts have to be prepared of the rate of investment, both public and private, the level of exports; and public expenditure on goods and services as indicated by the budgets of the central government and local authorities. These can be regarded as the major (more or less autonomous) influences on the level of output and income. But the forecast must also embrace the other elements in final demand: the flow of consumer spending and the rate of stock-building. The first must be consistent with a plausible view of the probable course of personal saving; and the second should tally with previous experience in similar circumstances and reflect the degree to which the stock–output ratio diverges from the normal[1].

The forecast, once prepared, allows the government to judge whether effective demand is mounting in relation to current output and creating inflationary pressure, with its accompanying shortages and bottlenecks, or whether effective demand is lagging behind and likely to yield a lower level of employment and income. It is then possible for the government to devise measures, whether budgetary, monetary or administrative, to adjust the pressure of demand and keep it within acceptable limits. The fact that

---

[1] For an elementary treatment of the problems of economic forecasting see A. Cairncross, *Essays in Economic Management* (Allen and Unwin, London, 1971), pp. 122–158. For a discussion of some of the models used see Demand Management (ed. by M. Posner, Heinemann for NIESR, London, 1978), especially Chapter 7 by Professor M. H. Peston.

the measures, in Britain at least, are rarely described as a plan and more commonly as a budget or a 'package' should not conceal the identity between the procedure followed and the procedure characteristic of planning. Indeed, it is hardly too much to say that what really matters in planning is not the periodic preparation of something that can be described as a plan but the continuous practice of forecasting and standing ready to take any necessary measures to secure the major objectives of policy.

Development programmes

Longer-term planning usually aims at accelerating economic growth, although it is only comparatively recently that the two ideas have become closely associated with one another and the extent to which planning does or can accelerate growth remains highly controversial.

There is not much doubt about the desirability of planning public expenditure. Where the expenditure is such that it can be varied at short notice the annual budget is an adequate instrument for this purpose. But most public expenditure is not of this kind and represents a continuing commitment over several years ahead. Expenditure on education and health, for example, cannot be quickly expanded or reduced except within comparatively narrow limits. Similarly defence expenditure, generally the biggest single item, does not lend itself to variations up or down at short notice. To make appreciable changes in expenditure of this kind requires major decisions of policy that are slow to affect the flow of expenditure on current output. Given this inflexibility of public expenditure from year to year, it is obviously necessary to relate decisions about its scale and composition not to the situation expected over the next twelve months but to an assessment stretching over a much longer period. It makes more sense to have a programme or plan of expenditure covering a number of years and registering the commitments that the government has already entered into or expects to have to shoulder during that time. Such a plan not only allows of a more rational allocation of funds between different public services but also makes for consistency between the different schemes being financed: for example, between the plans for school-building and the plans for teacher-training. On the other hand, the plan cannot be a completely firm one unless it is intended that public expenditure should contract out of any adjustments that the government is obliged to make in the management of the economy from year to year.

From planning public expenditure it is a fairly short step to planning the public sector as a whole. The central government, the local authorities, and the industries in public ownership are more likely to keep in step with one another if they are working to a common plan. But – and this can be a very material qualification – the more agencies have to be coordinated and the more diverse their functions, the greater the danger that the effort of planning and coordination will lead to over-centralization and secure consistency at the expense of initiative and enterprise. Where this happens, growth may be jeopardized instead of being promoted. The art of successful planning is to achieve the right balance between centralization and decentralization.

This becomes a point of major importance when planning extends to the whole economy and embraces the private as well as the public sector. The place of the private sector in most long-term plans tends to be highly ambiguous. The public sector, in principle at least (in practice, things are by no means quite so simple), can be made to conform to the plan. But there can be no guarantee that the private sector will do what the plan postulates. Exports, which come almost entirely from the private sector, may not grow at the rate required. The public may not save as much as the plan assumes. One industry may expand too fast and another too slowly. The success of the plan may turn on a big increase in industrial investment and private industry may hang back.

This last possibility is perhaps the most awkward of all. The nub of a development plan is generally the investment programme. But most of the public investment undertaken is not directly productive and helps to accelerate growth only by providing an infrastructure for industrial expansion. The plan may take for granted a concomitant increase in private industrial investment. But no one can be sure in advance that it will take place; and the funds which were assumed to flow into industrial investment may flow instead into property development or out of the country.

The government is by no means powerless in relation to the private sector. It can try to make its plans effective by a whole series of controls – import controls, rationing, building licensing, and so on. It can offer various incentives to industry such as tax concessions, cheap credit, or output subsidies. It may also find industry anxious to be cooperative, happy to share in the preparation of the plan, and willing of its own accord to work for the implementation of the constituent parts of the plan. But when all is said and done, a plan for the private sector has a different significance from a plan for the public sector; and the more rigorously the government tries to control the private sector, or the more eagerly the private sector tries to transform itself into a quasi-public sector, the greater the danger referred to above of over-centralization and a loss of managerial drive.

A long-term plan, like plans to keep the economy in balance, rests on a good deal of economic forecasting. But since the object of a long-term plan is usually to bring about important changes in the economy, not just to preserve balance, the forecasts are dependent on policy decisions. The outcome is a series of programmes reflecting the decisions which, taken together, make up the plan.

The function of a programme is to summarize policy, to register both expectations and decisions, to set out what is likely to be the course of events *taking into account* the action that the government has set or will set on foot. A programme mingles in one set of figures the government's view of what it would like to happen with its consciousness that its powers to influence what will happen are limited. An export programme, for example, might show a rise of only 10% over the next year, although the government would welcome an increase of 20% and would be prepared to take all necessary measures to facilitate the larger increase. The rise of 10% would then reflect the government's assessment of the outcome of the efforts of traders to export, aided or bullied by all the expedients that the government was proposing or had already devised. The programme would be a recognition of the difficulties of bringing about as large and as rapid an increase in exports as the government would like to plan. An export programme constructed on this basis would be quite different from an export *target*. The 'target' might be no more than a calculation of the increase in exports necessary to wipe out a current adverse balance of payments without any indication of the measures by which the increase was to be accomplished, the speed at which it was likely to take place, or the reactions on other sectors of the economy through the employment of additional resources on exports.

The preparation of a development plan is symptomatic of a transformation in the attitude of the state to economic activity. The state is engaged in shaping economic activity, not just in regulating it. It is no longer, for example, in the position of taking the size and distribution of the national income for granted and adjusting its own plans to autonomous changes in the national income. It is itself one of the determinants. The size of the national income, indeed, is one of the first items that the state attempts to plan. The full employment of the country's resources, their allocation between competing claimants, their productivity however allocated, are all objects of state planning and policy. The distribution of the national income is also the subject of direct government decision. It is not merely that about half the national income passes through the hands of the government and that some redistribution of income inevitably takes place in the process. It is also that the government sometimes operates directly on incomes, freezing wages and dividends or entering into something like a compact with trade unionists and employers as to the changes in existing rates of pay that can be treated as compatible with public policy.

Chapter 31

Some problems of economic policy

The most important problem with which economics has to grapple is how to ensure a continuous improvement in the standard of living without wide fluctuations in employment. This calls for full and stable employment of the country's manpower, an enlargement of its stock of productive assets and a progressive improvement in productivity. It calls also for stability in the value of money and this forms a second objective of policy in its own right. A third is to take full advantage of trade with other countries and so obtain a better return from productive effort, but without paying too high a price in instability of employment. A fourth set of problems is associated with the allocation of resources between different uses in the most satisfactory way. Producers have to be given reliable indicators of resource costs and consumer preferences and incentives to respond to those indicators both in deciding what to produce and in the choice of technique when there are alternative methods of combining different resources for a given purpose. This group of problems embraces that of ensuring that new and better techniques will be sought out, experimented with and widely applied. Finally, there are the problems associated with inequality of income and opportunity: the need to relieve poverty and insecurity and to prevent the abuse of economic power.

On the one hand, these problems present themselves in terms of industrial organization: for example, there are the dangers of slackness and inefficiency arising from monopoly and of duplication of effort arising from competition. On the other hand, the problems concern the effectiveness of prices as instruments of allocation: market forces direct resources into channels cut by prices but these may act slowly and harshly in conditions of structural change when an accelerated response, or one that tempered scarcity or over-production, might be brought about by direct controls.

Some of these problems have already been discussed in earlier chapters; a full discussion of them all would take at least another volume. We may, however, pick out for further comment three of the most important: those relating to unemployment, industrial organization and inequality.

Stabilization policy

In a managed industrial economy, the prime aim of economic policy has tended to be full employment. This is not because it takes precedence as an aim over rapid economic growth (although it is perhaps its most important prerequisite); it is largely because there is a body of economic theory that explains how the aim can be achieved. We know comparatively little about the way to faster growth, but we know a good deal about how to get full employment.

Economists brought up in the tradition of Keynes would argue that full employment is matter of demand management. They would dispute Say's Law that supply (or production) creates its own demand (or expenditure) and submit that, with some reservations, and under conditions where there is still some 'slack' in the economy, the truth is the other way round: demand can be relied upon to generate its own supply. By periodically injecting or subtracting purchasing power, governments can regulate the pressure of demand through so-called 'fine tuning'.

Economists holding these views have been forced to recognize, however, that the matter is not quite so straightforward. There are interactions between supply and demand that make it impossible to represent the process of expansion as a smooth progression along a more or less horizontal supply curve of output. An increase in demand pressure will spend itself to *some* extent on rising costs and prices or on increased imports and lower exports rather than on pushing up output; and the more this is expected to happen the more likely it is that it *will* happen. Expectations of inflation may be reinforced by the development of bottlenecks at critical points and by an overflow of these expectations on to the foreign exchange market, with a consequent fall in the exchange rate and rise in import prices. Domestic costs and prices may thus receive an upward jolt at a point in the expansionary process difficult to foresee in advance. The maintenance of full employment can also be complicated by sharp changes in relative prices unrelated to effective demand, as for example when there is a harvest failure or a doubling of oil prices by OPEC.

Other economists go much farther and dismiss 'fine tuning' altogether. Monetarists of different vintages would unite in regarding demand management as illusory. In their view, the private sector of the economy is self-regulating and government intervention would merely aggravate the inescapable, but milder, oscillations that would otherwise occur.

First, we have to examine how demand management works and the problems that arise because employment policy may be in conflict with other parts of the government's policy. We can then go on to discuss the instruments at the government's disposal in seeking to achieve full employment – the budget, monetary policy and administrative controls – and some of the practical difficulties encountered in the use of these instruments.

Demand management and economic potential

To a Keynesian, the object of demand management is to maintain a steady pressure of demand at the highest sustainable level. Given such a steady pressure under conditions of continuous full employment, output will grow from year to year at a rate in keeping with the economic potential of the country. With existing resources and technology, there is a ceiling to the rate of expansion that is sustainable even if everything else goes well (e.g., if there is little or no inflation of prices, the balance of payments does not deteriorate, no important bottlenecks develop, and so on). Since it is unlikely that everything will go well, the actual rate of growth may not reach economic potential except for short periods, but will probably oscillate below it, bumping up against the ceiling from time to time. On the other hand, the ceiling may turn out to be rather elastic and be pushed up by the bumps. If we look back at past rates of growth (in productivity) and find that on the average they do not seem to change greatly from decade to decade so long as full employment or something like it is maintained, we are apt to think of economic potential as equally stable and perhaps equate it with the long-term realized rate of growth. It is as well to remind ourselves, therefore, that the conditions governing economic potential are by no means fixed and unalterable, that they include expectations formed in the light of past rates of growth, and that as growth accelerates economic potential may accelerate too.

We also have to recognize that if employment falls below the level consistent with full economic potential, the drop in output will be larger proportionately than the rise in unemployment. Some of the fall in employment will not show up in higher unemployment but earlier retirement, return of married women to home duties, and so on; while at the same time employers may be slow or reluctant to cut employment in proportion to the drop in output. It is no easy matter to gauge from the conflicting information available at any point in time how much slack there is in the economy and by how much demand could be expanded within the limits of economic potential. Even if this were the sole objective of policy it would need skilful and imaginative management.

Conflicting objectives of demand management

But in fact the government has to take account of other objectives of policy in its efforts to regulate the pressure of demand. There are even times when it may be obliged not to stabilize but actively to destabilize demand. It cannot be assumed that the only source of instability is the behaviour of domestic demand: fluctuations may be communicated from abroad or reflect the militancy of organized labour. In these circumstances governments may elect to restrict demand by domestic deflation so as to reduce the pressure on the balance of payments or on money wages. In the United Kingdom there have been several occasions on which the government has adopted a policy of this kind. There has been an alternation of 'stop' phases followed by spells of 'go' in which demand was allowed to expand again, until another 'stop' was applied. In most other industrial countries there have also been abrupt 'stops' from time to time because of conflicts between the objective of full employment and some other objective of government policy. There is nothing unusual about such conflicts, and it is one of the major tasks of economic management to resolve them satisfactorily.

There are number of conflicting objectives which have somehow to be harmonized in employment policy:

1. First of all, there is the need to reconcile full employment with a reasonable degree of stability in the value of money;
2. This is associated with the need to avoid running into balance of payments difficulties that may interrupt the process of expansion;
3. These objectives will be promoted by an even pressure of demand throughout the economy and thwarted by the emergence of bottlenecks in capacity in particular industries or localized unemployment in particular areas;
4. If full advantage is to be taken of the opportunities of growth and development, the necessary level of investment must be maintained.

(a) Price stability

We have already discussed inflation at some length in Chapter 23. We saw there that different economists have different prescriptions for controlling inflation based on different diagnoses of the causes.

Followers of Keynes would distinguish between demand and cost inflation and prescribe for the latter direct intervention by the government through some form of incomes policy. They would also recommend that, to avoid demand inflation, the pressure of demand should be limited by demand management. This does not mean that there is a straight choice between full employment and the avoidance of inflation, or even that there is a simple trade-off between the two. But it does imply that the danger of inflation is more acute the nearer the approach to conditions of full employment.

Monetarists, on the other hand, have no use for an incomes policy either in principle or on the basis of past experience of such policies. They do not accept the distinction between cost and demand inflation; and they regard long-term steady monetary growth at a pre-determined and published rate as the key to price stability. They are against 'fine tuning' and anxious to limit the discretion of the monetary authorities. They regard any attempt to raise output by monetary expansion as self-defeating. Lowering interest rates will be ineffective, except in the very short run, since as soon as the market becomes aware of the inflationary implications of monetary expansion, heightened expectations of inflation will force interest rates up again in compensation. Fiscal policy will have equally little effect on economic activity unless it involves a faster growth in the money supply. If it does, the effect on production will be transitory. If it does not, increased government borrowing to finance additional expenditure will simply 'crowd out' an equal amount of private borrowing. Thus in strong contrast to the Keynesians, monetarists believe that while in almost every other respect governments are powerless or untrustworthy, they do have it in their power to control inflation.

Experience suggests that it is much more difficult to wring inflation out of an economy once it has taken hold than to keep it within moderate limits from the start. The monetarist route to greater stability can involve serious risks, first to the level of employment, then to the solvency of industrial and (even more serious) financial undertakings, and finally to industrial (and even international) peace. Is there any alternative?

Incomes policy   An alternative exists only if it is possible to operate on prices directly rather than by demand management alone, whether through the use of fiscal policy or monetary targets. Reducing the pressure of demand means increasing unemployment; and unemployment can increase a long way without any marked slowing down in the rate of increase in wages and prices. But there are drawbacks and difficulties in trying to influence wages and prices directly. In particular it means trying to establish a new framework for collective bargaining arrangements.

What changes in the framework of negotiations are called for? The short answer is the adoption of an incomes policy. But since the phrase 'incomes policy' has become a cliché it is necessary to point out that it can mean entirely different things, from an effort to secure voluntary restraint on the part of the trade unions at one extreme, to the statutory fixing of prices and wages by the state at the other. Moreover, while some people think in terms of a series of expedients that are not intended to do more than damp down inflation from time to time, others have in mind some 'final answer' to the problem. For example, some think of a six months' price and wage 'freeze' as an incomes policy, while others think of it as the antithesis of an incomes policy.

There is a further ambiguity. An incomes policy can relate either to money incomes or to real incomes. If it accomplished its purpose of slowing down the rise in money wages all round and to an equal extent, the effect on real incomes would probably be almost entirely transitory. Prices would gradually reflect the reduced pressure on costs and at that stage real wages would return to their previous level. But the average worker has little confidence that this will happen and takes it for granted that incomes policy is designed to restrain a rise in *real* wages. To some extent he may be reassured if some form of price and dividend control is introduced simultaneously. Unless such control is very skilfully administered, however, it is likely either to be largely cosmetic if it does not bite or damaging to efficiency if it does. There is a danger that wage-earners will seek compensation at the expense of profits for sacrifices which they do not make. There is also a danger that when sacrifices *are* called for because the policy is designed to reduce or restrain real wages, the sacrifices will be seen as much larger than they really are.

There is a sense in which the state has always had an incomes policy: that is, a policy about the distribution of *real* income among different social groups. Such a policy was traditionally a budgetary matter rather than one of wage determination and it operated through taxation, welfare services, and so on. If the community wanted low incomes to be increased this meant action in relief of poverty; and poverty (as distinct from low wages) was something to be dealt with through public expenditure on social services. There was a second and quite different approach that might also have been labelled 'incomes policy' and took the form of seeking to alter the play of market forces with a view to obtaining a more advantageous outcome in higher wages. The state itself might take action to strengthen the legal position of trade unions, or set minimum wages as a means of safeguarding the position of weak and disorganized groups of workers. The economic environment within which the trade unions operated was also highly material to their bargaining power. Full employment added to it enormously. The trade unions, with the support of their members (and sometimes under strong pressure from them) could hardly be expected to refrain from taking advantage of this reinforcement. Particular unions cannot afford to claim less than other unions have already obtained: all the more, because they tend to be judged by their members in terms of the cash increase negotiated – which is what the wage bargain is about – rather than the real increase – which registers the outcome of a complex of wage bargains, including the repercussions of each successive bargain on the purchasing power of the money in which the bargain is expressed.

Thus two independent mechanisms affecting the distribution of income are at work simultaneously and independently of one another: one highly effective, over which the trade unions have no control, and another that is more effective in generating inflation than in anything else, in which the trade unions occupy a position of great strategic importance.

It is conceivable that these two mechanisms could be directly linked. This would mean giving the trade unions a say in the macroeconomic bargaining process that takes place through the budget, and would involve an important limitation on the powers of the government to manage the economy as it saw fit. This might be a price worth paying if it guaranteed an end to inflation. But so long as wage negotiations remain fragmented, no pact between the government and the TUC would of itself remove the inherent instability in wage determination. For this usually results from the freedom of individual unions to strike the best bargain they can in the interests of their members; and this freedom cannot effectively be held in check by other unions (or the unions as a group) so long as the rank and file are determined to press their claims. The unlimited powers of minority groups to strike in support of pay increases may operate as the principal and enduring source of cost-inflation. When it does so, it may be necessary to qualify that power. But this obviously raises political problems of the first order and requires some form of reassurance as to the circumstances in which the exercise of industrial bargaining power will be limited. This reassurance has to go back in the end to acceptance of the equity of existing arrangements, and hence to the macroeconomic mechanism governing the distribution of income. If there is no direct link, there has, at least, to be some indirect link between the two mechanisms.

It is clear that the handling of cost-inflation takes us well beyond the realms of pure economics and raises problems in several allied disciplines, not least politics and sociology. But the economist has a responsibility to put forward suggestions on the basis of his knowledge and experience. He can at least help to guide public opinion, or any agency set up to give a lead to public opinion, by sifting the facts, applying agreed criteria and pronouncing on the public interest in individual cases.

(b) External balance

Some of the most acute dilemmas of policy arise in trying to reconcile the requirements of the domestic situation with the need to maintain external balance. There are three contingencies against which it is particularly necessary to provide: in each case a disturbance in the balance of payments poses a threat to domestic stability. First of all, the country's competitive position may be weakened in relation to that of other countries so that, at the current rate of exchange, exports fail to keep pace with imports. Secondly, a sharp recession abroad may reduce the market for exports and throw men out of work, first in the export trades and later in other industries. Thirdly, a movement of capital may drain away the country's reserves without any simultaneous change in the domestic market.

(1) A decline in competitive power   The first situation is one that should normally be dealt with by depreciating the currency and holding money incomes steady. Depreciation will help to restore the country's competitive position whether it is deteriorating because of a more rapid increase in prices than in other countries, or because of a less rapid increase in productivity. The fall in the rate of exchange will tend to make exports cheaper abroad and imports dearer at home and so help to bring the two into balance. Since the cost of living will have risen while money incomes have not, the level of real income will be somewhat reduced (relatively at least to the normal upward trend – it may be sufficient to mark time for a year). If the country seeks to avoid this reduction in real income, depreciation will bring only transitory advantages: money incomes, including wages, will follow prices up and the competitive advantage of a lower rate of exchange will be wiped out.

The first type of situation may arise, not because of a divergence in costs and prices from costs and prices in other countries, but because of an increase in income and employment. The rate of exchange that keeps exports and imports in balance when unemployment is at 10% is not likely to be the rate appropriate to conditions of full employment. Even if costs are comparable with costs elsewhere, it may be necessary to make imports less attractive and to give exports an additional stimulus, in order to prevent the increased purchasing power of the home market from flowing too heavily towards imported goods or goods that might be exported.

If a country is unwilling to depreciate under pressure of a persistently adverse balance, it has three possible courses of action. The first is to abandon the struggle to maintain full employment and deflate. This will allow it to bring its accounts into balance at a lower level of activity, with less income, lower imports and more unemployment. This is a desperate solution: but if countries are not prepared in an emergency to accept some check to the growth of real income – such as tends to follow depreciation and an adverse movement in the terms of trade – it is what may easily happen. The second course of action is to live on its reserves and on foreign borrowings in the hope that, given time, the balance of payments will begin to pull round. This course is only possible, however, if reserves are large and if the country's credit is sound.

A third line of action is to limit imports by quotas or 'quantitative restrictions'. These restrictions, so long as they do not react on exports, will reduce the payments to be made to other countries without any need to alter the relative price of imports and exports. The government simply decides that the country can no longer afford to buy certain things (or more than a certain amount of them) and takes steps to prevent them from entering the country. There are important disadvantages to this way of putting things right. It inflicts an arbitrary injury on the trade of other countries and may provoke retaliation. It is obviously not very appropriate if the root of the trouble is that the country's prices are getting steadily out of line with prices abroad, so that more and more imports would have to be restricted or banned in an effort to make ends meet. While it provides a powerful instrument to reinforce either or both of the first two courses of action, when the restrictions are eventually withdrawn their effects are reversed, so that they are worth while only if maintained for a considerable time.

(2) A decline in demand abroad   The first type of situation is dangerous because of the financial pressure which it exerts; the second type of situation does not merely threaten unemployment but causes it. Workers lose their jobs in the export industries and if no action is taken unemployment will spread to industries making for the home market. The action that the state can take depends first on the state of its reserves. If it has large reserves it can ignore the loss of foreign exchange as its exports fall, and create additional purchasing power without fear that this will aggravate an already serious balance of payments problem. If it has only moderate or low reserves it will not be able to pursue an expansionist policy without first restricting imports. The quickest way of restricting imports is by quantitative limitation. In a major depression this is one of the weapons that the state will almost inevitably use, but it is a weapon to be used with care. If every country uses quantitative restrictions, each will merely add to the others' difficulties; but if the restrictions are concentrated on imports from countries with a large favourable balance (while other countries are exempt) this will help to bring creditors and debtors more quickly into balance and allow the debtors to maintain trade with one another instead of being obliged to make cuts over the whole of the trade. Such discrimination against the countries with a credit balance, however, is not likely to be welcomed in those countries, especially if they are already wrestling with unemployment problems of their own. It will be desirable to have their agreement to such discrimination on the grounds that, since they are free from balance of payments anxieties, they are in the best position to pursue an expansionist policy. By pressing on with such a policy, they can give international trade an upward thrust that will help to remove the grounds for discrimination against them.

The scope for quantitative limitations depends upon the structure of a country's imports and the controls over consumption that it already uses or could institute. It is not necessarily sufficient, for example, to stop importing luxuries, for these may be a small fraction of the total or obtained from countries that would have no option but to retaliate if their markets were cut off. It may be necessary to limit imports of foodstuffs and ration them; or to allocate imported raw materials. A further problem arises from the supposed temporary character of the slump in exports. Quantitative restrictions are protective and, like tariffs, are easier to impose than to remove. When the slump ends, an assortment of new industries may have come into being under cover of arrangements originally designed to effect an emergency cut in imports. Fresh arrangements (e.g., higher tariffs) may confirm these industries in the protection they enjoy, and as they are not likely to be export industries, international trade will undergo an enduring contraction.

(3) Capital flows   There may be an outflow of short or long-term capital, involving a transfer from sterling (to take the example of Britain) to other currencies. The outflow may be due to distrust of sterling or it may be due to higher rates of interest or higher yields on investment abroad. Where the cause is lack of confidence a rise in interest rates will help to check the outflow only to the extent that higher interest rates are interpreted as a demonstration that the authorities will take decisive action to maintain the value of the currency. Where the cause is a disparity in the return on capital, however, a rise in interest rates can remove the disparity and stop the outflow. The disadvantage of such a remedy is that it condemns the monetary authorities to aligning their rates with rates in foreign money markets when credit conditions in Britain may make it appropriate to pursue a different policy. There may be good reasons for not making money dearer in Britain when rates are rising abroad.

The same line of argument applies, *mutatis mutandis*, to capital inflows. These may occur for reasons quite unconnected with domestic economic policy or the domestic economic situation: for example, because of uncertainties about the exchange parities of other countries. The inflows may be on a very large scale and may distort money market conditions in spite of efforts by the central bank to 'sterilize' them. With floating rates of exchange, capital inflows might be discouraged because the rate would be temporarily forced up as capital flowed in until fear of a subsequent drop in the rate halted the inflow altogether. But such undesired fluctuations in exchange rates can be just as unsettling to the domestic economy as undesired variations in interest rates or money market conditions.

It might seem that an easier solution would be to control capital movements. In fact, however, control is by no means easy. Quite apart from any evasion of regulations, there is always a large volume of commercial credit outstanding in favour of exporters or due by importers, and if there is any distrust of sterling or large differential in interest rates between London and other centres there is no obstacle to an acceleration of payments in one direction and a delay of payments in the other ('leads and lags') so as to increase the net credit due in foreign currencies[1]. This increase represents a net loss to the reserves since more foreign exchange has to be paid out and less is paid in. There is presumably some limit to a shift of commercial credit of this kind but it can be sufficiently large to alarm other holders of sterling and start off a withdrawal of banking and other funds held in London.

While there are various technical devices by which credit policy can be to some extent insulated from credit policy in the other leading financial centres, the fact remains that so long as there is any freedom of movement of international credit and capital, a persistent movement in interest rates in one centre restricts the freedom of action of the authorities in other centres, particularly if they maintain fixed rates of exchange.

---

[1] British importers will make payments more promptly in sterling because they expect foreign currencies to become dearer and exporters will delay bringing back earnings of foreign exchange for the same reason. An interest differential exercises a similar effect by bringing more money to the London market and inducing holders of London funds to move them elsewhere.

The need for international action   All this is on the assumption that each country has to act on its own. If the major countries take joint action, however, the problem can be greatly eased. Two or three countries have it in their power, by maintaining stability in their own economy, to make full employment an attainable goal for most of the others; if the big countries fail, the others will almost certainly fail, too. The efforts of international agencies and concerted action by the leading countries can do more to remove the danger of unemployment than the single-handed efforts of each.

(c) Avoidance of bottlenecks

The greater the pressure of demand, the greater the danger that it will bear unevenly on the available resources and create acute shortages in some directions while there are still surpluses in others. In such a situation, there may be demands for higher wages based on the shortage of labour in some areas and industries while localized unemployment persists in others. There are likely also to be sharp increases in the prices of some products which may threaten the stability of prices generally. To allow demand to increase further would be to intensify the lack of balance in the economy without initially absorbing the surpluses. What is required in such circumstances is action to divert demand away from the bottlenecks to products for which there is still some unused capacity and to districts in which there are pockets of unemployed labour.

Such action is not easy; and without some leverage from the price mechanism it is likely to be futile. A rise in prices where there is a bottleneck helps to divert the demand of consumers to substitute products and a rise in costs in districts where labour is scarce helps to direct orders more quickly to other districts. It is a mistake, therefore, to try to prevent *any* response of this kind in relative prices. But there is little to be gained and a great deal to be lost if the swing in prices and costs is violent. If the lack of balance seems unlikely to be enduring, the government, being itself a large consumer, may be able to switch some of its orders so as to relieve the pressure or it may allow or encourage additional imports for the same purpose. If the lack of balance appears to be more deep-rooted, it can offer financial and other inducements to firms that are prepared to create capacity in the appropriate areas and industries. In dealing with localized unemployment it can offer to build factories on behalf of firms willing to establish themselves in the areas affected and limit factory-building elsewhere. In the same way, it can try to alleviate industrial bottlenecks by encouraging or subsidizing expansions in capacity. But no *quick* results can generally be hoped for from intervention along any of these lines and the total result, even in the long run, is often disappointing.

(d) Control of investment

In the management of demand, the government has to some extent a choice between operating on investment or on consumption. It might seem natural to pick on investment as the more unstable of the two. But it is often difficult to act on investment, especially private investment, except through consumption. A large part of investment takes place in response to fluctuations in consumption, as we have already seen in discussing the accelerator principle[1]. Moreover, investment is rarely the outcome of an instantaneous decision. It may need careful consideration extending over a long period of time; and even after the decision is taken little spending may take place for several months while land is being acquired, tenders prepared, and orders placed.

Apart from organizational difficulties, investment does not lend itself to quick changes. This is particularly true of many forms of public investment. Some kinds of construction simply cannot be postponed (for example, the building of warships or the replacements of condemned bridges); others can be postponed only at the risk of a public outcry (slum clearance, for example); others again must, once commenced, be carried through to completion, boom or no boom (major schemes of road improvement, bridge building, the construction of docks, harbours, electric power stations, and so on). Moreover, it is not always easy for a local authority or a central government to foresee its requirements over the next five or ten years, since new duties may be imposed upon it, new types of equipment may become available, and changes may take place in the size and kind of population for which it has to provide. Plans which have been prepared in advance, therefore, may prove to be in need of complete revision just when it would be desirable for such plans to be implented at once.

On the other hand, consumption responds quickly to fiscal changes, whether on the side of taxation or government expenditure. In Britain, for example, the government can make use of the regulator to reduce indirect taxation across the board by up to 10%, and this can have a powerful influence on consumer spending within a matter of weeks. Action on government expenditure can be equally effective if, for example, it takes the form of a change in pensions, family allowances, unemployment benefit, and so on. Action to limit consumer credit through hire purchase restrictions is also highly effective in checking or stimulating sales of consumer durables. It is in fact *too* easy to operate on this last element in demand, since it unbalances a few industries in which stable market conditions are particularly important, and subjects them to wider swings in demand than would otherwise occur.

The strength of the case for operating on consumption is that this is by far the largest segment of total economic activity. The proportionate size of the check or stimulus required is correspondingly smaller, and any harmful side-effects less pronounced.

But of course if the object of employment policy is to achieve stability at the highest sustainable rate of growth, there can be no presumption that government action should concentrate exclusively on consumption. This would be highly paradoxical if consumption was inherently stable and the sources of instability lay in investment or the trade balance. The object of the government must be to find the most effective means of stabilizing demand, *taking into account* the long-term as well as the short-term consequences of stabilization policy.

[1] Above, pp. 305–307.

Rapid growth and high investment

Even if demand is stable and sufficient to preserve full employment, the government has still to decide whether it should try to change the balance between investment and consumption in the interests of faster growth. It is not easy to judge how far economic growth could be accelerated if a larger proportion of current income were saved and invested. But where there is clear evidence that capital is an important limiting factor, the state may decide that it should relieve the shortage and take special steps to encourage investment. This means that it may have to offer tax and other inducements to private industry or prod the nationalized industries to increase the size of their investment programmes. Very often it means no more than that policy should be directed to ensuring that savings are adequate to finance the desired volume of investment – for example, by running a large budget surplus – or that it should be willing to permit borrowing abroad, or if necessary, borrow itself.

The problem is not just one of seeing to it that total investment is high but rather of ensuring that it is high in those sectors of the economy where it is essential to rapid development. It is a mistake, therefore, to treat the problem purely in terms of budget surpluses, foreign borrowing, and so on; encouragement may have to be given to particular forms of investment while others are delayed or discouraged. Policy will also differ according to whether the areas of heavy investment lie in the public or in the private sector of the economy. In some countries an active investment policy automatically involves the government in raising additional capital, and this may pose awkward financial problems that would take quite a different shape if the capital were being raised by private concerns.

The government, for example, would have to raise the money by the issue of bonds at fixed rates or interest while private industry would be likely to rely mainly on issues of equities. Similarly, in an underdeveloped country, high investment in the public sector may be particularly urgent in order to improve the transport system and lay the foundation for later development: such investment, in view of the absence of an organized capital market, would be far more likely to lead to foreign borrowing than an equal amount of private investment in, say, commercial property.

Savings and investment are no longer matters for private persons only. The state can exercise a major influence on both. If the public is too thrifty the state can be 'unthrifty' and let the national debt take up the public's savings. Similarly with investment. An ever larger proportion of investment is undertaken by the state or by bodies prompted or controlled by the state. Thus it is by administrative decision rather than by reference exclusively to interest rates and prospective yields that investment is coming to be determined. This of itself helps to stabilize investment. But it also puts on the state an added responsibilty for judging what level of investment is socially desirable in order to maintain stability and at the same time promote further growth.

Policy instruments

In pursuit of these conflicting objectives of policy, governments can make use of three main instruments of policy: the budget; monetary policy; and a variety of administrative controls. These may be used either separately or in combination. Let us take them in turn.

Budgetary policy

Until a generation ago, it was almost universally held that the budget ought to be kept in balance in all circumstances and that unbalanced budgets were inherently wrong. In view of the proneness of governments to overspend, this may have been no bad rule in ordinary circumstances, especially at a time when the central government was a relatively small element in total demand. So long as the economy was in balance or did not depart from balance, there was no need to unbalance the budget and indeed to have done so would have been to unbalance the economy. But in conditions of boom or slump, when the economy was out of balance, the budget offered a means of redressing the balance of private spending and saving by an appropriate shift in the balance between public spending and saving. Not that such an idea was in fact advocated at a time when the very existence of the trade cycle had yet to be discovered, and economic fluctuations were still thought of in terms of panics and crises. Even if fiscal weapons had been employed to stabilize economy activity, they might well have been comparatively ineffective so long as the flow of central government revenue and expenditure remained a very small fraction of GNP as was true in peace-time in the nineteenth century. The smaller the budget, the bigger must be the variation in the flow of revenue or expenditure to offsct a given swing in the pressure on resources generated by private demand (including demand for exports and capital formation as well as for consumer goods).

Whatever may have been true under nineteenth-century conditions when it would have been natural to rely primarily on monetary policy as an economic stabilizer, the expanding role of the government in the twentieth century makes the use of fiscal weapons indispensable since the budget is the natural means for harmonizing the spending plans of public authorities and private households (taking into account fluctuations in business outlays on capital equipment and structures and any unwelcome gap that is in prospect between imports and exports and goods and services).

Nevertheless, the maxim that the budget ought to be balanced is still widely held, usually because false analogies are drawn with behaviour in private life or in business. In a democratic community this may limit or condition the use of fiscal weapons since without public understanding and support governments hesitate to act.

On top of this, there is a great deal of confusion as to what precisely is meant by balancing the budget. For example, is a budget only in balance if the government does not have to borrow money? Does this hold even for borrowing to finance the building of power stations? If they are excluded what about roads? Or a war? If the government can borrow for these purposes without giving rise to a deficit is there some other kind of borrowing for other purposes that does correspond to a deficit?

The fact is that budgetary balance is highly ambiguous and depends on the conventions used in presenting the constituent items on both sides. In the United States, for example, there are three quite different ways of measuring a budget deficit that have been given official recognition. First comes the cash deficit – the excess of cash payments to the public over receipts from the public – irrespective of the way in which the deficit is covered by borrowing. The second definition is in national income terms: it excludes transactions in existing assets (e.g., sales of land) and is on an accruals basis rather than a payments basis (expenditures are recorded as goods are delivered rather than when they are paid for). Yet a third definition brings in social security and other payments and receipts which do not form part of the administrative budget but lie within the control of the government.

To an economist these alternative measurements are much less important than a calculation of the economic impact of the budget designed to show whether the proposed changes in the flow of government expenditure and revenue over the coming year will be expansionary or contractionary and if so, by how much. An economist would attach even more importance to an assessment of the economic consequences of the *changes of policy* introduced in the budget, and would try to evaluate the net expansionary effect of these changes in, say, six or twelve months' time.

These changes in what is usually referred to as 'fiscal stance' can be measured by comparing the expected surplus or deficit provided for in the budget with the surplus or deficit that would accompany an unchanged level of employment. If this level was higher than the level of employment allowed for in the budget, tax revenues (at existing rates of tax) would also be higher and there would be some diminution in governmental disbursements (e.g., on unemployment benefits). The change in the constant employment surplus (or deficit) from one year to the next would provide a more accurate guide to the change in fiscal stance than would a comparison between successive budgets presented to Parliament.

The constant employment surplus makes it easier to judge how far a change in the budget surplus or deficit reflects deliberate government policy rather than a fluctuation in the level of activity. But it does not tell us what effect the change in 'fiscal stance' so revealed will have on the economy. Governments continue to present their budgets as if the size of the cash surplus or deficit was all that really mattered and economists holding monetarist views would probably agree with them. There is rarely any published attempt to evaluate the full economic effects of changes in taxation or expenditure or to assess the speed with which these effects will show themselves, if only because calculations of this kind are bound to be open to dispute. Nobody really knows with any precision what the impact of a particular budget will be.

Moreover, different ways of spending the same sum have quite different effects on employment and output. If additional government expenditure is on pensions, there may be a simple transfer from the taxpayer to the pensioner with little or no change in employment. Similar expenditure on new road construction would immediately add to the level of employment even if paid for out of taxation rather than borrowed funds (the spending of those who were newly employed offsetting the reduction in spending by taxpayers). An increase in corporation tax has quite different effects from an increase in tobacco duty. And so on. The translation of flows of revenue and expenditure into demands on resources is not something that can be done unequivocally and automatically. Assessment of the economic effect of budgetary changes is inevitably a rough and ready affair.

Monetarists would argue that the main significance of the budget lies in its effect on the money supply. They would treat expenditure financed by long-term borrowing as non-inflationary even if the size of the government's borrowing requirement was high; but a cash deficit they would regard in a quite different light, whatever the make-up of total revenue and total expenditure. They might also be concerned that a large public sector borrowing requirement (PSBR) would create financial difficulties for the government and tempt it to refrain from seeking to finance all of it through the capital market. But their main emphasis would be on the need to concentrate on the monetary impact of fiscal policy while Keynesian economists would regard this as subordinate to the effect on effective demand.

All this may reasonably suggest that those who make use of fiscal weapons are in some doubt as to the outcome of their use. But one should not push scepticism too far. There have been plenty of illustrations of the successful use of fiscal policy to stimulate or curb expansion and governments can usually form a fairly accurate picture of what is called for, even if they can never be quite certain how fast the medicine will work or whether the dose will prove excessive.

Fiscal weapons have the advantage of great flexibility since they make it possible to inject additional demand in a wide variety of ways so that the stimulus (or curb) can be applied to different sectors of the economy and so as to take effect quickly or over a considerable period of time. The budget furnishes not just one weapon but a whole armoury of weapons that can be combined to promote several different aims of policy simultaneously.

It must be admitted that there are also considerable limitations to the use of fiscal weapons. They may bring with them large and unwelcome changes in the money supply that complicate the task of the authorities both in the short run and, more obstinately, when the time comes to change direction. There may be long lags between budgetary decisions and the reflection of these decisions in economic activity, so that what seemed sensible at the time proves ill-advised in the event. In many countries there is the further difficulty that tax changes cannot be made between budgets: the most appropriate fiscal weapons may then only be brought into use intermittently and at intervals too long for efficient management of the economy. Then there is the political problem of obtaining parliamentary approval both for what may be called 'the budget judgement' and for each and every element in the budget itself: acceptance first of the net change in economic pressure at which the budget aims and at the same time – what is by no means the same thing – acceptance of the individual tax and expenditure proposals that are designed to produce that change.

Monetary policy

Let us turn next to monetary policy which has a much longer history as an instrument of economic control. Monetary forces used to come into play almost automatically to check expansion or contraction. Expansion, for example, put increased pressure on the money supply and at the same time helped to throw the balance of payments into deficit and set up a drain on the gold reserves which led to a curtailment of the money supply and increased pressure on sources of finance.

Although monetary forces are not allowed to operate in quite this way nowadays, there is a common feeling that there ought to be a more automatic mechanism for checking inflation and deflation; and it is the semi-automatic characteristic of monetary forces that makes some people argue in favour of greater reliance on monetary weapons. Sometimes this attitude reflects little more than distrust of governments, but it is usually also associated with disenchantment with the use of fiscal policy or with disbelief in the potency of fiscal measures.

At the purely technical level there is still plenty of controversy about how monetary policy actually operates. There are, however, one or two points on which there would be fairly widespread agreement.

First of all, if monetary and fiscal policy are being used in combination with one another, they are more likely to be effective if they are pulling in the same direction than if they are pulling in opposite directions. But since the two kinds of policy serve different purposes there are bound to be times when to some extent they pull against one another. For example, monetary conditions abroad may make it desirable to maintain tight money at the same time as slackness in the labour market points to the need for a stimulus administered through the budget.

Secondly, no one familiar with monetary history would ever dispute that monetary policy can be extremely powerful. What is open to dispute is whether the resolute use of monetary policy would have consequences that are both unnecessary and undesirable. For example, pressure on liquidity may conceivably have relatively modest effects on demand until things build up to a liquidity crisis with consequences for economic activity and business solvency of a quite different order.

Thirdly, monetary policy tends to have strong directional effects. It tends to operate by cutting off or seriously curtailing the flow of credit to particular types of borrower. For example, in 1966 it was very apparent in the United States from the big drop in housing starts that private housebuilding was particularly vulnerable to tight money conditions. It has always been accepted that smaller firms, with few alternative sources of finance outside the banking system, are more affected than larger firms with access to a wider range of facilities.

Fourthly, there is no way of avoiding having a monetary policy since monetary conditions are changing all the time and inaction on the part of the monetary authorities is just as much an expression of policy as actual intervention. Money markets are functioning continuously and monetary policy cannot therefore be an intermittent affair like fiscal policy with action held up for many months at a time by the need for parliamentary approval. In other words, monetary policy does not lend itself to detailed political control but requires the devolution on the monetary authorities of very wide responsibilities. This does not mean that things are left to the central bank since central banks act in increasingly close conjunction with Ministries of Finance. But it does mean that there is usually more flexibility in the use of monetary weapons than of fiscal.

Administrative controls

A third means of regulating demand is by administrative devices such as licensing, rationing, and so on. But these devices are not very useful in checking *total* demand unless they are used on a vast scale: and even then, they are highly inefficient because they give rise to queues, black markets, and so on. They can play a useful but modest part in special circumstances when the pressure on the economy is particularly acute at a limited number of points, for example in the building industry. When this happens, the inflation of demand in a single industry may increase costs there in a way that affects the whole of the rest of the economy and leads to a general cost inflation when the economy would otherwise remain in reasonable balance. Experience shows, however, that except in war-time when there may be serious shortages of specific materials, rationing devices are not only clumsy but ineffective. In the case of the building industry, which is perhaps the most obvious candidate, the public sector is itself the source of a large part of the demand on the industry and it should be as easy to exercise control by limiting orders from public authorities as by introducing a system of licensing calculated to bear almost exclusively on the private sector.

There may in addition be various ways in which the government can influence specific forms of activity by tax allowances, subsidies, etc. In principle, for example, it should be possible by varying investment grants or investment credits to influence the level of investment, and various experiments have been conducted, notably in Britain and Sweden, in accordance with this principle. It is not very clear, however, how far the action taken by the government (in Britain at any rate) has been successful in influencing the volume or timing of investment as part of a general programme designed to stabilize demand.

Deficiencies of economic information

Given these instruments, the government next requires to arm itself with the information necessary for their proper use. But here it encounters a problem fundamentally different from that facing anyone seeking to control the natural world. It has to reckon with the fact that it does not know and never can know exactly what is happening either at the moment when it is happening or indeed much later. It can never identify all the economic forces currently at work – only those whose operation is reflected in statistics of the past. In deciding what measures of control to take it is inevitably out-of-date, ignorant and uncertain.

This is so for a number of reasons. First of all, the information available relates to a period which may be several weeks or months or even years back. It takes a long time for these statistics, collected from individual producers or consumers, to be aggregated, processed and fed through a bureaucracy to those on whom rests the responsibility of seeking to manage the economy. For example, they cannot possibly tell until long afterwards what is happening to productivity in the sense at least of the steady improvement from year to year in the average efficiency of industry on which it is possible to reckon in the normal industrial country. It is rare to know with any degree of accuracy the changes taking place in the level of output and employment and still harder to form a judgement of the forces lying behind any apparent change of trend.

Even information that seems at first sight to be entirely reliable may turn out subsequently to be totally misleading because, after fuller consideration, the original figures are substantially altered. This has happened on several occasions in the United Kingdom and it happens in the United States as well. One example is that of the statistics of British exports which were suddenly increased retrospectively by 2–3% because it emerged that exporters were no longer filing returns as faithfully as they had done earlier. An error of 2–3% may seem small, but it may make all the difference between a balance of payments surplus and a quite substantial balance of payments deficit.

Moreover, even when the figures undergo no change they may come to have a quite different significance when taken in conjunction with other information. Without any change in the basic information relating to the production of steel, electric power, textiles, etc., the statisticians may suddenly announce that what previously looked like an increase in total production was in fact a decrease because they feel obliged to change the relative weights attached to different outputs or to make different seasonal adjustments to the data, or for some other reason such as fuller information about changes in prices, or a different allowance for the outputs of smaller firms not making returns. The longer one handles economic information the more apparent it becomes that what are at first sight hard facts are not hard at all but of a degree of softness at which one is obliged to guess.

The picture that one forms from the available information has also to take into account inconsistencies in the statistical data where by definition no inconsistencies ought to arise. It is well known that there are three ways of measuring the total volume of economic activity: from the side of output; from the side of income; and from the side of expenditure. In principle these three systems of measurements should yield the same result but they never do. It is quite easy to find a year in which one measure rises, another falls and a third shows little or no change in either direction. The fact that statisticians, faced with this problem, seek to evade it by adding up the three figures and treating their average as their last word on the subject does not make for much confidence in their verdict. There are plenty of other examples of this sort of thing with just as little chance of establishing once and for all which figures are right and which wrong.

Economic development complicates control

All this is very distressing to anyone seeking to exercise precise control over the economy because it means that no one can say without fear of contradiction what has been happening, is happening and is likely to happen. Economists are in fact in a position like that of historians rather than in the happier position of natural scientists. Not only are they working with limited data that can be made to support alternative hypotheses, but the events which they are seeking to interpret are unique and by their nature non-recurrent. The economic system, unlike the natural order, does not stay still and repeat itself; it changes through time and our awareness of the changes that are taking place necessarily lags behind the event.

Hence it is not possible to work with fixed parameters and identify by a process of closer approximation each of the relationships governing the behaviour of the system as a whole. Even the inclusion of a trend term does not overcome this difficulty since the economic system need not evolve in some inherently predictable way as new elements are introduced into the system by technological development, population changes, political conflict, and so on.

The contribution of economic analysis

Against these limitations on our power to control the economy – weaknesses in the instruments of control, deficiencies in the available information, dependence on popular support for the action proposed – must be set the great advances in economic analysis over the past generation. We now have what we did not have in 1929 – an intellectual apparatus with which to face fluctuations in the economy. We are more alive to the questions that need to be asked, the information that needs to be collected and the methods by which statistical information can be made to yield useful results. We know a great deal more about what is going on in the economy and about what to do about it. We have, for the first time, trained staffs of economists whose job it is to help governments to get ahead of events through the preparation of systematic economic forecasts.

The greatest single gain is in the more scientific character of economic analysis. Efforts to regulate activity now rest on unifying concepts which at least provide a calculus of action. One can reduce the forces operating on demand to a common denominator and express their interactions in terms of a series of equations or so-called economic model. Econometrics – an entirely new branch of economics – can be used to assign values to the parameters and enable us to estimate how an initial change in any one element of demand will affect the other elements and in turn the level of demand in the aggregate. Rough calculations can then be made of the probable outcome of particular governmental measures, subject of course to a wide margin of error, both as to the time over which these effects will show themselves, and the degree of reliability of the forecast. We can add up what the government is doing in all kinds of different ways and express the answer in terms of a single variable – the expected net change in pressure on the economy.

Control of industry

The relationship between the state and industry rests partly on expediency, partly on broad issues of principle. Of the issues of principle the one which has given rise to most controversy (except, perhaps, amongst economists, who have rarely worked themselves into much of a passion over it) is nationalization.

Nationalization

The case for nationalizing an industry can be rested either on the local circumstances of the industry or on the more universal grounds of social philosophy. Until some years ago the arguments commonly advanced fell mainly under the second heading. It seemed natural to many people that if private enterprise was unsuccessful or unjust as an economic system, the state should step in and run industry instead. This would have meant wholesale nationalization, not selective nationalization of particular industries.

There was a good deal of black and white in the background to this point of view and not much grey. It implied, for example, a sharp antithesis between full state ownership and control and private enterprise without government control; it dwelt on the defects of the one without developing any theory of how the other could function or the difficulties that it would be likely to encounter. It assumed that there was no other way of remedying the defects of the capitalist system: of maintaining full employment, reducing social inequality, and controlling monopoly. It was sometimes linked with the idea of confiscation as a means of 'soaking the rich'; this puts the stress on the *ownership* of capital. At other times it was linked with the idea of workers' control and syndicalism – of handing over each industry to the men engaged in it; this put the stress on the *control* of capital. Other ideas were also associated: the idea that the state should have more control over the economic system and be able to plan it without having to face the opposition of existing owners or alternatively allowing them uncovenanted benefits in order to have its way; the idea that it was less degrading for men to work in the service of the state than for the private profit of the capitalist; and so on.

There is no doubt that although some of these ideas are now less fashionable, they are still widely entertained. Nationalization enjoys the backing of egalitarian sentiment even when full compensation is paid; the fact that it does nothing to promote social equality is submerged by the memory that it was once advocated on those grounds. Politicians still talk of 'citadels of power' when they already exercise at least as much control over an industry as they can hope for after nationalization. Workers still assume that they will enjoy more say in the running of a nationalized industry even when it is operated on commercial lines with instructions from the state to cover its costs (including interest charges)[1]. But opinion lags a long way behind recent developments. The fact is that the state (in Britain at least) could bring about nearly all the changes in industry that it could desire by using the powers that it already possesses or could readily assume. Nationalization *en masse* is largely an irrelevant issue; the real issue is what the state would like industry to do and what controls are necessary for that purpose.

When we come down from the high plane of social philosophy to the selection of particular industries as candidates for nationalization, the

---

[1] This feeling is well illustrated by the Durham miner who complained bitterly that what he wanted was 'nationalization and no more state interference', and the Scottish miner who told a fellow citizen that the mines 'are no yours, they're oors'.

problem becomes one of deciding what degree of control over an industry is necessary in the public interest and what form it should take. There are some industries where a strong case can be made. It can be argued, for example, that the British coal industry was in need of the kind of jolt given to it by the *act* of nationalization and that, in private hands, there would have been insufficient investment of capital to maintain efficiency, or bad labour relations at a time when these could not be afforded. It can be argued also that it was right to nationalize the railways because the state makes great use of them in emergency, cannot afford to see their rolling stock and other equipment deteriorate, or might wish to sink money in fresh capital expenditure on them in times of slump, when private companies might be hesitant about their future. Nationalization of some industries, that is, can be defended on strategic grounds; or as relieving a long-standing antagonism between employers and employed; or as giving the state more room for manoeuvre in controlling capital expenditure. It may also be the most appropriate way of ensuring a continuous and efficient service or of ensuring that where powers of monopoly exist, these are not abused. Monopoly, however, takes many forms and so do the best ways of dealing with it.

Control of monopoly

The importance of monopolistic elements in modern industry has repeatedly been emphasized. On the one hand, the imperfection of the market results in duplication of services and of plant, the insulation of inefficient firms from competitive pressure, and the excessive multiplication of brands and types of product. On the other hand, the increasing scale of enterprise leaves a few giant concerns to divide the market, with no guarantee to consumers either that the monopolists are really efficient or that the benefit of reductions in costs will ever be passed on. The state has thus a double motive for intervening. It may be able to organize industry more efficiently than private enterprise, and it may try to divert monopoly gains from private to public hands. The wastes of imperfect competition might be eliminated by extensive rationalization – by shutting down redundant plant, standardizing output, and concentrating production in the most efficient firms. The extortions of monopoly might be prevented by setting up public corporations, aiming, not at maximum profits, but at efficient public service.

At this point, however, two important reservations must be entered. First of all, monopoly powers are much more restricted in an open economy than in one where competition from abroad is hampered or prevented by tariffs, quota limitations, and other protectionist measures. It has often happened in the past that monopoly was nurtured by just such measures, that the government had itself to blame for any resulting damage to the economy and that control of monopoly needed little more than the withdrawal of protection. In such a situation the government is caught between its desire to maintain or build up some industry and the concentration of the industry into a monopoly under the protection afforded it. This situation is common in countries undergoing industrialization, but it can arise also in industrialized countries.

Foreign competition is sometimes put forward as a reason for not taking seriously the danger of monopoly in modern industry in the absence of protection. Indeed it may be urged that foreign competition *requires* businesses to merge or enter into restrictive agreements with one another in order to survive. In Britain, for example, large business units have been encouraged to merge on the grounds that this is indispensable if they are to be able to face competition from still larger businesses from abroad[1]. After the merger the enlarged unit remains exposed to foreign competition. But this does not completely exorcise the danger of monopoly. Since foreign competition is unlikely to be of equal force in all branches of the combined business, it may be quite consistent with the development of quasi-monopolistic powers in some of those branches where previously there was no danger of monopoly.

The second reservation is one of practicability. It is much easier to decide that something ought to be done than to find a way of doing it. There are serious limitations to what the state can usefully do to improve industrial efficiency and these limitations include the weaknesses of the government machine itself.

Public corporations, for example, are not likely to improve efficiency except where there are large economies of scale and where their market coincides with some convenient administrative unit. Where there are strong economic forces – the need for energetic and resourceful management, for instance – making against large-scale enterprise, or where, as commonly happens, the optimum unit lies midway in scope between the central government and a local authority, a public corporation is beset with difficulties from which private enterprise is likely to be free. Prices may still be reduced, especially if the danger of monopolistic exploitation is serious, but the gain to consumers will accrue out of the excessive profits of the monopolist, not from the greater efficiency of the public corporation. To enjoy the best of both worlds, it might be easier to leave the monopolist, with his more flexible organization, in control of production, and, at the same time, to fix maximum prices for his output.

Where a private monopoly is replaced by a department of state or by a municipality, the gain is still more dubious. Democratic governments and their officials are constantly under the necessity of explaining and defending their decisions. But sound practical judgements are not always easy to explain; they may be intuitive and incapable of exposition in a speech or on paper. At the same time, speed of decision is sacrificed to quality of decision. The need for a policy that can be publicly defended inculcates an excessive caution. Large risks, however justifiable, must result in occasional failures which can be seized upon to discredit a democratic government.

When a government ceases to be democratic or where, as in war-time, it has a single aim to which everything is subordinated, many of the above considerations lose much of their force. The achievements of dictatorships

---

[1] For a sceptical view of this argument see A. Sutherland, 'The Management of Mergers Policy' in *The Managed Economy* (ed. by A. Cairncross, Blackwell, Oxford, 1970).

or of war-time governments cannot be readily compared with those either or private enterprise (competitive or monopolistic) or of democratic governments; for the sacrifices to which people will submit, or which they willingly accept, under a dictatorship or in war-time are immensely greater than those which a democracy would contemplate in peace-time. The task of economic organization, for example, is enormously simplified by the sweeping aside of vested interests and the suppression of internal conflicts. A dictatorship can plunder whatever classes can be represented as enemies of the people, can conscript labour whenever it sees fit, and can, by suitable propaganda, represent as a resounding success what in a democracy would be denounced as a shocking muddle or a costly failure. In any discussion of government operation of industry, therefore, we must be on our guard against arguments based upon experience in other countries or in war-time.

If we think it unwise of a democratic government to try to operate more than a limited sector of industry (including the public utilities and other activities that are peculiarly subject to monopoly), we are left with the alternative of regulation and control. The state may try in various ways to limit the exercise of monopoly powers: by making restrictive agreements illegal, by taking powers to break up large units in order to restore competition, by referring all mergers between the largest companies to the Monopolies Commission, by supporting consumers' organizations, that can set a countervailing power against the monopolist. A programme of this kind must be based on a clear definition of the practices that are to be regarded as anti-social, and there must be provision for investigation of monopolistic behaviour, and powers to enforce decisions. It is not enough to set up a statutory body like the Monopolies Commission and leave it to rely on mobilizing public opinion against the grosser abuses of monopoly power.

There are other ways in which the state could check the arbitrary exercise of monopoly powers. It could become a shareholder in the larger business units, not so as to participate in the profits but to rid them of monopoly elements. It could take powers to nominate one or more directors to the boards of public companies. It could threaten to enter into direct competition with monopolistic units.

There is a danger that in concentrating on ways of curbing monopoly a greater danger may be overlooked. The prime need is to make competition work where there is scope for it and to make it work so as to raise productivity. There is no great virtue in competition if it does not improve industrial efficiency. But in some of the most competitive industries such as agriculture it is doubtful whether improvements in technique are brought about as effectively by competition as in other ways. Extension services which convey to the farmer the fruits of research and experiment may make him aware of ways of reducing his costs of which competition would leave him in ignorance. In other words, it may be more important to encourage technical progress than to introduce more competition. Competition is not an infallible instrument for generating technical progress, although it is more likely than monopoly to work in favour of technical progress and this is, or should be, the main plank in an anti-monopoly campaign.

Inequality and social welfare

If every man is free to earn what he can, in a world which offers large profits to the enterprising and the fortunate, it is to be expected that some people will earn much more than others. These inequalities, especially when they are clearly due to luck or inheritance, and when the many still go in fear of unemployment and poverty, arouse envy and resentment; in a democratic community, where everyone is equal in voting power, it is felt to be inconsistent to permit wide differences in purchasing power.

Before the war the top 5% of income-earners in the United Kingdom received about 29% of personal incomes before tax and about 25% after tax[1]. In 1973/4 these percentages had fallen to 17 and 14 respectively[2]. It is difficult to be sure that more recent figures are comparable but there is no doubt that a substantial shift has taken place in a relatively short time. It would appear, too, that the shift was still in progress over the last two decades. One reason for the change is the diminution in the post-war period in the share of income from property in total national income. In the mid-1970s only about 5% of personal incomes before tax took the form of investment income while earned income formed 93%. But for the top 1% of income earners, investment income came to 30% and before the war to 60% of taxable income. This suggests that inequality of income is to a considerable extent the outcome of inequality in the distribution of capital and of the inheritance of property by which this inequality is perpetuated. Capital is, in fact, much more unequally distributed than income: in 1973/4 5% of the adult population owned about half the marketable assets of the country and 1% of the adult population owned over a quarter. But if occupational and state pension rights are added in, these shares are cut by about a third to about 33 and 17% respectively. The shares are also appreciably lower than 20 years ago and still lower in relation to the pre-war period.

Inequalities in the distribution of wealth are to some extent no more than a reflection of inequalities between old and young. Property accumulates in the hands of the old, while the young own little or nothing. Before the war there were three times as many men between 25 and 55 as there were over 55; but, of those dying in 1938, the older men owned more than ten times as much as the younger. The figures for women show an even greater concentration of wealth in the higher age groups: of the women who died in 1938 and left estates of £10 000–50 000, for example, 60% were over 75 and less than 2% under 45[3].

There is nothing abnormal about inequality of income or wealth; all social systems permit some measure of inequality, and in many of them inequality has been greater or harder to justify or has taken far more pernicious forms. But in a democracy the complete equality of voters cannot in the long run be consistent with extreme inequality of consumers.

[1] H. F. Lydall, 'The Long-term Trend in the Size Distribution of Incomes', *Journal of the Royal Statistical Society*, Vol. 122, Part 1, 1959.

[2] Royal Commission on the Distribution of Income and Wealth, Report No. 4, 1976, p. 12.

[3] These figures are calculated from tables in: Kathleen M. Langley, 'The Distribution of Capital in Private Hands in 1936–1938 and 1946–1947', Bulletin of the *Oxford Institute of Statistics*, December 1950.

This is not a matter of moral rights and equity. It is a simple corollary from the proposition that voting power outweighs purchasing power. Once the mass of the people want economic equality, the only real issue is how to secure it, or at least to remove gross inequality, without serious injury to economic growth and without sacrificing some other social objective such as justice or freedom.

Reducing inequality is a task that occupies the state in a variety of ways. Taxation can limit the growth of large fortunes and the net income drawn from them; subsidized social services can raise the real income of the poor by reducing the cost of things of special importance in their budget or by assuring them of services that they could not otherwise afford.

Progressive taxation

The first method by which the state can make its influence felt in checking inequality is by taxation. It can play Robin Hood by taking from the rich and giving to the poor. By heavy death duties the state can prevent the passing of large estates intact to private persons by the accident of birth or favour; by steeply progressive rates of taxation (that is, rates which are higher, the richer the taxpayer) it can keep earnings, after payment of tax, within relatively narrow limits; by creating a system of social services, it can guarantee a minimum standard of living. All this within a social framework in which the flexibility of private enterprise can still, in great measure, be preserved. It is just such a compromise that is in process of being worked out in Great Britain.

This 'compromise' involved a revolution in the theory of taxation. In 1900 a progressive income tax was still something of a novelty, and to suggest that it might be used deliberately to procure greater equality of income amounted almost to economic heresy. Economists defended progressive taxation on other grounds. They cited the rather oracular pronouncement of Adam Smith that people 'ought to contribute towards the support of the government, as nearly as possible in proportion to their respective abilities', and undertook to prove that ability to pay increased more than in proportion to income. Or they put forward an 'equality of sacrifice' theory and engaged in philosophic discussions on the rate at which the income tax would require to increase as income increased in order to involve rich and poor in an equal measure of sacrifice.

Whether their slogan was 'ability to pay' or 'equality of sacrifice', economists found arguments to justify progressive taxation. But they did not regard it as part of a comprehensive policy for checking the growth of large fortunes and financing a system of social services. The theory of progressive taxation was rather like that of discriminating monopoly – mathematical rather than ethical. The question posed was: given the revenue to be raised and the number and relative incomes of the taxpayers, how much should each pay in tax? But there is, of course, a more fundamental question to which this leads: What incomes should people be left with after the state has raised and spent its revenue?

Our answer to this question depends upon the importance which we attach to ability and need as alternative principles of distribution. Men are both producers and consumers; and the distribution of income which spurs them to the greatest effort as producers may be grossly unfair when we look at the needs which have to be met out of the unequal earnings. But whether rewards should be related to ability and effort or to human needs, neither principle can justify the prevailing extremes of poverty and wealth. Rewards are obviously not in accord with needs. Neither are they proportioned uniformly to ability and effort. They depend also upon the wealth or opportunities bequeathed by one's parents; the efforts which are rewarded do not always confer a benefit on society, but may be directed to anti-social ends; and it is highly unlikely that the highest incomes are a necessary spur to the efforts and sacrifices for which these incomes are paid. It is possible, therefore, for a progressive income tax simultaneously to bring income and need, and income and effort, closer together. Moreover, the incentive that controls effort is frequently gross, not net, income; we are often content with the shadow of purchasing power while the government makes off with the substance. Hence taxation may go very far towards lining up income and need without doing damage to the relationship between income and effort.

But not indefinitely far. There are limits to the usefulness of taxation as a means of redistributing income. In the first place, a high rate of tax affects people's inclination to work, and hence the supply of labour. Since the highest rate of tax is paid on marginal earnings, there is a natural temptation to work less hard, do less overtime, retire earlier from business. A skilled workman or professional man who is paying income tax at 50p in the £1 on part of his earnings will naturally reflect that every £1 that he is offered for overtime work is worth only 50p net of tax. If there is a fixed net income which he is determined to earn, he will have to work all the harder because of the tax which he has to pay. But he will generally be inclined to react the other way and sacrifice the 50p for the sake of some leisure. After all, it is because he is fairly well off that he is liable to income tax at so high a rate; and since he is well off he is likely to be less rigid in his idea of the income that he wants to earn.

High taxation reacts on savings in a similar way. It reduces the surplus out of which people save; and it penalizes saving more than expenditure, since the income set aside to be saved is taxed at the time, and when dividends are paid on the capital sum they, too, are taxed. On the other hand, when people are determined to make provision for a given *net* income from investments at some future time, the higher the rate of tax the more they will be forced to set aside. It is not a *necessary* consequence of high taxation, therefore, that it should reduce private savings; but we are pretty safe in concluding that in practice it does, on balance, have this effect.

This is of special importance when we are thinking of business profits. The traditional method of financing extensions to a successful small business is out of profit; but if a large part of the profit is drained away in tax, growth is retarded and the attractiveness of founding a small business is greatly reduced. One effect of a high income tax, therefore, is to fortify established businesses against competition from young and expanding rivals.

An additional reason why this tends to come about is that high taxation penalizes risk-bearing. What was previously an even chance is now more likely to be a loss since tax is deducted from any profit earned, but no compensating refund is made for a loss. If, for example, there was formerly an equal chance of a profit of 10% or a loss of 2%, the effect of an income tax of 50p in the £1 is to turn this into an equal chance of a net profit of 5% or a net loss of 2% – obviously a much less attractive proposition. The established concern, whose risks are limited, gains once again by comparison with the young and struggling firm pioneering products or methods which have yet to be tested.

These limitations to taxation are obviously elastic and can be largely offset by other measures. If private savings diminish, the state can use public funds for capital construction. If the enterprise of young firms is checked, the state can foster new methods of industrial finance designed to put capital at the disposal of new and expanding businesses.

Whatever the theory of the matter, since the beginning of this century Britain has moved from a state of things in which the largest incomes did not pay more than about 5% in tax and the lowest incomes paid at least as much, to one in which the largest incomes pay up to 90% in tax and the lowest incomes receive much more from state subsidies and services than is taken in tax. This change has been associated with the change in the electorate from the middle-class monopoly of the nineteenth century to the universal suffrage of the twentieth; and it has been greatly accelerated by the three costly wars which have been waged since the century began. It has been brought about, not by Socialist governments pledged to 'soak the rich', but mainly by Conservative and coalition governments in need of enormous revenues and anxious not to antagonize the wage-earner.

The social services

The state is concerned not only to prevent the accumulation of economic power in private hands, but also to get rid of poverty by establishing a minimum standard of living for all citizens. This it tries to accomplish by means of what have come to be called 'the social services': free education and health services; retirement and widows' pensions; social insurance against unemployment and sickness; family allowances and child welfare services; assistance to those in need; and a host of other services, the aim of which is by no means simply to relieve poverty.

Expenditure on the social services has increased rapidly since the beginning of the century (*Table 31.1*). The total rose from about £1 per head of population in 1900 to £10 per head of population in 1939 and approximately £80 per head in 1980. Even if the rise in prices and in the real income of the country over the past 80 years is taken into account, it is a phenomenal expansion; whereas in 1900 the social services absorbed one-fiftieth of the national income, in 1980 the proportion had grown to over one-fifth.

The entire cost of these services is not borne by the general taxpayer. Part is met from contributions by those who benefit from the expenditure. National insurance contributions, for example, cover most of the current outlay on pensions, sickness and unemployment benefit. The net transfer of income to those who use the social services – mainly wage-earners –

TABLE 31.1. Current expenditure on social services by British public authorities

£m

	1900	1946	1960	1970	1979
Education and child care	20	203	801	2237	9 070
Health services	2	92	866	2047	9 116
Nutrition services	–	44	85	171	544
Family allowances	–	20	136	351	2 701
Pensions (including war pensions)	–	232	854	2100	9 404
Other national insurance (including administrative costs)	8	73	324	1015	3 219
Social security (supplementary benefits)	12	94	172	517	2 156
Housing subsidies	1	45	120	312	1 971
	35	803	3358	8740	38 081

Source: National Income and Expenditure, 1980.

through state expenditure on the social services falls short, therefore, of the gross outlay. But the social services do undoubtedly make an addition to working class income which is large, if difficult to quantify; and this addition is mainly at the taxpayers' expense even though the benefits are open to all.

The social services are exceptionally cheap to administer where, as with insurance, pensions and family allowances, the size of the service is an advantage, the conditions of benefit are relatively easy to define, and the work of administration consists largely of simple book-keeping. The social services are more difficult to administer where, as with the national health service, there are personal relations (between doctors and patients), business relations (between government and doctors) and administrative relations (between one hospital and another) all mixed up with one another.

The great merit of the social services is that everyone is treated alike on a basis of need. On the one hand, benefit is drawn as of right without the stigma or humiliation of charity; the state lays down the terms upon which the service is made available, and so long as those terms are complied with, anyone may apply. On the other hand, society has the satisfaction of ensuring that minimum needs are covered and that, while gross incomes may be fixed in relation to productivity rather than need, in the final outcome the social services restore the balance sufficiently to give every-one a minimum of the essentials of life and liberty.

The limits of redistribution

The changes that have already been brought about by state action are striking. But they rest above all on one thing: the willingness of people to pay their taxes. If people sought to evade taxation on a large scale the system would be in serious danger of breaking down. The British social system is pre-eminently a system for honest taxpayers. There are other dangers. One is that the tax system should become unintelligible (as the income tax is already) and ill-devised, so that the raising of revenue causes needless dislocation, destroys valuable incentives and penalizes innovation (on which, more than anything, the industrial future of Britain depends). Another is that in an excess of zeal for equality, the tax base is kept too narrow and an increasing load heaped upon the superstructure. There is a limit to what taxation can squeeze out of the higher incomes.

However much can be done by levelling, moreover, it is only by an increase in the total national income that the *average* standard of living can be improved. An extra 1% per annum in the rate of growth of the national income would soon contribute more to working-class incomes than a once-for-all redistribution in their favour of the whole of the sum paid to private persons in rent, dividends and interest, which does not amount to more than about 5% of total personal income before tax.

Sources of British economic statistics

For annual and quarterly data covering most of the post-war period, *Economic Trends Annual Supplement* is strongly recommended. For longer runs of annual statistics readers should consult:

> *Second Abstract of Historical Statistics*, by B. R. Mitchell and H. G. Jones. Department of Applied Economics, University of Cambridge
>
> *The British Economy. Key Statistics 1900–70*, Times Publishing Co.

Similar volumes of *Historical Statistics* have been issued for a number of other countries such as the United States and Canada.

For the immediate past, the most comprehensive annual and monthly series of official statistics appear in:

> *Annual Abstract of Statistics*
>
> *Monthly Digest of Statistics*

Annual data on the national accounts over the past decade are to be found in *National Income and Expenditure* (published yearly in the autumn). Preliminary estimates appear in the White Paper, *Preliminary Estimates of National Income and the Balance of Payments*, published just before the Budget. *National Income and Expenditure* is usually referred to as the 'Blue Book'. An official commentary, not on the statistics, but on the economic changes in progress, is published annually with the Budget in the *Financial Statement and Budget Report*.

Quarterly estimates of the gross domestic product and the components of final expenditure (consumers' expenditure, export of goods and services, fixed investment, public authorities' consumption, stockbuilding) are made public about twelve weeks after the end of the quarter, and revised estimates are issued later together with estimates of personal income and expenditure. The full set of *quarterly* national accounts is given in:

> *Economic Trends* (monthly)

and also appears in:

> *Monthly Digest of Statistics*

Quarterly details of the accounts of various sectors are given in:

> *Financial Statistics* (monthly)

Statistics on the balance of payments are published annually (September) in the *United Kingdom Balance of Payments*. Preliminary estimates are given in the pre-Budget White Paper. Quarterly statistics on the balance of payments are made public in *Economic Trends* (March, June, September and December), with a long-run of quarterly figures in the September issue. Monthly figures of the official reserves are released on the second working day of the following month and are reproduced in *Financial Statistics* (monthly).

The main statistics relating to the Budget are published on Budget Day, in the *Financial Statement and Budget Report*, the *Memorandum on the Estimates* and the White Paper, *Loans from the National Fund*. These should be interpreted in conjunction with the full text of the Budget speech by the Chancellor. The supply estimates (covering most central government expenditure) are published in the *Defence Estimates* (February) and *Civil Estimates* (pre-Budget). The financial transactions of local authorities appear in *Local Government Financial Statistics* and *Local Financial Returns*. The Blue Book analyses public expenditure over a long calendar-year run; and financial details for social services and housing appear in the *Monthly Digest of Statistics* (May).

Financial Statistics brings together all the key financial statistics, including indicators of the money supply and domestic credit changes. Figures of transactions in financial assets, and liabilities between different sectors of the economy, are also to be found in the *Bank of England Quarterly Bulletin*. Quarterly estimates are given to indicate the extent to which a surplus in one sector's capital account is channelled to finance the deficits of other sectors.

Unemployment and vacancies statistics usually call for cautious interpretation, and these figures – together with data on incomes and prices – may be found in the Department of Employment's *Gazette* (monthly). A convenient source for changes in employment and unemployment is the Labour Market Quarterly Report issued by the Manpower Services Commission.

Trade statistics are presented monthly in the *Report on Overseas Trade*.

The form and timing of official statistics change from time to time and provisional figures are inevitably revised. These revisions make it necessary for readers to be careful when trying to interpret and use current statistics on the economy. Estimates of some key statistics, such as those of consumers' expenditure, are issued in a preliminary form (at constant prices and seasonally adjusted) ahead of the main estimates and are then subsequently revised in *Economic Trends*. Provisional estimates of the index of industrial production are compiled monthly but these too are subject to revision (e.g., because the seasonal allowances are modified).

As part of its programme to help users of statistics find their way around British official sources, the Central Statistical Office (CSO) has issued a useful *List of Principal Statistical Series and Publication* (1972). This is kept up-to-date in the CSO's quarterly *Statistical News*. A summary of current economic changes may be found in the monthly *Economic Progress Report*, prepared by the Information Division of the Treasury and made available (free) through the Central Office of Information.

Unofficial and less inhibited commentaries are included in the quarterly *Economic Review* of the National Institute of Economic and Social Research

This is indispensable to anyone wishing to keep abreast of professional analysis of the current economic situation; there is a special, low subscription rate for students.

Among other official and semi-official sources of British economic statistics, the following are useful for commentaries and comparisons from international standpoints:

OECD, *Economic Survey of the United Kingdom* (annual)

OECD, *Economic Outlook* (quarterly)

Bank for International Settlements, *Annual Report*

An important source for comparative data on members of the European Economic Community, published monthly in Brussels, is:

General Statistics, Statistical Office of the European Communities

For international statistics the most useful sources are:

United Nations Statistical Year Book

United Nations Monthly Bulletin of Statistics

OECD General Statistical Bulletin (monthly)

International Financial Statistics (monthly)

A detailed guide to British national income statistics is:

National Accounts Statistics: Sources and Methods, ed. Rita

Index